D0886677

The Wild Horse
Controversy

Other Books by Heather Smith Thomas

A Horse In Your Life
Your Horse and You
Horses: Their Breeding, Care and Training
Horses; A Golden Exploring Earth Book

The Wild Horse Controversy

Heather Smith Thomas

SOUTH BRUNSWICK AND NEW YORK: A. S. BARNES AND COMPANY
LONDON: THOMAS YOSELOFF LTD

A. S. Barnes and Co., Inc.
Cranbury, New Jersey 08512

Thomas Yoseloff Ltd
Magdalen House
136-148 Tooley Street
London SE1 2TT, England

Library of Congress Cataloging in Publication Data

Thomas, Heather Smith, 1944-
  The wild horse controversy.

  Bibliography: p.
  Includes index.
  1. Wild horses—The West. 2. Horses—Law
—United States. 3. Donkeys—The West.
4. Donkeys—Law and legislation—United States.
5. United States—Public lands. I. Title.
SF284.U5T48   1979   333.9'5   77-84588
ISBN 0-498-02191-2

\

PRINTED IN THE UNITED STATES OF AMERICA

to my mother, Betty Smith,
whose interest in and enjoyment of history and research
has finally rubbed off on me.

Contents

Preface

I've been interested in the wild horse situation for a long time, but until recent years my interest was confined to discussing the subject with friends, and reading a few items here and there. Then in the summer of 1975 I decided to write some articles about the wild horse controversy, and discovered that my well-organized and history-minded mother had been saving newspaper clippings for a number of years on several interesting subjects, including wild horses. She sent me all of her wild horse clippings, and these, along with information I gleaned from several other sources, got me launched.

I sold several wild horse articles to various horse magazines. But I discovered that I really couldn't do justice to this subject in short articles; I wanted to really dig in and cover the whole subject thoroughly. The only solution was to write a book.

This project has been immensely interesting, and has led me along paths of research I might not have otherwise traveled. The further I dug into the wild horse issue, the more the subject unfolded, and new roads beckoned me on in several directions. What started out as an outline of 8 chapters soon blossomed into 10, then 15, then 18, then 20. The wild horse issue was much more complex and bigger than I thought. And after chasing down the many aspects of the wild horse controversy, I feel I gained a much broader understanding and perspective than I had when I began. Writing this book has been not only fascinating, but also an educational experience for me, and I wish the same for my readers.

Acknowledgments

I owe a great debt of thanks to many people who helped make this book possible. Most of all, I want to thank my mother, who meticulously collected news clippings and other sources of information for me. She already had a good file of wild horse items collected before I began this project, and without this help I might not have ventured forth on this book. I'm a very disorganized researcher myself, and had let many interesting items slip by me in the past, whereas she had a massive amount of information already filed away over the years—how did she know I would someday want to write this book?

I also want to thank the people at our Salmon BLM office who provided me with information, especially Jim Englebright, wild horse specialist— who helped me when I started writing articles about the wild horse issues and about our local Challis herd—and later his successor, Robert Larkin, who continues to work with the Challis horses. I want to thank Harry Finlayson, BLM District Manager, and also Don Smith and Sally Gregory, Challis Area managers, who took a very full day to show me and my husband through the Challis wild horse area on a cold November day in 1976, and who have helped me in numerous ways since then.

I also want to thank the many District Managers and other BLM people in several western states who corresponded with me and sent information and photographs.

And I especially want to thank Dr. Floyd Frank, head of the Veterinary Science Department at the University of Idaho, for loaning me his file on wild horse material gathered during his years on the national wild horse advisory board.

Other people whose help was greatly appreciated are our librarians at the Salmon Public Library (whom I pestered a great deal), the many, many people who gave me information through interviews or correspondence, my brother Rockwell Smith who processed many photos for me, Beth Yost and my husband Lynn, who proofread my manuscript, and lastly, my children who were patient with me and stayed out of my way while I wrote this book— during a busy summer when I should have been outdoors helping with the haying and starting three green horses under saddle.

Many people helped supply photos for this book. For the photos that I did not supply myself, I wish to thank the following:

Bureau of Land Management, Salmon, Idaho
Bureau of Land Management, Nevada State Office at Reno
Denver Public Library, Western History Department
Bureau of Land Management, California State Office at Sacramento
Charlie Thomas
Chester Bowman
Lynn Thomas
Heidi Smith
Jeff Edwards (Wild Horse Research Farm)
Peg Freitag (Spanish Barb Breeders Association)

11

James Englebright
Robert Larkin
Lamar Taylor
Jan Bedrosian
Bob Goodman

National Wild Horse Advisory Board
California Department of Fish Game
And I want to thank my brother, Rockwell Smith, for developing a great deal of film.

Introduction

The wild horse controversy is probably the most misunderstood environmental issue of our time. It is uniquely controversial and confusing because of the intense emotion generated—on both sides—over the issues of protection and control of free-roaming horses and burros. It is also confusing because of the common over-simplification of the wild horse issue and its problems.

The wild horse situation in America today has many more complexities and implications than most people realize. It's easy to take sides on an issue if you think that one side is all wrong and the other side is right. But most things in life are not that black-and-white, and if we look a little closer and dig a little deeper into any controversy, we usually find that the extremist positions are lacking in full understanding of the problem.

Most differences of opinion can be helped toward resolution if the extremists on each side can make an honest attempt to objectively learn more about the issue, and try for even a short while to stand in the other fellow's shoes. There are usually fragments of truth on both sides of any serious argument. The beginning of reaching better understanding in any

emotional, deeply felt issue like this one, is to try for better communication—for a better knowledge of all the facts, and a realization of why the other side feels the way it does. When communication improves, often the antagonists discover that their deepest feelings about the issue were not really so oppositely opposed after all. And the wild horse issue in our country will not be adequately resolved until this happens—until the American people can sit down together and realize that we share more common feelings and ideals than we thought, and until we become aware of the great responsibility that we all have to try to resolve the problems in the best interests of this whole great country of ours.

A few years ago I was one of the extremists. But if a person cares enough about any issue, he will take the time and effort to find out more about it, and find out the facts. This is what I have tried to do, and this is what this book is about. I've tried to portray the whole broad picture of the wild horse issue from its very beginnings, and all the complications along the way. It is my hope that the reader will come, as I have, to a fuller understanding of the wild horse and his place on our ranges.

The Wild Horse
Controversy

1

A Brief History
of the Horse in North America

The horse, as we know him today, is not native to North America. He is an introduced animal, a domesticated creature brought here by man. The progenitors of the first "wild" horses on this continent were escapees from Spanish stock brought here by early Spanish settlers.

But the horse had prehistoric ancestors that roamed these lands. Most scientists agree that the forerunners of the horse evolved here. After the age of dinosaurs and giant reptiles was past (about 60 million years ago), small mammals began to appear. One of these small mammals, Eohippus (a Greek word meaning "dawn horse"), was the early ancestor of the horse. Eohippus was the size of a small fox, with four toes on his front feet, three on his hind feet, an arched back, and an egg-shaped, sheep-like head on a thick neck. All of his toes were equipped with pads of heavy cuticle, and shaped like miniature hoofs. Fossils of Eohippus dating from about 55 million years ago have been found in the central plains of North America.

Though most people use the name Eohippus for the rodent-like little dawn horse, his correct scientific name is *Hyracotherium*, because early scientists who in 1838 discovered his fossil remains near Suffolk, England did not realize he was related to the horse. The fossil animal closely resembled the Hyraxes—rock rabbits—which are similar in size and external appearance to rodents, and the scientists named the fossil after them. By the time some similar fossils were discovered in America, scientists had established certain principles of evolution, and the fossils were recognized as ancestors of the horse. Charles Marsh of Yale University gave the name Eohippus, "early horse", to these fossils, but since *Hyracotherium* is the older of the two names, it is the correct term under the rules of zoological nomenclature.

Little Eohippus lived in North America and Europe at the same time. He was able to do this because for awhile the British Isles and North America were attached, as part of the supercontinent or landmass called "Laurasia" (which also included Greenland, and Europe north of the Alps and east to the Himalayas). Europe was separated from Asia by a sea, and joined to North America via Greenland and Iceland, and all of this landmass had a tropical climate.

Eohippus appeared in Laurasia at the very beginning of the Eocene Epoch (Greek "eos" meaning

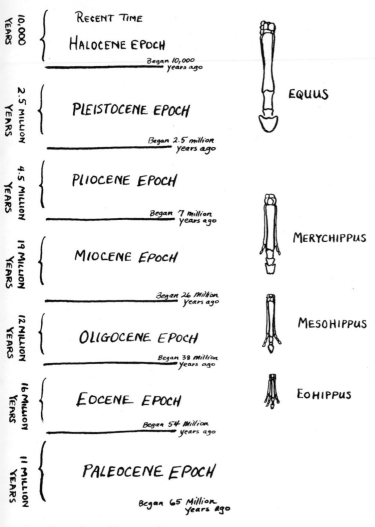

10,000 YEARS
2.5 MILLION YEARS
4.5 MILLION YEARS
19 MILLION YEARS
12 MILLION YEARS
16 MILLION YEARS
11 MILLION YEARS

RECENT TIME

HALOCENE EPOCH

Began 10,000 years ago

EQUUS

PLEISTOCENE EPOCH

Began 2.5 million years ago

PLIOCENE EPOCH

Began 7 million years ago

MERYCHIPPUS

MIOCENE EPOCH

Began 26 Million years ago

MESOHIPPUS

OLIGOCENE EPOCH

Began 38 million years ago

EOCENE EPOCH

Began 54 Million years ago

EOHIPPUS

PALEOCENE EPOCH

Began 65 Million years ago

Time chart of horse evolution.

"dawn"), which began 54 million years ago and lasted 16 million years. This Epoch was the dawn of recent life. During the Eocene, all the major divisions (orders) of modern mammals appeared. There were several species of Eohippus at that time, varying in size from about 10 inches tall to 20 inches tall. Then the little dawn horse, for some unknown reason, became extinct in Europe, which had by this time separated from North America. The evolutionary line that was to eventually produce the horse continued on in North America.

The little pre-horse was in the process of evolving from a browse-eater to a grazer. At the beginning of the Paleocene Epoch (about 65 million years ago) the habitat that the emerging dawn horse came into was swampy and lush with leafy vegetation. Little Eohippus was well suited to this environment, with his four splayed toes that did not sink into the mud, and his short teeth for browsing on the soft leaves of the shrubs and swamp plants. He scuttled around the forest floor, or fed on plants in the lowlands bordering the underbrush of dense forests. He resembled his modern-day relative, the tapir, with three toes on his hind feet and four on his front, with pads to rest the toes like a dog. His tail was long, and held in a curve, like a cat's. He was not as fleet as his larger descendants, and had to stay constantly alert to avoid the large predatory birds and other enemies that sought to eat him. When frightened, he scurried to cover, much like a rabbit does today.

But as time went on and the swamps gradually gave way to drier plains, little Eohippus had to change, too. The little dawn horse evolved into Mesohippus, an animal as large as a collie dog, possessing an enlarged skull and brain, and only three toes on each foot. Remains of Mesohippus have been found in abundance in the Badlands of South Dakota, and in northeast Colorado, where the barren plains were laced with winding streams and wooded valleys. Feeding on leafy plants, Mesohippus inhabited the brushy streambanks. The bunch grasses had not yet appeared.

But by the Miocene Epoch, beginning 26 million years ago, the vegetation in many areas had changed to grass, which contains silica, and which can wear down teeth. The climate became drier and more seasonal, as the tropical zone receded toward the equator. Grasses which had formerly been inconspicuous and scanty suddenly flourished, underwent rapid evolutionary changes, and spread all over the earth, replacing some of the forests. A new environment appeared—grassy plains instead of barren open spaces with no vegetation or sparsely dotted with plants. There were now wide areas with continuous grass cover.

As grass became more abundant (this had been determined from fossil grass seeds), many browsing animals were unable to adapt to this new food (grass is tougher and more fibrous than leaves) and became extinct. But the little pre-horse thrived. He had become larger, and more ready to assume his role as a traveling grazer instead of a small browsing, hiding-in-the-bushes swamp animal. He was about the size of a small donkey, with an increase in the length of his cannon bones enabling him to run faster and to better survive in the open prairie country. Now called Merychippus, he had become adapted to his new environment by developing long, high-crowned, harder-layered teeth which were capable of uninterrupted growth. Thus he could graze the grasses for a long life-span without wearing his teeth out. His tooth pattern altered to permit grinding, and he could now eat almost any kind of vegetable matter, including the harsh grasses. This change in his teeth developed during the Miocene and has not changed much since then.

As his teeth changed, his eyes changed too, becoming larger and wider spaced so he could see danger on the wide horizons of the plains. His feet adapted, and became more suitable to hard, dry ground; he still had three toes on each foot, but only the enlarged middle toe reached the ground and carried his weight. Eventually all external signs of his outer toes disappeared (except for the vestigial "splint bones" on each side of his cannon) and by one million years ago the horse had become very similar to what he is today, becoming *Equus caballus*, the true horse.

But this final evolution took place in Asia. No fossil remains of horses have been found in North America for the Pleistocene Epoch (which covered about 2.5 million years)—the Great Ice Age. Either the fossil remains were washed away in the great floods after the ice melted, or the horse vanished in North America. However, by this time there were horses in other parts of the world; they had spread to Asia by crossing the land bridge which connected Alaska and Siberia at that time. Horses appeared on all continents except Australia and Antarctica, and the final evolution of the horse into *Equus caballus* took place in Asia. Changes in conditions, perhaps, brought the horse back to North America at about 600,000 B.C. and fossil records dating from about that time to about 8000 B.C. have been found in many places in North America. About 25,000 B.C. the last ice sheet in North America began melting, and by 15,000 B.C. it was gone, leaving large new areas covered with grass, which became occupied by horses. What is now the Southwest and northern Mexico became drier and desert-like, but there were still plenty of grassy prairies farther north.

But after about 8000 B.C.—about 10,000 years ago—the horses again vanished, along with several other species of large grass-eaters, including the camels. Various theories have been advanced to try to explain this disappearance. Why the horse disappeared in both North and South America and not in Asia is not known, but some people feel it could have been a combination of hunting pressure (from the early Indian tribes that crossed the Asia-Alaska land bridge and came into North America about 10,000 years ago, spreading southward into both continents) and perhaps some epidemic disease, or parasite such as the tsetse fly. Or could it have been due to extra radiation in this hemisphere from a super-nova or star explosion? There have been seven of these super novas in history that were intense enough to be seen in the daytime, and there were probably some that occured in earlier times also. Scientists feel that this radiation could have changed the genetics of certain animal species,

making them incapable of reproducing. The offspring would be so mutant they could not survive. This could explain the sudden disappearance of the dinosaurs, and later, 10,000 years ago, the sudden disappearance of the horse and camel in the western hemisphere. Radiation is responsible for many mutations, making evolution possible, but excessive radiation could wipe out a species by altering the genes and chromosomes too much.

The melting of the last ice sheets in Europe created an increase in grassy plains there, too, and there the horses thrived instead of disappearing. Our world would have been without horses, if it hadn't been for the earlier prehistoric migrations of some of these horses into Eurasia and Africa, where the line of development continued, producing our modern horse as well as the zebra and donkey. Our modern species of horse descended from ancestors in north central Asia. The evolution of the horse was not marked by slow and steady change, but went in fits and starts, and in several directions. While the environment stayed the same, so did the horse; when it changed, the horses did, too; taking advantage of new conditions, responding to the changed environment.

Near the end of the Ice Age, prehistoric man was hunting the horse for food, as is evident from remains of horse bones at camping and cooking sites. In the limestone formations of central France there are many caves eroded out of solid rock; they are shallow caves that were used by Cro-Magnon hunters thousands of years ago. Deep in the winding limestone caverns, Cro-Magnon medicine men painted pictures of the animals the hunters pursued for their living, probably hoping that the magic of the pictures would help assure a successful hunt, or bring the pictured animals in plentiful numbers for the hunt. These vividly colored pictures have not faded through the years, and give good descriptions of the wild horses of that period—about 18,000 B.C. according to carbon 14 dating methods. The horses in the cave paintings are dark red with black points (black legs, mane, tail and ears), or light colored and covered with dark spots.

As Europe warmed after the Ice Age, forests encroached on the vast grasslands, forcing the grazing herds of wild horses to move eastward onto the vast steppes of southern Russia and western Asia. Tribes of Paleolithic hunters, in small villages along the woodland fringes of the prairies used the horses for food. In time they became semi-nomadic, following the horse herds across the rolling open country in summer, and returning to their huts for winter. They had hunting dogs, and by 5000 B.C. had domesticated the onager, a small wild ass.

By about 4000 B.C. several types or subspecies of horse had developed in the grasslands of Eurasia. *Equus caballus* came with some color variations, according to the colored cave paintings in central France, but the most common color pattern was dun, with a black dorsal stripe, tail and lower legs. The Tarpan was a distinct type found around the Black and Caspian Seas. Scientists have called him *Equus ferus silvestris* (the forest Tarpan) and *Equus ferus ferus* (the Steppe Tarpan). He was mouse-grey with a thick head, dished face, long ears, short frizzy mane and a dorsal stripe. He was a very small horse, with the base of his tail short-haired. The first domesticated horses were probably Tarpans, several thousand years ago.

This wild European horse survived in small herds in remote areas of central Europe up until recent times, becoming extinct in the early part of the 20th century. As the grasslands were plowed up over the centuries and domestic animals competed for the grazing lands that remained, the Tarpan herds were pushed back and steadily decreased in number. The last Tarpan died in 1918 in captivity in the Ukraine. Since then the Tarpan has been "re-created" on a small scale; the Munich Zoo produced a Tarpan-like type of horse by selective breeding of domestic horses that were thought to have Tarpan ancestry (during the last few centuries crossbreeding took place between the Tarpan and the domestic horses of the area, and wild herds often ran off with domestic horses).

In Mongolia (or Manchuria) another type— Przewalski's horse (*Equus ferus przewalskii*)—was found; he is considered by some people to be the forerunner of the domestic horse. This subspecies was discovered in western Mongolia in the late 1870's by the Russian explorer N. M. Przhevalsy, and is a small stocky, dun-colored animal with a dark mane and tail (upright mane and no forelock) and dorsal stripe. He has a light muzzle, narrow white rings around his eyes, short hairs at the root of his tail, with the dorsal strip starting onto the tail. This horse, the last of the true wild horses, may now be extinct except in captivity.

A third type, the large "forest horse," inhabited western Europe and became the ancestor of the heavy horses used by the armored knights of the Middle Ages, and later the modern-day draft horses. A type of forest horse existed in the wild state in Polish forests up until the middle of the 18th century.

The origin of our domestic breeds of horses has long been a subject of guess and conjecture, and there have been several popular theories. In 1949, Bengt Lundholm, a Swedish zoologist, came up with a theory that helped explain the dissimilarities of domestic breeds. Rather than stemming from just one wild type, as some people had supposed, he became convinced that the domestic horse we know today sprang from at least three types of wild horses. He studied skulls of horses dug up in southern Sweden (some dating back from Neolithic times or earlier, and others more recent, from the Bronze Age, when the horses were domesticated) and other fossil remains in western Europe. He found that the early wild horses could be divided into two groups, the main difference lying in the relative size of the second and third molars. The eastern group of horses had a third molar larger than their second molar. This group included the Tarpan, Przewalski's horse, and today's Exmoor pony and Polish konik pony (a descendant of the forest Tarpan). It also includes several fossil types, all found east of the Alps, that are no longer in existence today.

The western group of horses had molars the same size, and could be further divided into two types—a large horse (the Germanic type) found mainly in the area of the Rhine, and a much smaller type of horse which Lundholm called the "Microhippus group." The large Germanic type became the forerunner of the big "forest horse," the heavy draft horses, and some of the Swedish and Gotland horses. The smaller "Microhippus" type was the forerunner of the Celtic ponies, Fjord ponies and the Arabian horse. This group diversified, as some of them stayed north (the ponies) and some migrated south, becoming the ancestors of the Arabian. One of the early domesticated horses in Switzerland was of this Microhippus group, while other early domesticated Swiss horses (Bronze Age), along with most of the domesticated horses of eastern Europe and central Asia were clearly of the Tarpan type.

Lundholm's study was the first evidence, from fossil data, that there were several different types of wild prehistoric horse in Eurasia, and that these different types gave rise to different domestic types in the locations where they existed. If there were several horse species during the Ice Age, capable of living in the same environment without competing for food and habitat and without interbreeding (this can be surmised because of no intermediate fossil specimens found to suggest interbreeding), then we can easily see where the diversity of our domestic horses came from.

Early peoples domesticated their local variety of horses and then traded them around (some horses being better suited for draft, others for riding) and selectively bred them to be better for their work— either draft, riding, racing, or as sturdy ponies or pack horses, and so on. Horse breeding spread gradually among the various tribes and peoples. As trade links were established between peoples, different groups learned more about other domestic horses, finding that some from one area made the best pack animals, some from another area were better draft animals, and others best for riding. Thus, different types of horses were bartered and exchanged, and eventually selectively bred and crossbred by innovative peoples trying to improve their usefulness. With selective breeding and inter-breeding of the different types, the domestic horse breeds (starting from different initial potentials) soon became even more diversified as man bred them for his own purposes.

Before recorded history, some of the western group of Microhippus horses went southwest into Asia Minor and eventually into all of North Africa and the northern shores of the Mediterranean Sea. This southern group of horses underwent dramatic changes in a relatively short time, becoming finer boned, fleeter, and "hot-blooded" (with more red blood cells per cubic centimeter of blood, and therefore more oxygen-carrying capacity). Some of this change was undoubtedly due to their domestication, and man's selectively breeding them as swift war-horses on the desert, breeding them for tremendous endurance under hot and adverse conditions. These hot-blooded Arabians and Barbs (an offshoot from the Arabian) eventually became the source of breeding for almost all domestic horse breeds except the draft breeds and some ponies. The Barb has been called the "African Arab," the name Barb coming from the Barbary states—the old north African countries west of Libya—Algeria, Tunisia, Morrocco, Tripoli and Fez.

We don't know exactly which tribe of people was first to tame the horse. Our ancestors were eating horses long before they rode them. There are indications that the horse was first domesticated several thousand years ago by an early civilization in the Middle East, using forerunners of the Arabian-type horse. About the same time, Indo-European peoples tamed a few of the Tarpan-type horses, which they used at first only for religious purposes.

These Indo-Europeans had invaded the steppes of southern Russia and western Asia, displacing the Paleolithic hunters who had previously roamed there following the horse herds. The invaders became known as the Red Earth people, from their tradition of coating the bodies of their dead with red mud before burying them in mounds of earth.

The Red Earth people did some trading with tribes in the Near East, via the Black Sea and the straits linking it to the Mediterranean. In the Near East's Fertile Crescent they found that their trading friends had domesticated sheep, goats, cattle and onagers (wild asses). These innovative people used wheeled carts and wagons pulled by their oxen and onagers. The Red Earth people quickly borrowed all these good ideas for their own use, and trained a few of their Tarpans to pull carts in about 4000 B.C.

Other peoples eventually tamed some of the native wild horses in their different locales. It is not known exactly when man stopped eating the horse and started using him as a beast of burden, but it was much later than his domestication of the dog and the cow, and the horse was used in harness long before he was ridden. The horse-drawn chariot dates back at least to 2000 B.C. in actual records, and there is evidence to suggest it had been in use for at least 1000 years before that. Yet the use of horses for riding didn't become a widespread practice until later.

When man domesticated the horse it re-volutionized his life, making him more mobile. All of the great and powerful early civilizations of Europe and Asia used the horse. The Red Earth people may have been the first horseback riders. They had converted some of their horse-drawn carts into sleeping quarters, and became truly nomadic, traveling over the steppes with their horse herds in search of game, and grass for the horses. To handle their horse herds in this open country, they needed a few mounted men to keep the herds from straying, and to bring horses into camp when fresh teams were needed for the wagons and carts. These nomads on horseback were such a strange sight to the Greek traders who came to the Black Sea region that at first the visiting traders thought the horse and rider to be some strange animal, a centaur, half horse and half man. This parallels the American Indians' first reactions to the Spaniards, who were the first horseback riders they had ever seen.

The nomadic caravans with their horse herds, wagons, and horsemen, eventually reached the foothills of the Asian mountains, where the native people they met quickly adopted the use of the horse. But, in the mountain country this tribe of people found horses more useful as mounts and pack animals than in harness, and soon became expert horsemen. Whole villages learned to ride, becoming nomads—the life of the group centering around their horses, which furnished mounts, pack animals, and food. Mare's milk became a part of their diet.

Like the revolutionizing of the western American Indians' lives and culture a few thousand years later when they acquired horses, horse culture swiftly changed the way of life for people in Europe and Asia. Use of the horse spread north and east into Mongolia, and hundreds of thousands of people changed their life-style and became nomads. Over the centuries, these mounted nomads moved out onto adjacent lands to conquer vast areas, pasturing their horses on the grasslands.

These nomadic horsemen invaded the settled valleys of the Near East, the first wave of horsemen pouring down from the Iranian plateau into the fertile lowlands of Mesopotamia in about 2000 B.C. They were followed in the next century by other bands in sufficient numbers to gain a strong foothold in that area. These Mongolian horsemen were fierce fighters and excellent horsemen, and had no trouble overrunning the country using chariots as well as mounted warriors.

By about 1600 B.C. the Mitanni had taken over a large area in Syria and set up a strong kingdom, dominating the region for about two centuries, and an earlier tribe of invaders had set up the nearby Hittite kingdom. The Hittite king, greatly respecting the Mitanni horsemanship, hired a Mitanni expert to set up a training program for his own warhorses. This training program was written on clay tablets, which have survived until the present time, the earliest known work devoted entirely to horses and horse training.

While the Mitanni and Hittites were setting up their kingdoms, the Hyksos, another band of horsemen with chariots, overran Palestine and Egypt, bringing the first horses into Africa about 1700 B.C. Not long after that, a sea-going people shipped horses across the Mediterranean to Libya. From these early horses in Egypt and Libya, all of the northern part of Africa west to the Atlantic had horses by 1000 B.C. Many of the North African tribes, especially the Moroccans, Algerians, Numidians and Moors, became excellent horsemen and bred exceptionally good horses, which soon attracted the attention of the Romans. Later, as the armies of Rome conquered one country after another, all the good horses of the Mediterranean became available to the Romans.

As the use of horses spread around the Mediterranean world, horse breeders tried to produce special types of horses for specific purposes, and often imported stallions from other areas to use in their breeding programs. The Roman conquerors took advantage of the various types of horses, and bred horses for riding, racing, cavalry and chariots.

Then after civil wars had weakened the Roman Empire, Germanic tribes from the north broke through the frontier guards and poured over the Roman Empire. These tribes—Goths, Vandals, Franks, Visigoths and so on—were large men who preferred the large heavy horses of the northern forests.

To backtrack a little, the early peoples in what is now Spain (Greek and Phoenician colonists) were using the horse by about 1000 B.C. These horses came from the north, and were small and stocky. They were used more for pulling carts and chariots than for riding. As time went on and Spain was influenced successively by the Celts from the north, the Romans who ruled for several centuries, and then the invading German tribes, the horse became used for war as well as a beast of burden. But the early Spanish war horse was a heavy horse, like those developed in Germany, France and the British Isles for carrying armored knights. These were big, cold-blooded horses, descendents of the heavy forest horse and the dun and striped Norse horse brought by the Visigoths. After the Visigoths conquered the area, and became the landed nobility, they bred sturdy easy-gaited horses that were better suited for comfortable riding than for war.

When the Muslims (Moors) invaded Spain in the 8th century, mounted on agile little north African desert horses of Arabian and Barb breeding, the Spanish knights on their ponderous horses were no match for them, and the Muslims took over Spain. A few centuries later, when the Spanish were finally able to throw off Muslim rule, they did so because they had adopted the swift desert steed for themselves (along with the Arab style of riding, weapons, and battle tactics). From that time on, Spain improved the quality of her horses by importing more of the hot-blooded desert horses to cross with the larger native stock. This method produced good riding animals that were slightly larger than the desert horses. It was these cross-bred Spanish horses which were later to become the first free-roaming horses in the New World.

Soon after Columbus discovered America, other Spanish explorers and adventurers sailed across the sea to the New World, and many of them brought horses. But it took at least 150 more years before free-roaming feral herds sprang up in North America.

Columbus brought the first horses to the New World, bringing them to the island of Santa Domingo in 1493 on his second voyage, as seed stock for the ranching colonies he was to establish. The Spaniards always rode stallions, but on this voyage the king decreed that 10 mares be brought along also, to establish breeding stock on the island. Here, and on other islands in the West Indies, royal and privately owned ranches sprang up and were soon raising horses. Velaquez brought horses to Cuba in 1511. Royal horse breeding farms were operating in Jamaica by 1515.

By 1519 Cuba furnished the 16 horses for the

conquest of Mexico. The West Indian islands furnished horses for Mexico, Florida and South America as Spanish exploration and conquest gained momentum. Ponce de Leon took horses from Cuba or Puerto Rico to the coast of Florida in 1521. Cortez took horses on his famous expedition, discovering the Aztec civilization in 1519. Peter Mendoza took horses to South America in 1535.

During the early years of Spanish exploration, horses were sent in nearly every ship that left the home ports. So many horses were transported to the New World that the king of Spain eventually forbade shipment of horses to the colonies; the home stock was becoming depleted. At one point horses were in such short supply on the West Indian breeding farms that horses were imported from North Africa, adding more Barb blood to the strain.

De Soto took 237 horses and some "freight animals" to Florida in 1539; some of these also went on his expedition in the Middle West in 1544. These were butchered for food by the survivors of the expedition or killed by Indians. Coronado took horses on his trek in 1539 and lost many of them to Indians; no horses from these early expeditions survived to go wild, even though popular legend would have it so.

The whole story of the introduction of the horse to North America actually begins in the 8th century after the Moors invaded Spain. The legend began that a Spanish bishop had fled from the Moors, over the western sea, and had set up the Seven Cities of Ciepola. In the Spain of the 16th and 17th centuries, people still believed in the mythical Seven Cities, and after Columbus discovered this New World across the sea, Spanish explorers came eagerly searching for the Seven Cities. The legend grew after Fray Marcos de Niza, a Spanish missionary, traveled north of the early Spanish settlements in what is now Mexico, and asked the Indians about the Seven Cities. The Indians were very obliging and helpful, and Fray Marcos returned to his Spanish settlement with news of the Seven Cities of Ciepola where there was lots of gold, and the streets were paved with precious stones.

This is why Coronado set out in 1539 with a large company, including 250 horsemen, to try to find the Seven Cities. The "cities" turned out to be just the Indian pueblos of Zuñi. Coronado didn't give up easily and he looked from California to Kansas for Ciepola before he turned back. But the Catholic world didn't give up the dream. Seven years later, Gastaldi drew up a map of the known Americas, and near the mouth of the Colorado River he drew in the Seven Cities, with little cathedrals marking them. Fray Augustin Rodriquez went back in 1581 to find

the cities Coronado missed but with no luck.

Romanticists have envisioned the wild horse herds in the western United States as springing from strays and escapees from these early Spanish explorers, and even until recent years historians and anthropologists accepted this theory. The favored choice for the supposed source of wild mustanges was either the expeditions of Hernando de Soto or Francisco Vasquez de Coronado. Both of these expeditions reached the Texas plains during the years of 1541 and 1542; De Soto's trek ended when he died of fever near the Mississippi River in 1542. The rest of his party traveled west and south to Texas, trying to get back to Mexico overland. They failed, and came back to the Mississippi, where they built boats. They started down the river in the boats with 22 horses, which, after losing many to Indian attacks, sickness and accident, were all that remained from their original number of 237. They killed these remaining horses one by one for food until only 5 or 6 were left. Reaching the mouth of the river, they turned these horses loose.

Legend and theory would have it that these six horses became the ancestors of vast herds of horses on the Texas plains, provided that the six could have made it back to Texas through miles of swamps and mile of desert, eluding all the natural predators along the way. A couple of facts pretty well settle the issue, however. First of all, one of the Spaniards in the party later said that some Indians came out of the bushes and shot the horses full of arrows even before the boat had gone around the first bend in the river. Secondly, the horses the Spanish rode were stallions. Even if some had survived, they could not have reproduced and started the wild herds, for there were no mares among them.

Coronado's horses didn't fare any better. He took more horses to begin with, but lost many to Indian arrows, starvation and sickness. Some were gored by buffalo on a buffalo hunt; some fell into a ravine during the chase. Only two of the horses taken on the expedition were mares, the rest were stallions. Even if any of these had strayed, they apparently did not survive, for Spanish explorers and buffalo hunters from the later Santa Fe settlements did not find any wild horses.

Before the horse could even begin to survive as a species in North America, the Indians of the Southwest had to learn about him and consider him useful to ride, rather than as an enemy to destroy, or food to kill and eat. The first horses seen by the Indians were terrifying to them. Indians often thought the horses were gods, or that the horse and rider were one creature. "Horses are the most necessary things in the new country because they frighten the enemy most, and after God, to them belongs the victory," said one of the Spaniards.

And after bad treatment at the hands of the Spanish, many Indians considered the Spanish horses their enemies also. After once finding out the horses were mortal, the Indians killed many. Until the Indian learned to use the horse himself, stray horses had no real chance of survival in the New World. A few scattered stray horses would have been like scattering a few juicy white men here and there among the cannibalistic tribes of New Guinea—a few might survive, but their chances of establishing a large population within 100 years are hardly worth looking at. But the Indians did eventually learn how to use the horse, for 200 years after Coronado, the Indians were mounted, and stealing horses.

Juan de Oñate was indirectly responsible for the Indians becoming mounted. Oñate was born in Mexico in the mid-1500's. His father had fought Indians with the Coronado expedition of 1539-1542. In 1595 Oñate made a proposal to the king of Spain, offering Spain a new empire north of the Rio Grande. Up until that time, the Spanish ranching frontier stopped abruptly just beyond the northernmost Mexican mining camps, for the mining camps were the major market for livestock. A few prospectors had made excursions across the Rio Grande into what is now Texas, and in 1581 a missionary enterprise reached the pueblo Indian villages on the upper Rio Grande, but were soon killed off by the Indians.

Thirteen years later, Oñate made his proposal for settlement. He would take an expedition north and make a settlement in the upper valley of the Rio Grande del Norte, where the Pueblo Indians lived in farming villages. The king thought it was a great idea, so in the spring of 1598 Oñate set out with 130 soldiers and 400 settlers and their families and slaves. He took with him on this colonizing trip several thousand head of livestock, including more than 100 mares and foals, along with the regular assortment of stallions and mules. They settled down about 30 miles northeast of the present Santa Fe. The settlers added to their horse herds with steady traffic from Mexico over the next years.

After they had established themselves, they sent out many exploring expeditions into the surrounding plains, making written reports on the geography, plant and animal life of the region, and on the Indian's way of living. The Indians used dogs as beasts of burden and there were no horses among them, and none wandering loose. Oñate explored the land from Kansas to California in his travels, and found no horses and no traces of horses—no bones, no manure at the water holes, no Indian traditions of horses, no evidence at all. There were no surviving strays (or their descendents) from either de Soto's nor Coronado's expeditions 50 years earlier.

Oñate's settlement prospered, forcing the Pueblo Indians to work as serfs in the fields they once had owned. A few years later the colony branched out and started another settlement at Sante Fe. During these years the surrounding Indians learned a great deal about horses. The Apaches raided some of the herds, eating the first horses they took, as well as the stolen cattle. Here was a source of food much handier than the buffalo herds, and the Spanish stock was tame enough to be driven to their camps for butchering.

Some of the Pueblo Indians learned to ride. The Spanish had brought herds of cattle, sheep and horses, which had to be herded near the settlement, because there were no fences. There was no material available on these lands for building fences (until the invention of barbed-wire 2½ centuries later) and the livestock herds had to be tended, to keep them from straying and to keep them out of the growing crops. Indian boys could herd the sheep and goats on foot, but handling the semi-wild cattle was a job for horsemen. Spanish law was decreed that no Indian could own or ride a horse, so the job of cow-herding initially was done by Spaniards.

Then the Spanish got careless. The Indian serfs did almost all of the menial work, taking care of the horses ridden by the Spanish, acting as grooms and stable hands; the Indians quickly learned how to handle and take care of the horses. Sometimes a Spaniard would send an Indian boy to help round up a herd, or he might take a few Indians with him on a long ride, to take care of the camp chores and handle the spare horses. Thus, in just a few short years, some of the Indians learned a great deal about horses and riding.

Horses began to trickle into the hands of the surrounding tribes. The first documented use of horses by Indians occurred 61 years after the establishment of Oñate's colony; in 1659 the governor of Santa Fe sent an official report to Mexico about a raid by a group of mounted Apaches. And when in 1680 the Pueblo Indians rose up against their masters, killing many Spaniards, they took the Spanish horses and knew what to do with them. No longer was the horse a fearsome god, but a useful beast of burden and swift means of transportation. The Spaniards who survived the massacre fled south to El Paso, leaving all their livestock in Indian hands. Thus, the beginning of the general spread of horses over the plains can be dated from this 1680 massacre. When the Spaniards came back to the

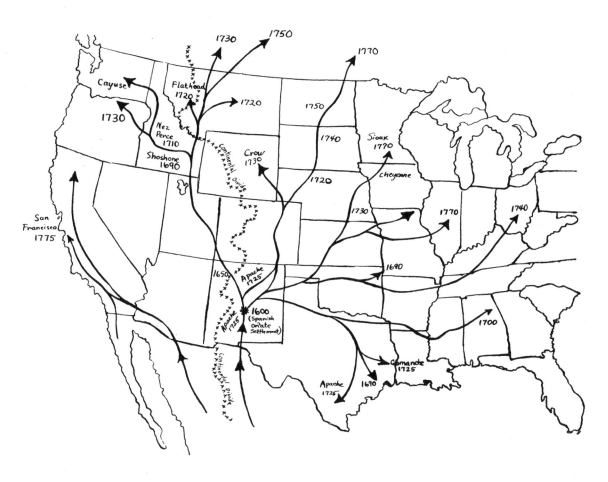

Northward spread of horses among the Indian tribes.

southwest from Mexico they found the Indians mounted; in 1601 the Indians had no horses, but in 1682 they had plenty of horses.

The Pueblo Indians didn't need as many horses as they found in their possession after the Spanish were routed, and were willing to trade some of them to the Plains tribes to the northeast, and to the Utes and Navahos to the northwest. The Pueblos also lost horses to Apache raiders. By 1690 all of the plains tribes in Texas had horses. Each band or village traded horses to their neighbors, slowly spreading horses over the plains. But it took another century for horses to reach the northern limits of the Great Plains.

The Missouri and Kiowa Indians had horses by 1682; the Pawnees farther east were well mounted by 1704; the Comanches by 1714; the Osages by 1719; the Iowas by 1724; the Assiniboines, Cross, Arikaras, Mandans, Crees, Snakes and Tetons by the late 1730's. And so on, as the horses spread from tribe to tribe over a larger and larger area, spreading eastward and northward. By the early 1700's there

were horses all over the Southwest, and some of these horses were destined to become the forerunners of the feral herds of "mustangs".

The grasslands of the plains provided an ideal habitat for the horses, and they thrived. As can be expected when any species moves into a vacant ecological niche, there was soon a population explosion in free-roaming horse bands. Many "wild" horses got loose as a result of Indian attacks on outlying Spanish missions and ranches. The Indians did not always stop to round up all of the livestock after a raid, and by the time the raid and massacre was discovered by the closest neighbors, much of the livestock had wandered away. Sometimes whole colonies were wiped out, or ranches abandoned, leaving the livestock on their own. Wild horses and wild longhorns were the result, and they began to spread over the southwest.

A new era had begun. This was the era of "horse culture" among the Plains Indians, and the beginnings of the vast herds of wild horses that would eventually roam the Southwest.

2

Mustangs and Indian Horses

The Indians had horses for only a couple of centuries, but in those two centuries their traditions and culture were dramatically changed. The Plains Indian's way of life came to depend so greatly on the horse, and he made such excellent use of the animal, that even today when the modern American thinks in terms of the historic Indian, he invariably thinks in terms of a mounted Indian.

The Plains Indians, before the coming of the Spanish horses, were nomadic and warlike and not as settled and agriculturally oriented as some of their brothers to the east. And with their acquisition of the horse, these nomadic and warlike traits were intensified. They were now more mobile, and this made it much easier to hunt and to raid their neighbors. Buffalo hunting became a sport instead of a duty, horse stealing became the chief occupation of young braves, and warfare became more deadly. In earlier times, the battles fought often ended with few or no casualties—the men lying behind their shields at a respectable distance from one another. But after the Indians went horseback, skilled riders dashed at their enemies—armed with war clubs, lances, bows and arrows. The sedentary horseless tribes had to retreat from the plains into more protected wooded areas. Eventually some of these tribes acquired horses, too.

Horses transformed the farming tribes along the edges of the plains, enabling them to range farther from home for several months of the year while the hunting was good, subsisting more on meat and less on corn. Added mobility, and the fact that a horse

The Plains Indian adapted so thoroughly to a horse culture in the short time that he had horses, that today when we think of the Indian, we invariably think in terms of a mounted Indian.

could pack much more than a man could, greatly increased the range of their trading area and gave them a greater variety of goods. Some of these agricultural Indians gave up their settled lives entirely and became wanderers on the plains. Horses recast the Cheyennes from crop-tenders to boundless drifters, limited only by the winds and snow of winter, the seasonal drift of the buffalo and the fruiting of berries. Horses turned war into a game, and food-gathering into the sport of the chase. Indians counted their wealth in horses. With horses they bought their wives and paid their debts. And an Indian's wealth and family were decided by the number of his horses. Next to strength and bravery in battle, skill in horse stealing was regarded as the greatest virtue an Indian could possess.

And the mobility of the horse, the ease with which the Indian could hunt, gave him more time to develop other aspects of his culture. Now his time was not solely devoted to the work of survival, and he had more leisure time for art and pageantry, gambling, warring, horse racing and horse stealing.

But before the Indian thoroughly adapted to a horse culture, he used the horse merely as a curiosity. As horses were introduced to each new tribe, the tribe might have at first only one or two horses in the village, kept merely as pets or for show. The horses were led around on festive occasions. Then later the Indians practiced riding them, and gradually a full-blown horse-oriented society emerged, the Indian depending on horses for social as well as practical purposes.

None of the plains tribes were truly nomadic before acquiring the horse, for each tribe had a permanent wintering place that it lived in for at least three months of the year. Bands from the Texas panhandle moved west and visited the friendly Pueblo Indians in New Mexico during the winter. The Comanches took refuge in the foothills of the Rockies when cold winds drove the drifting snow across the prairies, living in places where they had stored their food reserves—seeds, nuts, dried meat from their big fall hunt. Apaches of western Kansas

Use of the horse changed hunting into the sport of a chase, as well as making food-getting easier.

followed buffalo several months of the year, but raised gardens and corn for the lean wintertime. The Mandans lived a similar existence. The Pawnees and Osages lived along the eastern edges of the plains in permanent villages raising corn. But after acquiring the horse, all of these tribes began to follow the buffalo herds year around.

One of the primary wandering tribes was the Sioux, but before they got horses, they were a sedentary people. The Sioux are usually considered the typical northern Plains Indian tribe, yet even as late as 1766 at least one large band of Sioux was still horseless, living near the lakes and swamps of Minnesota, having bark huts for homes and canoes for transportation, and wild rice for food. During the 1770's they became mounted, leaving their canoes behind, and became buffalo hunters instead of rice-eaters, moving westward to the grassy plains of North Dakota.

This late introduction to horses by the Sioux illustrates the relatively slow northward spread of the horse on the plains. It took thousands of horses to supply the various tribes. Horses were always being traded off, horses were killed and eaten in times of famine, and harsh winters and predation by wolves took a heavy toll, especially on the foals. Some horses died on buffalo hunts and some were killed in battle. Most of the Indians were poor horse-breeders and didn't provide their horses with optimum conditions for reproduction. Pregnant mares were sometimes run to exhaustion on buffalo hunts or worked too hard on long pack trips while their foals were very young, causing heavy losses among both mares and foals. The Indians depended more on new stock from Spanish ranches of the Southwest than on their own horse breeding for increasing their herds. Stolen and passed from tribe to tribe (either by trading or theft) there were horses with Spanish brands all over the plains and even to the north.

West of the Rocky Mountains, the use of horses spread rather swiftly. The southern Navaho passed a few to the Utes, who in turn traded some to the Shoshonis farther north by 1670. From the Bear River, north into the upper Missouri drainage, the Shoshonis controlled the whole region, and it was good horse range. Soon horses were spread to the Crow Indians down the Yellowstone River, north to the Blackfeet and Flatheads, and west to the Nez Perce and Cayuses in the Columbia Basin. These tribes all had a few horses by 1730. Yet the horse acquisitions among the Plains Indians had barely reached as far north as the Platte in Nebraska by then.

Along with stolen horse gear, the Indians' first horses came from the Spanish, some Spanish tack finding its way as far north as Alberta by 1790. Later the Indians learned how to make their own. A Frenchman traveling through the Arkansas River territory in the early 1700's found the Wichita Indians mounted on very fine horses and using Spanish bridles and saddles. When ridden to war, Pawnee and Comanche horses were protected by leather armor, like that of the Spanish.

Later, after wild herds became more numerous, some of the Indian tribes added to their herds by capturing wild stock. Capturing wild horses became sport. Indians had two main methods for catching horses: the relay and the "grand circle hunt". In the relay, a group of riders would scatter over the range, taking turns chasing a band until the wild ones were nearly exhausted. At that point the pursuing Indians would rope some of the wild ones. The horse would be choked down or thrown, and while down the Indian would tie his feet, then loosen the choking rope and fix it around the lower jaw of the horse for more control. By the early 1800's, the rope or lariat became the conventional Indian sign for wild horses. The Osages used a noose at the end of a pole for "roping" horses.

In the circle hunt, many Indians rode out to look for horses, and after finding a band, they widely circled the horses, posting groups of Indians at intervals around the circle. When the horses became alarmed, they ran, only to discover more horsemen in front of them. They would turn back and the Indians would keep them running across and around the large human enclosure until they were exhausted and the circle would be tightened and the horses captured. Many Indians used a braided rawhide rope for catching horses—about 40 feet long, with a slip knot noose at the end. When a horse was roped, it was choked down until a halter and lead rope could be put on.

The Nez Perce Indians of the Northwest were somewhat unique in their horse culture, for they were really the only tribe to practice selective breeding and gelding. By trading off inferior horses and gelding some of the poorest stallions, they kept their breeding stock of good quality, raising better and larger horses than most of their neighbors, and much larger horses than those on the plains.

The Nez Perce did not get the horse until the 1730's. These Indians had been a fishing tribe, living in small permanent villages along the Snake River and its tributaries. But after they got horses, they branched out and traveled eastward over the mountains annually, to hunt buffalo in Montana more than 100 miles away. There they met the Crow and Blackfeet Indians, and later the Sioux, and borrowed so much of their Plains culture that they

The Indian used the horse when moving camp.

had more in common with the Plains Indians than with their fishing neighbors. The Nez Perce tribe bred the speckled Appaloosa horses, a color phase that originated in China, coming to the New World via the Spanish horses.

The Blackfoot tribes (Piegans, Bloods and Blackfeet proper) were among the first of the northern tribes to have horses, getting their first horses from the Snake (Shoshoni) Indians. At first the Snake Indians took advantage of their horseless neighbors. One old Piegan chief gave this account to the explorer David Thompson, the incidents he was speaking of occurring about 1730:

> We had more guns and ironheaded arrows than before, but our enemies the Snake Indians and their allies had Missitutin (Big Dogs: horses) on which they rode swift as the deer, on which they dashed at the Peeagans, and with their stone Pukamoggan knocked them on the head . . . This news we did not well comprehend and it alarmed us, for we had no idea of horses, and could not make out what they were . . . We were anxious to see a horse of which we had heard so much. At last we heard that one was killed by an arrow shot into his belly . . . numbers of us went to see him, and we all admired him.

This same chief told of the Piegans finding a camp of Snake Indians who had all died or were dying of smallpox—their horses wandering loose. The Piegans therefore took the horses. After that the Piegans and the other Blackfoot tribes began raiding to the south to get more horses, and raiding the Snakes, Flatheads and other tribes that did not yet have firearms.

The Mandan Indians had horses by the late 1730's and used them for hunting. They locked the horses in their own dwellings at night to keep them from being stolen by their neighbors, the Assiniboines, and took them out to graze during the day, watching them closely. The Mandans didn't have enough horses, and they guarded the few they had very carefully.

The Crows had many horses and were good horse traders. They had so many horses that their women didn't have to carry any of the loads when moving camp, which was unusual among the Indians of the Northwest. The Crows obtained horses cheaply from the Flatheads and sold them at great profit to the Gros Ventres and the Mandans.

Spanish horses were a great enticement to the Indians, and were acquired by the Plains Indians by trading or stealing. The Comanches, who raised no crops, quickly adjusted to a completely nomadic life, following the buffalo herds with their newly acquired horses. By the early 1700's the Comanches were taking many Spanish horses and ranging far south of their customary "stomping grounds" in order to get them. In the beginning this tribe traded a few buffalo robes for horses, but soon they were stealing horses, and in large numbers. The Comanches boasted that the only reason they allowed the Spaniards to remain in Texas, New Mexico and northern Mexico was to raise horses for them. The Comanches and neighboring tribes took horses from every Spanish outpost from Louisiana to the upper Rio Grande, and while the French were in Louisiana, the Indians traded horses to them for guns, knives, trinkets and other goods. For almost a third of a century, Comanche warriors made an annual trek south into the ranches and mining camps, clear down into Mexico, to bring back great herds of cattle, horses and mules.

The Assiniboines were also great horse stealers, probably the most renowned in the northwest. They, too, got most of their horses in raids as far south as the Spanish settlements, and many of their horses wore Spanish brands.

While horses were being spread across the West from the Spanish colonies in New Mexico, a similar movement of horses occured east of the Mississippi, but on a much smaller scale. Franciscan missionaries established a chain of missions in Georgia—more than 20 missions by 1615—where local Indians learned to handle horses. After a time, these mission farms were a source of horses for Indians to the north, (especially the Creeks, Cherokees and Chickasaws, who learned about using horses from the mission Indians). These tribes were farming people living in permanent villages and did not become nomads like the Plain Indians, but did use horses for riding and as pack animals, packing deer hides to trade with the whites, and selling horses to the settlers.

There were no wild horses when Indians first began riding, and wild horses did not become plentiful until after the Indians were well mounted. The Indians themselves added to the wild stock. Sometimes they turned exhausted or sore-footed horses loose, figuring to recapture them after they had recovered. Another tribe might gather them up, but some of them joined wild bands, and some were not recaptured. Mules, and horses with Indian ear-marks were often seen among the wild horses. The smallpox epidemic that decimated numbers of some tribes in the Missouri drainage in 1837 left many horses to run wild.

But there were very few wild horses in the northern plains or mountain country until the mid 1800's. There were lots of Indian horses, but no wild horses before that. This fact is well documented by the early explorers and fur trappers who went out into the Pacific Northwest in the early 1800's. Indian horses were often available when white men were desperate for new mounts or for meat, but wild horses were not common.

After President Jefferson acquired the Louisiana Territory for the U.S. in 1803, he sent out several expeditions to explore this new land. The most successful and famous of his expeditions was the one led by Meriwether Lewis and William Clark, who traveled up the Missouri River to find its source and to determine the limits of the United States at the Continental Divide. Then they were to go on into foreign territory beyond the divide and explore through the mountains to the Pacific. The success of this daring expedition (traveling more than half the width of the present United States and back) depended a great deal upon the available horses among the Indian tribes in the Rocky Mountains, for although they traveled by river for most of their journey, they had to leave their boats at the headwaters of the Missouri's Jefferson Fork in southwestern Montana and travel on through the mountains. They needed pack horses to carry their scientific equipment (writing materials, instruments, gathered plant and animal specimens, etc.) and trade goods, for the men themselves could not carry anything more than their own clothing, blankets, weapons, ammunition, and food.

The expedition was able to trade for pack horses with the Shoshoni Indians, thanks to Sacagawea, the Shoshoni wife of the expedition's interpretor, and obtained a few more from the Flathead Indians. The horses enabled them to successfully cross the mountains. When they again reached the navigable waters that would take them to the Pacific, they left their horses with the friendly Nez Perce Indians who took care of them over the winter, returning the horses when the expedition retraced its steps on the return trip.

The journals from the Lewis and Clark expedition are one of the earliest records pertaining to horses in the northwest:

There are no horses here which can be considered as wild; we have seen two only on this side of the Muscleshell (Musselshell) River, which were without owners, and even those, though shy, showed every mark of once having been in possession of man. The original stock (speaking of the horses owned by the Shoshoni Indians) were procured from the Spaniards, but now they raise their own. The horses are generally very fine, of good size, vigorous, and patient of fatigue as well as hunger.

Other exploration and fur trapping parties that followed in later years came into the area up the Missouri River and then traded for horses when they got to the mountains—Zebulon Pike in 1806, Wilson Price Hunt and a party of fur trapper in 1811, and then many more.

While explorers and fur traders were opening the Missouri drainage and the northern Rocky Mountains to travel, other Americans were trekking across the southern plains to Spanish settlements in New Mexico, looking for a source of trade. Some of them brought back mules, which were much in demand on the sugar and cotton plantations of the South and they also brought back donkeys for breeding, so they could raise more mules themselves. These Spanish donkeys soon made Missouri the mule-breeding center of the United States. The trading trail to the Southwest led through Comanche country, but the Indians were not a serious problem. The Comanches were continually raiding the Texas and Spanish settlements for horses, but they kept their northern borders peaceful so that they could trade with the Americans for guns and ammunition. Other tribes did occasionally raid the horses on these trading expeditions.

This was the era in which the wild horse numbers were reaching their peak. The number of wild horses that grazed the Great Plains will never be known exactly, but the wild horse population reached its peak during the late 1700's and early 1800's and has been estimated at various figures.

Wild horse numbers reached their peak in the early 1800's, numbering about 2 million as the ever-increasing herds spread northward.

J. Frank Dobie, a well-known authority on wild horse history, guessed the peak numbers to be about two million. He felt there were no more than one million at any one time in Texas and about another million scattered over the rest of the West. The greatest numbers were in the Southwest; the most densely populated ranges were in west central Texas. There were never as many in the North, partly because the northern Indian tribes were late in acquiring horses, and there was not time for the buildup of large feral herds. The wild herds that sprang up in the northern parts of the West came later, partly from Indian herds, but predominantly from stray horses belonging to white settlers. Thus there was never the concentration of Spanish blood among the northern wild herds that there was in the Southwest, where horses had been wild longer and had originated from feral Spanish stock.

As long as any unbranded young animal was still with its branded mother, it belonged by law to the owner of the branded mother. But after it grew up and left its mother, there was no way to claim ownership; it belonged to anyone who could catch it. The word "mustang" is an English corruption of the Spanish word *mesteño*, which comes from the word mesta, which means a group of stock raisers. The first Mestas dated back to 13th century Spain, as organizations of sheep owners. On the long drives between summer and winter ranges, sheep often became lost, and these stray sheep were called *mesteños*—which meant "belonging to the Mesta." Some were also called Mostrencos, from the verb mostrar, which means to show, to exhibit. The strayed sheep had to be "mostrado" (shown) in public, to give the owner a chance to see it and claim it. The term "bienes mostrencos" meant goods lacking a known owner.

A later form of the word *mostrenco* is *mestengo* and seems nearer to the sound of "mustang" than does *mesteño;* some etymologists think it might be the origin of the term mustang. But according to J. Frank Dobie in *The Mustangs*, English speaking people in the Southwest were not aware of the existence of the word *mostrenco* or *mestengo*. According to Dobie, the term mustang was first used in the early 1800's.

Wild horses caught on the southwestern prairies were sometimes better animals than the typical Mexican stock from which they had sprung. This was due in part to the fact that the Mexicans did not practice selective breeding, and did not try to improve their stock. The Spanish rode stallions and did not geld their riding animals, but the Mexicans gelded their best colts for use as saddle horses and left the poorer ones as stallions. A general degradation began occurring in most of the Mexican herds, resulting in many poorly bred Spanish-type horses averaging only about 650-800 pounds and not larger than 13.2 hands in height (as compared to the original Spanish horses being 900-1000 pounds and at least 14 hands tall or taller). In the wild, only the strongest and most courageous males gained harems and sired the foals. Also, the wild horses had a vast amount of country over which to roam, and were able to move to better feed when grass ran out on their home range; they were not confined to a certain area like the domestic stock, nor caught and ridden too hard too young.

Texas was the great reservoir for the wild horses that spread over the Southwest. The first mission settlement by the Spanish was at San Antonio in 1718, consisting of seven families, a military detachment, and missionaries. They brought 548 horses along with the usual cattle, mules, sheep, goats and chickens. Other missions, and privately owned ranches soon sprang up along the San Antonio River. Domestic horses left on the wide ranges were constantly reverting to the wild. When José de Escandón started some settlements along the Rio Grande in 1747 he found a few wild horses on the Texas side of the river. Eleven years later an official inspector reported thousands of horses, mules and burros in herds in the Texas country.

In 1777 Fray Morfi, a Franciscan missionary, made observations in his diary about the vast numbers of mustangs. He wrote that the wild horses north of the Rio Grande "are so abundant that their trails make the country, utterly uninhabited by people, look as if it were the most populated in the world. All the grass on the vast ranges has been consumed by them, especially around the waterings."

In 1804 a Spanish judge who rode out to inspect land on the lower Nueces River reported that mustangs were so numerous that settlers there could not raise any horses; all of their horses went away with the wild bands. The large numbers of horses in the Rio Grand-Nueces River territory had become the wonder of travelers, and on maps of Texas drawn in the early 1800's, this vacant space in Texas was usually marked as "Vast Herds of Wild Horses."

Crossing the Texas plains in 1846 with a column of soldiers, Lt. Ulysses S. Grant came upon great herds of horses and wrote, "As far as our eye could reach, the herd extended. There was no estimating the animals in it." Another man described the trampling of their hoofs as sounding like the roar of the surf on a rocky coast.

But the wild horse population had reached its peak. After the early 1800's came the inevitable spread of civilization as the United States grew westward. The prairies where the wild horses roamed were soon to change. Farms and cities would someday spring up where once the wild horse and the buffalo grazed, and it was inevitable that the vast herds would disappear.

3

The Wild Horse Versus Civilization

The buffalo went first. These great shaggy beasts were killed by white hunters for their hides, and later just for sport, so ruthlessly that long before the first railroad was built across the West in 1869 the herds had begun to vanish. The Plains Indians presented an obstacle to settling the American frontier, and it was felt by many Americans that if the buffalo were destroyed, the Indians could be controlled. The railroad finished the job, for it brought cheap transportation for the meat and hides, and brought the professional hunter to the plains. With cheap transportation, the hides could be sent east to commercial tanners, and the buffalo herds presented an adventurous opportunity for profit in the "Wild West." The plains were overrun with eager hunters, whose guns boomed from dawn until dark while freight wagons hauled the piles of dried hides, pickled tongues and cured hams to the nearest railroad boxcars. In just two decades the buffalo herds dwindled from 20 million to a few thousand; by 1885 the plains were cleared of buffalo, and the Indians were pretty well penned up on reservations.

The wild horse was next. He had enjoyed almost 200 years of free roaming in the Southwest, his numbers gradually but continuously expanding his ranges, as more feral horses joined the increasing wild herds or strayed from their Indian or frontier

When the white man encountered the Great Plains and its vast buffalo and wild horse herds, he used them to suit his own purposes. The buffalo went first. . . .

masters. Wild horse numbers reached their peak in the early 1800's, reaching approximately two million, with most of these in the Southwest. But then the encroaching white man's civilization began to spread onto the prairies, taking up the land that had been the habitat of the wild horse. Because the horse is a large, mobile animal that imposes heavy demands on the limited amount of space and food available, he immediately suffered when human demands for these same resources began to increase. As civilization marched out onto the Great Plains, the wild herds went. Many wild horses were

As civilization encroached upon the prairies, the wild herds were killed off or pushed out, escaping to the mountains and high deserts where the white man had not yet settled.

directly exterminated by the white men pushing into his domain, and eventually those that were left escaped to the mountains and high deserts where man had not yet settled.

The wild horse is essentially a prairie animal, like the antelope. It was on the prairies that he evolved into his present form; grasslands are his natural habitat and the environment to which he is best suited. A wild horse does not like to go into heavily wooded country or into a brushy creek bottom or canyon, except for water or shelter from the elements. And even then, he prefers a ridge or hill as a windbreak, rather than trees or thicket. Being pursued by man, he took to the brush and the rough mountains as a last resort, but his natural place was the prairies where he could run, where he could see his enemies from a distance. He relied on his swiftness and his keen eyesight for survival and his liberty, not cover or thicket in which to hide.

But the introduction of barbed wire and fencing marked the end of the wild horses on the plains,

and also reduced their numbers elsewhere. By the end of the 19th century—the late 1890's—most of the wild horse concentrations that were left were west of the Rocky Mountains. The Great Plains wild herds were diminishing fast; the wide open spaces were becoming farms and ranches, cities and roads.

Some of the wild horses ended up under saddle; others were shot to get them off the land. Like the buffalo before him, the wild horse was fair game. The United States government tacitly approved the removal of both, because most people felt that the only way the Indian could be completely dominated and halted from his vagabond ways was to get rid of the two animals he depended upon for this nomadic existence—the buffalo and the horse. The expanding United States would not be satisfied until the Indian was tamed and confined to reservations, where he could no longer make war on settlers and could no longer claim the choice lands that the settlers wanted.

By the end of the 19th century the buffalo were already gone and the wild horse herds were diminishing. The wild horse would never disappear completely like the buffalo, however, because the horse was more adaptable. A feral domestic animal like the horse was more versatile than a truly wild animal, and could shift his range and his eating habits more readily without ill effects. The buffalo had his traditional ranges that he had migrated to and from for the last several thousand, perhaps million years. When these ranges were hunted by the professional buffalo hunters, the buffalo did not move from their grounds—they were killed. However, the feral horse had no such instincts, and he was more flexible, and many of his numbers survived.

Mustangs never migrated from north to south and back like the buffalo. The genuine wild species like the buffalo are migratory. But the mixed races of feral horses, having several thousand years of domestication behind them, were not truly wild. They wandered erratically to different grazing regions rather than to a point of the compass. Drought, scarcity of grass, and later the hunting pressure from the white man, caused the wild horse bands to shift irregularly from place to place. And spurred by intensified hunting and pursuit by man, some of the wild horse bands forsook the prairies completely and took to the mountains.

But many of their number were captured or died on the plains. Some ended up as saddle ponies for the cowboys that had the fortitude and cunning to catch them. But the popular notion that the wild herds served as a great source of "cow ponies" for the American cattleman and that the mustang was highly prized as a saddle horse, was not entirely true. Some of the best ones were caught and used as cow horses, but most of the mustangs were looked upon as pests—a nuisance animal to get rid of.

There were actually more well-bred domestic horses used as saddle stock on the early southwestern cattle ranches than mustangs. The early Texas ranchers took good horses with them when they settled, and also purchased horses from neighboring Spanish ranches. According to Frederick Remington, noted western painter of the 1800's, the domestic ranch-raised horses of the Americans were not as stunted as the wild mustangs that were "set back" because of the hard cold winters on the plains.

Yet a great deal of "mustanging" went on, for the outstanding individuals in the wild horse bands were a lure to the cowboys who had hopes of catching one. Wild horses were caught by early Texas settlers and cowboys for sport and profit. When broke to ride, the ones that didn't get killed in the process of capturing or breaking were worth $10 to $12, only about a tenth of what a good "American" horse would bring. But the low price for the mustangs didn't deter their would-be captors, for it was good sport, and there was always a chance of getting a really good one for their own use, and if they did round up some that were salable, it was mildly profitable.

The cowboys on the big cattle outfits enjoyed trying to capture the wild horses now and then, but their employers did not always appreciate the mustangs. To the cattleman the wild herds were worse than a nuisance, for they ate the grass needed by the cattle, and drank the water in an arid land that had little water. The horses drove the cattle away from the salt, broke up water troughs, milled around the springs and dirtied them, and galloped through herds of cattle, knocking them down and killing calves. Because of the wild bands, night herders were needed to guard the saddle stock at every cow camp, and the wild stallions had a bad habit of stealing valuable ranch mares. Also, the horse ate grass as closely as a sheep, and his sharp feet cut up the sod. A horse, with his upper and lower front teeth, can bite off the grass close to the roots, whereas a cow, with no upper front teeth (just a hard palate) wraps her tongue around a bunch of grass and breaks it off with a twist of her head. She cannot crop the grass as closely as a horse.

The rancher shot and captured wild horses, and he also lost some of his well-bred imported horses to the wild bands. During those days of the open range (a ranching tradition that began in the Southwest with the Spanish settlers, because the arid land and sparce forage made vast areas necessary for pasturing livestock; it took a lot of acres to feed each animal) the ranchers' and settlers' domestic stock were pastured out in the unfenced regions and some of these strayed to the wild herds, adding to the remnants of the Spanish and Indian feral stock.

Some of these strays were saddle stock and many were work horses. Many of the wild herds, especially in the North—where there were few, if any, Spanish mustangs to begin with—were made up entirely of stray ranch stock. Ranchers' horses diluted the Spanish blood of the wild herds in the Southwest, and made up many of the northern wild bands entirely. These bands were initially just domestic horses turned loose to graze, rounded up periodically by the ranchers and settlers when they needed them, or wanted to bring in the young horses to train or sell. But as time went on some of these horses went wild, either because they wandered into remote areas where the ranchers had trouble gathering them all, or because some of the ranchers left them out there, not bothering to gather them. Wild horse numbers fluctuated several times, in reaction to certain conditions (which included the price and demand for horses, the numbers of domestic stock turned loose, and so on), but never again reached the vast numbers that had existed in the early 1800's.

As settlers came into an area, the characteristics of the local wild bands soon changed, domestic blood of all types mixing with the already-wild herds. The wild horse of today is no more related to the Spanish mustang than today's ranchers are descendents of the old-time Texas cattle drovers. The old-time cowboys disappeared, like the mustangs, when the conditions that made their existence possible disappeared. The mustang, the tough, hot-blooded descendent of the Spanish horse, disappeared almost entirely by the end of the 19th century.

The tide of settlers coming westward caused the first major dilution of the mustangs, for hundreds of domestic horses became lost or stranded, abandoned along the way because of lameness or exhaustion, or merely turned loose to range. Many of these strays or cast-offs joined wild bands and bred with them, and the characteristics of the wild bands began to change.

One horseman in Texas in 1870 noted that horses on the Texas panhandle grew larger than the mustangs in southern Texas and wrote that some of these larger stallions weighed 1000 to 1100 pounds, a good 400 pounds heavier than the average mustang. He attributed these heavier horses to "American horses lost or stolen by Indians from emigrant trains going to California."

This same conclusion was reached by Thomas

Dwyer, writing in 1872, that some of the Texas wild horses were not only larger, but had a certain power and symmetry that he felt came from "American stallions and mares, which, from time to time, escape their owners and join the mustangs."

Frank Collinson, who worked on a horse ranch in Texas in the 1870's said that the mustangs in northern Texas were not entirely of feral Spanish breeding because the Indians had been stealing good ranch horses in east Texas and from emigrant trains, some of these horses getting loose and mixing with the mustangs. He knew a cattleman in Colorado who bought blooded stallions every year from Kentucky; some of these got away when used to breed range mares. In fact, by the time Collinson came to the plains in the 1870's, the area was "alive with the biggest and best bred mustangs I ever saw, and the fastest. Some that were caught and taken East were the foundation for some of the fastest horses on the Eastern race tracks."

In the Far West, in California, Titus Fey Cronise, while studying the natural resources of California in the 1860's, said that the native Mexican-Spanish horse, "while of great endurance, lightweight, and excels in steady liveliness, was not suited to the demands of American settlers, and American and half breeds [American horses crossed with Spanish horses] are fast supplanting the native stock." The settlers wanted a larger horse that could pull a plow and work in harness as well as being ridden.

What happened in California, with the gold rush and American settlers pouring in, was soon repeated on the Great Plains. James Cook, who lived for 50 years on the frontier, said that by 1880 almost all the Spanish mustangs had disappeared from the plains, and just a few were to be found among some of the Indian herds. But by 1885 even some of the Indian horses were undergoing change. The mustang blood was fast becoming diluted.

For a century before the Civil War, range-raised horses of Spanish breeding moved from the Southwest across the Mississippi at Natchez and St. Louis to help supply the need for horses created by fast growing farm and city populations. These horses were strong and hardy but considered too small for draft, or even for good riding horses. But when mated with larger stallions, the Spanish mares produced good big foals, partly because of the sires and partly because of better pastures, away from the harsh conditions of the range. The western mares were often used to raise good mule foals.

And during the quarter century after the Civil War, probably a million range horses were trailed out of Texas, going east of the Mississippi to pull plows and wagons for cotton farmers, or going to the plains to break sod for homesteaders. Some of these horses were wild mustangs, but many were range horses out of branded Spanish herds, basically the same type of horse in either case. During the 1830's and 40's there were great drives to the east. Then the discovery of gold reversed the flow, as more livestock was needed in California to supply the miners.

But the Spanish mustang did not disappear by being rounded up and driven away. He disappeared through crossbreeding and castration. For a long time, ranch breeders wanted Spanish mares to breed to Morgan, Thoroughbred, Quarter Horse and other types of stallions, and after a while there were no more Spanish mares left.

Thomas A. Dwyer, a lawyer who came to Texas in 1847, mentions that most of the wild horses were undersize—about 13 hands, "showing generally good points in the forequarters, and rather poor in the hindquarters." But some, the result of crossbreeding with escaped American horses, were over 15 hands tall and showed good breeding, "a vast improvement in height, weight, power and symmetry were observed immediately. This visible result induced me, as well as others, to breed fine American blooded stallions and jacks to Mexican mares."

This kind of decision was influenced not only by the good results obtained by crossbreeding good domestic stallions with mustang or Mexican mares, but also by the price of obtaining the brood mares. It would cost a horse breeder $100 for an American-bred mare, compared to $10 or less for a Mexican or wild mare. And the mustang mares, bred to good stallions, had exceptional offspring. As Dwyer pointed out,

> "Evidently the Mexican stock came originally from the south of Spain, where there is a good deal of Arab blood, degenerated if you will, from breeding in and in, etc. but still showing some fine points such as small heads, full bold and lustrous eyes, wide nostrils, small ears, delicate withers, well set shoulders, and flat bones from the knees and hocks down, which signs of good blood are wholly wanting in common American and common European horses."

Recognizing the money to be made by using wild or Mexican mares as broodmares, many people like Thomas Dwyer bred them to blooded American stallions, or to jacks to produce mules.

The Spanish mustang was thus bred out of existence just as the Spanish longhorns were bred out of existence, bred to beefier bulls. The domestic Spanish horses were bred up, and the wild ones were gathered, killed off, or mixed with stray horses of other breeding, until the Spanish type was gone or diluted. The 1870's and 1880's were good days for the mustang hunters, and then as the plains were fenced, the mustangs were killed off or run into New Mexico. Most of the wild horses caught on the northern Texas plains were driven to Kansas, sold there, and shipped East.

There were a few wild horses left in southwest Texas as late as the 1880's, and one large bunch ran free until 1902, although in a large fenced pasture of 130,000 acres (it was fenced in 1881). The wild horses had been fenced in inadvertantly, and remained there, hiding in the brushy areas. As this country was settled and fenced, the wild horse took to the hills and the brush, like the deer and the coyote. And also like the deer and the coyote, he managed to stay longer in the midst of civilization than most other wild animals. The mustangs in the fenced pasture in Live Oak County thrived for two decades, though they were chased by a number of people and some of them captured. In 1902, part of the land was sold, and the new owner hired several different parties to try to round up the wild horses. Eventually the bulk of them were captured and the

Range horses—1910. photos courtesy Chester Bowman.
Range horses being corralled—1905.

rest shot. There are no wild horses in southwest Texas now. These last wild horses had degenerated so badly that they were hardly worth capturing.

By the time Nevada was starting to make her history, the history of the Spanish mustang was almost finished. Nevada was one of the last areas of the continental U.S. to be explored and settled. It had not attracted Spanish settlement. And the Spanish horse did not make it to Nevada via the Indians. The tribes that lived in the inhospitable Great Basin were some of the most destitute of all American Indians, scattered over the desert in small isolated bands and lacking large-scale social organization. If they had encountered a horse, they would have been more likely to eat it than to put it to any other use. Thus there were no wild horses in Nevada when white explorers and early settlers went there.

The wild horses that spread over Nevada were horses from the East, American horses. Some of them carried the blood of heavy draft horses— Percherons, Belgians, Suffolks, Clydesdales and Shires—and some were crossed with lighter breeds such as the Thoroughbred, Hackney, Morgan, and coach horses. The demand for horses was great as mining towns sprang up, and the need for big horses to pull freight wagons and stagecoaches and ore wagons was increasing.

Ranchers brought their own horses to Nevada and turned them loose to pasture on the range, harvesting them when new mining booms created a demand for them. And when hard times came, many ranchers, instead of feeding their work stock, turned them loose also. The wild horse herds that sprang up in the West in the early 1900's were as much a melting pot of breeds as were the settlers and ranchers who established their homes there.

Sturdy mares from Oregon (brought to Oregon by settlers, for use as harness and work horses) and stallions from Kentucky built the free-roaming herds in Arizona that later found a ready market in the Boer War. The stockmen who went into northern Arizona between 1878 and 1880 found no wild horses, but within a few short years their own domestic horses on the range had multiplied so much that they numbered in the tens of thousands. In other areas of the Southwest there were already Spanish mustangs, and the settlers turned loose good mares and stallions with them, using the offspring later when they could catch them.

The first settlers in the Pacific Northwest found no wild horses except for the Indian horses. The wild bands that subsequently grew up here and there in the Northwest were stray settler's and ranch horses, saddle stock and draft animals mixed. In the rough country, mountains and deserts, especially of

Arizona, Nevada and Oregon, wild herds flourished from about 1885 on. There were perhaps 100,000 horses in Nevada as late as 1910—more horses than citizens.

In California and Oregon, horse raising got a boost after the discovery of gold. California had had horses for a long time. Right after the Seven Years War (1756-1763, in which England defeated several European powers and seized French colonies in America) Spain made a great effort to colonize California and hold back encroachment by other nations. Spanish ports and settlements were established at San Diego, Monterey, and San Francisco, and a string of 21 missions was created along the coast. The first breeding stock for these mission farms was brought from the older missions in Lower California. The coast range from San Francisco to Los Angeles was excellent pasture for livestock, with mild winters and very few predators. Livestock prospered and filled the grazing lands around each mission, and by 1800 the missions had a total of 24,000 horses, 74,000 cattle and 88,000 sheep, averaging more than a thousand horses for each mission—more than were needed for the farm work and cattle herding. As the range horses multiplied, some wandered into the hills or into the swamplands of the central valley and became wild. When the wild horse bands became so large that they ate the grass needed for the cattle and sheep, people killed them by the thousands.

From 1800 until the gold rush in 1849 the California ranchers consistently raised more horses than they needed, even though there was no real market for the extra horses, and these were often allowed to go wild. The Indians in the Sierra mountains to the east stole some of the horses to eat. Trapper explorer Zenas Leonard wrote about the California prairies swarming with horses during the early 1830's.

A few years later, James H. Carson, a '49er who worked at several diggings and wrote an account of California during the gold rush, said that the San Joaquin Valley "perhaps contains a larger portion of wild horses than any other part of the world of the same extent. On the western side of the San Joaquin (River) there are to be seen bands from 200 to 2000."

John Birdwell, one of the first Americans to settle in California, wrote that some wild horse herds in the San Joaquin Valley were 20 miles long. Ranchers exterminated thousands of wild horses during drought years to save the grass. In one great drought during 1828-1830, about 40,000 head of horses and cattle died. Some horses were driven off the cliffs into the ocean at Purisima and Santa Barbara.

The greatest number of wild horses in California roamed the coast hills and west side of the San Joaquin River. Wild horses east of the river and into the Sierra Nevada Mountains got a later start, when ranch owners drove their horses over there, evading government edicts to slaughter their horses during a drought. But the ranchers never went back, and the horses multiplied.

Then with the gold rush, and the upsurging population of prospectors and miners, the market for horses increased, but it was mostly a market for larger "American" horses instead of the small Spanish wild horse. Some of the Spanish horses from California were brought to Oregon by two early ranchers, where they were crossed with American breeds. These crossbreeds, mixed with Indian horses, were the start of the large wild herds in Oregon.

E. R. Jackson expresses this in *The Oregon Desert*, stating that there were no wild horses in Oregon when the settlers first went there. While the wild horses were reaching their peak in Texas, there were still no wild horses in Oregon, even though it was probably more settled than any other western state of the mid 1800's. When Lewis and Clark went through it in 1805, most of the Oregon Indians still didn't have horses—just the Nez Perce, Shoshonis, Cayuse and Snake Indians had horses, indicating that the horses of these tribes came directly north from New Mexico, and not up the coast from California. Horses didn't appear on the Oregon desert until it was settled, and it wasn't really very settled until after the last of the Indian wars in 1878.

Speaking of Indian wars, I might just mention that one of the reasons it took the Americans so long to subdue the Indians was that their early cavalry was often out-done and out-distanced by the scrubby little Indian horses (a fact that was often a sore spot with the Army officers). The main problem was the Army's theory about conducting war on horseback. Instead of adopting the Indians' tactic of traveling light and fast, the Army officers liked each soldier on active duty to carry along enough gear to be ready for anything. It was a nice theory, but it was a burden to the horse. Therefore, cavalry warfare needed a large, strong horse to carry all that gear—tack, weapons, ammunition, mess kit, canteen, overcoat, blanket, bed sheet, halter, picket rope, rations, feed bag and oats.

To get the large horses needed for this sort of excursion, saddle mares of mixed breeding were bred to draft horses to increase the size, and the results bred to a Thoroughbred to increase the speed. Thus, the typical cavalry horse in those days was half Thoroughbred, a quarter draft horse and a quarter mixed saddle stock, and averaged 16 hands

The typical western horses of the late 1800's and early 1900's were large animals—horses that could be ridden or worked in harness. (photos courtesy Chester Bowman)

tall and 1100-1200 pounds. Thus he needed more feed than a smaller horse, and often grain, in order to keep up with the Indian pony. The Indian war party on the other hand traveled light, with the horses carrying merely a bridle and saddle pad, weapons, a small robe and a parcel of dried meat. Thus the small horses weren't overburdened, and being tough and conditioned to rough country and conditions, they outran the U.S. cavalry time and time again.

After Oregon was settled, many of the early pioneers raised horses, some of them counting their horses in the thousands. All of the homesteaders who owned horses pastured them out on the desert part or all of the year, and during hard times or low horse prices, many of these horses just stayed out there, maybe 10 years or more. The stallions gathered harems, the mares had foals, and these feral herds just kept increasing.

The characteristics of wild herds of this period were sharply altered by crossbreeding with domestic stock, comprised primarily of heavy horses for pulling and farm work, rather than saddle stock. The

typical "American" horse was a product of the multi-purpose needs of the farmer, and the needs of a growing commerce; the horses had to be big enough to work in harness for pulling all the various freight and delivery wagons and conveyances. And on the farm, a horse had to be able to pull a plow, pull a spring wagon for a trip to town, or to be ridden to round up the cows from the back pasture.

Big horses were much in demand to work in harness, so much of the domestic stock turned loose to run with the wild bands were draft horses. Many a purebred Percheron or Clydesdale stallion was turned out in the hills to sire future pulling horses among the range herds; the offspring of the draft horse and the small wild mares often made good light teams, ideal for harness or farm work or for haying. Some of these crossbreds also made excellent bucking horses if they turned "outlaw", having the power and strength of the work horse and some of the toughness, agility and spirit of the wild horse. Before the days of the open range were over, the mustang blood had been diluted, and the wild horse could, in most cases, no longer be recognized as a descendent of Spanish stock.

As horse ranching in the West increased after 1870, the prices of horses decreased and soon they were not profitable to raise. From 1870 til the 1890's, there was an increase in the wild horse populations, because many ranchers just let some of their stock roam, no longer bothering to brand the offspring or round them up. Saddle horses were hard to sell at any price, and the ranges filled up with unbroken, and often unbranded, horses. In Oregon between 1895 and 1900 many stockmen neglected to brand their range animals and the wild horse herds grew—herds that were to become very numerous in southeastern Oregon by the 1920's.

But when the Boer War broke out in South Africa, creating a large demand for horses, westerners again became horse breeders, and also started rounding up the range herds. Since many of these horses had never been ridden, and buyers wanted only broken horses, cowboys made a few dollars "gentling" them. The British government had men in ten western states buying horses by the thousands, to send to South Africa. Sound horses 5 to 9 years old were worth $40 each, cash. Thousands of wild horses were caught and shipped, and since some of them died en route and many were killed in action, the strong demand for horses continued until the war ended in 1902. By that time the range herds had been reduced and the country was recovering from hard times. But wild horses were again worthless; their quality had deteriorated badly because the best had been captured. From 1903-1914, when a good domestic two-year-old brought only $5 to $10, no one bothered to capture the wild ones.

In 1898, the same time as the Boer War, the U.S. Army mounted troops for the invasion of the Spanish possessions, turning to contractors and subcontractors who bought horses all over the U.S. and some of the horses bought were wild ones. After the turn of the century, the government took a hand in horse breeding for the first time, mainly because of the difficulty in getting horses for the Army. In 1910 the contract system of buying horses was supplemented by the establishment of several remount breeding establishments, using well bred mares and stallions. But even then there were not enough horses, especially after World War I cut deeply into American horse numbers. The United States supplied over a million horses to France, England, and so on, before mechanized forces became so important.

This had a great effect on the wild herds in the West. Ranchers again began to round up their unbranded stock and to turn good stallions and mares loose on the range to produce more horses. During World War I, amateur and professional mustangers in Rocky Mountain regions found they could sell all the wild horses they could catch, and make a fair living selling horses for $30 to $40 a head.

About this time the Army started the Remount Service, putting out Thoroughbred, Arabian and Morgan stallions maintained at the expense of a private individual. The army reserved the right to purchase any young horse sired by these Remount stallions, but did not guarantee to buy it. In this way, good quality half-bred stock could be raised for the Army. Many of the western ranch horses and saddle horses were upgraded this way, and some of the wild herds along with them. More than a few ranchers who kept a Remount stallion turned him loose on the range to run with privately owned range mares, to produce good half-bred foals. And of course, a few of the offspring ended up going wild.

Some of the better quality "wild" horses of today can trace their ancestry back to a good Remount stallion or privately owned purebred saddle-type stallion on the western ranges a few years back. For instance, in the 1930's an Oregon rancher imported a good Thoroughbred stallion from England to cross with his mares. The horse was temporarily infertile after the trip from England and the rancher thought he was no good, and just turned him out on the range. The next year lots of good half-Thoroughbred foals cropped up among the wild range mares. The rancher and his friends tried to recapture the stallion but were unsuccessful; he was too swift. He stayed on the range and sired good foals for many years.

After World War I the wild bands increased again, especially on the northern ranges. Farm horses were replaced by tractors, and since there was no market for work horses, many were simply turned out on the range in "retirement" to take care of themselves. In 1925 there were more than a million "wild" horses. The "wild" blood was further diluted during the depression of the 1930's when many farmers and ranchers went out of business. When the wheat farmers of the northern plains moved out, many draft horses joined the wild bands.

Montana, for instance, did not have a range problem with wild horses until the wheat farmers turned loose their horses after World War I. Horses were then worthless, and no one bothered to round up any to sell. The range was already overstocked with domestic livestock of all kinds (ranchers had been agitating and badgering Congress for some kind of control and regulation of livestock grazing ever since the 1880's, but so far Congress had done nothing about it) and now had the extra burden of unwanted and unclaimed horses. Many of the poor conditions still existing today on some of the Western ranges are considered by many range experts to be a direct result of the large uncontrolled horse herds in the late 1920's and 30's—herds that outgrew their range capacity and ate the plants into the ground. With more controlled use of the range in subsequent years it has improved, but in some areas still has a long way to go.

A few horses found a market during the 1920's. The pet food industry was getting started, and horsemeat was also used to some extent in chicken feed and as human food. Also, there was an increase in the use of horses by the southern farmers; cotton prices had dropped and tractors were too expensive for them. A few of the horses that were shipped South as work horses were rounded up off Western ranges. But these few markets were not large enough to make much of a dent in the expanding wild horse populations of the 1920's.

Farmers in western Kansas complained in 1929 about the unclaimed stray horses running loose, tearing down their fences, and trampling their spring wheat. But the situation was even worse in the Western range states. Montana and Wyoming had the largest stray horse population. The agricultural development of these areas before the War had brought thousands of immigrants to the Western states, all of them bringing horses. Many of these horses were soon replaced by tractors. Then when the dry years came, and agricultural prices dropped and farmers went broke, most of them picked up and went East, turning loose their horses, because they were mortgaged for more than they were worth. More than one hundred thousand unclaimed horses wandered over the public lands in these states, breaking through fences into private farm and pastureland, and inhabiting the mountain regions and inaccessible border areas and Missouri River breaks.

These horses had become a serious menace to the livestock industry, and the cattlemen of Montana were the first to really organize countermeasures. The Montana legislature authorized the gathering of the wild herds by the stockmen through county roundups. The first of the roundups began in 1925, and in subsequent years roundups were held in 26 of Montana's 56 counties. Each roundup was advertised in advance, so that any horse owner who might have stray horses in that area could come and claim his branded horses, after paying his share of the roundup costs. The remaining horses were sold to horse buyers, who in turn sold them as light work teams or to rendering plants.

Soon after Montana started trying to reduce its stray horse herds, Wyoming followed suit, authorizing county commissioners to conduct horse roundups. One buyer shipped 22,000 horses from Wyoming's Big Horn Basin during 1933 and 1934.

In eastern Washington and Oregon the abandoned domestic horses had also become a nuisance. In Washington the worst problem was near the Yakima Indian reservation, where wild herds were made up chiefly from the reservation's escaped horses. There was no legislative action in Washington, but the cattlemen organized locally and removed most of the horses, selling them to a Yakima dog food plant.

The range conditions were much worse in eastern Oregon. The mustangers and ranchers hadn't been able to capture the horses in the rough country bordering Nevada and Idaho, and these had increased almost unchecked. World War I prices for horses had encouraged mustangers in eastern Oregon, but after the price declined again many ranchers let their range herds go unbranded and ungathered. In 1928 there were estimated to be at least 10,000 horses on the Oregon desert in the southern part of Malheur County.

Mustangers had already reduced Nevada's wild horse population, (some of them had even sold branded horse-hides to the hide dealers, which resulted in a state law preventing the removal of wild horses from the range without permission from county authorities) so not much wild horse removal went on in the 1920's or early 30's. In 1897 the legislature had passed a law permitting the killing of unbranded horses because of the over-population of "worthless" horses (horse numbers in Nevada at that time far outnumbered the people), but it was repealed in 1901 and mustangers now had to obtain

permission from county authorities and post a bond guaranteeing that they would take no branded horses from the range.

Southern Utah had more than 15,000 loose horses in the late 1920's, and Colorado had a few, but there was not as much roundup activity in these states. Texas had eliminated its wild horse problems by the early 1900's. New Mexico ranchers began rounding up feral horses in 1925 when drought conditions on the range made it necessary. The Indian reservations in New Mexico were a constant source of feral horses on the surrounding ranges. The Forest Service at this time began gathering horses in that state, and thousands were sold to Texas rendering plants. There they were made into fertilizer, cat and dog food and fish food at about $2 to $3 a head. The drought also forced Arizona cattlemen to start rounding up horses at about the same time.

By then the ranges were in sad shape, except in the few areas where local ranchers worked together to control overgrazing. In many places where there was open range, the nearby ranches and farms pastured their cattle, their dry milk cows, their sheep and their work teams. Many ranchers who did not "farm" the soil still had to have work teams to put up their hay, and pastured these teams on the range except when needed during haying season.

The federal government had done nothing to regulate grazing, and some stockmen in the late 1800's had made attempts to try to regulate and improve it themselves. Some tried to halt the overgrazing by buying, leasing or filing upon the watering places, and putting in fences to control the use of them—whereupon the Department of Interior declared the fences illegal. Government land management practices (or lack of them) at that time were unknowingly geared to increase rather than decrease the stress and overgrazing of the public lands.

It was almost impossible for the ranchers to regulate and control the overgrazing by themselves. Even if several ranchers in an area held their cattle off the range in early spring to let the grass grow, there was always some unscrupulous neighbor who turned his out early anyway and got the grass. Anyone who attempted to practice good range management just didn't get his share of the grass. In spite of continuous attempts by ranchers to introduce bills in Congress that would allow leasing or some kind of permit system (to keep a few greedy people from turning out more livestock than the range could support), grazing on the public lands outside the national forests was entirely unregulated until the Taylor Grazing Act, which became law on June 28, 1934.

This act of Congress, named for Edward Taylor

—a veteran spokesman for the stockman and irrigation farmers—set up a system of controls to keep the range from being misused like it had been since 1890. It allotted each rancher a certain number of cattle, sheep or horses that could be turned out to graze on federal lands. Rules for seasonal use came into being. In the northern parts of the West that did not have a year-long growing season, the grazing animals could no longer run at large all year-around. The stock was to be taken off the range for winter and kept off through early spring when the hillsides were thawing and soft. At this time large animals could easily tramp out the root systems of the bunch grasses or eat every spear of green before it had a chance to grow. A large animal like a horse or cow, grazing on a thawing or spring-rain-soaked hillside, could sink into the mud at each step, gouging out the grass and leaving deep slide-marks and trails that hastened erosion. Range use by domestic livestock was to be only in the late spring through fall, after the grass had gotten a start.

Regional offices, each managed by a trained range specialist, were set up in key cities in the western range states. Grazing districts were drawn up, and range use was granted by grazing licenses and paid fees, under carefully prescribed conditions that assured the range would not be overgrazed. The "carrying capacity" of each range area was evaluated, and the various ranchers who used it could only turn out a certain number of livestock. A rancher could not turn out more livestock than he could put up winter feed for on his home place.

Part of the grazing fees went back into improvements on the range—water developments, crossfencing for controlling and rotating the grazing and so on. Under these regulations, the depleted ranges slowly began to come back. The Taylor Grazing Act brought a long-needed sense of order to domestic livestock grazing on the federal lands, helping to prevent future misuse of the range, but also spelling the end for the large herds of feral horses.

Now that the emphasis on federal lands was placed on management and controlled use of the grass, rather than lack of control and further degeneration of soil, watershed and native plants, the range experts looked upon the wild horse as a menace to the range itself, as well as a nuisance to the stockman. The wild horse, living on the range year-round, damaging the ground and the new plants in the spring, ate more grass than two cows or ten sheep.

Range studies in the northern climates, where plants are dormant part of the year, showed that yearlong grazing is damaging. Survival and growth of plants is dependent upon stored food reserves

In many mountain areas of the Northwest, deep snows at higher elevations force horses to spend their winters at lower elevations, concentrating the horses at lower elevations and overusing that part of their range.

This hillside is showing evidence of early erosion. Much of the plant cover is gone, due to overgrazing, and the soil is not held very well.

(carbohydrate reserves in various parts of the plant). The important grasses in a horse's diet have stored most of their carbohydrate reserves by the time their seeds are ripe. If some fall regrowth occurs because of a wet fall, some of these reserves are used up and decreased. Food reserves are produced in the above ground parts of the plant, primarily the leaves, by photosynthesis.

Defoliation—having the leaves eaten off—is most harmful when the reserves are lowest. This is usually in the early spring when the plant is starting to grow most rapidly. Studies showed that defoliation of plants in early spring is much more detrimental than late in the fall. Horses grazing the plants closely in early spring, when the plants are starting to grow, greatly reduces plant vigor and can lead to killing out these overgrazed plants if it happens several years in a row.

On the great prairies, before the land was taken up by the white man, the wild horse roamed with the seasons, confined to no particular area, moving on to better grass. He ate out the areas around the waterholes in dry seasons when water was scarce, but in general he did not stay overlong in any one place and did not seem to permanently damage the majority of his habitat. But in the mountain regions (most of them farther north than the original great herds of horses on the southwestern plains), where the last of the wild herds was forced to go, and joined by herds of more recent strays, the situation was not as well suited to year-round grazing by large bands of horses.

In some of these isolated mountain retreats, the wild horses had limited grazing area and were forced to overuse parts of their range. In the northern regions, where winters were hard, deep snows at higher elevations forced the horses to winter in lower, less expansive parts of their range where feed was more accessible, thus overusing that portion of their habitat. And when spring came, the wild horse often damaged the thawing hillsides and overgrazed the new green grasses because he was half-starved.

The wide-open spaces of the prairies were no longer his for the roaming; the wild horse was confined now in more remote mountain and desert ranges, away from the farmland of the valleys and the population centers. And if his herd numbers outgrew his isolated areas' feed supply, he overgrazed it. And if on part of his range he was also competing with domestic cattle and sheep and wildlife, he was resented for his use of the grass and his damage to the range, and he was often hunted down.

After the Taylor Grazing Act, ranchers had to have a permit (and pay grazing fees) for any of their own horses pastured on federal land. And these horses were not supposed to be out there all year, as many ranchers' horses had been in the past. Horses were to stay off the range in winter and early spring when they were most apt to damage it. But some ranchers, especially those who had been pasturing horses on the range for many years, resented the new regulations and left their horses out, sometimes running unbranded ones on the range in order to avoid grazing and "trespass" fees. The Grazing Service sometimes served trespass notice on owners of branded unlicensed horses, threatening arrest unless the horses were removed. And if the grazing officials had to round up the trespass horses, the owner of the branded ones could not get his horses back without first paying the trespass fine. If no one claimed the horses, they were sold at public auction.

When the Taylor Grazing Act was passed, there were approximately 150,000 wild horses and strays on public lands in 11 western states. But range managers considered the wild horses a threat to the range, and ranchers were now reluctant to share their assigned (and paid for) grazing areas with wild horse bands. A more concentrated effort was launched to reduce the wild horse numbers. Ranchers, professional mustangers, and the government agencies in charge of the federal ranges cooperated on roundups.

By 1940 there were a few trespass stray horses in eastern Montana, but no more unclaimed, abandoned or wild horses in that state. In Wyoming many wild horses died during the drought of 1934, and many more were rounded up; 4000 were removed between 1936 and 1940. By February, 1940, the official number of unowned horses at large in that state was about 14,000. The Grazing Service cooperated with local ranchers in removing horses in Idaho, and in some areas the wild horse populations were greatly reduced or eliminated.

After the Taylor Grazing Act made it mandatory for ranchers to pay a grazing fee and have a permit to graze their horses on public land for 7 months of the year (they had to be at home on private pasture or on feed the other 5 months), feral horses were greatly reduced in Oregon. Before that, there were more than 25,000 running on the public domain, 40% of them unbranded. There were many cowboys who had no ranches, but who owned brands and ran horses on the Oregon desert.

After the Grazing Service came into existence, a person had to have base property on which to keep his stock for part of the year. Consequently these cowboys and horse raisers had to quit; some of them left, and left their horses running loose. Eventually many of these horses were rounded up by ranchers and stockmen's organizations, and the Grazing Service. By 1940 there were only 11,682 licensed horses on the ranges in southeastern Oregon, and only about 1000 unbranded wild horses left, running the range in scattered bands.

Wild horse numbers in the other western states were also reduced during the late 1930's. Local stockmen's organizations had used airplane roundups fairly successfully in Utah, though there were still wild bands in some of the more inaccessible areas. Cowboys and mustangers in Nevada gathered some horses, and in 1935 the Federal Bureau of Animal Husbandry removed about 500 because of dourine—a serious contagious venereal disease of horses (characterized by local swelling, then progressive anemia and emaciation, and finally paralysis and death). But in most of Nevada there were still wild horses. Colorado, New Mexico and Arizona had all reduced their wild horse numbers considerably.

World War II brought a temporary halt to wild horse roundups, for people were too busy with the war to bother with the wild horses. But after the war was over, horse gathering again gained momentum. In 1946 the Grazing Service became the Bureau of Land Management, continuing the same basic policies of range management and trying to enforce the rules for range use. Part of this policy was to remove the feral horses, and to get the trespass horses off the range.

But the biggest factor in the reduction of the wild horse herds during the late 1940's and early 1950's was not the government policy nor the ranchers' dislike for the wild horse's abuse of the range, but the market for horseflesh. During the 1940's and 50's more than 100,000 horses were removed from Nevada rangelands and smaller numbers were taken from other states. The use of horsemeat for chicken food began in the 1920's in California. The railroads for awhile shipped horses at a special "chicken feed" rate; by designating them as chicken feed they were under no obligation to feed or water the horses en route. Thousands of horses went to California this way, bought for one cent a pound or less off the range as far east as the Dakotas. This was almost the only market for scrub wild horses when prices for horses were low.

Then along came another market—the canned cat and dog food industry. It had its small beginnings in 1934, and by 1945 had become a $25,000,000 industry. It is a billion dollar industry today, with $2,604,000,000 worth of pet food sold in 1976. In 1945 there was one dog for every 10 people (number of cats unknown), and this number has undoubtedly increased. By 1935 there were about 200 firms in the U.S. making dogfood. Records in the USDA, tabulating the number of pounds of dogfood canned each year, show the greatest increase during the years the wild horse herds were being reduced in the early thirties. Not all the horses processed into pet food came from the wild herds, but the majority of them did at that time. A report written in 1939 stated that wild horses were ground into dog food and chicken feed at the rate of 100,000 or more per year. The USDA inspection dealt with 30,000-130,000 each year for several years during the 1930's.

The American public did not protest, for times were different then. The horses were not "wild mustangs" but merely stray ranch horses or degenerate scrubs. To quote Walker D. Wyman in his book *The Wild Horse of the West* (published in 1945), "rather than preserve degenerate estrays, it is better to look backward to that which once was, and cease thinking of perpetuating that which does not exist"—speaking of the disappearance of Spanish mustangs. In an earlier chapter of his book he stated that, "nobody except the tourist wanted this (stray) horse on the range . . . starvation produced an unattractive, stunted horse no larger than a child's pony. Not only economic but humane considerations sent this animal to the cauldron." The average American's feelings on the subject of wild horse slaughter for pet food were more practical than emotional, and many didn't care. The few protests that were raised fell upon deaf ears.

Another industry that reduced the wild horses during the late 1920's and early 30's was the processing of horsemeat for human consumption. Horse slaughtering and processing plants under federal jurisdiction grew in number from 1923 until 1930. During this period thousands of wild horses were disappearing from the western ranges, and export figures for that period show the same trend—an increase in the pounds of horsemeat in the form of cured meat, chopped and smoked meats and sausages being shipped to Europe.

Some of the horsemeat consumed by humans was not inspected, however, as during the depression years many a poverty-stricken American family supplied its protein needs by eating horsemeat intended as pet food. Many of the pet food canneries, though not federally inspected, had high quality and sanitary standards. They put out good-quality edible meat with no waste, cooked and ready to serve, at 10¢ or less for a one-pound can. The strong demand for low-grade horses for pet food cleared out the scrubs from domestic pastures, and reduced the numbers of wild horses on the western ranges.

Thus, the era of the wild horse was nearly over. His ever-fluctuating numbers were now in sharp decline. He had had his heyday on the vast prairies before the white man's expanding nation grew westward and pushed him off. Now the mixed descendents of the little Spanish horses, the tough but runty Indian horses, settlers' plow horses, ranchers' cowhorses and farmers' work teams—the modern day feral horse of mixed type and ancestry, of all shapes and sizes and colors—was making what some people considered his last stand in the more remote and inaccessible mountain areas of the West. He had been met by civilization, reshaped by it, and as always (but now more than ever) used by it. And it began to look like the wild herds would soon be gone.

4

The Mustangers

The catching of wild horses is a sport almost as old as history. Until the machine age, man was dependent upon the horse, and wherever there were wild horses, he helped himself. Wild horse catching was never easy, however, and the enticement of it was as much the challenge as it was the end product. Even after the advent of the machine age, there was interest in catching wild horses, not only for the economic gain involved, but for the challenge. And much romance and drama has been centered on the capturing (or attempting to capture) wild horses. Many a piece of fiction and many a western movie has used this theme. Many a youngster and many a dreamer has wistfully romanticized about catching wild horses.

But in recent years there has been a shift of feeling about this subject. Because of the declining numbers of free-roaming horses over the last thirty years; because of the sometimes inhumane methods of the mustangers who chased them; and because of the increasing trend for Americans today to think in terms of conservation, preservation and protection of the wild horse; mustanging has taken on a different meaning. Among the majority of Americans, wild horse chasing is no longer romanticized. Instead, it is often looked upon as wicked, inhumane, cruel and bloody.

Yet mustanging had been a respectable activity for 300 years. The original wild horse chasers in North America were the Indians. They already had Spanish horses and had learned how to use the horse, so they began to capture some of the horses from the growing wild bands to add to their own herds. Indian methods of capturing wild horses were discussed in Chapter 2. Some of the white man's methods were similar. California cowboys, riding with only a bridle and surcingle (to which a long rope was tied) chased and roped wild horses.

In the late 1840's and 50's, Mexican families in the Rio Grande watershed made their living capturing wild horses and wild cattle. Some of these Mexican ranchers traveled into wild horse country in the early spring, camping there with their families and chasing horses until fall. Some of them specialized in capturing young horses, sometimes catching as many as 100 in a season. Some rode bareback, with a lariat tied to a well padded rope around the horse's neck, while chasing the wild herd, and roping and tying the young foals that fell behind. These were picked up by other members of the party following behind, and taken to camp. The caravan included milk cows and burros, and the foals would be fed milk from the cows.

On the "Wild Horse Desert" of Texas, cowboys

rode bareback, tying lariats around their horse's necks and roping wild horses when they could get close enough. This was dangerous sport, especially if other running horses got mixed up in the rope.

Jack Thorp, a New Mexico cowboy, told about a mustanging family in the late 19th century who made annual treks up from Mexico to capture horses. The younger, lighter members of the family, two girls, mounted on good horses, would chase the wild ones. When one of them got up alongside one of the wild ones, she would slip from her horse onto the back of the running mustang, taking with her a hair rope about 10 feet long, which she looped over his head, making a makeshift halter. Her sister would catch the horse she had departed from and bring it back to camp. After letting the wild horse run until it was nearly exhausted, the mounted captor would eventually stop him, using the rope, turn him and bring him back to camp. The younger children of the family were kept busy herding the newly-broken wild horses during the day, and they were kept penned at night. After the family caught about 50 mustangs they would head back to Mexico to spend the winter, selling their catch on the way or after they got home.

The term mustanger has come to mean any person who makes his living, for at least part of the year, capturing horses for profit. But many of the horse chasers down through history, including recent days, were horsemen who did it for sport. Many a cowboy went after a bunch of wild horses, trying to catch a particular animal that had caught his eye—a horse that he wanted to own. Mustanging was a form of recreation and adventure. To capture and ride the wildest, most fleet and beautiful mustang in the herd was the highest ambition of many cowboys in those days, when every man used horses. Most men prized fine horses, just as today they take pride in a fine automobile, and the wild horses could be obtained by anyone who had the patience and skill to catch them.

A method sometimes used by wild horse catchers was snaring—using a loop of rope on the ground by a water hole or salt-lick, or a loop in a brushy trail where a horse might be caught by the head. These tricks were not always successful, for it was difficult to hide the loop so that the wild horse would not detect it. The foot trap was developed in Nevada in 1911, made from a small wooden box that was carefully buried in a horse trail going to a water hole, and the loop in the box then tied to a log or tree. A spring trigger was attached to it with light twine. When a horse stepped in the trap, the twine snapped, releasing the trigger and causing the rope to fly up and encircle the horse's leg. When the

horse jerked back, the rope tightened. If tied to an immovable object, the horse might break its leg, so it was usually tied to a log. The horse could drag the log, leaving a trail to follow.

But most mustangers used more active methods, attempting to rope a wild horse from horseback, or to drive a band of horses into a hidden corral. Some mustangers roped individual horses after they had come down to a waterhole to drink, being able to catch up with the wild horse easily, because it was full of water and not able to run as fast. The mustanger might throw and tie the roped horse, and immediately take off after another member of the herd. A good roper could sometimes capture 4 or 5 horses from a water-logged herd this way. Many mustangers felt that the best "trap" was a fast horse and a long rope.

The earliest account of corraling wild horses came from Mexico in the mid 1700's. Apache raiders had taken most of the horses and mules from Sonora, so the settlement built sturdy corrals at the water holes, with wings leading to the corral made from cut branches, ready to catch wild horse bands coming in to water. At the approach of wild horses, riders burst out from hiding places behind them, driving them into the corral. People on foot hid along the wings, adding to the commotion as the horses were driven toward the corral, frightening the herd in the proper direction.

The first American mustanger was Philip Nolan, who made four trips into Texas from Louisiana between 1790 and 1800, capturing wild horses. On his first trip he lived with the Comanches and captured 50 head, and on the second trip he brought back 250. He brought even more from his third trip (having bought part of them from the Indians), but on his fourth trip he was killed by the Spanish.

Wild horses roamed the Texas plains in great numbers by 1800, along with many herds of range horses belonging to the Spanish ranchers. American mustangers claimed they captured nothing but wild horses, but the Spaniards were certain some of their tame ones were also being driven off. The captured horses found a ready market at Natchez, or went to sugar plantations near New Orleans. New settlers west of the Allegheny Mountains were able to buy work horses caught from the plains cheaper than they could buy eastern horses that were being bought up by the stage lines, freight companies and other non-farm operations.

The process of penning wild horses developed with time and local conditions. By 1870 hundreds of corrals had been built by the Mexicans between the Nueces and Rio Grande Rivers. Some were simple pens around water holes, where a night watcher waited, hidden, to shut the gate on a band if they came in to drink. This type of corral worked only if water was scarce. All other water holes in the area would be "spooked" by putting rags or upturned sagebrush around them—anything to make the horses suspicious and keep them from watering there. Eventually the thirsty horses would use the only water hole available—the one with the trap.

The larger catches were made in big corrals with wings, into which many men would attempt to drive several bands. The big corrals were often built in spiral form, or in the shape of a figure eight (double circle) to keep the horses from doubling back when they came into the corral. The "spiral" corral was circular, but built so that when the horses ran in at the gate, following the fence, they would be directed by the inward curve of the fence toward the middle of the pen when they came back around to the gate. Instead of trying to run out the gate again they were deflected toward the center and would continue to mill about the corral. These corrals were usually 50 to 60 feet in diameter.

Corrals were strategically located so that the horses would not see them or suspect a trap until too late. Sometimes a corral was built on a well-used trail or at a creek crossing, places that the horses used regularly. These corrals often had a gate at each end, so that the horses could go through them and become accustomed to the corral, until the day of the roundup, when one end would be shut. The unsuspecting horses would go right in, only to find the other end blocked.

The professional mustanger usually built his corrals in trees or brush for concealment, making it circular so the horses couldn't stampede into a corner and break it. Sometimes a corral was built by digging a trench where the fence was to go, then placing sturdy posts upright in the trench and tamping dirt around them. Then the tops of the posts were well tied together with strong strips of rawhide. This made a fence that was strong and hard to break, yet somewhat elastic if a horse hit it. Wing fences were usually made from brush or treetops; one wing was often a half mile or more in length, the other shorter. Often the gateposts were carefully hidden by brush.

When ready for the chase, a rider would be stationed and hidden at each wing-end, and the other horsemen would run a band in the direction of the corral, turning them down the long wing as they approached. The rider from the short wing would appear, keeping the horses running against the long wing toward the gate. As soon as the horses were in the pen, a man would quickly put up a pole or two across the opening and throw a blanket across them

Wing fence, tied into a rock outcropping. This fence was used to guide oncoming horses into a concealed corral in the timber at right, built along the horses' trail to water.

Part of the old corral in the timber, using trees as corral posts.

to serve as a gate. The horses would not try to crash the solid-looking blanket. Then the horses could be roped, sidelined (front leg tied to hind), allowing only about 12 inches stepping space, and then driven to water or grazing. When driving the herd to market, they would be unhobbled a few at a time as they learned to drive and stay with the bunch.

In rougher country, catch corrals were often made in a canyon, or around a bend in a brushy creek bottom. But on the plains, concealing a corral or making wings to it was more difficult. Furrows were sometimes plowed out for half a mile or more from the corral each way to serve as wings, because the wild horses feared the line of upturned sod and would not cross it. Wire hung with rags was also used for wings in areas that had no brush.

Another way that wild horses were caught was "walking them down". Usually two or more riders relieved each other, taking turns following a wild band over a period of several days, never letting them rest. Eventually the horses became too tired, footsore or indifferent to put up much resistance and could be gradually headed toward a corral. Even one person alone was often able to "wear down" a wild band if he was persistent. The horses would spook and run, nervously aware of the rider trailing them, not able to relax and graze. The man, keeping after them at a slow but steady pace, could usually ride them down after a few days, for he and his horse did not travel as erratically in speed or direction.

Gradually the wild horses would become accustomed to the following rider and lose some of their fear of him, letting him get closer, and eventually allowing him to stay with them. After a few days a good hand at this could even ride among them without disturbing them, and in time he could begin to drive them, drifting them slowly toward a mustang pen, where he would plan to have other riders help him chase them in at the last moments. It usually took about 8 to 10 days to "walk down" a herd in this way, if everything went well.

This kind of walking down wild horses was done many times in early days and was possible because the wild horse, being a feral animal and not truly wild, had a ready acceptance of man's presence. The horse had been a close companion of man for several thousand years and hundreds of generations, and this sense of companionship and security in the presence of a lone rider easily returned. The wildest of the wild horses could be gentled much more easily and become more completely "domesticated" than any of the truly wild animals.

Walking down a band of horses was usually made easier by the fact that the horses tended to stay on their home range, eventually circling back. Thus, the following horseman, coming back to near where he started the band, could change horses, or riders could be stationed at strategic points to spell each other. After finally wearing the herd down, the mustanger could easily rope one, or drive the whole herd into a corral.

Some would-be horse catchers took a chance on a quicker, yet riskier way to capture wild horses, attempting to "crease" or "nick" them with a rifle ball or bullet. If a shot was aimed carefully—just through the top of the horse's neck at the base of his mane and in front of the withers—he was supposed to be momentarily stunned. There is a nerve center in this area, and a shot correctly placed might make the horse fall to the ground, paralyzed, for a moment or two. Then the horse hunter could rush forward and tie the horse with ropes.

Very few people had any luck with this method. If the bullet went high, the horse ran off. If it was too low, the horse died instantly of a broken neck. It has been estimated that probably about 100 horses were killed for every one successfully captured by creas-

ing, and the odds were probably even greater than that; in all the accounts I have read about "creasing", I did not run across ANY that were actually successful.

The most common way to gather large groups of horses was to use the circular corral with wings, driving the horses into the corral. This method has been used by mustangers successfully for two centuries. An innovation on this method was developed by Pete Barnum in Nevada about 1910; he used a portable canvas corral. It had several advantages. The rolls of canvas could be easily packed into inaccessible back country, and the corral and wings could be put up quickly and noiselessly, before the horses in the area knew what was going on. The old method of constructing a corral of poles was noisy and usually took several days, and the horses in the region would become alarmed and suspicious. The canvas corral did not injure the horses if they crashed into it in their fright, as a wire or wooden corral might, and they rarely tried to crash it because they couldn't see through it.

Barnum used two pieces of heavy canvas, long enough and wide enough to make a corral about 100 feet in diameter and eight feet high. He took these rolls of canvas into the wildest parts of Nevada where Mustangers had never been successful before. He also used 3500 yards of cloth for his corral wings. Cottonwood poles were peeled and canvas for the main corral was hung and stretched on them. Two corrals could be joined together like a figure eight, the back one serving as a holding corral, while more bands were run into the front one. If a group of horses dodged the trap and got away, becoming too suspicious to return, the portable set-up could be dismantled and moved to a different place, where it could be put up again in about two hours' work. After using it a few times, Barnum learned how to place it, hidden by the terrain so that an oncoming band of horses would not see it until too late to turn back. At other times he might place it along one of their main travel routes. Barnum and his crews captured 7000 horses in Nevada in a six year period, and about 15,000 altogether during his 15 years in Nevada.

Mustangers came and went with the upswing or downswing in the price they could get for the horses, but a few of them enjoyed it so much that they stuck with it, even when the horses were practically worthless, attempting to make a living of sorts running wild horses. Before the mid-1930's, a number of men made their living capturing horses on the Oregon desert. Some of them worked part-time for cattle outfits and ran wild horses the rest of the year. The Oregon horses were domestic range horses, many of them branded. They ranged

Early day horse roundup. The horses were gathered into a corral and then roped. (both photos courtesy Denver Public Library—Western History Department)

on the desert and multiplied; their owners could actually be called horse ranchers, using the rangeland to pasture their horses. But gathering them was a challenging job.

The mustangers who gathered these horses usually owned several brands in the course of their career, buying another brand now and then from a rancher who was going out of the horse business, or from someone who had branded horses out on the desert but didn't want to gather them. After the mustanger bought the brand, he legally owned any of the horses out there that wore it, and could sell any of the animals that he could round up wearing the brand. Sometimes in a band of gathered horses there would be several brands, and the horse runner would have to notify the various owners and find out what they wanted done with their horses. Sometimes the owner wanted to come and get his horses, or wanted them turned back out on the range again. Or sometimes he just wanted the captors to sell his horse or horses along with the bunch, and be given the money.

Reub Long, cowboy co-author of *The Oregon Desert*, and a partner, gathered and sold more than 3000 head of horses in southeastern Oregon be-

tween 1928 and 1936. Their type of operation was typical of the horse runners of that time and locale. They usually had several other riders working with them (usually a crew of five when gathering horses to sell). Sometimes there would be as many as 20 riders, if they were rounding up many horses for a group of owners. They didn't do much roping in the open country, preferring to run the horses into corrals. The horses always ran in bands, and if one was roped, the others would get away. So the men usually gathered the band into a corral, then roped individual horses—branding the young ones, castrating stallions, and sometimes throwing a horse down to check him more closely for a brand. Out of a corral-full of about 100 horses, usually over half would be their own horses. Another 30%, carrying various brands, might belong to other owners, and maybe 10 head might be wild horses—unbranded and unclaimed. If a branded horse's owner couldn't be located or contacted for instructions on what to do with his horse, that horse was turned back out on the range again.

Another man that ran horses out on the desert at that time was Jim Bailey, who spent 1930 through 1936 riding part of each year for the Jordan Valley Grazing District, a locally managed grazing association. The ranchers hired extra range riders in the spring, to help keep the sheep off their cattle range when the sheep bands were traveling through to higher country in Nevada. The rest of the year Jim ran horses, and owned several brands. Horses were only worth 1¢ a pound for chicken feed at that time, but the $7 or $8 per horse was fair money then. The better horses were sold as saddle stock and brought a better price.

These horse runners occasionally used traps in canyons or along the river, building them out of brush and wire and piled rocks. But they had their best luck out in the open, running the wild bands into a group of tame, loose-herded horses, called a *parada*. One or two men would loose-herd the horses during the day, letting them graze, and their partners would run a wild bunch into the herd. Then the whole group could be easily driven into a corral. Usually four or five riders would run the wild bunch, one person in the lead, the others behind and at the sides of the group, hazing.

When Jim first went into that country he tried to help some ranchers catch an ex-racehorse for its owner. The big gelding was very wild and running with three other geldings, and very hard to get. The men had no success at all for 2½ months, and then caught the wary group by accident. One day the group of geldings, upwind from the riders, grazed right into the group of loose-herded horses, not realizing the men were there. After joining the group, the geldings were easily herded into the corral with them.

Jim told about one big brown horse they never could catch—a horse with a long curly mane and tail. One time Jim was running him, and the horse went into rough country, finally going right off a 30-foot bluff without even slowing down. Down below, the steep hillside was rock-strewn, but the horse managed to miss the boulders, landing in the loose shale and sliding down, and he kept right on going. In the six years that Jim rode that desert the brown horse was never caught. Some of that country is exceptionally rough, with rimrocks and bluffs and only a small level area on top of the rimrocks about five miles long and 1½ miles wide. The range horses raised in that country were extremely agile, running in the steep rocky country from birth. They could run downhill top speed through treacherous country and never seem to stumble—pouring down over the boulder-strewn hillsides like running water, while a

There is nothing more agile than wild horses when pursued, whether they are running pell mell over a rock-strewn hillside or leaping the brush in their way.

pursuing rider would just about have to pull up and watch them go.

One day in 1935 Jim and his friends had 15 head in a bunch, bringing them down out of the rough country, and along the way picked up 20 more. They stopped at the first ranch they came to, to corral the horses, and happened onto a horse buyer from Missouri who wanted to buy horses for the cotton fields at $25 per head. This was a real bonanza, and the horse runners gathered 90 head for him, to be shipped south on the railroad.

Some good horses were gathered off the desert. In the early days, some of the ranchers turned loose very good stock, including some "copperbottom" horses, and one man turned out an imported English Thoroughbred stallion. There was some inbreeding in these range herds, and the really inbred horses got very small, some of the inbred copperbottom strain not reaching more than 600 or 700 pounds at maturity (the same strain, not inbred, would normally weigh about 1100 pounds). But on the whole the horses in Oregon were fairly good. The riders gathered them often, castrated the poorer stallions, sold the worst horses for chicken feed, and tried to leave just good stock out there to multiply.

The Taylor Grazing Act put these horse runners out of business. Under the new law, a person had to have base property for his stock and a permit to pasture horses on the federal land. The men who owned horses out on the desert, but no ranch land, were wiped out; they could no longer legally have horses out there. Many of them had to leave some of their stock out there; they weren't able to gather them all. Later the government tried to gather these "trespass" and abandoned horses, but didn't have much luck at first. An airplane was tried, but was not successful. The horses got used to the airplane and would go up against the rimrock, staying there instead of coming down out of the rough country.

The first airplane roundup was tried by Archie Meyers, who had been running horses in the area earlier. Meyers helped remove about 8000 horses from the Oregon desert altogether, coming into the area from the Pacific coast in 1928. He rented a ranch, and then set out to earn some money catching horses, buying from most of the area's horse owners the right to all horses caught. Within two years he had caught about 3000, a third of which were unbranded. In 1930 he hired an airplane in an attempt to run the horses down out of the rough country into more accessible country, but this attempt was a total failure. From 1930 to 1935, he (like Reub Long and Jim Bailey and others of that period) ran them on horseback and captured another 5000.

A subsequent airplane venture was more successful. From 1936 to 1938 Floyd Hansen flew several aerial roundups in a one-motor plane, with the help of mounted cowboys who took the horses on down to corrals after Hansen hazed them out of the rough country.

After the Taylor Grazing Act, the government worked to exterminate the feral horse and thousands were taken off the ranges. In Wyoming, between 1936 and 1940, about 4000 were removed. Oregon estimated in 1940 that about 1000 unbranded horses still ran wild, after 10,000 had been cleared out. Old timers that ran range horses are still bitter about having to give up their horses under pressure from the government, and many felt that the government men were brutal in the way they handled the removal. One man remembers a government plane chasing horses off a 400 foot cliff. Others resented the attitude of the Taylor Grazing personnel, who warned ranchers to get their horses off the range, stating that branded horses would be shot along with the unbranded. On the other side of the coin, Taylor Grazing officials sometimes had to put up with cheating horse owners who ran more horses on the range than they had permits for.

Western fact and fiction have romanticized some of the horse-catching methods used by the early cowboys and mustangers. One method that was not glamorous, but easy and humane, was sometimes used by people who wanted to catch a few horses for saddle stock or breeding purposes. This method was to catch foals. In early fall, about the time the foals were old enough to wean, riders would go out on their best horses and run a wild bunch. After a long run some of the foals would begin to tire and drop back, and some of the riders would drop back with them. In most cases it wasn't even necessary to rope these young horses, because the youngsters were lonely and desperate, left behind by their mothers. They would generally stay with the riders' horses, wanting security and companionship. Thus, the cowboys could gently work back toward camp, with the wild foals going along with them, content to stay with the group of horses.

Wild foals captured this way often grew out to be good horses if given good feed and care, and were not as stunted as they would have been if left in the hills to struggle through a hard winter. When bred to good domestic stock, the results of the cross were often outstanding, gaining quality from the purebred stock and retaining hardiness from the mustang ancestry.

In most range areas in the West, some local ranchers, cowboys or mustangers made a living or increased their income by running horses on the range, periodically gathering up horses to sell. In

"Boots"—mustang mare, caught as a 5-day old foal on the Wyoming desert in 1939.

many instances the horses were their own horses, or descendents of horses turned loose by their fathers, grandfathers, or other ranchers of the area.

Charlie Thomas, who ran wild horses in Wyoming in the northwestern part of the state, herded sheep in the late 1920's and early 30's. He spent the summers with the sheep in the mountains, and down on the desert with them in the winter on the Granger lease, which was originally railroad land. This is part of the checkboard land patterns in Wyoming where every other section was railroad land interspersed with the federal land. This particular area was winter range for sheep, the sheepmen leasing the railroad lands.

There were lots of wild horses on the desert, and when the sheepherders were wintering there with the sheep, they often spent some time catching wild horses, which was not too difficult using their grain-fed saddle horses. A good roper could rope and hobble several horses out of a bunch and then go back and lead them home. Sometimes the horses would stand behind the sand dunes out of the wind and a horse hunter could sneak up on them and get fairly close. A good horse, broke to saddle, sold for as much as $10.

There were some good horses, some of them in that region tracing their ancestry to a good Thoroughbred stallion that got loose and ran on the desert for 15 years. He was so fleet that no one could catch him, and too smart to ever be lured into a corral.

But there were also some poor horses. There were runty inbred scrubs weighing only 500-600 pounds. Some of the inbreeding showed up in deformities; it wasn't unusual to see a horse born with only one eye, or just one front leg. And Charlie saw several that were cloven-footed on one front foot. Some of the horses starved to death in the winters; the conditions could be pretty harsh some years.

One of Charlie's best horses was a mare that he caught as a baby on the desert when she was only about 5 days old. He was after her mother but couldn't catch the fleet mare. But he did catch the baby and brought her home to raise on a bottle, with cow's milk. The baby thrived, and grew up to be a good all-around ranch horse. Named "Boots", all of Charlie's children learned to ride on her, and the mare was a favorite in the Thomas family until she was humanely put down at the age of 32.

A lot of the ranchers in the Northwest could not really be termed "mustangers" because the horses they periodically gathered off the ranges were their own. One family that came into the Salmon, Idaho area in 1912 had been a horse-raising family for several generations. Jim Bowman and his son, Jesse, had been nomad ranchers in the Wood River country near Shoshone before Idaho was a state, keeping their livestock in the low country in the winters and driving them up to summer range in the Sawtooth mountains in the summers.

After coming to Salmon, Jim Bowman ranged 500 head of his own horses in the hills. He raced some of his best horses and was interested in well-bred stock, bringing the first Thoroughbred stallion into the Lemhi valley. Jim and his son and grandson gathered the range horses every fall and wintered them at home on their ranch, branding the young ones, and selling some of the older ones. Some went to the Remount program, some were sold to the Forest Service, and some of the poorer quality ones to a killer market. A buyer from Butte, Montana came over the hill every few years and paid $20 a head, then trailed his purchased horses, 200 or so in a bunch, over the mountain to Montana.

After Jim Bowman died in 1929, his son and grandson gathered up most of the horses. His grandson, Chester, was in the 8th grade then and was riding a good horse that had been trained to run wild range horses. Chester says he vividly remembers those wild rides, and still has nightmares about them; the horse was surefooted and knew exactly what to do, hazing the wild running horses down out of the hills. Many of the horses had been born out on the range and hadn't been gathered and worked after his grandfather got old, and were hard to get down out of the hills. As his horse jumped gulllies and rocks at top speed, Chester just dropped the reins over his neck and hung onto the saddle horn for dear life—sometimes so scared that he was bawling—with his dad yelling at him, "Come on, this will make a cowboy out of you!"

There were still a few horses out there in the early

One of the old corrals near Challis, Idaho, used for catching range horses 60 years ago. The corral was built on a trail to water, with the ends left open except when the horses were to be caught. Part of a tree was left rooted in the center of the corral as a snubbing post to tie to when roping the horses.

1930's, and about 1935 Chester and his Dad gathered the last of them, for the Forest Service was getting stricter on trespass livestock. On that particular range, the days of the "wild horse" were over.

But in other areas the free-ranging horses were never completely gathered up, becoming the source of our present day wild horses. Such was the case at Challis, Idaho. This country was settled right around the turn of the century, and some of the old ranching families are still there. One of them, the Bradshaw family, has raised horses for two generations. Ray Bradshaw came into that country in 1910 as a freight driver, and he raised big Percheron and Belgian horses for his teams, owning two good stallions. He and his sons pastured a lot of horses on the range, on the East Fork of the Salmon River, in the same area where the Challis wild horse herd exists today, as did many of their contemporaries.

The Bradshaws and their neighbors got together for horse gatherings, and would trail 400 to 500 head of horses down to Blackfoot, Idaho in the southern part of the state. This was a distance of about 150 miles by a direct route over the hills and desert, and would take the men about six days on the trail, camping at night and night-herding the horses. Crossing the desert took three days. There was no water on the desert, but the men stopped at the train station with their horses for water.

The horses sold at Blackfoot mostly went as work horses, but in later years there were also some good light stallions added to the range herds—American Saddlers and Hambletonians—and some of the offspring made good saddle horses.

Some ranchers pastured their good broodmares on the range, turning them out after they were bred at home to the ranch stallions. One man had more than 500 mares that he rounded up every spring, putting them in his fields to foal and be bred to his own stallions, then turning them out again in the fall. He was raising foals the way he wanted them bred, yet still using the range for pasture. But many of the range mares bred indiscriminately on the range, and some of the offspring invariably went wild. The wild herds were also enlarged during the drought of

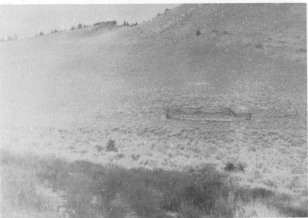

Two views of another old corral in the Challis area, used 50 years ago for catching horses. Originally this corral had wing fences to direct the oncoming horses into the corral.

1934-1935, when some of the ranchers in the area went broke and departed, leaving their horses out there.

The elder Bradshaw made his living during the 1930's with his horses. Every year, in the early summer (June and July) before haying season started, he and his sons rounded up horses to sell. They built a corral near the ranch on Herd Creek. Some of their own gentle range stock, about 100 to 150 head, were grazed in the nearby hills during the daytime, and the men would run wild bunches into them, maybe six to ten horses in a bunch. Then the whole group could be taken down to the corrals at night. The captured horses would be sorted out, and the gentle horses taken back to the hills in the morning to graze again. After enough horses were gathered to sell, they would be trailed to market, sometimes taking some of the gentle range stock along with them to make them easier to drive.

Some of the two and three-year-olds they caught and gentled as saddle horses made excellent mounts. They had endurance and staying power and agility from running in the hills. They were easy to tame—just like any other horse—as long as you were close to them. But because they had been born and raised in the hills instead of at the home ranch, they were unpredictable if they ever got loose; they went back to the hills instead of home to the ranch like a ranch-raised horse. If one of these range-raised horses got loose from his rider out in the hills, chances are the rider would never get him back again without running down a wild bunch. One of Bradshaw's neighbors had a horse get away with a saddle on and the horse wore the saddle out in the mountains for two years before he lost it. The horse was captured again several years later in a bunch that was gathered by airplane.

During the 1930's and 40's and early 50's the local cowboys rounded up wild stock for the Clayton rodeo every year, for some of the wild horses made good buckers. But some didn't. One old stallion they caught for the rodeo had apparently been a ranch horse at some time in his earlier days, for when the chute opened and he was supposed to come bucking out, he merely came out calmly and walked across the arena with the rider on his back. After the rodeo the horses used were turned back out on the range.

Ken Bradshaw recalls that the hardest bunch they ever gathered was a group of 9 or 10 horses that were up on Forest Service lands. The Forest Service got strict about trespass horses during the 1930's and wanted the horses off, so the Bradshaws spent 8 days straight running those horses—three men using 10 saddle horses—and finally got the trespass bunch down to the home corral. These men were good horsemen and running range horses was their favorite way of life. In all the years that they rounded up and handled wild and semi-wild range horses, only one horse was killed—breaking its neck hitting the corral fence.

Another family that ran horses in the Challis area was the Gosseys. Ray Gossey has lived in that area for 75 years, since 1902. Local ranchers have been pasturing and gathering horses on that range for a long time. He recalls one man taking out 400 horses more than 50 years ago. These horses were all fairly tame and easy to handle. But over the years some of the horses got wilder, partly because the domestic herds multiplied and some were not gathered; some were born out in the hills, and they and their descendents became quite wild. Also, after being run by the ranchers a few times, some of the horses that got away or were left out there to reproduce, became more wary about being chased and captured. They got wilder and wiser. A man who came into this country from Nevada in the 1950's to catch horses—a professional mustanger—declared that these Challis horses were the toughest bunch he had ever tried to get.

In the early days, the horses used the Forest Service lands as well as the lower country that is now administered by the BLM. At the higher elevations, the snows got very deep in winter and some of the horses got snowed in each year and winterkilled. Don Gossey, Ray's son, tells of one group of 13 head he found one spring, dead of starvation, with their eyes sunken in and their manes and tails eaten off. A nearby pine tree had been eaten down to a stump. As the horses became weak and died, they apparently had just sunk down into the deep snow; when Don found them that spring after the snow melted, the carcasses were kneeling upright.

The wild horses often didn't seem to want to come down to lower country when the snows came; their natural inclination was to go higher. The ranchers usually had to ride up into the high country before the deep snows came, to push their range bands down to lower elevations, because they would not come down on their own. After the creeks froze over, the horses would not cross the ice to come down out of the high country. The Forest Service has since cleaned out all the free-roaming horses that used to graze that area, and the BLM range where the present Challis herd exists is a little better in wintertime for horses, but even there a few have starved to death at higher elevations.

The Gosseys did their horse gathering in the fall, when the foals were big enough to stay with the bunch, and the mares were not yet too heavily pregnant. Horse roundups in springtime invariably

Capturing and breaking wild horses (photo courtesy Denver Public Library—Western History Department).

left a few young foals behind. The mares wouldn't go back for their foals, because the harem stallion would not let them. So fall was generally the best time of year to run horses.

During the early 1950's, the Challis wild horses had increased to the point that their range could not support them, and some winterkilled. So the local ranchers, with permits from the BLM, reduced the numbers down to about 100 head, gathering over 1000 to sell. Some of these were sold as saddle stock and the worst ones were sold for pet food. The Bradshaws gathered nearly 300 horses during 1952, and "Chug" Utter, a Nevada mustanger with an airplane, captured 587 in 1953, using a camouflaged corral and trained horses. He had six trained horses that he "planted" near the camouflaged corral, and when he, with the airplane and the local cowboys on horseback, ran a wild bunch to them, the trained horses would mix with the wild bunch and head for the corral. The six horses were held on ropes, by a man hidden in the brush nearby. When he could see the wild bunch coming, he turned them loose and they would drift to the corral.

The corral was made of lumber, camouflaged with sagebrush, and the whole thing was built on cables so that it would give if a horse hit the side. When flying the airplane and bringing in a bunch of horses, Chug Utter always hazed them downhill, never uphill. If they have to head uphill, a tired bunch will split and go in every direction; the only way to keep them together was to run them downhill.

After 1953 the horse herd was controlled to around 100 head. Don Gossey roped a few each winter, helping keep the numbers down, and a few riding clubs came in occasionally from southern Idaho and Washington to rope wild horses. They usually captured a few foals and older mares. The local ranchers, being horse people themselves, and who enjoyed the range horses and the sport and profit from gathering them now and then, did not ever want to see the horses eliminated, and always kept enough out there to multiply. These horses were a part of their life. Yet they also did not want them to starve to death because of lack of winter feed, and tried to keep the numbers down to what the range could support.

The rancher-mustangers, in many instances, considered the horse herds their own, especially if much of the stock had been domestic or was offspring of horses they themselves had turned out on the range. And because they considered these horses their own, they cared about them, tried to manage them, and handled them with understanding. They were horsemen, with a love of horses as deep as any man can have, for horses were their life-blood and recreation, as well as their livelihood.

Many a rancher in the mountains depended upon a good horse to get his work done, looking after cattle or horses, and in rough country chasing cattle or horses he often depended upon a good horse for his very life. A poor one could easily stumble and fall and break the rider's neck as well as its own. Appreciation for a good horse with lots of stamina, agility, "heart" and spirit was deep in many of these men, for it was an appreciation gained over years of experience working with and handling horses. They loved their horses with a love that cannot really be put into words, a love that tied in with their love of Old Mother Nature and living things. They thrived on the rugged mountain country upon which they eked out their living, and the freedom of being their own person out in God's great outdoors, limited only by time and the seasons.

These horsemen—the cowboy on the Oregon desert, or the Wyoming desert, or the Nevada desert, or the Utah desert, or the Idaho mountains, or anywhere else—all had some things in common. They used the horse for their own ends, but they also admired and appreciated his freedom. Though capturing horses was part of their life and their living, there was something intangible about the free-roaming horses that was soul-stirring, and the last thing in the world most of these old cowboys would have wanted to see would have been the end of the wild horse. It might seem contradictory to say that the wild horse runners admired the wild horse's freedom, but it is true. They were addicted to the thrill and challenge of catching horses just as the skier or Kyacker is addicted to his sport, and yet they felt there was something natural about horses being wild. The mustanger always wanted to leave some out there for next time. The challenge to conquer a mountain or a frontier or to tame a wild horse does not preclude a love of wilderness or wildness. Often the person who does this sort of thing is out there doing it because he does love wildness and freedom even though he is taming it. Maybe this is one of the paradoxes of man's nature.

As long as the "mustangers" were predominantly horsemen and ranchers, there was never any danger of the wild horse being totally exterminated or pushed off all the ranges completely. Many of these ranchers had some of their own horses out there and most of them felt there was something natural and good about having a few wild horses in the hills. Under this kind of "management" and loose sponsorship, the wild horse in many places had a pretty healthy future.

But there were other mustangers on the scene, increasing in number now that the demand for pet food had raised the price of horseflesh. The machine age had recently supplied the airplane and the truck for easier capturing and hauling. A new crop of mustangers arose, men who were not horsemen, men who thought of each free-roaming horse only in terms of dollars and cents and the cheapest, easiest transport to the slaughtering plants. And sometimes horses were seriously injured.

In the words of one BLM man, "Any time you have a lot of people with varying degrees of knowledge about what they are doing, involved with anything that is both dangerous and exciting, whether it's motorcycles, or boats, or chasing wild horses, you always have some who get out of hand. The sad part of this situation is that a lot of good people, and some great horsemen, who were conscientious and knew how to do the job and did it well have been thrown into the same barrel with the few rotten apples."

There are some aspects of the mustanging picture, of both yesterday and today that have not been pretty—in long years past as well as after the advent of "pet-food" mustanging. Throughout America's pioneer history there have been instances of mass slaughter and extermination of wild horses, as they were pushed off lands wanted for other purposes, or their numbers reduced in areas they had over-run. No history of a pioneering effort is completely pretty, for there are always some things that have to go to make way for the new use of the land. Some of the chapters of "progress" are sad. Progress is a mixed blessing. We look back on some of the things that took place in American expansion across this continent and we regret them, and yet, we cannot wholly condemn, or we are being foolish and unrealistic dreamers.

To sit where we are today, in this great land that feeds us, clothes us and enables us to pursue our hearts' desires, and condemn the means by which we got here is childish. We don't have to like or condone some of the evils in our history, but to say that the results are all bad, or that the pioneering effort should not have been made is ridiculous. That's as two-faced as the lazy hippie cursing the establishment while letting it support and feed him. There have been evils and greed and exploitation of our great land, but through the march of history has come good as well as abuse.

Most of us demand the very comforts and material blessings that are the products of what some people term "abuse of the land." To wish that the vast American wilderness had never been "spoiled," that the buffalo had never gone, or that the wild horse had not declined is as ridiculous as wishing that your father or grandfather or great-grandfather had never come to America. Most of us Americans wouldn't be where we are now if "progress" hadn't carried the pioneers across North America, changing the landscape and its resources to fit their evolving needs.

And part of that pioneer movement reduced the wild horse herds, and pushed them away until the Great Plains (which had originally had the most numbers) had practically no horses left. The western mountains and deserts (which at one time had the fewest, and in many localities, none) had the remaining horses in fair numbers. The wild horses made way for civilization—put to work by it as work horses or saddle stock, used by it as commercial products (pet food, chicken feed, fertilizer, hides, and so on) or exterminated by it.

The pet food industry is part of that American "progress." As the American population became less rural and more urban, the pet food industry boomed. The farm cat or dog subsisted on table scraps, butchering scraps, extra milk from the family cow, and self-sufficiency—catching rodents around the fields and barnyard and haystacks. But his city cousin had no such bounty, and his city cousin's master started buying prepared pet food. The demand soared, and pet food production is a billion dollar business today.

There may be less horse meat in pet food today than there was when range horses were gathered up and sold to the canneries; the pet food companies have probably had to find substitute ingredients for part of their product. But those wild horses fed a lot of American pets. Many of the very people who recently bemoaned the fate of the wild horse and came to his support for protective legislation were the same people who bought the pet food and made it worth the mustanger's while to gather the horses. How many sentimental American wild horse enthusiasts have cats and dogs, and what have they been feeding those cats and dogs for the last forty years? Ironic, isn't it, but just another instance of the complexity of the system in which we live. The American public cannot really place the total blame on the mustanger or the rancher or the government land agencies for the decrease in the wild horse numbers during the 1930's through 1960's. We must also blame ourselves.

5

The Mustang Registries and Organizations

People interested in the Spanish horse-gone-wild began to get concerned a few years ago that the remnants of these mustangs would soon be gone. Spanish blood had been in the process of being diluted by other breeds for more than a century and a half, and very few horses, if any, left running free today can be positively traced back to Spanish stock. With the many range horses rounded up during the past few decades, the chances of any Spanish-type horses being left out there were getting smaller and smaller. So a few horsemen who had a liking for the original Spanish feral horses set about to try to preserve some, realizing even as early as the 1920's that the Spanish mustang, as a distinct type, was vanishing.

One of the chief promoters of the Spanish mustang, Bob Brislawn, was born in 1890 in Spokane, Washington, to pioneer parents. He spent 31 years as a packer with the U.S. Topographical Survey, then retired to his Cayuse Ranch in Oshoto, Wyoming. Bob and his brother Ferdinand were probably the first to concern themselves with the disappearing Spanish mustang and to do something about it. In 1925 they began to search for horses that looked like they might still carry some Spanish Barb blood. They purchased some horses from the Cheyenne Indians, and captured others from wild bands. They

found some on the Bookcliff range on the Green River between Utah and Colorado, some in the mountains of Oklahoma, and on the deserts of Arizona, New Mexico and Nevada. These horses

Robert Brislawn, mustang breeder and founder of the Spanish Mustang Registry.

they captured and took home to their Wyoming ranch.

The type of horse they were looking for was small, under 14 hands, weighing about 800 pounds, with low withers, deep narrow chest, a low sloping croup and hind legs set well underneath the body. The horse had to have a short back with 17 pairs of ribs and only 5 lumbar vertebrae (in back of the ribs). Some of these horses would have a 6th vertebrae fused into the 5th, but never 6 distinct vertebrae. The head should be small, not over 18 inches from poll to end of nose bone. Ears should be small and rimmed with black hairs. This type of horse, called the primitive Spanish Barb (an attempt to trace its ancestry to the north African Barb, which was an offshoot of the Arabian, but somewhat coarser featured and having more "primitive" characteristics, somewhat similar to the Asiatic wild horse like the Tarpan or Przewalski's horse) is usually solid colored or roan or grulla (this term applies to colors shading from slate blue-gray to mouse-brown),

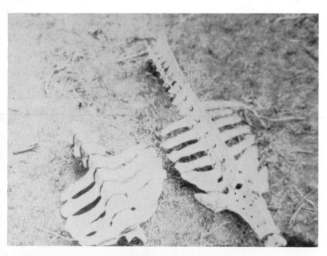

Bob Brislawn and his associates studied a horse's bones after death, to determine whether that horse was a Barb or Andalusian or of some other breeding, by counting the lumbar vertebrae.

including duns and buckskins. The mane, tail and hoofs are black, and the legs are black from the knee or hock down. The mane and tail are full and long, and the hair at the back of the legs is not straight, but grows in a "curl and comb", and the fetlock hair is curly.

In 1957 Bob Brislawn and other interested people set up the Spanish Mustang Registry, Inc. to try to preserve the Spanish mustang by registering some of the better authenticated animals and trying to raise offspring from them. Bob and his sons kept some of these Spanish mustangs on their Cayuse Ranch, roaming free on 4000 acres. Then in 1969 a severe winter storm killed half the herd. In 1971 Bob shipped 14 horses to Porterville, California, where he formed a partnership with Jeff Edwards, creating the Brislawn-Edwards Spanish Barb Research Farm, selling the Wyoming Cayuse Ranch to his son Emmett in 1973. Some of the Spanish Barb horses are still at the Wyoming ranch.

The Spanish Mustang Registry was set up as a nonprofit venture, with its purpose to perpetuate the Spanish wild horse. "We're trying to restore a breed, not create one," said Robert Brislawn. "We are not like other horse breeders and we are not trying to compete against them for show or for ribbons." This registry is very strict with its registration procedures and absolutely will not allow the introduction of horses of other breeding to try to "improve" the Spanish mustang. As of mid-1977 the organization had registered about 650 horses, many of which are now dead.

Other mustang registries have been formed in more recent years and have slightly different objectives. The Spanish Mustang Registry is based upon preserving the purest possible descendents of early Spanish horses of both Barb and Andalusian types, not making any distinction between them, except to refer to them as the light type (Andalusian) and heavy type (Barb).

The American Mustang Association was created in the 1960's by a different group of people "to unite the owners and admirers of the American Mustang into an active, enthusiastic force for the preservation and promotion of the American Mustang through registration and an intelligent breeding program." After careful study, breed characteristics were established. These were determined by studying writings of people in the early days of this country who had described the mustang in detail, and by studying material gathered from several South American countries whose governments were registering the South American counterpart of these feral Spanish horses. The American Mustang Association developed an inspection procedure for determining

Barb stallions at the Wild Horse Research Farm at Porterville, California (photos courtesy Jeff Edwards).

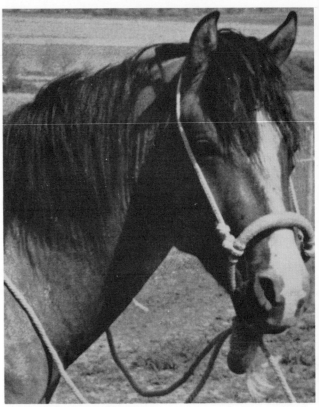

Quien, SBBA P-19, buckskin stallion sired by Scarface SBBA P-1. Spanish Barb stallion owned by Susan Banner of Hot Springs, S.D.

Spanish Barb gelding owned by the W.D. Banners of Hot Springs, S.D. (photos courtesy Peg Freitag).

whether or not a horse would be eligible for registration, based on conformation and measurements of various parts of the horse. While almost any horse will fit some of the requirements, the American Mustang Association feels that no horse will be able to fit them all unless it IS a mustang, having all of the necessary proper proportions.

In order to pass inspection, a horse must show no evidence of outside breeding. If a foal from registered parents crops up with improper characteristics when he is inspected for adult papers after his third birthday, he cannot be registered as breeding stock, and his parents will be investigated to try to track down where the outside blood came from. The responsible parent will then be dropped from the registry as breeding stock.

Another association, the Spanish-Barb Breeders Association, is dedicated to the restoration of the true Spanish Barb horse, and was incorporated as a non-profit organization in 1972 by Peg Cash and Susan Banner. After being associated with the other mustang registries and seeing the variety of horses registered, they decided to form their own organization for restoring ONLY the Spanish Barb strain. Foundation stock for the SBBA was picked very carefully, and the bloodlines are perpetuated through selective breeding and linebreeding.

One strain of Spanish Barbs, the Scarface horses, was an isolated strain that had been kept pure on a ranch in New Mexico that had been in one family since the mid 1800's. These horses are considered by

SBBA to be the purest blood in the U.S. The Romero ranch that kept this breeding intact was purchased by Weldon McKinley in 1957 and he has continued to breed Spanish Barbs. His stallion, Scarface, is SBBA's foundation sire, P-1.

Foundation sire number 2 is from the Ilo Belsky bloodlines in Nebraska. This buckskin stallion is Rawhide, P-2, and is now owned by Peg Freitag. Ilo Belsky has been raising Spanish Barbs from selected bloodlines since the early 1900's.

As of October 1976 there were 74 Spanish Barb horses registered in the SBBA, and in order to perpetuate a breed with so few individuals, very careful breeding programs are practiced—in strict conformance with the registry's breed standard. This standard is based upon documented descriptions of Spanish Barbs in the 15th through the 18th centuries.

There are several other associations that are interested in the mustang, but not in the capacity of breeding and registering these horses. The National Mustang Association, based in Utah, is not a breed registry but a club whose members are interested in preserving the traditional wild horse. Before the passage of the Wild Horse and Burro Act which prohibited capture of the wild horses, the NMA was interested in the sport of "mustanging", chasing and capturing wild horses for their own use. The animals captured were then evaluated and graded according to how much Spanish blood they seemed to have.

The NMA was organized in 1965 for the purpose of having areas where the wild horses, and other wildlife, could live in their natural habitat without fear of extinction. The organization was founded by Tom Holland of Newcastle, Utah, and is dedicated to protecting, preserving and perpetuating the wild horse in its natural habitat. The NMA purchased a 600 acre ranch near Barclay, Nevada, and in 1977 purchased the grazing rights which adjoin the ranch, paying two sheep ranchers $60,000 for their grazing rights on 22,500 acres. This area produces enough forage to support about 100 horses year-round.

Another group that is interested in preserving the wild horse is the International Society for the Protection of Mustangs and Burros (ISPMB), which was organized in 1960 by Velma B. Johnston ("Wild Horse Annie"). This group is interested in protection and humane treatment of wild horses, regardless of their bloodlines. Incorporated in 1965, ISPMB was the first organization formed exclusively to carry on the battle for protection and preservation of wild horses and burros; before its formation, all efforts in behalf of these animals were on an individual basis.

Then, after the passage of the Wild Horse and

Spanish Barb filly. Spanish Barb mare, Coche Tres SBBA P-10, with her younger half-brother. Spanish Barb mare, Coche Tres (courtesy Peg Freitag).

Burro Act of 1971, an additional wild horse protection group, WHOA (Wild Horse Organized Assistance) was formed, with Wild Horse Annie becoming its Executive Director and Chairman of the Board. WHOA was created to provide surveillance patrols to assure the safety and well being of wild horses and burros and to insure humane treatment for them. Other purposes of this group are to assist in providing care and protection of these animals, conducting research and field studies on wild horses and burros, providing scholarships for student research studies, supplying educational material on wild horses and burros, and any other necessary projects to help the cause of the wild horse and burro. WHOA and ISPMB have been very active in all legislative and judicial matters pertaining to wild horses and burros.

Another group of wild horse enthusiasts is the National Wild Horse Association, formed in the early 1970's by about 50 Las Vegas citizens who were interested in the welfare of the wild horse. This group spends its time checking and repairing water holes, packing salt out to the horses, and helping the BLM with its present Adopt-A-Horse program. They also screen applicants, help transport horses and work on the roundup arrangements and facilities. Instead of spending its time, money and energies on legal battles or promotion of its organization, this group spends its time and effort out in the field trying to help the horses, or putting on trail rides and gymkhanas to raise funds for their water developments and other practical projects.

6

The End of the Wild Horse?

The wild horse population in America has fluctuated greatly over the past century, and public sentiment about the horse has also had its ups and downs. The controversy over wild horses simmmered rather quietly for many years, the waves of emotion (beginning back in the late 1880's) alternately rising and falling. At the beginning of the present century, rancher-conservationist Roy Wright predicted of the 1000 wild horses on the land surrounding his ranch that "if you are back here ten years from now, I doubt if you'll find a single horse in this valley. They're facing their last stand." But obviously the wild horses hung on for 70 more years and are still with us.

Public opinion concerning the plight of the wild horse gradually increased, gaining momentum after the 1930's as more people became aware that wild horses were being ground into pet food and chicken feed, capture and transport methods not always humane. A few articles in national magazines began to appear, regretting the decimation of the horse herds, extolling the virtues of the better mustangs, reminiscing about the old West, and so on. The reduction of the great herds of wild horses was looked upon as necessary, but most people who wrote about the subject at that time wrote with nostalgia and a regret for the passing of the era of the wild horse.

An article by Andrew Boone in *Travel* magazine in 1933 ("The Wild Herd Passes") estimated the remaining wild horse population at 50,000. He praised the wild horse for its stamina and discussed the horses in general. But at that time there was as yet no great outcry from the public to halt the further reduction of the horse herds. That was to come later.

During the early history of ranching in the West, the horse herds had been viewed several different ways. On the plains, wild horses generally had to make way for cattle and grazing and settlers. The early cattlemen viewed him both as an asset and a liability. Cowboys and range riders admired and appreciated the wild horse and often tried to catch him, but some of the cattlemen looked at the horse as a range robber that ate valuable grass. Some of these cattlemen exterminated a lot of horses.

The situation on range areas west of the Great Plains, in the mountain regions, was a little different, for the wild horse herds were not so numerous when the settlers arrived; most of these herds sprang up from the settlers' own stock. It wasn't until later that the wild herds in the mountains became numerous enough to be considered detrimental. After that happened, several factors took a hand in reducing wild horse numbers. It's hard to say just when the local ranchers in these areas stopped thinking of the wild horse as an asset (as range horses to gather periodically for their own use) and started to consider him a pest.

This change in attitude was tied to several things. The population in the West had increased and the open land was pretty well filled up except for marginal range land that would not support a homestead. With the coming of cars and tractors, the value and usefulness of the horse as a necessary part of man's way of life was decreased. With no big market for horses as saddle, harness and work animals, the "worthless" horses were not rounded up for this market, and their numbers increased. In some places these wild herds became serious competitors with domestic livestock for range grass. So, for these reasons, the ranchers' way of looking at the wild horse changed, and between 1920 and 1960 some ranchers would shoot a wild horse on sight, considering him a worthless pest that ate too much grass.

It was during this period that the wild horse became an economic asset as pet food, and it was this factor, more than the rancher's attitude, that was to spell doom for the large free-roaming herds. The wild horse now fell prey to commercial hunters for the pet food processing plants, and within a short span of years these commercial mustangers did what the rancher and his occasional shooting of wild horses hadn't been able to do, seriously depleting the wild horse numbers in every state that had them.

Because these mustangers were paid by the pound for the horses they delivered to the processing plants, and had to bring in many pounds of horseflesh to make a living, some of them felt they could not afford the extra time required to handle the horses humanely. The horses were, after all, going to slaughter anyway. And most of these men were gathering horses for profit, viewing them as a commodity—horseflesh—rather than as animals to be appreciated.

These men, for the most part, were not horsemen. Some regretted the methods they used, but it was "one of those things." There really wasn't any other way, they felt, to bring in large numbers of horses and get them to the slaughtering plants quickly. Humane considerations had to fall by the wayside. And at first, these commercial hunters had the public's approval. What they were doing was "progress"—clearing the ranges of excess horses, and providing a much-in-demand product for the American people in the form of canned pet food.

As late as 1945 the Department of the Interior's Annual Report boasted that 20,000 excess horses had been removed from the public ranges that year. The report went on to say that "Action under the Secretary's orders of March 16, 1943, and January 29, 1944, resulted in the removal of about 100,000 surplus horses from grazing districts and adjacent lands during the past three years. Steps are needed to encourage purchase and shipment of excess horses by appropriate agencies for food and farm purposes in devastated countries." This was following World War II and there was a use for horses and horsemeat in war-torn Europe. The people who rounded up the horses and the ones who ordered it or let it happen were responding to conditions and national attitudes that were far different from those of today. The wild horse was being looked at as a serious competitor for the grass needed to produce beef and mutton for a hungry world. These excess horses, Americans felt, should be rounded up and removed from the ranges. If they could then serve a useful purpose, so much the better.

So for awhile, public opinion condoned the roundups. The news media and national magazines carried occasional stories about the reduction of the wild horse herds, but viewed it as progress, or carried interesting accounts of wild horse roundups. The American people had a nostalgic regret for the passing of the Old West, and with it the wild horse, but as yet there was no real move to try to keep the wild herds.

An article in the *Illustrated London News* in 1949 showed pictures of a Wyoming roundup that used aircraft for gathering the horses. In 1946 *The American Cattle Producer* carried a story about the Yakima Indians rounding up more than 5000 wild horses in the Fort Simcoe and Medicine Valley areas. Nostalgic articles like that of J. Frank Dobie's in the *Saturday Evening Post* ("The Murderous Mustang of the Plains," December 1951) gave exciting accounts of past wild horse experiences and observations about wild horses. Typical of some of the nostalgic articles was Ross Santee's "The Last Run" (*Arizona Highways*, November, 1958), depicting the "good old days" of wild horse chases and roundups.

And then the articles began to take a more serious turn. The modern mustanging methods were not as romantic as the old ways and the exciting "wild west" experiences, but instead were sometimes bloody, brutal and repulsive. At first, the abuse of the captured horses concerned only a small group of people. A few strong voices began to rise, condemning these methods and also condemning the uses for which the wild horses were being rounded up. The "forgotten" wild horse began to come to view and the American people's conscience began to stir, sluggishly at first, and then more fully aroused. The fight to save the wild horses, begun by a handful of individuals, began to gain momentum. In time, the wild horse protectors grew in number and their protests about inhumane treatment of the horses destined for dogfood began to attract national attention.

As early as 1950, photographer Verne Wood began promoting a plan for a state controlled wild-horse refuge in Wyoming, using his wild horse pictures for publicity. This plan, which had begun in Verne Wood's mind in the late 1940's, was publicized in an article in *Nature Magazine* ("A Kingdom for Wild Horses"). The proposed refuge would be controlled by fish and game wardens and "some four hundred head would be permitted to live without danger of being rounded up by professional horse-hunters." The article went on to describe the horse roundups, and concluded by maintaining that the refuge would become a great tourist attraction. Only it never became a reality.

In 1953 an article by Gus Bundy ("Rounding up Wild Horses") appeared in *National Humane Review*, describing the early truck and airplane round-ups which were common in Nevada in the late 1940's and early 1950's, and the article was accompanied by vivid photos. Even though the photographs were staged and posed, similar to scenes used in the motion picture *The Misfits*, they illustrated the type of brutality that often accompanied this kind of roundup.

Robert O'Brien, in the December 1957 issue of *Reader's Digest* ("The Mustang's Last Stand"), gave a brief description of wild horse history and legends and then described the efforts of people like Verne Wood, Edward Gladding and Mrs. Velma Johnston ("Wild Horse Annie"), who were at that time trying to arouse public sympathy and enough support to get some legislative protection for the wild horses. We'll take a closer look at Mrs. Johnston and her efforts for the wild horse cause in the next chapter, for she was the strongest driving force behind the wild horse protection crusade, and accomplished the most in getting legislation passed to protect them.

But during the 1950's there was still no protection of any kind for the wild horse, and numbers continued to dwindle. As Will C. Barnes of the U.S. Forest Service stated, as early as 1924, ["With every man's hand against them, these wild horses will eventually be exterminated. In the meantime, any red-blooded man thirsting for adventure, excitement, and some Wild West riding can get plenty of it chasing these unwelcome residents of the Western ranges. There is no closed season on them at any time in the whole year, for they are classed with the wolves and coyotes as predatory animals, marked for slaughter."]

A similar statement was made by Archie D. Ryan of the Department of Interior Grazing Service in 1939: "A wild horse consumes forage needed by domestic livestock, brings in no return, and serves no useful purpose." Thus it seemed as though the wild horse's doom was sealed. He was being pushed off the land to make room for civilization and domestic livestock, except in some remote areas where he was under the loose sponsorship and protection of the ranchers themselves. And now that the market in horseflesh was profitable, he was being hunted down by professional horse-hunters even in these remote areas. A western newspaper in the 1950's stated that "the true picture of a wild horse is a runty, moth-eaten, mangy little scrub critter of no value anywhere outside of a can."

Pet food processors (a billion dollar business by the 1960's) paid 6¢ to 7¢ per pound for live horses delivered at the packing plant, and that meant $50 to $60 a head for the average-size wild horses. Many of the horses used in the "canneries" were old retired domestic horses, but the wild horses found their way there, too, having the advantage of being cheap. The only cost involved was rounding them up and getting them there.

The cheapest way to gather wild horses in quantities large enough to make the enterprise profitable was large-scale airplane roundups, hazing the horses to corral sites where they could be trucked out. Shotgun blasts from the airplane were sometimes used to keep the horses moving or turning in the proper direction. Then when corraled, the horses were jammed into trucks with no regard for their condition; there might be a horse or two with bleeding shotgun wounds, or a horse with part of his face shot away, or a broken leg, or a ripped abdomen. Some of the horses, after being run down out of the hills with airplanes to open, level ground (such as some areas in Nevada) were not corraled, but run down by trucks or four-wheel drive vehicles and roped.

One method was to lasso a horse with a rope that had a big tire on the end of it. After dragging and fighting the tire for a while, the horse was so worn out he could then be handled and loaded into a truck by several strong men. Many horses were injured in the process. But as long as the horses were still alive, the packing houses would take them.

After becoming aware of some of these inhumane methods of capture, public apathy about the wild horses began to crack, and then to shatter. In this jet age in modern America, a remote and forgotten "pot" began to boil. Not only just outraged westerners, ranchers and horsemen and sportsmen, but also some Americans who had never even seen a wild horse—ones who had no notions whatever about wild horses except what they had read in paperbacks or seen at the movies—were suddenly waking up to the problem and adding their voices to the cry that "something should be done" about the plight of the dwindling wild ones.

The wild horse had long been a romantic and sentimental favorite, but once the West was "won" with pavement, ranches, wheat fields, parking meters and progress, the real wild horse had been almost forgotten. He was hunted for the canneries, and hunted just to remove him from the ranges, but most people, going their own way in our modern-day fast-paced civilization, were not aware of the wild horse in his remote hide-outs. The western range was fenced and crossfenced, with the wild horse always on the outside. The dwindling wild bands retreated into areas more remote and inhospitable—desert mountain country that often had little feed or water. Some of the small scrubby wild ones became smaller and scrubbier due to poor forage and inbreeding. And even in some of these remote places, the airplanes chased them.

In the eight years following World War II, due to increasing use of commercial pet food, wild horse roundups accordingly increased and approximately 100,000 horses were captured in Nevada alone. In 1958 the Department of the Interior estimated that there were only about 20,000 wild horses in the West. Tom McKnight, in his article, "The Wild Horse Today" (June 1959, *Desert* magazine), assistant professor of geography at UCLA, estimated wild horse numbers in 1959 as being somewhere between 15,000 and 30,000, after his year and a half study of feral horses in the U.S. and Canada. Nevada had the largest number, with several thousand in the northern and central regions and several hundred in the southern part. California's main herds were in the east, bordering Nevada. Arizona had just a few widely dispersed remnant herds, the main concentration on the Fort Apache Indian reservation. New Mexico was second only to Nevada in wild horse numbers, with Colorado and Utah and seven other states having fewer numbers.

McKnight described the physical appearance of the wild horses as having little resemblance to the famed mustangs of earlier times, due to inbreeding and scanty grazing. He termed them as runty, big-headed and coarse, but still possessing agility and stamina. Occasional individuals had good conformation and pleasing appearance, but these were the exceptions. Their most common nickname was "broomtail". He maintained that if left alone by man, the wild horse would probably multiply rapidly, having no other major predators. But man

had a strong controlling influence at that point, keeping the herds reduced to scanty numbers. McKnight concluded by saying that wild horse numbers would continue to slowly decrease until only a few thousand wild horses were left in widely scattered locations. And he felt that this remnant would survive indefinitely.

But other people didn't feel so confident. Concern that the dwindling wild horses would disappear altogether unless something was done to protect them prompted some people to suggest that refuges be established for them. Articles continued to depict the gory roundups and brutal handling of captured wild horses.

Nancy Wood, writing in *Audubon Magazine* (November 1969, "The Wild Horse—Heritage or Pest?") said, "The wild horse is a tormented creature who never really sleeps. His death lurks in every daylight hour. If he is to escape to the beginning of one more night, he has to keep on the move." She described him as having no place or purpose and as being one of America's most ruthlessly hunted animals. She went on to say that no one knew exactly how many wild horses were left, the most reliable estimate at that time being the BLM's figure— 17,300 in 9 western states (California—2,300, Colorado—300, Idaho—100, Montana—150, Nevada—8,700, New Mexico—50, Oregon—1000, Utah—600, and Wyoming—4100). "Neither pretty nor practical, the wild horses are creatures that no one wants except a handful of horse lovers and an occasional rancher who will break one for use as a cow pony. For nearly 50 years their destination has been the dogfood companies, and they have been rounded up by the tens of thousands for this purpose."

Some didn't go to dog food companies, however. A wild horse roundup in May of 1964 in central Montana had gathered 1200 head, most of which were sold in a special bucking horse sale at Bozeman, Montana. Charlie Pike, associate editor of *Western Livestock Reporter*, participated in the roundup and said it was the "largest band of wild horses since 1926" to be rounded up and shipped out of central Montana. "We would expect to see this type of drive on a TV western," he added, "but here we were seeing it and participating in person."

Anthony Amaral, in his article "The Wild Horse—Worth Saving?" (*National Parks and Conservation Magazine*, March 1971), mentions the last massive roundup of feral horses in the U.S.—when about 70,000 wild horses in Nevada were taken off the public range in the early 1950's. There wasn't much public outcry over the fate of those horses partly because there wasn't much publicity about the roundup; the state and federal agencies did not want a lot of public outcry. The free-roaming horse numbers in Nevada at that time had reached a high figure, and some of them had to go. The government managed the removal.

E.R. (Hank) Greenslet, who was then the Nevada State BLM director, supervised this Nevada roundup and said,

This program was carried out without cost to the government except some assistance in building holding corrals and truck trails when needed. We herded the horses humanely with a plane. It can be done, expediently, and far easier on the horses than attempting to herd them by men on horseback. After we thinned the herds—and we did leave seed stock wherever we saw a herd led by a decent-looking stallion—private interests took over. They used planes and flat-bed trucks to rope the horses. Some of these operators allowed that technique to become callous and brutal, and a lot of horses suffered miserably. That was when public ire was aroused, through Velma Johnston, resulting in a federal law outlawing mechanical means to capture wild horses. Now (1970) when the BLM tries to help out the range by thinning the herds, and allowing ranchers and sheepmen to get their full measure of range privileges, which they pay for, the public steps down on us.

Public protests grew loud over any threat to wild horses, and the BLM, formerly in the position of trying to keep feral horse numbers under control, to keep the range from being overgrazed, suddenly found itself as the reluctant guardians of the remaining 17,000 horses that roamed the West. Nevada, the state with the most horses, seemed to be the scene upon which the stage was set for enactment of the drama in the emerging controversy over the wild horses.

Several different ideas about wild horses had emerged. One group, including many stockmen and range managers, considered the wild horse merely a feral domestic horse, a range horse, and considered it a nuisance, detrimental to the range. Another group favored native wildlife, and where the horse competed with native wildlife for feed and habitat, this group felt the horse should be removed or rigidly controlled. And then, the newest emerging group, which quickly became the largest group, viewed the wild horse as a symbol of the Old West and the embodiment of freedom, feeling that the wild horses should not be molested nor controlled. A more moderate view leaned toward multiple use of the public lands, with healthy condition of the rangeland as the first priority, and subsequent use of the range by all animals (wildlife, livestock and horses) inasmuch as they did not abuse the range.

But the moderate views were quickly drowned out in the first acts of the drama, as the battle lines were drawn between the extremist positions—the voices for removal or strict control of the horses, and the voices wanting complete protection and no

Afraid that wild bands like these were headed for a last roundup, an outraged public came to their defense, demanding protection for them.

control for the wild horses. An outraged American public was finally reacting to the plight of the wild horses. The trickle of articles and stories in national magazines and the news media became a stream, then a torrent. Millions of people who had never even heard of wild horses became concerned, appalled, and vocal. Many began writing letters to their elected representatives, urging them to enact legislation to protect the horses.

In 1959 the "Wild Horse Annie Law" was passed, prohibiting use of aircraft or motorized vehicles in capturing or killing wild horses, and prohibiting the pollution of waterholes for the purposes of trapping the horses. This was a step in the right direction, but the law was hard to enforce. Some Nevada ranchers still wanted to keep range horse numbers low with periodic roundups, and other individuals, attempting to make a profit from the market for horseflesh, continued to gather horses to ship to rendering plants in California. By the early 1970's there were many people who felt that the wild herds were on the brink of disaster. Estimates of wild horse numbers were at a record low of approximately 16,000 head, and some people were sure the actual numbers were even lower than that. Doom for the wild bands seemed close at hand.

7

Wild Horse Annie

The most persistent and dedicated person in the fight to save the wild horses from brutal destruction was Mrs. Velma Johnston, better known as "Wild Horse Annie." Her story is a case in point to show that one persistent person can ultimately change conditions they do not like. She began the movement, almost single-handedly, that was eventually to change the nation's thinking about wild horses, and give them protection and a permanent place in our nation's future.

Her untiring efforts to protect the wild horses spanned three decades. But her interest in them went back farther than that. She was born Velma Bronn, daughter of hardy pioneer parents. Her grandfather was foreman of a silver mine at Ione, Nevada, and when the mine closed down in 1884 he and his wife, with a brand new baby boy—Velma's father, Joe Bronn—headed across the desert to California in a wagon. One of the mares in the four-horse "mustang" team had a new foal, and it was milk from the mare that kept the baby boy alive on the long journey.

Joe Bronn grew up, married, and was a mustanger and freighter when little Velma was born in 1912. He lived in Nevada, near Reno, and freighted goods back and forth over the mountains to California. Velma was an outdoor child and loved horses, but when she was 5 years old she became ill with polio. After several years of wrestling with the disease and a twisted spine—and spending some time in a San Francisco hospital in an upper-body cast which left her face disfigured—she was able to lead an active life again. She helped her father with the freight horses and had her own special horse, named Hobo. Later she married a neighbor boy, Charley Johnston, and Charley bought the little ranch from her father. They named it the Double Lazy Heart Ranch, and in the summers on weekends they ran it as a dude ranch for children, along with raising hay. Velma also had a secretarial job in Reno, 26 miles away.

It was on her way to work in Reno one day in 1950 that she happened to see something that was to change her life and spur her into active concern for wild horses. Ahead of her on the highway was a large cattle truck, and as she followed it she realized it was full of injured horses, wounded and bleeding. She surmised that these were wild horses that had been captured in an airplane roundup, on their way to a slaughterhouse. For years she had known about the capturing of wild horses in this manner, but because it had not touched her life directly she had ignored it, pretending it did not exist, hoping it would go away. Sickened by the sight of the mutilated horses

Velma B. Johnston, "Wild Horse Annie"

crammed in the truck, she could no longer ignore the brutal facts, and she determined to try to do something about it.

Instead of going to work, she followed the truck off the highway and down a narrow, dusty road to a rendering plant in an isolated spot. The horses, some of them hobbled, were pulled off the truck and into the building, where at last their suffering would end. In a rage, Velma snapped pictures, and then as an angry man approached her car, she spun it around and sped away.

The next problem was how to go about halting these abuses. First, she urged her local newspaper to report the brutality of these roundups. Next she found out that the local BLM office gave permission and permits to pilots to round up wild horses. The BLM condoned the wild horse gatherings, because they kept the wild horses from multiplying and using range that was designated for cattle, sheep and domestic horses. Letting the airplane mustangers round up the horses to sell to processing plants solved the BLM's problem of keeping the horse numbers in check, at no cost to the taxpayers.

In mid-June of 1952, Mrs. Johnston learned of a proposed airplane roundup of wild horses in the Virginia Range of Storey County, near her ranch. Permission had already been granted to the mustangers by the BLM district office. Finding out that the airplane mustangers had to apply to the County Board for their permit, required by Nevada state law, Velma and Charley and some of their friends began a crash program to inform and seek the support of as many people in the county as possible, and went to the board meeting at Virginia City, where two pilots were to apply for the permit.

As it turned out, the men who hired the pilots, explaining the need for the roundup by posing as sheepmen who needed the range cleared of horses, were the men who owned the processing plant. Edward Gladding, postmaster of Virginia City, presented a petition signed by 147 people protesting the permit; Velma showed the photos she had taken of the battered horses in the truck, and after a lengthy discussion, the permit was denied. The first victory had been won. The Storey County board of commissioners subsequently banned the pursuit or spotting of wild horses by plane for roundups in their county.

Thus, measures to prohibit the capture of wild horses by using aircraft had its first success June 12, 1952 in one Nevada county, and though it was a small, localized victory, it was the beginning of a larger one. Velma and Charley sent copies of a magazine article about "mustang murder" to each Nevada legislator, along with a letter stating the need to stop airplane mustanging everywhere in the state. Then with the help of Mr. Gladding, they wrote a bill to make it unlawful for anyone to hunt wild horses or burros with airplanes or motor vehicles, and also unlawful to pollute water holes for the purposes of trapping these animals. Next, they started their letter-writing campaign, sending letters to newspaper editors, riding groups, humane organizations, prominent citizens, civic organizations and friends. In the letters they tried to convince people that this bill needed passing, and that their support must be voiced through their legislators.

In 1955 a bill similar to the Storey County law was introduced by state Senator James Slattery in the Nevada state legislature in Carson City at Velma's request, but with an amendment exempting the public lands in the state—86% of Nevada. Other bills that had been backed by concerned individuals in the past had failed to get out of committee due to public apathy, but Velma had done her homework, educating as many people as she could. Her efforts to enlist help from the news media had failed except for an occasional "letter to the editor" which got printed, but the writer of one weekly horseman's column helped in many ways. And Velma's other letter-writing efforts had paid off. Her bill passed with almost no opposition, the first statewide measure ever enacted to prohibit the airborne and mechanized pursuit and capture of wild horses and burros.

It was a beginning, but still the mustanging went

on. On a couple of occasions Mrs. Johnston had tips on horse gatherings from a sympathetic truck driver, and she was able to get photographed evidence, once of corraled horses being loaded at night (she stood on her truck cab and used a flash-bulb) and once of an airplane roundup. She notified law enforcement officers about the roundup and the next day they released 400 wild horses that had been gathered without permission from the BLM or county officials.

At a hearing on her "mustang bill" in Carson City, she got her nickname, "Wild Horse Annie," a nickname given in derision, but which she has proudly carried ever since. Today probably more people know her by her nickname than by her real name.

"Annie" and her friends could not be satisfied until protection for the wild horses could be extended to the federal lands. The wild horse controversy began to take on the aspects of an old-time range war. Mustangers, and some of the ranchers, wanted to be able to continue to round up horses. It seemed to reach a climax in 1957 after a big California newspaper, the *Sacramento Bee*, published a series of front page features on the struggle to save the wild horses (February 21, 1957); thousands of encouraging letters poured in. Velma and her friends continued to try to inform as many people as possible, telling them that effective protection for wild horses and burros would require federal legislation. Velma and Charley posted spotters in strategic desert locations to notify the sheriff's deputies of any signs of illegal gatherings, and many Nevadans volunteered to serve on "Annie's Patrol."

Meanwhile, Wild Horse Annie's crusade was reaching far beyond Nevada. Magazines and newspapers began to carry feature articles about her efforts. In April of 1958, Nevada's Congressman Walter S. Baring introduced her bill in Washington D.C.—a bill that made it illegal for anyone to use an airplane or truck to capture wild horses. But Congress adjourned before action was taken on the bill, so Velma and her husband renewed their crusade wtih determined vigor, trying to reach even more people in the interim before Congress convened again.

More publications carried the story (*Desert* magazine in June of 1959, *Sierra, Western Horseman*, and *Time* in July) and the mail poured in. To each inquiry of "What can I do to help?" Velma replied, "Contact your delegations in Washington." Velma wrote to schools all over the country, telling the children about the wild horses and what was happening to them, ending with a plea for them to write to their Congressman to help save the mustangs. And Congressmen began to receive letters and petitions from children.

The neighborhood children and his own two children brought a petition to Congressman James Wright at his home in Fort Worth, Texas. That night Mr. Wright dictated the following in his weekly newsletter to constituents: "Any Congressman is likely to receive a petition every now and then, but this week I got one which really struck home . . . Am I going to be susceptible to pressure? Am I going to be influenced by a bunch of children? Am I going to support this bill because kids—mine and others—are sentimental about the wild horses? You bet your cowboy boots I am!"

In January of 1959, Congressman Baring reintroduced his bill (H.R. 2725), the "Save the Mustangs Bill." The storm of letters was reaching its peak; Mr. Baring told Velma that Congressmen had never had so much mail over any one bill before. An Associated Press release (July 15, 1959) stated, "Some Congressmen hope the matter will be settled soon. Seldom has an issue touched such a responsive chord in the hearts of their constituents. Their offices have been overwhelmed by mail."

And Velma flew to Washington to be there when the judiciary committee held their hearing on the bill. She presented each member of the committee with a portfolio of wild horse history and problems, accompanied by photos taken by Gus Bundy. Her testimony was based on 9 years of research and effort, and she had two very compelling arguments: first, that the efforts of the commercial mustangers had so reduced the wild horse numbers that they were no longer a significant competitor to domestic livestock on the public range, and second, that the inhumane methods used to capture and transport the horses were an affront to humanitarian values.

The Department of Interior's BLM presented a strong case for amending the bill to allow use of aircraft and motorized vehicles by the BLM or other authorized individuals for management of horses on the public lands, but Mrs. Johnston, so thoroughly appalled by what misuse of the airplane had done in the past, argued against it, refusing to agree to the amendment. The committee, after a few days of deliberation, recommended passage of the bill as it had been originally introduced, without the BLM's amendment. Thus, on September 8, 1959, President Eisenhower signed the bill into law. It was a major victory for the wild horse lovers, not only in Nevada, but across the nation. This was the first federal legislation enacted to protect wild horses and burros and the 20,000 remaining wild horses would be safer.

But things didn't really get any easier for Velma Johnston. Her husband Charley had emphysema, and was getting steadily worse. For a year, he owed his survival to oxygen tanks, and then in 1964 he died. Her loss was hard, but Velma carried on her fight for the wild horses bravely, alone.

The second problem was that wild horse roundups still continued, and some of these gatherings were using illegal methods—airplanes. There was difficulty in enforcing the 1959 law. In one Nevada trial the defendants admitted use of an airplane and did not deny using a gun during the roundup, claiming that they were merely gathering their own horses. A county sheriff and deputy brand inspector who saw the roundup claimed that the horses were unbranded, yet the jury's verdict was not guilty.

One of the problems was that dishonest mustangers would turn a few of their own branded horses loose, then round up groups of wild horses with the branded ones, claiming that they were merely gathering their own horses, for it was legal to round up domestic, branded horses with aircraft. In 1968, 725 horses were rounded up in Lander County, Nevada and transported out of state to a processing plant owned and operated by members of the family on whose ranch the roundup had been made. Of the 725 horses, 469 were not branded, but no charges were brought against the captors.

Mrs. Johnston checked the state records during the late 1960's and found that during one six month period, 4,332 head of horses were taken out of Nevada, of which about half were unbranded, and she began to wonder if aircraft had been used in rounding them up. Enforcement of the wild horse law rested in the hands of local officials, and conflicting opinions sometimes arose over the term "wild" horses, for many free-roaming horses were loosely claimed by ranchers because these horses ran with, or were offspring of, their own branded stock. Some owners released domestic horses on the range without grazing permits, and sometimes these horses were not kept branded (offspring were not periodically rounded up to be branded), thus confusing the identity of which horses were "wild" and which ones were legally owned.

In Colorado an unsuccessful attempt was made to change the designation of wild horses to a protected species. State BLM director Ed Rowland was in favor of setting aside a wild horse refuge in northwestern Colorado, but at that point nothing came of it.

The BLM, previously more concerned with livestock grazing—looking at the feral horses as strays and trespass horses to eliminate from the range—in 1967 acknowledged the public's growing interest in the wild horse bands and changed its policy to include wild horses in its ideas of multiple use of the public lands, taking on preservation and protection duties. It was a belated move in the direction of protection, but understandably so, because up until that point (the passage of Wild Horse Annie's law to prohibit aircraft roundups) the American people had had no real interest in the wild horses and had not considered them worth keeping. But now the public was apathetic no longer. Suddenly awakening to a desire to protect and preserve the horses, Americans found it hard to change the traditional views of the mustangers, range users, and government agencies overnight.

But the process of change had begun. And once begun, it kept moving. The BLM now recognized the wild horses and would provide feed for them, taking the horses into consideration when management plans were made for grazing in those areas in which they roamed. But because ownership of wild horses and burros rested with the separate states under the state estray laws, the BLM often lacked jurisdiction to provide a comprehensive control program for the wild bands.

To whom did the horses belong? The states claimed ownership, yet the horses for the most part lived on federal lands. In most states, the local county commissioners had the final authority on issuing permits to people for capturing horses. These county commissioners often issued permits to local ranchers who wanted to reduce the horse numbers because the horses ran on lands leased by the ranchers. The ranchers were paying for the grass eaten by the horses, maintaining the water troughs from which the horses drank, and packing salt out for cattle that was also utilized by wild horses. Thus the wild horse was in political limbo. Not being a native wildlife species, he could not be protected as wildlife. Technically, he was stray livestock, but because he had escaped human control and was unclaimed, he did not fall under livestock regulations for grazing. Herds of horses that had lived free in the mountains for several generations held an appeal, a special something, for most Americans, and they wanted to see these horses left free, rather than rounded up and disposed of as stray livestock.

The 1959 law referred to "horses and burros existing in a wild or free state on public lands . . . this classification does not rest upon the origins of the horses in terms of bloodlines or similar technical limitations . . ." This leaves an uncertain borderline area in the definition—an area in which exist the privately owned range horses whose owners haven't branded them, or haven't paid grazing fees on them, all mixed in with the wild horses on the same ranges.

For example, a few years ago the Oregon BLM estimated that approximately 1000 horses, 850 of which were privately owned but trespassing without permit, were grazing in one Oregon district. And not all of the "wild" horses are on public lands. Nobody knows exactly how many wild horses exist on the various Indian reservations, or on the large tracts of private land whose owners do not mind the horses being there. Some of the last wild horses left in Arizona are on an Indian reservation along the Gila River.

There was nothing in the 1959 wild horse protection law to determine whether the horses were the responsibility of the Federal government or the states, so for many years the status of the wild horse was uncertain. And since the horse had no definite legal status on the range, the BLM had no real authority to make allotments of forage for wild horse use, nor any other provisions for wild horse needs. Politically, the wild horse was in a sort of no man's land.

Public interest and concern continued to mount, along with a growing recognition that some sort of federal management program for protection and control of the horses was probably necessary. The feeling grew that the wild horses belonged to all Americans, not just to those people whose lands they inhabit, or those who were responsible for turning the horses out on the range in the first place. Thus there came a strong push for changing the responsibility for the horses from the state and local agencies to the federal government. The 1959 Wild Horse Annie Bill had given the horses some measure of protection, but it did not solve the problems. It failed to establish a legal status for the wild horse and failed to provide a program of management for the wild herds.

In 1965 Wild Horse Annie formed an organization called the International Society for the Protection of Mustangs and Burros (ISPMB), and pressed on harder than ever in her crusade. To help slow down the horse gatherings for dogfood processing (from the Nevada area at least) ISPMB helped California state senator Anthony G. Beilenson put through a new law in 1970 to prohibit the sale of wild horses, dead or alive, in California. Since most of the "canner" horses from Nevada went to processing plants in California, this slowed the traffic a bit.

Subsequently, the ISPMB worked toward getting passage of federal legislation to give the wild horses real protection. Their efforts were largely responsible, with the help of other individuals and organizations, for the eventual passage of the Wild Horse and Burro Act of 1971, an Act which will be covered in more detail in a later chapter.

After the passage of this protection act, Wild Horse Annie and her associates formed another organization to help in providing surveillance patrols, research and field studies and other activities to insure the effectiveness of the new law. So, although Velma Johnston already served as president of ISPMB, she took on another task as well. The new organization, Wild Horse Organized Assistance (WHOA), was founded on the condition that she become chairman of its board and executive director, which she did. Both organizations strive toward the same goal, protecting wild horses and burros. WHOA was established at the insistence of friends who knew of Velma's need for funds to continue her crusade.

But that crusade was not easy. It won her enemies as well as friends and supporters. Shortly after the Wild Horse and Burro Act was passed in late 1971, a letter to the editor of the *Nevada State Journal* said, "I predict that Wild Horse Annie will be called Dead Horse Annie in a very few short years."

And in the August 24, 1972 issue of the Pioche *Record* there were statements disagreeing with Velma's position of preserving the wild horses. The first was signed by the Board of County Commissioners of Lincoln, County, Nevada, wanting the 1971 protection law repealed because they felt the wild horse was not a symbol of the pioneer spirit of the West, did not contribute to the diversity of life forms of this nation, and did not enrich the lives of the American people.

The second statement, signed by three men, stated:

There were a few individuals that were somewhat 'wild' in deportment, but the pioneer is not characterized by a spirit of wildness and adventure. The pioneer came west to improve his economic status—the commendable and major ambition of civilized man. He left home, friends, relatives, and security, with little but his courage and ambition, to suffer hunger, hardship and peril to attain his purpose. Such was the historic spirit of the pioneer . . . The wild horse was one of the major 'perils' of the pioneer in his trek to the West. His horses—draft and saddle—must get their food by being allowed to graze during the night with as little restraint as possible. This necessity, in wild horse country, exposed them to the enticement of the wild horse herds . . . When at last the pioneer reached 'the one hundred sixty' where he settled, the wild horse 'peril' was increased. His meager resources were generally exhausted. There was no money for shelter or fences. He made a cave in a side of a hill (the dugout) to protect his family from the elements, but his horses must be unfettered on unfenced pasture where they were again the unprotected prey of the wild horse. Not the least of the chronicled struggles of the pioneer was his injury by 'free-roaming' horses. Perhaps he fought no greater pest; as the loss of even one horse from his team sometimes spelled his failure. It would take a distorted imagination to arrive at a conclusion that the wild horse is a living or any symbol of the spirit of the pioneer. The toil, labor and privation of the pioneer's tame horse would more nearly symbolize the spirit of the pioneer . . . Feed that now produces a significant portion of our beef and mutton supply and supports useful wildlife is wasted on animals that are of no value aesthetically or otherwise.

The supervisor of Utah brand inspectors, John Chugg, was quoted as saying, "Which is more important, to allow herds of wild, useless mustangs to deplete the mountain plains and rangeland . . . or to intelligently manage the grasslands so that food—beef and mutton—can be produced for the survival of mankind? The law that was pushed through Congress by busybody Women's clubs and elementary school children is ridiculous, unrealistic and dangerous to our environment and economy."

Mrs. Johston's crusade, which led to the wild horse protection law, not only drew opposition from mustangers and livestock men, and skepticism and concern from range managers, it also drew a few threats. One day in the mail she received an envelope containing a large yellow poster of a coiled snake, and written beneath it a warning: "Don't Tread on Me; the Vigilante Committee of 10,000".

But in spite of opposition, Wild horse Annie continued her efforts, being instrumental in establishing the wild horse refuges at Nellis Air Force Base in Nevada, and in the Pryor Mountains along the Montana-Wyoming border, and doing her part on the national advisory board for wild free-roaming horses and burros after the passage of the federal law protecting them. She was a dedicated and sincere woman, doing her part to make America better, doing what she believed in.

8

The Wild Horse Refuges

The first refuge for wild horses in the United States was created in Nevada in December of 1962 by the Department of the Interior in cooperation with the Department of Defense. The refuge is a remote 394,000 acre expanse of desert and mountain country in the northwest corner of the Nellis Air Force Base practice range, northwest of Las Vegas. The horse range is located within, and is part of, the Air Force Bombing Range. When the Bombing Range was withdrawn from public range land for military use, the government purchased all the livestock grazing rights from the local ranchers who had used it earlier.

The wild horse range was established, because of pleas from concerned individuals throughout the country, to protect the diminishing horse herds in the West; about 200 wild horses were therefore granted sanctuary in the Air Force Base lands. Unsuited for domestic livestock because of military uses and scarcity of water, the Nevada wild horse range was nevertheless a piece of land large enough to maintain bands of free-roaming horses, and due to the vastness of the area, the danger to the horses from military uses was quite remote. The area was used occasionally by the Air Force for gunnery practice, and the public was not permitted to enter it.

Secretary Udall announced the establishment of the Wild Horse Range to the public, saying, "One of the biggest problems faced by the department in its search for a suitable refuge is competition between wild horses and other stock. Since the Air Force Range is already a military withdrawal where domestic animals are not permitted, wild horses and wild game have shared this area in recent years . . . Preserving a typical herd of wild horses may prove difficult, but we will make the effort to assure those of us who admire wild horses that there will always be some of these animals."

Another news release from his office stated that, "the Refuge was established in answer to pleas from thousands of admirers of the free-ranging animals . . . To many people, the wild horses are a symbol of an inspiring era in the West."

It was originally planned to develop the horse range into a national park type of attraction, at the same time providing for research and evaluation of resource management practices for wild horses. It was optimistically hoped that the military requirements for the area would lessen, but this did not happen. Because the Air Force had to increase its use of the area, public access was not allowed.

The Las Vegas district of the BLM has jurisdiction over the Wild Horse Range, and put in water developments to help sustain the herd. Like many areas in the southern deserts, water is sometimes scarce in the horse range. Improved watering places aided survival of the horses, and helped to better distribute them over a larger portion of the range, increasing the amount of usable forage available to them.

Cattle from adjoining grazing districts have occasionally wandered onto the wild horse range, and in 1977 a boundary fence was built across the northern end, intended to exclude range cattle from the horse area and save the forage for wild horses and wildlife. The wild horse herd had increased since the creation of the refuge gave sanctuary to 200 head in 1962. During the winter of 1976-77 more than 1000 horses were counted on the Wild Horse Range and adjacent areas.

In 1977 the BLM, Energy Research and Development Administration, Nevada Department of Fish and Game, U.S. Air Force, and the U.S. Fish and Wildlife Service met to discuss plans for the Bombing Range. This area includes the horse range, for which a management plan was proposed, considering the vegetation of the area, the wildlife, and the wild horses. At the time of this writing, inventories of the vegetation, wildlife and wild horses were still being made, after which a management plan would be written, giving some guidelines for management and control of the wild horses and wildlife in the area.

The next wild horse range established by the government was in the Pryor Mountains, named after Sergeant Pryor of the Lewis and Clark Expedition. This is an area on the Montana-Wyoming border. The events leading up to the creation of this wild horse range were more controversial than those surrounding the creation of the Nevada wild horse range; the news media splashed the Pryor Mountain controversy across the nation, increasing public pressure in favor of saving the horses.

This area used by the Pryor Mountain horses ranges from cool, timbered highlands, down through rocky plateaus to scrub desert at the lower elevations. Deep, steep-walled canyons, isolated grassy plateaus, and foothill slopes characterize this country. Wind keeps the high ridges free of snow most of the winter. The Custer National Forest forms the north boundary, the Bighorn Canyon National Recreation Area lies to the east, private property borders the southern part, and public land lies to the west across a deep limestone canyon carved by Crooked Creek.

The Pryors have a long Indian history, with signs of Indian culture still in evidence. The plateau just across Crooked Creek from the wild horse area has more than 100 teepee rings and was a camping area for nomadic tribes. Some of the teepee rings are small, indicating the size of the teepees that could be carried on an Indian's back or dragged by dog travois; archeologists believe these smaller teepee rings were made before the Indians had horses. Other sites in the Pryors have petroglyphs and pictographs, carvings and paintings of early man. One cooking firepit in the area is believed to be more than 10,000 years old.

It is not known exactly when wild horses first appeared in the Pryor Mountains. Some of the local residents claim that the horses were introduced into the region by the early settlers. Others claim that there were already wild horses there. William Hamilton, an early trapper, roamed through the Pryors in 1848 and recorded many of his observations. He did not report seeing wild horses, but this does not necessarily mean there weren't any. Horses may have strayed from the nearby Crow Indian reservation into the Pryors during the latter part of that century. These small bands were probably added to by early settlers' horses; the first white settlers came into the area in 1894, bringing horses with them. A photo of a roundup on the Dryhead about 1910 is the earliest definitive record available, and it can be assumed that horses existed in the surrounding country for some time before that date.

Later, after 1934, a local rancher, Lloyd Tillet, was licensed to graze 20 horses on the south slope of the Pryors. Time, and a rugged terrain that made roundups difficult, saw those horses increase. The free-roaming bands increased in number until there were about 200 horses by the mid-1960's. Some of

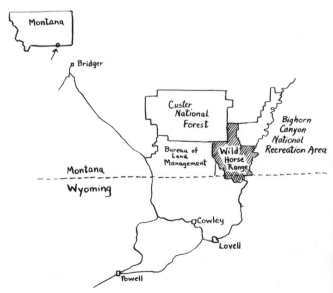

Location of Pryor Mountain Wild Horse Range

the privately owned horses were eventually gathered.

Whether or not the first wild horses in the Pryors came with the first settlers or were already there doesn't really matter; whatever their origin, local people in that area wanted to see some of the horses remain as an historical attraction.

The controversy over the horses developed because of poor range conditions; the Montana game officials felt the horses were eating browse needed by the deer, and the BLM contended that the horses were overgrazing the plant cover needed to hold the soil in place. Vegetation was deteriorating, resulting in increased erosion and a dwindling food supply for the horses and wildlife. The horse's favorite plants were severely overgrazed and dying out, and the horses were beginning to compete with deer for rabbit brush, mountain mahogany and other browse plants. Edible vegetation was so sparse that some horses were pawing and digging away the soil to get to the plant roots to eat. Water was another problem. The major watering places were two springs near the south boundary and a mine tunnel waterhole on the west side. Some horses had to travel up to ten miles between water and available feed. The BLM, alarmed over the deteriorating range and subsequent soil erosion, decreed that the horses should be reduced or removed.

But some of the local citizens didn't want the horses removed, and in the town nearest the wild horse area—Lovell, Wyoming, population 2700— the Chamber of Commerce organized a campaign to keep the horses from being destroyed or removed. A report in the *National Observer* (April 11, 1966) told about the smoldering controversy, and almost immediately, letters of protest poured in, criticizing the BLM policy. People wrote to the governors of Montana and Wyoming, the BLM, their congressmen, and local Wyoming officials, demanding that the horses not be removed. In the face of such opposition, the BLM postponed the decision about the fate of the horses for two years, until the controversy could be resolved.

The controversy actually began some years earlier, growing out of very ordinary circumstances, typical of situations in the West where feral horse herds were part of the history of an area. In the Pryors, the horses had increased to the point of competing with domestic livestock and wildlife and the range was seriously overgrazed. But many of the local ranchers did **NOT** want to see all the horses eliminated. One rancher, Lloyd Tillet, was dead set against the BLM plan to remove the horses. He and his brother Royce, and his 80 year old mother Bessie, ran the 9000 acre TX cattle ranch, which

forms the southwestern border of the wild horse area. The Tillets ran cattle on the public range, the number controlled by their BLM permit. They also had a permit for 20 horses.

Bessie Tillet's parents homesteaded there in early times, less than 20 years after General Custer's famous defeat over the next ridge east. Wild horses were a part of their landscape then, and in those early days some of the ranch stock came from the wild bands. The ranchers rounded up others to sell as rodeo bucking horses, and others were left to run free. As in many ranching areas in remote mountain areas, the ranchers appreciated the wild horses and held them in a loose sort of sponsorship, making sure that there were always some out there.

But times changed, intensive land use came into being, and the wild horses were looked upon by some as a nuisance and a detriment, damaging the range. By the early 1960's it looked pretty certain that the horses had to go. The BLM considered all of the free roaming horses in the area (which was rangeland) subject to the permit for 20 horses, and told the Tillets to cut down the herd to 20 head, the number which could legally graze there. But the Tillets declared that the extra horses were truly wild, not just loose range horses, and thus should not be counted for the permit. There were already wild horses in the area when the Tillet family settled there in 1894. The BLM maintained that the horses were damaging the overstocked range and must be removed.

So, to prevent the rounding up or outright shooting of the horses, the Tillets in early 1966 were forced to claim ownership of them, thus protecting the herd temporarily.

This of course earned them a trespass notice from the BLM, warning them to get their illegal horses off the range; they had no permit to let that many run out there all year around. And when the Tillets did not round up the horses, their BLM grazing permits for their livestock were suspended—for both their cattle and horses—leaving them just a short time to get their stock off the range or pay a stiff fine. It was at this time that the controversy exploded into print, and people across the nation set up a cry to save the horses.

The BLM retreated and set up a range survey to study the problem. The Tillets gave up their claim to the wild horses, got back their grazing privileges, and the Pryor Mountain horses had a temporary reprieve. The BLM, in defense of its position on horses and burros, issued a publication called *Fact Sheet: Wild Horses* in May of 1967. The Bureau acknowledged that it shared with many people an interest in preserving and protecting the remnants

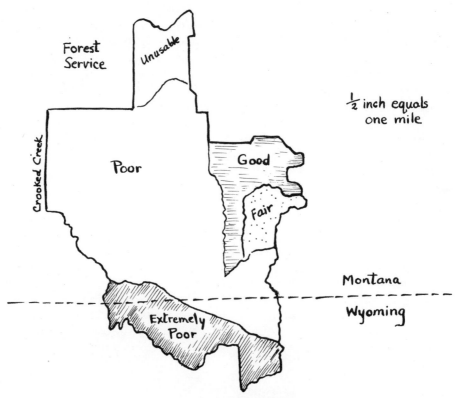

Forest
Service

Unusable

½ inch equals
one mile

Crooked Creek

Poor

Good

Fair

Montana

Wyoming

Extremely
Poor

General Range Condition in the Pryors.

of the wild horses. It defined any horse roaming free and uncontrolled as wild, and estimated the numbers of wild horses on the public domain at 17,300 (along with 8,100 burros). This fact sheet concluded by saying that solutions to wild horse problems would be found when all concerned people could work together.

In the meantime, newspaper and magazine articles reported periodically on the Pryor Mountain wild horse controversy, including an article in the April, 1967 issue of *True* magazine. As more and more people became aware of the Pryor Mountain situation, protective efforts for the horses increased.

In a nationwide news release in September of 1967, the BLM announced a policy which assured that positive efforts would be made for the preservation of wild horses and burros. This policy provided for a planned management program where the aesthetic value of wild horses or burros was determined to be a public asset. Where feed and water were limited and the wild horses or burros competed with livestock or wildlife, the BLM would work with interested groups to try to solve the

problems. Where reserved forage was set aside for horses or burros, the BLM would establish cooperative agreements with the state and local authorities and other interested groups. Where horse or burro numbers became too plentiful, the BLM would work with state and local authorities in gathering excess animals to reduce the herds to manageable levels. This news release was concluded by the BLM director stating, "We feel that the public has amply demonstrated its concern for these animals and look upon them as representatives of a colorful and historic chapter in the story of the West."

But as soon as the BLM policy statement was issued, the Montana Livestock Commission went into action, resolving on December 4, 1967, that the ownership of livestock (including horses and burros), without specific responsibility, was contrary to the policy of the Livestock Commission of the State of Montana, and that in the creation of any refuge area (such as in the case of the Pryor Mountains), state lines should be fenced, in order to determine jurisdiction and eliminate confusion of responsibility and policy. In other words, the public could not

Pryor Mountain Wild horses

"own" the horses, because these horses were stray livestock and under the jurisdiction of the state estray laws.

After the expiration of the two year reprieve the BLM had given the horses, the Bureau held public meetings and presented three alternatives for managing the Pryor Mountain wild horses. These alternatives included maintaining the greatest number of horses the area would adequately support (about 60 head), after reducing the excess; maintaining fewer horses to further reduce competition with deer (reducing the herd to about 15 head and letting them grow back up to about 30 head as the range improved, managing the horses so a healthy deer herd could be maintained). The third alternative involved complete removal of all horses—managing the area for wildlife, including reintroduction of bighorn sheep.

These alternatives were referred to by *Newsweek* (May 13, 1968) as a choice of "remove, remover, removest" and Royce Tillet was quoted as saying, "No one disagrees that the land is overgrazed, but we want a herd large enough—say 100 head—so they won't inbreed and spoil the mustang blood." The article went on to say that the controversy had become increasingly bitter, the BLM implying that the Lovellites were more interested in tourism and publicity than the fate of the land. The mustang preservationists on the other side labeled the BLM as "armchair naturalists" and "horse haters."

Several newspapers and magazines, in stories about the Pryor controversy, ignored the fact that the BLM had proposed several alternatives, and stated that the Bureau planned to trap all the horses and sell them for dogfood. For weeks, newspapers, radio, and TV stations blasted the BLM, and hundreds of letters were written accusing the BLM of

inhumane treatment of wild horses. Actually, the only thing the BLM had done that directly affected the horses was to build a fence across the southern border of the wild horse area. This was built to keep them off private lands and to keep cattle and sheep from wandering onto the horse range.

Headlines about the "nearing mustang slaughter" spread across national newspapers, magazines gave the story top priority, and TV coverage topped it off. Because of all the national publicity, public outcry grew increasingly bitter. One BLM spokesman said ruefully, "We're the guys in the long mustaches and black hats." By June, the BLM had received thousands of letters and had held 24 public meetings.

In a news release dated June 16, 1968, by the Billings, Montana BLM district office, District Manager Dean Bibles said, "While we have been urged to establish a wild horse refuge in the Pryor Mountains, no group has volunteered to sponsor the horses so far. Because of the requirements of Montana livestock law, someone will have to assume responsibility for them." Someone would have to claim the horses and "own" them, because by Montana law stray horses belonged to the state unless they were branded or otherwise subject to valid claims of ownership. The BLM was responsible for the land resources, but had no legal jurisdiction over the horses. The BLM planned to reach a final decision about what to do with the horses by August, 1968.

Upon announcement of this requirement of sponsorship for the horses, residents of the area and volunteers from other parts of the country formed the Pryor Mountain Wild Horse Association, interested in sponsoring the horses. The five requirements for sponsorship, outlined by Dean Bibles of the BLM, included the stipulation that the horses would have to be purchased from the states of Wyoming and Montana, and would have to be branded by the sponsor with a properly recorded brand in both states. Otherwise the states would claim the horses as strays. Other specific requirements were to be worked out in accordance with the BLM's wild horse policy. The sponsoring groups would have to manage the wild horses, annually round them up and brand the young stock, and keep their total numbers at a certain level. But the newly formed group that was interested in sponsoring the horses did not want to comply with the branding requirement, feeling that this went against the idea of the horses being wild.

In the meantime, the BLM began construction of a corral-type trap at one of the horses' major water holes on the Wyoming side of the mountains; water trapping would be the most humane method of capturing the excess horses. After trapping, an auction would be held to get rid of the surplus animals, and the rest would be branded before being released again.

Two television networks produced programs on the Pryor Mountain horses, including a feature by Hope Ryden (a writer and producer of documentary feature films for television) for ABC, in mid-July of 1968. And national magazines, including *Life*, sent staff members to the area to take pictures and prepare articles about the problem. After the television news feature on ABC revealing the possible plight of the wild horses just six weeks away, the BLM and ABC were deluged with mail, telegrams, and phone calls from an outraged public, renewing pleas on behalf of the horses.

Work on the BLM trap continued in spite of the many protests, for it was obvious to the range managers that SOME horses would have to be removed to halt range deterioration. But the general public could not understand this kind of thinking, and determined to stop the BLM from rounding up ANY horses. Shortly after her television news feature was aired, Hope Ryden went to Washington D.C. to register a personal protest against the removal of the horses. BLM officials told her that no decision had been made yet regarding the horses, for indeed, no one knew how many horses would be removed or retained in the Pryors.

As the trap neared completion, many individuals and organizations joined in the effort to halt the plans for removing horses. Some of those organizations were the International Society for the Protection of Mustangs and Burros, the National Mustang Association, American Horse Protection Association, Animal Welfare Institute, the International

Society for the Protection of Animals, and the Humane Society of the United States. Many ABC viewers called and wrote letters, wondering what they could do to help save the horses. People who contacted the BLM received fact sheets and information explaining that the horses were being removed to protect the forage, and to save the animals themselves from inevitable starvation. Hope Ryden, along with Mrs. Pearl Twyne of the American Horse Protection Association, and Mrs. William Blue of the Animal Welfare Institute, conferred with senators and congressmen, asking them to look into the situation.

Efforts to stop the BLM failed, so in late August, 1968, the Humane Society of the United States (an eastern-based organization, not the older American Humane Society), and rancher Lloyd Tillet of Lovell, Wyoming, filed suit against the Secretary of the Interior and other officials of the BLM to bring the proposed removal program to a halt. At the hearing on the application for a restraining order, BLM officials stated that they had no intention of destroying the horses, and that if any decision were made, there would be plenty of time and opportunity for everyone to be heard. Upon this assurance, the temporary injunction was dismissed on the grounds that it was premature, but left standing was the petition for a permanent injunction, which would enable the Humane Society to reopen the case at a moment's notice, if the BLM announced a decision to remove wild horses from the Pryor Mountains.

Because of the furor, BLM director Boyd Rasmussen visited the area for a first-hand look at the problem, and recommended to the Secretary of the Interior that the Pryors be designated as a wild horse refuge. Plans for trapping the horses were abandoned, and on September 12, 1968, Secretary Udall established the 32,000 acre Pryor Mountain Wild Horse and Wildlife Range, "to give Federal protection to a herd of wild horses whose future has aroused nation-wide attention for several months." Because the BLM's ultimate boss, the American people, had requested it, the wild horse herd in the Pryors would be maintained; the BLM accepted the challenge to provide a permanent and healthy home for them.

In a BLM news release, Director Boyd Rasmussen said that the question of how many horses would be allowed to inhabit the new Wild Horse Refuge was still being studied, and stated that,

it is essential that we move ahead immediately to designate these lands to provide federal protection for this national heritage, and as quickly as possible to establish long-term management for both horses and wildlife, including a mule deer herd. After signing this designation, Secretary Udall has authorized me to appoint a special Advisory Committee to help us study humane and practical means to operate this range and to advise us of a suitable method to arrive at a balance between the horses and deer and the food available to them. . . . Another factor is that forage on 8000 acres of this area was identified years ago as important for mule deer. Thus I want the best advise possible from a wide range of interest within this committee before developing a multiple use program for the area with our State Directors in Montana and Wyoming.

But this statement was misunderstood by some wild horse lovers, including Hope Ryden, to mean that the BLM might try to reduce the herd drastically to a number which threatened survival.

The advisory committee consisted of eight members: William G. Cheney, Executive Director of the Montana Livestock Commission; Dr. C. Wayne Cook, Chairman of the Department of Range Management at Colorado State University; Dr. Frank C. Craighead, Jr., wildlife naturalist from Moose, Wyoming; Frank H. Dunkle, Director of Montana Fish and Game Department; Mrs. Velma B. Johnston ("Wild Horse Annie"), president of ISPMB, Reno, Nevada; Clyde A. Reynolds, Mayor of Lovell, Wyoming; Mrs. Pearl Twyne, President of American Horse Protection Association, Great Falls, Virginia; George L. Turcott, Chief, Division of Resource Standards and Technology, BLM.

This committee held its first meeting October 16-20, 1968, at the wild horse range, and at Billings, Montana and Lovell, Wyoming. On October 17th the group was flown over the Pryor Mountain range. Range conditions, condition of the horses, and other factors were noted. At this first meeting, the BLM emphasized that its primary job was to protect the soil and watershed from destructive usage. The BLM "seeks to enhance aesthetic values while it manages the land to produce the maximum in usable resources." No action would be taken by the BLM to reduce the horse herd until the BLM had received a full report and recommendations from this committee.

Experts from the Denver Federal Center performed a series of soil and weather studies, as agreed by the committee. This resulted in a 70 page report on range conditions and the conclusion that "none of the area within the horse range is in good condition. About 3,500 acres are in fair condition with the remainder classed as poor . . . If the potential of the range is ever to be achieved, grazing control that will allow periodic rest to the vegetation is a prerequisite."

The advisory group met again in early spring of 1969 and flew by helicopter over the range to see how the horses had stood the winter. Many were very thin. They also listened to individuals, representatives of clubs and organizations who had opinions to voice about the horses. Then, they spent long hours hammering out preliminary recommendations. The range carrying capacity for deer and horses had to be considered, along with territorial preferences and feeding habits of the horses. Future management of the range might require water developments to distribute the horses better, reducing grazing pressure on the areas near the existing waterholes. The problem of free-roaming, branded (privately owned) horses that compete with the wild ones had to be considered, and the question asked whether or not the branded horses should or could be removed. How could the wild horses be protected from people who might want to round them up and sell them?

These and many other questions were thoroughly discussed at the conference table, and eventually a set of recommendations emerged to be presented to Director Rasmussen—recommendations that could be used as a pattern for other wild horse refuges, if and when established. The recommendations were:

1. The BLM should manage the range for the benefit of the horses through cooperative agreements with state Fish, Game and livestock agencies concerned.
2. Ultimate size of the herd should be reached through three steps. Branded, claimed, old, sick and deformed animals should be removed first. Water developments should be used to improve distribution of horses on the range, with priority given to northwest and northeast corners and central ridges of the area. Effects of removing some animals and improving water and grazing use shall be studied before additional horses are removed. The committee recommended every effort be made to retain at least 100 horses.
3. Limited roads into the now inaccessible area should be provided to allow tourists to visit in passenger cars, but disturbance of natural values should be kept to a minimum. Off-road vehicles would be restricted.
4. The entire boundary should be fenced horsetight, and all gates should be locked. Auto gates should be used to provide entrance for visitors.
5. Additional management studies should be conducted, including studies on characteristics and behavior of the horses.
6. Roundups should be handled in small groups, with no more than one stallion or "harem" in a corral. Methods other than corralling, such as use of tranquilizers, should be tried.
7. Animals requiring disposal should not be knowingly sold for pet food uses, and surplus animals should be sold on the range if possible. Animals unfit for sale should be destroyed on the site in a humane manner,

and the carcass disposed of under state sanitary statutes.

8. Supplemental feeding should be used only in dire circumstances when survival of the basic herd is threatened; the committee recognized that routine feeding by man would destroy the wild nature of the herd.

9. Branding of animals should be avoided unless marking for protective identification becomes essential, then an inconspicuous lip tatoo should be used.

10. Selection of animals for herd quality will be based on the roan, mouse and buckskin coloring characteristics of the small compact horse now found in the Pryor Mountains.

11. The committee urged that management agencies give adequate financial and administrative support for maximum management possible, and that the wild horse range be given a high priority among agency programs.

All of these recommendations were adopted by the Secretary of the Interior in 1969, and the committee was retained for a follow-up study in 1970. According to Velma Johnston, speaking of the committee, "Each of us, to the best of his ability, held to his knowledge and beliefs and each had to give a bit here and there." The many viewpoints of the eight committee members, all very qualified in their particular fields, were, in the end, beneficial to the future of the wild horses and their habitat.

The new Secretary of the Interior, Walter Hickel, made this statement: "I am firmly convinced that the public interest is always best served when people can sit down together and seek mutually acceptable solutions based on the very best information available."

And Velma Johnston felt that with the establishment of the advisory committee for the Pryor horses that one of her major aims (and efforts of the past 10 years) had been reached. Wild horses had become a dimension of quality, nationally recognized, and in whose behalf the public had forcefully expressed itself. Their future, at least in the Pryors, was now to be decided only after the most careful consideration by acknowledged experts in their fields.

To keep the horses on the range and the cattle off, the committee recommended fencing the wild horse range, and it was fenced by the BLM in areas where there were no natural barriers. For management purposes, the boundaries conformed to natural barriers where possible, and feasible fencing routes. Lands outside the meandering boundary were subject to existing domestic livestock grazing. Within the horse range, the horses were free to roam at will, but the boundaries would prevent them from moving into new territory as their population increased. Under natural conditions, a group of wild horses

Pryor Mountain Wild horse band.

would expand into new territory as their numbers grew.

Consequently, one of the first problems faced by the BLM, in the management of the Pryor Mountain herd, was the horse range's overpopulation. Like any animal on a limited range, the horse has the reproductive capacity to outrun its food supply, and once this point is reached, the animal literally starts to destroy the environment that sustains it. The biological wisdom inherent in a high reproductive rate is negated when artificial factors are introduced. In a completely natural environment, the horse is preyed upon by predators (cougars, wolves), disease, harsh climate, and the mortality rate is high. A high reproduction rate is nature's way of offsetting these losses from natural causes. But when man enters the picture, his best intentions often do more harm than good. By the Autumn of 1971, this was what had developed in the Pryors, and had been developing for many years. Man had eliminated the predators, as well as some of the horse diseases in our country that might have affected the horse in the wild.

Now man had fenced the ever-increasing herd in a limited area. With natural population controls decreased, the herd now faced a more serious and deadly threat—overpopulation and eventual starvation. Every hill had signs of overgrazing: numerous deep trails, pedestalled plants, and invasion of undesirable plants such as halogeten, Russian thistle, broom snakeweed and others that tend to come into an area after the perennial and better forage plants are killed out. Nineteen "range trend" plots had been established after 1968 to compare the fenced plots with the grazed areas adjacent to them. Almost all of the plots indicated a downward trend in range condition after three years. A BLM range study was done in the area in 1958, and again in

1963, and showed a sharp downward trend in range condition over those five years. So the range deterioration in the Pryors had been going on for some time, and was still continuing.

Biologists estimated that the Pryor Mountain range, in its 1970 condition, could produce enough feed for about 85 horses. At this population level the horses would get enough to eat to be able to go into the winter in good condition, and the majority would be expected to survive. But by the fall of 1971 there were more than 160 horses, or twice as many as the range could support.

One of the insidious things about overpopulation is that its harmful effects are not immediately apparent. To the untrained eye, conditions might still look all right, at first. There are a lot of animals and they seem to be in good condition, but the danger signals are subtle. The plants eaten by the horses adapt themselves over the years to a periodic loss of part of their foliage.

When a grazing animal eats a bite of grass or leaves, the plant has a reserve of tissue and energy that enables it to recover and to replace its lost foliage eventually, benefitting both the plant and the grazing animals on a balanced range. But when too many grazers eat on a plant too often, the plant soon has no reserves left to restore itself, and in time it dies. The first thing that occurs on an overgrazed range is the disappearance of the best forage plants—the ones the animals like best and eat first. These are sometimes called the "ice cream" plants by range managers. As these favorite plants are overgrazed and killed out, less palatable ones, usually annuals, take their place. To the untrained eye, however, the range still looks good because it is green and covered with vegetation. But to the grazing animal, in this instance the horse, the pickings are becoming increasingly slim.

Eventually the horses have to start eating the less palatable plants, in their hunger eating the ones that they would not ordinarily eat. As the range continues to deteriorate, the horses are forced to become less and less choosy, and many of the plants they now have to eat are low in food value. They start to show signs of malnutrition. As the overgrazing continues, the vegetative cover of the soil is depleted until there are not enough plant roots to hold the soil and it begins eroding.

But even on an overgrazed range it is rare for horses to lie down and die of simple starvation. They die of other things first because of their lowered resistence to disease and to extremes in climate. Because they are weakened from malnutrition, an infection that a healthy animal would throw off becomes fatal, and a cold spell or rainy season that would only be a minor inconvenience to healthy horses might take a heavy toll in an undernourished herd. Stress that a healthy horse can handle—such as foaling, or nursing a foal, or changes in climate, or a hard winter—may easily prove fatal to the thin and undernourished horse. This kind of disaster is often misinterpreted by the public, who will generally think of the death loss in terms of an epidemic disease or "winterkill", when actually the real killer is overprotection.

Recent studies have shown that some animals have a sort of self imposed population regulating factor that is density dependent. As the number of animals in an area increases, physiological and possibly psychological factors affect the reproduction rate and population level. These ideas have been picked up by some people and superimposed on the whole spectrum of animal populations, and some proponents of this idea recommend letting the "balance of nature" solve the horse population problem. But this "balance of nature" idea is misunderstood and misused in this context. If a "balance" in nature actually exists, it is a precarious one, at best. About the only thing that is "constant" in nature is change.

Glen Cole, of the National Park Service, says there is a "theory that in essence says that an animal cannot progressively destroy his habitat in a closed ecosystem. That is, if all the components are available in a natural system, then the system will be self perpetuating." But in the Pryors, as in many other areas of the West where wild horses exist, the horse is an "exotic" animal that did not evolve in the area that it is now occupying. It does not have "natural" conditions; it does not have the vast space of the prairies for wide roaming, or changing its range if one area becomes grazed, nor does it have natural predators. Some people argue that because the horse was here on this continent up until 10,000 years ago, he should "fit in". But are the predators of 10,000 years ago that kept him in "balance" then, still here? The "natural" situation in our American West has changed a very great deal since then.

The horse is a large and extremely competitive herbivore, that in the Pryor Mountains had no regulatory factors besides disease and starvation. Poor nutrition results in some regulatory factors (slower maturity and later breeding age, shorter span of reproductive years, possible resorption of embryos in undernourished pregnant mares, shorter life span, higher death rate among foals, and so on) but these factors are not harsh enough to be adequate for timely regulation of the wild horse population.

Studies have shown that animal condition lags

behind a decline in range condition. In other words, the range will be seriously hurt before the animals grazing it suffer enough to slow their reproductive rate. All indications are that this lag is extreme in wild horses, because they are highly mobile and can decimate a lot of range before they themselves suffer seriously. In an area like the Pryors, the horses cannot move on when their favorite feed runs low. They are confined to one range and keep grazing it until irreversible damage is done to it. By the time the horses themselves are in bad shape, the range is terrible, and may take decades, or even centuries to improve again.

Nature and her cycles often work in terms of thousands of years. The geologic tearing down of mountains and production of soil is very slow. Once the soil is eroded and gone in places, the chances of range improvement in those areas in our lifetimes is practically nil. A limited area of 33,000 acres was available to the horses in the Pryors and the soil resource had been seriously depleted in the past. If this continues, the number of horses that can be supported in the area will continue to decline. If the philosophy of "allowing the horses to seek their own population level" is adopted, we will ultimately destroy the animal that we are trying to perpetuate.

Thus it developed that by 1971 the Pryor Mountain horses were threatened by their own numbers. But because of the widespread public outcry about the horses earlier, the BLM wasn't too sure how to approach the problem of overpopulation and the obvious need to reduce the herd, without arousing more public wrath.

But at its final meeting in Billings, Montana, in September, 1971, the advisory committee strongly recommended an immediate reduction in the numbers of wild horses, fearing that the foals from that year would have a very poor chance of surviving the approaching winter. The committee suggested removing ALL of the foals, to keep them from dying during the winter, and to give their mothers a better chance of survival with the meager feed available; the mares would not be stressed as hard if they were not nursing their foals. Feeding hay would not be considered as a solution, for it would destroy the wild nature of the horses.

The suggestions made by the advisory committee at this final meeting were:

1. Expansion of the wild horse range to include some of the bordering areas.
2. Employing a man to permanently police the wild horse range.
3. The proposed loop road should NOT be constructed (during 1960-1970 the BLM had made plans for a recreation complex in the wild horse area—a loop road

with overlooks and picnic sites so that people could come and see the horses—but these plans were later abandoned after collecting more data on the wild horses and realizing that too many roads and too much human contact would destroy their "wildness").
4. No further improvements on roads. No BLM roads were planned within the horse range, but the National Park Service was constructing a recreation road along Bighorn Canyon, creating a hazard for horses that had to cross the road to water; the only existing recreational development at that time was the Devil's Canyon Overlook, built by the National Park Service. The BLM was surveying a site adjacent to the horse range for a visitor center and overlook, which would all be outside the horse range.
5. Because of declining range conditions, it was recommended to reduce wild horse numbers to be compatible with their food supply, with allowances for range recovery.
6. Reduction: a. This year's foals to be taken off and cared for by support from private funds, and an effort made to find good homes for them. b. Sale or giving away of horses with the stipulation they cannot be slaughtered. A lip tatoo will help guarantee this. c. Surplus bachelor stallions to be given to the Crow Indians, but can't be sold for slaughter. d. Old, sick, or crippled horses to be disposed of humanely and left on the range.
7. It was recommended to continue intensive studies on horse behavior, food habits, horse geneology and condition and trend of range. Intensive soil and site survey should be carried out to determine if there are areas suitable for artificial rehabilitation as a means of increasing forage.
8. Continue lip tatoo practice.
9. Due to starvation crisis this winter, the 33 ranchers who trail cattle through the range (following the Dryhead Road through the horse range to other ranges in the spring, and back home in the fall) should use no more than a day, or truck the cattle through, not allowing them to drift and graze along the way.

All of these recommendations were adopted by the BLM. Several water developments had been made, for water is the main distributive factor for the horses in spring, summer and fall. In winter the horses eat snow and are able to utilize all of the wild horse range. During April through June, before the weather gets hot, the horses will travel quite a distance to water, but in late June through August many of the horses concentrate around the water sources, eating out the available forage in those areas.

In early October of 1971, after consultation with the advisory committee, local citizens and concerned national organizations, the BLM decided to remove as many surplus horses as possible, starting with the foals, for it was unlikely that any of the foals would survive the winter. Some had already died.

The remaining 16 were captured by seven horse-men, bucking chest-deep snow. The better feed is back in the snowy country under the overhang of the tall mountains, but when the deep snows of winter come, the horses can be trapped there and starve to death.

Each foal was roped from its parent group and led to where it could be trucked out of the wild horse range. Wild Horse Annie's organization, WHOA, asked to be allowed to provide a foster home for the foals until they could be placed with carefully selected private individuals, and this plan was approved by Secretary of the Interior, Rogers C.B. Morton. Corrals to accommodate the foals were arranged for in Lovell, Wyoming, near the horse range, and corral rental (along with all other expenses in connection with the "foster home") paid by WHOA, such as supplemental feeding and veterinary care. Two of the foals, unable to be brought down out of the high country due to deep snow, were flown out by helicopter. The foals were cared for by a veterinarian in Lovell during the winter, and then given away in March and April of 1972.

With a crew of seven men and 20 horses, the November 1971 roundup spanned 18 days, removing a number of adult horses as well as the 16 foals. Of the 79 horses rounded up, two branded horses were returned to their owner, and 28 bachelor stallions were given to the Crow Indian tribe at Pryor, Montana. Approximately 130 horses were left on the range.

The 1971 roundup was merely a stopgap emergency measure, and only a partial success. It did comply with popular demands, reducing the herd without sacrificing the horses, and it did reduce the herd to a point where the remaining animals could survive the winter. But it did not reduce the herd to a level that would bring grazing pressure into balance with the carrying capacity of the range, nor did it establish any workable procedures that could be followed in future years for sound management of the herd. More roundups would be necessary in the very near future to keep the herd from disaster.

Rex Cleary, who was district manager of the BLM in Billings, Montana for four years, said later (at the Wild Horse Forum in April of 1977):

I would simply like to express a note of caution relating to refuges. After managing the Pryor Mountain horse range for the four year period, we had the population problem well under control. We had our base population down to the sustained yield level and from that point on we were in the highly desirable position of simply needing to go out and capture a few excess colts each year. The colts were easy to catch and easy to give away and we didn't take out any older animals. We were able to leave the older animals to die a natural death and would just leave enough colts to offset the death loss and maintain a stable population. Very low expense and a lot of public appeal for the excess animals.

What we hadn't done yet was to bite the bullet on management of the land. The horses were still grazing year-long on the Pryor Mountain Wild Horse Range. There was a large share of the range—I would estimate maybe half—where the water sources were, that the horses concentrated on for the most part of the year, grazing on the vegetation yearlong. Here, the halogeton was invading at an alarming rate. The land was continuing to deteriorate and someday the Bureau is going to have to bite that bullet. In setting up refuges there can't help but be pressure on the agency to stock the refuge somewhere near capacity for wild horses. So the refuge manager has the problem of worrying about how to manage the land, how to rotate the horses to provide periodic rest similar to (land grazed by) domestic livestock.

Another wild horse range was created in the Bookcliff area in Colorado in 1974. This area had been inhabited by wild horses for several decades, roaming within a 46,000 acre range which was also used by domestic cattle.

In 1972 a range survey was conducted, and results indicated that the range was in poor condition and needed to be better managed. With year-around use, the range was not able to support the number of horses and cattle that used it. In 1973 the Grand Junction District BLM Manager issued a decision closing the area to all livestock grazing, and the ranchers who had grazing licenses for using the area appealed this decision.

Following the passage of the Wild Horse and Burro Act, P1 92-195, in 1971, rules and regulations were issued providing for the claiming of privately owned horses on the public lands (after all the branded and claimed trespass horses were gathered, the remaining horses on federal lands would be classified as wild and protected under the new law), and the rancher on whose range allotments the Bookcliff wild horses roamed, filed a claim for all of the Bookcliff wild horses. This claim was ruled invalid by the Colorado Brand Commission.

Because of continuing conflicts and difficult management problems, the BLM agreed on March 28, 1974, to divide the area into two portions, moving all the wild horses onto a 27,225 acre parcel and leaving the remaining 19,000 acres for domestic livestock use. The rancher who had claimed the horses formally withdrew his appeal and claim to the wild horses at that time. Thus the Little Bookcliff Wild Horse Area was established, to preserve and protect the wild herd.

To accomplish the separation of the wild horses and domestic livestock, a fence was required, and it was decided to build pole fence instead of wire, to be safer for the horses. The terrain in the area had many places that could serve as natural boundaries, including some sheer canyon walls. By tying in the ends of the pole fences to these canyon walls, less than five miles of actual fencing was needed to enclose the entire 27,225 acres for the wild horse area. Youth Conservation Corps crews built the stretches of pole fence.

There was a need for water developments within the wild horse area, because there were no streams. Five big springs were developed, to establish permanent watering sites and to provide for better distribution of the horses. There were approximately 85 horses in the Bookcliff range, roaming in dense stands of pinon pine and juniper and in the deep canyons. After the fence was completed and the watering improvements made, the next step was to move the horses, for only about half of them were in the designated wild horse area at the time the fence was completed; the other half needed to be moved into the area.

On August 15, 1975, a contract was awarded to move the 50 horses remaining outside the wild horse range into their new home, and movement of the horses was begun on August 28. An observer for WHOA (Wild Horse Annie's Wild Horse Organized Assistance group) reported:

In all fairness to the contractor, I have never seen a more conscientious man and that goes for all the cowboys he has hired to do the job. I spent the day watching them work with their own horses and the wild ones. I was very much impressed . . . when they stopped for an hour, the saddles were pulled and the horses rubbed down . . . I'm glad it is this bunch of men doing it. I watched those wild ones trying to elude the horsemen and they were running so easy. They (the riders) must just be hoping for the wild ones to go in the direction they point them. The legendary Devil's Pride (one of the dominant stallions in the area) is not going along with their plan. They do have a couple of expert ropers hired and I understand they were close enough to Devil's Pride to have roped him. However, the contractor would not let a rope be used except as a last alternative.

Devil's Pride was eventually captured, but he managed to elude all efforts to capture him until two of his mares headed for a fenced enclosure that was being used as part of the capture plan, the big stallion following them in. Thus he was caught and transported, with his band, to his new home in the wild horse area. The horse gathering and moving project was completed on September 18, 1975, and the Little Bookcliff Wild Horse range was launched.

9
Wild Horses

Perhaps we should take a moment and spend a chapter on wild horses. We've outlined the history of the wild horse in America, told of his decline in numbers and of some of the efforts to protect and preserve him, but we haven't actually said much about the wild horse himself. What is he like?

At the beginning of this discussion it is important to understand something about wildness. Any American wild horse, be he Spanish mustang or abandoned plow horse, is descended from domestic stock with a history of possibly 6000 years of association with, and dependence on man. But the horse, or almost any other domestic animal, will revert to the wild state very soon after escaping from human control. A domestic animal turned loose and gone wild is said to be "feral." But the feral horse can, in just one or two generations on its own, become almost as wild as if its ancestors had never known human contact, fending for itself very adequately. The reverse is also true. The horse was probably domesticated in the first place because it was a highly social animal that was amenable to human presence and control. After capture and proper handling, a wild horse soon adapts to the presence of man.

The ability to live in the wild has never really been "bred out" of the horse as it has been in some breeds of domestic dogs, for instance (some of the purely

The feral horse can, in just one or two generations, become almost as wild as if its ancestors had never known human contact.

show dogs and pampered pets with their very short legs and selectively-bred body conformation might have a hard time becoming effective predators again). The horse, although he has been refined and changed somewhat in outward appearance and athletic ability by domestication and selective breeding, is still basically the same fleet and timid animal that man first domesticated some 6000 years ago. The horse depends on his good eyesight, sense

A harem band usually consists of a stallion and a few mares. The stallion is the alert one who senses danger first, but the band is usually led by a wise old mare.

range and the boundaries are well defined in the animals' minds. Home ranges for several bands may overlap. Two or more bands may use the same water hole, for instance, but never at the same time. Thus, wild horses do not establish "territories" in the true sense of the word, for the definition of territory is a specific area over which an animal or group of animals establishes exclusive jurisdiction. It is defended against intruders and is mutually exclusive of other animals of the same species. People studying wild horses do not use the term territory, but home range, which commonly overlap among the horse bands. For instance, in the Pryors, during the summer of 1972 at least 17 bands used the same piece of country at least part of the time.

The home ranges of most wild horse bands are seasonal, and vary in size, depending upon the available forage. In the spring they leave their winter range and wander to summer range, following green grass, but the amount of movement depends somewhat on the geography of their area. In some areas seasonal movement is not pronounced, and in some bands, where there is adequate feed all year around, seasonal movement is nonexistent. Many bands do not move more than four miles during any time or season of the year. As snow comes, the bands in some areas seek lower elevations and move onto a "winter range" where the snow is not so deep. Others choose to remain at higher elevations, grazing on wind-swept ridges as long as possible (sometimes the grass runs out on these ridges and the horses literally eat them into the ground, pawing out the grass roots and eating them, too).

In winter, especially in areas where the bands tend to congregate on winter range to avoid deep snow, many bands will use the same area, and be within sight of one another a lot of the time. This is usually the case with the Challis, Idaho wild horses and the horses in the Pryor Mountains. As Ron Hall, BLM wild horse specialist who studied the Pryor herd, said, "During the winter especially, applying the concept of 'territory' would be stretching it." He prefers to call it a "sphere of intolerance." Bands tend to use the same areas, but mutually avoid each other, avoiding confrontations. If one band is at the water hole when another approaches, the approaching band will wait some distance away until the watering horses are through and have moved on.

There seems to be a pecking order among the bands of an area. The dominant band will drink first if two groups approach the water hole at the same time. The dominant band will water, and feed around the water hole until ready to leave, the less dominant band waiting their turn a good distance

of smell, and ability to run for eluding his enemies; he is highly mobile and able to utilize the forage plants over a wide area.

In the wild state, or after having gone wild, horses generally band together in small groups dominated by a stallion and led by a wise old mare. The stallion may have just one or two mares in his band, or many, depending on his ability to win and keep them, defending his band against all challengers who would steal them from him. A band of 20 is unusually large in this day and age and not very common. The average band size in most wild horse areas is five or six mares. Average band size in the Pryor Mountain Wild Horse range is three or four. The term "herd" means all the horses (or burros) in a given area or land management unit, while the term "band" means the individual harem units—the stallion (or jack) and his mares.

"Home range" means the general area traveled during the normal daily and seasonal activities of the band. Each band in an area establishes its own home away. And during some times of the year, especially in winter, even this sphere of intolerance is absent, and animals from more than one band will graze almost side by side.

In some situations bands may actually join together, showing mutual toleration, one of the stallions taking over the dominant position for both bands. In his studies of horses in Nevada, Steven Pellegrini noted that during one winter, two bands and one lone stallion grouped together. They later broke up into their original bands when spring came, and the lone stallion went his solitary way again. During the rest of the year, especially during the breeding season, the harem bands tend to stay apart, the stallions warding off all intruders.

Daily movement of wild horse bands is related to their water supply. During late spring, summer and fall, the horses usually water at least once a day, moving to water in the evening or early morning. After watering, they usually feed out, traveling a mile or more, and then repeat this pattern the following day. During the winter in many areas, daily movement decreases, partly because the horses can subsist on snow and do not have to travel to water, and partly because living space is reduced in areas with deep snow.

Although the home ranges of several bands often overlap, some actions of wild horses seem to be territory-related. Stallions mark their area with large piles of manure, called "stud piles" and it is believed that these mounds serve as some kind of "scent post" as a marking of territory or an assertion of rights. A stallion, upon going near such a manure pile, will always check it out, smelling it, to see if the freshest manure is his or that of another horse, and will then deposit some fresh manure of his own on top of it.

Sensing a challenge, the stallion is alert and inquisitive. If the intruder is another stallion, he will whistle and snort and strut out to meet him.

The stallion is naturally a somewhat aggressive and domineering animal, having a very high opinion of himself and his superior strength. This is nature's way of enabling him to keep and hold a band of females together, protecting them and keeping other stallions from taking them. The strongest, boldest stallions are able to keep their mares the longest, and thus pass on their superior traits to more offspring, whereas the weaker, more inferior stallions are less apt to be able to win or keep a harem at all.

Always alert, the harem stallion first scents, or sights his enemies, then gives a warning whistle which is neither neigh nor whinny, but an indescribable sound. His mares are instantly alert, poised and ready for flight. If the danger is a challenging stallion, the harem stallion will whistle and snort, arch his neck, strut and prance out to meet him, and the mares will relax and go about their business, waiting for the outcome of the encounter. Two

A "stud pile"—a pile of manure used by the dominant stallion as a sort of "scent post" or territory marker.

stallions go through a ritual of posturing with heads and necks, displaying their arrogance and strength. With arched neck and tail and stiff-legged prance, they confront one another until one of them backs down. Often this threat display is all that is needed, and a real fight is avoided; the challenger may just leave. But if the challenger presses the issue, a fight is inevitable.

But if the approaching danger is a man or predator, the alert stallion may whistle his warning, and watch for a moment to determine the exact danger. Then, as the mares turn and flee, he will challenge the intruder briefly, giving the mares time to get moving, then turn and run after them, urging them on. This is the indescribable heart-stopping beauty of wild horses, as they flee in swift-flowing, sure-footed flight. The lead mare chooses the direction of flight, and the stallion brings up the rear, sometimes stopping to look back and challenge a pursuer, then hurrying to catch up with his mares again.

Although the domineering stallion is bold and brave when it comes to jealously guarding his harem against rival stallions, he is not always so bold and brave when it comes to protecting his band from other kinds of danger. Most stallions will drive their mares away from danger, herding them and nipping at the stragglers, but if the danger gets too close or threatening, such as when a group is chased by man and is close to being captured, corraled or cornered, the stallion is usually the first to take off and save himself, deserting his harem. This was noticed repeatedly during the Pryor Mountain wild horse roundup in November of 1971 when the herds there were being reduced to enable the remaining horses to survive the winter.

The aggressive behavior of the stallion reaches its peak during the breeding season (early spring and summer) for this is the time that other stallions will be challenging the harem stallions. There are always young "unattached" males hanging about, teasing the harem stallions and hoping for a chance to steal a mare or two. These young bachelor stallions have been driven out of their parental bands and wander about, either singly or in loose-knit groups, ever hoping for a chance to win some mares.

Young males are driven out of a harem upon maturity—whenever the dominant stallion begins to feel that the young male is a threat to him. Because young males reach sexual maturity at different ages, depending partly upon individual maturing rates and upon feed and nutrition, some young males may be driven out of the band as yearlings, while others, especially in poor range areas where growth of young horses is somewhat stunted, may not be driven out of the band until they are three years old.

The stallion is the rear guard, nipping at stragglers and urging them on.

The stallion pauses to look back and challenge the pursuer.

In the Pryor Mountain range, due in part to poor feed and malnutrition, most young colts do not develop sexually (testes descending) until they are about three years old. Fillies also are late developing on this range, not showing signs of first heat until they are three, whereas in many other areas fillies will come in heat and breed as two-year-olds, or even as yearlings in some cases.

The young males, after being ousted from their parental bands, often wander alone for awhile, perhaps following the band dejectedly (or trying unsuccessfully to join another band) until the dominant stallion has fully impressed upon the youngster that he must leave. Then, because the horse is a highly social animal, and seems quite dependent on group living for his mental well-being and security, the young outcast usually joins a fellow outcast, or joins a small "bachelor" group that is already established. These bachelor groups are not as stable as a harem band, but are usually bossed by the most dominant of the young stallions, who "herds" the

This young stallion shows evidence (the scar on his rump) of being severely bitten, probably when he was driven out of the band by the harem stallion.

These two stallions . . . share this harem, in the Challis wild horse area.

others as though they were a harem group. In all groups of horses, both wild or domestic, there is a pecking order—a firmly established series of rank. The stronger, bolder ones lord it over the younger, weaker or more timid ones, and each horse has his specific place in the order.

Thus it is in the bachelor group, the strongest young stallion happily herding and bossing the more passive younger ones. But in the bachelor band this dominant role may be precariously enjoyed, for sooner or later the younger or more passive males in the group begin to develop the same drives, the same desire to be dominant, the same masculine image of themselves as superior and self-sufficient.

A bachelor group, or a pair of young friends, may suddenly or slowly find their way of life disrupted or their friendship strained, either by the opportunity to add some females to their lives, or by the budding desire of the passive one to be dominant. It is not unusual for two stallions to share a harem, possibly because they were bachelor friends who acquired the harem together. But this is not a stable situation and eventually the drive for dominance forces them to break up the alliance. As they compete, first in mock battle, as friends, and later more seriously, sooner or later one of them definitely gains the upper hand in rank and the other one must leave.

The young stallions in their bachelor groups enjoy a kind of carefree playful existence, staging mock battles, . and amusing themselves by threatening older stallions with harems. As time goes on, these young stallions gain the maturity and experience to win and keep mares for themselves, but few of them are strong enough or experienced enough to gain harems before they are five or six years old. An older stallion that has been defeated by younger rivals and driven from his harem usually spends the rest of his life alone; even the young bachelor groups will not usually let him join them.

The pecking order is very evident in every harem band. The stallion is dominant and bossy (especially during the breeding season), but he is not the king in all matters. The lead mare is the strongest, highest ranking mare, who has earned her top place in the herd by her superior age, wisdom, experience or strong personality. It is she who decides where and when the band will travel, dictating the normal daily activity of the group. She chooses the grazing area, decides when to go to water, and leads the flight to safety if the band is spooked by enemies. She leads the band and the stallion brings up the rear, herding and hurrying the stragglers. In the matter of feeding and watering, she usually has higher rank than the stallion, she and her foal watering first at the spring.

Horses are gregarious and social animals, happiest when with a group. The instinct to follow another horse is very strong, and if for some reason a horse becomes separated from the band, he may become disoriented. For instance, one time in the Pryors, a band was trapped in a corral, but the lead mare escaped. The horses, without the lead mare for them to follow, stayed in the corral for two days, even though the gates were open. The lead mare's social role seems to be as important to the band as that of the stallion.

In most wild horse areas, breeding takes place in the spring and early summer—April through July—and since the gestation length for the horse is approximately 11 months, foaling takes place March through June or July, with most of the foals coming in May or early June. But a few foals are born in late summer and fall, and these have less chance of making it through the winter.

In her book *Mustangs; A Return to the Wild*, Hope Ryden states that wild mares come in heat only in the spring and early summer, one month after they foal (which is incorrect, because many mares have their first heat cycle 7 to 10 days after foaling, and are rebred at this time). She points out that domestic mares are irregular in this respect, some of them coming into heat even in the fall or winter, and she claims that all wild mares breed between April and July, due to natural selection and a higher survival rate of foals and mares at this time. But this is not really true. The domestic horse does not revert that quickly and readily to prehistoric breeding patterns, for essentially he is still a domestic horse that can and will breed any time of the year, nutrition level permitting.

At first glance, breeding and foaling in the spring seems to show that the horses have "adjusted" to the wild, when actually it is due to nutritional improvement (green grass) in the spring, which brings the mares into better condition to cycle and breed. Green grass of spring and the lengthening days have an effect on the mare's endocrine glands and she gets ready to breed. It is more natural for any horse, wild or domestic, to breed in the spring, but if feed is good, both wild and domestic horses can also cycle and breed other times of the year. Hope Ryden's supposition that wild horses have, through natural selection, reverted to true wild breeding habits, is in error, for in many wild horse areas, including Challis, Idaho, a few foals are always born in late summer and fall.

The pregnant mare usually leaves the band shortly before foaling, seeking a secluded spot for giving birth. This is a mare's natural instinct, to seek privacy at foaling time, whether she is wild or tame. The dominant stallion seems to understand her need at this time, or else is put in his place by the determined female, and he lets her go. She usually chooses a secluded spot on a south slope (which gets more sunshine) free of wind, and does not seem to

Half-grown foal.

A lone stallion peers over a ridge.

seek shelter in brush or trees (any open slope away from the wind and away from other horses will do). Privacy at foaling time is important, for in the first hours of the foal's life he must get to his feet and nurse, establishing a firm relationship with his mother. Interference by other horses at this crucial time in their lives may prevent the establishment of this relationship, and the foal might not survive. After the foal is strong and able to travel, the mare brings him back to the band.

The mare nurses her foal all that summer and through the first winter, weaning him just before she is ready to give birth to a new foal the next spring. Many observations have been made of a new mother and tiny baby, with the preceding year's big yearling following her. If for some reason she does not have another foal the following year, she may not wean her present foal until even later. Thus one can see that in range areas where nutrition is poor, especially during winter, mares with foals have a heavy burden on them. For instance, in the Pryor Mountains, the sex ratio for many years has been roughly 60% males and 40% females, the lower number of females indicating a higher mortality among the females who are producing foals, due to the greater stress placed upon them during the winter when they are nursing foals. The pregnant mare who is still nursing a foal has a tremendous drain on her system, especially if she is not receiving adequate nutrition, and during a hard winter she may die, or be so weak by spring that she dies foaling.

The small size of wild horses in some areas is due in part to poor nutrition, hard winters, and inbreeding. The fillies start producing foals from the time they are sexually mature. Whether this first foaling occurs at age two or is delayed to age three or four due to poor feed and slow development of the filly, the filly is not yet full grown in terms of her potential for mature size. And because of the subsequent drain on her—pregnancy, nursing, and further pregnancies—she never really has a chance to gain her full size, remaining stunted the rest of her life.

As for inbreeding, there are some wild horse enthusiasts who claim that wild horses do not inbreed, and that the dominant harem stallions chase their own fillies out of the herd at the time of the filly's first heat cycle. I have traced this theory to only two sources. Hope Ryden, in *America's Last Wild Horses* and *Mustangs: A Return to the Wild*, mentions this expelling-fillies-from-the-band theory, as reported to her by Robert Brislawn, founder of the Spanish Mustang Registry. It is also mentioned briefly by G. C. Robinson in "Mustangs and Mustangers in Southwest Texas" (*Mustangs and Cow Horses*, edited by Dobie, Boatright and Ransom). Most people who make claims that wild horses do not inbreed quote from one or the other of these two sources (Robinson or Brislawn), sometimes second or third hand, to substantiate their claims.

Some kind of "natural instinct" to thwart inbreeding may be a factor in some instances, as has been reported by Robinson and Brislawn, but this does not seem to be the general rule among wild horse bands. There are innumerable reports to the contrary, and ample evidence that wild horses do inbreed. Almost any of the old-timers who had a lot of experience with wild horses can give you descriptions of inbred horses that they encountered (see Chapter 4).

And even if a stallion DID drive off both his sons and daughters, what was to keep one of his sons from picking up daughters—which would be half, or possibly even full sisters of the younger stallion—for his own harem? An ousted son, growing up in the same range area and eventually gathering his own band of mares might very easily, over the years, pick up a few fillies that might be his own sisters, if they were ousted by "the old man". Inbreeding, to some degree, is inevitable among wild horses.

Inbreeding, the mating of closely related animals such as father to daughter, brother to sister, tends to double up certain qualities, good and bad. Recessive traits (for color, or for defective conformation, or anything else that is controlled by a recessive gene) will often crop out in an inbred animal, because of the doubling up of the recessive gene received from each parent. A recessive gene is often "hidden" in a normal animal, masked by a dominant gene that produces a dominant trait. The animal will physically show the dominant trait, but carries the recessive in his genetic makeup, which can be passed on to the offspring; it will crop out visibly if the offspring receives the same recessive gene from the other parent. And this is more likely to happen if the other parent is closely related. If two animals are mated that carry the same recessive gene, this recessive trait can show up in the offspring, even though it may not have been obvious in the parents.

Outstanding individuals can sometimes produce very outstanding offspring with inbreeding, through the doubling up of the good qualities. But few horses are this perfect. Inbreeding much more commonly brings out inferior or even crippling characteristics, by doubling up the weaknesses of closely related horses. The traits held in common, both good and bad, are magnified. But the bad traits tend to show up as deformities when doubled this way, which wipes out the value of doubling up the good characteristics.

When overgrazing and poor range condition is added to the problem of inbreeding, there are even more defects in the offspring, because the animals have nutritional deficiencies as well as hereditary deficiencies. This can be seen in the horse herds on some Indian reservations (such as the Navajo reservation in Arizona), where the horses live in a semi-wild condition on poor range that is also overgrazed (because of excess horse population). Many of these horses show both hereditary and nutritional problems.

Steven Pellegrini, in his study of Nevada wild horses in the Wassuk Range, mentioned that these horses are "crude looking beasts: small, shaggy and Roman-nosed, but they are, at the same time, a reflection of a crude environment. These animals are in every sense 'broomtails' and 'jugheads', descriptive words frequently expressed in a derogatory manner, but in reality words which reflect adaptations to a harsh environment."

Inbreeding frequently causes a progressive stunting of the offspring. The opposite of this condition is hybrid vigor—the production of larger, stronger individuals by mating two totally unrelated animals, or animals of different breeds. Another thing that sometimes crops out with inbreeding is more white coloring on the body—offspring with higher and higher white leg markings, more white on the face, or body patches. But the worst thing that inbreeding can do is produce deformities, and freaks that cannot survive.

Jim Bailey, who ran horses on the Oregon desert in the 1930's described some tiny inbred horses there that weighed only 500 pounds. Ted Barber, in an article "Wild Horses on Welfare" in *Western Horseman* (April 1974) described one group of 500 horses that were corraled from an overcrowded range in Nevada in early years—horses that were so underfed and inbred that their average mature weight was under 500 pounds. Charlie Thomas, who spent some years herding sheep and capturing a few horses in Wyoming in the 1930's tells of runty horses there, weighing 500-600 pounds, that showed deformities due to inbreeding. He saw some horses that had been born with only one eye or only one front leg, and horses with one cloven (split) hoof. The hoof deformities he observed were not injuries from running in the rocks, but defects the horses had been born with. The Gossey family at Challis, Idaho, recalls some of the inbred horses that showed up on their range—horses with big long heads, heavy fuzzy legs, and crooked, bowed legs.

The reports go on and on about the freaks and stunted horses that were undoubtedly the results of inbreeding. A strong stallion can hold his harem for a number of years, and within that time he may be siring foals from his own daughters, then from his granddaughters out of his own daughters, or even worse. He may be an exceptional stallion, but by the time his offspring are this inbred, undesirable traits are bound to crop out if there hasn't been a change and some mare-shuffling in his band.

In earlier days, the inbreeding in some wild herds was kept to a minimum by sporadic roundups which took out the young stock for use as saddle or draft animals, and by occasionally turning out domestic stallions to upgrade the wild herds, adding to the gene pool. Some ranchers gelded or shot inferior wild stallions, and the practice of rounding up the horses periodically broke up the stability of the harem bands and reshuffled some of the mares.

In her book *Mustangs: A Return to the Wild,* Hope Ryden mentions that some stallions show preference for mares of a certain color, having a harem of mares that are all the same color. But she does not feel that this suggests that some of the mares might be the stallion's own daughters, as other people feel. She cites instances of stallions being a different color than their solid-colored harem, pointing to a herd of bay mares that was dominated by a brown stallion for her example, attempting to show that the mares, therefore, are not his daughters. But this example does not prove her point, and merely serves to show her lack of knowledge in horse color-genetics. Brown (a color characterized by black mane, tail and legs and a coat sometimes so dark that it appears almost black, only distinguishable from black by the lighter hairs around the flanks and muzzle) is a variation of bay, actually just a dark, dark bay, and brown horses very regularly produce bay offspring. Her brown stallion, mated to bay mares, would naturally produce bay offspring; thus some of the bay mares in his harem could be his own daughters.

Inbreeding can produce a variety of results, as already mentioned. Perhaps another result might be a tendency to revert back to a more primitive type. Some of the inbred horses are freaks and cripples, and in the end, mother nature takes care of them, for they are handicapped and not likely to survive or to produce offspring. But the ones that do survive— runtier, coarser, bushy-maned, jugheaded, and toughened by a harsh existence—after a number of generations begin to look more like the small, coarse, heavy-boned, big-headed and ill-proportioned, animals that man first encountered, before he improved them with selective breeding. These runty, ugly horses are not exactly the type of horseflesh a horse lover would admire, and this kind of throwback would never be selected as a likely candidate for the Olympic jumping team, the Kentucky Derby, a cow-cutting contest or a 100 mile endurance race. He simply has lost the finesse, the special characteristics, the athletic ability that centuries of selective breeding have given the well-bred domestic horse. He may be tough (if he has not inherited too many weaknesses or bad legs from the compounding of structural faults due to inbreeding), but he is ugly and short-legged and sometimes reminds a person of the prehistoric type of horse, especially if he happens to be a dun color. His hooves grow thick and tough from running over rocks and dry deserts (moisture tends to make a hoof softer, and dry conditions make it harder) and nature begins to fit him to his environment. Through inbreeding and poor feed, successive generations become smaller, adapting to a scantier food supply. The ones that aren't hardy don't survive.

Nature continually culls her wild animals, and it is truly "survival of the fittest". The survivors are generally the animals most capable of living in a harsh environment. The thin-skinned, pampered, modern purebred may not be as able to withstand a hard winter—severe storms and lack of feed—in the mountains as the thick-bodied, coarse and woolly-haired, bushy-maned mongrel. The purebred can do a better job than the coarse mongrel in the field he was bred for (running the mile, turning the barrels, jumping 6 foot fences or winning a 100 mile race in 8 hours riding time), but he can't begin to subsist on or endure the conditions that the coarse little horse takes in stride.

As body type reverts back to an earlier type due to inbreeding and lack of selective breeding, coloration tends to revert back also, with a few more duns and buckskins cropping up, along with leg stripes and dorsal stripes. The "coyote dun" is so named because of his dorsal stripe; like the coyote and the wolf, he has a darker shade running along his spine. According to J. Frank Dobie, the Spanish people began the tradition of the dun, feeling that dun horses had a primitive kind of toughness, the dun color being a relic of the prehistoric undomesticated horse.

Darwin concluded that all domestic horses stem from wild species "of a dun color and more or less striped", to which modern descendents "occasionally revert". All the known primitive horses had, or have, the dorsal stripe, and most of them are dun colored or a variation of dun—Przewalski's horse, the Tarpan, the eel-backed dun of Norway, the Kattywar breed of northwest India, the linebacked duns of ancient Prussia, Hungary and Spain, and so on.

Dobie felt that generations of life in the wild tend to push horse type back toward the primordial, and to the dun color, with a dark line down the back. The dun possesses the black mane and tail, black hoofs and lower legs, occasionally horizontal dark stripes around the upper legs, and sometimes a transverse stripe over the shoulders. The dun color and stripe are always waiting to come back, all other colors (except roan and gray) being recessive to dun. The terms buckskin and claybank are other names for dun. Grullo is a slate or mouse-color, shading into blue. Like the dun, the grullo often has the dorsal stripe and zebra marks on the legs and occasionally a line over the shoulders.

Primordial tawniness is probably the most protective shade in nature, and rings and stripes add to the camouflage. The line-backed dun Tarpan of the Asian steppes was hunted by the striped, tawny tiger, and the dun horse of the American plains was hunted by the dun puma. As stated in *Tropical South Africa* by Sir Francis Galton, the zebra "might seem conspicuous with his stripes, but on a bright moonlit night you can't see him. If the black stripes were more numerous, he would be seen as a black mass; if the white, as a white one. The stripes are proportioned to exactly match the pale tint which arid ground possesses when seen by moonlight."

Arabian horses are never dun (perhaps because they are the oldest domestic breed and have been selectively bred by man the longest) but most bay Arabians have black mane, tail, ear tips and legs, and a few have the barest hint of a dorsal stripe. A few of the earlier Arabians had even more hint of the dun color. Dun color has been suppressed in the Thoroughbred breed also, but in the first volume of the Thoroughbred stud book, dating back to 1738, dun color was frequent. Striped or unstriped, the dun colored horse is not necessarily devoid of Arabian blood in its background. There are no purebred dun Arabians today, but a few Arabians have just a suggestion of the dorsal stripe. After the dun color is bred out and the dorsal stripe has faded, the terminals of that line sometimes linger, and in some horses the shadow can still be seen between the mane and tail. Other breeds today, newer breeds that have not been selectively bred for so long, especially the Quarter Horse, still carry the primitive dun color.

Selective breeding, taking advantage of a few natural deviations in color, conformation, or type, and mating these individuals with those that possess similar desired deviations, can, in time and many generations, produce animals that look very different from their original type. They will possess qualities far different from those of their ancestors (more muscle and meat in meat animals, more milking ability in dairy animals, and so on). This kind of selective breeding produced horses that were larger, stronger, swifter, more beautiful, more adapted to man's purposes than their wild predecessors. The various breeds were diversified still further from original type, each breed with its own special qualities and purposes.

But feral life and indiscriminate breeding creates a "melting pot" of breeds and types of horses, the subsequent mongrelization and haphazard inbreeding destroying in a few generations what selective breeding had taken centuries to create. Just as mongrelization in the dog tends to "smooth out" the drastic differences created by selective breeding, producing an animal that may look like his primitive ancestor, the nondescript wolf, so does mongrelization in the horse tend to sometimes minimize the differences created by selective breeding, and produce animals that seem to revert to an earlier, unrefined type of horse.

It might seem plausible that in time this sort of melting pot in the wild might eventually create a

No matter what he looks like—noble descendant of Spanish mustang, abandoned plow horse, stray cow pony or degenerate inbred "scrub"—the wild horse is here to stay, as an American symbol of freedom.

animals, but the many-generations-wild horse—a mix of many types, with some inbreeding thrown in—is more often jug-headed, runty, and ugly. Some of these horses look bad even at a distance. Others, running pell mell over the hills, look like decent, admirable animals, but when caught and looked at more closely (as many a mustanger of yesteryear discovered to his disappointment) do not have the qualities necessary to make good saddle horses, and are not so good-looking after all.

So, by preserving the wild horse in a truly wild state, without adding fresh domestic blood now and then to improve the horses and thwart inbreeding (as was done sporadically throughout the West for the last three centuries), we are not perpetuating the fleet and beautiful dream animals of many people's romantic ideas; we are perpetuating a melting pot of feral domestic horses—from draft horses to cow ponies—that will invariably create some misfits and a few freaks.

But as long as the American people understand and accept this, maybe it doesn't matter. The important thing is that the American people have decided to perpetuate the wild horse, in all his various forms of domestic degeneration, because he is a symbol of our western pioneer heritage and a symbol of freedom. Though he may be crude in form, and ugly in close-up appearance, there is still a beauty in him as he high-tails it over a far ridge, and a ruggedness and determination about him that has enabled him to survive and thrive under all sorts of conditions. For that reason, most Americans feel strongly that the wild horse deserves to stay free and deserves a place on our western ranges. As Will James once said, in his often-quoted phrase from "Piñon and the Wild Ones" (*Saturday Evening Post*, May 19, 1923), "For they really belong, not to man, but to that country of junipers and sage, of deep arroyos, mesas—and freedom."

fairly uniform type of "wild horse" similar to the prehistoric wild horse. Only a scientist well versed in animal genetics could answer that question, but it appears obvious that it would take hundreds of years or more for any such tendency to exert itself. Even then, the results would not be uniform because of the different varieties of feral domestic horses in different areas in the West. In the meantime there would be just some ugly, stunted, inbred horses produced, a few of which might remind a person of prehistoric type.

It should be evident from this discussion that the typical wild horse of today is not any one type of horse, nor is he necessarily beautiful. The romantic notion that many people have about wild horses being beautiful, noble animals, the kind of horses that any horse lover would desire to own or ride, is based on fiction, not fact. The feral horses that are only one or two generations away from some rancher's good saddle stock are still good looking

10

The Mustang Campaign

After the establishment of the Pryor Mountain Wild Horse Range in 1968 and the national controversy that led to it, public pressure began to build toward the creation of some kind of national policy for wild horse protection—not just in a few scattered refuges, but on all western ranges where wild horses were found. In the late 1960's the BLM estimated that there were about 17,000 wild horses roaming free in the West, with a few thousand more on Indian reservations.* The wild horse numbers had been steadily dropping. Wild horse enthusiasts felt that the only thing that could save the wild herds from complete eradication was immediate federal legislation, and they worked hard toward a federal protection law.

The wild horse was not protected by any existing law except the Wild Horse Annie Law (1959), which prohibited use of aircraft or motorized vehicles in roundups. He did not qualify for protection under any wildlife laws, because he is a feral animal—a domestic stray. There was no closed season on horse

*Since then, it has been discovered that there are more Indian-reservation horses than originally thought. Approximately 70 reservations in the 11 Western states have horse problems. A questionnaire was sent to them, and by April, 1977, 32 had responded—with surprising results. There were more than 46,000 unbranded horses and some 30,000 branded horses—approximately 76,000 head—on these 32 of the 70 reservations with horses. It might be interesting to know the exact total.

hunting. The free-roaming horse had no legal classification that could protect him from harvest by ranchers or by mustangers for the horsemeat market. And in localities where he competed for forage with wildlife or domestic livestock, his presence was not appreciated by some of the people concerned with game management or livestock range management.

The very term "wild horse" was vague, and there was often conflict over definition. Were certain horses in question actually "wild", or were they some rancher's trespass range horses that should be removed from the range? Many horses on the western ranges fell into a questionable category, for they were ranchers' range horses or offspring of ranch horses. Should they be rounded up and removed from the range to prevent overgrazing, or should they be protected as "wild horses"? Public opinion, which tended to think in terms of all free-roaming horses as "wild", did not agree with the local stockmen's associations and ranchers, who thought of the horses as stray domestic livestock. The growing opinion was that the wild horses and burros belonged to all Americans, not just to the people whose areas they inhabit, not just to the men who had in earlier years turned the horses out to roam. The mounting public pressure pushed for

95

some kind of federal management and protection for free-roaming horses, instead of leaving the responsibility for the horses in state and local agencies.

According to Wild Horse Annie, and other wild horse enthusiasts like Hope Ryden, the stockmen's organizations and state estray laws were the major obstacles to wild horse protection. These state laws, which generally held that all stray unbranded animals belonged to the state stock commission, or the county, were originally created to settle disputes and ownership claims. With many different ranchers using the same common range, there were invariably some arguments over livestock ownership. Every rancher branded his own stock, but there were always a few cows that calved out on the range after the spring branding, and range mares that foaled on the range. It was an unwritten law of the West that any unbranded young animal still following its branded mother was the legal property of the man owning the branded mother. But what about the weaned yearling—bovine or equine—who followed no mother anymore and who was somehow missed in last fall's roundup? Ownership disputes over these "slicks" or "mavericks" could be pretty bitter. Thus the problem was solved by the state or county commission having legal claim on the "slicks". Any profit from the sale of such animals usually went into school funds.

But these estray laws, which were very necessary to the open range country, were thought by the horse protectionists to be outmoded, and detrimental to the wild horses. Hope Ryden, in her book, *America's Last Wild Horses* (a book in which she paints the plight of the diminishing wild herds and urges people to press for federal legislation to protect the remaining herds throughout the West), stated that the estray laws were the biggest remaining obstacles that kept concerned horse lovers from finding a way to protect and manage wild horses like wildlife. Individuals who wanted a law passed to keep the horses "from being completely exterminated", were thwarted because the western free-roaming horses, by legal definition, were not unowned. As she pointed out, these horses were the property of the appointed livestock commissions in each state, and thus could not be protected by any wildlife law.

The stockmen bore the brunt of Miss Ryden's condemnation in her campaign to save the mustangs, for she felt that many stockmen arbitrarily resented any person who advocated protective legislation for the horses. Livestockmen who depended upon the range for their living and the continuity of their ranching operations were naturally cautious and suspicious when it came to talking about a law that would completely protect the horses, with no provisions for periodic roundups and control. These ranchers had seen the fluctuations of the wild horse numbers in the past, and knew that the horse herds could quickly increase to the point of damaging the range, if left totally unchecked.

Their fears and cautions, however, were hard for the wild horse lovers to understand, because people like Hope Ryden could think only in terms of the dwindling herds of very recent times and could only think of the horse as a badly abused and vanishing "free spirit". Hope Ryden, and many others like her, felt that the wild horse, like the buffalo, would soon become extinct, and she interpreted the stockman's attitude as one of callous disregard for the wild horse.

In her book, Miss Ryden is also highly critical of hunters and sportsmen's organizations, for opposing legislation that would give the horse a change in status and a permanent, protected place on the range. The individual states have traditionally had jurisdiction over the wildlife within their boundaries, and the fish and game department of each state has set up the game laws appropriate for each area, and managed the native wildlife. But because these state game departments are funded from the sale of hunting and fishing licenses, Miss Ryden found it "not surprising" that "nontarget" animals such as wild horses, were neglected or endangered by the attitude and management programs of the game departments. She felt that "target animals" had increased in number as a result of this kind of management, while other kinds of animals have dwindled, or even disappeared.

The two exceptions, at that time, to state jurisdiction over wildlife were animals within the National Parks (which come under the federal protection of the U.S. Department of the Interior) and animals on the endangered species list, which could be claimed and managed by the United States Fish and Wildlife Service under the Migratory Bird Treaty Act. The Migratory Bird Treaty Act was an international agreement intended to protect Canadian birds that migrated across the United States. Included in the Act was a clause to permit the federal government to manage and protect any native animal in danger of extinction.

But the wild horse could not be protected under either category. The National Parks protect only native animals. The Migratory Bird Treaty Act applies only to endangered species and to native animals, and the wild horse did not qualify on either count. He is not in danger of extinction (he is merely a feral domestic horse, and all it would take to start more wild horse herds would be to turn some more omestic horses loose) and he is not native.

In spite of these obstacles, the National Mustang Association drew up a bill in 1969, trying to fit the wild horse into the "endangered species" clause by claiming that the Andalusian and Spanish Barb breed of wild horse was becoming very rare and would soon be extinct unless appropriate steps were taken to protect them. The bill was introduced into the U.S. Senate in the spring of 1969 by Senator Frank Moss of Utah. But this bill (S-2166) aroused controversy and conflicting feelings among individuals and organizations that were pushing for protection of wild horses. Many wild horse lovers opposed the bill, fearing that its shortcomings would help bring on the destruction of the wild horse. Consequently a bitter controversy between the National Mustang Association and the International Society for the Protection of Mustangs and Burros began.

The conflict arose over some of the points of the proposed law, especially these points:

(1) The Spanish Barb and Andalusian wild mustang are endangered species threatened with extinction. (2) These animals are to be included in the 1966 Endangered Species Act. (3) All horses are to be rounded up, with the Barb and Andalusian separated out to be preserved, protected and propagated, and placed on selected areas. (4) The rest of the horses are to be disposed of (in the public interest).

Senator Moss had prepared the bill from material furnished by the National Mustang Association, and much enthusiasm and support for the measure had sprung up among part of the wild horse enthusiasts. But other wild horse lovers, particularly those associated with ISPMB, feared that the bill, if passed without what they felt to be necessary alterations, would only create more problems for wild horses instead of solving them. Some felt that the bill was potentially dangerous, because it would cause the destruction of all wild horses that weren't of Spanish bloodlines; the unwanted extra horses would probably be purchased for horsemeat. Only a very few "pureblooded" mustangs would be released after the mass roundups, and granted protection.

The bill was also misleading, and not consistent with the scientific basis of concern for an endangered species. In the first place, the Spanish Barb was not in danger of "extinction" because there were already a fair number being bred by the Spanish Mustang Registry, and secondly, and most importantly, these horses could not technically be placed under the endangered species act. They are not a native species, and they are artificial "breeds" created by man; none of our modern day horse breeds are unique or a separate species, for all of them belong to the same species. The differences in breeds reflect variations in type created by man's selective breeding.

Rounding up and "sorting" the wild horses on the basis of bloodlines was very distasteful to many horse lovers, and some felt strongly that it could ultimately lead to the destruction of all wild horses. Some accused the National Mustang Association of creating the measure so that its members could help round up the horses. Wild Horse Annie, president of ISPMB, did not feel this way, and acknowledged the bill as a sincere effort on the part of the NMA to find a legal way to give the wild horses protection and management under the federal government. But she did object to the bill, because she feared it would be used by anti-wild horse factions to get rid of the wild herds.

And this was a good point, because technically there could be no "pure" mustangs left. All of the horses could have been condemned as being of mixed breeding. And what, actually, constituted the first "mustangs"? There is a lot of conjecture as to what the bloodlines and origins of the original free-roaming horses were. The early descriptions of Indian horses and cow-horses that were caught from the wild herds do not uniformly conform to descriptions of what the Barb and Andalusian mustangs looked like.

In the intervening two centuries, so many domestic American horses mixed with the wild herds (or made up the wild bands entirely, especially in the northern areas where most of our remaining wild herds today exist) that there is strong doubt that anyone could find much more than a trace of "Spanish" breeding left. Some of the wild horses may show a hint of Spanish blood, but it is more likely they exhibit just the similar characteristics that might have come through some Arabian breeding in the American domestic horses. One should not forget that the Arabian was used in the creation of almost all domestic breeds, except a few of the draft breeds.

According to Dr. George Gaylord Simpson, an authority on the evolution of the horse, most people agree that the Barbs and Arabians had a common origin (the Barb is considered to be an offshoot—with some other bloodlines added—of the Arabian). The horse brought to Spain by the Arabs was probably a mixture of Arabian and Barb. And the Andalusians, later brought to the New World by the Spanish, were thought to have been developed from a mix of these Arab-Barbs and some coarser European blood from the north. Dr. Angel Cabrera feels it was descendents of these Andalusians that were

brought to America, and has described Andalusian conformation from old paintings and records.

Many of these points of conformation are common to other light breeds of horse, and some are different from the characteristics set forth by the Natonal Mustang Association. Therefore, if a person takes into consideration the controversy over what the first mustangs looked like, the amount of mixing with later wild horses of other bloodlines, and the variations that environment and breeding in the wild (both selective breeding due to natural factors, and inbreeding) could give a group of horses, it is obvious that there are no "pure" mustangs, and to base a protection program on wild horse "bloodlines" is ridiculous as well as fallacious. A strict interpretation of Senator Moss's bill would spell the end of ALL wild horses, and many wild horse lovers feared that opponents of the movement to protect the horses would be quick to take advantage of this.

Dr. Michael J. Pontrelli, who was then the Assistant Professor of Biology at the University of Nevada and a man who worked closely with Wild Horse Annie for several years, suggested that a bill for wild horse protection should include protection for wild burros, and that they be under the jurisdiction of the federal government and protected as a national heritage. He felt that more areas should be set aside for wild horse ranges, and that in the other places in the West where wild horses and burros

Wild Horse Annie urged people to support a horse protection bill, fc she felt it was up to our generation to work out an arrangement the would benefit the wild horses long after we are gone—so futu generations can enjoy them.

exist, they should be included as part of the rang and managed along with the other animals there in multiple use concept. Also, there should be prohib tions against releasing domestic horses on publi lands for the purposes of later roundups. He felt tha studies should be done to make sure that manage ment of the horses could be on a sound ecologica base, and he also wanted a national advisory board responsible to the public, to advise the governmen agency (probably the Department of Interior) whic had jurisdiction over the horses.

Other concerned individuals sought means b which the wild horses could qualify for managemen on the state level. In Colorado, Senator Georg Jackson and Congressman John Fuhr co-sponsored bill to reclassify wild horses in Colorado as wildlife placing them under the management of the Col orado State Game, Fish and Park Departments. Bu this measure died in committee.

Meanwhile, however, momentum was buildin and the movement for wild horse protection wa gaining strength. It would be only a matter of time now, before some kind of protective measure would be passed nationally. Clyde Reynolds, mayor of Lovell, Wyoming, and who had served on the Pryor Mountain Wild Horse committee, wrote a bill which would grant the Department of the Interior authority and funds "to protect, manage and control free-roaming horses and burros on public lands." It would also punish "any person who allows a domestic horse to run with, or takes possession of, or molests free-roaming horses or burros," with a penalty of a $1000 fine or imprisonment of one year. Mr. Reynolds had hopes that this bill would be sponsored by some member of Congress.

This bill had the support of the ISPMB, along with other animal-protection organizations. Wild Horse Annie expressed hope that serious attention would be given to the measure before it was too late for the horses, saying, "I strongly feel that it is up to our generation to work out a permanent arrangement that will inure to the benefit of the Wild Ones long after we are gone and forgotten. Having lived with this situation for more than 15 years, I am firmly convinced that it will not be the Utopia that all would like for them. Idealist that I am, I would like to see them left alone. But realist that I must be, I recognize the fact that we are running out of resources for all forms of life, including human, and in order to maintain every species properly conservation and level-headed planning are called for."

Clyde Reynolds's bill was introduced in the Senate on January 30, 1970, by Senator Clifford P. Hansen of Wyoming. It was read twice and referred to the Committee on Interior and Insular Affairs, where it died without a hearing. Senator Hansen did not press for a hearing, and when asked the reason by journalist Hope Ryden, he replied that he had found his constituents to be antagonistic to any bill that would give further control of public lands to the federal government.

After the introduction of that bill, Wild Horse Annie was invited to meet with a specially appointed committee of the American National Cattleman's Association and the National Wool Growers' Association, to review the provisions of the Hansen Bill, and if possible, to work out recommendations for legislation that would be acceptable to all users of the public lands. She invited Dr. Michael Pontrelli, professor at the University of Nevada, and director of a wild horse research program, to attend the meetings with her. Over a period of 14 months this special committee held meetings with representatives of the BLM, the Nevada Fish and Game, and the U.S. Forest Service.

In October of 1970, Hope Ryden's book, America's Last Wild Horses was published, and public response to the plight of the wild horses grew louder. Miss Ryden was deluged with mail and was asked to tell the wild horse story on several television programs. In November the New York Times carried a story on its front page: "A Devoted Few Strive to Save Wild Horses." In response to this article, the "Country Art Gallery in Locust Valley, Long Island," contacted Miss Ryden and offered to hold an art benefit for the wild horses. The benefit raised enough money to send a copy of her book to every senator in Washington and to 100 representatives. Also as a result of the Times article, Miss Ryden did several stories and articles for My Weekly Reader, a current events magazine for elementary school children, which touched off a flurry of response from children across the nation. At the same time she did articles for National Geographic ("On the Track of the West's Wild Horses", spinning a tale of the dwindling herds' fight for survival on "harsh and inhospitable public lands" and how the wild horses would soon disappear unless laws were passed to protect them), Children's Day, The Reader's Digest, and other magazines, all telling the same story.

In Washington D.C., Mrs. Pearl Twyne and Mrs. William Blue, active in horse protection organizations, systematically kept calling on Congressmen and Senators in behalf of the wild horses. In Nevada, Wild Horse Annie had a full schedule of speaking engagements.

Livestock interests in the West favored state, rather than federal, legislation for protecting the wild horse, but the state legislation seemed doom to failure. For a year, bills for horse protection were introduced in Colorado and Nevada and Oregon, only to be defeated. The Oregon bill was initiated by a fourth-grade elementary school class in Roseburg, Oregon, and was the first protection bill introduced in that state. The Roseburg class, led by their teacher, Miss Joan Bolsinger, had learned about the wild horses through the Weekly Reader articles done by Hope Ryden. The bill was defeated, but the children then turned their efforts toward trying to get a bill passed by the federal government. Children all across the country had begun a "pencil war", writing to congressman and senators. Congressmen, some who had never even heard of wild horses, began getting more mail on that subject than on any other single issue. One senator received 14,000 letters about wild horses, 9,000 of them from children.

Twelve-year-old Gregory Gude, son of Maryland's Representative Gilbert Gude, had gotten a copy of Mustang: Wild Spirit of the West (the story of Wild Horse Annie's efforts, written by Marguerite

Henry) for Christmas, and began badgering his father about a bill to save the wild horses. As a result, on January 21, 1971, Congressman Gude was the first to introduce legislation in the new session of Congress for wild horse protection. Passage of the bill, Gude said, would show young people that Congress "will respond to their legitimate concerns."

In the Senate, Senator Gaylord Nelson introduced a similar bill, and soon after that other senators (Mike Mansfield, Frank Church, Frank Moss, Mark Hatfield and Henry Jackson) drew up other wild horse protection bills. The Jackson bill proposed no fewer than 12 wild horse sanctuaries to be established on public lands. All in all, there were no less than 54 wild horse protection bills put before Congress.

Miss Bolsinger, Roseburg teacher, and one of her fourth grade pupils, Lynn Williams, appeared on an Oregon radio show urging people to write to their congressmen about the wild horses. And Senator Mark Hatfield was deluged with mail; in just one day he received 25,000 letters.

Most of the wild horse organizations and wild horse enthusiasts chose to support S-1116, the bill introduced by Senators Henry M. Jackson of Washington and Mark Hatfield of Oregon, and H. R. 5375, introduced in the House by Walter S. Baring of Nevada. These two bills were very strong, and were very close in content to a sample bill that had been drawn up by Wild Horse Annie and Dr. Michael Pontrelli. These recommendations had been offered to interested lawmakers as an example of what they thought necessary in a protection act. This legislation, if enacted, would create an entirely new category for the wild horse, designating him as an aesthetic resource and a national heritage species.

With such a tremendous interest in this issue coming from the American people, the wild horse situation could no longer be ignored by lawmakers, and hearings were scheduled in both houses of Congress for committees to hear arguments for and against the bills that had been introduced, and witnesses were invited to testify before the Senate Committee on Interior and Insular Affairs and before the House Subcommittee on Public Lands, on April 19 and 20, 1971. A record number of witnesses representing the many interests involved testified at the House hearings on April 19th, and at the Senate hearings the next day. Among those testifying were Wild Horse Annie, Mrs. Pearl Twyne, Joan Bolsinger and Lynn Williams from Oregon (who had been invited by the American Horse Protection Association), Dr. Michael Pon-

trelli, Dr. James Naviaux, Gregory Gude, Hope Ryden, and many others.

Most of the people presenting testimony supported the legislation, but some opposition came up in subsequent committee meetings. One opponent was Representative Wayne Aspinall of Colorado, who pointed out that the wild horses compete with sheep and cattle on the range, and if protected, might easily overrun the range. He also pointed out that these wild horses are not the strong free symbols of the Old West that many horse lovers believe them to be, but small, ugly inbred animals.

Another problem concerned the claiming of privately owned horses on public lands. Many ranchers had permits to pasture their horses on the range, and some had stray horses out there that they wanted to round up. What would be the status of these privately owned horses after passage of the wild horse protection law? Would these privately owned horses be considered "wild"? Would their owners ever be able to claim them? Some of these horses were not branded, but had other characteristics of domestication (such as saddle marks, tatoos, man-created blemishes, or were gentle and trained to lead or ride, or were gelded, or the current offspring of a mare that was known to be privately owned, and so on). The original text of the Senate bill did not recognize claims by individuals to unbranded horses or burros on public land, so the word "unclaimed" was added to the definition of a wild free-roaming horse or burro, to give recognition to valid claims of private individuals.

And a new section was added to the Senate bill:

. . . to emphasize the ability of an individual to prove ownership of a horse or burro on the public lands under the branding and estray laws of the State in which it is found. It is certainly not the intent of the committee that the right of the individual to claim and prove ownership under the respective State branding and estray laws be abrogated, nor that the appropriate State or local body should not exercise their statutory authority and obligation if the question of private ownership of a horse or burro should be raised. (June 25, 1971)

The House also dealt with the same problem in September. Chairman of the Subcommittee on Public Lands, Mr. Baring, said in his report:

Many privately owned animals are unbranded, and merely because of this lack of visible markings the ownership of such animals should not be placed in doubt .

The Senate bill contained basically all of the recommendations set forth in the special committee analysis drafted by Wild Horse Annie and Dr. Pontrelli, plus a few additional provisions designed to strengthen it. It passed the Senate without a dissenting vote on June 29, 1971. But the House bill, although similar to the Senate bill, was more bitterly contested and would never have emerged from committee without the dedication of its sponsor, Congressman Baring. After being amended and redrafted, and with approximately 200 co-sponsors, it passed the House unanimously on October 4, 1971. Then, after the differences in the House and Senate versions were resolved in conference committee, the consolidated measure passed both the House and the Senate and was signed by President Richard Nixon on December 15, 1971, becoming Public Law 92-195. Now, for the first time, a national law protected the wild horses, and they had a special classification and legal status all their own.

11

Federal Protection for the Wild Horse and Burro

With the passage of Public Law 92-195 (known as the Wild Free-roaming Horse and Burro Act), the wild horses and burros of the West were given a measure of protection they had never known before. (See Appendix for text of PL 92-195)

Section 1. of the Act states that

"Congress finds and declares that wild free-roaming horses and burros are living symbols of the historic and pioneer spirit of the West; that they contribute to the diversity of life forms within the Nation and enrich the lives of the American people; and that these horses and burros are fast disappearing from the American scene. It is the policy of Congress that wild free-roaming horses and burros shall be protected from capture, branding, harassment, or death; and to accomplish this they are to be considered in the area where presently found, as an integral part of the natural system of the public lands."

Section 2. of PL 92-195 defines "wild free-roaming horses and burros" as all unbranded and unclaimed horses and burros on public lands of the United States—any lands administered by the Secretary of the Interior through the BLM or by the Secretary of Agriculture, through the Forest Service.

The new law closed out all the long-standing arguments between the public agencies, individuals and organizations as to whether or not the West's wild horses should be protected, eliminated, utilized commercially, or forgotten. From now on the horses had a legitimate place on the range. The person most responsible for getting the new law passed was Velma Johnston (Wild Horse Annie), and on June 15, 1972 she was awarded the Interior Department's Public Service Award by Secretary Rogers C. B. Morton. She was honored for "leadership which contributed to a statutory solution to a public issue which will permit the Department of Interior and Department of Agriculture to manage and protect wild free-roaming horses and burros within a larger context of ecologically sound management of the public lands."

The Secretaries of Agriculture and Interior were henceforth responsible for wild horse and burro management and protection (and given the broad responsibility and authority to issue whatever regulations they felt necessary to carry out this management and protection) and the fate of the horses would no longer be dependent on local officials. The free-roaming horses and burros were now classified as part of the public lands in a program designed to achieve a natural ecological balance. If advisable, specific horse ranges could be designated as sanctuaries (similar to the Nevada and Pryor Mountain Wild Horse Ranges), but would not have to be created. To date, only one wild horse range, in the Bookcliffs of Colorado, has been created since passage of the Wild Horse and Burro Act.

Indiscriminate reduction programs were prohibited, but humane destruction of old, sick or lame animals could be ordered in an overpopulated area. Other excess animals could be captured and removed for private maintenance under humane conditions. The remains of any deceased wild horse or burro could not be sold for any consideration, directly or indirectly, nor could they be processed into commercial products. Only a federal marshal or agent of the secretary could authorize the removal or destruction of a wild horse or burro that strays onto private land. Any person violating the terms of the Act is subject to a $2000 fine or up to a year's imprisonment, or both.

The law provided for the Secretaries of Interior and Agriculture to appoint a joint advisory board of not more than 9 members, to advise them on any matter pertaining to wild horses and burros and their management and protection. The law also provided for private owners to be able to recover their own horses or burros on public lands, under the brand and estray laws of the State in which the animal is found, after filing a claim with the Secretary. People who graze horses without a permit must get authorization from the BLM to round them up.

In the opinion of the wild horse enthusiasts, the new law was only a beginning, and left several loopholes that needed to be closed. Wild Horse Annie felt it was unfortunate that the recommendation to prohibit grazing permits for domestic horses on the open range was not included in the legislation. But in the eyes of many westerners, particularly those that understood range management, the new law brought with it several unanswered questions, and several possibilities for future problems. In fact, the law seemed to have some built-in problems. There was really nothing to spell out how the law should be administered, especially as to the problem of population control, and there was no plan for maintaining and protecting the habitat of the herds.

The BLM, the administrator of the lands upon which most of the wild horses and burros exist, got most of the problems. And they were problems of a new nature; range managers had never before had to deal with the situations created by this Act. The wild horse, previously thought of as a feral domestic animal, was now suddenly in a new category—a category of animal that had never before existed. The horse was not wildlife, nor livestock, but a "national heritage species" (non-native, at that). And this category had no precedents for management.

In Section 1. of PL 92-195, Congress notes the significance of the wild horse as a desirable resource, and, in spite of his historic status as an introduced species, declares him "an integral part of the natural system of the public lands." To some biologists and scientists, this was a little bit like playing God (thrusting an exotic, non-native animal into the western ecology and calling him a natural part of it) as well as giving the BLM some new and different duties. The BLM had never before had clear responsibility and authority for the management and physical welfare of animals on the range, either wild or domestic; this agency's primary responsibility had been management of the habitat—the land and its vegetation—keeping it healthy and flourishing so that it could support the maximum number of animals, wild and domestic.

PL 92-195 also required some adjustments in other quarters. Responsibilities previously assumed by various state and local agencies were now taken from them, and private landowners could not move so independently against wild horses and burros trespassing upon private lands, and some people could no longer assume that their claims of ownership on free-roaming range horses could be assured. Also, wildlife interests could no longer assume that horse and burro competition with wildlife would stablize or continue to decrease.

There were also some legal problems in defining the wild horse, managed by the federal government, as part of the natural system of public lands. These will be discussed in a later chapter. The terminology of the Act resulted in a significant jurisdiction problem as to whether the BLM can actually have jurisdiction over the animals at all. Section three assigns the responsibility for wild horse and burro protection and management to the Secretaries of Interior and Agriculture. Sections 5 and 6 authorize the Secretaries to enter into cooperative agreements with the states for the management of them and the recovery of claimed animals, under the conditions set forth by the estray laws of each state. Acting for the Secretary, the BLM entered into such agreements with each state where it had to manage wild horses, and this led to a legal battle over the legal status of wild horses. The administrative responsibility of the BLM in regard to authority given by the Wild Horse and Burro Act was questioned.

Until these legal problems were worked out, the

BLM was not really able to make many management decisions; Congress and the BLM both had to take a "wait and see" attitude. In the meantime, very little was done in terms of management or control of the wild horses and burros, and no long term funding was given for wild horse and burro management.

This lack of funding was a major problem hindering the BLM management programs. In Wild Horse Annie's words, the most serious gap in PL 92-195 was the elimination of the appropriation of funds to carry out the provisions of the Act. The BLM was under-funded to begin with, and the additional obligation to protect, manage and control wild horses and burros on public lands in the 11 Western states tremendously increased BLM responsibilities. The BLM was now faced with the impossible task of shouldering this additional responsibility on a budget already strained to the breaking point.

Section 3 of the Act describes the means by which the BLM can dispose of excess horses to avoid overgrazing, and it is this section, more than any other, that posed the biggest problems in management of the wild horses and burros. The BLM and Forest Service were prohibited, by the Wild Horse Annie law of 1959, from using aircraft or motorized vehicles in rounding up the horses. This left as the only alternatives shooting them with tranquilizers from the ground, rounding them up on horseback, or destroying them by shooting. And since public sentiment is against the destruction of excess animals, this left only the first two choices, which were extremely expensive and time consuming.

In early management and control attempts, the BLM found tranquilizing to be impractical and unsatisfactory; horse tolerance to tranquilizer drugs varied so much that proper dosage was almost impossible to determine. The amount that might work for one horse could be totally ineffective for another horse of similar size and weight, or even lethal for a third. So the only workable means for rounding up excess horses was by horseback round-ups. And the cost of the capturing, feeding and finding homes for the excess horses came to about $800 to $1000 per captured horse in the BLM's first roundup attempts.

Section 9 of the Act limits the alternatives even farther by prohibiting the introduction of horses into areas they did not inhabit before passage of PL 92-195 (December 15, 1971). Section 3(d) clinches the problem by prohibiting the commercial use of excess horses which must be destroyed, and by outlawing the sale or transfer of ownership (from the government) of the excess horses taken off the range.

These prohibitions were written into the Act to show that wild free-roaming horses and burros belong to all the American people, and to insure that excess horses would not be sold to private buyers for slaughtering and processing into commercial products. But they created a real problem for the agencies responsible for disposal of excess animals. Section 3 (b) permits humane methods of destruction, in recognition of the difficulties of gathering the animals from wild herds, but this solution is really not acceptable to the public. Section 3 (b) also permits capture and removal for private maintenance under humane conditions and care. The Secretaries may authorize such maintenance under specified conditions, the animals retaining their status as "wild and free-roaming horses and burros". Thus the Act made it legitimate for the Secretaries to turn over extra animals to private individuals' care but only on a custodial basis, with title of ownership remaining with the government.

Thus began the wild horse and burro "adoption" program. But because the number of people willing to accept a horse under these conditions has proved limited, the BLM has been caught between a rock and a hard place. The way the act was written, the only economically feasible means of regulating wild horse populations was to shoot them, which was unacceptable. And the limitations on uses of the carcasses left the BLM no alternative on destroyed horses but to leave them on the public lands to rot and provide food for scavengers, or bury them.

Therefore the BLM was faced with an impossible task—to protect, manage and control the wild horse herds, but with almost no funds for the job, and so many restrictions on how to go about it that most BLM managers honestly did not know how to begin. The first two years after passage of PL 92-195, almost nothing was done in the way of actively managing the horses and burros. The animals were protected but no control programs were started. A lot of things had to be ironed out before the BLM could begin "managing" the horses, and as a result, the protected herds began to increase again, increasing as much as 20 to 30% per year in many areas.

The Forest Service was responsible for the horses on FS lands, but since most of the wild horses and burros are on BLM lands, for all practical purposes we shall be speaking mainly about the BLM. One can, in most instances, assume that the same statements apply to the Forest Service problems but on a much smaller scale.

1972-1973 estimate of horse and burro numbers on BLM lands in 10 Western States

State	Horses	Burros
Arizona	115	7,510

California	265		2,500
Colorado	456		*
Idaho	257		8
Montana	264		*
Nevada	17,972		454
New Mexico	7		13
Oregon	2,925		16
Utah	658		60
Wyoming	3,247		20
	26,121		**10,581**

The first thing the BLM and FS had to do was draw up some management regulations needed to carry out their responsibilities (as set forth in Section 9 of the Act: "for the furtherance of the purposes of the Act"). These regulations were mainly a restatement and definition of various points of the Act. Then, in order to comply with the National Environmental Policy Act (NEPA), the BLM and FS had to issue an environmental impact statement on the effects of these regulations. The first drafts of these environmental impact statements were released in late December of 1972, and public comment was invited.

The statement contained an estimate of free-roaming horse and burro numbers on BLM lands (see accompanying chart) and a map of the areas in the West in which the herds were located. The text of the BLM-proposed regulations is contained in the appendix in the back of this book. In the explanation of these regulations in the BLM's environmental statement, the basic policy proposed is to:

". . . manage wild horses and burros under principles of multiple use, sustained yield and environmental quality, to protect them from unauthorized actions, to manage their habitat in a manner to achieve and maintain an ecological balance and a population of sound and healthy individuals. Full participation by the public and cooperation with States, local governments, and others are required."

The over-all management considerations for wild horses and burros is described:

Planning in accordance with the Bureau's multiple use planning system is proposed as essential to determine location, population and other management actions for wild free-roaming horses and burros. This system applies principles of multiple use, sustained yield, and environmental quality to the management of specific tracts of land.

The principle of "multiple use" means the management of the national resource lands so that they are utilized in the combination that will best meet the present and future needs of the American people; and

harmonious and coordinated management of the various resources, each with the other, without permanent impairment of the productivity of the land or undue damage to irreplaceable values, with consideration being given to the relative values of the resources, and not necessarily the combination of uses which will give the greatest economic return or the greatest unit output.

The principle of "sustained yield" means the achievement and maintenance in perpetuity of a high level annual or regular periodic output of the various renewable resources of land without impairment of the productivity of the land and its environmental values.

. . . management activities must be consistent with the free roaming behavior of the animals coupled with the multiple use concept.

Reservation and allocation of habitat to wild horses and burros will be based on the biological requirements of the animals and the nature of the habitat. Wild free-roaming horse or burro numbers and other uses may be adjusted to maintain proper balances. . .

Provision is made for establishment of specific ranges for wild free-roaming horses and burros if such action is necessary for their protection and preservation. . .

Procedures are established for the removal and relocation or disposal of wild free-roaming horses and burros where such action may become necessary. Relocation of the animals on public lands is limited to the areas inhabited by wild horses and burros on December 15, 1971. Provision is made for custodial care under terms and conditions needed to carry out the purposes of the law.

To preclude illegal takings and to maintain responsibility, only authorized officials or agents will be permitted to destroy wild horses and burros. Criteria for destructions including justification, methods, and disposal are listed.

Specific prohibitions are provided to prevent commercial exploitation and preserve identification of any animals placed in private custody.

The regulations do not restrict a private party from allowing wild free-roaming horses or burros on his private lands. However, he must not remove or entice the animals from public lands. If a private person wishes to actively maintain such animals on his lands, he must enter into a cooperative agreement with the BLM.

The regulations provide that where private persons wish, in accordance with the law, to have wild horses and burros removed from their private lands, the authorized Federal official shall do so upon request provided the animals are within an area that contains a "legal fence" as defined in the regulations. In "no fence districts" or other areas where fences are not required by State statute to protect private property, the authorized officer will remove wild free-roaming horses and burros from private property at the request of the landowner.

Subpart 4713 provides procedures for removal of private animals from the national resource lands.

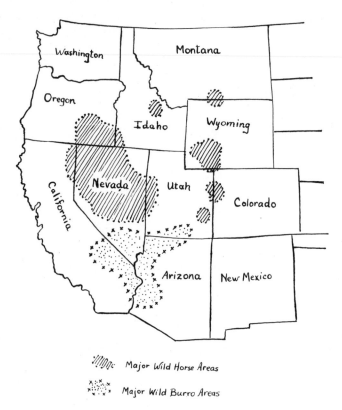

///// : Major Wild Horse Areas

x.x.x : Major Wild Burro Areas

Wild horse and burro areas in the West.

The major portions of this BLM land are utilized to some degree by domestic livestock and many species of wildlife. The domestic livestock—cattle, sheep and horses—are authorized to graze the public lands under the provisions of the Taylor Grazing Act of 1934 which was an act "to stop injury to the public grazing lands by preventing overgrazing and soil deterioration; to provide for their orderly use, improvement and development; to stabilize the livestock industry dependent upon the public range; and for other purposes." Many of the lands presently occupied by horses and burros have many other uses in addition to wildlife and domestic livestock, including recreation, hunting, fishing, sight-seeing, rock-hounding, photography, etc.

Under the environmental impacts of the proposed wild horse and burro regulations, the BLM listed as beneficial impacts the fact that PL 92-195 ended the legal questions as to the authority of the Secretary to manage wild horses and burros, and would permit the BLM to bring management of horses and burros into ecological balance with "all members of the biotic community of the national resource lands".

With typical government optimism, and faith in its own ability to perform miracles, the statement goes on to say that with the creation and use of grazing management systems that recognize

"the life needs of the plant and animal communities recovery of the national resource lands from past abuse will be hastened. At the same time, animal communities will function more efficiently under improved habitat conditions. Implementation of planned management practices can improve vegetative composition, ground cover and vigor. Water quality can be improved and erosion further controlled. Improvement in forage, water and other habitat requirements should improve the health and vigor of wild horses and burros, wildlife, and other animals using the area."

These statements sound like government optimism at its best, and are asking a great deal of the wild horse and burro regulations, seemingly looking at these regulations as capable of solving all of the range problems.

Under the section on detrimental impacts, the BLM environmental statement mentioned that protection and preservation of wild horses and burros would require manpower and funds, which might in turn reduce the time and funds available for management of other national resource land values. Wild horses and burros would compete directly in most areas with domestic livestock and some species of wildlife; burros and bighorn sheep were given as an example. The successful existence of wild horses and burros in the natural environment would de

Claims must be submitted within 90 days after the adoption of the regulations and must be based upon acceptable proof of ownership. Authorization and conditions for recovery of such animals will be prescribed by the authorized officer and ownership established in accordance with the criteria as cooperatively agreed upon between the BLM and the appropriate State agency administering the State branding and estray laws. The fundamental concept of the agreement will be that the proof of ownership must be found acceptable by both BLM and State officials before removal will be authorized by BLM. . . Capture and removal of future estrays will be permitted only upon written authorization by the Bureau.

Subpart 4714 establishes the procedure for enforcement of the act and the regulations.

The next section of the statement is a description of the environment. Only 16 percent (approximately 25 million acres) of the Western public rangelands where wild horses and burros exist were rated in good condition in terms of watershed quality. About 26 percent (42 million acres) of the more deteriorated lands are in the "frail lands" category and can stand very little concentrated use. The major wildlife species which compete to some degree with wild free-roaming horses and burros are listed.

pend on the BLM's ability to manage and control them in a way that would maintain an ecological balance with other resources and values. BLM opinions might be opposed by members of the public who have strong views on methods of management, and this kind of opposition could prevent or delay BLM efforts to protect the other natural resources.

Other detrimental impacts could be the fact that wild horses and burros might become a reservoir or source of disease for domestic livestock, due to the impossibility of a disease prevention or control program in the wild herds.

In some of the closing comments of the environmental impact statement, the BLM made this statement:

"There have been no programs for the protection and management of wild horses and burros on national resource lands. As a result of this and past excessive use by domestic livestock, there are thousands of acres of rangeland which have been severely abused. In many instances livestock use has been dramatically curtailed to cope with these conditions. In some areas, however, uncontrolled and unmanaged grazing by wild horses and burros year-round negates the efforts made to manage livestock and these areas continue to be abused. The proposed regulations provide the means for sustaining wild horses and burros in keeping with the multiple use concept of land management. Such management will enhance the national resource lands."

Because of a lack of basic information about wild horses and burros, and lack of management plans for each separate area, the BLM's statement had to be rather broad. A copy of the draft statement was sent to a large number of groups and individuals (including federal agencies, wild horse and wildlife organizations, livestock organizations, and the 10 states affected by the proposed regulations) and public comment was invited. Many interest groups, including the Sierra Club, attacked the statement as being too general, and for not following the NEPA directive to "initiate and utilize ecological information in the planning and development of resource-oriented projects".

The Bureau of Sport Fisheries and Wildlife found the BLM's statement "most difficult to evaluate in terms of the impact . . . on fish and wildlife resources," due to lack of specific information on proposed actions. "The statement should comment on the anticipated increases or decreases of forage available to big game species as a result of management practices affecting horse and burro population levels."

A comment from Idaho's state land commissioner

found the BLM study at fault in not clearly describing the areas of state endowment land which qualify as wild horse habitat to be protected by the proposed regulations: "State endowment lands constitutionally must be managed for the financial benefit of the institutions they support. Designation of surrounding federal lands as 'Wild and Free-Roaming Horse Range', with any subsequent reduction in domestic livestock carrying capacity, would reduce the income-producing capabilities of the involved state lands."

He also questioned the assumption that the proposed regulations would result in better land management than already existed on the involved range lands, stating that the mere fact that a management plan would be written for wild horse range does not insure that "animal communities will function more efficiently under improved habitat conditions." In his words, a relatively uncontrollable animal was being considered. Management plans which had proven effective in improving vegetative conditions have used deferment or periodic seasonal rest of certain areas. As he pointed out, this is possible with domestic livestock, but impractical, if not impossible, with the wild horses.

He went on to say that many of the poor range conditions existing in his state are considered by many range authorities to be a direct result of the large uncontrolled horse populations that roamed the ranges during the late 1920's and early 1930's. He felt that reduction of horse numbers had not improved these ranges because the perennial grasses had been killed out. Many areas have not been productively grazed since then, and he said, "A look at our history will substantiate that free-roaming horses in substantial numbers have never been a positive factor in range management." He recommended that thorough studies on horse population dynamics and related forage and nutritional requirements of wild horses be conducted, the results incorporated into the proposed regulations. He also mentioned that the potential impact of large horse populations on native forage plants, particularly browse on winter big game ranges, could prove disastrous.

The Oregon State Department of Agriculture commented on the BLM's EIS by saying that the project did not have significant environmental impact description, and remarked that no range can stand year-around grazing; "probably within ten years much of the open range area used by these (so called) wild horses will be depleted."

The director of the Oregon Division of State Lands questioned the validity of the broad generalizations in the BLM statement and he also wondered what approach the federal government intended to take towards state-owned lands. Were state lands to be considered the same as private lands in that the state could elect to support wild horses or have them removed?

Unrestricted horse herds reproduce at a rate of about 25% per year, and the BLM regulations' provisions for eliminating surplus horses gave no indication of what would be considered an excess number. Did the BLM intend to maintain the approximate level of horses existing at that time and eliminate 25% per year? Or is surplus considered to be anything in excess of the maximum capacity the site can support? If so, then how did the BLM intend to restrict expansion of horses into an area not now used by them, especially adjacent, unfenced state-owned lands? And, how many horses are needed to create a recreational or aesthetic experience?

The Oregon land commissioner went on to say that

"according to the Department of Interior, horse and burro numbers and *other* uses may be adjusted to maintain proper balance. Horses are extremely aggressive and competitive, and when left unchecked, could more than likely completely dominate many sites. Horses, like livestock, are introduced species whereas various wildlife species are native. In determining proper balance, where does the Department of Interior intend to assign their priorities? It is obvious that horses will have a priority over livestock in most cases. What priority will horses have in relation to rare and endangered species or other *native* wildlife? . . . The study doesn't say much about the local impact on cattlemen, except that in some area domestic livestock may be excluded. There are several areas in Oregon where this may very well be the case. If this happens, then cattlemen using those ranges will, in effect, be wiped out. How does the Department of Interior intend to compensate those individuals for the loss of their livelihood?"

The Oregon State Game Commission pointed out that the BLM regulations stated that ranges for wild horses and burros may be maintained "exclusively" for them and that this exclusive phase of philosophy was not in keeping with the intent of PL 92-195 (Section 3-a) which states that any adjustments in forage allocations on any such lands shall take into consideration the needs of other wildlife species which inhabit those lands.

Comments on the BLM's environmental statement by Velma B. Johnston (Wild Horse Annie) questioned the mention of competition between burros and bighorn sheep as a detrimental impact, asking if this claim had any substantiation outside Departments of Fish and Game, which "have tradi-

tionally supported occupancy of public lands by target animals, rather than a non-target species, as it is upon the hunting and related industries that Fish and Game Departments depend for their support." In referring to the bighorn sheep as a "target" animal, perhaps she was not aware that in most of the localities where burros compete with them, the bighorn is an endangered species, and is *not* hunted, but protected.

She also commented on the section that dealt with contagious diseases, which stated that wild horses and burros could become a reservoir or source for a disease outbreak. She pointed out that sleeping sickness (equine encephalomyelitis, which was one of the examples given) is carried by birds, transmitted by mosquitoes and that horses are a dead-end host, except in the Venezuelan strain, in which there is a brief viremic stage during which the horses blood stream is infective. She was probably correct in assuming that the wild herds would have very little role as a reservoir or source of this disease.

She mentioned two other diseases for which the wild horse may become a reservoir—dourine and equine infectious anemia ("swamp fever")—but then went on to say that "domestic horse owners through inoculation of their own animals, have controlled the spread of these diseases." Here she was in error, because neither one of these diseases are yet controllable; there has never been a satisfactory vaccine developed. Neither disease can be controlled through inoculation, and there is also no real cure for either one of them. The only means of control is destruction of carrier horses.

Dourine is a venereal disease of horses caused by a protozoa, causing swelling, paralysis and eventual death, although sometimes a carrier horse may live several years before dying. Many drugs have been tried in treatment, but most cases are unresponsive to treatment. The disease can be eradicated only by testing a herd and destroying the carrier horses. This dread disease has been virtually eliminated in the United States, but only because of a concentrated effort by the Bureau of Animal Industry. Wild herds were affected by dourine more recently than most people realize. When the Bureau of Animal Industry made sample tests among the wild horses at the Apache San Carlos Agency in 1930, they found 17% affected with dourine, and later tests showed that as high as 80% of the Indian horses in the high country had the disease. In the removal program that followed, about 8000 horses were destroyed. And in Nevada in 1935 about 500 horses had to be removed and destroyed by the Federal Bureau of Animal Husbandry because of the presence of dourine. We cannot be sure that this might not happen again.

And equine infectious anemia (EIA, or "swamp fever") is a debilitating disease caused by a virus and spread from horse to horse by biting insects or by careless use of hypodermic needles or surgical instruments. The horse may suffer an acute attack and die, or have a long, chronic illness. A few apparently healthy horses as well as chronically sick ones can act as carriers and spreaders of the disease. There is no known cure, and the only way to control spread of the disease is to blood test the horses with the Coggins test and destroy the infected horses and carriers that react positively to the test. Most states have laws prohibiting a horse entering the state unless the horse has a recent negative Coggins test report. EIA is far from being eradicated in the U.S. and all indications are that this disease is increasing. Therefore it is naive to assume that wild horse herds could never be a source of infection.

In her comments, Wild Horse Annie takes the position that wild horses and burros should be granted a "dominant use" of the BLM lands occupied by them at the date the Act was passed. "Since the wild horses and burros, because of encroachment, harassment, and commercial exploitation have already been driven to the extremes of inhospitality as to habitat, occupying areas that are not conducive to domestic use and have subsequently been able to adapt, I can see no reason why theirs should not be the dominant use of said areas . . . the only limitation to be in terms of the over-all welfare of these animals themselves."

But the Act itself states that wild horses and burros will be protected, managed and controlled on BLM lands under the multiple use concept. Dominant use by horses and burros would reduce the variety of animal life in those areas, with subsequent adverse effects on the variety and balance of vegetation; usually the greater the variety of animals in an area, the greater the chance for ecological stability. Taking away the domestic livestock and the major forms of wildlife in an area, and giving it dominant use by wild horses or wild burros, is no better than having dominant use by livestock or by a certain "target" species of game animal. Abuse of the habitat by a dominant user is not good for the land nor ecology, be that user cow, deer, or horse.

The BLM statement was also reviewed by the National Wildlife Committee of the Sierra Club, and the Sierra Club commented that the legalization of this new category of animal (the feral horse, which had now been given symbolic and historic value) offers the BLM "a pioneer opportunity to develop a new set of concepts for animal management on the public lands."

Because PL 92-195 emphasized managing the wild horses and burros in such a way as to maintain a thriving ecological balance, the Sierra Club felt that the main object of all management regulations should be the soundness and good condition of the environment. The Sierra Club felt that part of the new concepts of animal management developed by the BLM should deal with the phenomenon of a feral (introduced, non-native domestic species gone wild) animal that has been incorporated by law into the natural environment it now inhabits. The new law states that the historic and symbolic value of the wild horse and burro—an aesthetic land "use"—must be incorporated and managed within the broad framework of multiple use planning. The Sierra Club hoped this kind of non-consumptive use would not be overshadowed by more tangible and materially productive uses.

"Wild horses are not a breed but a state of being," said William Brandon in a *Sierra Club Bulletin* (September 1972), "a state of wildness, a state precisely opposed to control in any way exploitive." And in the Sierra Club's opinion, management of horses and burros must strive to maintain this "state of being"; the BLM's goal must be to maintain this state of wildness within a balanced environment.

In general, the Sierra Club felt that the BLM's regulations and environmental impact statement were moving in this direction, but felt the statement inadequate because it failed to use ecological information, and was too general and inconclusive. Wild horse and burro research was felt to be strongly needed before any effective management could take place.

> Management by myth and presumption is something that cannot be tolerated, and yet—to some degree—this appears to be what BLM plans to do in the absence of adequate ecological information . . . it appears that BLM is seizing upon PL 92-195 as an opportunity for intensified management in areas inhabited by wild horses and burros . . . quite out of keeping with the spirit of PL 92-195 which states 'All management activities shall be carried out at the minimum feasible level,' presumably because the writers of the law sensed that unduly managed horses and burros cease to be wild, *by definition.*

The Sierra Club questioned whether a single impact statement could be adequate, and recommended that the BLM submit 102 statements on their management plans for each region, feeling that "the present statement suffers badly from the grandeur of generality"—as an example: the attempt to describe the environment of the public land of 10 western states in slightly more than three pages.

Comments on the environmental statement from

the Environmental Defense Fund stressed that wild horse and burro populations be controlled, so that they do not put pressure on native animals such as the pronghorn antelope and bighorn sheep. The bighorn and the Sonoran subspecies of the pronghorn have been steadily declining in number, and would obviously suffer if heavy competition for forage from too many horses and burros became a reality. This organization felt that careful ecological studies would be needed to insure that this did not happen, for it was vital to maintain viable populations of our native large mammal species.

Comments from the Society for Animal Protective Legislation were directed at prevention of cruelty to animals involved in roundups, and in making sure that none of the horses would ever be used for commercial purposes. The group consented to destruction of animals by shooting rather than roundups, and stressed that enforcement of the wild horse and burro protection laws should rest with the federal government rather than the states.

The various comments on the BLM's proposed regulations and environmental impact statement from the different interest groups and individuals were very indicative of the differences in thought across the nation about wild horse management, containing a good cross-section of various aspects in the controversies involved.

In August of 1972 the Forest Service planned to round up about 10 wild horses from Lee Canyon area 50 miles north of Las Vegas, Nevada, because the horses were interfering with skiing and camping. Wild Horse Annie halted the roundup, reminding Secretary Earl Butz that the Secretary must consult with the advisory board (Section 3-b and Section 7 of PL 92-195) before destroying or removing wild horses, and she said, "Not only has the advisory board not been consulted, it has not even been appointed. On the grounds that the FS plans are premature and in violation of PL 92-195, I respectfully request that you immediately instruct your FS office to cancel plans for the removal operations." The roundup was cancelled.

Section 7 of the Wild Horse and Burro Act authorizes the Secretaries to appoint a special advisory board, "to advise him on any matters relating to wild and free-roaming horses and burros and their management and protection." A set of administrative procedures was drawn up to govern the advisory board (things like membership and qualifications). There were to be 9 members, none of them employees of the federal or state governments, and each having specialized knowledge in one or more of these fields: protection of horses and burros, wildlife management, animal husbandry, natural resource management. At least one of these disciplines was to be represented on the board at all times. The first advisory board was appointed in November of 1972 by the Secretaries of Interior and Agriculture. Many of the members had earlier served on the Pryor Mountain advisory committee. The board was composed of the following people:

Dr. Floyd Frank, Head of the Veterinary Science Department at the University of Idaho

Mr. Ben Glading, retired Chief of Game Management, California Department of Fish and Game

Dr. Roger Hungerford, Biological Sciences at the University of Arizona, specializing in desert wildlife studies,

Mrs. Velma Johnston, "Wild Horse Annie", of ISPMB and WHOA

Mr. Ed Pierson, Larimer County Horseman's Association, Colorado, and retired state director of the BLM in Wyoming

Mr. Dean Prosser, Jr. Wyoming Livestock Association, and past president of the National Livestock Brand Conference

Mrs. Pearl Twyne, American Horse Protection Association, Virginia Federation of Humane Societies, and past president of Defenders of Wildlife.

Mr. Roy Young, Nevada Cattleman's Association

Dr. C. Wayne Cook (Chairman), Head of Department of Range Science, Colorado State University

The first advisory board meeting was held in Salt Lake City, Utah, January 12-13, 1973. Mr. George Turcott, Associate Director of the BLM, was present as representative of the Secretaries of Interior and Agriculture, and Frank Smith, Director, Division of Range Management, represented the Chief of the Forest Service.

Mr. Turcott welcomed the board, saying:

You have been selected because of your talents. You

First National Wild Horse and Burro Advisory Board meeting, January 12-13, 1973, at Salt Lake City, Utah.

are not representatives of any special group or interest. Your advice is needed from the full scope of your talents, and cannot be limited by past or present affiliations. We would like to emphasize to you that we feel that you have a tough job ahead of you. . . For your recommendations to prevail, it may not be enough for them to be judgmentally sound. They may need, in addition, persuasive supporting background and perhaps even documentation. Advice in the field in which you are asked to serve is particularly competitive, since the questions and problems involved in the administration of the Wild Horse and Burro Act cannot be solved solely by techniques and procedures. The American people's value systems are crucially involved. Some may argue that wild horses are not mustangs, but of some other order of genetic determination. The fact that many wild horse blood lines may trace back to ranchers' work horses of not so long ago doesn't mean a thing to a large segment of our population. We emphasize that the legislative history of the Wild Horse and Burro Act recognized this, and requires qualifications for status as wild horses and burros merely that the animals be unbranded and free-roaming. In our management and therefore, in your advice, you must give full weight to the values placed on these animals by the people as a whole. We cannot be unduly influenced by value systems of special groups of our citizenry.

This diversity of values creates a responsibility for the board to insure expression and documentation of diverse views. However appealing it may be to Board's aspirations for a successful mission, unanimous recommendations which conceal strong differences of opinion may not serve the Secretaries well. . . .

The Secretaries have to make the decisions. In the Act the Congress also recognized the need for the highest level of advice from qualified citizens. This is your job. . . A desire may arise for the Board to concern itself with the multiplicity of individual actions that must be taken in the implementation of the law, the regulations, policies and guidelines. We have viewed this Board as operating at the highest levels of program controls and not at the implementation levels. . . . Other systems provide for full public participation and interdisciplinary considerations at lower levels. . . . In accepting service on this Board, you have of course not given up your rights as individual citizens. In that capacity, you may individually wish to participate in the public participation process at the district, state and regional levels. You are all skilled enough to make it clear when you are acting in your individual capacities and when you are acting in your advisory role at the national level.

During the course of their first meeting, the advisory board discussed FS and BLM horse and burro inventories, the procedures for claiming and removing privately owned animals from public lands, opportunities for cooperative agreements with other government agencies as well as private landowners, priorities for various competing range and environment uses, and disposal of excess animals.

In the period for public comment, there was an expression that the capture of wild horses in the past had been accomplished by individuals and organized groups as a form of sport, and that this should be allowed to continue as a method of wild horse population control. Representatives of these groups wished to gain title to any animals captured. A suggestion was made to modify the bloodlines and characteristics of wild horses by introducing domestic stallions. Wild Horse Annie later told a reporter, "I was amazed that the people were more concerned about the recreational aspect than the economical aspect," and she was surprised there were so "many riding groups interested in chasing the animals."

The second meeting of the national advisory board was held in Denver, Colorado, March 21-22, 1973. The main purpose of this meeting was to make comments and recommendations on the agencies' proposed environmental statement and regulations. The group reviewed the regulations section by section and recommended a few changes in wording or amendments.

In the time allotted for public comment, Frantz Dantzler (Humane Society of the United States) regarded the recent Idaho roundup situation as a disregard of PL 92-195 and as a lack of responsible enforcement action by the BLM. Mr. Dantzler also expressed concern about the procedure for claiming privately owned horses on public land.

Belton Mouras (Animal Protection Institute of America) suggested "visual supervision" of all capture procedures to prevent undue cruelty to the animals. He favored the term "proven ownership" rather than "probable ownership" in the regulations for claiming procedures, and wanted a safeguard of 30 days' advance notice of any roundup, to allow review by concerned organizations.

Dr. Michael Pontrelli disagreed wtih the concern of some of the Board members that trespass action taken in claiming of privately owned horses was of a punitive nature and he pointed out that the provisions of earlier federal legislation such as the Taylor Grazing Act made it unreasonable to excuse trespass action. Requiring proof of ownership would also be reasonable under existing public land regulations.

Two letters were read from the ISPMB, which were critical of the regulations concerning claiming procedures and criteria for proof of ownership. Reference was made to the Idaho roundup at Howe as evidence of the need for stronger federal regulations, and ISPMB called upon the advisory board to require safeguards that would guarantee protection of wild horses and burros.

Velma Johnston read a letter received from the National Council of Public Land Users in Grand Junction, Colorado, which called for elimination of all permitted livestock grazing on public lands, citing the Idaho roundup as evidence that livestock operators do not respect the laws, administering agencies, or the public interest.

Mr. Ferris, BLM range conservationist, then read a letter received from Minford Beard, describing his experiences in running wild horses in Rio Blanco County in Colorado, and suggesting that regulated running of wild horses should be continued as a form of recreation, and as a way of keeping them wild in nature, free of inbreeding, and controlled in number.

Mr. Alan Kania of FOAL (Feral Organized Assistance League) read some interviews on mustanging and horse roundups showing disregard for the animals. He also read an interview with an unnamed individual giving a viewpoint on BLM and FS aims and objectives, giving a picture of gloom if these federal land agencies remain in control of wild horses and burros.

Then William Wright, of Deeth, Nevada, described his life as a rancher and mustanger from the time of his boyhood. He spoke sincerely and from an immense fund of experience in handling wild horses, explaining the various ways horses may be gathered by horseback and by use of an airplane. He made a strong case for use of a plane, when properly handled, as a humane method of management. This view was shared by several board members, and there was additional discussion about the provisions of the law prohibiting the use of aircraft; it was moved and seconded that the BLM and FS have their lawyers review the 1959 law prohibiting the use of motorized vehicles and aircraft to see if aircraft might be used for wild horse management.

The third meeting of the advisory board was held in Billings, Montana, July 16-17, and one day was spent on a field trip touring the Pryor Mountain Wild Horse Range. The second day was spent in discussing previous recommendations submitted to the BLM and FS on their proposed regulations for administering PL 92-195. They formally approved the regulations and recommended they be published as soon as possible. The board felt that its further views should be reflected in suggested changes to the Act itself, rather than in regulations.

The question of transferring title of excess horses was also discussed, and parts of a letter (of Feb 13, 1972) to the Chief of Forest Service from the General Counsel of the Department of Agriculture regarding transfer of title, were read:

Section 3(b) of the Act does not authorize the Secretaries to sell, convey title, or transfer legal ownership of the animals . . . The FS should act as a trustee to protect the animals from inhumane abuses or harassment, not as an owner and breeder of horses and burros . . . If protection under the Act creates an excess of animals, the surplus must be disposed of when overpopulation occurs . . . Section 3(b) permits humane methods of destruction in recognition of the difficulties of gathering the animals from wild herds. Section 3(b) also permits capture and removal for private maintenance under humane conditions and care. The Secretaries may authorize such maintenance by some instrument and under specified conditions. Animals so maintained must retain their status as wild and free-roaming horses and burros . . . The Secretaries will have a continuing responsibility for animals placed in private maintenance. The private maintenance concept is also developed in Section 4 of the Act. Animals in private maintenance under Section 4 must be kept in a free-roaming state.

Mrs. Johnston disagreed with that interpretation, stating it was the intent of the drafters of the bill that distribution to private ownership could be made, and that the Secretary of the Interior would be the custodian—the interim guardian—until such time as these animals could be placed in ownership of someone else.

Mustanging was discussed, for during the public comment period Kent Gregerson of the National Mustang Association proposed mustanging as a way to reduce excess horses. But the board at that time did not wish to recommend amendments to include mustanging.

The Pryor Mountain horses were discussed, along with possible range expansion (which was later done), the poor range conditions and too many horses, and disposal of the horses through cooperative agreements with individuals. Some of the extra horses were rounded up later that year and given out for adoption.

The advisory board formally recommended that the Secretaries seek an amendment to the law to explicitly permit transfers of surplus horses to private ownership, with adequate provisions for the welfare of the animals. Other recommendations were that the Act be amended to permit the Secretaries to designate other lands (such as national parks, wildlife refuges, Bureau of Reclamation lands, etc.) under their jurisdiction for administration of wild horses and burros, that the Secretaries request adequate funding for research on wild horse and burro management, that supplemental feeding of these animals not be resorted to, except in extreme emergency.

The board recommended, with Wild Horse Annie dissenting, that legislation be sought to allow use of aircraft, including helicopters, in the inventory and removal of excess wild horses and burros, provided that each aircraft have an employee of one of the Departments in it.

The board also recommended, with Wild Horse Annie and Mr. Prosser dissenting, that the two Secretaries seek an amendment of Section 3(b) and Section 8 of the Act to "permit carcasses of animals designated for disposal to be rendered in the customary manner, including commercial rendering plants, provided that any costs or any income resulting from such disposal be a responsibility of the federal agency concerned, and that no money, in any way, go to any third party."

Wild Horse Annie did not support this motion, and gave her reasons in a minority report. She pointed out that the horses are usually located in rugged, inaccessible terrain and that it would be necessary to round up or trap them, driving the ones to be destroyed to corrals adjacent to roads. The most humane procedure would be to destroy them where they are found, in their own habitat, and from there it would be impossible to move the carcasses to processing plants.

She also gave her reasons for not supporting the motion recommending use of aircraft, based on her own observations of the abuses in airplane roundups in the 1950's. She felt that amending the law would completely destroy its protective effectiveness, not being sure of the humaneness in the use of aircraft. The motion required that each aircraft have a BLM or FS employee in it, but she said that such a requirement would be no guarantee of humane treatment, looking at the past record of abuses in carrying out horse clearance programs authorized by government personnel. "As I have done for the past 14 years," she said, "I shall continue to oppose efforts aimed toward restoration of the use of aircraft and motorized vehicles to collect wild free-roaming horses and burros."

What would the wild horse population increase be after the passage of the federal protection law? No one really knew.

Wild horses and burros had been under federal protection for two years, and the agencies responsible for their welfare were beginning to work out policies by which to protect and manage them. The whole program was unique, and much trail blazing still needed to be done. Finding the acceptable path to follow, amid strong extremes of opinion about wild horse management, was not always an easy task, some of it almost falling into the category of trial and error. Federal protection for wild horses and burros was an entirely untried concept, and no one really knew what the problems would be, or the best courses of management to follow.

No one really knew what the population increase rates would be under total protection, or to what degree the horses and burros would compete with other animals. Much research needed to be done on grazing habits, mortality, population dynamics, and other factors. The BLM shouldered the new responsibiltiy somewhat gingerly, but with determination to follow the spirit and letter of the new law. It was a careful middle road to be traveled, and the controversies were not yet over. On one hand, some of the ranchers using range permits felt strongly that grazing privileges and forage for wildlife should take precedence over allowances for wild horses and burros, that the BLM should have authority to give permits for allowing capture of excess horses, and that the BLM be authorized to use aircraft or any other mechanical means necessary in the management, relocation or control of wild horses and burros.

On the other hand, wild horse enthusiasts who had pushed hard for the federal protection wanted strict assurance that the horses WOULD be protected. Some of them wanted even stronger measures to insure that the herds would not be "controlled" too much, and to insure that the wild horse had a rightful place on the range, even at the expense of domestic livestock and native wildlife.

Wild Horse Annie summed up her own feelings about it this way:

> Legislation to protect and manage wild horses and burros by placing them under federal protection has followed a tenuous path, with public interest and action finally prevailing. Those of us in the forefront of the battle only showed the way. We did not achieve all that we set out to achieve, and we are not yet sure that what has been gained will provide an adequate program; we must wait and watch. The people of America have fought hard to save this colorful remnant of two animal species that so uniquely represent the American spirit—freedom, pride, independence, endurance, and the ability to survive against unbelievable odds. Should the future of these animals remain in doubt, the fight will go on.

113

12

The Howe Massacre

One of the most unfortunate incidents to occur since passage of PL 92-195 was a roundup of range horses in the Lemhi Mountains near Howe, Idaho in 1973. Several things went wrong on the roundup and several horses died. Following so close on the heels of the new wild horse protection act (a little more than a year), and with the national publicity it received and the subsequent public outrage, this incident probably did more to widen the gulf between the western ranchers and the wild horse lovers than any other single event. It shook the horse protectionists' faith in the BLM's ability to administer PL 92-195 as a protection for wild horses, and heated up the controversy over the status of some of the West's free-roaming horses.

According to the ranchers who rounded up the Idaho herd, these were privately owned horses. But the wild horse enthusiasts considered them "wild and free-roaming" and subject to protection under the Wild Horse and burro Act. And some of the extremists in the campaign for wild horse protection took the incident, distorted it to suit their own purposes, and used it to fuel the fire of public emotion and outrage. They employed it as a means to smudge the image of the western rancher, to paint him as an irresponsible "bad guy" who greedily uses the western range for his own benefit, even to the

point of getting rid of wild horses in a brutal manner. And they used the incident as a means to gain more support for their own purposes in the wild horse campaign. As a result, the "Howe Massacre", as it came to be called, is one of the most misunderstood incidents in the whole wild horse controversy, and one that has probably been responsible for a great deal of the bitter feelings on both sides of the wild horse issue.

To get an accurate view of the Howe roundup, we have to go back to the initial actions. There was no doubt in the minds of the men conducting the roundup, or in the minds of the local people of that area, as to the ownership of the horses. They were all privately owned ranch horses, but had been in "trespass" for a number of years. In other words, the ranchers had let them run free on the range year-round, without a permit or without paying grazing fees.

This kind of situation is probably hard for a person to understand unless he is familiar with the history and traditions of western rangeland. People in the East often look accusingly at the western rancher, because of his use of "our" public lands as summer pasture for his livestock. This is especially so since the controversies of the past decade over the wild horses and the related lobbying by many horse enthusiasts for recognizing more of these lands for wild horse use.

But this kind of resentment is bewildering to the average rancher on a couple of counts. First of all, his traditional use of the range stemmed from pioneer days, when he took up homesteads in which the use of the rangeland was granted to him as a "right", as compensation for the lack of productivity on his homestead. And secondly, the "wild" horses are merely his own or his father's or grandfather's horses—just ranch horses turned loose. It is hard for him to understand the type of thinking that in one instance accuses "trespass" horses of grazing illegally ("get your dirty rotten domestic horses off our public land"), and then turns right around and fights a bitter battle to "protect" these horses as "last remnants" of "wild, free-roaming horses". In many instance these are the same horses.

Let's take a closer look at the rancher's view of the range. When western lands were homesteaded under the Homestead Act of 1862 (an act which sought to help settle our frontiers), 160 acres was the size of a homestead. But there was a lot of difference between the 160 acres of flat fertile land in the East or mid-West or in a few of the wider river-bottoms (almost 100% farmable land), and the rough 160 acres of a brushy, dry, rocky, steep western homestead situated along a little creek. On the western homestead there might be 20 acres out of the 160 that a person could ditch water onto to grow something, if he was lucky. The rest of it was steep hillsides.

The administrators of this homestead plan in the West realized the inequities of 160 acres of good prairie farmland compared with 160 acres of rough Rocky Mountain land of mostly steep hillsides— good for a bit of pasture, but nothing else—and tried to get Congress to change the Homestead Act to allow 640 acres in the western homesteads. As a compromise, the act was changed to allow the western homesteader a "range right" so that he could pasture his livestock on the abundant federal lands near his ranch during the summer months. He could then irrigate, and grow hay for winter feed on his few "farmable" acres at home. The federal lands he used for summer pasture were good grassland, but not suitable for homesteading—maybe too steep, maybe not enough water, perhaps high mountain slopes or semi-desert.

In order to get a hay crop at home, he turned his livestock out on "range" for summer pasture. The range use, therefore, was a very necessary part of the ranch. This is why western ranchers still feel very strongly about the range today and feel they have a "right" to use it. The grazing privilege is not a nebulous thing, nor a subsidy, nor a use of "our" public lands by "big business greed" as claimed by some wild horse protectionists. But rather it is a very necessary and integral part of many western ranches, especially many smaller ranches, which could not exist without grazing privileges. Without the range, the rancher could not continue to operate; his home acres are necessary for growing winter feed for his cattle. If he had to pasture all his cattle at home, on his hay meadows, he would be forced to cut down to such a small number of cows that he would be out of business.

So the ranchers' traditional view of the rangeland he uses is that it is an essential part of his ranching operation, almost a part of his ranch. Indeed, the Internal Revenue Service considers the range as part of the ranch, substantially taxing it as part of a rancher's estate.

These are just some of the reasons that ranchers are bewildered and angered by the well-publicized ideas in recent years that belittle his claim to these lands and call his use of the range a "rip-off", or a subsidy, or a monopolistic use of "your land and mine."

We have a traditional use of the range by ranchers. In the early homesteading days, there were no regulations about how many head of stock a rancher could run on the public lands he used, and many ranchers overgrazed the lands they used. This was partly because there were very few fences yet in those days, and many ranchers ran their livestock in the same areas. There was no real way to manage the range, because somebody always ran more cattle or sheep out there than he should. The only way to get your share was to get your animals out there first. With no regulations, it was only human nature that some livestock owners took advantage of others and got more grass. It didn't do much good for the conscientious ones to try to protect the range by good management practices, leaving some grass to go to seed, because invariably some of their neighbors came along and used all the grass.

Finally, in self defense, the ranchers (who had been agitating for some kind of range control since the 1880's) succeeded in getting the Taylor Grazing Act passed in 1934, to regulate use of the rangeland and keep it from being overgrazed. The average rancher is conscientious and conservation-conscious, because he has to depend on Mother Nature and her continuing bounty for his livelihood. But just as in any other business or walk of life, there are always a few who need regulations, or they tend to spoil it for the majority. Thus, rules of range use were sorely needed, and finally came into being.

Soon after the Taylor Grazing Act the Grazing

Service, and then its successor, the BLM, became the overseer, the manager of the range and enforcer of the range rules. Range surveys were made, overgrazed areas were restricted in use, cattle and sheep numbers that certain ranchers could run were reduced (or in some instances after range improvements warranted it, increased). But by and large livestock numbers were reduced by the changes. In the early days of the BLM's existence there were fewer personel, and they spent most of their time "out in the field" instead of in the office, doing range surveys, helping ranchers put in range improvements such as water developments and cross-fences to improve grazing management.

But the BLM, like all other government agencies, has suffered from the typical government-office syndrome—increasing the number of personnel to do the same amount of work or less. And as the years went on, more and more BLM men were employed to do more and more office work. Ranchers chuckled (and shuddered) at the way some of the new "smart" young BLM men did their work. For instance, on a range condition survey done in 1964, BLM researchers walked across the rangelands in straight lines, throwing out a circular device every so often and counting the grasses in it. The ranchers, scratching their heads and smiling over the government men and their "hula hoops" pointed out that no self-respecting cow took that kind of a route over the range (straight lines would take you over the rock outcroppings, through the dense brush by the creek-bottoms, over the alkali flats, and so on); she went wherever the grass was. But they didn't chuckle when the results of the newfangled survey chopped their grazing permits even more.

Ranchers had mixed feelings about the BLM range managers. Many ranchers had concern for the health of the range and its vegetation, and were willing to take cuts in permit numbers in order to improve a range; they were willing to work with the BLM in any way necessary to make the range better or to minimize the overgrazing of parts of it. But at the same time, most ranchers had a basic distrust of government bureaucracy—or of green young kids or fresh transfers coming in and telling them how the range should be run. Most of the BLM men coming into the offices in later years had no experience with livestock and didn't have a glimmer of an idea about range cattle habits and grazing patterns. They might propose to relocate some of the rancher's grazing area, or put in some new fencing project that disregarded cattle grazing and travel habits, creating a worse problem, and so on. A good range manager has to be able to think like a cow in order to best take care of a range area, to be able to utilize its full potential while yet improving it and not abusing it. But many modern BLM employees fall short in this responsibility.

So it is no wonder that many ranchers tend to have a little distrust of the government agency in charge of their grazing permits, an agency whose decisions sometimes seem capricious, or dictatorial. Because of this distrust of government bureaucracy, some ranchers, especially those of the "old school" who preferred the way things were run on the range before the government became involved, had few qualms about doing things a little differently from the way the BLM office would have them done. A rancher who allowed his horses to run year round on the range in trespass (in violation of BLM range rules, or in excess of his permitted numbers) probably didn't feel he was doing anything criminally wrong; he was merely doing things the old way, or the way his father did it. He couldn't get by doing it that way with his cattle and sheep, but he could with his horses, because horses can fend for themselves in the wintertime. They'll paw through snow to grass, and are mobile enough to stay in the rough back-country, where they are elusive and hard for a government employee to check up on.

Most ranchers didn't do this, and most resented the irrresponsible rancher who had this kind of disregard for the range, grazing it year-around. But most can also understand the thinking behind this sort of sloppy activity, understanding the feeling that the range actually belongs to the rancher, federal management agency notwithstanding.

So, we come back to the Howe situation. Before 1945 a large herd of horses, numbering about 200, ranged in the Badger Creek area in the Lemhi Mountains. Periodically, these horses were rounded up and sold or used as saddle and pack horses by the local ranchers. After each roundup, a few horses would be turned loose again, to keep the herd going. But in about 1945, all of the herd was rounded up and sold. For at least six years, there were no free-roaming horses in that area.

Then, in the early 1950's several local ranchers turned out range horses—some of their own ranch stock. They pastured them on the range most of the time, bringing them in during some winters to feed them hay, rounding up the group occasionally at other times of the year to capture some for their own use or for sale. But they left a reservoir of range horses out there to draw from whenever they needed them. They were definitely not wild horses, but ranch stock owned by two local ranches and their families. One of the ranchers stopped applying for and receiving a grazing license for his horses in 1953. The other rancher was licensed up until 1968. Both ranchers stopped branding the foals during the early 1960's. By leaving the young horses unbranded they attempted to avoid any trespass action by the government, for if the BLM could not determine ownership of the horses, the ranchers would not have to pay a trespass fee. But the ranchers periodically gathered and protected the horses, breaking some for saddle horses and selling others as bucking stock or for other purposes. The ranchers were all natives of the Howe area, and until recent years raised horses as a major part of their ranching operations.

With the change over in BLM employees in the district office at Idaho Falls, the new range managers who were not familiar with the circumstances considered the unbranded horses as unclaimed horses, and thus did not make much effort to try to establish ownership. The ranchers, in the words of a later BLM district manager (who had been in the area earlier and who DID know the circumstances behind the Howe herd), were trying "to pull a fast one". The range horses "were privately owned horses, deliberately put out there without brands so we couldn't identify them so we could trespass them. The ranchers had been getting grazing land for free." The roundup that occurred in January and February of 1973 was just the climax of a situation that had been building up for 20 years. After the passage of PL 92-195, the ranchers realized they would have to get their horses off the range, or due to the changing laws, the horses might be declared wild and free-roaming.

In the late fall of 1972, one of the ranchers who owned part of the horses, William Robison, contacted Bill Yearsley, of Blackfoot, Idaho, and asked if he would be interested in gathering the herd. The roundup was planned to take place on Thanksgiving weekend, and Yearsley began his preparations for the roundup. Robison contacted the other ranchers that had horses in the herd, and asked them if they would relinquish their ownership to him. One rancher had turned out seven fillies and a stallion in 1955, another had lost a mare and stallion in the area.

On December 19, 1972, a BLM advisory board meeting was held in Idaho Falls, Idaho, at the district BLM office, and attended by two of the ranchers from Howe. One of the items discussed at the meeting was the Wild Horse and Burro Act. The two Howe ranchers left the meeting with the impression that if the herd of horses (which had now grown to about 50 head) in the Badger Creek area was not removed from federal lands within 90 days, they would be declared wild free-roaming horses. The BLM district manager had this same understanding. Copies of the proposed BLM regulations and copies of PL 92-195 were given to all the advisory board members at this meeting. These proposed BLM regulations had been amended in December 12, 1972, but the regulations that were given to the advisory board members did not contain the amendments.

On December 28, Robison and Frank Hartman, another Howe area rancher, visited with the BLM district manager, discussing the possibility of removing the band of about 50 horses from the federal lands. The district manager, Ed Jones, advised them that if the horses were theirs, they should remove them, and suggested they contact the county attorney and county sheriff concerning their proposal to gather their claimed horses, which they did.

The next day, a water board meeting was held at the Howe school, and one of the topics of discussion among the ranchers at the meeting was the gathering of the band of horses in the Badger Creek area. Early in January, the BLM district manager contacted the Forest Service Supervisor of the Challis National Forest (which is adjacent to the BLM lands in the area) and advised him that the ranchers at Howe were going to gather their horses at Badger Creek. The Forest Supervisor answered that as long as the horses being gathered were on land administered by the BLM and were privately owned, the Forest Service would not be involved.

The first roundup attempt was made by Bill Yearsley with a helicopter piloted by Sam Buckley of Mountain States Helicopter Service, Rigby, Idaho, trying to corral the horses in a set of corrals commonly known as the Badger Creek corrals, owned by Frank Hartman. Only one horse, a stallion, was captured, and was kept by one of Hartman's hired men.

Between January 6 and January 20, 1973, Yearsley asked Max Palmer, of Sugar City, Idaho, to help him gather the horses, and Palmer agreed, on condition he would get half of the horses captured. A second helicopter attempt was made in late January, but was unsuccessful. Later, with the assistance of several other individuals on horseback, some of the horses were driven into the corrals at the Badger Creek ranch, and others were roped. About this time (mid-February) the assistant area manager for the BLM contacted Robison to tell him the BLM had received an inquiry from Idaho's Senator Frank Church concerning the roundup. The men involved in the roundup discussed Senator Church's inquiry on the evening of February 16 and decided to continue their attempts to gather the horses. They were under the impression that any horses left out there would be classified as "wild" and protected under the new law, and might eventually multiply to the point of interfering with their livestock grazing.

After several days of continuous chasing, the remaining horses had become quite wild and could not be driven anywhere near an enclosure. On Feb. 17, in the effort to get away from their pursuers, some of the horses climbed up on the west slope of the mountain range between Birch Creek and the Little Lost River, and traveled across a very rough and rocky slide consisting of large, loose rocks. In crossing the slide-rock, three of the horses got their feet caught in and between the large rocks, then panicked and struggled to get free, injuring their legs.

After going across the rock slide, the rest of the horses found themselves on a 30-40 foot high rocky ledge from which they could not escape without coming back through the rock slide. The pursuing horsemen, after seeing the three struggling horses in the loose rocks, wondered what to do, for by this time the struggling animals had compound fractures of their feet and legs. Since none of the men had a gun to end the horses' suffering, and as it was too late in the day to obtain a gun, it was felt that the most humane and merciful thing to do would be to cut the horses' throats. This they proceded to do.

Because it was too late in the day to do anything more with the captured horses, the men made a makeshift corral by felling a tree across the horse's escape route, trapping them in an area surrounded on one side by a rock wall and snowbanks and on the other side by the 30-40 foot cliff. After leaving the area, the men discussed several means of controlling the horses so they could be moved down out of the mountains. They consulted a veterinarian in Rexburg, Idaho, and he advised them to partially close their nostrils with hog rings.

On the morning of February 19, 36 hours after the trapping of the horses on the ledge, Yearsley and Palmer and several others went back to get the horses. Four of the horses had fallen over the ledge to their deaths. How or why these horses went over the edge is not known. The ranchers thought that a cougar might have frightened the horses, since fresh cougar tracks were found near the area; two cougars had been recently killed in that vicinity that winter. Some thought that perhaps a stallion milling around in the small area among the horses might have crowded the four horses over the ledge.

The remaining horses had to be trailed back through the same route they had gone in, over the rock slide. But they would not come out over and past the bodies of the three dead horses that had had to be destroyed earlier. Because the dead horses were frozen solid, and it was impossible to get their

Bodies of several horses lie at the base of the cliff after the "Howe Massacre."

legs loose from the rock crevices, their legs were cut or sawed off to free the bodies, which were rolled over and down off the rock slide.

This is where the story got started that the horse gatherers deliberately ran the horses over a cliff, and sawed off their legs with chain saws. The emotion-packed gruesome story spread by the American Horse Protection Association and other wild horse protection groups implied that it was LIVE animals that had their legs sawed off. By twisting the unfortunate facts a bit, and leaving out parts of the episode, editing it to make it sound even worse, the horse protectionists soon had the whole nation up in arms over the "deliberate brutality" and gory "spectacle" of the Idaho roundup.

Four or five of the wildest horses were caught and their nostrils stapled together in a way to restrict their breathing so the herd could be driven down off the mountain without running away again. The horses had to be brought down off two miles of rugged country, and then across three miles of flat country to get to the Badger Creek corrals. The mountain slopes were steep, with shale rock covered by slippery ice, as well as strewn with down timber. Hobbling the horses or leading them out tied to saddle horses, which could easily result in injury to the men and horses, was ruled out because of the rugged terrain.

The horses with hog rings in their nostrils were able to travel, but couldn't open their nostrils wide for the air necessary for hard running. Only a portion of the horse's breathing capacity was restricted; room was left in each notril for a man's two fingers. According to the ranchers later, the rings did not restrict the horses inhumanely; even with the rings the horses traveled well enough that it was difficult for many of the riders to keep up with the herd coming down off the mountain.

The horses were then driven to the corrals (February 19), where they were fed, and the rings taken out. A few more horses were captured later. Seven of the horses were kept by various individuals, and 37 head were shipped from the Bish Jenkens stockwards in Idaho Falls to a packing plant in North Platte, Nebraska.

After the horses were captured and removed from the valley, one man who was involved in the original plan to keep unbranded horses in the area took it upon himself to notify the Humane Society and horse protection groups about the roundup. These groups were waiting for just such an opportunity, and in the words of one local man, "they got in on it for all it was worth, which was considerable." The ranchers became the targets of horse protectionists seeking a cause around which to rally emotional followers.

On February 26th, Mrs. Velma Johnston (Wild Horse Annie) received a telephone call informing her of a roundup of wild horses in a remote area in central Idaho. The caller said that some horses had been stampeded over a cliff and lay dead at its base and that others had been shot. An undetermined number were reportedly on their way to slaughter at a processing plant. Wild Horse Annie immediately called two top BLM officials in Washington D.C. and asked for intervention. She then called Harold L. Perry, a wildlife authority and field representative for the Humane Society of the United States (HSUS), borrowed him for a special assignment, and put him in contact with her informant in Idaho. She had him arrange for a helicopter, to be paid for by WHOA, to get him and the informant into the area as quickly as possible to take pictures.

Perry later reported that there was blood all around the cliffside and seven mangled horses at the bottom of the "200-foot cliff" (reported by the BLM-FS investigation later as being nearly 40 feet high). The next morning, with the use of a two-way radio, Perry directed Frantz Dantzler of the HSUS, along with an NBC-TV crew, to the scene of the roundup.

In Wild Horse Annie's view, "There is little doubt that the horses captured and slaughtered in the roundup came well within the definition of 'wild unbranded free-roaming' and thus are protected under the 1971 Act, as old-timers in the area say they have existed in that rugged habitat for decades and have always been considered to be wild horses." She expressed this view in spite of the fact that all the horses were cleaned out of the area in 1945 and no free-roaming horses existed there for at least six years—until more ranch horses were turned out to range there in the early 1950's.

The Idaho Humane Society heard reports that ranchers in the Little Lost River area had used helicopters and snowmobiles to round up privately owned horses on public lands, and began investigations. State BLM director Bill Matthews said that reports of helicopter and snowmobile use came to him when the roundup was all over. It was his understanding "they were used primarily the first day, but after that the horses moved into rough country and that kind of equipment wasn't of any use to the people conducting the gathering operations."

Yearsley admitted using a helicopter for one day, and snowmobiles at other times, but claimed their use was not inhumane. "The horses just weren't afraid of the helicopter," he said. "The snow machines made it a lot easier on them and on our horses. You can just zip along on a snow machine and stay above them, herd them down into the flat. That's all those boys did."

But wild horse protectionists were adamant in condemning all other aspects of the roundup. "I would call it a massacre," said Velma Johnston, and Harold Perry agreed, saying, "This is one of the most cruel and inhumane things I've ever seen in my life."

Leo Amy, one of the ranchers who arranged the roundup, owning some of the horses involved, disagreed with the charges of inhumanity, saying that the men who participated in the roundup "did it in the best way possible. They were serious and they were horse lovers. Nothing went on that hasn't gone on for a hundred years in the horse business."

Hindsight is better than foresight. The best laid plans can still go astray. Looking back over the entire situation, there were things that could have been handled differently, but at the beginning who was to know the way things would turn out? In Robison's words, "The men in the roundup were doing a difficult job and no maliciousness was done or intended."

Leo Amy argued that the horses could not be considered wild. "They were domestic horses that ranchers turned out or lost in the 1950's and that started to multiply. They were all branded horses there in about 1960. This thing has been blown out of proportion." The only recognized wild horse herd in central Idaho is located in the drainage of the East Fork of the Salmon River, near Challis, at least one mountain range away from the area of the Howe roundup. The horses at Howe had always been considered domestic range horses.

The ranchers and the BLM officials of that district agreed that the BLM had given verbal permission for the ranchers to gather up the horses they owned; the BLM felt it was illegal, under provisions of the Wild Horse Act, to graze domestic horses on public lands without a permit. "The horses were owned, and in trespass," according to the district manager. But there had been no written permission, nor proof of ownership required. The district manager said, "The ranchers claimed them because they turned their horses out there. Whenever anyone else would go up there after the horses, the ranchers would run them off, so I'm sure they owned the horses." Only about 14 of the horses had brands; the rest were offspring of the original range horses and had never been branded.

BLM assistant state director, Clair Whitlock, said that if the horses were privately owned, "in our view they are not in our jurisdiction except when run on BLM land, and then they're in trespass." He mentioned the problem of enforcing the Wild Horse Act, since "no regulations have been promulgated pursuant to the Act which spell out how to administer the Act." He said problems arose because the specific regulations had not yet been passed by the National Wild Horse Advisory Board.

Wild Horse Annie felt that the roundup was an example of loopholes in the Wild Horse Act. The Act originally provided that ranchers could remove horses from wild horse herds if they could show the animals probably were theirs. "I believe this terrible thing that happened in Idaho is proof there has to be more than just the probability of ownership. I want federal regulations to require definite proof of ownership before a horse can be removed from public lands—and a collection of grazing fees for that horse when it is captured." Wild Horse Annie wouldn't say how she heard about the roundup, but the issue was first brought to public attention when a Howe rancher, Bill Stauffer, wrote to Senator Frank Church in February, complaining about the roundup.

The federal government investigated the roundup, sending three Forest Service investigators and two from the BLM. The roundup began on BLM lands, but ended on FS lands after the horses climbed up into the mountains. In a meeting March 6th, FS and BLM officials agreed to pool existing facts about the Little Lost River herd and to conduct all further investigations on a joint basis, developing a joint investigation report.

Bill Matthews, Idaho state BLM director, said, "At this point we are getting some conflicting information and it is difficult to sort them out and get the facts." Humane groups and horse protection organizations were eager to "make an example" of the unfortunate roundup, and were playing up every aspect they could find to suit their purposes, blowing up some of the details and making them sound worse than they were.

Many different stories about the "massacre" began circulating. The number of "murdered" horses varied, depending on who you talked to. Horse protectionists called the horses "one of Idaho's last herds of wild horses." Details of the roundup varied, depending again on who you asked. The facts got twisted with several tellings, especially if the tellers were outraged wild horse enthusiasts.

Robison and Yearsley, who were involved in the roundup, emphatically criticized the television coverage of the incident. "They came up and took some pictures," Robison said, "And didn't ask anybody anything. I think that's a poor practice for any TV station to do." Some of the horse protection groups, and HSUS, contended that the roundup was inhumane and malicious, but these groups never, at any time, tried to learn the truth about the roundup from any of the men who were involved. Nor did they have any desire to learn about the whole situation. None of these groups ever considered the possibility that the horses were privately owned, always stubbornly taking the attitude that these were wild horses.

"Everyone felt terrible about the horses that were killed," Yearsley said. "I love horses. We were trying to help them, not hurt them." The state BLM director said one of the reasons the horses were being rounded up during the winter was that the "range had been severely depleted and from a humane standpoint it was desirable to get them on feed." The ranchers also felt it would be easier to gather them, because they were ranging down near the ranches at lower elevations that time of year, and felt they could gather them easily. But plans backfired when the horses climbed back up into the mountains. That the horses were short of feed and in poor physical condition was an undeniable fact. "They were skin and bones," Robison said.

Action taken by the BLM and FS officials resulted in the tracing of 29 of the horses to a slaughter house in North Platte, Nebraska, where they were awaiting killing and processing. The two federal agencies assumed custody of the horses, providing feed and veterinary care for them while waiting in the North Platte corrals for the outcome of the investigation (of the rancher's claim that they owned the horses).

Confirmation that the horses were starving and in poor condition came after the horses were located. Duane Struthers of the Central Nebraska Pack Company confirmed statements by the Howe ranchers that the horses were very thin. Struthers, who held the horses, feeding them "good alfalfa hay and supplements"—to be reimbursed by the government—said in a telephone conversation with reporters that the horses which were trucked into his plant March 2nd "were emaciated and starving." He said five of the horses died of stravation on the way to the packing plant.

Yearsley had earlier stated that the horses were thin. "Sure, a lot of them would have survived the winter. They would have gone on." But some would have died. Is malnutrition and starvation humane? By the wild horse lovers' standards, the roundup was cruel. But is freedom to starve, or to be hungry all winter really humane?

A few people questioned whether the roundup might have violated a state law (no. 25-2314 of the Idaho code) which says that "all animals over the age of 12 months ranging upon what is known as the public range and bearing no marks or brands, may be taken up by the finder thereof, and when so taken up, such animals shall be delivered to the constable of the nearest precinct, who shall dispose of said animal in the same manner as is now provided by law for the disposition of estray animals."

The estray laws require the sheriff or other officer to make inquiries after ownership, and if no owner is found, to sell or destroy the animals, with the proceeds to go to the county public school fund. The county sheriff, Richard Lords, said that he did not believe that the ranchers violated the code. "The law doesn't apply in this case," he said. "Those horses up there were privately owned. The people knew who the horses belonged to and they had a right to go in there and take them."

A report that came out on March 7 said that if any charges were filed, much of the case would probably hinge on the definition of what makes a legally wild horse. The 1971 act defines wild horses as "all unbranded and unclaimed horses and burros on the public lands of the United States." The ranchers at Howe, and the BLM officials, declared that the horses were all claimed. But the Humane Society and Wild Horse Annie and others argued that because of the length of time the horses were running freely on the range, they were wild.

Yet advocates of wild horse protection, while feeling strongly that the Howe horses were "wild", at the same time kept verbally condemning "trespass" unlicensed horses on the public range. For instance, Wild Horse Annie, in her WHOA newsletter of June 1973, asked her members to "not be misled by 'technical terminology' when numbers of unlicensed free-roaming horses on our public lands are quoted. On at least two occasions, the results of an inventory of *unlicensed* horses has been interpreted by the news media and by individuals to mean *free-roaming* horses, which in turn has led to the belief that there is an extreme over-population of wild horses. As a result protectionist efforts have been severely criticized by other users of the public lands, and the credibility of protectionists themselves has been questioned."

She went on to define licensed horses as those for which a permit has been issued, and upon which the owner pays a grazing fee, and which are identifiable as being privately owned. She described unlicensed horses as those for which no permit has been issued, no grazing fees paid, and which must be removed by their owners. These are considered in "trespass". Wild horses are those not privately owned, which have lived in a wild free-roaming state and are not required to be licensed. She warns her WHOA members that it is "impossible to give any reasonable estimate of the number of wild horses UNTIL SUCH TIME AS THE PRIVATELY OWNED *UNLICENSED* HORSES ARE REMOVED."

On the one hand she is strongly advocating all trespass horses be removed, yet on the other hand she is appalled and up in arms over the removal of just such trespass horses at Howe, urging everyone interested in the fate of wild horses to write to the governors of the western states, to request a revision of state laws to (1.) require positive proof of ownership of horses running at large, (2). require concurrence of federal officials as to the validity of the claim, and require 30 days public notice before any roundup.

The HSUS investigators met with the BLM officials in Washington in early March and began considering taking legal action "against the BLM for illegally giving permission for the roundup, and against the two men who claimed they owned the horses." Frantz Dantzler, HSUS regional director, said that all information gathered by HSUS would be turned over to the U.S. Attorney. The American Horse Protection Association (AHPA) offered a $500 reward for information leading to the arrest and conviction of anyone involved in "an illegal roundup and slaughter of approximately 60 wild horses on the public's land in south-eastern Idaho."

And threats began to rain down on the Howe ranchers, and were to continue for two years. Hundreds of hate letters came in, many of them abusive and some of them direct threats to the ranchers' lives or those of their families. Most of the letters were turned over to the local sheriff or to the FBI, for although most of the threats were considered to be from misinformed and unbalanced individuals, since the ranchers' families were involved, they had to take the threats with some seriousness.

The Butte County Sheriff received a call that was traced to Los Angeles, California, threatening his life as well as the lives of the ranchers at Howe. The caller mentioned that he had just received literature and information from a major horse protection association concerning the Howe roundup and he informed the sheriff that since justice was not being carried out, he was prepared to take the law into his own hands.

Part of the problem was that confidential information had been given to the news media and to the horse protection groups, who then used bits and pieces of it to suit their own ends. The BLM and FS investigation of the Howe incident included conversations with the ranchers which were made in strict confidence; it was the opinion of the ranchers that these conversations could only be used in a court of law. But later (in April, 1974) a federal judge in Washington D.C. ruled that these government investigation reports be made public. This meant that the various horse protection groups would have access to them, and subsequently many newspaper articles and horse protection group bulletins (such as the AHPA) rehashed the Howe incident in very slanted terms by taking sentences out of context; this is how the AHPA and other groups were able to apread the widely publicized misconception that LIVE horses had their legs cut off with chain saws, and so on. This sort of publicity brought an influx of more abusive letters and phone calls to ranchers at Howe.

According to Pat Woodie, one of the ranchers' wives,

Because of one now-regretted phone call to Wild Horse Annie by an angered rancher in Howe, a situation that had already been resolved in our own area erupted into national focus, and Howe, Idaho, became a household word. However, I personally feel that the ranchers did their very best to go through proper channels (the BLM had never considered the horses as anything but privately owned, and the sheriff assured the ranchers that the estray laws did not apply to privately owned horses). And they acted in good faith. Not being accustomed to the easily aroused anger of the public, they were very nearly mentally destroyed by the flood of abusive mail they received. The sound of a man's faith in humanity being shattered can be very heartbreaking when they discover that liberty and justice for all does not apply to them in any way!

On April 5, 1973, the American Horse Protection Association and HSUS filed suit in U.S. District Court in Washington against the Secretaries of Agriculture and Interior and 13 other officials to seek court review of the Howe incident. They wanted to compel the federal government to enforce laws for protecting wild horses, and to keep authorities from encouraging more horse roundups. The suit asked $10.3 million in penalties and damages from federal officials, who, in the opinion of the horse protection

groups, allegedly failed to fulfill their responsibilities, under PL 92-195, in allowing the roundup.

Dantzler of the HSUS said, "We specifically did not name any of the ranchers involved, since we felt the prosecution of the ranchers is the responsibility of the federal government. We are hoping this suit will cause the federal government to begin procedings against all those involved. However, we are still continuing our investigation and we are considering other legal actions against them." Mrs. William Blue, vice-president of AHPA, was one of those who went to Idaho to investigate the roundup.

The horse protection associations requested of the USDA and Department of Interior that the grazing licenses of the ranchers involved in the roundup be revoked, and also requested that the Badger Creek Area of the Little Lost River be made into a national horse refuge. WHOA launched an appeal to the public to return the "survivors of the Idaho carnage" from Nebraska to their former habitat in Idaho. As Wild Horse Annie stated in a letter to the associate director of the BLM, the ranchers and BLM district manager who authorized the Howe roundup would probably not be receptive to having the horses returned, and their attitudes would present a threat to the safety of the remnant of the band.

Consequently, in order to provide safeguards for the future of these horses, WHOA requested that the area where the horses formerly roamed, with an extension of that area to the southwest, be designated a national wild horse sanctuary, dedicating it as "a lasting memorial to the wild horses that were run to death here by those engaged in rounding them up during February, 1973, and to the surviving remnant of those once proud bands that roamed this land."

In the meantime, the remnants of the "wild horse band" awaited their fate. The horses were in such poor condition when trucked to Nebraska that some of them died on the way, and about 14 died while under veterinary care at the Nebraska packing plant. Plant officials said they were too thin to be used for commercial horsemeat; the firm processed meat mainly for human consumption.

The horses were cared for by a Nebraska veterinarian, Dr. William Burford. In the spring, two of the mares gave birth to foals, but some of the pregnant mares aborted. One of the two live foals was bitten by a stallion and died. Burford said that the plant processes only about 1% of its horses for dog food; the hindquarters were usually shipped to Europe, with some of the choice cuts going to the east coast to be sold for human consumption. "These horses wouldn't be alive today if they had been in killing condition when they arrived," Dr.

Burford said. "The only reason they weren't killed is because they were just skin and bones."

H. B. Stewart, superintendent of the Central Nebraska Packing Company, which had been caring for the horses since March 2, 1973 (to be reimbursed by the government $1.50 per horse per day for feed expenses) received word in October that the government was planning to move the horses back to Idaho while the federal officials determined whether or not they could be claimed as private property.

The Justice Department announced on October 11th, that it would not prosecute the individuals participating in the roundup. "The case lacked prosecutive merit in our opinion", said Larry Westberg, assistant U.S. Attorney in Boise, acting on the investigation filed jointly in April by the BLM and FS. So, although the AHPA and HSUS had lost the first round in their attempts to penalize the Howe ranchers, they proceeded with their suit against the BLM and FS. That case was under the jurisdiction of federal District Judge Thomas Flannery in Washington D.C., but the FS and BLM requested a change of venue, so that the case could be tried in federal District Court in Boise, Idaho, where most of the witnesses were. This request was rejected, however, and the rejection was a victory for AHPA and HSUS, who wanted the trial conducted in Washington D.C., where their own headquarters were, and where the top BLM and FS officials are based.

Under the federal protection law and subsequent regulations for wild horses and burros, people had until November 15, 1973, to file formal claims of ownership for loose domestic horses running on federal lands without a grazing permit. Bill Matthews, Idaho State BLM Director, said that the horses at the Nebraska packing plant were to be returned to southeast Idaho so that the ranchers could make claims, or so the horses could be turned loose again if not claimed. "It appears that some are old saddle and work horses, so they presumably could be claimed," he said, mentioning that some of the animals had old saddle marks.

In early November, 1973, the 18 horses and one foal were trucked back to Idaho, stopping overnight at Rawlins, Wyoming, to be fed and watered. A BLM official supervised the loading of the horses from the packing plant corral, and Frantz Dantzler of HSUS and Dr. William Burford, veterinarian who had been caring for the horses, accompanied them on the trip. The horses were put into a corral near Idaho Falls, in the Idaho Falls Livestock Auction Company yards, still under custody of the federal government until the question of ownership could be resolved.

The "Howe horses", shown here in corrals near Idaho Falls after being trucked back from North Platte, Nebraska.

The national advisory board for wild horses and burros at their fourth meeting rejected the motion by Velma Johnston that prosecution of the Howe ranchers be demanded. The board rejected that proposal on the gounds that further action in the case should await a hearing to determine if the horses were privately owned.

Mrs. Joan Blue of AHPA said later, "We thought naively that once we had the Wild Horse and Burro Protection Act, the wild horses would be safe. We couldn't have been more wrong. The Interior Department encouraged and permitted this roundup. And, now to save face, they are permitting the ranchers to claim the horses that are left. They are not safe anywhere in this state. We are holding the Interior Department responsible for this. We've started a letter writing campaign already. And we plan to go through the Senate and House next week to initiate hearings on the Interior Department's action."

She went on to say that her association would seek a temporary restraining order to keep the ranchers from obtaining custody of the horses. "They have until November 15 to file claim, and they personally told us they are moving to do so."

The horses, after being fed and cared for for eight months, had gained weight and appeared in good condition when they arrived in Idaho Falls, and were not very wild. A boy from Nebraska who had accompanied the horses on the trip slipped a twine around one horse's nose and rode it bareback around the feedlot corral. Dr. Burford said they encountered no problems on the truck trip. The horses were unloaded, fed and watered on their overnight stop without incident, traveling and handling as nicely as domestic stock. Traveling from Cheyenne, Wyoming to Idaho Falls with the horses was Jens Jensen, range management specialist with the BLM.

Dr. Burford said he doubted if the horses could be put on the range and survive until spring, after having been fed in feedlots for the past 8 months. Of the 18 horses brought back to Idaho, about half were mares; the others were stallions, along with two *geldings* (these were "wild"?!). If not claimed, the horses could be released again in the spring.

Mrs. Blue said she would stay in Idaho Falls until she was "sure those responsible for the Howe massacre don't get their way. We think it is ironic that the horses are being brought back to Idaho at the taxpayers expense, to the same jurisdiction (BLM) that sent them out in the first place. I have traveled 800 miles, which would not have been necessary if the Departments of Interior and Agriculture had done their job by enforcing the law in the first place." Lawyers for the horse protection groups said they weren't worried about having the BLM looking after the horses, but Mrs. Blue said, "It bothers me a whole lot" to have the people she is suing guarding the horses she was trying to protect.

Mrs. Blue, in a letter to her AHPA members said,

It has been suspected for many years, and known in specific cases, that the BLM has considered itself the guardian of the grazing rights of private ranchers on public lands. Until the 'Howe Massacre', none of us knew the extent to which the BLM would go to help ranchers reduce the competition for grasses for their domestic livestock. While we continue our fight in our present lawsuit, AHPA v. Department of Interior, the BLM continues to set dates for other roundups in every state where wild horses and burros roam free. They are making plans to fence off the public lands in certain areas to keep these wild horses and burros from competing with the precious domestic livestock of these ranchers . . . Our fight in the present case takes on additional significance when we consider what will happen if we win, or in the alternative, if we lose. If we lose, the BLM will feel justified in continuing their roundups and their fencing and they will feel justified

While the debate over ownership of the horses continued, the horses spent the winter in the Union Pacific Stockyards near Idaho Falls, being cared for by the BLM.

in their protective attitude toward ranchers and their private livestock grazing on public lands. However, if we win, we will have forced the government to enforce the law of the land and to finally protect and preserve wild horses and burros against the brutal and malicious treatment which the horses in Idaho suffered at their hands.

The letter ended with a plea for contributions to help the AHPA continue the fight.

Max Palmer, of Sugar City, Idaho, who had helped to gather the horses on the condition that he would get half of them, filed a claim for the foal and 13 of the 18 horses held at Idaho Falls. The BLM district manager at Idaho Falls said that other claims would be accepted in his office up until 4:30 p.m. on November 15th, the deadline for claims to privately owned horses on public lands. All claims would be sent to Boise, where the state office of the BLM, along with the Forest Service and State Brand Department would determine their validity.

At the 5th national advisory board meeting, many of the public comments concerned the Howe Round-up. Mrs. Blue of AHPA was highly critical of the advisory board and the departments of Interior and Agriculture, along with their respective managing agencies, in the administration of the Wild Horse and Burro Act, and dwelt at length upon the Howe roundup. She gave her interpretation of the law and regulations.

Mr. John Hoyt, president of HSUS, outlined his Society's investigation and findings, saying "all of these actions were in apparent violation of federal laws." Mr. Hoyt suggested that the advisory board be disbanded "if this appalling situation cannot be brought under control. As currently operating, the advisory board appears to be little more than a front for bureaucratic deception and maneuvering."

Yet the advisory board had agreed unanimously that it was "appalled" by the Howe roundup, and urged the Secretaries of Interior and Agriculture to state their positions on the incident, acting on a motion by Ben Glading, and calling upon the Secretary of Interior to appoint to local grazing boards "persons knowledgeable and sympathetic to the purposes of the Wild Horse and Burro Act." Mr. Glading and Dr. Floyd Frank teamed up on a resolution calling for more money to be spent on research by the BLM, after hearing from Kay Wilkes of the BLM that the agency was seeking $700,000 for enforcement of the Wild Horse law in the following fiscal year, but planning to spend only 5% of it on research.

Meanwhile, the Howe controversy dragged on. U.S. District Court Judge Thomas Flannery in June told the lawyer for AHPA, Robert McCandless, that the lawsuit was taking too long to get to trial, and directed him to produce within a few days a list of the witnesses he needed. McCandless was taking too much time and had opened the session with a plea to expand the AHPA complaint so that it could involve not only the 1973 roundup at Howe, but also some actions by federal officials concerning wild horses in Oregon, New Mexico, Colorado and Nevada.

"It seems to me you're bringing a lot of new facts into this case," Judge Flannery told McCandless. "This case started out as a roundup of horses in Idaho, and now you're bringing in Colorado, New Mexico—this is getting out of hand. Where's all this going to end?"

McCandless replied that the incidents in the other states, details of which he didn't have, would show that the BLM and FS had failed to enforce the law in other localities, too. They would help bolster the argument that the trial should be conducted in Washington, D.C. instead of in Idaho, where the federal authorities claimed it belonged. "The gov-

ernment has never taken this law seriously," McCandless said, referring to PL 92-195. "The ranchers and the defendants [BLM and FS] have a cozy relationship . . . the law says these horses are to be protected, but the people think they are chattels."

Judge Flannery told McCandless that he would put a limit on the time available to question witnesses before the trial. "I'm going to have to cut if off, and that's it. This case has got to come to a conclusion."

Robert Werdig, assistant U.S. Attorney representing the Interior and Agriculture Department officials being sued, pushed for a ruling on his motion to dismiss the case. "I come not to praise the horses, but to bury them," he joked, and Flannery replied that he would get to that motion after McCandless finished his pretrial questioning of witnesses. Werdig said he had recently taken testimonies from "two lovely ladies who can't manage five horses but have subjected us to ridicule for trying to manage millions of horses." Werdig said that the women (whom he later identified as Joan Blue and Pearl Twyne, outspoken officials of AHPA) "are concerned about the horses, but they refer to people as 'Those people out there . . .'"

McCandless objected to Werdig's remarks about his clients, but Judge Flannery said, "I understand lawyer talk. I used to practice law myself."

While lawyers fenced over the possibilities in the horse protectionists' suit against the government, plans were underway for a hearing to settle the question of ownership of the horses, and an "oversight hearing" was held before the committee on Interior and Insular Affairs June 26, 1974. Earlier that year, Senator Henry M. Jackson, of Washington, asked the Senate Interior Committee, which he headed, to investigate the administration and enforcement of PL 92-195. In a statement to Mrs. Blue, Senator Jackson said, "I have had many reports about the way the Wild Horse and Burro Act has been administered and perhaps abused. I believe that sufficient time has elapsed since the law was passed to merit an examination of its administration by the Senate Interior and Insular Affairs Committee." He had several reports of possible violations of the act and was concerned with the apparent slowness with which the act was being implemented.

The Oversight Hearing was held June 26, 1974, to receive testimony from BLM and FS witnesses regarding their actions and intentions under PL 92-195. In his opening statement, Chairman Jackson said, "There has been widespread concern regarding a roundup of horses which occurred in Idaho last year. The questions surrounding that incident have not been answered. The purpose of today's hearing is not to fix the blame, but rather to determine how, under PL 92-195, this type of activity was allowed to occur. The intent of Congress in adopting this act is clear—these horses are to be protected, not managed to extinction. Concern has been expressed that the administration is, in fact, using the act to confine these horses and burros or to rid the range of them altogether."

Several newspaper articles about the "Howe Massacre" from the *Washington Post* ("Their Fate May Depend on Courtroom", "Wild Horse Protectors Win Their First Round", "The Bloody Roundup—Wild Horse Slaughter Detailed", "Wild Horses: A Bill Trampled"), the *Chicago Tribune* ("The Roundup That Became a Slaughter"), and the *Sunday London Times* ("The Last Sad Roundup"), were read into the record.

Jack Horton, Assistant Secretary of Interior, explained the BLM's efforts up to that time in enforcing PL 92-195 and managing the horses. Aerial inventories had been completed in many districts, showing substantial increases in the wild horse population. He told of the difficulties encountered in gathering claimed horses, and in managing wild horses in general; no real "management" attempts had been begun yet. Two amendments to PL 92-195 had been proposed to make management easier (to allow use of aircraft, and to allow transfer of title on captured horses), but nothing had come of them yet. Wild Horse ranges, adoption of wild horses, and various other problems involved in the wild horse issue were discussed by the committee.

A statement by Mrs. Blue mentioned the pending lawsuit over the Howe incident and said,

The Government has tried everything they can to get the suit dismissed or get the venue changed so that the suit is moved to Idaho. So far, we have been able to maintain the suit in this jurisdiction and we are hopeful that the suit will be tried this Fall . . . one significant consequence from our lawsuit has been the forcing of the Government to turn over to us and to this Committee the Joint Investigative Report conducted by Interior and Agriculture after that bloody slaughter out in Idaho . . . we have heard the Department of Interior and the Bureau of Land Management testifying for additional funds and additional personnel. We have heard them complain that the law is too vague and too difficult to administer. Their story never changes. Instead of trying to administer the law and protect the wild horses, the Bureau of Land Management would rather continue their cozy relationship with the cattlemen and sheep growers at the expense of the protection of the wild and free-roaming horses and burros.

We oppose the ill-served and inhumane request by the Bureau of Land Management to be able to dispose of so-called excess wild horses. We believe that nature can handle that much better than the present occupants of the hierarchy of the Bureau of Land Management. This committee is aware of the senseless slaughter of a herd of wild horses in Idaho last year. That slaughter, Mr. Chairman, occurred after the statute had been on the books for almost a year and a half. Instead of learning a lesson from their wanton and destructive conduct in Idaho, the Bureau of Land Management has had the audacity to schedule additional roundups, and has asked for funds to help destroy the so-called excess wild horse population and to otherwise continue to ignore the law as it is now written . . . in the time of Watergate when all of us citizens are looking for honest and good government, the Bureau of Land Management continues to give government a bad name. They are responsible for the destruction of that herd in Idaho. They tried to cover it up. They do not believe that the wild horses should be protected.

The Joint Advisory Board has members on it who by law should never have been appointed to the board. They lie with their figures . . . they do not care, Mr. Chairman, what you or I think. They basically do not believe that we have any right to have an opinion about wild horses since we do not live out there. They believe that the wild horses are their exclusive province to be protected or killed, rounded up or driven off particular ranges at their discretion, and as they think best.

Mrs. Blue went on to suggest changes in the horse protection law to make it stronger, "since we can no longer expect the Department of Interior or the Bureau of Land Management to uphold the law as it is written."

Meanwhile, a two-day hearing was held in late June at the Butte County Courthouse in Arco, Idaho (not far from Howe), to determine the question of ownership of the Howe horses, and was held by J. Burns Beal, Idaho State Brand Inspector. The hearing was intended to determine ownership claims, and according to Beal, would probably be the first step in resolving one of the key questions in the lengthy controversy—whether or not the horses were ever legally wild. Max Palmer had filed claims arguing that the animals were NOT wild, and that they belonged to him since he bought them from the ranchers who owned them.

Senator James Abourezk, South Dakota, and U.S. Representative Gilbert Gude of Maryland, had claimed the horses "on behalf of the American people", arguing that the horses were wild (their claim was legally invalid however, having been filed after the deadline for claims). Senator Abourezk and Representative Gude were represented at the Arco hearing by Robert McCandless, the lawyer for AHPA.

In an interview before the hearing, Beal said that testimony would be restricted to proof for or against private ownership, and would not be allowed to stray into other controversial parts of the issue, such as the legality of the roundup, or whether or not it was conducted humanely. "Neither of those two issues bear on the problem we have before us," Beal said. "Our jurisdiction is only in evidence pertaining to ownership."

After all testimony was recorded, Beal said it would be transcribed and studied by officials in his office; a decision would be made within 30 days. But that might be only the beginning of the process, for either side could appeal the decision to the district court, and beyond that, "as far as anybody's got money enough to take it."

If the eventual decision held that the horses were wild, they would be turned out on the dry rolling hills near Howe where the roundup began. If the brand inspector ruled that the claims of private ownership were valid, the horses would be returned to the ranchers, but not immediately, because the BLM (which had jurisdiction over the horses) would have the final word.

"We'd like to go along with the brand inspector's ruling if at all possible," Jensen, of the BLM, said. "But it has to be a pretty good case, a pretty clear case, if they're entitled to ownership." Any ruling the brand inspector made would be incorporated in a BLM report and sent to BLM headquarters in Washington D.C. "We may not make the final decision here," Jensen said.

If Palmer's claims of ownership were upheld, he and the other ranchers might have to pay more than just legal costs; they might have to foot the expense of keeping the animals while the horses were in government custody, and in addition might be charged trespass fees for the years the horses spent on the range at Howe. And the average trespass fees—the fines a rancher has to pay for having an unauthorized animal on public range—run about $4 per animal per month. If the hearing established that the horses were roaming in trespass for several years or more, the cost of ownership could be high.

The first hours of the hearing were filled with legal sparring between the three lawyers representing Max Palmer, and Robert McCandless, representing Senator Abourezk and Representative Gude. But by mid-afternoon of the first day the hearing had settled down to an almost friendly discussion of the owner-ship issue, due to the easing of tension caused by the abrupt departure of McCandless. He left after a debate over whether his clients' claims were valid and whether or not he could practice law in Idaho.

McCandless arrived at the hearing with no license to practice law in Idaho, and no contact with an Idaho Attorney—a seemingly minor point, but one

required by Idaho law. Palmer's lawyers conceded the latter point, but stuck to their complaints about the congressmen's complaints, calling McCandless' clients' claims untimely and unnecessary (the hear-ing was just to determine ownership claims, not other points of controversy). The lawyers for the ranchers decided to waive the requirement about the Idaho law license, and invited Mr. McCandless to stay and cross examine if he desired. But he did not desire, and he and Mrs. Blue and Frantz Dantzler staged a dramatic walkout.

"My claims are valid to the people of the United States," McCandless said as he left, "and I do not see any reason to continue while the objection to them is still in the minds of the counsel for Mr. Palmer." After the departure of McCandless, Blue and Dantzler, there were no further objections to the proceedings.

Among the witnesses who testified in favor of private ownership were the man who organized the roundup, several long-time residents of the area, and a BLM official who had worked in eastern Idaho since 1944. In the years he worked in the Little Lost River area, the BLM official said he often saw small bands of horses in the area, and because of their build and their lack of fear, he knew someone owned them, but no one in the valley would tell him who. The reason for the secrecy was that the owner of the horses could be fined (trespass charges) for having livestock on public land without a permit.

Robert Amy, a lifelong resident of the area, admitted the deception. "We winter some of them and turn them out in the spring," he said. "We thought as long as those horses were running out there unbranded that we're not liable. The BLM can come and look at them and if there's nobody's brand on them, they can't trespass them."

He testified that since 1942 he either knew of or participated in several roundups. The last of these was in 1964 when he and others rounded up and sold most of the horses, but let nine go back to the range. "From that time on to the spring of 1973 we just more or less let them build up."

None of the remaining horses from the roundup wore brands, so the lawyers representing the ran-chers concentrated on showing that the ranchers exercised constant dominion and control of the horses. "Was there ever a year that went by that some responsible party didn't check and take re-sponsibility for those horses?" one of the lawyers asked Amy.

"I don't think so," Amy said. "Just driving up from Howe, you could see them. We'd slow down there and look at the horses from the road."

During the second day of the hearing, one of the

lawyers said, "It's not the money, it's not the property involved in this case. I'm convinced these people are concerned about their reputations, their integrity and their very humanity." He sought to prove that the horses had never been abandoned by the men who owned them. "What you had there," he explained, "was a pooling of horses by their owners in an informal arrangement by which some of them, for the benefit of all, exercised dominion and control." Key testimony, he told Beal in his final statement, was that which showed the horses had never been abandoned.

"Certainly the absence of a brand has nothing to do with whether or not a horse is abandoned," he continued. Witnesses had repeatedly testified that at least 60% of Idaho's domestic horses were not ever branded. "The fact that a horse may be trespassing on public lands doesn't mean a man foreits owner-ship. The question turned on intent." And to prove the intention of the ranchers, the lawyer drew testimony about roundups and about times when the ranchers had fed the range horses over the winter.

He also emphasized what he called the constant surveillance of the horses by the man he said owned them. A key to proof of ownership was a "general knowledge in the community" that, in the words of one witness, "if you went up on the hill after those horses, you'd have some gentleman up to see you." This protective attitude, the lawyer said, could hardly be interpreted as abandoment. "How better can you indicate to the world than to have a general knowledge in the community to that fact?"

The Idaho State Brand Inspector, in accordance with State law and the cooperative agreement between the State, BLM, and FS, has the responsi-bility for determination of ownership claims under the provisions of Section 5 of PL 92-195. On September 3, 1974, State Brand Inspector Beal declared in a 14 page decision that all of the Howe, Idaho, horses in the government's possession at Idaho Falls were domesticated horses, and not wild, feral, or wild free-roaming horses. He said in an interview that "we think that the evidence produced at the hearing and the history through the years would indicate that the horses were not wild and free-roaming and without care."

Reaction to this decision from the wild horse protectionists was swift. "We are very disappointed with the decision," said McCandless. "It seems to me to be a very specious decision. We'll try to find a way to appeal this ruling."

Wild Horse Annie said she was stunned by the decision. "Those ranchers didn't have much to go on," she commented. "I will confer with my attorney right away."

Mr. Dantzler called the decision "incredible." "I'm amazed," he said. "As I understand Idaho legal history, the way to go about establishing ownership is not by letting animals run unbranded and unat-tended." The protection groups were going to try to appeal the case in state District Courts.

Warren Felton, Deputy Idaho Attorney General, said he was not sure the Congressmen's claims to the horses "in the name of the American people" were valid, since they were filed after November 15, 1973, the deadline for claims, set by the wild horse law regulations. Felton also said that the state estray laws probably do not apply in this case, because the Butte County Sheriff told the ranchers before the roundup that the estray laws did not apply; these were owned horses.

Before Palmer could take the horses out of the corrals where they were being held by the BLM, someone had to pay the trespass fees. "We'll prob-ably submit a bill based on what our attorney thinks we can collect," said Jens Jensen, a range manage-ment BLM specialist.

In November, U.S. District Court Judge Thomas Flannery took under advisement the Justice De-partment's request that he throw out the civil suit brought by horse protection groups against the federal officials involved. Robert Werdig, U.S. Attorney representing Interior and Agriculture De-partments, argued that Beal's September ruling establishing private ownership of the horses was sufficient reason for the court to dismiss the lawsuit. Robert McCandless, lawyer for the horse protection groups, argued that it couldn't be left up to state officials to decide whether or not the horses are eligible for federal protection.

Judge Flannery said he thought the law was "silent on who shall determine ownership."

McCandless replied he couldn't see how the 13 or 14 western states can each make its own decision on who owns the horses grazing on the land we pay taxes to support." He insisted that the decision to label horses wild or domestic was "not given to the state."

Judge Flannery countered that, "It was not with-held from it either" in the law.

Werdig said he thought a state official would be ideal to settle the question of ownership. "Who can have been a more neutral arbiter than a state official?" he asked.

McCandless retorted, "What is going on here is a cover-up!" and said that federal officials "couldn't cover up a massacre of horses, so they turned it over to the state, for a ruling in their favor."

In a November 8 hearing, lawyers for the horse protection groups contended that the horses were wild and that it was federal, not state responsibility, to determine their ownership. McCandless said it was never the intent of Congress to allow ranchers on federally owned land to herd horses to a "bloody demise" with snowmobiles and helicopters.

Justice Department lawyer John E. Linskold told the court that the state clearly had the authority to determine ownership under the law, and told his opponents, "All we have here are people who are disappointed with the state administration on the law."

On December 2, U.S. District Court Judge Flannery dismissed the suit and said that in his opinion the Howe roundup was ruthless and inhumane, but on a very narrow point of law, legally correct. He said the strict legal issue was whether the state of Idaho had authority under federal law to determine ownership of the horses. He ruled that the state did. Flannery pointed out that there was "clear support" for the federal agencies' defense, "that Congress intended state agencies to continue to play a key role in determining claims to horses found on federal land."

Section 5 of PL 92-195 states that "a person claiming ownership of a horse or burro on the public lands shall be entitled to recover it only if recovery is permissible under the branding and estray laws of the State in which the animal is found."

The horse protection groups wanted to appeal this decision, "but we have to canvass our members first because it's so costly," Mrs. Joan Blue told reporters. "No matter what the judge said, the horses were unbranded and unshod." She said that unless further protective action is taken, the survivors would be sold for slaughter. "We're loath to quit and to leave those horses to have died in vain."

Max Palmer, who claimed ownership of the horses, said he planned to sell them at public auction, not send them to slaughter. He telephoned Wild Horse Annie and Mrs. Blue, to invite them to the auction. "There's been a lot of public comment," he said, "that these horses are going to a slaughter plant. The main point is that they are NOT going to any dog food plant. They will just be sold to local farmers, ranchers, or whoever wants them."

On December 7 the AHPA said it would appeal the court action dismissing the suit, and Mrs. Blue said AHPA lawyers would also seek a temporary restraining order banning sale of the roundup's surviving horses. She told a reporter she had offered Max Palmer $2000 for the horses and that he had laughed in our faces". Palmer said he hadn't laughed at the offer, but that he told Mrs. Blue's lawyer, McCandless, that he couldn't accept any offers yet, since he had promised months ago to hold an auction for the horses and many other parties were interested. He said he did laugh at an earlier offer from the lawyer for $500 for the entire herd.

Palmer said that McCandless proposed on behalf of AHPA, that if the rancher would sell all of the horses to AHPA and exclude all other bidders, the horse protection group would drop further legal action. "I don't know what that sounds like to you," Palmer told a reporter, "but to me that sounds like a bribe."

The horse protection groups appealed the court's decision that ownership claims could be determined by the state and not the federal government, and the case dragged on. The horses, meantime, were still in the custody of the federal government in corrals near Idaho Falls. Lack of exercise and standing around continually on the concrete-floored feedlot caused many foot and leg problems to develop. Hoof care was nonexistent, and long, breaking feet added to the leg problems.

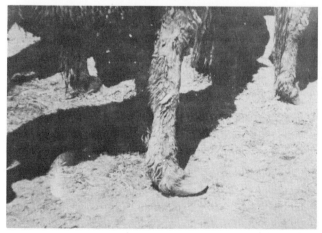

Feet grew long, and winter coats matted and muddy, during the long stay in corrals and feedlot. A horseman would be appalled at this kind of neglect, especially when realizing these horses were subjected to this subtle cruelty under the guise of "humane treatment"—so they wouldn't end up as dog food. Dog food might have been a kinder fate.

Who would stick their neck out and take responsibility for trimming this bunch of horses—a costly, time consuming and risky job, considering that many of the horses had never had their feet handled. The federal government could not possibly give the horses the individual care that a private owner could; all the government could do was see that the horses were fed, protected, and major health problems taken care of. Even at that, the cost to the government of maintaining those horses came to more than $24,000.

The horses were kept in custody, awaiting the results of the legal hassles over them, for a total of four years. Four long years in corrals, with a minimum of exercise and individual care. Very few private owners neglect their horses this badly. This kind of neglect is a form of abuse, because the horse is an athletic animal of wide open spaces. If confined, he should be exercised every day. Total confinement is hard on a horse mentally as well as physically; he gets bored and his disposition suffers.

It is ironic that the Howe horses were subjected to four long years of this quiet abuse because of the battle over them by several horse protection and humane groups, *in the name of humanity*. Where were the humane organizations during those four years? Why didn't THEY provide a few services and care for the horses? If they were actually interested in the horses, it seems like they would have insisted on doing something for them. It almost seems as though the horse groups and humane organizations were actually more interested in wining the legal battles (pushing mainly for weakening the state and local jurisdiction over the horses), thereby increasing their own power and influence, than in actually caring about the horses. Perhaps the horses were merely innocent pawns in a larger struggle.

Oral arguments on the appeal were finally heard on January 14, 1976, in the Circuit Court of Appeals, District of Columbia. In early February, the federal appeals court reversed the earlier decision and ruled that the federal government, not state branding commissions, must determine ownership of horses grazing on federally owned western lands. Under the 1971 law, unbranded horses on federal lands are protected from roundup unless a rancher proves he owns a horse. The law specifically states that state branding and estray laws will apply to ownership questions, but did not specifically say whether federal officials in the Interior or Agriculture departments should decide ownership, or whether it was to be left for state officials.

The AHPA had filed suit, contending that only federal officials had the authority to decide ownership, although state law would be used, and three judges on the U.S. Circuit Court of Appeals unanimously agreed. Circuit Judge Spottswood S. Robinson said that PL 92-195 was passed in the first place because state officials had been lax in the past in protecting wild horses and burros. "A state vulnerable to pressure from cattlemen and other groups could defeat the congressional purpose of saving wild horses, simply by pressuring state branding commissions to find horses privately owned," he said. Since poor state protection was responsible for the federal legislation in the first place, "we cannot believe that Congress intended to abdicate to state officials final determinations" of ownership under the law, Robinson concluded.

Finally, in May of 1977, the issue was at last resolved. The local ranchers at Howe reached an agreement with the AHPA and the BLM to relinquish all their claims to the horses. In return for gaining custody of the horses, the AHPA agreed to drop its $10 million suit against the BLM and FS. The out-of-court settlement was reached at the request of a district court judge in Washington D.C. and ended the bitter dispute. The horses were shipped to the east coast for adoption under the Wild Horse and Burro Act, going to members of the AHPA in Maryland and Virginia under the BLM's "adopt-a-horse" program.

At Howe, the ranchers were glad the issue was finally resolved. But outside of Howe, it seems the bitterness still lingers on. As late as Christmas of 1976, three families at Howe received anonymous letters, the writers saying "They want us to know they haven't forgotten, and that they know where we live," Robert Amy's wife said. She has a scrapbook full of unsigned letters and threats, some of them from as far away as New Zealand.

Mrs. Blue of AHPA claimed that some westerners still feel that hunting and corraling wild horses without permits is legal, though forbidden by the 1971 act. She claimed that BLM officials sometimes "look the other way" when they hear about illegal roundups.

But just the opposite is true. Larry Woodard, Associate State Director (Idaho) for the BLM disagreed with her, saying "I know of no such incidents in Idaho in the past several years." Because the issue is still "sensitive", BLM personnel have bent over backward to check out all reports of wild horse roundups even though most turn out to be false. The BLM, after the lengthy lawsuits, is extra careful, and so are the ranchers. After the Howe hassle, there are probably none who would dare risking the same kind of public condemnation and tromping by horse protection groups. In fact, there are more than a few ranchers who still have branded range horses at large, but who are afraid to try to claim them. Those old cow horses and work horses will probably spend the rest of their days "trespassing" on public lands, thanks to the "Howe massacre"; no rancher in his right mind would consider trying to round up his stray property now. It's not worth it.

Another blow had been struck at individual rights. The traditional law of the West recognizing the fact that any man could lay claim to his own property, was overshadowed. The Howe incident, and its legal repercussions, was to have far-reaching implications. It was perhaps the pivotal event in the wild horse controversy, giving a victory to the horse protectionists who had been looking for just such a test case to force the rancher to his knees. Winning this battle and setting a precedent for federal jurisdiction over ownership claims, instead of state jurisdiction, was a major victory for the horse protection groups and other eastern-based organizations that wanted more control over western lands. And this was just the beginning.

13

Claiming Problems

One of the problems the BLM faced in enforcing PL 92-195 and putting it to work was the fact that scattered and mixed with the wild free-roaming horses were many privately owned horses. Before the wild horses could be properly protected, managed and controlled, the unlicensed (trespass) privately owned horses had to be rounded up. The Wild Horse Act states that a person claiming ownership of a horse or burro on the public lands would be entitled to recover it only if recovery was permissible under the branding and estray laws of the state in which the animal is found.

But since many privately owned horses are unbranded, and since the brands on many branded horses can be difficult to see at a distance, these claims usually could not be fully validated until the animals in question were gathered and physically examined. Advocates of wild horse protection did not want the horses rounded up until proof of ownership was established, but often substantial proof of ownership could not be certain until the horses were rounded up and examined.

And since federal law prohibited the use of aircraft or motorized vehicles in the capture and removal of wild horses or burros from public lands, and since many privately owned horses were mingled with these federally protected "wild ones", the only method that could be used for gathering claimed horses was horseback roundups. This method was not always successful, and at the beginning of the efforts to clear the privately owned horses from the ranges, BLM officials estimated that it would take several years to complete the gathering of all the private horses that had been claimed under the provisions of PL 92-195.

The Wild Horse Act and its legislative history indicate that Congress intended decisions concerning private ownership claims to be made according to state estray laws and by the appropriate state agencies. This becomes evident when a person considers that Congress considered and rejected more than 20 bills which provided for the proving of title "to the satisfaction of the Secretaries". Congress had considered vesting the power to determine private ownership with the federal agencies, but rejected the idea in favor of allowing the responsibility for deciding private ownership claims to remain with the states (ironic then, that later court case overturned this idea—such as in the case of the Howe horses, stating that only federal officials could make the decisions in ownership claims).

State estray laws were to remain applicable in determining ownership, insofar as they did not conflict with PL 92-195. For example, the federal wild horse law states that wild free-roaming horses and burros (unbranded and unclaimed animals on federal lands) are under the jurisdiction of the Secretaries of Interior and Agriuclture for purposes of protection , management and control. Therefore, if any state law made a similar assertion of jurisdiction over these animals on public lands, or in any way interfered with the Secretaries' authority to manage, protect and control them, it was superceded by the federal law.

The FS and BLM entered into a three-party cooperative agreement with each state for examining ownership claims within the state. Federal regulations established a 90 day claiming period in which people could file their claims—a claiming period which expired on November 15, 1973. If a claim showed evidence of ownership, the FS or BLM issued an authorization for gathering the range horses in question. Final release of the horse to the private claimant was given only after the horse was captured, examined, and private ownership verified in accordance with the state brand and estay laws and the cooperative agreement between state, BLM and FS. Public meetings were held in the various BLM and FS districts to discuss the regulations of the Wild Horse and Burro Act and to explain the claiming procedures. Included in the regulations pertaining to claiming procedures were these stipulations:

All claimed horses using public land that are not authorized by the BLM to be out there are included in the category that comes under the claiming procedures.

Proof of ownership must be made. Although a brand is the only prima facie evidence of ownership, ownership can also be determined by affidavit and claim, bill of sale, valid inspection certificate and other evidence, such as pictures. Documents must fully describe the claimed animals.

Authorization in writing by the BLM district manager is required to round up claimed animals.

The forest supervisor must authorize removal of horses from national forest lands.

Ownership claims for all unauthorized horses and burros must be filed by November 15, 1973. A reasonable but specific length of time is allowed for gathering claimed animals.

Use of aircraft or motor vehicles is prohibited in capture of wild horses and burros.

Authorization to gather animals will include necessary stipulations to minimize stress on any associated wild free-roaming horses and burros and to protect other resources. This means requiring the presence of BLM personnel during the roundup.

Close BLM supervision is given to see that capture is done in a humane manner, and that any wild free-roaming horses are released back onto public lands. The procedure would take several years to complete because of the number of claims, the location of the range horses involved, and the BLM's lack of manpower and funds. Capture was authorized during periods of the year in which stress to wild horses would be minimized.

The BLM and state brand inspectors from Idaho and Nevada supervised a roundup of 115 permitted horses on federal range between the Jarbridge and Bruneau rivers (Nevada-Idaho border), to make sure that no unbranded horses were taken, and that the roundup was humane. The horses—owned by the Prunty Brothers of Charleston, Nevada, and used as dude and rodeo horses—were grazing on a permit from the BLM in an area where it was presumed there were also wild horses. Even on a routine yearly range horse roundup like this one, bringing the horses in after their allotted time on the range, BLM officials must supervise the roundup because of the 1971 Wild Horse law.

A public notice was published by the BLM (in compliance with regulations) stating that the roundup would take place, and giving concerned people a chance to voice their views. Bob Krumm, manager of the Idaho BLM district involved, said that the only person who called about the roundup was a humane society representative. But when invited to send along an observer, the society caller decided that no one in the organization was a good enough rider to go along on the roundup.

The first efforts to gather stray trespass horses were not very successful. In Arizona, an authorization was given to gather 16 horses. The applicant and 15 riders spent three days trying to capture them and caught only two horses. Ownership of one of the horses was verified, but the other horse was released as wild and free-roaming. An authorization to gather 150 claimed horses was approved in Wyoming. The roundup crew of 5 men and 28 saddle horses was completely exhausted trying to corral the claimed horses in the rough and rocky terrain. The crew spent some time learning the country, and repairing fences. They planned to drive the horses into a small canyon, and staked 10 head of saddle horses as decoys just outside the opening. They tried to gather bands of various sizes and guide them through the opening out of the big pasture into a smaller, lower elevation pasture. The riders tried for three days to corral the horses, with no success. Every time the horses neared the fence they sensed danger and turned back, running through the riders. One observer concluded that 50 mounted men could not have turned the horses.

As the roundup proceeded, three of the slower horses were roped. The crew spent three 12-14 hour days trying to gather the horses, pushing themselves and their horses to exhaustion, and the futility of the roundup became obvious. On the evening of May 8th it was decided to quit. All 28 of the saddle horses had been ridden to the limits of their endurance, some were lame, and the men did not want to permanently cripple or kill any of them riding them further. Only three horses and four foals had been captured.

Later in the summer the owner of the horses hired another man to round up the horses, and the second gathering attempt was approved by the BLM. Early in that roundup the hired contractor roped a large stallion and his saddle horse was thrown onto its back, injuring the rider internally. The roundup was halted until about three weeks later. After the contractor recovered, 68 horses were gathered, all of them privately owned. But this constituted only half of the claimed horses in that area. Similar poor results were reported on roundup attempts for claimed horses in Oregon.

During the 90 day claiming period, only seven claims were filed (for a total of 42 horses) in Idaho, and only 24 claims (totalling 1,310 horses) on the more than 5500 horses roaming eastern Oregon. In the Vale district in Oregon, George Gurr, district manager, said there were between "1200 and 1300 horses that are either wild or abandoned". Most of Oregon had been closed to licensing of domestic horses. In one area there were 125 privately owned horses whose owner decided not to file a claim, because the gathering would be restricted to horseback roundups; the owner felt he could not do the job without an airplane and he didn't want to try.

About 75 Nevada ranchers filed claims to 6,800 horses (wild horse numbers in Nevada alone, as of that year—January 1974—were 21,174). Several ranchers in Eureka and White Pine Counties in Nevada received federal permission in January, 1974 to gather their horses, so that the remaining wild horses and burros could be identified and protected. The authorized roundup was to end August 30, 1974, after which any claimed as well as unclaimed, horses and burros left on BLM lands there would be considered "wild" and protected as such. The ranchers were allowed to lure the horses into corrals with hay, trap them by fencing off water holes, or round them up on horseback. No aircraft or motor vehicles could be used. After the horses were corraled, a BLM man and Nevada brand inspector were to examine them and determine which ones belonged to the ranchers. The ranchers would have to pay trespass fees on all the horses they owned that were captured on federal lands.

Which of these horses are wild and which are privately owned? It's hard to tell, unless you can get them into a corral where they could be examined more closely.

Horse owners were given until November 15, 1973 to file claims, but even after the deadline an owner could still file a claim to a stray horse if the horse was branded, and if the owner had proof that the horse escaped AFTER the deadline. Any person that loses a horse on the range must have permission from the local BLM office before he makes any attempts at recovering it.

By early 1974 wild horse numbers were beginning to increase to the point that ranchers, wild life experts and government officials in charge of the public lands began to get concerned. The BLM as yet had no real way to control the increasing wild horse population legally or effectively. Wild Horse Annie herself admitted that the horses were multiplying, but adamantly claimed that any shortages of grazing lands was due to poor management and overgrazing by the ranchers. To her, the wild horses and burros had as much right to the land as anything else, and should be permitted to expand naturally. The 1971 law provided that once the ranchers had claimed what they could prove were their stray horses—or the offspring of their own horses, the federal government must control, protect, and manage the rest. And therein lay the loophole, according to Wild Horse Annie.

She felt that ranchers were claiming every wild horse and burro that they wanted eliminated from the public lands, and that it was nearly impossible to dispute their claims. In Nevada, as in several other Western states, the men verifying the claims were themselves ranchers, former ranchers, or members of ranching families, hired because of their familiarity with livestock. There was no strict horse branding law when PL 92-195 was passed; only a sworn statement and an animal description were required to substantiate a claim. In Wild Horse Annie's opinion, the Wild Horse Act was no guarantee of safety to wild horses during the claiming and gathering in areas where "private commercial interests predominate to the extent that their influence over state and federal personnel takes precedence over the Congressional mandate."

As of December 20, 1973, a total of 1661 claimants had filed claims of ownership to 17,165 horses and burros on the range in ten western states. And in a direct challenge to the Wild Horse and Burro Act, the New Mexico Livestock Board notified the BLM that it claimed ownership of all free-roaming horses and burros in the state, under the estray laws of New Mexico (about 7520 horses and about 85 burros). Director of the Livestock Board, Lee Garner, said he was acting for the state and "in behalf of ranchers and a lot of public officials who are not at liberty to say how they feel," and filed the assertion the day the BLM's 90 day claiming period ended.

Yet in other areas of the West, owners of stray horses were not so eager to claim them. Many ranchers were afraid to claim their horses, because they did not know what the trespass charges would be. When filling out the claiming application, the claimant had to describe the horse, where the horse had been ranging, how long he'd been out there, and had to sign the paper in front of a notary. A minimum trespass charge of $10 was specified but there was no mention of a maximum amount, so many ranchers were afraid to claim their animals. If a high trespass fee was charged against them, more than the worth of the horse or horses, they did not feel they could afford to get their horses. As a result, many branded horses are still out there on the range.

Some ranchers gave up on getting their horses back. For instance, as of January 1975 there were six recognized claims for 1241 horses within the Battle Mountain, Nevada, district (1050 of which were claimed by two parties). But as of January 15, 1975 only 10 claimed horses had been gathered. High gathering costs, trespass charges, and grazing fees,

along with the fact that most of the claimed horses are unbranded and hard to prove legally owned, make it impractical to gather the claimed horses. It is doubtful whether very many will be actually gathered. In the Battle Mountain district, for instance, no further extensions of time for gathering were allowed after the last gathering authorization expired June 30, 1975.

The state of Oregon questioned the federal government's "ownership" of the wild horses, contending that the government has not gained this through due process of law. Dean Clark, of the Oregon Department of Agriculture, said,

We have heard the argument that after previous claiming periods had expired, all owners of free roaming horses had abandoned such horses and that therefore, possession, if not ownership of such abandoned horses is now vested in the federal government. We would agree with this argument if the abandonment had been voluntary. But we contend that the abandonment, at least in Oregon, was involuntary, and that therefore title, in and to, or ownership of all such horses remains vested in Oregon citizens. Our contention of involuntary abandonment of these horses by Oregon citizens is based upon numerous complaints to the Oregon Department of Agriculture, that in many cases the trespass fees were so large that owners either could not afford the trespass fee, or the trespass fee exceeded the value of the animal.

Some BLM districts did not bother to try gathering the trespass horses if the ranchers themselves did not wish to claim them. But other districts attempted to get the horses off the range. For instance, in the Vale District in Oregon, the BLM had long been bothered by trespass horses, and had had several long-standing trespass violations. At first, the BLM managers tried to identify the horses and persuade their owners to remove them, but this proved ineffective. Trespass charges were filed against the horse owners who had livestock grazing permits, but no license or authorization for grazing their horses out there. But only a few of the horses belonged to ranchers who had BLM grazing permits, and BLM trespass procedures do not apply to people who don't have grazing permits.

During the summer of 1973, fences in the area were improved in the hopes of stopping the movement of stray horses, but without results. So, in the spring of 1974, Archie Craft, BLM State Director, closed the entire Star Valley unit to licensed horse use. Any horse found in the unit during 1974 would then be in trespass. In late October, Barry Stallings, the southern area manager, found 27 head of horses grazing within the "closed" area, and BLM officials took action to gather and impound the horses. They were able to gather 24 of the horses and transport them to the McDermitt (Nevada) rodeo grounds, where Oregon state brand inspectors identified the horses. Owners were notified that they could pick up their horses at the rodeo grounds after the trespass and impoundment charges had been paid. Unclaimed horses were to be sold at public auction. Twenty-one of the horses were redeemed by their owners at a cost of $1,206, and three other branded horses were not claimed; they were then sold through the Vale, Oregon auction ring.

With it being illegal for private owners to gather their range horses with an airplane (even when there is no question about the ownership) is is often too difficult to gather the horses. A rancher may be fined for having too many horses on the range, but he cannot use an airplane—often the only way to gather them—for fear that some may not be branded. If he tries to gather his own horses that may be running with a wild bunch, he risks a fine or a jail sentence. He has no real choice but to leave the horses out there. To many horse owners, this represents government confiscation of his property.

Privately owned horses on the range in areas where "wild" horses also roamed were a problem—a problem to the ranchers who wanted in most cases to get them off the range so they would not fall into the designation of "wild", and a problem to the BLM officials who really could not begin to inventory, manage and control the wild horses until the tame ones were gathered up.

Horse protection groups were usually ambivalent in their views about privately owned horses. On the one hand they wanted them off the range so they wouldn't interfere with wild horse management, or eat the grass that wild horses might use. And on the other hand, they often lumped them with the wild horses and protested their removal. Some of the horse protection groups went so far as to demand removal of ALL domestic horses from the range, even the licensed horses—the ones that had permits to range out there.

It is little wonder that many ranchers were bewildered and angered by the demands of the horse protection groups. Traditional range use had been by cattle, sheep and horses owned by the ranchers, and some ranchers still have grazing permits for horses—summer pasture for brood bands or ranch stock that is not needed for work at home. To take away these grazing privileges for ranch horses just because of the furor over "wild" horses (just so the "wild" ones could be managed without having to worry about being mixed in with privately owned stock) seemed like a bunch of nonsense and grossly unfair as well. Especially since the "wild" horses were in most cases merely second or third generation ranch horses anyway.

Because of the problems in differentiating between wild horses and permitted range horses, as of 1974, all domestic horses and burros turned onto BLM range were required to be branded as one condition of their license, lease, or permit. Some ranchers questioned the BLM regulations under the Wild Horse Act and declared the regulations would not work—and that the time requirements for the ranchers to claim their horses was not a part of the Wild Horse Act. The BLM regulations denied people their own property (their range horses) without due process of law or compensation, and prohibited the ranchers from just going out and getting them. To the people that lost their horses this way, this was big government trampling the little guy, and very unfair.

The wild horses now had a well-defined legal status, and the federal government had the official responsibility for them.

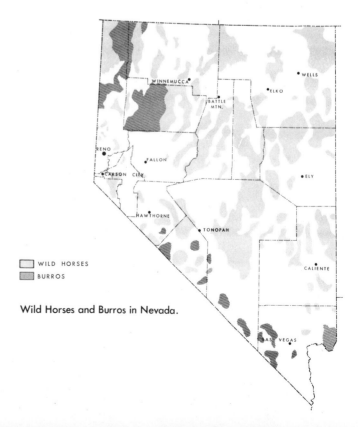

WILD HORSES
BURROS

Wild Horses and Burros in Nevada.

14

BLM Management Attempts

As mentioned earlier, the Wild Horse and Burro Act gave the BLM a new and difficult responsibility—protection, management and control of free-roaming horses and burros on its lands. Congress had shown its continuing concern and recognized a deep interest on the part of the public for the wild horse. PL 92-195 brought a new concept to official attitudes toward wild horses on the public range-land. First, it established the legal status of wild horses by making them the official responsibility of the federal government. Second, it decreed the horse an integral part of the natural system in which it was found and gave it the right to a place in the ecology of the range. Now the managing agencies could allot a part of the public range forage for the use of the wild horse. Third, it eliminated any possibility of making a legal profit from wild horses, by prohibiting their sale. Fourth, it extended and strengthened provisions prohibiting the capture, branding, harrassment or death of any wild horse on public land. Fifth, it established an Advisory Board composed of prominent citizens who were charged with responsibilities for advising both Secretaries on matters concerning managment and protection of wild horses.

The new law provided for protection of the horses wherever they were found on public ranges and provided for a system of range management that recognizes their presence. BLM officials could see some problems ahead, and predicted that more legislation would be needed in future years for proper wild horse management, but they also conceded that at last the place of the wild horse on the public lands was firmly and rightfully established.

The Wild Horse and Burro Act itself limited the BLM's means for controlling the population of the wild herds. For the first few years after passage of the Act more effort was given to trying to amend certain parts of the bill for workable management than in trying to incorporate the management restrictions into a Bureau-wide management plan. With the BLM's limitations in manpower and money, this was about all they could do.

The first action the BLM and Forest Service took was to issue interim instructions to all field offices about the new responsibilities of PL 92-195, and Secretaries Morton and Butz sent letters to the governors of all the Western states requesting state cooperation in administration of the new act. Notices were published advising the public that unbranded, unclaimed horses and burros on public lands were now protected by law. Federal regulations were prepared by each Secretary for administration of the law on BLM and FS lands. The draft regulations were published in December of 1972 for general public comment and review. Many people concluded that wild horses would not be protected until the regulations were finalized, and others expected the regulations to have details to cover any conceivable situation, but this was not so.

The national advisory board for wild horses and burros made recommendations for some revisions, and the revised regulations were adopted and became effective August 15, 1973. The BLM and FS worked out cooperative agreements with other agencies in areas where wild horses or burros overlapped onto lands under the jurisdiction of state or other federal agencies. For instance, the BLM worked out an agreement with Hill Air Force Base and the Army's Dugway Proving Grounds in western Utah, and with state Fish and Game Departments.

A few attempts were made to round up excess horses, beginning in 1974, more than two years after passage of PL 92-195; not many management attempts were made until after working out the environmental impact statement and the federal regulations for enforcing the Act. But even these small efforts were time consuming and costly. The division of range management overran its cost estimates for the horse removal program in 1974 by $300,000.

In 1973, $100,000 was budgeted for wild horses and the actual costs to the BLM were above $400,000. These costs included operation of the wild horse and burro advisory board, field surveillance, investigation of reported violations of PL 92-195, feed and veterinary costs for the horses in custody at North Platte (the Howe horses), initial population inventories, and management of the Pryor Mountain Wild Horse Range.

In 1974, $400,000 was budgeted for wild horses, and 10 new positions were created in the BLM for wild horse and burro work. The actual costs were expected to exceed $600,000, which they did ($687,123). The budget adopted for 1975 was $700,000, while the actual costs came to $1,314,306. The budget for 1976 was $1,000,000, while the actual costs were $1,271,833. The budget for 1977 was set at $1,850,000, and actual costs were $2,679,000, $450,000 of this going for drought relief. The 1978 budget was set at $3,077,000.

The wild horse and burro act, in giving the BLM new responsibilities, also created the need for a new field of study and expertise. More knowledge was needed about the wild horse: his habits, his population dynamics, his relationship and impact on his habitat, and possible competition with other animals using the same lands. Before a reasonable management program could begin, the BLM personnel responsible for managing the wild horse and burro had to learn more about the animals they were to manage. This research and learning process is still going on.

Every BLM district in the West that had wild horses under its jurisdiction wrote up a wild horse management plan and environmental analysis reports dealing with their district wild horse program. Some districts integrated their wild horse management proposals with their overall district or area management plans. Wild horse specialists were trained and assigned to districts having wild horses; they study the horses, write up the management plans, help with herd reductions, and so on.

The optimum number of wild horses and burros that can be maintained in each area is determined as part of the BLM planning system process. This number is determined by suitability of the area, historical use, public recommendations and other values. Many people were quite concerned as to how the BLM would arrive at the numbers they would consider excess, and what approval would be required before the field offices could start proposing removal programs. Normally the BLM would view these decisions as being within the responsibility and authority of each district manager, subject to review by the State Director. But because of intense public interest and the request by the 1974 Oversight committee that the Secretary require review of any roundup proposals by the Washington Office, the BLM did agree for a period of time to review these proposals at the Washington Office level.

When the field offices submit a gathering proposal, they have to have a good inventory of current horse numbers in that area and a good estimate (if they don't have the actual figures available) of what the populations were in that area at the time the Wild Horse and Burro Act was passed. They submit information pertaining to range conditions, any of the conflicts that have arisen with other legitimate uses of the public lands, conflicts with wildlife, domestic livestock and so on. Additionally, they prepare an environmental analysis, which is used as a basis to determine whether an environmental impact statement is needed prior to action on the removal proposal. There is a lot of ground work that has to be done before the proposal is approved, sometimes involving a review from the BLM Solicitor's Office. If any of the information is deficient, the field office must supply more information to meet the full requirements. Then authorization is given from the Washington office for the State Director and District Manager to go ahead with the gathering proposal.

The BLM's goal was to try to maintain horse numbers at the 1971 levels until they could complete the necessary planning process for arriving at the optimum numbers for each area, taking all of the resource uses of that area into consideration. But because of the time it took to get the program rolling, and the many difficulties involved in gathering horses, the BLM fell short of this goal and horse numbers continued to grow. As of May 1, 1975, there were over 49,000 wild horses and more than 5,000 burros inventoried on public lands. This was after 205 excess animals had been removed by the BLM (from the Pryor Mountains and several districts in Oregon), and 2,240 privately owned claimed horses had been removed and returned to their owners.

Any proposed removal receives widespread publicity, and wherever possible, the BLM meets with interested groups, presents the information to them and gets their views and recommendations.

The BLM investigates all reported violations of the Wild Horse and Burro Act. These investigations are carried out by a trained investigator, and the BLM also has an agreement with the Fish and Wildlife Service and uses their investigators to help them. Some of the investigations also involve the FBI.

At the September 5, 1975 national advisory board meeting, the members passed a resolution stating that since feral horses were increasing 10-25% each year, the Secretaries should act immediately to reduce the horse populations where BLM management plans were current, and that the other populations be reduced to the 1971 level. Another recommendation stated that any public relations program issued by the Secretaries stress that horses and burros are exotic animals and not part of the natural system—since populations of exotic animals have adverse affects on native species and if uncontrolled, can lead to extinction of native species.

No roundup of excess horses can take place unless it is under the supervision of a BLM representative, who must be present at all times during the actual roundup. First of all, after the roundup is approved, notices are sent out to interested contractors who must file statements of qualifications, references and background experience. Those found suitable are invited to submit contract bids. Once the roundup is in progress, the BLM has the right to stop a contractor at any time if he seems to deviate from the established standards and requirements.

Some of the BLM's management attempts have been attacked by horse protection groups as "unnecessary herd reductions". Some of these groups question the BLM's population data and rate of increase figures, and call them unsupported conclusions based on insufficient data. Other groups, such as WHOA (Wild Horse Annie's organization) have tried to work *with* the BLM in most cases, trying to figure out and do what is actually best for the wild horses.

As a result of the complete protection of wild horses and burros following passage of PL 92-195, the herds increased, some of them by as much as 20% to 30% per year. Since the horse and burro are not native species, and have no significant predators, it was very unlikely that the herds would establish "an ecological balance with their environment" in a few years. Man had been the only real predator, the only regulator, for these herds, and after the protection given by the 1971 law, the horses increased unchecked except for a small death loss from winterkill among the very old or sick, or a small foal mortality during an unusually bad spring.

When one considers the life span of a horse (an average of 20 years or more as compared to about seven years for a deer), and that some fillies will breed at one year of age and almost all by two, to foal at age three and continuing to produce foals into their late teens and sometimes even longer, it is not hard to see why the horse herds are increasing.

Some people felt that certain herds were in trouble from overgrazing as early as 1973. In August of that year, Kent Gregerson, vice-president of the National Mustang Association, said, "There are areas in the West where the horses are in trouble now. When winter hits, some of the horses are going to die of starvation unless something is done, and done fast. At the same time, the overpopulation of horses in some areas has the potential of destroying the range and making it a wasteland for years to come."

He also questioned the BLM's ability to respond to public comment. In the BLM planning process there is supposed to be "full public participation," but the BLM districts have used different degrees of public participation in their decision-making process. A common activity prior to public hearings is a BLM evaluation of the situation, and then the presentation of management alternatives. Some BLM decisions are made and the public "informed" rather than involved in the actual decision. As Gregerson mentioned, "It's apparent that the government agencies aren't really about to take advice anyway. They make up their minds, then ask for advice, and do as they please."

There is often no distinction made between the public being informed and the public being involved. If some people are then not satisfied with the decision, the BLM personnel may then be confounded by the public's apparent inability to agree with the "logical" point of view; the disgruntled portion of the public is reinforced in its view that the only way to change the BLM's decision is through legislative or judicial action.

Yet it is difficult to combine all the elements of diverse public views and wishes along with basic range management policy. In some cases it is impossible to combine a high level of range expertise and maximum public involvement. As BLM Director Curt Berklund said in 1975:

Why are our programs so controversial? Because we don't have a primary use. Take the Park Service, Sport Fish, and to some extent the Forest Service. They are basically dedicated to three programs. Ours is strictly multiple-use, a mix of all programs. Everything is controversial. When we make a decision, no one is completely happy. There is a trade-off in nearly every decision that comes before us. We have public participation in our management framework plans. After these plans are made, we still find that there is opposition to some segments. You can't get a unanimous decision on any of these plans. So we still have controversy.

BLM Assistant Director George Turcott said at an advisory board meeting for wild horses and burros, "We know that one resource cannot be developed to its full potential while we ignore possible conflicts with other resource uses. Planning, like politics, is a matter of compromise, give and take. But if we have full public participation in our planning process and sound recommendations from the public, we feel that we can assure the people of the United States that their public land and resources are used wisely."

On the problem of wild horse overpopulation, Kent Gregerson of NMA had visited the Pryor Mountain Wild Horse Range in 1973 and declared it to be in terrible condition, with too many horses for the available forage. He also mentioned the Nevada Wild Horse Range at Nellis Air Force Base, which at that time had 2500 horses when it was capable of supporting less than 500.

In the Fall of 1973 it was planned to remove about 30 excess horses from the Pryor Mountains and adjacent Forest Service areas. Lowell Brown, BLM area manager for the Pryor Mountain Wild Horse Range, said that the combined areas were capable of maintaining 110-120 horses. The herd had grown to 150, even though the past two winters had been harsh, with a substantial loss of young horses. Sixty-six applications were submitted from individuals and groups interested in caring for the excess horses. The herd reduction was accomplished successfully, and all the horses were given out for "adoption"—none had to be destroyed. The horses

Wild horses gathered in Oregon in 1977, awaiting adoption in the holding corrals at Vale, Oregon.

were captured by water trapping (using corrals around the water holes and closing the gates when the horses enter to drink) and by horseback roundup.

By 1974 it was obvious that BLM districts in wild horse areas had to start some kind of management and control programs. By January of 1974 there were more than 20,000 wild horses in Nevada alone and by the end of that year there were more than 25,000. In Oregon in 1974 the Vale District alone had over 2000 horses, 25% of which were foals from that year. Oregon as a whole had only 2925 horses in 1971 when the Wild Horse Act was passed; by the spring of 1975 they had increased to 6928. Utah in 1972 had 658 horses, and by 1974 there were almost 1400. The herd near Challis, Idaho had 156 horses in 1971; by 1975 there were almost 450. By the summer of 1975 there were more than 50,000 wild horses and burros in the western United States in spite of some reduction attempts by the BLM during 1974. These management attempts could not begin to keep pace with the increases.

Wild, Free-roaming Horses and Burros in Nevada
(based on 1975 inventory)

District	Horses	Burros
Elko	3,202	—
Winnemucca	7,044	120
Carson City	3,203	111
Ely	2,137	—
Las Vegas	2,424	600
Battle Mountain	4,249	11
Susanville	3,158	207
	25,417	1,049

"In some cases it appears livestock will have to be removed to make room for horses," commented Ross Ferris, a BLM wild horse specialist in Nevada. One Nevada rancher looked gloomily at the future, saying, "You're going to wind up with 50 million wild horses and not enough room to put a single cow."

BLM and Fish and Game Officials were worried that if wild horses began to crowd out deer, elk, and mountain sheep, they would also start to cut down on recreational lands available to the public. "A lot of other public land uses will probably have to be sacrificed in a trade-off for protection of wild horses and burros," Ferris said, mentioning also that the BLM had no idea yet how to control the booming horse population effectively and legally.

Congress was warned in mid-June, 1974 (in the report submitted to Congress by Secretaries of Interior and Agriculture), that the wild horse numbers were increasing so rapidly that some might have to be destroyed in the future. Controlling this expanding population "is considered the most difficult and controversial problem associated with wild horse and burro management."

In an article in *Field and Stream*, Ted Trueblood warned sportsmen of the detrimental impact of expanding horse and burro herds on native wildlife, and called PL 19-195 a "greased slide to disaster" unless amended. The law, in his words, was an "all time classic example of legislation stemming purely from emotion." He felt that the federal protection laws would lead to extermination of two endangered species of native wildlife—the Sonoran pronghorn and the desert bighorn—and a decline in other wildlife populations including elk, mule deer, California bighorns, antelope, upland game birds and small mammals. He felt that the overgrazing from expanding horse and burro herds would damage watershed, leading to siltation of streams and reservoirs; flooding and drought; loss of fish, waterfowl and habitat; and a decrease in water supply for arid parts of the West.

The national advisory board for wild horses and burros met in September of 1974 (their 6th meeting) at Reno, Nevada, and the first day was spent on a field trip southeast of Reno near Tonopah, to observe wild horses by plane, helicopter and bus. At the meeting the next day, many concerned individuals made statements. The president of the Nevada Wool Growers Association mentioned that drought conditions in Nevada caused the forage to be at an all time low. His association did not want the horses eliminated, but controlled. Dean Rhodes, of the Public Lands Council, recommended amendments to PL 92-195 to allow use of aircraft in wild horse management, and to allow the Secretary to sell or donate excess horses or burros without restriction. This was the general feeling of almost all the speakers, including the Director of Nevada Fish and Game Commissioners, the National Wild Horse Association of Nevada, the California Cattleman's Association, Salmon River Cattleman's Association, National Wildlife Federation and others.

George L. Turcott, Associate Director of the BLM, told the board that the outlook for the future was not good. It boiled down to a need for legislative changes in the Wild Horse Act (as Dean Rhodes had already described), "because we can't be responsible ultimately for every horse and burro that may be given away."

These two critical issues—use of aircraft, and passing title to the excess horses—were reviewed with Senator Jackson and the Interior and Insular Affairs Committee at the hearing in June, but at that point no legislation had been introduced. Part of the problem was that wild horse enthusiasts were frightened that if use of aircraft were allowed, the BLM and FS would be deluged with claims for most of the animals out there, once there was a workable means of capture. They did not take into consideration that the ever increasing trespass charges on claimed animals were mounting as time went on, and that most people could not afford to claim the horses.

Carl Rice, range management specialist in California, spoke to the national advisory board about disease problems among wild horses and burros, mentioning that diseases are one of our most serious management problem indicators. He explained that often diseases go hand in hand with population overcrowding, poor habitat, poor forage conditions, and other factors. Starvation has a direct relationship with the susceptibility of an animal to disease, whether it is parasite infection, bacteria, or virus. A healthy environment means a healthy wild horse population.

Some people could not understand why all of the "excess" horses could not just be moved to other federal lands. Senator Abourezk (South Dakota) asked this question at the June oversight hearing and suggested amending section 9 of PL 92-195 to allow the horses to be moved to other federal lands. Secretary of Interior, Jack Horton replied by saying, "Would there be any limit? You have an upward growth curve that continues. Would the solution simply be to create new areas?"

Senator Abourezk said, "There would obviously have to be a limit somewhere, somehow, but as it is with other wild animals, do they not have a natural thinning out?"

Horton replied by saying, "Natural predators and hunting seasons. The elk in my state have a 30-day hunting season. The deer have a six-week hunting season and the antelope have a six-week hunting season. They are also encroached on by things such as coyotes and mountain lions. With the 1971 Act we have totally taken away natural and artificial predation for wild horses, therefore the resultant population growth. We have to have a better solution than the ones we have."

Abourezk agreed we have to have a better solution, but he did not particularly like the solutions available to the BLM, suggesting that amendments to PL 92-195 limit the reduction of horses to only those that are sick and lame.

Geroge Turcott, Assistant BLM Director answered by saying,

It will not solve the problem unless we want to lie to ourselves about what is sick or lame. What we have is a vastly increasing population situation where we have a growing biological base. Right now, with these two protective acts . . . the animals are increasing rapidly . . . There is a vast number that may be involved if we have anything like an 8 to 10 thousand increase a year. The act is very explicit in two or three places. It is one of the best statements of ecology and wildlife management I have ever seen concerning the point that the animals be kept in a thrifty, hardy, virile condition and in balance with their habitat. But with increases, such as we are experiencing, this will not happen. Not only will the horse herds be decimated, by disease and other problems abhorrent to us, but the basic range values, the forage, aesthetic values, domestic livestock and wildlife values, the watershed itself, would be destroyed. I have seen evidence that it is occurring now. It has occurred in some of the burro areas and it was surely occurring in the Pryor Mountains of Montana until management was undertaken.

These are biological principles that cannot be avoided by the Congress, by us and especially be me, as a professional land manager. I want these animals protected. I want a viable, thrifty herd. I want them where they occur in the several states, but they must be managed, otherwise we are back in the dark ages. We

are not using the science we know. There have been evidences of such situations in Australia, where everyone could not face the abhorrence of thinning out animals, of selecting animals and reducing their numbers to the point where devastation could be avoided. Then means had to be taken that are even more abhorrent than you can imagine.

Over-population, overgrazing, malnutrition and starvation would be the destiny of some wild horse herds until better means of control could be employed. About 75 wild horses were gathered near Burns, Oregon (Kiger Gorge, on the Steens Mountain range in southeast Oregon) during July through October of 1974 by the BLM to preserve the rest of the herd, which was starving. It was an emergency situation. The rancher in that grazing allotment was fencing about 1200 acres of his own private land that the horses had been previously using. The herds would have to be reduced so that the remaining range would support them.

Willard Phillips, area manager for the BLM, said he had found horses dead from starvation on that range. "They eat up the grass and the brush and when they can find nothing else, they eat the hair off one another's manes before they die," he said. Overpopulation is a vicious cycle; the increasing numbers of horses damage the range by overgrazing and killing out the plants, decreasing the productivity of the land so it can support even fewer and fewer animals.

This group of horses, called the East Kiger herd, was the first herd of excess wild horses to be controlled after passage of PL 92-195, except for the Pryor Mountain horses. The Oregon roundup was conducted by BLM personnel on rented cow horses, with the help of volunteers from nearby cattle ranches. The horses were difficult to corral. Ray Naddy of the BLM described their difficulties and said, "There just aren't a lot of wild horse runners around. Even the ranchers used to drive them with planes, but under the act we can't do that. It's really tough. Even those cow ponies are not used to that hard riding along the rimrock."

Public participation in this roundup was high; the public had been informed in advance about the roundup and interested persons invited to attend. Three major TV networks filmed the event and 35 reporters were present, along with representatives from the Humane Society and the AHPA. A thorough briefing was held the day before the first roundup attempt, explaining the objectives of the roundup and pointing out the potential hazards that exist in working with wild horses. The first day's attempts brought in only 8 horses. On the second try, a band of 12 horses being brought into the corral

143

spooked and broke through the fencing. One wild horse and one saddle horse were injured and had to be destroyed, and ten of the wild horses escaped.

It took the men about four months to corral the 96 horses, 20 of which were turned loose on the range again. The excess horses were given out for adoption, the first one given away (a small black six-month-old colt) to a 13-year-old boy for his birthday. The boy, Sid Ridling, of Salem, Oregon,—a victim of osteomyelitis—had always wanted a horse of his own. Four of the horses went as far away as Maryland, the first wild horses to be given out for adoption on the east coast.

In another desert area not far from this herd, wild horses had adapted well to the rough and jagged terrain of eastern Oregon (and the tip of southwestern Idaho) and the nearby Owyhee Breaks of Malheur County, Oregon. But lack of water in this desert area is a problem. Grant Baugh, public affairs officer in the BLM Vale District (Oregon) stated in the fall of 1974 that the horses' adaptability and flourishing numbers in this area would eventually spell disaster for the herd in Malheur County, as well as for some of the wildlife in the area, including the California bighorn sheep.

Baugh had been keeping close track of the horses and wildlife in the Owyhee Breaks and claimed that these animals were "headed for an ecological battle which none can win and the ultimate price could be paid in terms of destruction to plants, soil and watershed. There is very little annual precipitation in the Breaks, and therefore very limited vegetation and drinking water. According to Baugh, "the battle for every little waterhole, and every clump of grass is a problem of disastrous potential."

In 1974 there were 234 wild horses in the Breaks and BLM officials estimated that the herd was growing at a rate of 20% per year. Thus there could be 670 horses in the Owyhee Breaks by 1980, Baugh said, unless their numbers are controlled. On the other hand, the California bighorns number between 75 and 100, but they won't increase because their numbers can be controlled through permit-type hunting.

But control of the horses is difficult. In 1949, before strict measures regulating roundups, 7000 horses were taken out of the Squaw Creek area in that same county, and that part of the county was just a dust bowl from overgrazing. The BLM wants to keep that from happening in the Owyhee Breaks.

A hard winter in 1932, combined with an over-population of horses, killed thousands of horses in northern Nevada and southern Idaho on the Owyhee Desert. Horses were seen eating each others' manes and tails after they had chewed the sagebrush down to stumps. In one canyon off the Owyhee River, the entire canyon floor was covered with carcasses in the spring, and for many years afterward the ground was covered with horse bones.

Under PL 92-195 the BLM had two ways to control the horse population—rounding them up and giving them out for "adoption", or destroying them. The first method was most favored, of course, but not the easiest, requiring long, hard days of dangerous horseback chases through very rugged terrain. For instance, at the BLM roundup near Burns, Oregon, it took a week of hard riding just to catch 7 horses out of the 96 head they were trying to catch, and two horses were hurt when a wild horse fell down in front of a rider in a fast chase. The accident injured both horses and the rider was very lucky to escape injury.

The difficulties in this kind of roundup are not the only problems. Giving the horses away is another. There were 250 requests for the 70-odd available horses at Burns, but the BLM still had trouble getting rid of the horses. When the applicants were notified that the horses were corralled, many failed to appear, and some took one look at the horses, turned around and left. Murl W. Storms, BLM director for Oregon, said that the number of people interested in taking these horses is dwindling. About half the people who applied for a horse through this adoption program then decided against taking one.

Most applicants who want a wild horse for adoption want a young horse, but there are also old stallions and mares that need homes. In the East Kiger roundup there were 27 older stallions—which are hard to break and train—that nobody wanted. Some of the horses had foot deformities from running in the rocks, and some were just not riding-type horses. Many are inbred, reverting to a coarser type, or are of poor quality with bad conformation. The BLM has to destroy the excess horses that cannot be placed in "foster homes" and this is not a pleasant job.

And if the BLM is lucky enough to have someone take the excess horses, the problem doesn't end there. The BLM has to retain legal title to the animals, according to the Wild Horse law, and the citizens who keep the horses are only keeping them for the government; the horse cannot be sold or used for any commercial purposes. Persons receiving a wild horse must sign a private maintenance agreement with the BLM which specifies they must care for the horse under humane conditions. Terms of the agreement prohibit transfer of the horse to another person without BLM authorization.

If a person finds out he can't take care of the horse, it goes back to the government, putting the BLM right back where it started—with an excess horse. If that happens, the BLM first tries to find someone in the same region who will take the horse. If not, and the "foster parent" does not volunteer to return the horse, the BLM has to go and collect it, and then find another home for it somewhere else.

Gene Nodine, BLM district manager at Battle Mountain, Nevada, said, "I've been surprised at the lack of experience with horses that is obvious in many of the people who come to claim horses, and I'm sure that some of these horses are going to come back to us. Through injuries, broken legs in trailers, a runaway in downtown Las Vegas that put two legs through the windshield of a car, already 5 or 6 have been put down since adoption (that was in late 1975). Some people have come and found the horses weren't what they expected. One woman called asking us to come after a mare, but will keep the foal. The mare was too much for her, and I'm sure we'll have more requests like that, hopefully before the people receive serious injury."

As one Nevada rancher put it, "To let a horse go to unknown people and stand in a little corral with sometimes not enough feed, and his feet getting long is cruel, especially if they dwindle away to nothing and have to be put away by a veterinarian" or have to be reclaimed by the BLM—all at a cost to the taxpayer.

According to the wild horse law, the BLM must supervise all the horses kept in foster homes. The BLM is not sufficiently staffed or funded now to retain permanent supervision over wild horses placed in the care of individuals—it is a task that will mushroom in the years to come, as more and more excess horses must be rounded up, unless the law is changed. In Oregon alone the BLM will have to round up about 1400 horses each year just to keep the numbers in balance with their food supply.

Curt Berkland, BLM director, made the statement in 1976 that to handle the wild horse numbers by placing them in private custody, and keeping track of them, would create a welfare program as big as some people welfare programs in some states. At the 1976 wild horse population level and with the rapid rate of increase, at least 8000 to 10,000 horses would have to be removed annually just to keep the horse numbers static.

An example of the problem faced by the BLM is that not only do some people change their minds and decide they can't take care of the horse, but also a few horses have to be "repossessed"—the BLM responding to complaints of neglect or inhumane care, and going to get the horse. Two horses that had been in the care of a Nampa, Idaho man for four months had been so ill-cared for that complaints reached the BLM from both the Nampa police and an organization called Pet Haven. One of the mares had foaled, and none of them were being properly fed and watered. The foal, 1½ months old, died. Jerry Wilcox, wild horse specialist, said the mares at the time of adoption were in "typical range condition, not fat", but after four months of neglect looked like walking skeletons.

The two Nampa mares were the first in Idaho that the BLM had to reclaim, but a total of 16 others across the country had been voluntarily returned after complaints of abuse. Wilcox said that returned horses are "fattened up" and given out for adoption again if possible.

Having to repossess abused horses is a problem that will grow. As of January 1978, the Boise, Idaho district had received 50 complaints and had taken back 17 horses. Other states were having similar problems. Some people who adopt horses in the summer when pasture is available are not able to feed them in the winter and cannot keep the horses. The BLM estimates it costs a private owner in an urban situation about $1400 a year to keep a horse, and many adoptors do not realize what they are getting into.

According to BLM officials, there is little protection in the wild horse law for horses placed in the private maintenance programs; all the BLM can do is confiscate the horses. As Wilcox pointed out, there are strong penalties for abusing wild horses in the wilderness, but these do not apply when the horses are transferred to foster parents. As cases of neglected adopted horses became more numerous, the BLM began working with local law enforcement officers. When extreme neglect is evident, the BLM seeks prosecution under state humane laws, working closely with the local humane societies and the county sheriff.

The screening process for adoption applicants involves only selection from written requests. "It is impossible to go out and check on all these applications to find out the applicant's credibility or to check their facilities," said Wilcox. "And there are no funds to check on the horses once they are placed for adoption." The BLM has to rely on wild horse protection groups and local humane societies to report incidences of neglect or cruelty, just as they relied upon some of the wild horse groups to help screen the applicants in the beginning of the adoption program. Now all applications are processed through the BLM's Washington office, and the names of qualified applicants are sent to the automated data processing system in the Denver Service Center.

Ever since the beginning of the adopt-a-horse

program, an appeal has been made across the nation for horse lovers to apply for the horses. The BLM's adoption program works like this: each year, through well planned and humanely conducted roundups, a pre-determined number of horses are taken from overgrazed areas and made available to individuals who can provide proper care. These capture and adoption operations are monitored by horse protection and humane organizations. A central application system allows the selection of suitable "foster" parents who are screened for such things as where they will keep the horse, their facilities for keeping a horse, their ability to care for a horse, to provide adequate feed, and so on. The BLM has an application form that the prospective horse-keeper ("custodian", in BLM language) fills out.

The captured horses are inspected by a veterinarian and given the necessary Coggins test and vaccinations. A fee of about $17 to cover the test and vaccinations is paid by the person adopting the horse. He also must arrange for transporting the horse from the BLM's capture site or central holding facility to his home. The horses as such, are given away "free" to the applicant, but the adoptor is henceforth responsible for all costs in keeping the horse. The "foster parent" may train the horse for riding or other non-commercial uses. The government remains the legal guardian of the horse, but any offspring of the adopted horse would belong to the person taking care of it; only the original adopted horse is owned by the government.

In its beginnings the BLM adoption program was aided by volunteer work by interested horse groups, especially WHOA, helping the BLM process and screen the applications. The BLM still depends on this kind of help by interested persons and organizations, but now the applications for adoption all go through a central BLM computer. Excess applicants names are kept on file in the computer and called upon when needed. The computer matches the applicant to the description of the horse or horses he would like to obtain, and the applicant is then notified to get in touch with the appropriate BLM office where the desired type of horse or horses are located following capture.

So far the BLM has had fair success in placing horses through the adoption program, especially during the summer months when people are more able to travel and come pick up the horses. The state BLM office in Nevada reported that about 80% of the applicants notified actually come to take their horses, during summer months. But in winter the figure drops to about 20%.

By late 1977 the BLM was working on an attempt to put together large group shipments of horses,

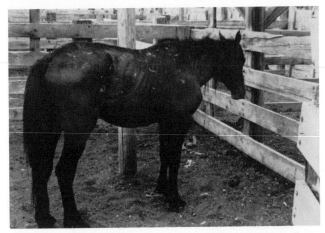

One of the stallions rounded up in Oregon in 1977; he has scars all over his body from fighting other stallions, and is emaciated because of drought and poor range conditions.

Horses awaiting adoption at Vale, Oregon.

sending them to central points around the country so that the people who wanted the horses wouldn't have to travel so far to get them. With an eastern distribution point, quite a few more horses could be placed with foster parents.

People adopt wild horses for various reasons. Some do it out of a sincere concern for the plight of these animals, wanting to give some of them a good home. Others do it as a means to obtain a horse for their own use. Still others do it partly because of the novelty of having a "wild horse." Many of the people who have adopted horses out of sympathy have been well pleased, feeling that in some small way they are personally helping solve the wild horse problem. Some who have taken orphans or emaciated animals from the drought areas have had a real struggle to nurse their animals back to health, and have felt a great deal of gratification when their efforts have been successful.

For instance, Alan and Gail Beers of Reno, Nevada, took a three week old orphan colt in late summer of 1977. When the BLM picked up the colt, it was starving and had been without food for a few days. Gail and Alan took the colt home that same day, fed him Foal-Lac and stayed up with him all night, feeding him small amounts frequently. When the BLM called them up the next morning to see if the foal was still alive, Gail realized how critical his condition must have been.

But he survived. They took him to their veterinarian and he was given antibiotics. At first the foal was so weak he couldn't bend his head down to drink water; the water tub had to be held up for him. But the constant attention and loving that he got from his foster parents helped to pull him through and he became strong and playful. The Beers family named him Ricochette No Bars, because he was a wild horse with no pedigree. By late fall of 1977 he was tame enough to try to go into the house, wanting to play games with his people, and was learning to lead. The foal was dearly loved—one of the family—and the Beers were glad they adopted him.

Frances Fischer of Carson City, Nevada, adopted a little wild filly on December 21st, 1976. The filly was in very poor condition and loaded with ticks, she had an injured chest and a swollen leg, and pneumonia. Keeping her alive was a struggle, and Frances almost lost her more than once. But the filly, named Bingo, survived.

It took her awhile to become tame however. She was terribly afraid at first and fought like a wildcat. But good food and loving care won her over and she became a well-mannered, confident filly. She was something of a celebrity, for she appeared on television three times, including the Today Show, and was also filmed by a camera crew from Hollywood for a documentary on mustangs.

But the first month Frances had her, keeping her alive was a major effort, and brought a $500 vet bill. At one time the filly was so far gone that the BLM gave Frances permission to have her humanely destroyed, and said that if she didn't want to do it, they would come out and do it themselves.

The expenses incurred in keeping the filly alive were very high and Frances began to realize she couldn't afford it. She wrote the BLM's Washington office, wondering what could be done. The BLM in turn notified WHOA of the problem, and Dawn Lappin of WHOA got in touch with Frances, telling her about a retired woman in Ohio, Miss Heppe, who was sympathetic to the plight of the wild horses. She would sponsor one that needed financial assistance. Miss Heppe had no facilities to keep a wild horse herself, but wanted to help someone else keep one. She sent Frances a check for $500, which was used to build a bigger area for the filly, and sent a

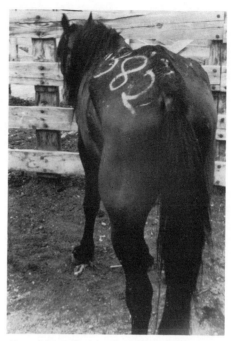

One of the stallions gathered in Oregon in 1977.

check every month to help with Bingo's feed, foot care and veterinary expenses. In return, Frances sent photos of the filly and Bingo's progress, and Miss Heppe compiled a large scrapbook on the little black filly.

Speaking about Bingo when the filly was a year and a half old, Frances said, "She is the smartest, most lovable horse you could ask for, and she will give me great pleasure as long as she lives. There has been a special bond grow between us and she treats me at times like I was her mother. If she's frightened, even now at her age, she'll run to me and stay there till I talk to her. She trusts me completely. And I feel so good to see her run and play. When she came here she could not, as she was too poor and sick. She will make it through this winter with no problem." But Bingo's early habits as a young starving foal in drought-stricken Nevada stay with her. She still digs up roots to eat and chews the bark off sagebrush, even though she has plenty of good food now.

Frances adopted another wild horse in the fall of 1977—a three month old orphan foal. But even though she worked diligently with it for 15 hours straight, she couldn't save it. It had pneumonia and was too dehydrated, and died. Frances feels there is a purpose in her efforts, and if confronted with another down-and-out case that needed her, she would probably take it home and try to nurse it back to health.

Some people travel a long way to pick up their adopted horses. Steve and Charlene Pyron, of

Atlanta, Georgia, traveled to Nevada in September of 1977 and picked up five horses, taking them home to Georgia in a 4-horse trailer and pickup truck. They adopted a grey mare, her four-month old colt, a big red five-year-old gelding, and two sorrel yearlings, a colt and a filly. They had an eventful trip home—flat tires, a short in the wiring to the trailer lights, and a few hassles with the wild horses. When at last they unloaded the horses in Georgia, the animals were glad to get out of the trailer and delighted to see some green grass. They were thin and had runny eyes and noses, but immediately started gaining weight on the good feed. They had all been rescued from drought and poor range conditions in Nevada. The Pyrons planned to breed their adopted horses, start a "mustang ranch" and build a riding stable. They hope to make at least one more trip to Nevada to pick up some more horses.

All of the "foster parents" I talked with agreed that if a person can get the horses young enough, these wild ones can soon be won over with feed and attention. As Frances Fischer put it, "If you get them before they're a year old, and give them good food and comfort, they become your friends for life."

Sandy Gaston of Reno, Nevada, adopted a yearling filly in February of 1977. At first the filly was wild and dangerous because she was so afraid. It took Sandy two weeks to get the filly to eat grain, because she didn't know what oats were. Sandy poured the oats over her alfalfa hay but at first the filly would sort out the hay to eat and leave the oats. It was a full month before Sandy was able to walk up to the filly without the horse running away, and a full three and a half months before the filly calmed down completely and accepted Sandy.

The filly, named "Fancy", had to be moved to a new place soon after Sandy got her, and it took four people 2½ hours to get the horse into a trailer. She broke ropes, kicked, lay down, and bloodied her nose, refusing to go into the trailer. But after frequent handling, she gentled down.

During the severe drought conditions in 1977, many wild horses were in serious trouble, especially in Nevada and eastern Oregon where there was not enough water and feed for them. The BLM intensified its roundup efforts during the summer and fall of 1977, trying to keep pace with the expanding herds and trying to save some of the horses from dying. By the summer of 1977 there were over 40,000 wild horses in Nevada alone (and more than 70,000 wild horses, total) and year-around gathering programs were started in some districts. The central corral and holding facilities for wild horses gathered in Nevada is at Palomino Valley in the Carson City district, and by October of 1977 many horses had been adopted out and 700 more were awaiting adoption in the corrals. Throughout the fall of 1977 there was no rain to break the drought in Nevada and horses were weak. Some were dying in the gathering process. Those that were too weak and ill to be adopted were humanely destroyed and buried out on the desert.

In Oregon more than 900 horses were rounded up in the Vale district during the summer of 1977, and about 700 of these were adopted out. Sixty of the others had to be destroyed because of diseases, disability or injury. That left about 140 older stallions that no one wanted to adopt, the BLM having to destroy them.

The adoption program gained momentum during 1977 as more and more of the excess horses were rounded up, and horse lovers across the nation responded to the need for homes for most of them. But as more and more horses need to be taken off the ranges in years to come (the BLM still isn't able to

Wild horses captured during the Owyhee Desert roundup in September of 1977 (photo courtesy the BLM—Jan Bedrosion, photographer)

Sixteen-year-old Pam Henstock of Winnemucca, Nevada with six month old adopted horse, "Sheba" (BLM photo, Bob Goodman-photographer)

gather enough to bring population growth to a standstill) the numbers of people needed to take them will become tremendous. In Nevada alone, 5000 horses per year will have to be gathered just to keep the wild horse population stable at 40,000 head. And more than 10,000 head will have to be removed across the West each year just to keep the numbers static at 70,000 head—a number that is much too high for what the ranges will support.

Wild burros can also be adopted in the BLM's program, and several BLM districts that have too many burros are rounding them up. The Bakersfield BLM district began rounding up burros in 1977 (there were over 2500 burros in that district) despite protests from the National Animal Welfare League of San Francisco. Other burro protection groups, including WHOA and ISPMB, supported the BLM reduction after touring the depleted and overgrazed desert ranges and seeing the desperate need for burro reductions. The burro gatherings began in September, 1977 and adoptions began in October. Six hundred burros were gathered in late 1977 from the Lake Almo region in Arizona, and all were adopted out by January of 1978.

Up through 1977 the response to the BLM's need for people to adopt excess horses and burros had been very good. But almost all of the people who have adopted these animals feel that if the wild horse law could be amended so that the foster parents could eventually own the horses or burros, it would be an improvement. More people would be interested or willing to take them.

Also, many people feel that shooting and burying the unadoptable horses and burros is a waste. If the law could be changed so that the carcasses of the animals having to be destroyed could be used for some useful purpose, or the unadoptable animals sold for use as meat, the management program could recover money that could help finance the program. As it is, millions of dollars are being spent each year to control the ever-increasing numbers of wild horses and burros, and this seems to be a great waste, when the program could be practically self-supporting. Gathering costs, plus feed and transportation costs make the wild horse program very expensive. In October of 1977 it was costing the Nevada BLM more than $500 per day to feed the 700 horses being held for adoption in the Palomino Valley holding corrals, to say nothing of the trucking costs from the various capture areas. Eventually the wild horse law must be amended to allow the custodians to own the horses, and to allow the BLM to regain some of its expense money through practical use of excess horses that must otherwise be destroyed and wasted.

By mid-1976, after the adoption program had been in existence two years, only about 700 wild horses had been captured and adopted. By the spring of 1977 a total of 2000 had been adopted. By the fall of 1977 this number had almost doubled, but the captured and adopted horses were still just a fraction of the excess horses that needed to be removed from western ranges. By late 1978 the total number of horses which had been adopted since the inception of the Adopt-A-Horse program totaled 9,100.

In early 1978, WHOA and ISPMB made arrangements with a California rancher, Peter Carey, to care for excess horses and burros. Many people had inquired about sponsoring an adopted animal, but did not have facilities themselves for keeping a horse or burro. Under the sponsorship program with the rancher, individuals wanting to save a horse or burro could pay the costs and the adopted animal would live on the 10,000 acre ranch at Alturas. The rancher cares for the animals, gives them vaccinations against diseases, gelds the stallions, feeds hay in the winter, and has the horses checked by a veterinarian once a month. The rancher picks up the animal from the BLM corrals and brings it to the ranch. An annual report and photographs of the animal are sent to the sponsor. The charge is $38.00 per month to sponsor a wild horse or burro. WHOA and ISPMB encouraged people to sponsor older animals that are hard to adopt. The sponsors and visitors are welcome to visit the ranch and see the animals. The first four burros sponsored were picked up and taken to the ranch in May, 1978. Sixty adopted horses soon followed.

Looking at the overall picture, the adoption program seems like a drop in the bucket, and doomed to failure as a reasonable way to get rid of all the excess horses. The BLM has been assisted in the placement of these horses by some of the horse protection and humane groups, but as Curt Berkland of the BLM once said, "these organizations will be called upon to play an increasingly large role in encouraging applicants, and also to help monitor the horses once they are placed, to assure humane treatment and adequacy of facilities."

Many people felt by 1977 that the adoption program was already nearly saturated; there are but a limited number of people who want or have the resources to take care of an adopted wild horse. Wild Horse Annie agreed that the adoption program is not limitless and that eventually the saturation point would be reached when no more individuals would want to take the horses. Her organization WHOA helped the BLM place the horses, and she said that WHOA has a moral responsibility to do it because the only other alternative to adoption is destruction of the horses. "When the saturation point is reached and the time comes that some horses have to be destroyed, we can say we've done everything humanely possible to avoid it," she said.

Part of the problem is the fact that the "foster parent" can never own the horse. There are a few people who are interested in the adoption program either out of sympathy for the plight of the wild horse or for the novelty of having one. But most would-be horse owners would prefer having a horse they could own, and more specifically, a well-bred domestic horse of their favorite breed. There are only a few horsemen who would desire to take home the typical wild horse of today.

One BLM district manager has said, "The adopt-a-horse program in my view is a genuine mistake. Asking people to care for horses that they do not own during these times of high land and feed prices is not right even if the people are willing to do it. Also allowing people who have no knowledge of horses and horse care to take custody of a wild horse is the height of folly and will eventually lead to disaster for the horse and the person who is responsible for its care."

As one of the information sheets on wild horse adoption points out, "these horses are wild animals. They may be dangerous to persons who are not familiar with horse care. As they come from the range, these horses are not suitable for children's pets. A period of breaking and training is required. Also, you may be liable for any damages the animal may cause to persons or property."

The information sheet goes on to explain that another "item which must be considered is the cost of keeping a horse. Recent estimates show the cost may exceed $600 per year for keeping a horse, depending upon your location, facilities and equipment available and how you plan to use the animal. This includes such things as veterinary expenses, vitamins, tack and transportation, in addition to pasture and food. Also caring for a horse, as with any animal, is a 365 day a year job."

On the requirements for hauling the wild horse home, under the section on two-year-olds and older, the instructions said that persons taking these horses "will pick up horses in a one ton truck or larger. Stock racks will be a minimum of 7 feet in height with open top. Cross bars over top are preferable. Certain types of goose-neck and other stock trailers are acceptable. If this type trailer has an open top, the sides must be 7 feet in height. If the stock trailer has a closed top, it must be at least 7 feet between floor and ceiling. Both truck and stock trailer racks must be solid construction from floor to a height of at least three feet."

Horses 2-years-old or older "*must not be hauled in ½ ton pickup. Horses hauled in ¾ ton pickup or regular type horse trailers will be haltered and tied.*" Also, stout halters and "a minimum of 20 feet ¾ inch cotton or ½ inch nylon tie rope will be required for each horse."

Another problem with the adoption program is that the government, legal guardian of the horse, might be liable for damage that the horse does. In taking the horse, the "foster parent" becomes an agent of the government and therefore has no recourse against the government if he himself is injured. But if a third party becomes involved—if the adopted horse injures someone else or destroys someone else's property, the government could be sued. These are the kind of headaches that make the program cumbersome and unsatisfactory in the BLM's eyes. A lot of problems would be solved if the people taking the horses could own them themselves.

And, if it gets harder and harder to give out more and more horses, it may mean taking a serious look at changing the law so that some of the less desirable horses could be disposed of for commercial purposes. One of the advisory board's recommendations was that when the horses are given away to private citizens, the citizens could gain title to the animal. This would allow the new owner to sell the horse if it proves too much for him to handle, if he finds he can't keep it, or it proves useless as a saddle horse.

Another recommendation from the advisory board was to amend the wild horse act to allow use of helicopters and airplanes in the management and control of wild horses. A helicopter can move in on the horses being gathered, at a slow speed that isn't dangerous to them, and reduce the danger to the horsemen taking part in the roundup. Wild horses tend to run faster and harder when pursued by horsemen than they do when being gently hazed along by aircraft.

Wild Horse Annie was the only dissenting voice on the advisory board concerning use of aircraft in wild horse management. She felt that making this change in the wild horse act "would send Nevada horses toward a 1940's type of slaughter." She supported the move to take domestic horses off the range because it would leave more feed for the wild horses, but she said that the use of aircraft would wipe out 24 years of effort to get protective legislation for wild horses.

But the people conducting the roundups of excess horses felt that the restriction prohibiting the use of aircraft was a severe handicap. In Oregon roundups during 1974 several horses were injured, two men were hurt, and one saddle horse killed. Speaking of these accidents, the BLM manager of the Burns district said, "We'll kill someone yet if we don't get relief from the present law."

In late 1974, the BLM began operations to round up horses in Malheur County, Oregon, where a herd of 70 horses had strayed from their "home range". Horse herds disturbed by hunters and by normal livestock operations, as well as herds suffering from space and feed limitations due to population expansion, tend to move out of their home territory and expand onto new ranges.

The April 1974 count of wild horses in Malheur county was 1,916 head; wild horses in Oregon had been increasing at a rate of more than 20% per year (there were more than 7000 horses in the state in 1975) and since some of the horse areas were getting crowded, some of the herds were moving into new areas. In late October the BLM, under the observation of Everett McVickers, a representative of the American Humane Society, moved one band of 10 horses back to their home range south of the Owyhee River in south Malheur County.

Another herd of 49 horses was gathered, transported to Burns, Oregon, and offered to the public for adoption. Jerry Wilcox, the BLM wild horse specialist, explained that these horses were being removed from the Stockdale Unit rather than returned to their home range because of extreme relocation difficulties. To go back to their range in the Barren Valley Unit, which already had a thriving herd of more than 1200 horses, they would have to be moved through 6 fences or hauled 20 miles by truck. This was an area that had too many horses already, and would have to have some excess horses removed in the near future. So it was decided to offer the 49 "straying" horses for adoption.

These wild horses that had strayed from the lands they inhabited at the time the wild horse act was passed, had to be captured or destroyed, and the BLM chose to capture the horses—a project that took nearly a month and cost more than $30,000, amounting to more than $600 per horse. Grant Baugh, BLM public affairs specialist for the Vale district, said that the growing numbers of wild horses might not be such a problem if "the law would give us some latitude in controlling them. Most of our herds in Oregon are still young. But we've got to round up 1400 horses each year to keep them in balance and we're overgrazing in some areas now."

In the Vale district's Barren Valley Unit—the desert land from which the horses had expanded and strayed—it takes about 200 acres to produce enough feed for each wild horse. Adequate feed and the horse population in that area were running neck and neck, with the horses getting ahead of the feed supply. Baugh also noted that the BLM was expect-

ing an adverse reaction to the adoption program from the horse-raising industry, resenting the giveaway. As one horseman put it, "Every one they give away eliminates one prospective customer who might purchase a horse that you or I might offer for sale."

The Oregon roundup to remove the 49 straying horses was the second wild roundup conducted by the Vale district. Everett McVicker, executive director of the Lane County Humane Society and associate commissioner of the National Council for Animal Protection, participated in both the summer roundup on the Steens Muntain range, and the winter roundup. He was building up a file, compiling information on the roundups from a humane standpoint. In talking about the BLM personnel and the ranchers hired to help with the roundup, McVicker said, "It's not just a job for them, they're really dedicated and concerned people. We've got to give them the tools to do the job humanely and properly. Controlled used of aircraft is vitally important. You've got to take into consideration these saddle horses are getting beat up."

Grant Baugh, BLM, said that "given the proper tools, horses are not that hard to manage. But here we are in the space age and we're reverting to the way the frontier livestock operator did it." The BLM leased saddle horses from ranchers in the Burns area because the gully-ridden rocky desert demands the use of a conditioned horse and the men doing the gathering needed horses trained in cutting and herding.

McVicker said that carefully controlled use of aircraft would have cut the roundups to the minimum in time and cost. On one typical day, the horsemen tried to round up 27 horses, employing 20 men and the leased saddle horses. Only nine horses were captured. The BLM paid for the men, the leased saddle horses, took the risk of injury to staff members, provided room and board, and planned expenses for at least another two weeks in hopes of capturing all 49 of the straying horses. According to the horsemen involved, the use of helicopter would have cut manpower at least in half, manhours in half or more, and would have eliminated the need for most of the saddle horses and riders, producing a more efficient operation.

Representatives of the Humane Society and the AHPA attended part of the roundup activities, and at the end of the gruelling and not-too-successful roundup, both agreed that it was more inhumane to take a saddle horse into the rugged rocky country and run the horses to exhaustion than to have used mechanical means to round them up.

Riders gathered 139 horses in the Vale district during November of 1976, at a cost of $17,300. They had hoped to gather 205, but ran out of money and good weather. The terrain was rocky and riders had to bring the wild horses 18 miles to the trap, an exhaustive effort for the saddle horses. In the process, wild horse specialist Jerry Wilcox was injured when his horse feel. He suffered a chipped bone and partially severed arm muscle.

The next headache in the roundup program was trying to get rid of the horses. A lot of inquiries had been received from people interested in adopting them, but when the people were notified that the horses were in Burns, many failed to appear, some said they would call back, and many of those that came, rejected the horses. "We had stallions, mares, and some colts—but not enough colts for the would-be horse owners," said Chris Vosler, manager of the Burns BLM district. "We had to kill five stallions because we had completely exhausted the stallion market. Two of those killed were more than 25 years old, two were more than 10 and one was about 8 years old. If we had more Black Beauty-type colts, we would have no problems, but that is not the case."

The BLM districts in Oregon that had wild horses to manage, gathered 344 more horses in various overgrazed areas during 1975 and 1976. Several shifts in livestock were made to accomodate wild horses, and BLM managers felt that more shifts and reductions of livestock use might have to be made in the future.

In January of 1976, the BLM advised cattlemen in the Burns district that fewer cattle than usual would be permitted to graze that summer, and that the grazing period might be shortened by as much as two months. The reason given was that overgrazing by wild horses had reduced forage on both private and public lands to levels which could not adequately sustain all the horses and cattle. The horses in that area had steadily increased, whereas the cattle numbers had remained stable. This action by the BLM, to cut the ranchers' grazing permits, led to a claim filed against the BLM by a cattleman for damages by wild horses to his private land.

Reducing livestock use in favor of wild horses has been one of the things that public pressure and various interest groups (horse protection associations and a few other animal and wildlife groups) have been pushing for. At the 5th national advisory board meeting, held in Washington D.C., March 1974, several individuals expressed these sentiments, including Steve Seater, field director for Fund for Animals, who asserted that wild horses and burros, as well as many native species, were suffering from severe grazing competition caused by excessive numbers of livestock on public lands.

Another presentation at that board meeting was made by Kenneth R. Hampton from the National Wildlife Federation. This group felt that management of wild horses and burros was lagging badly, because the BLM and FS were not pursuing their management responsibilities vigorously enough, and that the Act itself contained deficiencies which seriously restrict their management attempts. Mr. Hampton said that the Wild Horse and Burro Act, although a strong measure, did not succeed in changing the laws of nature. In his view, no matter how many reports are made to Congress, or how many bills become law, nothing is going to improve the range while protecting the animals until a deliberate management program is begun. "And before that can happen," he said, "the BLM and FS must conduct studies to collect data on horse and burro populations, rates of increase, vegetation and erosion effects—by themselves and in combination with other classes of domestic animals, wildlife and other uses on the public lands."

Mr. Hampton went on to say that some people claimed there had not been any significant population increase since PL 92-195 was passed, but he quoted surveys in California that showed wild horses were increasing about 20% per year, in areas that have numerous deer and antelope as well as seasonal cattle use. His statistics clearly indicated a trend in vegetative deterioration and erosion acceleration. He therefore felt there was an urgent need for an immediate control and management program, and comprehensive studies on competition between domestic livestock, wildlife and wild horses and burros.

He said the National Wildlife Federation is sympathetic to the problems the BLM and FS must overcome to effectively manage wild horses and burros, but that to perform any task effectively an agency must have two things: sufficient resources and a workable mandate. In this instance, in his opinion, the agencies, especially the BLM, have neither.

In September of 1974, Ben Glading of the national advisory board noted that Nevada had about 20,000 wild horses. At the rate those horses were increasing, there would be 30,000 by 1976 (and there were), and he figured there would be 151,000 by 1984 and 1,282,000 by 1990—just in Nevada.

National Advisory Board for
Free-Roaming Horses and Burros

1973-1974

Mrs. Velma Johnston—WHOA, ISPMB
Mr. Roy Young—rancher, past president of Nevada Cattlemen's Association

Mr. Dean Prosser, Jr.—Wyoming Livestock Association

Dr. C. Wayne Cook, Chairman—Range Science, Colorado State University

Mr. Ed Pierson—retired state director, BLM, Wyoming

Mrs. Pearl Twyne—AHPA

Dr. Roger Hungerford—Biological Sciences, University of Arizona

Dr. Floyd Frank—Veterinary Science, University of Idaho

Mr. Ben Glading—retired Chief, California Fish and Game

1975

Mrs. Velma Johnston
Mr. Roy Young
Mr. Dean Prosser, Jr.
Mrs. Pearl Twyne
Dr. Roger Hungerford
Dr. Floyd Frank, Chairman
Mr. William Reavley—National Wildlife Federation
Dr. Thadis Box—Utah State University
Mr. Arnold D. Ewing—Northwest Timber Association

1976

Mr. Roy Young, Chairman
Mrs. Pearl Twyne
Dr. Floyd Frank
Mr. William Reavley
Dr. Thadis Box
Mr. Arnold Ewing
Dr. Patricia Moehlman—Wildlife research
Mr. J. Melvin Coleman—Animal husbandry
Mr. Michael J. Pontrelli—Wild horse and burro protection

At the September 1974 board meeting, the board agreed that there was urgent need for immediate action on the problem of expanding horse and burro populations. They recommended that ten to twenty wild horse refuges be established throughout the West, and the rest of the herds outside these designated areas be removed. This would result in displacement of some livestock grazing and wildlife in the refuge area, but the rest of the public lands would be better off without the horses and burros. But so far, this idea has not received enough support from the general public to be put into practice. The wild horse and burro numbers continued to climb throughout the West.

Excess horses on the Pryor Mountain Wild Horse range were given out for adoption after roundups in 1973 and 1975, but not without some problems. Everything was arranged to assign the 1975 horses (25 head) to recipients immediately after gathering them in March. But the AHPA threatened the BLM with a lawsuit, claiming that the BLM was ruining the herd by removing ANY horses. With this threat from the AHPA, the BLM had to hold the 25 horses for seven additional weeks to review the situation

with their lawyers and the Department of Justice, and in the meantime it was hard on the horses. The BLM's facilities were not intended for such prolonged occupancy, and the weather was cold and wet. Many horses became ill and needed veterinary care, and the BLM spent $1100 extra on vet fees, $1000 extra for feed and $3000 extra for labor and manpower.

In 1975 some of the Nevada BLM districts began plans for horse reduction programs to control expanding horse populations that were contributing to declining range conditions. The BLM field offices were instructed to start plans to control the wild horse population at the 1971 level. The first roundup was planned for the Stone Cabin Valley herd in the Battle Mountain District, near Tonopah, Nevada—a rugged, isolated desert area with limited water sources. This area had been overgrazed for a long time, both by domestic livestock and free-roaming horses. As many as 200 domestic horses were licensed to graze here in the 1930's, but after the passage of PL 92-195 no domestic horses had been permitted.

Horse numbers had fluctuated over the years in the Stone Cabin area. Up until the late 1940's, local ranchers had introduced high quality purebred horses into the range herds and actively gathered the offspring up until 1959. Thousands of horses were harvested from this area during the 1940's. An estimate of wild horse numbers by the district BLM manager in 1957 was about 50 head. The herd had grown to 150 by 1966. In March of 1969, an airplane count showed 288 horses. A helicopter inventory of January 1973 showed 748, and another inventory in July of 1974 showed 917 horses.

One reason that the horse population in this area has "jumped" so much is that the horses drift onto and off of the Nellis Air Force Base Bombing and Gunnery range (where the Nevada Wild Horse Range is located) which is adjacent to the south, with no fences in between. There is some seasonal movement of the horses across this unfenced boundary, moving south onto the Nellis range during the winter and north into Stone Cabin Valley in the summer. For instance, the 1973 count showed 339 horses in one area between U.S. Highway 6 and the bombing range, in February. And in July of 1974 there were 640 horses in this same area.

In addition to the seasonal fluctuations of horse numbers, the total horse numbers there are steadily growing. By the early 1970's the range and watershed conditions were declining. Range studies showed that 56% of the range was in poor condition. There had been a recent succession of several dry years, combined with an increase in horse numbers, and a reluctance of grazing permittees to voluntarily reduce their cattle numbers on the range. Thus the range conditions, which had been poor for many years due to overgrazing, were becoming even worse, with the horse numbers in 1975 being much higher than they had been for 20 to 30 years.

The Battle Mountain district proposed to reduce the horse population and the authorized cattle use, monitor the range condition and trend with study plots, begin cooperative studies with the USAF to determine the extent of horse drift between Stone Cabin Valley and the Nellis Wild Horse Range, and build a fence on the Bombing Range boundary.

In May of 1975 the BLM began plans to gather 400 horses in the area, and took bids for the gathering project. The horses were to be captured in corrals built around water holes, but other methods would be used if the water trapping was not successful in capturing the 400 extra horses. A field trip to the area had been made in September, 1974 by the national advisory board, and the board agreed with the BLM's plan to reduce the herd.

Wild Horse Annie's organization, WHOA, did not oppose the wild horse reduction, but insisted that for the sake of the recovery of the range, there be an equal reduction in domestic livestock use as well. WHOA felt that the roundup of horses was necessary in order to protect the range and prevent starvation of the horses. Mrs. Dawn Lappin of WHOA was in charge of screening the applicants for adopting the horses.

A representative of Animal Protection Institute of America and four representatives of WHOA were on hand for several days of the roundup, which began on July 23, 1975. The other major horse protection group, AHPA, opposed the roundup, questioning the need for control of the horse population and taking issue with livestock management practices in the area. The BLM arranged a field tour for some of the AHPA's key people before the roundup, to acquaint them with the range conditions in Stone Cabin Valley, but this did not change their opinion.

In early July, AHPA sent two graduate students (Nancy and Howard Green, under professor David Kitchen at California's Humbolt State University) to study the horses in the area. Even though their findings agreed with the BLM on population figures (approximately 1000 horses in the area during the summer of 1975) and poor condition of some of the horses was noted, this AHPA study felt that the horse population had "stabilized" and that the range was still in "fair" condition.

Professor Kitchen said, "Even if the removal is appropriate, it isn't urgent. The government's own studies aren't adequate to merit the extreme policy at this point." AHPA felt that the BLM was merely a self-appointed servant of the ranchers' interests.

"Why should my tax dollars subsidize the ranchers at the expense of the horses?" asked Mrs. Chris Hawkins, a member of AHPA.

But other groups were in agreement with the BLM's roundup proposal. The livestock industry, conservation and wildlife groups had all been extremely critical of the BLM's failure to control the expanding horse numbers earlier.

Gene Nodine, BLM district manager of the area, refuted the AHPA claims of BLM partiality. "I could care less whether we reduce horses or cattle. The point is, something has to go." On a limited basis, the BLM had been able to obtain voluntary livestock reductions through cooperation with individual ranchers who used the area, and other reductions were made as well.

The BLM wild horse roundup program had the support of Nevada's governor, the director of the Nevada Department of Fish and Game, as well as Wild Horse Annie's organization, the Nye County Commissioners, the National Mustang Association, the National Wild Horse Association, and the First Nevada Cavalry. They all realized that the removal of excess horses would benefit the remaining wild ones.

The roundup received widespread publicity, and public reaction was favorable; the district received 2600 letters and telephone inquiries from people in 38 states indicating a desire to adopt a horse. Removal of 400 horses would leave a herd of 500-600 animals in a better balance with their food supply.

An experienced horse wrangler from Las Vegas, Nevada, received the BLM contract to gather the horses, and began water trapping in late July. Then on July 23 the AHPA filed suit in district court in Washington D.C., asking the court to enter an order permanently enjoining the Secretary of the Interior and others from authorizing or continuing any roundup of excess horses in the Stone Cabin Valley. Attorneys from the Justice Department and the Solicitor's Office of the Department of Interior appeared before Judge Sirica in U.S. District Court and obtained a change of venue to Nevada on July 24, but the AHPA stated that it would continue the suit in Nevada. By July 28, the contractor had captured approximately 80 horses and had them in a holding corral in Stone Cabin Valley, and about 30 people were on their way to Nevada to pick up their adopted wild horses.

Then, in a surprise move on July 28, the State Agriculture Director, Thomas Ballow, impounded the wild horses that had been rounded up, contending that they were state property under state laws covering unbranded and unclaimed animals running at large. He claimed that PL 92-195 giving the BLM jurisdiction over wild horses was unconstitutional (as the New Mexico state livestock board had done earlier). Ed Rowland, Nevada state BLM director, issued an order to stop the roundup, and the BLM contacted the Justice Department to see what action to take.

The state of Nevada intended to dispose of the horses as strays, and a notice to this effect appeared in the local paper at Tonopah on August 1. According to state law, the advertisement would again appear a week later. The Nevada state director of Agriculture planned to hold a hearing on August 18 to receive any private claims on the horses, and if not privately claimed under state law, the horses would be sold as estrays on August 25, ten days after the public notices appeared.

To comply with the state law, the BLM intended to turn three of the horses, which were branded, plus their offspring, over to the state as estrays. State BLM director Ed Rowland agreed that the state must be given enough time to make sure the horses were not diseased, and to allow for inspection of brands to find the horses among them that were privately owned. In return, Nevada's director of agriculture agreed to release the 75 horses already captured from impoundment, as long as they were not shipped out of state. Nevada agriculture officials claimed that there was no such thing as a "wild horse" and that any of the animals not claimed by individuals were state property. There had been some claims filed on the horses, but these had been waived before the roundup started.

The Nevada state officials requested that the BLM proceed with the roundup and waive all trespass and trapping charges against any privately owned horses caught—ranchers' horses that may have grazed on the public lands during the previous three years. Ballow said that the "wild" horses belonged to the state, and that some of them belonged to the local ranchers who were afraid to reclaim them. The BLM was planning to give the horses out for adoption, but some of the ranchers complained that many of the horses belonged to them.

Ballow stated that the ranchers were the victims of the BLM because they could not remove their own horses from the range, and yet would be charged fines if they tried to claim them after the BLM rounded them up. "The BLM is responsible for the trespass' ", Ballow said, for the BLM had declared that if the horses belonged to the ranchers, the ranchers would have to pay grazing fees for three years. According to Ballow, the ranchers were being threatened by the BLM with a reduction in their grazing permits if they did not cooperate.

The state requested that the BLM waive all trespass fees, but Rowland said he didn't have the authority to cancel the trespass fees on all of these ranchers' horses. While regulations can, under certain circumstances, be waived, this was not such a case; the possibility of a compromise depends upon the specific facts of an individual case. Rowland pointed out that the original plan (when the Wild Horse Act was being finalized) was to allow ranchers to collect their horses with no fees charged, but that the Interior Department had decided that the fees must be paid. Also, the BLM could not accept any proposal for a state sale of the unclaimed and unbranded stray horses, because such horses had been defined as wild horses in the 1971 Act.

Because of the controversy over what to do with the horses, the BLM opened the gates and released the 75 captured horses back onto the range on August 6, rather than keep them confined during what would probably be several weeks of legal hassle. Many people were disappointed, and afraid that some of the horses would do poorly. The best of the grazing season was already past, and many of the gathered horses were already in poor condition. But the BLM decided to turn them loose because it could not accept any proposal for the state to sell the unbranded strays. And the controversy over the procedures for disposing of the horses could result in months of confinement—which could lead to desease, injury or death for some of the horses.

The 1971 Act had no provision for turning unbranded and unclaimed horses found on BLM lands over to any state official. Other reasons for turning the horses loose were the high cost of keeping them in confinement, and the refusal of the state of Nevada to issue health and brand certificate clearance for the captured horses, without which the horses could not be transported out of state. The position taken by the Nevada state agriculture director was similar to that taken by the New Mexico Livestock Board—that PL 92-195 was unconstitutional and in violation of state's rights. But while a decision by the Supreme Court was pending, the Wild Horse Act remained in full force.

State BLM director Rowland was instructed to turn the horses loose by Assistant Secretary of Interior Jack Horton and National BLM Director Curt Berklund. Ballow, Nevada State Director of Agriculture, criticized the BLM for turning the horses loose, saying this move would show that the BLM wasn't sincere in its plan to improve forage for the livestock which graze the same range.

The rancher who had loaned the BLM the use of his corrals said, "Boy, I didn't want to see them go back out there. There's just too many horses."

Trapper Tom Warr said the horses would be tougher to get in the future. "They got caught this time. They'll be smarter next time."

On September 3, 1975, a cooperative agreement was signed between the Nevada officials and the BLM, clarifying procedures for disposal of wild horses, and this enabled the BLM to begin the round-up again. The agreement provided that branded horses would be taken by the state and returned to their owners. Unbranded horses would be adopted out by the BLM, and horses which had signs of being domestic—gelded, or having shoes, bridle or saddle marks, etc. but no brands—would be returned to the range. They would remain on the range until jurisdiction was decided in the New Mexico court case challenging the constitutionality of PL 92-195.

Gathering operations were resumed in Stone Cabin Valley September 10th. But on that day, the AHPA filed an amended complaint and a motion for a temporary restraining order in the U.S. District Court in Nevada to stop the BLM from rounding up the horses. On September 11th, the AHPA's motion for the restraining order was denied. A hearing was held on September 17, but no decision was made at that time, and the BLM continued to round up excess horses. Their roundup method, water trapping, was dependent upon the hot dry summer weather and any further delay would jeopardize the roundup's success.

Wild Horse Annie filed an affidavit declaring that she had had the opportunity to evaluate range conditions and that she was in agreement with the BLM's opinion that much of Nevada was overgrazed and that she had made two official field trips into the Stone Cabin Valley area, and that in her opinion it was in a critically depleted condition and could no longer withstand the heavy grazing pressures to which it had been subjected. She declared that in order to preserve wildlife habitat and to provide adequate forage for healthy wild horse herds and to allow for recovery of the range, that an immediate reduction in ALL grazing pressures should be carried out, wild horses and domestic livestock both, with immediate removal of all unpermitted domestic livestock.

But the AHPA continued to press its suit, using any means they could to try to stop the roundup. Two members of AHPA that had attended the earlier roundup operations, Chris Hawkins and Kim Fenner, claimed that the horses were being bruised, beaten and abused. Miss Fenner called the water trapping procedure "the most brutal, inhumane, cruel display that I have ever seen."

By contrast, other concerned groups and indi-viduals felt that the water trapping method was the most humane way of gathering the horses, for the horses came into the traps on their own, for water, and the gates were shut behind them. There was no running or chasing involved, and it was easy on the horses. Five horses were killed however—four horses spooked when the gates of the trap closed behind them and ran into the corral fence, breaking their necks, and a fifth horse slipped and fell in the corral and was fatally injured.

"Photographic evidence" of brutality was presented by AHPA in the court suit to block the roundup, but the photographs were deliberately staged. Freelance photographer William Marsik of Salt Lake City, Utah, said in a supplemental affidavit (to counter the charges made by AHPA) that his dog was coaxed over to a dead mare and a picture of the animals taken by Kim Fenner. Later the picture was introduced in court as evidence to show that a dog had been harassing the wild horses in the corral. Marsik said, "I heard Miss Fenner attempting to call my dog in closer to herself and the mare. The photograph was deliberately staged and a blatant misrepresentation."

Kim Fenner and Chris Hawkins had given affidavits earlier in the court action which said that the horses were being poorly treated. Samuel Rowley, area manager of the Tonopah BLM, said in a supplemental affidavit that Mrs. Hawkins was asked to get out of the horse trap after the horses became frightened and were being spooked. He gave this explanation in answer to Mrs. Hawkins' affidavit which said she was "ordered to leave after she questioned BLM wranglers about a foal which was suffering from convulsions."

Joseph L. Baker of the BLM said in another supplemental affidavit that he assisted in unloading horses at the Clifford ranch (where the BLM was using corrals for holding the horses). When all the horses were unloaded out of the truck except one colt, Rowley urged the reluctant colt out of the truck, put his foot on the colt's rump "and the colt went on down the ramp." Mrs. Hawkins had claimed in her affidavit that Rowley had kicked a frightened foal down the ramp of a truck after the young animal had been separated from its mother.

On October 2, Judge Roger D. Foley denied the AHPA motion for a preliminary injunction, and on November 11, 1975, the case was dismissed. The BLM captured 227 horses before fall weather made water trapping impossible. Trapping was continued during the spring of 1976, bringing the total of horses removed to 400, most of which were successfully given out for adoption.

Twenty-one of the horses were difficult to "give

away"—19 stallions, one old mare, and one gelding ("wild"?)—and the BLM thought they would have to be destroyed. But when it was announced in the news media that these horses would have to be killed because no homes had been found for them, all 21 were placed through the adoption program within 24 hours. The BLM started getting calls immediately, from as far away as Florida. The BLM warned the prospective adopters that the horses were all 10-15 years old and that the stallions would be difficult to handle, but the people didn't care, many of them taking the horses for sentimental reasons only. PL 92-195 authorizes humane destruction if the animals can't be placed in private homes, but that solution would have been challenged in court, according to a spokesman from one of the horse protection groups.

Earlier that same year, legislation was introduced in Congress to amend PL 92-195 to allow easier methods of managing and controlling the increasing wild horse herds. In the House, a bill was introduced in February by Congressman Whitehurst of Virginia, to give the Secretaries authority to use aircraft, and to sell or donate excess horses without restriction to individuals or organizations. These two proposed amendments to the Wild Horse law were similar to proposed legislation endorsed by the Department of Interior a year earlier.

In June, Senator Bob Packwood of Oregon also introduced a bill that would permit the use of helicopters in the rounding up of extra horses, and would also allow the federal government to transfer ownership of the horses to private individuals who give complete written assurance that the horses will be treated humanely. The use of helicopters for wild horse management was endorsed by the Oregon Cattleman's Association, the Oregon Environmental Council, the National Advisory Board for Wild Horses and Burros, and many other groups, including the Oregon Fish and Wildlife Commission, range consultants from the University of Idaho, the Oregon Farm Bureau, and even the Sierra Club. During 1976 there were seven bills introduced in Congress relating to the use of aircraft for capture or transferring title to the horses.

But horse protection groups opposed these bills, arguing that these amendments would negate PL 92-195. WHOA stated that to allow transfer of excess wild horses and burros to individuals and organizations without restrictions would make it possible for "killer buyers to acquire the animals for slaughter for pet food and other commercial products." Velma Johnston presented testimony in opposition to the Whitehurst bill, and Miss Joan Bolsinger, vice president of ISPMB, testified against the Packwood bill in a public hearing in Oregon. WHOA and ISPMB urged their members to write to their senators and congressmen to express opposition to these bills.

Mrs. Blue (AHPA) and Mr. Dantzler (HSUS) called the proposed amendments "inhumane". Mrs. Blue called the Whitehurst bill a "Deceptive device which in the guise of 'better management' would lead to the final extermination of the nation's wild herds."

Representative Gude (Maryland) called the bill a "sweetheart arrangement" by which the pet food companies would profit.

Meanwhile, the BLM conducted a few roundup operations, attempting to alleviate some of the wild horse numbers problems, while yet working within the restrictions imposed by PL 92-195. In Utah the BLM captured 19 horses out of 21 that had become a nuisance in the residential section of the Dugway Proving Ground, which was situated on the Army's chemical warfare testing ground. More than 300 wild horses roamed the proving ground (which is the size of Rhode Island), but 18 of the horses had been grazing at night on resident's lawns and gardens, and leaving their droppings. Three other horses were making themselves at home on the base golf course. Another horse had been killed when struck by the base ambulance on an emergency run.

The BLM spent a week capturing 19 horses. Thirteen were captured by enticing them into a temporary corral strewn with feed. The golf course horses were roped and the others trapped or roped, but one mare and one yearling refused to be caught. These two were chased ten miles north of the base; then the cowboy's horses gave out and the chase was abandoned. BLM director for the Salt Lake District felt that these two would probably not return. The 19 captured horses were checked for brands, and the unowned horses were given out for adoption.

In Oregon the BLM began a roundup to remove about 100 horses along the John Day River northeast of Prineville. This roundup was begun because the horses were straying onto privately owned ranch and range land, and competing with cattle for scarce feed and water. Larry Lee, spokesman for the BLM in Portland, Oregon, said that "all the water and the best vegetation is on private land" in that area. The roundup was under BLM supervision, but the ranchers were gathering the horses at their own expense, driving the horses into corrals. Then they trucked the horses to Burns, the BLM reimbursing them for trucking costs. At Burns, the horses were given out for adoption.

More horse roundups in Oregon were planned for late 1975. In September, the BLM attempted to

The more these horses are chased, the harder it is to catch the remaining ones.

capture more of the herd in the Malheur Cave area, where they had begun roundup operations the year before. A crew of five men on their own horses were trying to gather the horses, but one man was seriously hurt when he fell with his horse. Only two horses were caught and three others had to be destroyed because of injury. "The more you chase these horses, the harder it becomes to catch the remaining ones," one of the BLM men said. "They know the country better than we do and know we are after them."

The first routine horse roundups—as a management rather than an emergency effort—were planned for two other areas in Oregon for late 1975. These would be the first actual management attempts since the passage of the wild horse law in 1971. "Previously, wild horse gatherings have been the result of some type of emergency," according to Jerry Wilcox, the Vale District BLM wild horse specialist. "The BLM has been forced to gather the horses because they were in danger or starving during the winter, or they were outside the herd ranges as prescribed by law, or they were on private land and we were requested to move them. I have now completed wild horse management plans for both the Three Fingers and Jackies Butte areas, and we plan to conduct roundups in both areas every four years in order to maintain horse populations at the median levels of 120 for Three Fingers and 104 for Jackies Butte. Three Fingers now has 447 horses and Jackies Butte has 222."

He went on to say that homes were badly needed for the older horses, especially the stallions. "Experience in prior efforts to distribute horses under the private maintenance has shown that homes can be found for all the colts and young mares. Some young studs can be placed, but very few older studs or mares are ever accepted. In the past, where horses have come from over-populated ranges it has been necessary for BLM officials to destroy horses that could not be placed under the private maintenance program."

Roundup at the Three Fingers area started in October. The terrain there was formed by deposits of volcanic ash that eroded and weathered to make hundreds of canyons and washes, with rugged rock outcroppings and buttes which provide plenty of hiding places and escape routes for wild horses. Not many years ago the horses roaming these hills were not considered wild. As one BLM man explained, "They were a domestic crop" that ranchers in the area managed and utilized for their own ranching stock and business.

"I feel these horses were declared wild by law," said Grant Baugh, biologist and public affairs officer for the Vale BLM district. "Before the passage of the Act, we didn't think we had wild horses."

Thirteen riders chased the little groups of horses in the Three Fingers area, trying to corral them. One band of 25 head eluded the cowboys completely before they got to the trap. In another attempt, a big stallion slammed into a fence and on through it. Another little band was headed into the trap, but spread out at the last minute and ran away. Three were roped before they escaped. Eventually 40 horses were caught that day, and 15 the next day—a good start on the plans to capture about 500 wild horses from the Vale District.

The horses were hauled to Burns, where the branded ones would be returned to their owners upon payment of capture costs and trespass charges, or given out for adoption. Wild Horse Specialist Wilcox was not very optimistic about the owners claiming their horses, saying "They'll have to pay more than they're worth."

The BLM had planned to gather and remove

1,368 wild horses in Oregon in 1975, just to keep up with that year's increase, but the goal was not reached. Gathering stopped when money ran out. Only 400 horses were gathered in Oregon during an 18 month period in 1974-1975.

Another roundup was planned for the John Day country, in the Burns BLM district and Bear Valley Forest Service district, for 1976, reducing 200 head to 70. The roundup was planned for winter—February through April—when the horses would be concentrated in smaller areas and more open country. A summer roundup in this area is not feasible by horseback because of the roughness of the country and the heavy brush and timber in their summer range.

The January, 1976 helicopter census showed 210 horses, and the management plan was to reduce the herd back to 70 head every four years. During the summer and fall of 1975, the Forest Service constructed 8 wild horse traps and in February of 1976 contracted for the gathering. Some of the horses were bait trapped and some were corraled by horseback roundup. After being corraled, the horses were roped, haltered, and led to the Murderers Creek Ranch, to corrals that were accessible by vehicles. The traps were 4 to 7 miles from roads. The mature stallions were tranquilized (10 cc. Acepromazine) before being taken from the traps. Six horses in all had to be destroyed—one was injured in the roundup, one was deformed, and four were too old and thin to be adopted out. The greatest strain was on the saddle horses. This kind of terrain takes three horses for every rider, and the rough, rocky country was very hard on the horse's feet and legs. Several of the saddle horses were lamed, and all of them had bad cuts and bruises.

During 1977, roundup attempts in Oregon were more successful, due to legalized use of helicopters, and 1,397 horses were gathered at a cost of $200 a head. This was about $100 for the gathering and $100 to give them away—the cost of keeping them until adoption. It cost the BLM $3.00 per day per horse to keep them in the holding facilities. For the first time, funding for horse management was not a problem. There were funds available in Oregon to help relieve the horses in the drought situation. And because of helicopter use, this was the first time no cowboys were injured in the roundups. All but 7% of the horses were adopted out, going to most of the western states and also to Maryland, Iowa, Texas, Wisconsin, Michigan, Tennessee and Oklahoma.

In early 1977 the BLM completed a central holding facility for wild horses on a 160 acre site 8 miles west of Burns, Oregon. The facility accommodates about 300 horses, providing temporary quar-

ters for them until they can be adopted. A 265 foot well serves two 18,000 gallon tanks which supply water troughs in the corrals. The troughs are heated in winter to prevent freezing. The horses are fed a mixture of alfalfa and meadow hay, and foals are fed a special ration which includes a milk substitute. Horses are trucked to this facility from gathering points throughout eastern and central Oregon. Upon arrival, they are processed through chutes and holding pens where information about each horse is recorded. Then the horses are separated—mares and foals go into one section and stallions in another.

Wild horses in Nevada had increased to 25,417 by 1975 and several BLM districts had plans underway for management programs and future roundups (but by 1977 the number had grown to 36,000 wild horses and 1,510 burros in Nevada). The Battle Mountain district had rounded up 400 head from Stone Cabin Valley in the fall of 1975 and spring of 1976 as an emergency measure to protect the range and the rest of the herd, but had 21 other herd management areas that would need some kind of population control in the future. Some of these areas were showing evidence of overgrazing and range deterioration—forage depletion sooner in the year than usual, a general reduction in density of forage plants, and the fact that the animals were grazing unpalatable plant species. Consequently there was an increasing occurence and predominance of less palatable and "invader" plants in areas that earlier had good quality forage.

Several of the Nevada districts collected fecal samples of wild horses, deer and cattle in a study to determine dietary preferences of the various species and the extent of dietary overlap. Results of these studies will be discussed in Chapter 17.

The 1975 wild horse inventory in the Elko district showed a population of 3,325 horses, with the largest concentration in the granite ridge area southeast of Jackpot, Nevada. Many of the horses in this area are range horses turned out earlier by local ranchers, and a large portion of them were claimed as privately owned. As of January, 1977, 2,300 horses had been caught and removed from the range and efforts to gather the rest of the privately owned horses were still continuing. E. A. Moore, Elko District Manager, anticipated that about 700 horses would remain on the district in the category of wild, free-roaming horses at the end of the claiming process.

The Winnemucca District in 1974 had more than 7000 wild horses and 140 burros, which had increased to nearly 12,000 horses and 200 burros by 1977 and several areas were becoming overgrazed. For 1977 the district had 439,961 AUM's of forage available for consumption by herbivores. An AUM

(Animal Unit Month) is the amount of feed that one cow will eat in one month. Permitted domestic livestock in the district use 375,434 AUM's of forage, leaving 64,527 AUM's for wild horses and burros. But the present number of wild horses and burros (1977) would require about 146,000 AUM's, meaning that the range is short about 81,873 AUM's of feed. This doesn't count the amount of forage eaten by native wildlife. And, since wild horses and burros are usually found in localized areas, many of these areas were being severely overgrazed.

As in the Elko District, almost all of the wild horses and burros in the Winnemucca District were stray animals released by ranchers, miners and landowners adjacent to the federal range. The BLM allowed these people to claim their horses during a period of time in 1974 and 1975. But unlike the ranchers in the Elko District, most of the ranchers at Winnemucca chose not to gather their horses, because they would have to pay trespass fees for the length of time the horses had been out on the range—in many cases, a fee that was more than the horses were worth. It's possible that the Elko District gave more encouragement to ranchers to get their horses than did the Winnemucca District.

As of early 1977 the Winnemucca District had not yet been able to gather any excess horses. Funding was a slow process, and the district had not yet obtained the $2,540,000 which was estimated to be necessary to control the wild horse and burro population and reduce the animals in that district to a reasonable number. The district was able to begin their capture program July 12, 1977, and as of August 19, 1977 had removed 375 horses.

The Las Vegas District contains the Nevada Wild Horse Range at Nellis Air Force Base, which had about 1000 horses in early 1977. Another 1500 horses were scattered over the rest of the district. The National Mustang Association purchased the grazing rights for the Little Mountain Grazing Allotment (17,930 acres of rangeland) in the Las Vegas District, with the intention that the forage would be used for wild horses, the BLM maintaining management responsibility for the area.

A comment on this transaction by a rural newspaper editor was, "What about the management plan, the grazing scheme, and other wildlife considerations? What will be done on overstocking, range abuse, and so on? The wild horse people should be reminded, too, that these are 'our' lands and then dig into all of the phraseology that's been thrown at the cattleman to see if it would apply to the Mustang Sanctuary."

One of the four BLM planning units in the Las Vegas District, the Caliente Planning Unit, had 548 wild horses in May of 1974. During March and April of 1977, 840 horses, 15 burros and 8 mules were counted. No horse removal program had been started as of 1977, but a management plan was being developed.

The Carson City District had more than 3200 horses in 1975. From surveys done in 1973, 1975 and later, the BLM found that the horses were increasing at a rate of 15 to 20% annually. The wild horse specialist there explained that "wild horses will graze maybe 10 miles in one direction and six or seven in another, but as long as there is feed and water they will live and die within that area if they are left alone. But if they run out of water or feed, they'll look for a new home, and these horses are moving. We have wild horses in ranges where there were never horses before."

During 1977 this district began rounding up 174 horses in two areas north of Reno, because of feed shortages and complicated land ownership. There are many tracts of unfenced private land in that area, intermingled with public lands, and in order to minimize conflicts, the BLM removed some of the horses—leaving about 100 there that would be maintained in a herd management area.

In the Pine Nut-Markleeville planning unit in the Carson City District, increasing numbers of wild horses were raiding people's yards and haystacks because of lack of feed on their range. In the Fort Churchill-Clan Alpine planning units there were only 800 horses in 1971, increasing to more than 1500 by 1975.

Wild horses in the Ely District stem primarily from domestic stock used in past ranching and mining operations. Periodically some of the horses from the Spring Valley and Mount Moriah areas (in the northeast corner of the district) were rounded up and trailed into Utah, where the best ones were sold as saddle horses, or as draft horses to be shipped to Missouri for use by cotton farmers. The poorer ones were sold for chicken feed.

During World War I the Army provided Thoroughbred stallions to ranchers in Butte Valley, which were turned out with range mares. The offspring were gathered by the ranchers, under the Remount program, to provide horses for the military. More than 1000 head were removed from Butte Valley during World War I. Sources from the White Pine Historical Society show that in the 1920's and 1930's, Butte and Long Valleys used to have about 200 wild horses each, with another 100 each in Neward and Steptoe Valleys. At that time the horses stayed all year around in valleys, grazing primarily on the abundant winterfat plants (Eurotia lanata). But now they migrate to the mountains

Wild horses being gathered in Nevada, 1977 (BLM photo by Bob Goodman)

during spring and summer, coming down into the valleys to winter.

There were a large number of burros in Steptoe Valley in the early mining days, but not any more. Most of the ranchers in the area were mustangers in early times and turned their own horses loose to breed on the range, rounding them up to remove the young stock. Whenever the herds got too large, the ranchers would gather the excess and sell them.

In the 1940's horses became valuable for their hides for leather, and some of the wild and range horses were shot for their hides, which were worth about $10 each. Some of the ambitious hide hunters killed a lot of branded domestic horses as well as "wild" ones, which didn't make the ranchers very happy.

Mustanging continued into the 1950's. It is apparent from the quality and size of some of the horses remaining in the area that domestic breeding and mustanging (culling the herds) probably continued into the 1960's; many of the horses still have good domestic conformation and weigh 800-1000 pounds.

A complete aerial helicopter inventory of the Ely District in March, 1975 counted 2,137 horses in 18 herd areas. Of this total, 358 horses were claimed by ranchers in the district and 810 were claimed between the Ely and Elko Districts. Ranchers who submitted claims have had difficulty gathering their horses by on-the-ground methods such as water trapping and wing corral trapping, partly because, in the Ely District, the horses are in the mountains most of the year. There are quite a few springs in the mountains, which makes water trapping difficult or impractical; it is impossible to fence off all the other water sources. Wing corral trapping is also difficult, because most of the valleys are very broad and it is

impossible to close them with traps. Wing trapping in the mountains where the smaller canyons exist is difficult because of the steep, rough terrain and dense brush.

As of early 1977, only 500 horses had been gathered out of the 1,168 horses that had been claimed in September of 1973, and no action had been taken on several claims amounting to 156 horses. The presence of the remaining privately owned horses complicated the management of wild horses and the BLM planned to take steps to remove them if the owners did not.

Of the more than 60,000 wild horses in the West in 1977, more than half of these were in Nevada. The primary problem in most districts was the reduction of horses to manageable numbers. With many herd areas to manage (18 in the Ely District, for instance, 22 in the Battle Mountain District, and so on) it was a difficult job because of the continuing increase in wild horse populations. Several of the Nevada districts were considering consolidating their wild horses into two or three herd areas, removing the rest, and then managing the wild horse areas more exclusively for wild horses. This would mean only a few wild horse management programs in each district instead of so many.

With the passage of the Wild Horse Act in 1971, one of the basic problems concerning wild horse management was the lack of information available about the habits and biological requirements of the horses. To gather some of this information, two studies were begun in the Ely District in 1974. The first involved capturing and collaring a few of the horses to determine their movement patterns within the herd areas. The second was analysis of fecal samples from wild horses, cattle, sheep, antelope and deer to determine their seasonal and yearlong diets, as well as the degree of competition for feed among the different species.

Immobilization and marking of animals has been used by wildlife agencies successfully for many years and this technique was tried on wild horses using the Palmer Capture Gun. This gun is a 32 gauge single shot shotgun, designed to shoot darts with a drug in them. The drug, called succinylcholine chloride, causes temporary paralysis of the skeletal muscles. Once the horse is immobilized by the drug and lying down, the men involved in the capture install a color-coded canvas collar around the horse's neck for future observations. Then they put in a numbered ear tag, which identifies the horse if the collar is lost or destroyed. While the horse is down, they also check its teeth to determine its age; record its general body condition, color, markings, and a description of the other horses in the band, so that this information can be compared with future observations. After this information is noted, the horse is released to rejoin its band.

To determine its movement, and the band it is with, the horse is observed by people on the ground working in the area, or by low-elevation flights by helicopter or fixed-wing planes such as the Cessna 182. Since the summer of 1974 the Ely district has collared 14 horses and has been able to observe 10 of them. The information obtained indicates that horses within herd areas tend to have home ranges.

For instance, horses in the north end of the Sand Springs herd move within an area of 9.5 square miles during the year, while those at the south end use an area 55.8 square miles in size. Horses at the south end of the Buck and Bald herd move within an area only 1.7 square miles large. The vegetation in these different areas is about the same, but the horses that stay in the very small area have two permanent streams for water and don't have to travel. The horses in the Sand Springs herd have to depend on reservoirs and springs which dry up or decrease in flow during the year, forcing them to travel farther to water or to move to a different watering area.

The first wild horse management plan for the Ely District was completed in 1977, for the Monte Cristo herd (there are 18 herd management areas in the district, and a management plan will have to be written for each one of them), and this plan called for reducing horse numbers in this herd area from 142 to 72, with roundup of the horses planned for 1978. But no roundups were conducted because of a suit by AHPA and HSUS which halted roundups in Nevada during most of 1978. This suit will be covered in more detail in a later chapter. The district was also writing a management plan for the Fortification herd, and completing studies in the Sand Springs herd to determine what the manageable numbers should be. The main emphasis for several years to come will be studies to determine the desirable level of horses in the different herd areas, writing the management plans, and reducing the horses to a manageable level.

In other states, the BLM's attempts to manage wild horses have been similar. In the Craig District in Colorado, there are four wild horse herd units, and the 1977 count showed a population of horses in that district at 998 horses (before the foal crop), 10% to 15% being branded, domestic horses. As of January 1977, one management plan had been completed, calling for management of up to 140 wild horses in the Little Snake Resource Area. One other herd unit lies within this area, and the Management Framework Plan called for the total removal of all these horses (approximately 500 head). The other

two herd units are located in the White River Resource Area. Only one management plan will be written for that area, which contains approximately 360 horses (1977 count), and it is not yet known how many of these horses will have to be removed.

Two fecal analysis studies have been completed on wild horses in the Craig District, giving strong indications that there is considerable competition between the wild horses and domestic cattle, and only a minimal competition between the mule deer in the area and the wild horses. There is little competition between domestic cattle and the mule deer. Two forage inventories have been completed to determine the feed available for wild horses, domestic livestock and wildlife, the inventories covering 210,000 acres. Data on the foals, yearlings and adult horses are collected each year, and used to help determine the yearly increase in the wild horse population. In this district, the yearly increase has been from 18 to 22% per year, based on adult horses and on a 6.6% mortality rate. The mortality rate is an assumption; as yet there is no concrete data on mortality rates, but since the horse is a long-lived animal with no significant predators, the mortality rate is very low.

According to Bill Lawhorn, wild horse specialist for the Craig District, "Many of our problems are probably similar to those encountered in other areas where wild horses are found. Some of these problems are the high cost associated with removing and maintaining the wild horses, and too little forage for all the animals that ranchers and specific interest groups would like to have on the range . . . criteria needs to be established for determining the proper stocking rates for wild horses . . . there is a need for more detailed food habitat studies, a better understanding of the movement patterns of wild horses, and more and improved knowledge on population dynamics. Many of the decisions being made on wild horses do not have this type of information incorporated into them. Managing wild horses is not, or at least should not be, any different than managing any other wildlife species." The Bookcliff Wild Horse Range is in Colorado, also, and was established as a special wild horse range in 1974. See Chapter 8 for more details on the Little Bookcliff Wild Horse Area.

In the Rock Springs District in Wyoming there were more than 6000 wild horses in 1977, about 500 of them claimed by local ranchers. They were 2,300 horses in that district in 1971. Some of the difference in number may be due in part to error in the 1971 estimate, but part of the difference is just the high increase rate in the horses—20 to 30% per year. Most of these horses are located in rolling sagebrush country and high desert, areas that receive about 8 inches of precipitation per year. In years past much of the area was grazed by large bands of migratory sheep. Many of the ranchers in the area are now taking non-use of their grazing privileges, hoping to convert from sheep to cattle use. This temporary additional feed is being used by the large number of horses.

Much of the area has a checkerboard ownership, with over half of it being private or state land. The land owners have requested that the BLM remove the horses from their lands, and the Rock Springs District has started the removal program. This district is thinking of eventually having three large wild horse management areas and removing the small bands that are located in other places. This seems to be the most financially feasible method, offering a better potential for protection, management, and viewing of the horses. The BLM would keep the horses at a certain base number, reducing them when they exceed it, and then letting them build up again.

During 1977 the BLM gathered horses south of Little America, Wyoming, removing about 100 horses. They planned to gather horses in the checkerboard area north and east of the Bridger Plant. These checkerboard lands are within the old railroad land grants, and approximately every other section is under private ownership. There are four of these areas—the Rock Springs Lease (45% federal land), the Granger Lease (40% federal), the Carter Lease (45%) and the Cumberland Unit (40%). Most of the land is privately owned and managed by the Rock Springs Grazing Association, the Uinta Development Company, the Western Wyoming Range Company and the Uinta Livestock Corporation.

Requests to remove the wild horses from these private lands were received by the BLM from the Rock Springs Grazing Association and the Uinta Development Company and the BLM anticipated similar requests from the others.

The Rock Springs Grazing Association was organized in 1909, for the purpose of providing winter grazing for the livestock owned by its members, the grazing season being from December 15th to May 1st. The members of the grazing association keep their livestock off this winter range during the rest of the year to achieve maximum forage growth, but after passage of the Wild Horse Act in 1971 their management plan was defeated by the vast increases in numbers of unregulated horses grazing their lands and the intermingled BLM lands.

The Rock Springs BLM District wrote up a horse removal plan to comply with the removal requests, under Section 4 of PL 92-195, and to remove the horses with the least harassment and in the most efficient way at the least cost, trying to place the captured horses through the adoption program. Some of the problems facing the Wyoming districts in these grazing areas were the rapid increase in wild horse numbers, stallions stealing domestic mares, highway hazards in the wild horse areas (during 1974 more than 10 horses were hit by automobiles), recreationists complaining about wild horses chasing them, and so on.

The basic question of who owns the wild horses was still being debated. The BLM does not "own" the wild horses, and horses on private lands are not under the jurisdiction of the BLM. As custodian, this raises the question of the BLM's liabilities in the checkerboard areas for feed consumed, tourist injury, property damage, for situations where domestic horses are run off by wild stallions, and for public hazards on highways. Thus, the only real solution was to remove the horses.

The winter 1975 aerial inventory indicated 2,396 horses in the checkerboard areas (2,072 on the Rock Springs lease, 200 on the Granger lease, 43 on the Carter lease and 81 on the Cumberland Unit), a substantial increase over the 1972 inventory of 1,326 horses on these checkerboard lands. The winter 1977 aerial inventory showed 3010 horses.

The Rock Springs Grazing Association had indicated earlier it would enter into a cooperative maintenance agreement on the checkerboard lands it controls, if the BLM could show it could effectively control the horses in number—an agreement that the BLM felt was critical to the management of the Red Desert wild horse herd, which uses these same checkerboard lands as part of its winter range. But in March of 1977 the Rock Springs Grazing Association stated that they would appreciate the immediate removal of all wild horses on their checkerboard lands. A letter to the Rock Springs District BLM Manager from the Wyoming Fish and Game Department stated that they also would appreciate the immediate removal of excess horses.

These requests came because of severe drought conditions in 1977, and the subsequent increase in competition for feed and water between the wild horse, wildlife and domestic livestock, and because of the overpopulation of wild horses in these areas. Authorization was given to the Rock Springs District to remove about 1000 head of wild horses from the Checkerboard lands during 1977, and all of the horses on the Granger lease were to be gathered by July of 1977.

The removal methods were water trapping, hay trapping and dry trapping (corraling them on horseback). Water trapping consists of building a corral

BLM water traps.

Horseback roundups have proved dangerous and expensive. The Burns, Oregon district calculated the cost of their first horseback roundups at $785 per horse captured. Dr. Floyd Frank, chairman of the wild horse advisory board in 1975, commenting on the costs of roundups, said that the BLM and Forest Service have not been given the money for this. "In order to really handle the Wild Horse Act, the agencies have got to have funding."

Then there is the problem of what to do with the horses once they are captured. By the spring of 1977, only 2000 horses had been placed out for adoption in spite of an advertising program that reached three-fourths of the American population.

As of October 21, 1976, the use of helicopters for managing wild horses was made legal, approved by the 94th Congress. This roundup method has to be approved after public hearings in each state involved. In the new "Organic Act" (PL 94–579)—the Federal Land Policy and Management Act of 1976—under the portion on range management, Section 404 deals with the management of horses and burros and says:

> Sections 9 and 10 of the Act of December 15, 1971 are renumbered as sections 10 and 11 respectively, and the following new section is inserted after Section 8:
> Section 9. In administering this Act, the Secretary may use or contract for the use of helicopters, or for the purpose of transporting captured animals, motor vehicles. Such use shall be undertaken only after a public hearing and under the direct supervision of the Secretary or of a duly authorized official or employee of the Department. The provisions of subsection (a) of the Act of September 8, 1959 shall not be applicable to such use. Such use shall be in accordance with humane procedures prescribed by the Secretary.

around a watering place, with a mechanical device to close the gate when horses enter to drink. It is usually necessary to build a temporary fence around the nearby watering places to keep the horses from using them, forcing them into the traps for water. Water trapping was used successfully, in the area east of Rock Springs late in the summer of 1975, to remove 120 claimed horses.

Hay trapping is similar to water trapping, but is used during the winter months when snow covers the ground and the horses are short of feed. Hay is put into corrals to entice the horses into them. Dry trapping consists of herding the horses into a trap constructed where trails converge, along an established escape route, or in a location where the horses can be herded fairly easily. Herding the horses on horseback was used with limited success northeast of Rock Springs during the summer of 1975. One saddle horse had to be destroyed because of injury and two other horses were injured during the gathering.

As of October, 1976, helicopters could be used by the BLM for rounding up excess horses.

With the use of helicopters now allowed, many BLM managers feel that the problems involved in gathering excess horses will be lessened, and that these roundups will be made more efficient, cheaper, safer, and easier. Without the use of the helicopter (averaging $300-$400 per head to round up by horseback methods), it would cost more than $1 million each year to remove the extra horses. The helicopter alone cannot gather the horses, however, without the aid of some horseback riders, who will be positioned to help herd the horses at the crucial moments heading into the trap. With a helicopter, the horses can be herded one band at a time and at a rate of speed suitable to their endurance and slow enough that the foals can keep up with the group.

Because of the elevation, inconsistent weather conditions, and fast maneuverability required, the helicopter size should be a Bell 206 or equivalent, to reduce as many safety hazards as possible. A larger size can be used, but the price per hour would exceed the desired economics of the roundups. By using a Bell 206, the price per horse for capture is estimated to be below $100 per horse.

Fixed wing aircraft can be used for counting horses, observation and surveillance, but not for capture operations. Motor vehicles can be used in transporting captured horses, but not in chasing or herding them.

For any herd reduction plans, it was necessary to build adequate facilities for holding and dispersing the horses after capture. At Rock Springs, a centralized holding facility was built that could be used not only for that district, but for the state of Wyoming and perhaps Utah and Colorado. It is located about half a mile east of the Rock Springs District office on a county road. The corral is a complete portable unit built to hold about 300 horses, plus additional horses in additional portable pens. The corral was made from panels of 1½ inch square tubing, approximately 7½ feet high. Each pen will hold 50 to 75 horses and has hay bunks and an adequate water supply. The cost of the corral was $61,800 plus $3,900 for power to the corral, $4000 for the water lines and $2500 for miscellaneous items. Plans include a hay storage area and barn. The feeding and care of the horses are handled by the BLM wild horse staff.

The Susanville BLM District lies on the California-Nevada border with most of the district in northeastern California. Westward-bound settlers came through this country on their way to western California. A few horses were lost, turned loose or left to die along the Applegate Trail, becoming the forerunners of the earliest bands of wild horses in this area. The first settlers to take up land here came in the 1850's and 1860's, after many others had gone through on their way farther west. A drought in the San Joaquin and Sacramento Valleys in California was responsible for bringing many of the first settlers into Surprise Valley in the mountains of northeastern California; the ranchers, remembering the good grass along the Applegate Trail, took their herds up there for grass to save them from starvation in southern California, and later some of them settled the area.

Once the area was settled, the horse population grew proportionate to the needs of the region as horses were raised for saddle and draft animals, and then for sale to the Army. The closest Army market was Fort Bidwell, but ranchers trailed horses to other forts as well. There remained also a steady demand for horses from the homesteaders coming through to the West. Other markets existed for good horses and many of the early ranchers raised them as work teams for farming (32 head were needed on the early grain combines, for instance), and for the stage coaches and other means of transportation.

After the area was settled, the range deteriorated badly with the uncontrolled overgrazing by cattle, sheep and horses. Even after some of the bad winters encouraged settlers to bring in their cattle and sheep to feed them hay, the horses wintered out, pawing through the snow and grazing the ranges all year around. Horses increased in number until the ranchers had to have periodic roundups to keep their numbers down.

In Nevada the problem of wild horses was just as bad—so bad in fact, that in 1900 the state passed a law allowing unbranded horses to be shot, and 15,000 were killed. In 1910 there were more than 100,000 horses ranging over Nevada. Horses were the means of transportation, the work animals, and the source of economic stability for many people, but the horses turned loose to winter on the range contributed greatly to the overgrazing problem.

The present range conditions in the Susanville BLM District are poor. Only 4% of the area is in good condition, and only 8% falls into the category of stable watershed. The long range objectives of the Susanville district are to develop resource and herd management plans, to stop deterioration and improve habitat and watershed conditions in the herd management areas, and manage the horse and burro populations in balance with the other uses of these lands.

But because these long-range objectives can't be accomplished with the present limitations on funds and manpower, the short term objectives are less ambitious. They are to try to protect and manage these animals as components of the lands they occupied as of the first inventory (1973), and hold the rate of range deterioration back at the level that was occurring at that time. To accomplish this, the BLM will have to hold population increases to zero and reduce the horses to the level that existed in 1973, or 1,506 horses. This number had increased to 3,480 by August of 1975, and to 4,280 by 1976.

Range studies showed that 44% of the district was in poor condition, 52% in a fair condition, and 14% of the lands were still deteriorating. Domestic livestock had been reduced, but this action alone was not sufficient to improve the range, becaues the growth of horse and burro populations was more than making up for the reduction in livestock. Wild horses and burros were increasing 17% to 21% per year since the 1973 herd inventory.

Population control would be an interim measure until all the herd areas had been studied and individual management plans developed. Not all of the ten herd management areas would require the same degree of population control. The Susanville District planned to manage and protect not less than 1,545 horses and burros, and remove the rest. Domestic livestock were reduced; 13,304 head of permitted livestock were taken off, and intensive management plans for the remaining permitted livestock were begun. Habitat plans for the wildlife are being developed, along with multiple use management plans. In the meantime, a program for excess horse removal has begun, to keep range damage to a minimum. WHOA, the livestock industry, wildlife and conservation groups, as well as the district multiple-use advisory board had recognized the need for population control for the wild horses and burros in the Susanville District and were urging a beginning of some kind of removal program. The input from these various groups was used to help formulate the Susanville management framework plan for wild horses and burros.

The district received an increase in funds, and now has the necessary staff and equipment for the population control and management program. In June of 1976 the district requested authorization to remove excess horses, and this was received in August of 1976. Range technicians were hired to work with the wild horse specialist to provide the manpower force for the gathering program and for other range-related activities in a long-term program. The wild horse gathering is viewed as a long-term program, so the men were initially given the time to become thoroughly acquainted with the terrain and the location and behavior of the horses. A great deal of time was given to on-site visits by interest groups and news representatives.

In the first part of the gathering program, 135 wild horses and 16 branded horses were captured, along with 81 burros. Of the wild horses caught, there were 38 that were under a year old (23 colts and 15 fillies), seven yearlings, and the largest number of mature horses being in the 2 to 7 year old range (reflecting the protected increases since the 1971 Wild Horse Act). The youngest pregnant mare was only 2 years old, the oldest stallion was 20 years old and the oldest mare was 19.

Costs of the gathering program were as follows:

Long-term capital investment (this includes corrals, trailers, troughs, and other initial expenses) .... $69,900.
Gathering costs (includes salaries, vehicle costs, horse rental, hay, etc. incurred between August 1976 and March 1977 for gathering the horses and burros) .... 66,600.
Placement costs (includes salaries, veterinary expenses, film processing, telephone calls, etc. incurred to place animals with qualified applicants) .... 20,900.

BLM wild horse roundup, September 1977, on the Owyhee Desert in northern Nevada (BLM photo by Jan Bedrosian)

This gathering period was 60 days long, averaging 3 to 4 horses or burros caught per day (231 animals captured). The average cost per animal for the gathering, not taking the initial expenses for corrals and facilities into consideration, was $288 per horse. In addition, the average cost per animal for placing them out for adoption was $103. These expenses represented a total cost of $391 per horse.

This was the first gathering effort in California, and as was expected, it generated a high level of public interest. A lot of time was spent working on site with the news media, and humane, horse, and burro interest groups. This fact, coupled with the time it took to train the crew in horse gathering techniques, and the rough local terrain made the first gatherings quite expensive. But after the first four or five months, the efficiency of the gathering process increased.

The captured horses and burros that were not owned were placed with qualified individuals through the Adopt-a-horse program. Before the animals were released they were checked by a veterinarian and freeze-branded "C-2" (California, District #2) for future identification and follow-up. The BLM established informal working arrangements with humane organizations for follow-up on adopted animals.

Probably all of the BLM districts that must manage wild horses will make use of helicopters now in their population control programs, due to the increased efficiency and reduction of hazards to men and horses, as well as reductions in man-hours and costs. At a BLM-FS public hearing in Boise, Idaho on Wild horse management in March of 1977, all of the speakers who testified approved of the new federal legislation allowing helicopter use. This was a typical reaction. The amendment, and the public hearings required, provided an opportunity for ranchers, sportsmen, and conservation groups concerned over deterioration of rangeland to band together and voice their approval of helicopter use in the management of wild horses and burros.

15

The States Rights Issue

As in other states, the BLM and FS entered into a three-party cooperative agreement with the State of New Mexico through its Livestock Board. This agreement spelled out the way in which private ownership of horses and burros would be resolved—how privately owned claimed animals would be handled, as distinguished from animals known to be wild and free-roaming. This agreement was accepted and signed by the State of New Mexico on August 7, 1973.

Then, on November 15, 1973, the State, through its Livestock Board, advised the federal agencies that it was terminating the cooperative agreement. On January 15, 1974, the BLM was notified that the State of New Mexico would henceforth treat all unbranded and unclaimed animals as strays and would deal with them according to state law; all unclaimed free-roaming horses, mules, and burros on public land and private land in New Mexico would be claimed under the State's estray laws which give it authority to "regulate, impound or take up" stray animals.

This action was a direct challenge to the Wild Horse Act, the Livestock Board stating that it would exercise its right to sell the animals to private individuals if the impounded strays were not claimed after the publication and posting of notices.

On November 15, 1973, New Mexico terminated her cooperative agreement with the BLM and Forest Service, and notified the BLM that the State would claim all unbranded free-roaming horses under her estray laws.

The Board claimed its authority under a state law which says that all nonmigratory animals within the state belong to the people of the state, whether they are on federal or state land.

In letters to the BLM and FS, the Livestock Board Director Lee Garner said that the wild horses and burros are "not the subject of interstate commerce,

168

and are non-migratory, and since the federal government is not asserting the animals are damaging the federal lands, the government has no right to control, regulate or assert ownership of the animals."

He said that the federal law protecting wild horses and burros "takes away from the state the ability to control the livestock industry and poses a direct conflict with existing New Mexico laws. It is felt by myself, the board, and others that the law is dangerous. We are not objecting to protecting existing herds of what they call wild horses, but this law would create more herds. It could also deprive the livestock industry of grazing rights we've had for many years."

In answer to this challenge, Bob Williamson, of the Forest Service's Range Management Division, said the Forest Service would "enforce the federal law. We'll proceed as if the Livestock Board had never made its claim." He went on to say that "if the board elects to remove horses without permission we will take the necessary steps to prevent their removal if the horses fall under the Wild Horse Act."

Sections 1, 3, 4, 5 and 6 of PL 92-195 give certain custodial and management responsibilities for wild horses and burros to the federal government. The Secretaries of Interior and Agriculture are designated to perform the main administrative responsibilities for preserving wild horses and burros on federal lands. This assertion of federal power over free roaming animals (apart from federal treaty-making or interstate commerce powers) is unique to federal-state interactions in dealing with wild animal management. Throughout the history of the United States, the state governments have retained administrative control over wild animals on public lands within state boundaries.

In February 1974, a New Mexico rancher, Kelly Stephenson, saw several unbranded burros among his cattle on the range near Tayler Well, where his cattle water. The BLM made it clear when he contacted them about the burros that it would not remove them, and he then complained to the Livestock Board that the burros were bothering his cattle and eating their feed. The burros seemed gentle, not wild.

On February 11, under direction of the State Livestock Board, several individuals rounded up the 19 unbranded burros that had wandered onto a ranch at Three Rivers (north of Tularosa and near Carrizozo, New Mexico), impounded them and published notices. When no one claimed the burros, they were trucked to Roswell, New Mexico and sold at public auction in accordance with the state estray laws. They were sold on February 18 for about $35

apiece. The New Mexico Livestock Board approved the request for roundup and disposal. Jim Scott of Roswell bought 16 of the burros and Claude Foster of Corona bought the other three.

The BLM learned of the capture and sale of the burros through a newspaper article, and notified the U.S. Attorney that this appeared to be a violation of PL 92-195. The U.S. Attorney requested the Livestock Board return the burros to the federal lands because they were protected by the Wild Horse Act. This request was refused, and the New Mexico Livestock Board filed suit in District Court challenging the United States' action to administer wild horses and burros under the Act, charging that the Act violated state laws. The U.S. Attorney then directed the BLM to contact the buyers of the burros and request that the animals be held and cared for until the federal-state dispute over jurisdiction of the animals could be legally determined. The purchaser of the 16 burros agreed to do this, but the purchaser of the other three refused to make this commitment.

On March 4, 1974, a complaint was filed by the State of New Mexico in the U.S. District Court for the District of New Mexico against the Secretary of the Interior and against the United States for trying to keep the state from implementing the estray laws of the state of New Mexico. The State of New Mexico asserted that the Wild Horse and Burro Act deprived it and the citizens of New Mexico of their constitutional rights under the 4th, 5th, 9th and 10th Amendments to the Constitution, concerning jurisdiction and control over unbranded and unclaimed horses and burros in the state, and sought to have the court declare the Wild Horse and Burro Act unconstitutional.

Lee Garner of the Livestock Board said, "We're challenging the whole Act as applied to New Mexico because we already have laws covering them. We don't recognize wild horses or burros in New Mexico. They're all strays." He said the BLM defines a wild animal "as anything on federal lands that's not branded, and that's absolutely wrong." The 1907 estray law gives the state full authority over stray animals.

The BLM, by attempting to exercise powers not delegated to the United States by the Constitution was also, in the opinion of New Mexico, usurping powers reserved to the people and the states by the 9th, and 10th Amendments. The state felt they were also depriving the citizens of New Mexico of property without due process of law or just compensation, in violation of the 4th and 5th Amendments.

On February 28, 1975, a three-judge panel in Albuquerque, in the U.S. District Court for the

District of New Mexico, ruled the Wild Horse and Burro Act unconstitutional. The court ruled that the animals were not the property of the federal government simply because they were present on federal land, and said that ownership was vested in the states. The court ruled that the Act

conflicts with both the historical interpretation of the Territorial Clause, and the traditional doctrines concerning wild animals. . . . Wild horses and burros do not become 'property' of the United States simply by being physically present on the 'territory' of land of the United States. The doctrine of common law, dating back to Roman law, has been that wild animals are owned by the State in its sovereign capacity, in trust for the benefit of the people. This sovereign ownership was vested in the colonial government and was passed to the states.

The court decision described many of the legal complications associated with federal protection and management of wild horses and burros, and asserted that PL 92-195 is unconstitutional for two reasons. The Act represents a usurpation of state police powers and powers of control over wildlife. There is some question as to whether the power to regulate wild horses and burros is in accord with the Tenth Amendment doctrine of separation of powers.

The legal history of the doctrine of state control over wildlife goes back to Roman law. In English history, after the signing of the Magna Carta, English common law vested ownership of wildlife in the office of the king, to be held in sacred trust for the people. After the American Revolution and independence of the American colonies from England, the newly independent 13 colonies adopted much of England's common law. The independent states, each in their sovereign capacity, held the game and native wildlife in trust for their citizens.

In an earlier court decision, the court stated that "Undoubtedly, this attribute of government to control the taking of [wild] animals . . . which was thus recognized and enforced by the common law of England, was vested in the colonial governments, when not denied by their charters or in conflict with grants of royal perogative." Several other court decisions reaffirmed the passage of sovereign ownership from the king, to the colonial governments, to the states. Federal control over wild horses and burros would be in conflict with the traditional state jurisdiction over wildlife.

In addition to the historic sovereignty of the state over wild animals, state regulations for wildlife are supported by reference to the police powers of the state. This police power entitles the state to regulate the public health, safety and welfare of its citizens, and also to regulate the taking of game. The New Mexico court decision showed that federal control over wild horses and burros on federal lands conflicts with state police powers in regulating the taking of wild animals and the disposal of strayed livestock.

One of the main points in the New Mexico decision is that the federal government does not have the reserved authority to regulate wild horses and burros on federal lands. The phrasing of Section One of PL 92-195 suggests a reliance on the authority granted by the "Territorial Clause" of the United States Constitution which gives Congress the power to "dispose of and make all needful rules and regulations respecting the territory or other property belonging to the United States."

The New Mexico decision relies upon several court cases dealing with wildlife on federal lands to show that the powers granted by the "Territorial Clause" do not extend to federal control over wildlife management on federal lands. The only exceptions occur when federal regulation is granted by some other authority, such as treaty-making or interstate commerce regulating powers, or when federal control of wildlife populations is necessary to protect other values on the federal lands. PL 92-195 is aimed at protecting the wild horses and burros, not the land they live on.

The court found that since there is "no evidence to indicate that wild horses and burros are damaging public lands . . . the Wild Free-Roaming Horses and Burros Act cannot be sustained as an exercise of the power granted to Congress in Article IV, section 3 of the Constitution."

In the light of subsequent range damage due to the dramatic increase in the horse and burro population, this point might be questioned, but ironically the only reason the animals have increased to the point of damaging public lands is that they have been over-protected by the Wild Horse and Burro Act. In essence, the court suggested that the federal government had the authority to protect the land they live on, but not the horses and burros themselves.

The BLM claimed that PL 92-195 was constitutional, because it enabled the government to destroy horses and burros damaging federal property. But the potential damage to federal lands is a direct result of the Wild Horse and Burro Act, and not a purpose of the Act. Because of the problems that would be caused by the Act, it was necessary to include provisions in it to control the numbers of the protected wild horses and burros.

An attempt to justify the Act by the fact that it resolves a problem created by the Act itself is ridiculous, and cannot be looked upon as the purpose of, or a constitutional base for, the Act. If Congress had wanted to enact a Constitutionally sound law aimed at protecting the federal lands, it could have simply given the BLM and FS power to destroy the horses and burros or to control their numbers, whenever the public domain was being damaged or in danger of being damaged.

The opponents of New Mexico felt that if PL 92-195 was declared unconstitutional, other laws establishing wildlife sanctuaries would also be negated. But New Mexico pointed out that the statutes creating the National Wildlife Refuge System, the Wild and Scenic Rivers Act, and the Endangered Species Act all contain explicit language maintaining the traditional powers of the state over wild animals, or are otherwise distinguished: Congress provided for withdrawal or reservation of the lands for sanctuaries and refuges, and for wildlife protection in the National Parks. The National Wildlife Refuge System Act of 1966 states in part:

> The provisions of this Act shall not be construed as affecting the authority, jurisdiction or responsibility of the several states to manage, control or regulate fish and resident wildlife under state law or regulations in any area within the system.

In the Wild and Scenic Rivers Act: "Nothing in this chapter shall affect the jurisdiction or responsibilities of the States with respect to fish and wildlife." And in the Endangered Species Act:

> "The Secretaries may by regulation prohibit with respect to any threatened species . . . except that with respect to the taking of resident species of fish or wildlife, such regulations shall apply in any State which has entered into a cooperative agreement . . . only to the extent that such regulations have also been adopted by each State."

The Fur Seal Act of 1966 and the Marine Mammals Protection Act of 1972 are constitutionally sound, and different from PL 92-195, because within them Congress expressly states that the subject animal or its products move in interstate commerce.

The United States has obtained exclusive jurisdiction in other specific examples of parks or refuges because of an express cession of jurisdiction over that particular piece of land by the State to the United States. These statutes illustrate very well that Congress has meticulously observed the traditional constitutional and common law powers and rights of the States, with regard to resident wild animals, until the enactment of PL 92-195, which contains none of the "constitutional underpinnings" of the earlier laws.

As New Mexico pointed out, if the constitutionality of PL 92-195 was upheld, Congress would be free to nullify the conservation, fish and game, and estray laws of the respective states, infringing on state sovereignty as given by the 10th Amendment. In the western states, where the percentage of federal land is large (Alaska 96% federal land, Nevada 87%, New Mexico 34%, Arizona 44%, California 45%, Colorado 36%, Idaho 64%, Montana 30%, Oregon 52%, Utah 66%, Wyoming 48%, and Washington 30%), this would effectively end the traditional concept of state regulation and control, and trustee powers over resident wild animals. Several of these western states would, in effect, become federal property, with Congress becoming the "state legislature" for the major portion of the state. These states would have been admitted to the Union, not as equal members, but shorn of the legislative power vested in all the other states of the Union.

As pointed out by New Mexico and her friends in this court case, we need to keep a zealous regard for,

With PL 92-195 declared unconstitutional, Wild Horse Annie and other wild horse protectionists feared the horses would again be at the mercy of commercial mustangers, and that horses like these would once more be on the run.

171

and due recognition of, the powers belonging to the State, if we are to maintain the balance of the federal-state system as set forth in the Constitution. Quoting from *South Carolina v. U.S.*: "There are certain matters over which the national government has absolute control and no action of the State can interfere therewith, and there are others in which the State is supreme, and in respect to them the national government is powerless. To preserve the even balance between these two governments, and hold each in its separate sphere, is the peculiar duty of all the courts." And New Mexico argued that the subject of wild horses and burros is among those matters in which the state is supreme.

With the federal agencies apparently enjoined from managing wild horses and burros after the New Mexico court decision, the animals were nearly back where they were before PL 92-195 was passed. Conservationists had warned in 1971 that Congress was making a mistake by passing excessively restrictive legislation that would tie the managers hands in dealing with wild horses and burros. The Wildlife Management Institute had recommended that "those responsible for administering the resource should have flexible authority to control as well as to protect wild horses for the benefit of all natural resource values on the land."

But Congress yielded to the emotional demands from wild horse protectionists with an overly restrictive law which, in reality, prohibited proper management of the animals. The preservationists won, but the horses and burros lost. To many people, the New Mexico court decision was a predictable result.

But to the wild horse enthusiasts, the court decision was a giant step backward. Having PL 92-195 declared unconstitutional and restraining the federal government from enforcing it, aroused fears among the horse protection groups that the animals would again be at the mercy of commercial mustangers. Wild Horse Annie said that the court decision would lead to the slaughter of thousands of animals. "With horsemeat at 16 to 24¢ a pound I think we can look for a mass capture and slaughter," she said. "Wild horses and burros are unprotected at this time against any kind of capture or slaughter. I imagine they are piling up already."

The potential effects of the ruling were open to a wide variety of interpretations. Thomas Ballow, director of the Nevada Department of Agriculture, said people who wanted to capture wild horses would still have to obtain permits from local county commissioners under state law. Ed Rowland, Nevada state BLM Director, said he "would not expect a wholesale slaughter of mustangs" because of the ruling. Ballow stated that he expected ranch-

Who should have jurisdiction over these horses? State or federal government? On February 28, 1975 the wild horse law was ruled unconstitutional but the federal agencies appealed the case to the Supreme Court.

ers would "act in a responsible and reasonable manner so as not to antagonize the public."

BLM officials in Idaho and Oregon halted wild horse management attempts after the court decision. "As of Monday, when our office learned of the New Mexico action, we have totally stopped any wild horse management of any kind," Grant Baugh, public affairs officer for the Vale district in Oregon said. "It is a holding action until it is determined whether the New Mexico ruling applies to us or not."

In the confusion over the status of the horses, a few people took matters into their own hands and a few wild horses were shot. But on March 7, 1975, the three judge panel delayed implementation of its ruling and granted a stay of judgment at the request of U.S. Attorney James Grant, pending further court action. An assistant U.S. Attorney filed an appeal to the Supreme Court on March 28, 1975. The Wild Horse Act would remain in effect until the high court reached a decision, and management of the horses was resumed again by the BLM.

Jack Horton, Assistant Secretary of Interior said, "At this time we cannot predict how long this stay order will be in effect. However, until it is revoked, the BLM will continue to fully enforce the provisions of the 1971 Act." If the Act was reinstated on appeal, violators of the law in the interim period could be prosecuted under the Act by the U.S. Attorney's Office.

Mrs. Louise Harrison, a Colorado member of WHOA, said she was afraid "mustanging will start all over again," and that the individual states would be forced to assume the protection of the animals if the Supreme Court upheld the New Mexico ruling. Jim

Monaghan, an aide to Colorado Governor Richard Lamm, said the 1976 legislature would have time to pass a law protecting the animals in Colorado before the Supreme Court ruled on the appeal. Governor Calvin Rampton of Utah received about 300 letters asking him to enforce PL 92-195 until the Supreme Court decided the issue, for Utah didn't have a specific law relating to wild horses and burros.

Sixteen of the burros involved in the New Mexico case were placed under a maintenance agreement with the BLM on March 7, 1975, until the litigation between the State and federal governments could be decided. As of January 1976, the BLM had incurred the following expenses for maintaining the burros:

Veterinary expense	$712.00
Burial expenses for 8 burros that died shortly after capture	332.80
Feed and care	6,520.00
	$7,664.80

An additional bill was submitted by the purchaser of the 16 burros for the period of February 18, 1974 until March 6, 1975, totalling $9,060. Eight of the burros died soon after the roundup and three foals were born afterward, making a total of 14 burros remaining from the original 19.

The Supreme Court reviewed the New Mexico decision and heard arguments on whether the states or the federal government should regulate wild horses and burros which roam on public land. Attorneys for the state of New Mexico, supported by the Pacific Legal Foundation, the Nevada State Board of Agriculture and the State of Idaho, said the government was asserting an "exaggerated view of federal authority and power."

The government, appealing the New Mexico decision which declared PL 92-195 unconstitutional, said that similar reasoning could be used to invalidate legislation establishing federal wildlife sanctuaries. The government's position was supported in briefs submitted by horse protection groups, including WHOA.

The State of Idaho, supporting the State of New Mexico, was concerned over the State's continued ability to exercise its police powers in relation to the 19th Amendment of the Constitution—the ability to continue to enforce its laws, such as laws relating to brand inspection; animal disease control and quarantine laws; fish and game laws; and enforcement of its laws in general, both civil and criminal, in relation to persons on federal lands in Idaho. Therefore, in this case, much more was at issue than the validity of the Horse and Burro Act, for "if the Department of Interior is successful in this matter we believe that the way is open for eventual and complete erosion of any state jurisdiction over its citizens and persons generally on federally owned lands."

The federal government's jurisdiction, under the Property Clause of the Constitution, relates to management and protection of its property, and the mere fact that an animal comes upon federal property "does not and cannot, in and of itself, convert that animal forever after into an animal subject exclusively to federal protection throughout its lifetime." The State of Idaho brief went on to say, "If such were the case, under this same guise, any person having once ventured onto federally-owned land might thereafter for all time be declared to be part of the federal lands, and 'federal man', subject only to federal law to the absolute exclusion of all state law, whether or not the person thereafter remained on federal soil. This cannot be so. To go one step further, in fact the horses and burros under the Act in question do not even need to step on federal land at all, under Section 3 and 8 of the Act, in order to come within most of its terms. Of course, this is a ridiculous and absurd example. However, the Act in question here proceeds to claim and take absolute and continuing jurisdiction over all wild and free roaming horses and burros under just such a basis and declares them to be part of the land."

Section 3 of the Act states that "All wild free-roaming horses and burros are hereby declared to be under the jurisdiction of the Secretary for the purpose of management and protection in accordance with the provisions of this Act." And Section 8 says,

Any person who—
(1) willfully removes or attempts to remove a wild free-roaming horse or burro from the public lands, without authority from the Secretary, or
(2) converts a wild free-roaming horse or burro to private use, without authority from the Secretary, or
(3) maliciously causes the death or harassment of any wild free-roaming horse or burro, or
(4) processes or permits to be processed into commercial products the remains of a wild free-roaming horse or burro, or
(5) sells, directly or indirectly, a wild free-roaming horse or burro maintained on private or leased land pursuant to Section 4 of this Act, or the remains thereof, or
(6) willfully violates a regulation issued pursuant to this Act, shall be subject to a fine of not more than $2000, or imprisonment for not more than one year, or both. Any person so charged with such violation by the Secretary may be tried and sentenced by any United States commissioner or magistrate designated for that

purpose by the court by which he was appointed. . . .

Notice that only (1) is limited to the public lands. All the rest claim absolute and complete jurisdiction over all free-roaming horses or burros wherever they may be within this country, violating the Federal Interstate Commerce Clause of the Constitution.

The New Mexico brief stated that the Department of Interior's "extravagant view of federal authority under the Property Clause would create independent and sovereign 'federal states' within the States, if carried to its logical conclusion," and went on to point out that "the federal government is a body of strictly limited powers, and the powers which were not specifically delegated to the federal government were reserved to the sovereign States of the Union."

Many people watched this court case with interest and apprehension. An Oregon rancher said:

The Act attempts to set a dangerous precedent in that it gathers to the federal government exclusive jurisdiction over such animals even when found on private lands. Since the federal government owns one acre in two scattered in a checkerboard pattern throughout the eleven western states the next step could be a statute that gives the federal government exclusive jurisdiction over all species of wildlife to be also found thereon. Jurisdiction over migratory birds was upheld, in spite of the Tenth Amendment to the Constitution, by the U.S. Supreme court because their life cycle necessarily takes them across international boundaries coupled with a treaty with the Dominion of Canada and the Republic of Mexico.

If the Supreme Court decided in favor of the government, declaring PL 92-195 constitutional, it would be a "first" in federal control over a group of non-migratory animals within states' boundaries. This could establish a legal precedent that might result in increased federal control over wildlife. And a few narrow interest groups might then push for more federal regulation and control rather than state and local control. If this happened, it is conceivable that game management might then be regulated federally—by a bureaucrat in Washington D.C. rather than by in-the-field state and local game managers who are acquainted with wildlife biology and local situations. It is also conceivable that certain narrow interest groups (such as those opposed to hunting and fishing, for instance) could then gain control and dictate their desires over the whole area of wildlife management. A few Eastern interests could completely shape and direct the wildlife management, or lack of it, for the West.

This type of "centralized" wildlife management could spell disaster for many species and many habitats. No centralized regulator or his advisors could possibly be familiar with the biology of all the animals involved, nor the ecology of the areas they inhabit. Some species might need more hunting pressure, some more protection. A centralized control system, unfamiliar with local conditions and game biology, would be more apt to submit to pressure from interest groups at the national level, such as the advocates for NO hunting, and could easily do irreparable damage.

State game management programs are far from perfect, but they are much more suited to their task than a federal management program could be. The only way a federal program could approach it would be to break down its management and put it in the hands of local officials, merely duplicating what we now have. It would be of great cost to the taxpayer, creating another bureau and set of federal employees while losing efficiency and flexibility.

To put all of our wildlife under federal jurisdiction would be just one more instance of expanding federal control and uninformed "dictatorship" over local situations. Local control in government is usually better than remote federal control, in most instances, because the local government is usually much more flexible and able to adapt to local situations, conditions, and problems, making regulations that are more apt to fit the existing local conditions. But federal control, unable to be aware of all the vastly varying local conditions, cannot do this; federal control makes blanket laws and regulations that are much less likely to fit the multitude of local conditions. And then you have local dissatisfaction with the federal controls and regulations.

This trend in government—federal government encroaching more and more into what have traditionally been individual rights or local jurisdictions—is frightening to students of history and concerned individuals who cherish America's traditional freedoms. Once a trend of this kind is established, we all ask the question: Where will it stop? Who will it affect next? What restrictions will we be faced with tomorrow?

Perhaps the eastern city dweller could care less whether or not a farmer now has to have a permit before he can plow his fields, or whether the state or federal government controls the hunting seasons. But sooner or later, this trend toward federal regulation of our lives will affect us all, and much more than we'll want. There is a tendency in government to continually expand. It is difficult to "do away" with government controls once they are established, but it is very easy to acquire more and more government. Congress keeps passing more and more laws, but very seldom does away with any.

Someone once said, "That government is best that governs least," but we are already far past that point now.

In June of 1976, the Supreme Court upheld the constitutionality of PL 92-195, reversing the New Mexico decision, and remanding the case back to the lower court, with directions concerning additional proceedings. The State of New Mexico filed a petition for a rehearing. At that time, the burros in question were still in the custody of the individuals who purchased them at public auction.

Later the burros were all placed in foster homes under the BLM 's adoption program. The list of expenses the BLM incurred in care of the burros (payments to Jim Scott for caring for the burros from March 1975 until the court awarded custody of them to the BLM) amounted to more than $10,000. The additional $9,060 that Scott asked for, to cover the care of the burros from February 1974 until March 1975, was the obligation, the BLM felt, of the New Mexico Livestock Board.

The Supreme Court held that the Wild Horse and Burro Act was a constitutional exercise of congressional power under the Property Clause of the Constitution, which provides that "Congress shall have Power to dispose of and make all needful Rules and Regulations respecting the Territory or other Property belonging to the United States." (Article IV, S.3, cl. 2). The Property Clause, in broad terms, gives Congress the power to determine what are "needful" rules "respecting" the public lands. According to the Supreme Court decision, Congress' complete authority over public lands includes the power to "regulate and protect the wildlife living there."

Stu Murrell, regional conservationist for the Idaho Department of Fish and Game, commented later: "This ruling is contrary to several previous decisions by various courts that wildlife belongs to the States, and could negate States' rights, opening the way for federal management and a federal hunting license. The fallacy in the whole argument is that the wild horses are not true wildlife but feral animals. The International Association of Fish and Wildlife Agencies filed an objection with the Supreme Court based on this fact, but the court failed to draw a distinction between wild and feral animals."

"The future of Nevada and all the public lands states is in the gravest danger," commented John Marvel, President of the Nevada Cattleman's Association, referring to the Supreme Court decision upholding the constitutionality of PL 92-195.

"Every time a decision such as this . . . is handed down, Nevada becomes just that much weaker in controlling its own destiny. Throughout the course of this appeal, the livestock people tried to solicit the full power and support of wildlife interests, but they didn't realize the full significance and ramifications of the case."

Dean Rhodes, Chairman of the Public Land Council (a western state organization of public lands livestock operations, dedicated to the wise multiple use of all the public land resources) said, "We have been told by the BLM that their hands were tied on the wild horses until the Supreme Court decision was handed down, but it is imperative that they move now to control these animals by any method available to them while they still have forage left to manage."

In the Supreme Court case, the State of New Mexico argued that approving PL 92-195 as a valid exercise of Congress' power was sanctioning an impermissible intrusion on the sovereignty, legislative authority, and police power of the State, infringing upon the State's traditional trustee powers over wild animals. The Property Clause indicates that the power granted by it is of a protective nature, and not designed to intrude upon State authority; this has been clearly indicated in earlier court decisions (*Camfield v. U.S.*, *Kansas v. Colorado*, etc.).

But the Supreme Court stated that federal legislation under the Property Clause and the Supremacy Clause of the Constitution, overrides existing state laws. In other words, although PL 92-195 does not establish exclusive federal jurisdiction over public lands in New Mexico, it overrides the New Mexico estray laws in as much as the state law attempts to regulate wild horses and burros, which are now federally protected animals. "Unquestionably the States have broad trustee and police powers over wild animals within their jurisdictions . . . But as *Greer v. Connecticut* cautions, those powers exist only 'in so far as their exercise may not be incompatible with, or restrained by, the rights conveyed to the Federal government by the Constitution.' "

With the constitutionality of PL 92-195 thus upheld by the Supreme Court (though still questionable in the minds of many people), a new precedent of federal, rather than state control of animals on public lands was firmly established. Only time will tell how far this move will go toward replacing state and local jurisdiction with federal— over ALL wildlife management as well as the management of wild horses and burros.

16

The Feral Burro

Although this book is dealing specifically with the wild horse controversy, a mention should be made of the burro, for he is part of that controversy, being protected by the same law that protects the free-roaming horse.

The burro, like the horse, was brought to the New World by the Spanish. This little cousin of the horse was first domesticated by the Egyptians or the Libyans. From there he was introduced into Syria and Palestine, and for almost 4000 years was largely confined to the Mediterranean region (North Africa, Mediterranean Europe and Southwestern Asia). Pack strings of burros were used between Arabia and Egypt as early as 3000 B.C. The ox was not a good desert traveler, and the horse did not arrive until later, so the burro became the primary means of transport in this desert country.

Scientists are not sure just when the burro arrived in Europe, and some feel that there were burros there during Neolithic times. Spain and Portugal have long been the home of the burro, and some people claim that burros were native to Catalonia in northeastern Spain. There were burros in Spain during Roman times, and when the Moors invaded they brought more burros from North Africa.

The burro became important for transportation

Spaniards brought the burros to the New World, and for several centuries burros were used as pack animals in the West. Some strayed or were abandoned to run wild.

and as a pack animal throughout Europe as well as the British Isles. Burros went west across the ocean to the New World with the Spanish explorers and settlers and were used for breeding mules as well as for beasts of burden. Burros soon appeared in northeastern Brazil and in Mexico and were imported into Venezuela by 1535. They soon spread to Argentina and Peru. The trade route from Vera Cruz to Mexico City, established by Cortez in 1522, was important for three centuries, and burros and mules transported as much as 50,000 tons of goods a year over this route until the railroad came in 1873.

The first burros to come into what is now the United States probably came with the Spanish colonizer Juan de Oñate (see Chapter One). After that settlement was well established, pack trains of burros were moving between Chihuahua, Mexico, and the settlement in New Mexico. Later the burro played a role in the mining ventures that spread from New Mexico through the western United States from the 18th to the early 20th century.

There was not a high number of feral burros in the West until some point in the 19th century. Before then, Spanish missionaries, prospectors, miners, sheepherders and other pioneer travelers used burros as transportation or as pack animals (burros were better pack animals than horses, being able to carry heavier loads for their size, and able to survive on scanty desert forage). Only a few burros went wild—abandoned by their owners through misfortune, or left to fend for themselves when their owners died, or escaped from loose confinement. But later, after the advent of roads and better transportation, and then the decline in the mining boom, many burros were simply turned loose on the range. By the last quarter of the 19th century, feral burros became widely dispersed over most of the western states.

The impact of large numbers of domestic animals on the fragile desert ecology goes back over 100 years in some locations. One spring on Hunter Mountain in Inyo County, California, was depicted on a map with the name "Jackass Spring" as early as 1875. Mules were raised there for use in the mining industry. One mine in the Argus Mountain Range had as many as 500 mules transporting cord wood and charcoal for the mine. Some early camps had populations numbering into the thousands at the peak of the mining boom. Even though it was a roadless, harsh land, thousands of people were scattered over the desert before the turn of the century. Every one of these people had at least one animal for transportation and packing, and some had other livestock for food. When this use of the land is considered, it is not difficult to understand that the vegetation and animals today on the desert do not represent a natural condition. In 100 years of grazing by non-native animals, the desert ecosystem has suffered some drastic changes.

Burros are now found in arid, unpopulated areas of all the western states except Washington and Montana. The largest numbers of burros are found in California, Arizona, Nevada, and New Mexico. The greatest concentrations are in the drier, more desert areas, partly because these areas are somewhat isolated and not used by people, and partly because the burro is well suited to a desert existence.

Wild asses are desert animals. The burro has adapted well to arid regions with less than 6 to 10 inches of annual rainfall, little or no grass, and few perennial forage plants. As the burro thrived in arid regions of the West, he multiplied. During the early part of the 20th century, the burro numbers in some areas grew so high that naturalists became alarmed, noting how the burro dominated the desert habitat to the detriment of native animals. The burro's only predator, the mountain lion, was becoming scarce because of hunting pressure from man, and there was nothing to hold back the burro increase.

Burros are hardy and long-lived, with a life span somewhat longer than that of a horse. It is not unusual for a burro to live to be 40 years old. The females tend to live longer than males. Burros inherit the toughness of their ancestors—the wild asses on the deserts of Asia and North Africa—enduring intense heat in summer and freezing winds in winter. They are strong, tough, sure-footed, and swift for short distances. They are experts at conserving their energy and taking care of themselves. To illustrate their hardiness—after a severe drought on the Mojave Desert in California during the winter of 1922-23, cattle losses were 65%, horse losses nearly 50%, but none of the burros died. Cattle and horses on the range often get sore feet, but the burros never seem to get sore.

Burros are desert animals and have adapted well to arid regions with less than 10 inches of annual moisture, little or no grass, and few perennial forage plants.

Feral burro females usually start reproducing at two to three years of age, and produce a foal every other year or a little more frequently. The gestation period is 12 months, but can be as short as 11 months or as long as 13 months. It is not uncommon for a jenny with her 6 to 8 week old foal to be pregnant again, and having her earlier foal (about ¾ grown) following her also. Jennies mature at one year of age and many of them are bred by that time, dropping their first foal at two, and foaling every 13-18 months thereafter, for 30 years or more.

Removal of over 1000 burros in Grand Canyon in the early 1930's was done to protect the bighorn habitat. Steps were taken in several areas to reduce burro numbers during the first half of this century. More recently, in 1975, the National Park Service killed 52 burros in Bandelier National Monument (because the National Parks are not subject to PL-92-195 and the burros can be controlled at the discretion of the Park Service), but that same year there were 28 new foals out of the original 130 burros. In just one more year (1976) the 52 destroyed burros were replaced by the herd's natural increase in population.

A controversy over the feral burro's competition with native wildlife species has existed for many years, the most heated arguments for elimination or reduction of burros on public lands coming from people who are concerned about the survival of the desert bighorn sheep. The Desert Bighorn Council was formed in 1954, and has been concerned from its very beginnings with the impact that burros have on desert ecology. The Desert Bighorn Council is made up of people who are interested in promoting more knowledge about the bighorn. This group feels that burros should be completely removed from some of their areas in order to protect other biological values.

The burro has a detrimental effect on the bighorn, and has been accused of driving the sheep from their habitat, destroying vegetation and compacting the soil around watering areas, muddying and polluting waterholes with feces and urine, and forcing the bighorn to leave his traditional ranges and watering areas. Studies of burros and bighorn sheep since 1960 have shown that there are serious problems and that most of these accusations are true, but not to the extreme or universal extent that was earlier thought.

Because the burro is an introduced animal and not native, it can be expected that he will "upset the ecological balance," thriving more or less at the expense of the native plants and animals. He cannot be considered a beneficial addition to any natural environment to which he is not native. Studies have shown, however, that the burro is not a serious competitor with bighorns in every case; competition becomes serious primarily in areas where water and feed are scarce, and areas in which the burro has outgrown the food and water supply.

Burros do compete with bighorn for food, but where forage is abundant, direct competition for food is not serious. But it becomes serious during dry seasons and around watering holes. The burro consumes a greater variety of plants than does the bighorn, and sometimes damages the range by pulling plants out by the roots. Dense burro populations soon alter the make-up of a given geographical area by overgrazing, reducing the ability of the land to grow other plants, or to support other herbivorous animals.

T. J. McMichael, in studies of bighorn-burro relationships in the Black Mountains of Northwestern Arizona in 1964, concluded that there was enough overlap in food habits and summer range of burros and bighorns to keep the bighorns from reaching their maximum population potential in that area. Feral burros may eat up the bighorn's "emergency food supply" around the watering areas, which the bighorn use after traveling long distances to water through terrain where no food plants exist. A big problem is the depletion of vegetation near water, which is necessary for bighorn sheep with lambs.

Feral burros often congregate around desert water sources during the hot months. They sometimes totally take over small water supplies from both natural and artificial tanks as well as from small seeps and springs. When the water is in short supply they paw at pipelines and tanks and sometimes break them. When a waterhole is thus overused, they often foul it with such an accumulation of excreta that other animals in the vicinity either

Bighorn ewe and lamb—native desert animals endangered by the feral burro (Claifornia Department of Fish and Game photo).

178

California has the largest burro population, most of them living in the Death Valley National Monument.

leave the area or use the water only as a last resort.

Burro competition with other large animals, including mule deer and pronghorn antelope, is usually only a minor problem. Burros share the range with antelope in parts of Nevada, Arizona, New Mexico, Oregon and Wyoming, but the typical habitat used by each species is usually different. Competition is also very low between burros and mule deer. One study in Bandelier National Monument in New Mexico showed that the ranges of the mule deer and the burros in that particular area did not overlap.

In California, the largest concentration of burros is in the Death Valley region. More than 40% of the wild burros in California roam within the Death Valley National Monument (a little more than 2 million acres—the largest area in the National Park System in the southwestern United States). There were more than 1500 burros in the Death Valley Monument in 1973, their numbers increasing and range area expanding. In Death Valley, the habitat varies from barren valley floor (below sea level) to mountains over 11,000 feet high, and the primary vegetation is desert shrubs.

This national monument area is a nearly complete ecosystem—a valley between two mountain ranges. The burros range at various elevations (and in some areas come down out of the mountains at night to feed on farm crops in the valleys outside the Monument). Death Valley itself is the hottest, driest, lowest place on the North American continent. This unique geography and climate have resulted in some significant and unique biological situations. For instance, there are over a dozen species of plants here that exist nowhere else in the world, and several rare and endangered species of animals.

There are 51 native mammals in Death Valley, but

of greatest concern to biologists right now are the bighorn sheep, because their numbers and habitat are steadily declining. Their present range now occupies less than 380 square miles, in patchy, isolated areas, whereas their former range totalled 1,400 square miles and included all the mountainous areas of the Monument. It is estimated that there were more than 4,800 bighorns in that area before pioneer settlement, judging from the extent of the bighorn habitat. But their numbers had dwindled down to 915 by 1961 and to 583 by 1972.

In Death Valley, the feral burro has been introduced into a delicately balanced ecosystem that has a very low water supply, low annual forage production, severely dry climate, and occasional devastating erosive forces such as flash floods. This area supports a meager, low-level natural "balance" even at best, and cannot stand the addition of a new, large herbivorous animal like the burro who competes with the native animals for feed, water and space. Nowhere else on this continent does life balance so precariously on the thin edge between survival and disaster than it does in Death Valley, and nowhere else are ecological principles and dynamics so starkly apparent. This, in fact, is the very purpose in establishing the area as a National Monument. But when Death Valley National Monument was created in 1933, burros were already long established in all of the bordering mountain ranges. Indeed, in some areas burro damage was already severe, and burros were upsetting the precarious ecological balance.

For example, bighorn sheep used three major springs in the Cottonwood Mountains in 1939, but as burro use of the area grew, bighorn use declined, and there has been no significant use of these springs by bighorns in the last 25 years. A similar situation has occured in Cottonwood Canyon. And in the Panamint Mountains, bighorns were known to use Eagle Spring in 1935. Burros spread into the area in 1938 and the bighorn use dropped to zero. In Butte Valley, bighorns fed and watered there in the early 1930's, but by 1935 the bighorns were replaced by herds of more than 200 burros. Blackwater Spring was important to bighorns and free of burros in 1960, but burros have moved into the area and used it heavily, and now fresh bighorn sign cannot be found.

Smaller mammals, especially rodents, are also affected by the presence of large numbers of burros, and further study is needed to determine all the effects of habitat disturbance, such as destruction of rodent's burrows by trampling, reduced seed production and so on.

A study conducted by the National Park Service showed the amount of plant use and damage radiat-

179

ing several miles out from water sources. Ten plant species that are usually abundant in these desert areas were missing in this 1971 survey of Wildrose Basin in the Panamint Mountains, including four grasses. Many burro-grazed areas are now shrubland instead of shrub-grassland. The vegetation that is not actually eaten is often damaged by trampling or uprooting during feeding. Continued feeding on the same plant results in loss of plant vigor and eventual death in areas where burro concentrations are great. In overgrazed areas, flowering and seed production are severely reduced.

A conservative estimate of the amount of forage consumed by the 1500 burros in Death Valley (assuming the burros weigh an average of 319 pounds and eat about 9.7 pounds of feed each day) would be 14,500 pounds (7.27 tons) of food each day, or about 5,310,000 pounds (more than 2,650 tons) of forage each year. This is a very heavy defoliation of an area that doesn't produce much vegetation annually to begin with.

If edible material is limited, the carrying capacity of the area for these large herbivores will be reached rather quickly. Yet the burro population continues to grow, which means that more forage is harvested annually than is produced—the burros are eating material that has been "stored" over the many years that these plants have been growing. This means that plant vigor will be reduced and the plants eventually killed by this kind of heavy grazing. The expanding burro population is thus living off the stored plant reserves and is drastically altering the plant community.

Burro damage has resulted in a very low production of Bristlecone Pine on Telescope Peak in the Panamint mountain range, and down in the lower valley, the formerly abundant alkali sacaton grass has been so heavily grazed that many of the plants have died. This overgrazing and subsequent plant mortality has occurred since 1969. Creosotebush is being eaten in some areas of heavy burro use; this is an indication of range depletion, because creosotebush is an unpalatable plant that is rarely eaten by any animal.

The burros tend to congregate around the few waterholes, not traveling more than 5 or 6 miles away from water unless food is very scarce. The burros use the available water, leaving none for the native wildlife; most of the springs in this arid country don't flow enough to supply the needs of both the burros and the native animals. The constant trampling around the springs reduces the cover for birds such as quail and chukar (and small animals), pollutes the springs, and hastens erosion. This overuse of territory around the water holes affects all of the wildlife in an area, especially the smaller species that cannot range far from their water sources. Critical reductions in these species also affect the food supply, threatening the survival of predators and disrupting the entire community of living things.

Burro control began in Death Valley in 1939 when the burro population was about as high as it is now. By 1942, all of the burros had been removed from the mountains on the east side of Death Valley. Between 1939 and 1968 official records show that 3,578 burros were removed from Death Valley, but the number taken may be as high as 4,130, if the unofficial numbers taken by trappers in the area are added to the count. Then, in 1968, burro control activities were curtailed by state laws protecting the burros, and by 1972 the burro population had risen again to more than 1500. Live trapping was resumed in July of 1973 and a few burros were taken by permit holders.

The National Park Service management policy for natural areas like Death Valley states that:

> management will minimize, give direction to, or control those changes in the native environment and scenic landscape resulting from human influence on natural processes or ecological succession. Missing life forms may be reestablished where practicable. Native environmental complexes will be restored, protected, and maintained, where practicable, at levels determined through historical and ecological research of plant-animal relationships. Non-native species may not be introduced into natural areas. Where they have become established, or threaten invasion of a natural area, an appropriate management plan should be developed to control them, where feasible.

The plan proposed in 1973 for Death Valley Monument was to exclude the burros from the area, since they are non-native animals that are disrupting the ecology of the area. Parts of the Monument boundary were to be fenced to keep animals from adjacent areas from entering, and those inside the monument were to be trapped or destroyed.

But outside the national monument, on BLM lands, nothing was done for the first few years after passage of PL 92-195 that could be called management. The burro population had been increasing steadily on public lands in California, because for several years he had been protected by state law, even before passage of PL 92-195. Between 1953 and 1957 California had laws protecting the burros from indiscriminate killing. In order to kill or capture a burro, a person had to have a permit. But the only significant "management" results from this permit system were from livestock ranchers who controlled the burro populations in their own grazing areas. A lot of permits were issued to people who wanted to capture one or two burros for personal use, and if these animals had all been captured it might have had some effect on the increasing burro population. But few were actually captured. For instance, in the period from January to June 1970, 190 permits were issued to capture 420 burros, but only 5 burros were captured.

In 1967 the BLM issued a wild horse and burro policy statement, recognizing the burro in California as having some public value and proposing the development of management plans which would preserve the burro as one of many multiple-use objectives. A cooperative management effort was proposed, involving the California Department of Agriculture (the agency responsible for issuing the permits to capture or kill burros), the California Department of Fish and Game, the Bureau of Sport Fisheries and Wildlife, and the BLM. A cooperative agreement was signed, and these agencies developed common objectives for managing burros. But several things delayed completing the management plan and putting it to work.

One of the delays was caused by the BLM's planning system, which provides that a resource management plan can not be developed until all other resources in the area are inventoried, analyzed, and the conflicts between the various resources resolved. Also, there was a limitation of funds and manpower for the new burro management program; nearly all new money was being utilized to carry out the requirements of the planning system.

The California desert, where most of the burros in California are located, needed a special planning effort and the BLM created a Desert Planning Staff. In 1971, with passage of the Wild Horse and Burro Act, the BLM was instructed to use this existing planning system to develop management plans for the feral burro. One BLM wildlife biologist said, "It might be easy to blame our problems on the planning system or the requirements of the wild free-roaming horse and burro Act. In reality, the problem is the shortage of money and manpower necessary to inventory all the resources and develop plans necessary for management. The burro just happens to be one more resource added to our growing list of things that need management. Another problem is the nature of the beast. He has been portrayed as mischievous, unaffected and destructive. This image is probably true, because left to his own resources the burro has a knack for destroying everything around him."

The BLM was developing a burro management plan, with objectives consistent with PL 92-195, the first goal being to reach the population levels and distribution of the burros as they were in December, 1971. In some cases it would be necessary to reduce a certain population even below that level because of the deteriorated habitat. The only methods of control available were live trapping and killing. The first is most acceptable to the public, but also the most expensive. There is the added problem of finding and maintaining a "market" for the animals (remembering that this will be an "annual and forever" kind of program).

In talking with the National Advisory Board for horses and burros at their November 1973 meeting, Bill Radtkey, wildlife biologist in the BLM California State Office, said, "Regardless of how we carry out the management, the important thing is that we start immediately. Each year we delay makes the initial task of population control more difficult. It also poses the threat of destruction of the habitat of native wildlife and the burro."

He proposed an interim plan to prevent long-term or irreversible damage to the most severely over-populated areas. The requirements of the Act specify developing management plans using the planning system, and the BLM had already delayed two years since passage of the Act. His proposed interim plan was, in his words, "an attempt to justify killing burros in areas where permanent damage is occurring. If we are required to wait until a management plan is developed for the entire California desert, we will be facing an additional two or more years of delay."

Burros have also been a problem on the Naval Weapons Center in the Upper Mojave Desert near China Lake, California. Bordered by Panamint Valley and BLM lands, and almost bordered by Death Valley National Monument, this is a dry lake bed that probably dried out a million years ago. Death Valley is the termination of this chain of ancient lakes.

At the wild horse and burro advisory board meeting in November, 1973, Mrs. Bob Barling described the desert terrain and conditions found on the 17,000 square miles of the Naval Weapons Center (NWC) and mentioned that wildlife management on military bases is not unusual. She added that on the NWC it is done through cooperation with the Bureau of Sport Fisheries and Wildlife, and the California Department of Fish and Game.

She described the evolution of these desert lands that has determined the plant and animal life of these areas, and showed why the desert cannot tolerate the intrusion of an exotic species like the burro, that did not evolve in this system. Most of the desert vegetation is very sparce and very dry. Some of it is dead, and some of it is quite primitive. A lot of the shrubs take a long time to grow. The average precipitation at China Lake is less than three inches a year. At higher elevations there might be up to 9 inches, but some areas receive less than one inch per year. It takes a common sagebrush much longer to grow in a very dry climate than in an area that gets a little more rain. This is one of the problems encountered in adding a new animal to the desert vegetation system; the forage production is simply not there.

Burros are a problem over much of the military base, and Mrs. Barling said that the previous winter, after a drought period, there was not enough food for the heavy concentration of burros. She showed colored slides revealing the deep trails they had made and the absence of vegetation near the only available watering places. A March 1973 burro inventory showed approximately 430 burros on 50 square miles of the east side of the Slate range. The burro population on the entire NWC was approaching 1000.

Expanding burro populations have been a matter of concern for many years on NWC lands, and burro reductions have been conducted under permit from the California Department of Agriculture. During 1965–1966, 50 burros were removed, and in 1966–67 150 burros were removed, the reductions being supervised by game managers of the California Department of Fish and Game. In 1968-69 a permit for 200 more burros was requested and granted, but due to pending federal legislation affecting the burros, the permit was allowed to expire, unused.

Throughout the Mojave Desert, drought conditions prevailed during 1970 until late 1972 and food for wildlife reached a critical low point in late 1972. Personnel on the NWC observed many wild burros in poor condition in the Slate Range and southern Panamint Valley. Some were weak and stumbling, and some that fell had trouble getting back up. Fresh remains of dead burros were found near waterholes. Above normal rainfall came in late 1972 and brought out a good growth of annual plants, but the perennial plants that grew more slowly had been closely grazed during the drought years and could not make a normal recovery.

Without population control and management, the outlook for the burros in the future on the Slate Range-Panamint Valley would be one of marginal or near-starvation conditions. During 1973 and 1974 the burro population on NWC lands increased 30% each year. In 1975 another dry period reduced the available feed, and a number of carcasses of starved burros were found.

Living space and food are important things that are often scarce in the desert. In arid country where vegetation is scant and shrubs are few, the competition for shelter and nesting sites is often very keen between some species. And the highest level of competition involves food. There is a delicate balance on the desert, and in Mrs. Barling's words (in another presentation at the advisory board's 8th meeting—December 5-6, 1975, at the Naval Weapons Center, China Lake, California), "We have four factors we must consider if we are going to be managers. We must look at the producers, we must look at the consumers. We look at the variables that can affect this, and there's one sure thing you can say about the climate of this upper Mojave Desert—it is erratic. We may have 3 years with less than an inch of rain per year, then we may have 9 inches the following year and the natural ecosystems seem to be geared to keep up with this, provided they are not interfered with by human uses with the introduction of exotic species, or the invasive pollutants [smog] that seem to be spreading out farther and farther from the urban areas. . . . We get some of our precipitation in the form of snow in the higher elevations. We get about two snow storms a year above 5000 feet. A great deal of our precipitation comes from summer thunder showers—some pass over and some land on us, and when they do we have a little moisture in dry washes that is eagerly used by a whole variety of wild and feral animals."

Primitive peoples lived in this desert region since as far back as 10,000 years or more, and they left us some records of the animals they hunted or considered important to their way of life, in rock drawings. The desert bighorn sheep appears in almost all of the large petroglyph displays, indicating that this was a very important animal to the early people who inhabited these desert lands—not only in the Mojave Desert but in almost all of southern California and in Nevada where this rock art is found.

But then in the 1800's the miners started coming down through these mountains searching for gold and silver. They were seeking to make a living, and brought some of their livestock along. But when they left, they didn't take their burros with them. Some were turned loose, escaped, or were abandoned. And in several areas where the charcoal industry was thriving (to supply the mining and milling processes), there were farms where burros were raised to supply the pack trains for the charcoalers to transport the material from the charcoal kilns to the mining areas. And when no longer needed, a lot of these burros ended up loose on the desert. These burros, being clever and durable, thrived, becoming too successful for their own good.

The Slate Range is extremely arid, with only two

water sources—springs—that are 12 miles apart. The next nearest water is almost 22 miles away. Yet this area supports about 400 burros. And when this many burros concentrate on the water holes—it spells disaster. Every hill within 12 miles of these two springs shows deep trailing and diminished vegetation. When temperatures climb up during the summer, the burros shade up in the canyons during the heat of the day, milling around and trampling, destroying cover, food material and nesting sites for other animals. In hot weather the burros do a lot of rolling and wallowing on the ground to rid themselves of insects, destroying even more fragile plant life. The burros in this area gang together in bunches as large as 25 to 30, and their impact on their habitat is tremendous. Burros also use the major gullies and washes for shade, and as travel routes. Many small animals and birds use these washes, and the vegetation in them, as part of their habitat or for nesting. Unfortunately the burros ruin these washes for the small animals.

In 1972 the NWC Natural Resources Advisory Council and the cooperating agencies (BLM, Bureau of Sport Fisheries and Wildlife, and California Department of Fish and Game) unanimously decided to recommend immediate reduction of 200 burros in the Slate Range-Panamint Valley region. The emergency permit, a six-month permit to kill 200 burros, was granted after a first-hand look at the area by the biologist from the California Department of Agriculture. But the permit was not countersigned by the NWC Commander because of opposition to the reduction plan by a private citizen present at a BLM state advisory board meeting.

Starvation of the burros and destruction of their desert habitat is not the answer, and the NWC is seeking cooperation with the BLM and the Park Service for a management and burro control plan for the whole desert area, in order that the desert ecology can be restored to what it should be. But this goal is hard to accomplish as long as public pressure leans toward "leaving the burros alone" instead of controlling them.

Feral burros are so dense in some areas that they contest with cars for right of way on roads. In Alamo State Park in Arizona the burros are so thick that they are becoming accustomed to Park visitors, begging for handouts and raiding the garbage cans. There have been a few instances of park visitors being bitten by burros.

During a four year study of the bighorn sheep in California—a study conducted 1968-1972 by the BLM, U.S. Park Service and Calif. Department of Agriculture—investigations and observations were also made on the burros because of their impact on

Burros in California were protected by state law even before the passage of the Wild Horse and Burro Act.

the bighorns. Burro abundance and distribution were mapped. Fixed wing aircraft and helicopters were used, and much of the desert mountains were covered on foot. Seven of the 14 bighorn study areas in California have feral burros, and the burros have created problems in each of these areas.

In northeastern San Bernardino County it was found that burros have extended their range within the past 18 years, with a visible depletion of grass. At some springs, bighorn use has declined. Most bighorn sheep habitat that has had a heavy burro population for some years does not now have a resident bighorn population. Bighorn and burros, and deer and burros were observed at springs. The burros were dominant in each case, and the deer or bighorn sheep would not drink while the burros were near the spring.

In the Providence Mountains of San Bernardino County in July of 1969, a sheep and burro census was made, showing that 29 sheep and 47 burros came to water. The 1974 census at the same spring showed only 17 burros and 12 sheep. Because of extreme overgrazing, the burros (who had taken over this native home of the bighorn) were leaving. Sheep skulls and skeletons were found throughout the area, but very few burro remains were found. The burros had left the desert floor when it became overgrazed and had moved up to this rugged desert mountain where the feed was better—for awhile. After that feed, too, was gone, the burros moved on. But bighorn sheep do not move into new areas; they will not leave their ancestral home. They die first. A very vulnerable time is when the bighorn lambs are weaned. If feed is scarce, a lot of these weaned lambs don't make it.

In eastern Imperial County there is extreme

Burro area near Challis, Idaho; examples of soil erosion.

Light soil erosion on an overgrazed slope.
Intermediate stage of erosion—beginnings of gullies.

The desert part of northern Inyo County was designated as a burro sanctuary by the California legislature in 1957. Saline Valley and the mountain ranges that surround it have long had a dense burro population. The lower elevations have been wintering areas for bighorn in the past, as indicated by the presence of rock hunting blinds built by the Indians. Bighorn use the foot of the mountain ranges of similar topography in other areas. The conflict is not obvious in the Inyo Mountains, because at the present time there is very little overlap of burro and bighorn ranges; the bighorns have already left the lower elevations, where the burros are, and the burros are confined to these lower elevations by the nearly vertical cliffs. A remnant bighorn population of about 15 head range above the burros.

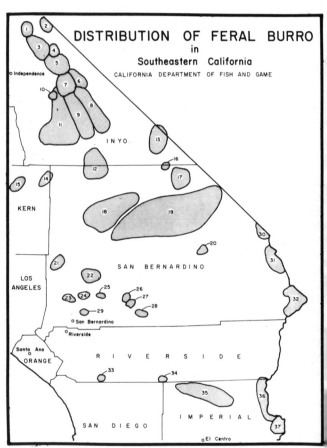

Distribution of feral burro in southeastern California.

competition between bighorn and burros, especially for water. The little bit of water in the area (in collection potholes, called *tinajas*, which hold a little rain water in the wetter winter months) is rapidly depleted by burros, after which they move on down to the Colorado River for the dry season. But bighorn, by their nature, avoid the dense brush near the river and are reluctant to leave the escape terrain in the mountains.

In northwestern San Bernardino and southwestern Inyo Counties there are two large military bases. Fort Irwin is free of burros while China Lake NWC has a large population, as already mentioned. The Avawatz Mountains at Fort Irwin have a good grass cover, a thrifty bighorn population, and no burros. The Argus Mountain Range in the NWC shows severe overgrazing and an absence of perennial grasses. No bighorn were seen during the investigation, and it is estimated that the population of bighorn is declining, with fewer than 15 remaining on that range.

In southeastern San Bernardino County the competition between bighorn sheep and burros is evident primarily in the areas near the Colorado River. The burros are continually expanding their range and in recent years have extended west of Highway 95 where formerly no burros existed. Areas where the burros have ranged are overgrazed and the

California—Feral Burro Inventory—1972

Map Area	County	Mountain Range	Area	Estimated Burro Numbers
1	Inyo	Inyo	Marble Canyon	25
2	Inyo	Last Chance	Sand Springs	25
3	Inyo	Inyo, Nelson, Saline	Saline Valley	350
4	Inyo	Panamint	Tin Mountain	100
5	Inyo	Panamint	Cottonwood, Hunter Mt.	500
6	Inyo	Panamint	Tucki	100
7	Inyo	Panamint	Wildrose	100
8	Inyo	Panamint	Butte Valley	350
9	Inyo	Panamint	Panamint Valley	150
10	Inyo	Argus	Panamint Spring	25
11	Inyo	Argus, Coso	China Lake, North Range	250
12	Inyo, San Bernardino	Slate, Brown Mt., Eagle Crags	China Lake, Mohave Range	200
13	Inyo	Nopah	Nopah Mts., Chicago Valley	25
14	San Bernardino	Lava	Lava	10
15	Kern	Sierra Nevada	Cache Peak	15
16	San Bernardino	Kingston	Kingston	3
17	San Bernardino	Clark, Mesquite	Clark, Mesquite Mts.	50
18	San Bernardino	Kelso	Kelso Peak, Old Dad Mt., Cima Dome	75
19	San Bernardino	Providence	New York, Granite	525
20	San Bernardino	Piute	Fenner Spring	25
21	San Bernardino	Kramer Hills	Kramer Spring	20
22	San Bernardino	Ord.	Ord Mts.	20
23	San Bernardino	San Bernardino Mts.		10
24	San Bernardino	San Bernardino Mts.	Rattlesnake Mt.	10
25	San Bernardino	San Bernardino Mts.	Box S Spring	2
26	San Bernardino	San Bernardino Mts.	Old Woman Spring	15
27	San Bernardino	San Bernardino Mts.	Mound Spring	15
28	San Bernardino	San Bernardino Mts.	Pioneertown	3
29	San Bernardino	San Bernardino Mts.	Slide Lake	5
30	San Bernardino	Dead	Dead Mts.	70
31	San Bernardino	Chemeheuvi	Chemehuevi	80
32	San Bernardino	Whipple	Whipple	100
33	Riverside	Santa Rosa	Rockhouse Basin	3
34	Riverside	Orcocopia	Dos Palmas Spring	4
35	Imperial	Chocolate	U. S. Navy Gunnery Range	30
36	Imperial	Chocolate	Palo Verde	50
37	Imperial	Chocolate	Picacho Peak	40
Not on map	Lassen County			100
				3,476

perennial grasses that are so important to the bighorn have been almost eliminated. During wet seasons the burros move onto the sheep range and compete with them for food and water, and then, when the water sources go dry, the burros retreat to areas next to the Colorado River. The bighorn sheep do not use the river and are thus forced to try to survive on depleted range and water, resulting in a smaller sheep herd.

In modern wildlife management practices one of the most important things is population stability. One of the factors that influences population stabil-

ity is competition with other species. The degree of competition that exists depends on the needs of the animal for survival and the availability of the basic substances required for survival. Many field biologists have studied the problem of competition between burros and bighorn sheep, and all of them agree that competition exists and is detrimental to the bighorn. As early as 1957, R.H. Bendt said that, "The most significant limiting factor affecting the sheep populations today (Grand Canyon National Park and Monument) involves the competition with feral burros for food and water."

That same year, R. E. Welles, studying the Death Valley bighorns, mentioned that "the question is often asked, what should be done to insure the status of the bighorn in Death Valley. The answer is simple: Remove all exotics and their influence from his biota and the bighorn will take care of himself . . . So the problem becomes one of how many burros and how much human encroachment can be permitted if a healthy status of the bighorn is to be maintained."

Richard Weaver, after studying the effects of burros on desert water supplies, wrote in 1959 that "burros can and do totally usurp water supplies. Natural and artificial tanks that depend on rainfall to replenish their water supply have been drained dry by the burro, leaving no water for other animals . . . In some instances the trampling of burros making heavy use of a spring may reduce or entirely stop the flow of water." Another biologist, after studying the effects of wild burros on Death Valley bighorns in 1959, wrote that "when a severely limited environment is invaded by a large, non-native animal with a fairly high breeding potential and no natural enemies, new pressures on the environment are inevitable. Some native plants and animals give ground. Such an invader is the wild burro of Death Valley, a region where the severe limitations of food and water are self-evident."

Studies in California conducted around springs have indicated that burros require three times as much water as bighorns, and also several times as much dry forage per animal. The bighorns prefer grass, and all ranges with good bighorn populations have good stands of perennial grasses. This grass is often eliminated within the range of the burros, especially if burro numbers are uncontrolled.

Welles and Welles, in a MS thesis on bighorns in Death Valley, (1959) stated that the "status of the feral burro is regrettably clear and has finally fallen into proper perspective . . . his effect on forage, vegetation, wildlife in general, erosion control and watersheds is increasingly and alarmingly clear. Some areas on the western slopes (of the Panamint Range) have already been so devastated that they will not recover in our lifetime."

In a later publication, they said that "without controls the burro population would logically be expected to exceed the carrying capacity of the range within a very short time. At this point a drought would turn a critical condition into an emergency, and under emergency circumstances, the burro becomes a desperate competitior with other wildlife species."

Feral burros use many of the same forage plants as the desert bighorn and the desert deer, as evidenced by studies conducted by examining the stomach contents of these animals. They use many of the same watering places and seek shade in caves and under ledges that were used by deer and sheep long before the first burro was turned loose in the desert. Where water is scarce, a herd of feral burros can rapidly deplete the supply.

According to John Russo of the Arizona Fish and Game Department, "This has been seen numerous times during my work with desert bighorn sheep. When the water supply is gone, the feral burros move off. Sheep, although placed in additional stress, can fend for themselves. Deer will generally stand around the dried waterhole and unless rain occurs, the deer will die."

Burros are having a clearly adverse effect on certain desert areas and unless we can get some good control of their population increase, these burros will continue to drastically alter the native desert ecosystems. Do we want these ecosystems preserved in a natural form or do we want to allow the burros to continue to modify them? We really have no choice. The burro populations will have to be managed, or the burro himself will ultimately starve. In the process, undernourished animals will be hit by disease, the vigor of the entire population will be reduced, and, of course, much of the native wildlife and plant life of these desert areas will be eliminated.

Obviously the living entities are not the only loss. Damage to soil and watershed are perhaps more irreparable losses. On the Bandelier National Monument, for example, it was estimated that 70,000 pounds of soil were being lost per year. The burro is a definite contributor to this sort of watershed, plant and soil damage and subsequent erosion. As stated by Dr. Milford Fletcher of the National Park Service, "there are renewable resources and there are nonrenewable resources, and the soil is a completely, totally nonrenewable resource. Once it's gone, you're out of business for a thousand years. We can't take that kind of damage."

Burros were first seen in the Bandelier National Monument in 1936 and had increased so rapidly by the 1940's that 50 out of about 100 were destroyed to protect the Park's natural features. By 1974 the burro population had increased again to about 130, research showing that there was a high soil loss and change in vegetative cover, primarily because of the overgrazing. Fifty-two burros were destroyed that year by shooting, and further research continued on the burros that remained.

Disturbance of desert soil in the form of heavy trampling and trailing accelerates erosion. Much of the rainfall that occurs in southwestern desert areas comes as severe thunderstorms that wash away disturbed soils. Bare soil in desert areas often forms a desert "pavement" which is a gravel or stone surface. This desert pavement, sometimes only one pebble thick, protects the underlying finer soil from normal wind or water erosion. Other soil binders are crusts of dissolved minerals, formed by evaporation. If the soil is disturbed by burro trampling, it is often opened up for erosion.

Soil compaction occurs in areas of heavy burro use, such as the sections of ground near springs, shady areas, or trails. Rainfall does not penetrate these compacted soils, and no plant cover can exist. The aridness of the desert is intensified by the burro. The amount of soil disturbance has been measured in some areas of Death Valley. Ninety-seven to 100% of the bare soil areas were disturbed in plots within one mile of Wildrose Spring. Five miles away from the water hole, 20 to 25% of the bare soils were disturbed. Compaction of soil near springs often reduces the water flow and has been known to dry up a water source.

The plants native to our Southwestern deserts evolved without the presence of a large aggressive herbivore, the burro. In the 100 years or so since the burro has been foraging in the desert, drastic changes have occurred to the vegetative cover. The burro's preferred plants are often eliminated near water sources and even for several miles around. Thus there is direct competition from burros with all sorts of animals, including rodents and ground-nesting birds, which need suitable cover for protection from predators.

Many concerned individuals who are familiar with desert ecology ask why these feral burros (in areas other than National Parks) are exempt from controls, being allowed to spoil the land and kill out the native plants and wildlife. The only reason is that well-intentioned, sympathetic groups of animal lovers, and a few conservationists who were not fully informed were instrumental in having the present protection law passed. Emotion and sentimentality do not enter into the management of domestic cattle, sheep, or horses on the public lands; the number allowed depends on the available feed and the needs of, and impact on, the native plants and animals. The feral burro should also be thus controlled.

The burro problem on our western deserts is a classic example of the natural ecology being disrupted by man's introduction of a foreign animal, and then giving that animal full protection under federal law. Fully protecting the burro and not controlling his numbers means wiping out the desert bighorn sheep and other native life in critical areas.

Burro area: severe erosion.

The continued existence of many reptiles, birds, rodents and other animals that have co-existed in the desert for thousands, maybe millions of years, are now seriously threatened.

In the words of Mary DeDecker, speaking for the California Native Plant Society, the southern California Botanists and the California Natural Areas Coordinating Council (December 1975 meeting of the national advisory board for wild horses and burros), several rare plant species are already endangered, and "the great amount of vegetation destroyed on water borders and on trails lacing the slopes is equally serious. The rapid acceleration of this damage is frightening because much of it is a permanent loss. Complete elimination of burros is recommended for most of the Southwest. They can be justified only in 'sacrificial sites' where limited numbers might be maintained for public interest. It reflects a sad sense of values which allows such abuse to the special habitats of this arid land."

At the same advisory board meeting, the California Wildlife Federation and its member councils, including Southern Council of Conservation Clubs expressed their concern with the impact of feral burros on the desert areas of southeastern California:

We view with frustration and a growing deep-seated anger the continued devastation of our land by the politically protected burro, a devastation that has continued unchecked for years after the seriousness of the problem had been officially and publicly noted. The competitive and destructive potential of the burro was not unknown in 1971. It had been testified to much earlier. Viewed from the ecological aspect in this light, the imposition of the present State and Federal laws restricting management of the burro in the southeastern desert ranges of California was a completely irresponsible act . . . Ecologically sound management of our land, water, vegetation, and wildlife resources requires that they be managed as a comprehensive whole, with each part relating in a balanced manner to each other part. Inflexible one-animal-biased management is ecologically unsound, and, in the case of the feral burro on our desert valleys and mountain ranges, clearly destructive to our other resources.

Miriam A. Romero, who with her husband spent 2½ years studying the burro situation in the American southwest—traveling thousands of miles looking at burro habitat, interviewing scientists, government agency personnel, conservationists and animal protectionists—also made a statement to the wild horse and burro advisory board:

I am convinced that the burro situation has reached crisis proportions in the Panamint Range in Inyo County, California. To delay control of burros in this mountain range would cause severe overgrazing to the extent that the land will take centuries to come back to normal, if indeed, it ever can again. While the National Park Service is moving ahead on plans for burro management, and the Navy has conducted environmental studies on burro habitats in the Naval Weapons Center, the BLM has not been implementing PL 92-195 in this area. While we do recognize the problems of manpower and funding, nonetheless, something must be done to eliminate the burros in the Panamint Range which are causing the ecosytem degradation . . . There are many areas in the Mojave Desert where burros have invaded bighorn habitat. I recommend that the BLM begin to clearly identify these areas and then begin planning for removal of burros from bighorn habitat areas . . .

PS 92-195 says that where the burro is that this land should be used 'principally, but not exclusively' for burro habitat and protection. I object to the word 'principally'. I do not think that the principal use of bighorn habitat should be for burros; nor do I think that the principal use of land where endangered species of native flora and fauna exist, or where there are sites protected under the Antiquities Act should be for burros. It is evident that the authors of the law did not know nor understand the geographical distribution of burros, nor the problems that the wording of the law would cause insofar as it deals with burros.

The Sierra Club has also shown concern regarding the adverse impact of burros on desert ecology and species like the bighorn, suggesting that the various agencies enter cooperative agreements for managing and controlling the burros in the Panamint Range, and give top priority for burro management in the Mojave Desert. The Sierra Club also recommended that the BLM immediately control burros in areas that are bighorn sheep habitat, since the bighorn in California is a threatened species. The

desert bighorns in California are fully protected and there is no hunting season on them, for they are becoming increasingly rare in the California desert. In the Sierra Club's view, the existing burro herds are the results of man's actions, a man-made problem. Therefore man must control the burro populations.

The Sierra Club recommended the use of firearms by competent federal agents or their appointees as a humane method of reducing burro populations, and that burro numbers be maintained at a level that would minimize their impact on native habitat. In the Sierra Club's opinion, the burros must be eliminated from all areas where they pose a threat to the habitat or to endangered plants or animals, and from all areas protected by the Antiquities Act, and from all National Parks and Monuments. The Sierra Club also recommended that PL 92-195 be amended to apply only to wild horses.

Mr. William Reavley, Regional Executive Director of the National Wildlife Federation, agreed. Burros, in his words, "are in no way indigenous to the American continent and are a part of the tremendous influence man exerts on a fragile environment . . . proper management must be based upon scientific fact and not upon prejudiced information or emotion . . . To do this will require changes in federal laws, and the expenditure of the necessary funds to do the job. It is a relatively simple matter. The small number of wild horses and burros removed from the range since the passage of the Act clearly indicate the federal law is too restrictive. In addition, there has been insufficient personnel and funds assigned to this project. As a consequence,

Many conservation-minded goups, including the Sierra Club, recognize the need for burro control in our western deserts, and strongly recommend burro reduction or elimination. The hardy burro outcompetes with native animals for food and habitat.

range deterioration has already taken place and destructive effects are inevitable."

Yet public opinion was outraged at the idea of getting rid of some of the burros. Not understanding the desperate need to control this exotic feral animal (and some of them probably not wanting to understand), people began to protest proposed control measures. The Wild Horse and Burro Act does not apply to the National Parks, and plans were made to begin destroying excess burros in several southwestern Parks and Monuments. The National Wildlife Federation in Washington, D.C. fully supported the National Park Service plan to reduce the burros. The reduction for the Grand Canyon was scheduled for February of 1977. But this program was delayed for an unknown length of time because of public reaction. Three private interest groups—the AHPA, the HSUS, and the Committee to Save the Grand Canyon Burros—filed suit in the U.S. District Court, seeking to hold up the plans for killing the excess burros.

"This outrageous act of extermination at the taxpayers' expense would turn the Grand Canyon into a giant butcher shop and cannot be permitted," said Joan Blue, president of AHPA. And ISPMB alerted its membership, urging them to write to the senators and representatives of Arizona and to the Park Service, protesting the "wholesale slaughter". A blizzard of emotional "save the burro" letters made the Park's burro control ranger an instant villain.

Because of the public reaction, the new Secretary of Interior, Cecil Andrus, suspended the shooting of the Grand Canyon burros, acknowledging the public's interest in the burros, as well as the widespread misunderstanding of the burro problem. Action would be delayed until accurate statistics and "proof of damage" could be gathered. The Grand Canyon National Park began putting together an environmental impact statement on the burros, and any control measures would have to wait until this was finished. The intensive study is costing about $1000 per burro in the park.

During the summer of 1978 several experiments were conducted for finding acceptable means of burro control. Rangers tried removing them alive, hoping to sedate them and fly them out of the canyon—at tremendous cost in time, money and manpower. One team of rangers, after considerable effort and a long day's work, managed to shoot three burros with an immobilizing drug, but two of the burros died. The third, slung in a cargo net, went for a $250 an hour helicopter ride out of the canyon.

In another experiment, cowboys rounded up 12 burros from one of the more accessible areas, and the animals were taken to an auction in Phoenix. They brought an average of $11 a head. It had cost $450 a head to round them up.

These experiments convinced the Park Service that there is still only one practical solution—the burros must be destroyed. But convincing the public of this fact is a tough job.

In 1977 Park Service officials went ahead with reduction of burros in Bandelier National Monument where a forest fire had destroyed more than a third of the area. Steady riflemen, chosen for their lack of what a federal official called "the Bambi complex," were dropped by helicopter into the wilderness of the Monument to shoot some of the burros. Burros, deer and elk had been driven by the fire to the lower canyons and mesas that dead-end at the Rio Grande River. Smoke was still rising from the charred area as 15 rangers moved in and reduced the burros.

The only real answer to the emotion-packed controversy over these animals is to acquaint more people with the facts about our Southwest, and the fragility of our desert ecology. Not until more of the public understands the crucial situation that is unfolding, and the responsibility we have as guardians and managers to protect this natural system (rather than destroying it with our feral animals)—not until then will we be able to truly control and manage the burro in a way that we can still leave some of the desert healthy and intact for future generations to enjoy. For until more people realize our urgent responsibilities in this area, any real attempts to manage the burro will only be thwarted at every turn by emotional, uninformed and very narrow interest groups. Only time will tell whether or not we can overcome emotion and begin to manage these animals in a sane and responsible manner. And time is running out.

17

Competition

We mentioned competition between feral burros and native wildlife in the previous chapter. Now let's look briefly at the problem of competition as it involves wild horses. Horses range in different areas, in most cases, and compete with different animals. The burro competes most obviously with the bighorn sheep. The wild horse competes most obviously with domestic livestock on the range, but also competes to some degree (and in some geographic areas, to a significant degree) with wildlife such as deer, elk, antelope, and occasionally bighorn sheep.

Wild horses cannot be considered and managed as a unique and separate entity on our ranges, but must be looked at as a part of the entire ecosystem in which they live: the soil, the grass and other vegetation, and all the other creatures that depend on that vegetation. The horse is non-migratory and may travel no more than a mile or maybe up to seven or eight miles from his home range. He moves to higher or lower elevation somewhat with the seasons, but basically grazes the same area continuously, leaving no chance for the plants to rest or to produce at their best. Confinement into restricted areas by the settlement and development of the West and other aspects of civilization has altered the

"natural" conditions for the wild horse and he can no longer change his range and move to new areas when one becomes overgrazed. These confined horse herds, although less healthy because of crowding and malnutrition, still survive long enough to destroy most of their range before they themselves would begin to die of starvation.

Any increase in horse numbers above the carrying capacity of the range is a threat to the wildlife and livestock with which the horses must compete for food. But the people who want the wild horse protected and allowed to increase without control are usually not alarmed over this kind of increase in horse numbers (not being aware of the balance that has to exist between the food supply and the consumer), and are merely happy to see the horses making such a good "comeback".

Horse protectionists want to leave the population control of horse herds up to Mother Nature, with no interference by man, but they don't realize that the horse is in an unnatural situation to begin with. Nor do they understand that Nature is indifferent and can be very cruel. She balances and takes care of everything, yes. But it may take awhile. She takes care of things in cycles, in terms of hundreds or even thousands of years or more. There may be some harsh situations in the meantime—like starved horses or wildlife.

By the time the horse's reproductive abilities are slowed down enough to limit his population growth (slowed by malnutrition and poor breeding conditions, affecting the mare's fertility and her ability to carry a foal to full term and then to feed it), many horses will be already dying, and few foals will survive. And most of the wildlife species that inhabit the same range, depending on some of the same feed, will already be gone. This is not a humane management method. The people who think we can have an increasing horse herd on our public lands without seriously harming our native wildlife populations had better take a closer look.

During the last few years several comprehensive studies have been done on competition, determining exactly what plants in a geographic area make up the horse's diet, and of what percent of his diet, at different seasons, these plants consist. Dietary overlaps have been studied, determining how much similarity and overlap exists in the diets of wild horses and other herbivores in the area, such as the native wildlife.

Several BLM districts with wild horses conducted dietary studies, collecting fresh fecal samples during the various seasons of the year. These samples were sent to Colorado State University, where they were analyzed under a microscope and the various plant particles (or cells) identified, under the direction of Richard M. Hansen, professor of range science at Colorado State University.

Some of the studies are still underway, but results have been obtained already on the studies conducted at several BLM districts, including the horses at Challis, Idaho; horses in southern New Mexico; in the Piceance Basin in Colorado, the Red Desert in Wyoming, and on the Granite Range near Elko, Nevada.

The number of free-roaming horses has been increasing since 1971. Consequently wherever there is a need to manage them it is helpful if their food habits are known—to prevent destruction of plant cover on their ranges and to keep up maximum plant production. One of the earliest dietary studies was done on the White Sands Missile Range in southern New Mexico, where wild horses share the range with exotic imported Gemsboks (*Oryx gazella*). The wild horse population was estimated to be between 150 and 200 during the spring of 1974. The herd originated from ranch horses and there are still some that wear brands. The horses roam widely during wet seasons when water is available in roadside ditches and shallow depressions, but during dry periods they remain concentrated near the only available water source—an alkaline stream flowing from springs.

Fecal samples for both horses and Gemsboks were collected from fresh manure each month from June 1973 through May 1974. There were 20 different kinds of plants and a few unidentified plants found in the diets of the horses. The most heavily used foods were Russianthistle (29% of the diet), dropseed (21%), mesquite (16%), Junegrass (12%), spangletop (6%), and saltbush (5%). Wheatgrass and grama were important foods in the horses' diets only in the spring and summer. Saltbush was eaten from fall through spring. Mesquite pods and leaves made up 53% of the diet in September and only 2% (just leaves) of the diet in March. Horses on the southern Arizona ranges seem to be fond of velvet mesquite beans and may contribute to the spreading and establishment of mesquite by passing the seeds in their droppings.

The horse diets in this study contained a lower percentage (50%) of grasses and grasslike plants than the horse diets from other areas, such as Montana, Idaho, Nevada, Utah, Wyoming and Colorado. This inclination exists probably because this particular range had less grasses. Up until recent years very little has been known about the food habits of range horses, and until more studies are done, the food preferences of horses cannot really be predicted for different types of range.

In the New Mexico study on the White Sands Missile Range, it was found that mesquite, grasses and Russianthistle were the major foods of both the Gemsboks and the horses. Without a managed herd size, the wild horses could become serious competitors with the Gemsbok for feed. During the 1973–1974 study it was observed that most of the mature mares had foals, the herd was healthy and increasing at a rapid rate.

In northwestern Colorado the diets of wild horses, cattle and mule deer were studied. Long-time residents of the area agreed that the wild horses were increasing and the mule deer numbers were decreasing; there is growing concern about the effects the wild horses and domestic cattle may have had on the declining deer population. Much of this geographic area is probably destined for oil shale development and subsequent reclamation. If revegetation is to provide food for the herbivores of that area, the important foods in their diets should be determined.

Five study areas were used at each of three different altitude-vegetation zones. Many plants occur in all three zones, but some plants are more abundant at either the highest or lowest level. Wild horses lived year-around in each zone. Cattle graze

In many areas wild horses compete with wildlife for feed and habitat. Mule deer on horse range near Challis, Idaho.

Elk on winter range. Elk and horses have very similar diets.

In the Red Desert in Wyoming it was found that there was more dietary overlap. Much of the same vegetation types were used by horses, cattle, sheep, elk and antelope, often in the same areas and during the same seasons. The study area was located in southwestern Wyoming, in the eastern part of the Red Desert, not far from Rock Springs. Aerial surveys and ground observations in 1975 showed that the area had about 800 wild horses, 850 pronghorn antelope, and 195 elk. Because it is a wintering area for elk and antelope, seasonal migration increases the winter population to about 1400 antelope and 475 elk. In addition, the BLM licenses 679 cattle and 27,000 sheep in this area. Much of the area is sagebrush and grass, saltbush, or rabbitbrush.

The average seasonal diet overlaps were highest between horses, cattle and elk. These three species were very similar in their diets, and not very similar to antelope. Sheep diets were most similar to cattle and least similar to antelope. Wheatgrass and nee-

On every cattle range where horses exist, the horses compete directly with the cattle for forage. These horses and cattle share the same range near Challis, Idaho.

on all of the areas from early July until late September. Resident deer herds occur in each zone from mid-April until early November. Migratory deer concentrate in the lower elevations from early November until mid-April.

The plant composition of deer, cattle and horse diets was determined by microscopic examination of fecal material, and similarity of the diets was calculated. Wild horses and cattle had much more similar diets than did horses and deer or cattle and deer, and diets of all three had more similarities when they were within the same vegetation zone than they did when in different vegetation zones. The only real area in which wild horses and deer ate much of the same food was in the mountain shrub zone (the highest elevation). It was concluded from these studies that the horse and cattle diets were not significantly responsible for the decline in the deer population in that area.

dlegrass each constituted 11% to 46% of the average annual diets of all of these herbivores except antelope. Wild horses, cattle and elk continued the same basic diet from season to season, whereas sheep and antelope had a more diversified diet, shifting in summer away from the plants that thickened and toughened when mature.

A large percentage of the diets of wild horses, cattle and elk were the same species of grasses and sedges. Saltbush was an important food in seasonal diets for all five of the animals studied. Each animal ate a variety of plants each season, but the bulk of the diet within a season usually consisted of less than six major plant species.

A diet study conducted in 1976-1978 on the Granite Range in northeastern Nevada found a 3% dietary overlap between wild horses and deer and a 17% overlap between horses and cattle. This area was selected for study because it was used by large numbers of cattle, horses and mule deer. Five hundred cattle graze the area from May until November. Approximately 200 wild horses were year-round residents at the start of the study in 1976, but removal of claimed horses from September 1976 to September 1977 reduced the population to about 160. Further reductions were carried out by the BLM with the use of a helicopter. The area is used as winter range by 400-800 deer.

At Challis, Idaho there is fairly strong competition between wild horses and domestic cattle during summer months when the cattle are on the range, especially around watering areas, in wet meadow areas, and in other habitat overlaps. These areas show heavy use and overgrazing. In competition between horses and wildlife, the fecal analysis showed the greatest dietary overlap between elk and wild horses. Elk generally use the horse area in winter and in early spring, and their diets consist mainly of grasses and shrubs during this time of the year, like the horses.

Competition between the wild horses and antelope is significant in the fall and winter when the horses are using less grass and adding forbs and browse to their diets. Deer and wild horses compete in the spring when the deer and horses both begin to eat the new green grasses, and a little in the winter when horses eat sagebrush. Idaho Fish and Game Department studies showed only 11 fawns per 100 antelope in the wild horse area in 1976 and only 9 fawns per 100 in 1977. Right across the highway on similar terrain except for the absence of wild horses, the counts ran approximately 50-55 fawns per hundred antelope. The Challis area was closed to antelope hunting in 1978 because of the decline in fawn numbers.

Antelope near Challis. Competition between wild horses and antelope on this range is significant in the fall and winter when the horses are using less grass and more forbs and browse.

In an article by Joan Blue of the American Horse Protection Association that was printed in a horse magazine in October, 1976, Mrs. Blue stated that there is "no reliable data to support the argument that wild horses pose a dire threat to rangelands or wildlife habitat," and went on to say that "what data there is indicates that wild horses never eat precisely the same foods eaten by cattle, sheep, antelope or other animals."

This is often the point taken by wild horse protectionists, attempting to justify ever-increasing horse herds on public lands. Either these horse protectionists are not aware of the in-depth dietary studies that have been going on since 1973, or they are ignoring them. The studies done by the various BLM districts, in conjunction with Colorado State University (supported by funds from Colorado State Universtiy Experiment Station and the BLM), identifying the various grasses, shrubs and other plants the horses were eating, and comparing the dietary overlaps with the other hoofed herbivores on the ranges, have been very comprehensive.

Several other wildlife experts in separate studies have also shown that there is dietary overlap between horses, elk, mule deer, antelope and bighorn sheep—especially in some geographic areas when the horses are on winter range. One of the men who has done considerable research in this field is James M. Peek, a professor of wildlife studies at the University of Idaho. He has had 19 years' experience in wildlife-habitat relationship studies in Montana (8 years), Minnesota (7 years), and Idaho (4 years), and has a Ph.D. in Wildlife management. During the past few years he has done studies in the Challis, Idaho, area—studying bighorn sheep ecology, responses of big game to a rest-rotation livestock grazing system, and becoming very familiar with the Challis wild horse range.

He has stated that the wild horse herd must be regulated to keep it compatible with other aspects of the complex range ecosystem, which includes the wildlife and the forage base they all depend on. In his words, "The potential for competition for forage between horses and the native big game is very great in this area, especially on winter and spring range. While numbers of big game are either precariously low, as in the case of the bighorn and are therefore completely protected, or are subject to judicious hunter harvest as in the case of deer and elk, wild horses have been allowed to increase without any checks, and without regard to the effects on indigenous wildlife. At a time when efforts to intensively manage livestock and improve rangeland conditions are being made, and when the data base on wildlife habitat relationships is being rapidly expanded, no management of wild horse numbers has been implemented."

From his studies he has determined that "grasses comprise a large component of the diet of elk, mule deer, bighorn sheep and wild horses. Bluebunch wheatgrass is a preferred species for all four at some time during the year. Big sagebrush is important in the winter diet of elk, mule deer, and horses. On our study area, we observe wild horses in winter and spring on range used also by mule deer in the spring . . . We thus have data establishing the presence of horses on critical spring and winter ranges for mule deer and elk, when use of the same forage species occurs.

Continuing expansion of horse numbers on presently used areas will become an increasingly critical factor in the survival of deer and elk. As competition for forage increases to where range deterioration occurs, associated wildlife species dependent upon the grasses and shrubs for nesting or cover, including the songbirds, small mammals, blue grouse, and sage grouse, and those species dependent upon the birds and small mammals for prey, including hawks and eagles, will inevitably also be adversely affected."

In the White Mountains, a desert mountain range on the California-Nevada border, a growing herd of wild horses in the Inyo National Forest is competing strongly with native bighorn sheep. White Mountain Peak is just over 14,000 feet high and wild horses range on the eastern slopes while the bighorn use the more rugged western slopes, but in the summer their ranges overlap on the crest. About 25 years ago, when there were fewer horses in the area, there were often sheep seen low down in the foothills on the east side, but now the sheep stay on the crest and the west side. This is a strong indication that the horses may be pushing the sheep back into a smaller area. Horses are found at all elevations on the east side, occupying all the vegetative types within that territory. Some of the ridges and sidehills get very heavy horse use and the vegetation and soil condition is deteriorating.

Studies were conducted 1972-1977 to determine horse numbers, distribution, rate of population increase, range forage condition, grazing capacity, and competition betwen the horses and other animals. It was determined that there were more animals than the range could support and it was deteriorating. In one area where overgrazing is severe, cattle numbers have been reduced, but before complete recovery can occur, a balance between horse numbers and forage must also be established. Capture of part of the 230 head was planned for late 1977.

A columnist in a Nevada newspaper criticized the BLM (August 28, 1976) for buying advertisements encouraging people to adopt a wild horse to keep them from starvation, while not mentioning that some of the wildlife are also starving to death. The people who got the Wild Horse and Burro Act passed "did not take into consideration the wild horse will consume 5 or 6 times what a deer will or 6 to 7 times what an antelope will, and so on down the line. The Federal Government was pressured into passing a ridiculous law by those who call themselves conservationists but who did not take the time to consider the impact on existing wildlife."

He mentioned that the Sheldon Antelope Range in northwestern Nevada was becoming critical, wild horses outnumbering the antelope nearly 2 to 1 and eating them off the range. He pointed out that the antelope herd will remain stable while the wild horses increase 20% per year. He asserted that Arizona is in danger of losing a large part of its bighorn sheep population because of the competition from wild burros. "In some areas of Arizona," he noted, "the burros outnumber the sheep three or more to one. Survival of burros he noted, on a yearly basis is near 100% while sheep survival is approximately 20%."

In district after district there are ample examples of competition between wild horses and wildlife. Dietary overlaps between horses and hoofed herbivores are well documented, but the smaller animals should not be overlooked either. Rabbit and rodent populations periodically increase to high levels and consume significant amounts of forage and plant seeds.

Some degree of competition for forage exists among all herbivores. Sage grouse habitat can be adversely affected by poor production of perennial forbs. And so it goes. The whole wildlife community is dependent upon a relative balance, with no one species, over-eating to the point of destroying its food supply and habitat and that of other animals.

A plant and animal community in nature develops slowly over a long period of time, under the controlling factors of climate, the geological materials, and the available forms of life. It may take centuries for a particular plant community to develop, and at each stage in its development there is a balance of some sort between the animals eating the vegetation and the vegetation using the soil. The animals that eat the plants determine in many ways the direction this developing plant community goes, depending on the diets and preferences of the animals.

The plant communities on our western ranges may have been relatively stable a few hundred years ago, with only the ups and downs of native animal populations that grazed them. But now we have a plant community that has the impact of an introduced exotic—domestic livestock. The horse is a feral member of this group of introduced exotics.

There are some definite changes that occur in any plant community when an exotic is introduced. This is especially so when the exotic population is allowed to increase rapidly in a short time. The plant communities begin to change because of the grazing pressure. The preferred plants of the grazing animal, if overgrazed, tend to lose vigor, very little growth takes place, and reproduction of the plant is lowered. These plants decline in number and the grazing animal has to change diet to a less preferred plant, and the process keeps repeating itself.

A difference between the wild and domestic animals should be mentioned. In most cases the wild animals do not have the ability to switch from one plant (if it is the major part of their diet) to another very rapidly. In experiments with deer, where deer and domestic livestock were put into strong competition, the livestock were able to change their food habits, but the deer did not and usually died off.

The domestic animal is the product of selective breeding and controlled evolution in recent times, bred to utilize a wide variety of forages and bred to do a wide variety of work. Some experiments with cattle in Texas showed that you can take cattle directly off the range where they've been eating native plants, put them into a feedlot to eat 9 pounds of grain-based concentrate a day for six weeks, and then put them back out on the range again, with very little adverse effect. Horses, too, can be switched fairly easily from one type of feed to another, and can utilize a wide variety of forage, as compared to our native wildlife.

The native animals have their ecological niche pretty well established, being well adjusted to their geographic areas and plant varieties that they have been eating for the past several hundred years. But if you suddenly add a large and highly competitive exotic to this habitat, an exotic who perhaps eats out the preferred plants of that species of native wildlife, the exotic will then shift to another plant type and survive, while the native animal cannot shift as well and usually loses out. Domestic animals usually outcompete because they have a much broader range of plants that can be eaten for survival.

The horse does very well on our western ranges. He can graze very close to the ground with his particular teeth structure; he can paw through snow in winter, and he can utilize a wide variety of plants and get by. He's also large enough to resist most of the predators. Dr. Thadis Box, wild horse and burro advisory board member in 1975-76, has called the horse a harvesting machine with "destructive poten-

Wildlife biologists, range managers and ecologists agree that we have a management responsibility—to control wild horses and keep them in proper balance with their range and with the other animals that use the range.

195

tial that is probably exceeded by no other domestic animal, sheep and goats included."

A controlled population that does not exceed the carrying capacity of the range does not destroy its range; in balanced numbers, this population does not reduce the carrying capacity of that range—the plants are not overgrazed and do not lose vigor, and continue to produce year after year. But as soon as the grazing animals exceed the carrying capacity, changes in the vegetation due to overgrazing start to appear, and the carrying capacity is lowered due to die-out of some of the preferred plants. If the population of grazers continues to grow, the plants left on the range are the ones that are least palatable, and some of the wild animals begin to be crowded out, dying off. The exotic grazer manages to survive awhile longer, being able to shift his diet to less and less palatable plants. But sooner or later he, too begins to suffer from lack of food and starts to die off, after overgrazing the various types of vegetation so badly that erosion, soil loss and watershed deterioration are pronounced. In the final analysis, the horse has the ability, both from an evolutionary standpoint and a practical management standpoint, to do himself in and completely decimate his range in the process.

As Dr. Thadis Box pointed out:

There is an argument going on in the scientific community the world over dealing with 'to manage or not to manage', 'to control or not to control'. This is going on in Yellowstone National Park with elk, it's going on in a national park in Kenya with elephants, it's going on the world over and you can find very reputable biologists on both sides of the argument. It depends upon what philosophical stance you take. But the point I am trying to make is that even though you have this argument with native animals, this same argument does not apply to a feral exotic population as we have seen with the goat in Hawaii, with the feral hog in the southeastern United States, and with the feral donkey and camel in Australia; the chances of habitat destruction and severe soil deterioration are much greater with a feral domestic animal than it is with a native wild animal.

Our management responsibility is clear. In protecting the wild horse (or burro) we must also protect him from himself, keeping him from overgrazing his range to the detriment of himself and all the other animals that share it with him. In areas that support competing forms of life we must make sure that we manage the populations so that there will be enough feed for all, and a continuing healthy range that will continue to support all of these forms of life in the future.

EXHIBIT A

Table 1. Comparison of diets for wild horses, mule deer, elk, and bighorn sheep on the East Fork Salmon River, near Challis, Idaho.

	% Browse	% Grass	% Forbs	Important forage species
Elk (winter 1975-76)[1]	29.9	67.5	2.5	Bluebunch wheatgrass, Idaho fescue, big sagebrush
Mule deer (March 1975)[1]	43.6	39.8	16.4	Big sagebrush, threetip sagebrush, bluebunch wheatgrass
Mule deer (May-June 1975)[1]	17.1	75.5	7.4	Bluebunch wheatgrass, bluegrasses
Horses (summer)[2]	4.1	68.6	23.3	Bluebunch wheatgrass, phlox, Idaho fescue
Horses (winter)[2]	13.8	61.5	29.7	Bluebunch wheatgrass, phlox, big sagebrush
Bighorn sheep (winter)[3]	7	82	11	

[1]Unpublished data of Craig T. Kvale, graduate assistant, College of Forestry, Wildlife and Range Sciences, University of Idaho.

[2]Based on data presented in Draft Environmental Impact Statement, Proposed Domestic Livestock Grazing Program for the Challis Planning Unit, BLM. June 1976. Page 2-124.

[3]From Lauer, J. L., and J. M. Peek. 1976. Big game-livestock relationships on the bighorn sheep winter range, East Fork Salmon River, Idaho Forest, Wildlife and Range Experiment Station Bulletin 25. University of Idaho, Moscow. (In press.)

18

The Propaganda Extravaganza

During recent years there has been a tremendous surge of interest in, and publicity about, the wild horses, almost all of it in a sympathetic vein. Most of the publicity has urged people to participate in the move to convince Congress, federal agencies and one another that the wild horse needs even more "protection" and that other interests on the public lands (particularly the ranchers who pasture domestic livestock out there, and hunters, sportsmen and wildlife interests who want to see the native wildlife managed in such a way as to ensure healthy, continuing herds) should move over and make more "room" for the expanding wild horse herds.

Many individuals and several different horse protection groups have been working for a number of years to insure federal protection for the wild horse and burro. But during the last few years the battlers for "wild horse rights" have split ranks, some of them trying to work with the agencies responsible for protection and management of the horses, and some of them charging along on an extreme course that still sees these government agencies as enemies to fight at every turn.

Some of the conscientious and concerned people who initiated the push for wild horse protection are now working hand in hand with the BLM and FS, in an attempt to manage the horses and burros in a way ultimately beneficial for both animals. But the extremists in the horse protection movement want NO management of these animals; they want "protection" for horses and burros at all costs—wanting to let the herds expand unchecked, to the detriment of all other public land values and ultimately to the detriment of the wild horses themselves. And they have set in motion a tremendous campaign to produce sympathy for the wild horses and financial support for their protection efforts.

Their emotional campaign is having far-reaching effects. Many of the people influenced by their crusade have no prior experience with horses, no knowledge of the problems on our western ranges, and are easily swayed to join the crusade. Wild horses have long been a romantic subject in our American heritage; we have a vast "western tradition" that idolizes the wild horse in western fiction, movies, children's toys, coloring books and so on. Horse books, movies and programs that are unrealistic but entertaining are what our younger generations have grown up on. "True West" cowboy stories, imaginary mustangs and Walt Disney adventures are fine—as long as they are recognized as entertainment rather than fact. But to our modern generation—who grew up after the advent of the automobile and the "passing of the horse" they are more often accepted as the real thing.

It's easy to understand why the American people

have been so easily influenced to jump on the bandwagon in support of the wild horse. The wild horse mystique holds a special something in our hearts. But the sad thing is that at the same time people are being influenced to be sympathetic toward the wild horse, they are also being encouraged to join ranks against his so-called enemies—the ranchers, wildlife enthusiasts, sportsmen, and government personnel who are doing their very best with very limited means to try to manage the ever-increasing wild horse herds.

Extremist horse protection groups like the American Horse Protection Association, based in Washington D.C., and the Humane Society of the United States (not the American Humane Society;* HSUS is a more fanatic, Washington D.C. based organization that has more extreme views, such as trying to ban rodeos, stop all wild horse roundups, and so on) imply in their campaigns that the wild horse is still endangered and that the wild horse controversy is simply a battle between horse lovers and horse-haters. The horse haters are of course the cattlemen, sportsmen, BLM men and so on. In actuality the wild horse issue is far from being that simple, and involves the whole ecology and future of our western ranges, and many other side issues. Groups like AHPA and HSUS have kept screaming for proper protection and handling of the wild horses, but at the same time they have harshly criticized all management attempts.

The wild horses, according to PL 92-195, are "living symbols of the historic and pioneer spirit of the West" that serve to "enrich the lives of the American people." This is true, and I'm sure that almost all Americans would agree that the wild horse has a certain historic and aesthetic value. With the increased public interest in the wild horse, and with the passage of PL 92-195, Americans have firmly made it clear that they want the wild horse protected and perpetuated.

But the AHPA, HSUS, and some other concerned organizations and individuals are pushing so hard for no controls or management of these horses that they are actually working to the detriment of a lot of other values out there that also enrich our lives (unique desert and mountain ecology, a variety of native

* According to Roger Van Teyens, field consultant for the American Humane Association, "American Humane considers itself to be a positive organization in that it tries to work with national organizations, local associations, and individuals to establish lines of communication that will allow us to have direct input into the humane standards that are necessary for the care and treatment of animals. American ·Humane considers a positive philosophy more effective in resolving animal-related problems than continuously raising a public outcry against injustices or hurling accusations and walking away without solving the problem or helping the animals."

The wild horse has been a romantic subject—part of our western tradition and American heritage. He has been idolized and held up to an almost mythical position in much of our western fiction and lore.

wildlife, a healthy watershed, a good crop of grass every year—one of America's most valuable renewable resources—and so on). They are working to the detriment of the horses themselves.

The horses and burros are already overgrazing their ranges in most areas where they exist, killing out the perennial grasses. In drought years, like the one we had in many western areas in 1977, some of these horses were doomed to die from thirst and starvation because of their overpopulation. And in the meantime they were destroying the habitat and food supply for the native wildlife that roamed the same areas.

The wild horse controversy is far from being a simple question of whether or not we should allow the horses to increase unchecked. The wildlife, the watershed, the endangered species of plants, the beauty of a land that is covered with healthy native vegetation instead of denuded by hungry horses—these are things that should be taken into consideration, too. The deer and the elk and the bighorn sheep are very much a part of our American heritage; they were here long before the feral horse. Must they go to make room for ever increasing herds of horses and burros—feral animals that are expanding beyond their own food supply and dooming themselves to starvation if not controlled?

The domestic livestock, the cattle and sheep that have grazed our western ranges for more than a century, are part of America too—part of the "historic and pioneer spirit of the West." The ranchers and pioneers that settled the West, and their descendents and modern-day counterparts who are growing food and fiber for our nation, are part of America's very backbone and foundation. Are the men who gave their lives fighting bad weather, blizzards, drought, and hard conditions—the early cattlemen and sheepmen who lie in dusty graveyards around the West—are they not a part of our western "historic and pioneer spirit" also? Are we going to glorify the wild horse that helped him win the West, but trample underfoot the hardworking rancher who today is struggling to make ends meet so that he can stay in business to produce meat for the American people?

Mrs. Joan Blue, in her articles and AHPA brochures that try to drum up support for wild horse protection, lumps ranchers and BLM personnel together as bad guys because they want to manage the wild horses. She should also include the fish and game and wildlife organizations and ecologists and conservationists in her accusations, because they also want the wild horses controlled. The biggest push in AHPA and HSUS campaigns seems like an attempt to discredit livestock interests and get them off the range. Some of the horse protectionists seem as dedicated to getting livestock off the range as they are to wanting the horses protected. The AHPA lumps all ranchers together as horse haters and claims that the ranchers want to take all the horses off the federal lands to make more room for their livestock.

What these horse protectionists are not aware of, or neglect to see, is that the livestock on our ranges are there in controlled numbers. The livestock numbers are static and are not going to expand; in fact, in most areas the livestock numbers have been reduced to prevent overgrazing, and in some places, more recently reduced again to make room for expanding wild horse herds. The horse herds in many areas (where the BLM is still far behind on up-to-date control programs) are expanding to the point that they are destroying their own food supply and that of domestic livestock and native wildlife as well.

In many parts of the Northwest, the limiting factor on how many horses the land can support is not the number of cattle that use the land during the summer months, but the condition of the horses' winter range, and how many horses it can support during the winter months. In winter the higher elevations are usually deeply covered with snow, and this limits the areas that the horses can find food. Horses during winter eat a lot of browse (shrubs and sagebrush) because there often isn't enough available grass. If horses overgraze their winter range, the herd may starve, even if the area might be able to support more horses during the summer months.

In spite of the hate campaign directed at ranchers by AHPA, and in contrast to some of AHPA's bitter accusations, most ranchers have sentimental feelings about wild horses. Many ranchers are still horse people (having a lot more knowledge of, practical experience with, and long years' appreciation for the horse than do most of the city-dwelling horse protectionists), with a soft spot in their hearts for the free-roaming range horses that are now called wild horses. Many of these "wild" horses are only a generation or two away from the rancher's own stock, or those of his father or predecessor, that were turned loose in earlier years when it was permissible to run horses on the range for pasture. The ranchers don't want all the free-roaming horses eliminated (as the AHPA implies), because these range horses are part of the ranchers' heritage. In many instances the rancher may have more valid protective feelings about certain wild herds than do the horse protectionists, because those horses are out there only because of the rancher, and he feels a certain kinship with them, and a sort of sponsorship. But the ranchers do want the horses controlled in numbers so that the western ranges can support other types of life as well.

During the 1970's it was fairly easy to follow some aspects of the wild horse controversy just by reading the letters to the editors in some of the national horse magazines. For instance in September, 1976, one woman from Virginia wrote to the *Chronicle of the Horse* saying, "Two recent articles discussed the predicament of our wild and free-roaming horses on public lands. The first, a letter to the editor, cited the claim by the Bureau of Land Management of an increased horse population on public lands and the supposed necessity for thinning the herds. The letter went on to urge us all to adopt a wild horse to help out the BLM. . . . It is the contention of the HSUS and the AHPA that the sole reason the BLM wants to remove horses from the public lands is to benefit cattle ranchers who graze their herds there at very low cost. The ranchers do not want the wild horses and burros competing with their cattle for forage. . . . So if anyone wants to save our wild horses, don't spend all that money and time trying to adopt one. Send your money to the Humane Society of the United States or the American Horse Protection Association, and spend your time writing to your elected representatives in Washington."

In an October issue of the magazine, another woman wrote a letter, saying:

the comparison of addresses of the correspondents about the wild horse issue tells more about the real story than the letter contents. Mr. Dahl lives with the problem in Nevada. Mrs. Burk in Virginia does not. I hope Mrs. Burk likes horsemeat because when the horses run the cattle off the range . . . perhaps she will be able to purchase from the government some excess coltmeat—for which we taxpayers are now paying approximately $500 a head to maintain. Cattlemen, of course, who are still getting the same price for beef that they did in 1950, are paying more rent per head for the use and upkeep of the BLM land. In addition, the ranchers are the people who with their own money put in water tanks used by wildlife as well as cattle, and it is they who do most of the range improvement for their cattle which also supports the wild horses as well as the nasty old cows that feed the country.

From a humanitarian standpoint, I see no purpose in growing vast herds of equines that display all of the characteristics man has carefully bred out of horses for over 200 years; nor do I think it's 'beautiful' to see 5 or 6 stallions maiming each other daily or undernourished foals stripping bare the few trees that Nevada can claim. I do not believe that one or two trips through rangeland makes an expert nor that out-of-state Humane societies whose members are not horsemen always have facts correct. Virginia is welcome to all the 'wild' horses they wish to support. It's a cinch that Virginia grows more grass.

In another issue an eastern woman gave her views on why people should NOT adopt wild horses, saying that the government—at the expense of the tax payer and the horse industry—was launching a huge campaign in behalf of the cattle industry to get the horses off grazing land desired by the cattle raisers. She felt that according to PL 92-195 the horses could stay on the range where they are; "undisturbed and unthreatened by the invasion of cattle to compete for grass, they are a valuable resource to this country". She didn't realize that the horses, where they are, are already competing with cattle and wildlife for feed.

She described the problems people will have trying to confine and tame a wild horse, and ends her statement by saying, "If you want to do something for the wild horse, write to your Congressman and tell him you want the horses to remain on their land, free and unmolested. Talk to your friends. Write to your favorite horse magazine. Whatever you do, DON'T adopt a Mustang!"

The AHPA and HSUS try to appeal to the emotions of an uninformed public, but they often talk out of both sides of their mouth to do it. For instance, in an article in 1976 in *American Horseman* magazine, Mrs. Joan Blue of AHPA said that the commonly accepted figure of 50,000 wild horses in the West (a figure that had grown to more than 60,000 by 1977) was inaccurate. She claimed that 14,000 of these horses were privately owned, along with an unknown number of branded but unclaimed privately owned horses, and went on to say, "So at best there are only about 35,000 true wild horses." She failed to mention that most of the "claimed" horses that could be gathered had already been gathered and that just about everything left out there would now be managed as "wild" horses.

Out of the other side of her mouth, in a letter she sent out from AHPA trying to convince people to contribute money to her organization, she claimed that the privately owned horses that ranchers attempted to round up a few years ago at Howe, Idaho (under BLM orders to get their trespass horses off the range) were indeed "wild" horses. According to Mrs. Blue that was why the AHPA filed suit against the BLM and wanted the ranchers prosecuted. In one instance a horse is "privately owned", so it can't be figured up in the total of wild horses out there, but at the next moment the horse protectionists will say it *is* a wild horse if anyone decides to round it up.

This is the most consistent thing about groups like

In spite of the hate campaign directed at cattle ranchers by extremists in the horse protection movement, most ranchers (being horsemen themselves) have sentimental feelings about wild horses.

AHPA and HSUS—their gross inconsistencies and manipulation of facts, figures, photos or what have you—anything to try to twist things their way and sway people to their point of view. When distortion and dishonesty must be used to gain an end, perhaps the goal in mind should be questioned. What, really, are their motives?

One of the main attempts of these horse protection groups has been to push for wild horse protection on the basis that there still are not enough horses out there, that the horses are still "endangered", in other words, and need more drastic measures for protection. Because they push hard on this line of reasoning, they therefore try to discredit any facts and figures that show that the horses are rapidly increasing. They want to keep the public believing that the horses and burros are persecuted animals that need more protection, not population controls.

When reading propaganda written by the extremists for horse protection, you might be led to believe that the horses still do need more protection, if you didn't already know better. Reading an article like "Attack on Freedom" by Jim Scott (September 1975, *Horse and Rider*) would make you think that all the wild herds were still being hunted by airplanes for horsemeat. He says it is a miracle that any have survived, and that the "last place to see wild horses today" is near Jackpot, Nevada. He apparently is not familiar with the status of today's wild horse, the restrictions on horse hunting imposed by PL 92-195, for he says it is now open season on wild horses again because they are threatening "the ability of public range and land agencies to produce the needed food" and "soon the plane attacks will be multiplying. Then it will be up to the wild horses to use their speed to escape to mountain hideouts, if they can." And so on.

The HSUS formulated a policy concerning wild horses and burros:

. . . to protect the remaining herds of western wild horses and burros from cruel exploitation and extinction and use its influence to ensure existing protective legislation is properly enforced and administered so that those concerned solely with exploiting these animals for profit, and those with conflicting interests, will not succeed in destroying these animals.

Further, the HSUS will continue to oppose attempts to weaken current laws that protect these animals, and will oppose vigorously use if improper methods of capturing and managing wild horses and burros.

F. L. Dantzler of HSUS presented this policy at the National Wild Horse Forum held in Reno, Nevada in April of 1977, and made a statement saying that the BLM's "management" was causing great concern to HSUS members and that the BLM was "over-managing" wild horses and burros in an effort to keep them at minimum accepted levels. He said that "while we realize BLM is subject to intense pressure from cattle and ranching interests, and also wants to keep operational costs down, we believe the agency has failed to adequately respond to the intent of the law." In his judgment, this was reflected by the BLM's "desire to conduct roundups of animals without developing and demonstrating sufficient data to justify reductions in animal populations."

He was also concerned that the use of helicopters in future roundups would add another element of abuse by "irresponsible personnel" and called it the "re-introduction of a practice so brutal and inhumane it drove the animals to the brink of extinction only a few years ago." He felt it would be "deterioration of the law that now gives animals some degree of protection."

He had hoped that with passage of PL 92-195 "other special interest influence would be reduced" in the management of wild horses, but he was disappointed. "It is quite clear that cattle and ranching interests continue to dominate management practices on public lands with a control completely disproportionate to their numbers and economic effect."

In an attempt to prove that there are really not enough horses out there, Mrs. Blue of AHPA insists that wild horses cannot reproduce as fast as the BLM had claimed. She cites one study conducted for AHPA in the Stone Cabin Valley in Nevada by two graduate students, Howard and Nancy Green. They found a relatively low foal crop of 9 to 10% for 1975, and that during that year most of the mares with yearlings did not have foals, showing that they were foaling every other year. Mrs. Blue tries to imply that this low reproduction rate holds true for all of the wild horse herds in the West, and that therefore the horses could not be expanding as rapidly as the BLM claimed.

Dr. James Naviaux, a veterinarian on the advisory council for WHOA, also feels that wild horses cannot reproduce rapidly. In a telegram he sent to the oversight hearing in 1974, he said, "I strongly question the probability of wild horses being capable of reproducing successfully at the rate of 20 to 25% annually. This opinion is based upon the fact that brood mares in general have a very low conception rate, the national average being under 55%, and only then under ideal nutritional and veterinary care. James Feist in his study of wild horse bands in the Pryor Mountains observed an extremely low foal crop. Established research indicates that one of the normal limiting factors in the reproduction of range horses is the low phosphorous dietary intake which is known to be a common cause of low fertility."

These views represent generalizations, and would probably apply only to horses on very poor range (which, in fact, is the case for the Pryor Mountain horses and the Stone Cabin Valley horses). Other independent studies prove that wild horses can reproduce much more successfully than this, concurring with BLM studies. For instance, a Master of Science thesis in zoology done by Jodean Blakeslee in 1974 at Idaho State University (on mother-young relationships and related behavior among free-ranging Appaloosa horses) showed that nearly all the mares foaled every year from their third year on, and that each year 96% of the mares had foals. This study was done on privately owned horses, but these were horses that ranged out in the hills all year around on large tracts of land leased from the State, under identical conditions of many of the wild horse herds, divided up into small bands of mares, each with one stallion.

Wild herds in different areas can vary in reproduction rate, and herds can vary from year to year, depending on the weather, the condition of the range, the nutrition and health of the horses. In a bad drought year when feed is short, some of the mares might be too thin to come in heat and breed, and in a late spring following a severe winter, some of the newborn foals might die. But under average conditions the wild herds have had pretty good reproduction rates.

In 1975 the herd at Challis, Idaho, due to a late spring and heavy snows and heavier mortality rate among the new foals, had only an 18% increase, but in 1976 the rate was up to 21%. This herd had been increasing 29% and 30% per year before 1975, but the horses are now overgrazing their range. As the mares suffer from malnutrition during winter months, this high rate of reproduction may drop a bit.

Mrs. Blue claims that 25 to 30% yearly increase in herd size seems "impossible to most equine experts" (and I suspect Dr. Naviaux is her equine expert). It may be impossible in a seriously overgrazed environment, where the horses are very thin and undernourished, but so far most of the horses in question have been doing all right. There is quite a lag in animal condition-habitat condition. If the habitat is the only significant limiting factor on the horses (no predators, no population control measures), the habitat will be severely damaged before the horse population is in bad enough shape to be "naturally" controlled through starvation, disease, reduced reproduction, and so on. In the Challis

herd, for instance, about 85% of the breedable mares have been producing foals, and what Mrs. Blue claims about wild horse mares breeding only every other year is not true.

Reproduction rate is probably even greater in the wild horse than in the average domestic breeding herd because mares have a better conception rate when bred naturally, at the proper time, with a stallion running with them, than do domestic mares that are hand bred (which most domestic mares are). Dr. Naviaux's figures of the national average (under 55% foal crop each year) for domestic horses is correct. And it should be admitted that domestic horses are bred under very unnatural conditions. This fact is well known by many western breeders who have the room to pasture-breed their mares. They get a much higher percent foal crop than other breeding establishments where the stallions are isolated and confined (and hand-bred) instead of being out with the mares.

No matter what arguments the AHPA and other horse protectionists might put forth to say the horses cannot reproduce rapidly, the facts are there. The horses in various management units have been counted. The yearly expansion rates have been well documented. The population explosion is fact, not fiction. The wild horse population has soared since the 1971 law protecting them, and they have increased from less than 20,000 to more than 60,000 in just six short years.

Mrs. Blue's organization doesn't seem to care about the wildlife that must share the range with the ever growing number of wild horses and burros, and plays upon the ignorance and emotions of people in its attempt to gather public support for non-control of the horses. But the AHPA propaganda is laced with inconsistencies, illogic, lack of facts, and distortion of facts. In the emotional letter that Mrs. Blue sent out in 1975 to encourage contributions to AHPA (this organization periodically sends out newsletter-type brochure soliciting money for their campaign), the "last wild horse" is described. Horses that numbered two million "at the turn of the century" (actually it was a little earlier than that) are depicted as being hunted down until they are all gone. "Even as recently as the 1970's the herd still numbered some 25,000", the letter states, then goes on to describe the last lonely wild horse. What the letter doesn't say is that in 1971 there were actually less than 25,000 horses, and that under the complete federal protection given them by the 1971 Wild Horse Act the horses increased, passed the 25,000 mark and soared on past the 50,000 mark by 1975 when that letter was written.

The brochure she sends out is entitled, "The Wild Horse: An Endangered Species—Endangered by

Big Business Greed and Big Government Bureaucracy". It says, "Among the canyons, sagebrush and cactus of remote parts of the western United States roam the last of our wild horses. Once they numbered two million—strong, beautiful, proud, swift, free mustangs, one of our most cherished symbols of our Old West heritage". Photo captions call them "direct descendents of the mounts that carried the Spanish Conquistadors through the New World" and "America's last wild horses have become noted for their intelligence, endurance, speed and adaptability".

Under a photo of the Howe horses, that spent several years in government custody in corrals because of the suit filed by AHPA, the caption reads, "Some of Idaho's last wild horses are penned in the Union Pacific Stockyards in Idaho Falls, Idaho, following one of the Bureau of Land Management's 'over-population' roundups."

Wild horses today are descendents of ranchers' saddle and work horses instead of direct descendents of Conquistador horses, and "Idaho's last wild horses" the Howe horses, were merely ranchers' range horses that were rounded up; Idaho's wild herds are at Challis, Idaho and in the Owyhee Desert in southwestern Idaho. But I suppose the truth doesn't persuade people to donate money for the protectionist cause like romantic emotionalism does: "Our funding is completely dependent upon people like yourself—people who love horses and cannot sit silently by, watching them being treated cruelly and destroyed senselessly by big business greed and big government bureaucracy. Are you angry enough? Willing enough? Are you one of us?"

Lorne Greene, vice president of AHPA, is quoted on the back of the brochure: "Without your financial support, the AHPA will not be able to continue its fight for humane treatment of our last wild horses. Nineteen horses at Idaho Falls live today because of the legal efforts of the AHPA and the support of concerned Americans like you. If we succeed in our other lawsuits and if the Horse Protection Act and the Wild Horse Act are strengthened, thousands of additonal wild horses will live, free and proud." And starving.

The AHPA, according to Mrs. Blue's statement at the oversight hearing in 1974, "thinks that the law as it is, if properly enforced, would be sufficient. But since we can no longer expect the Department of Interior or the BLM to uphold the law as it is written, the AHPA respectfully asks that consideration be given to changing the law in the following respects:

1. We recommend that the words "manage" and "management" should be deleted wherever they appear in the statute and that the words "preserve" and "protect" be substituted therefore;

2. PL 92-195 should be made specifically subject to the Administrative Procedures Act . . . the requirements of notice and of public hearings and the other protections built into the Administrative Procedures Act would cut down on frivolous claims for wild horses, reduce the number of roundups, and give all interested parties a sufficient amount of time in which to prepare to argue against a removal or a claiming procedure;

3. Sections 4, 5 and 6 should make it explicit that the horses roaming on the public lands of the United States are the property of all the citizens of the United States. If the case should arise where a horse or horses are claimed, the Federal Government should appoint a Federal Hearing Examiner to determine the merit of the claim. If the horse is found not to be the property of the Federal Government, then, and only then, should the state estray and branding laws be applicable to that animal;

4. PL 92-195 should explicitly require Interior and Agriculture to file impact statements prior to any roundup or other contemplated activities which involve wild horses;

5. The law should require that any rancher who requests a permit to graze a horse on public land should first have to brand or lip tattoo that horse and the FS or BLM should have to enter that brand or tatoo in their books . . . any horse not so branded or cateloged is indeed a wild and free-roaming horse;

6. Section 8 should be made much stronger as to the civil and criminal penalties. We would suggest that a separate section be made applicable to officials and agents of Interior and Agriculture if they fail to discharge their responsibilities under the law.

7. The Government has asked that they be allowed to use helicopters to make a survey of the herds of wild horses and burros. The AHPA would be absolutely opposed to that request. The law on the books now prohibits the Government or any private individual from harassing wild horses and burros from any motorized vehicle, including helicopters. The AHPA feels that if it is so important for the Government to make a survey of every last wild horse in the West, that they should find some other means of doing it more discreetly and less menacingly than to fly helicopters down over a herd of wild horses and thereby harass and perhaps injure those horses.

Mrs. Blue concluded her statement by saying that the AHPA was strongly against letting the government dispose of excess horses, "believing that nature has always been able to maintain its own natural balance among the herds of wild horses and burros. We believe that that balance is more logical than that so-called wisdom that the BLM would have you allow them to apply." Thus the AHPA wants no management, stricter protection laws, and would rather have the government not know how many horses are on the range. The AHPA attitude is leave the horses alone and let nature take its course, not bothering themselves with some of the facts of nature and the dire consequences of this kind of irresponsibility.

In spite of the wild horse law that has protected the horses so well that even the government agencies responsible for managing and controlling them have their hands practically tied (and have not been able to keep the horse population from soaring), the AHPA doggedly claims that the horses "are marked animals—marked for the slaughterhouse for pet and human food, for sport hunting and for mindless thrill killing . . . Because big business has persuaded government to look the other way. Because a few ranchers grazing cattle on public lands want all the forage on that land for their cattle. Because hunters would rather see the land populated with game animals for their shooting pleasure."

Mrs. Blue in her letters and articles takes a stab at ranchers who graze their cattle on public lands for $1.52 per month per cow (this was the 1976 fee; this is a grazing fee that is increasing). She calls this a subsidized grazing fee and feels that the cattlemen are enjoying a rip-off, and that the horses actually have more right to be on the range than do the cattle, which she considers to be a "commercial interest."

She says it "is important to ask whether vast roundups of wild horses are necessary at all. Few involved with the wild horse problem have considered a more fundamental issue: whether the federal public lands are to be held for the benefit of all Americans, or squandered to satisfy commercial interests. For too long commercial interests have been permitted to dictate how national resources should be allocated. Livestock have grazed on public land for years, at rates well below the prevailing commercial value of private grazing rights. This subsidy has come at the expense of the American taxpayer, and of animals such as the wild horse. The real 'problem' then, is who will control the future of OUR lands and OUR animals."

Yes, this is the real issue. Groups like AHPA and HSUS want more control of the public lands. They don't seem to care about the health or future of these lands, or the ecology of them; all they want is control. And they want the cattle and sheep off. Their feeling is that since this is "your land and mine", curtailment of "dominant uses" such as livestock grazing is long overdue.

According to Gail Snider of AHPA "Wild horses are not nuisance animals; they are a part of America's frontier heritage and must be recognized as such. AHPA believes that the Wild Horse Act gives these animals a preferred status in the multiple-use policy for the public lands. But the administration of the Act shows that the government, livestock operators, hunters and 'range management specialists' have failed even to afford wild horses consideration as a use of equal importance. This is the real issue in the whole wild horse controversy, and it is part of a larger debate: whether federal lands are to be administered for the benefit of narrow commercial interests, or for the public at large to enjoy, among other resources, a national heritage protected by Congress. The Bureau of Land Management can do more to protect wild horses. AHPA intends to see that it does."

Ranchers have been repeatedly accused by the horse protection groups of using the public lands for private gain, and accused of being more concerned about the welfare of their cattle than the welfare of the wild horses. To ranchers, this doesn't seem like a fair accusation, because they feel they are making a very legitimate use of the public lands they lease. They, too, have to make a living, yet horse protectionists stab at them time and time again as though the rancher were doing something dishonorable. In the words of Pat Woodie, a rancher's wife from Howe, Idaho,

Even the most dedicated teacher receives a paycheck. Certainly my doctor wasn't able to build a $100,000 home with his undying dedication only. Ranchers have a very complicated way to do it, but they are trying to make a living just like anyone else. . . . A cow is a very efficient and useful animal to have on the public land. Because of her unique digestive system she is able to convert forage into human food high in protein. . . . I admit we (the ranchers) are getting the most reasonable feed available for a certain portion of the year, but at least we put money back in the pot with the grazing fees we pay. Also, we pay our share of taxes on the land we own and on any profit we make . . . doesn't the tax-paying make us part of the public that demands control of the public lands? Strange that no one ever sees ranchers as part of the tax-paying body. I think people in general have an image of the wealthy rancher amassing his fortunes while taking advantage of the grass in the West. However, ranchers are one of the few groups who DO pay for the use of the public lands. If the horses do belong to the public as the horse groups have led them to believe, why not assess all taxpayers an extra $50-$100 a year for grazing fees. . . .

Ranchers point out that their time and efforts and money spent on range improvements benefit the wildlife and wild horses as well as their stock. And the ranchers are definitely not getting rich doing it. They had been getting the same low prices for their product for about thirty years, while paying more and more each year for all of their operating costs—feed, machinery, gasoline and diesel, fencing materials, taxes, farm rent, interest, and grazing fees. The 1966 Grazing Fee Study showed that federal livestock permittees were paying as much or more than private lease-holders when all factors were considered, and the grazing fees have gone up since then.

Some people contend that livestock producers who lease the range are not paying enough money for the grass. But this "leased pasture" on the range can never be equivalent to privately rented pasture in value, for several reasons. Ranchers do not feel it is fair to have to pay the going rates for privately owned livestock pasture—a dominant use of a piece of ground—when they do not have a dominant use. Out on the range, which has multiple uses, the livestockman has to contend with hunters (some of which accidentally or intentionally shoot livestock, or leave gates open, or cut fences), predators, recreationists, wild horses, poisonous plants, bad fences, poor water developments, and so on. Recreationists leave gates open, joyriders on motorcycles chase cattle and make trails up steep hills (causing erosion), picnickers leave litter (plastic bags, etc.) that may kill a curious calf that eats it, and so on. Regulations today tie the ranchers' hands in many areas if he wants to spray patches of poisonous plants or put in new water developments or fences. The rancher must share the range with many other land users and therefore cannot manage the range to its best potential for cattle. There is no way that our western rangeland, with its management for multiple use (which in some instances complicates or is detrimental to cattle use) can be worth as much as private pasture, which is managed solely for livestock grazing and contains optimum conditions for this exclusive use.

The typical rancher has a hard time making ends meet in these days of inflation, yet many Americans look at the price of beef in the grocery store and are not sympathetic. The price of beef has risen, and perhaps an explanation is in order. The cattle industry operates upon supply and demand; yet it cannot adjust quickly to changes in demand. When the auto industry finds they have a large supply of cars, they simply cut back workers and slow production. But in the cattle industry this is impossible. The cowman is dealing with a live product. He can't tell a calf not to grow, nor his cows to stop eating.

The cattle business goes in cycles. The supply of beef today (in 1978) is less than it was several years ago. High prices caused the market for beef to drop sharply in late 1973, and from 1974 through 1977 ranchers received very low prices for their calves.

These low prices didn't even cover the cost of owning and feeding the cow and many ranchers (and feedlot owners) went broke. Some of the ones that hung on sold off part of their cows in order to meet payments and costs of production to stay in business. As a result, the number of beef cows across the nation steadily dropped, until by 1978 beef was coming into short supply again and prices began to rise. Not only did the price of live cattle rise, but also, due to inflation, the costs of getting the beef to the consumer went higher. One of the largest increases in cost has been labor—the packer, the butcher, the retail store—demanding higher wages. Forty-seven percent of the price you paid for a cut of meat at the supermarket in 1978 was for labor, and that percent is climbing higher.

Because the price of beef stayed low during the years 1974–1977, it now appears to the consumer that the increase has "skyrocketed", yet beef prices are still below the costs of many other things. Other products have been steadily going up, while beef stayed low. It has not yet caught up with the consumer index, the average for products. People are still spending less of their disposable income for food (including beef) than at any time in the history of our country. Food prices have risen, but not as fast as many other things, including wages. From 1974 to 1977, the farm value of U.S. food costs showed little change, while the total marketing bill for food rose 38%. Labor costs alone, which have risen along with or ahead of the inflation rate, accounted for 50% of the increase in food costs during 1973–1977. In 1977, for the first time in history, the cost of labor involved in processing and marketing food exceeded the basic farm value of the food. In other words, a bigger share of the average food dollar now goes to workers in the food industries than goes to the farmers and ranchers who produce it.

In 1978 the price of cattle started back on an upswing. This, plus the added costs of labor and marketing, made the price of beef in the store look high. But the rancher shouldn't have to apologize for the price of beef. Beef is high—compared with what? Everything else the consumer purchases has risen also. And the stronger prices the rancher is now getting for his cattle have not yet begun to make up for the four years in which he tightened his belt or went deeper in debt trying to stay in business.

Therefore the rancher has a hard time understanding the negative feelings directed at him by an ignorant public, and the feelings that he is "getting something for nothing" by using the public range. The movement to push him off the range—by legislation, higher prices for grazing fees, or conversion of cattle AUMs to wild horses—makes him bitter and frustrated, for it strikes one more hard blow to his precarious existence.

This public land, "your land and mine," in our western states, has many uses, and an interesting history—its uses and usefulness changing as America's needs have changed. The BLM lands, called National Resource Lands, constitute the remainder of the public domain that once stretched from the Ohio River north and west all the way to the Pacific Ocean. This great stretch of land provided land for the State school systems, land grant colleges, transcontinental railroads, the National Forests, Parks, Wildlife refuges, Indian and military reservations. It provided homesteads for more than a million settlers, for thousands of people who earned land through their military service, and for miners who developed mineral resources.

From the original public domain of 1.8 billion acres, Uncle Sam has disposed of 1.1 billion acres for the various uses just mentioned, leaving 705 million acres. Later there were 55 million acres added to this, acquired for specific purposes—mainly in the East where there never was any public domain. Combined, the public domain and acquired lands now total 760 million acres. The National Forest System makes up 186 million of these acres. Another 450 million acres are the National Resource Lands. Originally, these were the lands that couldn't be farmed because of lack of water, lands unprofitable for a private owner because of low productivity, lands too remote from roads and towns and utilities to be attractive as homesites or business sites, and their official title was "the vacant, unappropriated and unreserved domain". The name "National Resource Lands" was adopted in 1972 to distinguish these lands from other categories of public-owned lands.

For 30 years, 1934-1964, the Interior Department, first through the Grazing Service, and then the BLM, administered these lands "pending their ultimate disposal", but the era of homesteading had already ended. The Classification and Multiple Use Act of 1964 gave the Secretary of Interior authority to classify public domain lands for a variety of purposes, or to sell the pieces better suited for private ownership. This was an interim authority which has now expired, but the Secretary may continue to make special designations for lands classified under that Act.

Thus, the lands nobody wanted during the long era of easy disposal of public domain are now National Resource Lands and have many uses that benefit our country—the mining of necessary metals and energy fuels, lumbering, livestock grazing that supplies much of our meat and wool, wildlife habitat, watershed, recreation, wild horses, and so on. These lands hold many practical and aesthetic values that are all vitally important to our country. The wild horses that inhabit portions of these lands are but one facet of the many, many benefits we all derive from the public land—an important facet, but one which needs to be in proper perspective for wise use of the land as a whole.

The horse protection groups who push for dominant use by wild horses, superseding all other uses of these federal lands, can only be called very selfish and shortsighted. To single out the livestock industry, because it is a practical use of the land, and condemn it for wanting wild horse numbers controlled, is ridiculous.

But there are many people other than Mrs. Blue who try to make the wild horse controversy into an issue involving the cattlemen as the main villains who want the horses controlled—the cattlemen as the only ones who suffer from the horses being out there, while in actuality, we all shall suffer if the horses are not managed wisely. Much of the West is desert or semi-desert and somewhat fragile, and if overgrazed, by any species, will not produce much forage at all. These lands must be well managed, with all grazers controlled in numbers.

Mr. Edwin Browne, in an article, "Destined for Oblivion" (March 1977, *American Horseman*), tries to imply that the cattlemen are the big villains. He tries to compare the demise of the buffalo with that of the wild horse, and blames the cattlemen for both, saying that "the cattlemen loaded down the range land with cattle, and to them the presence of the buffalo and the wild horse posed a threat . . . the fate of the buffalo is now history, but with the buffalo virtually extinct, still the cattlemen overgrazed the land."

And he goes on to say that the government came in with the Taylor Grazing Act to prevent ranchers from going broke. This is a misleading statement, because first of all, the ranchers had nothing to do with the slaughter of the buffalo; the buffalo were killed for sport and for their hides (and to "break" the Indian tribes that depended on them—the Indians who were giving the emigrant settlers and the U.S. Cavalry a bad time) and were already gone before the land they roamed was used for cattle. The vast slaughter of the buffalo herds was in full swing before the 1860's. The cattlemen that Mr. Browne blames for the departure of the buffalo never saw any.

Secondly, it was the cattlemen themselves who instigated the Taylor Grazing Act. They had been pushing for some kind of range management to control overgrazing ever since the late 1880's, but Congress wasn't interested in doing anything about it until the 1930's. Mr. Browne goes on to accuse cattle ranchers of using the range land as if it were their own (not understanding the history of the "range rights" that were part of the early ranches when they were homesteaded) and implies that we all would be better off if the public land were used for a "diversity of life forms, city tourists included."

This is what his position boils down to: "The issue isn't just the survival of the wild horses anymore; there simply are not enough wild horses left." He hasn't done his homework on wild horse numbers and he seems more concerned with ousting the rancher than with the future and well-being of the wild horse or the other values on the range.

Contrary to his claims and those of groups like AHPA, these public lands are already dedicated to multiple-use. But the complete protection and lack of control of wild horses, with no consideration for the other uses, or for the fate of the rest of the values on the range, is NOT multiple-use, but shortsighted and wasteful.

Mr. Browne says that public land produces less than 1% of the beef we eat. I'd like to know where he got his figures. Wild Horse Annie was more nearly correct when she gave the figure of public lands administered by the BLM (not counting the Forest Service) providing about 1% of the feed for all cattle in the U.S. and 6% of the feed for all sheep. There is a vast difference.

In talking about feed, you are considering all the livestock feed in the U.S., including feedlot concentrates. In talking about livestock numbers, you have to remember that the cattle on the range are predominantly mother cows, each raising a calf (a cow-calf unit is counted as one animal) and that the calves raised on these ranges are generally sold as weanlings, weighing 300-500 pounds each. These weanlings are sold to cattle feeders, many of them being shipped to feedlots in the mid-west. In the feedlots these animals are fed a high-energy ration for fast gains, and nearly triple their weight by the time they are re-sold to be butchered, as yearlings or long-yearlings.

In discrediting the importance of the range in our beef industry, Mr. Browne says that such a small amount of beef comes from the range that we don't really need it (while at the same time condemning the ranchers for overgrazing; he's claiming the numbers of beef cattle out there are supposedly so small we wouldn't miss them in our country's beef production if they were taken off, and at the same time says there are so many out there they are overgrazing our ranges). He says "the majority of beef we consume is commercially fattened in feed pens where they never see a blade of grass." This

statement is true, but he is not taking into consideration the fact that these feed-lot cattle had to come from somewhere. They were not born in those pens. Many of them were born on western ranches and spent the first months of their life on the range.

The total number of beef cows (mature calf-producing females) in the United States in 1976 was 43,746,000, and this number had dropped to 41,364,000 by 1977. The amount of mother cows that graze for part of the year on BLM lands is 3,587,159, or more than 3½ million. More than a million cows (1,095,178) graze on the Forest Service lands in the 11 western states, for a total of about 4 million cows that use the public lands (at least half of the cows that go onto National Forests have already spent some time on BLM permits). These four million cows produced nearly 10% of our feeder cattle that eventually become choice beef—four million range cows out of a total of 41 million beef cows in the nation. And when looking at the amount of beef produced by our western ranges, this is not counting the cull cows sold for beef after they become unproductive.

The sheep statistics are even more revealing. There were only slightly more than 10 million breeding ewes in the United States in 1975. This number had dropped to 9,359,000 by 1976 and is still dropping. More than half of the sheep marketed in the United States are raised on the public lands, for almost 4½ million (4,416,762) sheep graze BLM administered lands, with an additional 1,383,454 on the Forest Service, for a total of about 5 million sheep on the public lands.

People like Mr. Browne and horse protection groups like AHPA want the domestic livestock off the range to make room for more wild horses, but the domestic livestock that use the range represent a large portion of our total meat and wool produced in the United States. Calf numbers were down 7% in 1976 and dropped about the same amount again in 1977. If the cattle were taken off our western ranges, beef production would be even more drastically cut and beef would become such a luxury food that most people could not afford it.

The horse protectionists who feel that livestock raising and ranching aren't dependent upon public lands for grazing have not looked at all the facts. In the western states there are many ranchers who depend on the range for their continued existence, and most of them are small ranchers who pasture 30 to 200 cows on public lands during the summer. The range may provide up to 50% of their cattle feed, as summer pasture.

And if the ranchers could not use the range, they would be forced to cut down to even less than 50% of their cattle, because they would have to use their hay fields for pasture instead of growing hay. They would have to keep all their cattle at home on pasture during the summer, in the hay fields, and could grow no winter feed. Rented ranch pasture, and hay, would be almost impossible to buy; there would be such a fierce demand for private pasture and for hay that there would not be nearly enough to go around. Almost all of the ranchers that use the range would probably have to cut down to about one-fourth or less of their cattle if they could not use the range, and they'd be out of business.

More than likely a lot of the ranches that would be sold would end up as subdivisions instead of as ranch land, for no one else could make a living on them as ranches, either, without the range. And as subdivisions, these parcels of ground would contribute very little to feeding America. The impact of these ranchers going out of business might mean an even greater loss than 10% of our feeder beef, for there was always some beef raised on these western ranches that did not use the range. If the ranchers have to quit, and their ranches are subdivided, even these privately owned pasture acres will no longer produce beef either.

Shortage of meat won't be the only detrimental result we'll face if part of our livestock industry fails and we have less cattle to slaughter. There are many by-products that we have come to depend upon, which could get short if our total cow numbers are drastically reduced. There are many things we take for granted that we don't ordinarily associate with beef cattle; but that's where it all comes from. One of the most important by-products, perhaps, is insulin, which is made from the pancreas glands of slaughtered cattle. There are more than five million diabetics in this country, 1.25 million of which must use insulin daily, and it takes 26 pancreas glands to keep one diabetic alive for one year.

What do marshmallows, surgical sutures, steel ball bearings, leather and insulin have in common? In one way or another, all are derived from or use a derivative of cattle in their production process. The average 1000 pound steer yields about 500 pounds of steaks, roasts, and beefburgers. Do you know what happens to the other half of the animal? Very little is wasted. From the remaining 500 pounds we get a vast array of edible, inedible and pharmaceutical by-products. Most consumers are totally unaware of how many important products rely upon cattle by-products for their existence.

"Variety meats" are part of the edible by-products. The nutritive value of liver, heart, kidneys, brains, tripe, sweetbreads and tongue has long been acknowledged. Many gourmets esteem them as delicacies. Other important edible by-products

are less well known. Fats yield oleo stock and oleo oil for margarine and baker's shortening. Oleo stearine is also used in the making of chewing gum and certain candies. Gelatine from bones, horns and skins is used in making marshmallows, ice cream, canned meats, and gelatine desserts. Intestines are still in demand for "natural" sausage casings as well as for surgical sutures.

Inedible beef by-products affect the quality of our lives in many ways. Probably the best known of these by-products is the hide. Cattle hides give us three types of leather: latigo, suede and tooling. The beef industry provides us with almost all of our shoes. Even vegetarians usually wear shoes. The cowhide also supplies the material for making felt, certain textiles, and a base for many ointments. It yields binders for plaster and asphalt, and is a base for insulation material which is used to keep your house cool in summer and warm in winter. Hair from the hide is used in the production of insulation and rug pads. The fine hair from the ear is used to make artists' brushes, the so-called "camel hair" brushes.

From the inedible fats in the cattle carcass come industrial oils and lubricants, tallow for tanning, and soap. These fats also supply glycerine used in explosives, lipstick, face and hand creams, and some medicines. Fatty acids from cattle are used in the production of chemicals, bio-degradable detergents, pesticides and flotation agents. Stearic acid is used to make automobile tires run cooler and last longer; during the beef shortage of 1973 tire manufacturers had to cut back production because of the shortage of stearic acid.

Bones, horns and hoofs supply important by-products which include buttons, bone china, piano keys, glues and adhesives, animal feeds and fertilizers, neatsfoot oil, non-edible gelatin for photographic film, paper, wall paper, emery cloth, sandpaper, combs, toothbrushes and violin strings. Bone charcoal is vital in the production of high-grade steel ball bearings.

Cattle are walking storehouses for a variety of life-saving, life-improving drugs. More than 100 individual pharmaceuticals are currently in use, made from cattle by-products, and perform such functions as helping make childbirth safer, settling an upset stomach, preventing blood clots in the vessels of the heart, spurring a sluggish thyroid, controlling anemia, and helping babies digest milk. From adrenal glands of cattle we get epinephrine, a drug used to relieve some of the symptoms of hay fever, asthma and some forms of allergies affecting the mucous membranes of nasal passages. It is also used to reverse the effects of severe shock, to stimulate the heart under certain crisis conditions, and by dentists to prolong the effects of local anesthetics.

From the cow's blood we get thrombin, a drug which causes blood to clot. It is valuable in the treatment of wounds, particularly in cases where the injury is in an inaccessible part of the body such as the brain, bones or gastrointestinal tract (such as peptic ulcers). Thrombin is also used in skin grafting to help keep the graft in place and to "cement" gaps where tissues have been surgically removed.

Fibrinolysin (another drug from cow's blood) is combined with Desoxyribonuclease from the cow's pancreas to create a medicine that acts as a cleansing agent for infected wounds and which can speed the healing of skin damaged by ulcers or burns.

Liver extract from cattle is sometimes combined with folic acid and injected into the bloodstream to treat various types of anemia including pernicious anemia. Liver injections are also used to treat sprue, a long-term condition characterized by diarrhea, weakness, emaciation and anemia.

Ox bile extract from liver bile is used in the treatment of indigestion, constipation, and bile tract disorders resulting from disease or surgery.

Heparin, made from the lungs of cattle, is an important anti-coagulant. It is used to prevent blood from clotting during operations and to prevent blood clots within the circulatory system which might lead to heart attacks. Heparin is also used as a gangrene preventative in cases of frostbite, and as a burn treatment.

Insulin is probably the best-known pharmaceutical derived from cattle, and is used to treat sugar diabetes. Chymotrypsin is another product from the cow's pancreas; this is an enzyme used to clean wounds and to remove dead tissue where ulcers and infections occur. Glucagon (also from the pancreas) helps counteract insulin-shock resulting from overdose of insulin, or when a low blood sugar episode is caused by alcoholism. It also has a specialized use in the treatment of some psychiatric disorders. Trypsin is another pancreas by-product that can digest dead tissue without significantly affecting live tissue and is therefore used in cleaning wounds.

From cattle stomachs comes rennet, a mild enzyme, which is used to help babies digest milk, and which is also used in cheese-making.

From the parathyroid glands come parathyroid hormones, used for treating people who cannot naturally produce this hormone. Without it, parathyroid deficiency can result in convulsions, painful muscular spasms, or lead to a loss of calcium from the bones, abnormal tooth development, or cataracts.

The pituitary glands of cattle supply Corticotropin (ACTH), a valuable diagnostic tool. Its most important medical use is to assess the operation of the adrenal glands. It can also be used in the treatment of psoriasis, control of severe allergic reactions (rhinitis, bronchial asthma), eye inflammation due to allergies, certain respiratory diseases, anemia, infectious mononucleosis, and leukemia. It takes the pituitary glands from 10,000 cattle to produce one pound of this valuable drug.

Thyrotropin (TSH) is a hormone from the pituitary gland that stimulates the thyroid gland. It is used as a diagnostic tool to determine if a patient is suffering from hypothyroidism caused by anterior pituitary failure or by complete failure of the thyroid gland. In the event of anterior pituitary failure, this drug will stimulate proper functioning of the gland.

Vasopressin, from cattle pituitary glands, is used to control cases of excessive urination or in testing renal functions. It is also used to stimulate proper movement of material through the intestinal tract following operations, and to dispel "gas shadows" when making abdominal X-rays.

The drug cholesterol comes from the cow's spinal cord. This drug is essential in the synthesis of male sex hormones which are used when natural development of male characteristics does not occur. These synthetic hormones are also used to treat menopause syndromes and to prevent swelling of breasts and milk production when a mother does not nurse a new baby.

Thyroid extract from the cow's thyroid gland plays a major role in treatment of cretinism (a congenital absence of thyroid hormone which can result in physical deformities, dwarfism or idiocy).

In the case of some of these drugs, it has become less expensive to synthesize the product than to refine it from animal sources. But in some cases (as with male sex hormones) another animal product is crucial to the synthesizing process. In many cases, synthesis has been only partial, and animal sources remain extremely important. Such is the case with the protein drugs (insulin, parathyroid hormones and pituitary hormones) which are so complex that scientists shudder at the problems of attempting a synthesis.

This list of cattle by-products is far from complete. New uses for animal by-products are discovered every day. Cattle have always enriched our lives. Their importance to modern man's existence goes far beyond supplying a source of nutritious food. The people who feel that we could get along without beef, or without the portion of our livestock industry that uses the western ranges, had better take another look. Many of us are more dependent upon the cattle industry than we realized at first glance. Yet the conflicts over range use (whether wild horses or livestock should be given preference in areas where they compete) will continue, because many Americans see a cow only in terms of a grass-eater that exists only to make money for some rancher. Many Americans would prefer to think of the western ranges as populated by wild horses than by domestic livestock. The horse has traditionally been the underdog. The horse is a much more romantic figure than the more practical cow.

Mr. Browne's article, "Destined for Oblivion," in *American Horseman* describing the plight of the wild horses in the days when airplane roundups gathered them for the pet food industry, Wild Horse Annie's fight to save them, and her opposition from cattlemen, is almost a total rehash (in many instances, using the same phrases, even) of an article, "How the West Was Lost", by Richard Rhodes, in the May 1972 issue of *Esquire*. The difference is that Mr. Browne missed the main point of Mr. Rhodes' article and he forgot to use the last page. Mr. Browne ends by cursing the cattlemen and hurrying them off the range, and closes by saying we would have lost something if the horses had been hunted to extinction. "Although their numbers are depleted, is it not better that they remain as a reminder of the awesome wonder of all that is wild and natural and free?"

But the original article by Mr. Rhodes deals not only with the plight of the horses, and the efforts of Wild Horse Annie, and his own misconceptions about the cattle industry, but also with the paradoxes of our American frontier—the built-in paradoxes of our country itself. Rhodes feels that when the beaver were all trapped and the mountain men disappeared, and when the buffalo were wiped out and the buffalo hunters disappeared, we lost something. He says, "and now horse hunting is illegal and cattle raising on the open range less and less profitable, and eventually the horse hunters and range ranchers will disappear, too, but is it perverse of me to think that we all will have lost something by their disappearance?" He says that you have to see the ranchers in order to understand—men who spend their days riding herd on cattle up and down dusty valleys forty miles long and come in windburned and exhausted—and women like Wild Horse Annie who had the guts to fight 25 years for a principle that has only recently become popular, and then you have to see the wild horses themselves, and then you'll find yourself wanting "not a resolution of the triangle but a permanent continuation of its leverages, because if any side of the dispute were finally to give way then we would all be the less."

In his words, "We live on conflict, not on resolution; that is our dynamic in this unique land, that is what made us Americans, the conflict between loving the land and raping it, between becoming Indians and becoming shopkeepers . . . And there had better be at least one hard-bitten rancher for every ten preservationists, and at least one Annie for every ten ranchers and at least one horse for every ten Annies." He goes on to say that new problems come to replace the old, and gives this exchange of testimony between Congressman Dellenback of Oregon and Boyd Rasmussen of the BLM at the horse-protection law hearings as an example:

"Mr. Dellenback: If I may go back to this matter of reducing the population, I must confess we are having some concern as to what your bill would provide. You say on page 2 of your bill, 4-(c):
" 'The Secretary may reduce the population of the free roaming horses and burros in any humane manner; however, he shall not sell any free roaming horses or burros for use in rodeos or the preparation of commercial products.'
"Suppose you need to reduce the population? You could sell for any other purpose besides rodeo and commercial products. I don't know what those purposes might be. You might sell a few to a zoo or something. If you don't sell, I presume you could take them off and put them on other land, but I assume that doesn't really solve the problem of oversupply. Your third choice is to kill them. That means you go out and shoot them, poison them or do something else with them. What would you do with the carcasses? I don't know what you mean by reducing or controlling population.
"Mr. Rasmussen: I suppose we would bury the carcasses.
"Mr. Dellenback: You might go out and kill the horses and bury them?
"Mr. Rasmussen: Yes.

And Mr. Rhodes in his article concludes "that the government, on a lesser scale and more humanely, now will do what the horse hunters did before . . . For there is really no solution. Annie and her school children will have to contend with that." The federal government would be doing just what some private individuals were doing before, except that now the horse meat could not be sold—just wasted.

Thus Mr. Browne, in using Mr. Rhodes' article but failing to use the portions that show the problems will not be "solved" by protection and preferential range use, is guilty of the same kind of emotionalism and irrationality that plagues the thinking of most wild horse protectionists—not wanting to see the facts. He's completely disregarding them. And the dangerous thing is that by leaving out some of the facts, or twisting them to suit their own purposes, the horse protectionists are swaying naive people to their emotional way of thinking.

Our western ranges produce nearly 10% of our country's beef. Most of the cattle on the range are cows raising calves.

keep their expanding numbers in line with their food supply by rounding some up and giving them out for adoption, they found themselves blocked by court actions initiated by AHPA and HSUS and other horse protection groups. In some areas, management has become so hampered as to be nonexistent—the horses threatened now with the new danger of starvation.

The movement started by Wild Horse Annie has swung much farther than she herself would ever go. She was a lover of the wild horse, and could not go along with the extremist's wishes for no controls, for that ultimately leads to starvation and a fate more cruel than the slaughter for pet food that she fought so hard to halt. You didn't find Wild Horse Annie attacking the BLM's attempts to manage horses. She worked WITH the BLM, not against them, for she agreed with the BLM, the wildlife specialist and the concerned ranchers that these horses must be managed for their own good. It has been groups like AHPA and HSUS (which Wild Horse Annie was not

Save the wild horse and burro—at all costs—even if it means destroying some of the West so that our children and grandchildren will never get to see it except in a bare and damaged condition, even if it means pushing rare and endangered plants and wildlife over the brink into extinction, or bankrupting our western cattle and sheep industries.

Mr. Brown applaudes the efforts of Wild Horse Annie, saying that "Wild Horse Annie and her school children prevailed, and Congress listened. For that reason, if no other, Mrs. Velma Johnston must be considered a hero to horse lovers everywhere." This is true. But the interest and concern over the wild horses has backfired. The good cause that it started out to be has become warped. The crusade started by Wild Horse Annie has now gained a momentum and a fanatacism she never dreamed of. When the BLM began some attempts at managing the wild horses and trying to

Wild Horse Annie worked with the BLM to try to manage wild horses, to keep the range healthy and the horses themselves in good condition.

211

affiliated with) which have been fighting the BLM at every turn.

At first, many ranchers viewed Velma Johnston's crusade with alarm and considered her one of their worst foes. But as time went on and more extremist horse protection views took the forefront, it became obvious that Velma Johnston's voice was the most rational position in the tumult. She was against abuse of the land—whether it was by livestock or wild horses—and had no qualms about controlling the horses if that's what had to be done to insure the future health of the range and the horse herds. "Our only concern," she said, "is for the welfare of wild horses and burros, other wildlife, and preservation of the public land resource without which man himself, along with all other creatures dependent upon it, cannot survive."

In time, some of the ranchers began to realize that she was an ally instead of an enemy. Her position contrasted sharply with that of the AHPA, which opposes all forms of wild horse and burro control and which keeps trying to pressure Congress into giving horses and burros even more "protection" by eliminating domestic livestock grazing and by reducing deer and antelope herds if necessary. Faced with this kind of threat from a fanatical and influential eastern organization, some of the ranchers took a second look at Wild Horse Annie's more responsible position and her WHOA organization, which was now on the AHPA's blacklist. Wild Horse Annie cared about the horses, and it is questionable whether the extremist groups do; they seem more concerned with just getting the cattle off the range.

Velma Johnston reminded the livestock interests that PL 92-195 had the backing of responsible spokesmen of the cattle and sheep industries and also that, in drafting the legislation, she herself fought not only to protect wild horses but also to arrange for their control when that was necessary. She admitted that there are areas in the West where wild horses have become a serious problem, and need to be reduced. She warned that if the livestock people and wildlife interests don't unite behind the Wild Horse Act, things could get worse because of the shrill voice of AHPA, which has considerable influence in Congress; AHPA wants to throw livestock and wildlife off the ranges to accommodate the increasing wild horse herds. She warned that AHPA hopes to restrain the BLM from further horse roundups and to pressure Congress for a stronger horse protection law. "Should such an effort along these lines succeed," she said, "I think we all would be justified in being up in arms. The present wild horse and burro law provides control. I saw to it that it did. But until all of us work together, controlling only wild horses isn't going to get the job of range rehabilitation done, and man will be the poorer for it." She stressed the need for more control of domestic livestock overgrazing as well as control of overgrazing by wild horses.

Velma Johnston died in late June, 1977, of cancer, at the age of 65. Her death was a great loss to the people who have been fighting for a realistic approach to the wild horse issue. The BLM men who had worked with her on the problems of wild horse management felt that they had lost a close friend and associate. George L. Turcott, Assistant Director of the BLM, said in 1974, "On my first association with her, she did not have the full grasp, as a layman, of the management principles of western range forage land. She does now. She can get up and give as good a range management lecture as I can. I can assure you she does understand the management principles of western range lands."

She understood range management, and she strongly supported the humane and orderly round-ups of wild horses when their numbers needed reduction. With "Annie" gone, many people feel that the strongest rational and far-sighted voice in the wild horse protection movement is gone. Ultimately, we are all going to miss her.

Before writing this book, I corresponded with Velma Johnston a few times and had her support and best wishes for this project. I felt very badly that she died before I had a chance to meet her personally. After her death, a very good letter I received from Dawn Lappin, Secretary and Adoption Director for WHOA, had this to say:

"Every once in awhile an individual makes such an indelible mark on the meaning of 'life' that adequate descriptive praise is somehow impossible. Velma B. Johnston was such a person. She was and still is a tremendously tall person to those who knew her well. Unfortunately, the controversy allowed very few people to realize just 'what type' of person she really was. I can honestly state that she took into consideration a whole spectrum of issues when she fought her battles. When people really did get to know her they found out that her ideas and theirs were not so far off base as what they had previously thought. When I started out I was a 'gung-ho' livestock hater; she changed that attitude, not with force, but by example. Sometimes her intentions were misunderstood, misquoted, or blown out of proportion. We sincerely wish that more people had gotten to know her, but I am sure that eventually conservationists and humanitarians alike will come to recognize her views. Hopefully not too late."

Wild Horse Annie was not a sentimentalist, and she kept her emotions under firm control. "Often I want to lash out," she once said, "but I can't because I must not lose my power to reason. Even my detractors say I'm cold-bloodedly logical rather than emotional. I have never referred to the wild horses as beautiful noble creatures because they are neither. Today's wild horse is not the glamorous mustang of years ago. He is for the most part underfed, scrubby and inbred."

Annie was a superb lobbyist. She worked hard, got her facts together, and wrapped the package in a passion and an eloquence that was hard to resist. In 1959, testifying before a House Committee, she brought the entire room to its feet, describing the wild horse as a "symbol of freedom for us all. He is our American heritage, as meaningful to us as the battlefield at Yorktown or the white church at Lexington. Even more so because he is, a living symbol." She continued the fight for wild horse protection, capping her crusade with the successful lobbying for the Wild Horse and Burro Act that was passed in 1971. The merits of that Act are still being debated, but she defended it until the end.

A short while before she died, she opened the National Wild Horse Forum (April 4-7, 1977, Reno, Nevada) with a taped greeting. She was too ill to participate personally, but she wanted people to know what she thought the Forum was all about— "to bring people together, people with opposing viewpoints, and try to come to a common meeting ground."

Velma Johnston had an unswerving honesty and a dedication to what she thought was right, possessing the ability to back up her statements with cold facts. Emotion never outrode the truth. But the fanatics in the wild horse movement who are on the extreme end of the pendulum swing are doing a dangerous job of juggling their facts, or closing their eyes to anything but what they want to see. Their subtle (and some not so subtle) distortions will ultimately hurt the wild horse more than help him, especially if they get enough public sympathy behind them and do manage to cloud the issue enough to keep the wild horses from being properly managed.

President of ISPMB (one of Wild Horse Annie's organizations) said this in a newsletter:

There are several eastern organizations that oppose any type of reduction of the wild horses or burros. They state "let nature take its course". How humane can that be? If we want our wild horses and everything else too, then we must at least compromise with nature.

We (of ISPMB) have spent hundreds of hours in study, field trips, attending lectures, and on-the-site inspections, and that is why we feel we are qualified to approve or disapprove some of the ideas put forth, while an organization that has not done so should hardly

be in a position to take the stand that they have. They have not responded to the BLM plea for public input on new proposals and regulations for the very good reason that they have no expertise to offer in this area.

It is our position that much more can be gained through a cooperative effort between the land management agencies and all conservation organizations toward the restoration of the productivity of the public rangelands so that an equitable number of all creatures, including man, will be assured of sustenance in decades to come. . . .

It is all too true that when a movement gains national attention, as the wild horse and burro issue has over the past 26 years with Mrs. Johnston's leadership, others are attracted to it, oftentimes to the detriment of the entire program through lack of knowledge or other personal aims and purposes. Sensationalism is often times the tool used with which organizations increase their treasuries and their membership.

At the December 1975 meeting of the Wild Horse National Advisory Board, the board members were blasted by Pat Smith of AHPA for becoming a "rubberstamp" to the BLM's management attempts, and criticized for accepting the BLM's figures on horse population growth: "Figures such as 25 or 30% increases per year are bandied about in an attempt to demonstrate the supposed threat of too many horses. But no one really knows how fast horses reproduce, how much of a burden they place on range resources, or to what degree they compete with other animals for these resources."

AHPA completely ignores the fact that BLM districts have been studying these horses since 1971, have some accurate aerial census figures, and that some very comprehensive studies have been done on wild horse reproduction and dietary competition with other animals.

This AHPA representative felt that the BLM's management policy was "in reality a shorthand for wild horse extinction . . . that will eradicate the wild horse. . . . The costs of removal in dollars are ludicrously high—from $300 per head to $1200 per head. The cost in terms of permanently depriving Americans of a legislatively protected heritage by removal or destruction is even higher. . . . In the din that the BLM and livestock interests have created, the voice of the people of the United States has been lost. So, too, have historic aesthetic, and cultural values."

Nothing is said about ecological values. Or wildlife. Or watershed. Of the future ability of the range to support ANY herbivores, including horses. Are not a multiplicity of values on our ranges more worthwhile to try to keep than just one "historic, aesthetic and cultural" value—wild horses—which will not feed nor clothe us nor keep the rangeland healthy for our children to benefit from. Yes, let's keep the historic heritage, but let's not let it destroy the future.

A BLM document that played into the hands of the horse protection groups who are pushing for removal of domestic livestock from public ranges was the often quoted "Nevada Report". Six BLM men (none from Nevada) made a two-week study that has become highly controversial and perhaps very detrimental. The report, which covered a few districts in Nevada, indicated severe overgrazing and other aspects of poor range management on BLM lands. The researchers said there was consequent loss of wildlife habitat, destruction of cultural sites and erosion, and implied that these serious conditions were not isolated examples, but typical of range conditions throughout the West. This group, the Nevada Multipurpose Task Force to Evaluate Range Problems, felt that most BLM management decisions were made with the idea of maximizing livestock use of the public lands, with other resource values suffering accordingly. The Task Force felt that the BLM managers were so devoted to increasing the number of sheep and cattle on the range that "the objectives were dominated by, and oriented toward, satisfying the wishes, even dreams, of the livestock operators."

On the subject of wild horses and burros, the report said the BLM did not consider forage needs for them and they are thus forced to compete with livestock and wildlife, further depleting the productivity of the range. To correct this, the Task Force recommended that "proper allowance of wild horse and burro AUMs be allocated with appropriate reductions in livestock grazing AUMs."

And on wilderness values, the Task Force stated that "Range improvement work has had a devastating and widespread effect on the natural and primitive area values." The land is crossed with fences, roads, stockponds and other improvements. "Were it not for range improvements and the maintenance of old mining roads etc. for range purposes, approximately 90 % of the BLM lands in Nevada would probably be in a near natural condition."

Shortly before the infamous "Nevada Report", the BLM had been taken to court over its grazing program. In October 1973, the Natural Resources Defense Council (NRDC) and others singled out the issuance of grazing licenses and permits as a significant federal action impacting the human environment, under provisions of the 1969 National Environmental Policy Act (NEPA). The plaintiffs initiated a civil action in the District Court, District of Columbia, and sought a declaratory judgment against further issuance of grazing permits until the

BLM prepared environmental impact statements (EIS's) for specific areas where grazing is permitted.

The BLM responded to the NRDC complaint with affidavits outlining the BLM approach to grazing management through the planning process, allotment management plans, and environmental analysis procedures. At this time, the NRDC became aware of the Nevada Report and requested copies under the Freedom of Information Act. Upon receiving it, they immediately filed it with the court as supporting evidence that livestock grazing, as currently authorized, has a significant impact on the environment. They contended that more environmental statements were needed to comply with the requirements of NEPA. The court seemed to place great weight on the Nevada Report and on December 30, 1974, Judge Flannery issued his judgment in favor of NRDC.

Because of the magnitude and the many criticisms of the Nevada Report, another organization made a report on their research efforts on the same subject, called "Multiple Use of Public Lands in the Seventeen Western States." The organization that made this much more comprehensive study is called CAST (Council for Agricultural Science and Technology, with headquarters in Ames, Iowa), and was urged to make the study by members of Congress. This highly qualified organization selected 20 of the top scientists in the United States and prepared this report. Their researchers included specialists in agricultural engineering, animal science, fisheries biology, forestry, meteorology, plant ecology, plant physiology, range management, recreation, sociology, soil science, water resources, and wildlife biology.

In this report they examined the conflicts, the many different facts, and the difficulties in making these conflicts work together. They came to the conclusion that "RANGE CONDITION FOR LIVESTOCK HAS GREATLY IMPROVED THROUGHOUT MUCH OF THE RANGE AREA IN THE LAST SEVERAL DECADES." Nowhere in their study do we find the drastically overgrazed conditions indicated in the Nevada Report. Another report, by two prominent professors from Utah State University, that appeared in the *Rangeman's Journal* in April, 1975, stated that "the public ranges are in better condition today than they have been for 70 years."

Yet in the judge's decision in the NRDC suit he relied very heavily on the draft version of the Nevada Report. The court ruled that the BLM Programmatic Environmental Impact Statement for livestock grazing on National Resource Lands was inadequate, and that the BLM had a mandatory duty

The Challis range area—high desert, rolling foothills and steep mountains—was to be the first unit to have an environmental impact statement prepared on livestock grazing.

to prepare environmental impact statements in every area where livestock graze. The court ordered the BLM to meet with the NRDC to work out a schedule for developing these statements for all the local areas.

The BLM agreed to prepare 212 environmental statements—on groups of allotments with similar characteristics. The first EIS was to be prepared on the Challis, Idaho, Unit, and all the rest had to be completed by 1988. The environmental statements were to assess the effect of livestock grazing on other competing uses such as wildlife, wild horses and burros, and recreation, as well as on soils, vegetation, and water quality. They were also to discuss range management and examine reasonable alternatives to livestock grazing. Allotment management plans for livestock could not be implemented until after the EIS for that area was completed, and range improvement activities such as fencing, water developments, spraying, seeding or brush removal could not be undertaken before the completion of an EIS.

If the NRDC is not satisfied with the contents of the EIS's, then the judge has the power to keep the BLM from issuing the grazing licenses. And no more cattle could be turned out on the BLM. Even if the NRDC approves the EIS's, the BLM must still ask Congress for the millions of dollars to implement all these Allotment Management Plans. If Congress turns it down, the Judge could still say that the BLM can not give the ranchers permits until the money is received to improve those ranges.

The process of setting up the EIS's and then the Allotment Management plans seems very unfair to some ranchers, especially if they are in a unit that won't be started until 1988; they won't get any range improvement money or authorization to make any improvements themselves until after the EIS is made and an AMP developed, which won't be finished until into the 1990's. As one cattleman has said, "Environmental concerns are a must, but we must be wary of some people and the methods used to veto projects and the use of the national resource lands. We don't want this to hold up allotments, development and management. Most grazing users are ready and willing to work with the BLM on management plans, and good resource management should not have to wait for an EIS which might be years from completion."

The livestock industry in the West, in general, has always wanted to improve the ranges. Most ranchers would have been very willing to pay out of their own pockets for range improvements during the past 30 years, if they had had some kind of guarantee that they would have been able to continue to use the range. Dean Rhodes, a Nevada rancher, said that if the BLM had let the livestock producer spend more of his own money on these projects during the last 30 years, and had given the rancher some tenure and some sign of compensation, the ranges today would probably run a third more livestock and forage for wildlife would have also been increased. The rancher, knowing that he can come back to this same range year after year and knowing that nobody is going to take it away from him, will be a good manager, because he knows the land and knows that he must keep it producing well for his own future.

Rhodes said, "There is nothing wrong with cleaning up certain stages of our environment, but we can't agree with the courts that it should be an enormous project that will entail several millions of dollars, especially when it is going to reduce livestock on our public lands. Also what about an economic impact statement, what economic effect will this EIS have when thousands of cattle are removed from our public lands? What about the towns that livestock industry plays an important segment of their livelihood? What will happen to them?"

Nevada is 87% federal land. The other western states also have very large portions of federal land, much of which is used for livestock grazing. George Abbott, attorney, has pointed out that the livestock industries in these states are very dependent upon federal land. There is a 49% dependency on public land in Nevada, 28% in Utah, and so on. His point is that "the stable, economic factor for 300 to 400 counties in the West and 16 of our 17 Nevada counties has been our domestic livestock operations. There must be consideration of economic factors in any change that is made."

When talking about what the users are getting from public resources in preparing these environmental and resource studies, some mention should also be made about what these users are putting into the public resources. In most areas, the big game and native wildlife are dependent upon the private lands that border federal lands. For instance, in most Nevada counties the winter feeding areas, watering and nesting sites for these animals are on private lands. The farmers' and ranchers' lands in many areas provide a great deal of wildlife food and habitat. The rancher who is a public land user has been accused of having a priority interest. But in reality his continued existence is crucial to the stability of his community and to the stability of the native animal communities in his area. The resource users, the ranchers, who have historically used the public lands, cannot be abruptly disrupted without some tremendous adverse affects on the economy and upon the western ecology.

To quote an editorial in a western farm magazine in late 1977: "What some environmental organizations fail to recognize is that it does not benefit the livestock industry to abuse the range. Rather, it behooves the cattleman to take care of that range so he will have sufficient forage for his livestock . . . This concern for the range brought about the effort called the Range Improvement Program, a few years back. Users reached down into their own pocketbooks to finance many range improvements. They seeded, they fenced, they planted, they developed water and they rested and restored the range. No one has ever put a total dollar value on all the improvements the range users have invested. Nor has anyone ever compiled all of the donated time and effort that has gone into range improvements. And on top of all this, the ranchers have paid grazing fees."

The livestock industry is not opposed to range

improvements, for with proper management forage can be increased still further. But to spend millions of dollars (an estimated 55 million alone for just the studies, and at least one billion dollars by the time all the allotment management plans are completed) seems to be a waste of taxpayers' money. The NRDC and the court have created this future billion-dollar expense without any Congressional approval, thanks to the National Environmental Protection Act (NEPA) that enabled the NRDC to take the BLM to court. The ranchers feel that the livestock industry is almost a certain loser in the outcome of these monumental studies, suspecting that with the environmental standards that the NRDC group is going to require (slanted against livestock grazing) there won't be many ranches that will come out of these studies without a reduction of their permits. And in the end, we'll all be losers.

Lloyd Sorenson, a Nevada rancher, points out that in the context of a growing world food shortage, there isn't time for 13 to 15 years of making environmental impact statements. "We can't afford that kind of a deal—costing $55 million to make. If they would spend that $55 million on these lands, you wouldn't need an impact statement. It would take care of itself."

Most ranchers feel that the Nevada Report was unfortunate and unjustified, because in the last 40 years the range situation has been stabilized and in most areas improved under BLM management. In 1932 it was estimated that the western range had lost nearly 50% of its original productivity. Before the Taylor Grazing Act most of the range was deteriorating because of overgrazing. But the past 40 years' management attempts by the federal agencies and the livestock industry have slowed the decline and improved a lot of the range. There is still plenty of room for more improvement, but the domestic livestock grazing on public lands does not deserve the condemnation given it by the Nevada Report. The special interest groups would like to accuse the livestock grazers of being the worst "range damagers" and would like to see the rancher forced off this range.

To read the accusations of the horse protection groups (with the "Nevada Report" to back them up), you'd be easily inclined to think that the range has been deteriorating rapidly in recent years because of livestock grazing, when just the opposite is true. To bring the damaged range areas (that were severely abused before the Taylor Grazing Act) back to full production will take a long time, but movement, by and large, has been in the right direction for 40 years, wild horse and extremist environmental groups' accusations notwithstanding. Wild horse expansion in some areas has now become a very big

problem to contend with in further correcting deteriorated range conditions. In some wild horse areas, range management is losing ground swiftly.

Many individuals have been pushing for "wild horse rights" and opposing range management attempts. One of these people is Al Kania, a professional photographer and president of FOAL (Feral Organized Assistance League), and another is Hope Ryden, a New York Journalist who has written several books and articles about wild horses.

Al Kania is pushing a theory that the wild horses in North America are native animals rather than feral domestic stock (ironic, considering the name of his organization). He stresses this theory because he feels that the horses, as "natives", could then be protected and managed as endangered wildlife instead of considered to be stray domestic horses. Students of pre-history agree that the horse evolved in North America over millions of years and then mysteriously disappeared about 10,000 years ago. There is no fossil evidence of horses on this continent during the past 10,000 years.

But Al Kania feels that the horse did not disappear and was here all along, ready to greet and mate with the escapees from the early Spanish explorers. He bases his idea on the fact that there were two million or more horses in North America in the 1800's, a number that he feels is incredibly high to have stemmed merely from feral domestic stock of the Spanish and the later explorers and settlers. In his words, in order to multiply that rapidly by themselves, "the horses of the Spanish Conquistadores did not drop foals but had litters of babies instead." In his opinion, these great numbers of wild horses could not have been produced solely by the Spanish horses. He cites the fact that during the height of their explorations (1520-1542) not more than 600 horses were imported by the Spanish explorers, that most of these were stallions, and that many of these original Spanish horses did not survive.

This is all very true (see Chapter One), but what Mr. Kania does not consider are the many subsequent importations of horses brought for the later Spanish settlements in Mexico and the Southwest. It was from this stock, rather than from the Conquistadore horses, that the feral herds sprang up, beginning to trickle into the wilds and into the hands of the Indians by the late 1600's.

In his article "Wild and Free Roaming" in the July 1974 issue of *American Horseman* Mr. Kania says, "Isn't it amazing that these few survivors (mostly stallions of the Conquistadore horses) produced enough litters in an unfamiliar environment to produce four to five million offspring in the wilderness in less than 300 years?" He goes on to use J. D. Feist's Pryor Mountain wild horse studies as the basis for a low reproduction rate among wild horses, not taking into consideration the fact that conditions in the Pryor Mountains on the Montana-Wyoming border (lack of feed, overgrazing, harsh winters, etc.) are somewhat different from conditions on the southwestern Great Plains where there was ample grass and winters were milder.

But his biggest error is in thinking it impossible for the feral horses to reproduce as swiftly as they did, even though he stretches the time somewhat— they really had only about 200 years instead of 300, because the feral North American horses really date from Spanish settlements of the late 1600's rather than the Spanish explorations of the 1500's. But given 200 years (that's more than 60 generations of horses), even a small group of horses can expand astronomically, given fairly good conditions. The mustangs on the Great Plains had very good conditions; it was a natural environment, not an "unfamiliar environment".

When you stop to think that many fillies will breed as yearlings, and that the rest will all breed as two year olds, continuing to produce foals into their late teens or longer, it's not hard to visualize the rapid expansion of wild herds over the Southwest. The current rate of wild horse expansion since 1971 is a very good example of what can happen to a horse population in just a few short years; after federal protection the West's horse numbers have tripled in just 6 years. Think what the numbers might be, given 200 years in which to roam and multiply.

A major point that Mr. Kania fails to mention is that the Indians had not seen horses until the Spanish explorers brought horses to the New World. If horses existed as natives on this continent, why wasn't he part of any Indian traditions? The horse is found in the legends and mythology of almost every race except the American Indian; for him the coyote was the legendary animal instead. If horses already existed on this continent before the Spanish came, why didn't the Indians already have a name for the horse, instead of calling him a "big dog" when they were introduced to him?

The horse was a strange animal that the Indians were entirely unfamiliar with until the Spanish had been here for some time (see Chapter Two). The horse spread from the southern Spanish settlements northward, from tribe to tribe, the northern tribes getting horses as late as the 1770's. And there were no wild horses in these northern regions until after the Indians' and white settlers' strays took to the hills. If "native" horses existed, there would surely have been some in these regions already.

Another point that Mr. Kania has in error is the conformation of the "wild" horses. He claims that the Roman-nosed wild horse is a direct ancestor of a true wild prehistoric horse such as the Prezewalski horse instead of the "dish-shaped headed" Spanish Barb. What he doesn't realize is that the Spanish Barb is not dish-faced like his Arabian cousin; the Spanish Barb is slightly Roman-nosed. Today's wild horses, more than likely, got their Roman noses from some of the draft stock that was turned loose on the range during the last hundred years.

Mr. Kania says, "If the wild horses are merely domestic horses gone wild or feral, why have they resorted back to physical and behavioral traits only found in pure wild horses?" These physical and behavioral traits are also found in domestic horses; the horse has only been domesticated a few thousand years, and man has not been able to change him that completely.

In 1974 Mr. Kania protested the creation of the wild horse refuge in the Bookcliffs in Colorado, on the grounds that the horses should continue to use the whole area instead of being moved into the part that would be designated as a horse range. He condemned the BLM plans to move the horses, stating at the June, 1974 oversight hearing that

The route that approximately 25 horses will be chased down, is a narrow jeep trail 1-2 miles of which edge along the cliff dropping down into Main Canyon. Halfway along the trail there is a blind U-turn with loose shale rock underfoot. Galloping horses will not be able to slow down in order to negotiate the turn. . . . The Bookcliffs host the only forest dwelling horses in an extremely scenic location. Also, the horses are beginning to show physical characteristics of the pure Prezwalski and Tarpan horses. FOAL is striving to study the genetics of the horses in the hopes to further establish FOAL's theory that the Spanish did not return the first horses to North America—they actually remained native to the continent.

In order to study the horses with any degree of validity, the horses must remain unharassed within their normal migratory habitat without having to contend with government imposed fencing. By years' end, Grand Junction will either host the finest scientific refuge formed on a multiple based concept—with horses sharing the land with other wildlife, domestic cattle, and the public. Or Grand Junction will host a roundup that, like the Howe Idaho roundup, will reach world-wide attention for allowing as many as 25 horses to go over a cliff. The remaining horses will overgraze their abridged grazing grounds allowing the BLM to further reduce the wild horse population.

But the roundup was conducted without casualty; the horses were humanely moved without mishap. See Chapter 8, "Wild Horse Refuges", for more details on the Bookcliff area and that roundup.

Mr. Kania is like many of the people in the horse

protection movement—pouncing upon a few facts here and there to try to prove his point, but not looking at the whole picture. And this kind of dissection of facts can be very misleading. Another wild horse enthusiast who is very good at this sort of thing is Hope Ryden.

Miss Ryden has written several books and articles about wild horses for the purpose of arousing sympathy and more protection for them. She is good at stringing words together into vivid phrases that stir your emotions. She speaks in terms of the domestic horse as being "enslaved" and the wild horse as being beautifully free, even though he has been driven into isolated and inhospitable last retreats by man. But her history and biology are often in error; she writes like a novelist, instead of a historian or an animal scientist, and has not taken the time to get her facts straight. Her books are full of contradictions, because she twists history and biological facts around in an attempt to try to prove whatever point she is making at that moment.

And her photography, though beautiful, is also inaccurate and misleading. She has some lovely photos and has undoubtedly spent some time out in the hills getting these pictures, but her captions imply either a lack of knowledge of her subject, carelessness, or intentional deception. Several of her photos are incorrectly labeled. In *Mustangs: A Return to the Wild* her "lone gray stallion" that challenged her has another horse in the background. And the three "Juvenile Delinquents" in one photo are definitely not the same horses she calls the Juvenile Delinquents in another. A photo labeled as "young Blackie" is not the same horse she calls young Blackie in later photos—a different leg is white. And so it goes. There are numerous examples.

In her picture book for children, *The Wild Colt*, filled with photos taken on the Brislawn ranch in Wyoming, she portrays the life of a young colt in a wild band. He is dun with zebra marks on his legs, looking a little like his relative the wild zebra, she says, implying that wild horses are something unique—a wild species perhaps—and different from domestic horses. She talks about freedom, and implies that horse ownership is bad for the horse, inhibiting, enslaving.

Her photos are disappointing. She shows a horse pawing in soft dirt, preparing to lie down and roll, and says the horse is digging in a creek bed to find water (even though the area pictured is definitely not a creek bed but a weedy, grassy area). She goes on to say that after the horses have pawed and cleaned out a spring other thirsty animals come and drink, but the photo shows deer drinking in a fairly good sized stream—definitely not a place that the horses have dug up.

Then she shows the colt coming to a fence and says he is dangerously close to the territory of a rancher. Although she tempers this statement later by saying this particular rancher would not harm the wild colt, the damage has been done; it's this kind of double talk that helps poison the minds of children, encouraging them to take sides—to be for the wild horses and against the ranchers who are bad guys who are cruel to wild horses.

She puts irrelevant photos together to make a story, even though it is obvious that the horses are not really doing what she says they are doing. Her horse fight is merely one horse kicking at another, her "fleeing band" is merely trotting, and so on. The picture of the wild colt as a baby is actually a photo of a different foal, retouched—with zebra stripes carelessly painted onto the foal's legs.

The same kind of deception is evident in a lot of her magazine article illustrations. For instance, in a photo accompanying her National Geographic article in January 1971 ("On the Track of the West's Wild Horses") there is a photo of a foal lying down, with the mare standing beside it, captioned: "Unwilling to desert her offspring, the mother pushes the youngster into partial concealment." But all the mare is doing is bending her head down and rubbing the side of her face on her own leg, probably itching the flies off.

Her book *America's Last Wild Horses* is so full of major errors that I will not attempt to point them all out, but suffice it to say that her "history" is so garbled that a person wonders where she got her information. One example: she says that Lewis and Clark got their horses from the Mandan and Arikaras Indians in the Dakotas, whereas they actually traveled by boat clear up through Montana and dickered in Idaho for Shoshoni horses to take them through the mountains until they reached navigable waters again.

Her distortions of history go from bad to worse. By the time she starts talking about the settlers and cattle raising on the Great Plains, she's rewriting history to suit her own purposes. There is very thinly disguised hatred running through it all, directed predominantly at the cattleman, blaming him for the disappearance of the buffalo and for exterminating the game, denuding the prairies and causing the dust bowl of the 1930's (which was actually caused by homesteaders plowing up the prairies for farms). She even claims that the tough winter of 1886–87 wouldn't have wiped out so many cattle if the cattlemen hadn't waged such a war on wild horses the year before—in her opinion the wild horses could have pawed out grass for the cattle.

She feels that the "exploitive" attitude of the early stockmen set a precedent in the West for disregard of the land, the wildlife and the ecology (what about the fur trappers and all the other "exploiters" who came first?) and that because of this, Americans today continue to accept the destructive and inhumane practices of commercial interests as legitimate, as long as someone is making a profit. She thinks that while such a "materialistic view" prevails, wild horses or any other "noncommercial" animals won't have a chance of surviving.

She apparently doesn't realize that all of our American pioneers from the time of the very first colonists—the Pilgrims on the east coast to the Spanish ranchers in the Southwest—have been doing this same thing, going into a new land and making a living from it. If this is so bad, why doesn't she also condemn the easterners who settled the eastern part of our country so thickly that, in many places, there is almost no natural land nor native wildlife left? I suppose because that happened earlier, it was all right. But because the West, especially the Great Plains, was settled last, the people who came there to make a living from it and disrupted the "natural" setting are bad guys. Her book shows that she had little knowledge about the far West or its frontier history, and her views show a typical Eastern dependence upon government to solve all the problems. In her view, government should always be in control of things, not individuals.

This theme seems to run through much of the extremist preservationists' crusade—their desire to control through government. Perhaps the eastern city person secretly envies the natural good life and relative freedom of the westerner, particularly the rancher (even though in these times of inflation most ranchers are financially strapped and struggling hard—fighting for their lives). Thus the easterner must make laws to inhibit him. The rancher's free life—his ability to enjoy and use the wide open spaces of the West—must be squelched because others don't have this freedom. Because others chose a stable occupation and financial security instead of gambling against drought, bad prices, crop failures or livestock diseases.

It seems that many city people have gotten too far away from the good earth, having all the conveniences and comforts of life that most Americans take for granted. They are so far removed from the physical day-to-day struggle for existence that their ideas and values are somewhat distorted. Their spirits are so restless and hungry for the real meaningful challenges of life that they have to invent challenges, or

causes, to fight for. Instead of working along day by day for the essentials of life, working with his hands and with mother nature to accomplish this (as the farmer and rancher still does in a sense, for he is feeding and clothing the nation), the city dweller is often plodding through some artificial job he sees no real purpose in, and he is not satisfied. His soul is hungry. Instead of going to bed at night after a hard days' work well done (knowing that the work he is doing is important), the modern American may have some emotional hang-ups because of his artificial life and the consequent worries and mental frustrations.

Some city dwellers who are successful in a material sense, yet who are not totally satisfied with what they are doing, have the extra time and energy to put into "good causes" like that of saving the wild horse. Because they don't understand the circumstances and issues involved, and don't bother themselves with finding out (some do, but many don't), their well-meaning crusade may in the long run actually do more harm than good—not only for the horse, but for all the other natural resources and uses of these same western lands.

The move toward protecting and preserving the horse at all costs, because he has an aesthetic value and is therefore somehow "above" all the commercial and practical values, is shortsighted and dangerous. Granted, we should not ignore spiritual, aesthetic values. They are vitally important in our lives. But we cannot at the same time ignore or discredit our practical needs. There should be a happy balance. The modern American today may not be very concerned about where his meals and raw products are coming from ten years from now (we seem to be a nation of happy consumers who blithely consume along, not at all concerned with shortages until it hits our own pocketbook or stomach), but should be. We should use all of our natural resources wisely so that there will be some left for our old age, and for our children and grandchildren. And these resources include the wildlife; the grass that produces so much of our beef, mutton and wool; the watershed that is vital to our water quality and quantity—for our own personal needs and for irrigating the farms that grow the food we eat—as well as wild horses.

The idea that the wild horse should take precedence, by its "superiority" and "nobility," over cattle, sheep, or indigenous wildlife is somewhat ironic. The total denunciation of these practical and very necessary uses of the land (calling them "big business greed") smacks just a little bit of something not quite American. It is ironic, because that very pioneer spirit the horse preservationists talk about embodied the efforts of early Americans to come into a new country and subdue it, to make a living on it, to make it their own. This was just as materialistic as some of the present day uses of the land that the horse protectors are condemning so vigorously. This kind of freedom and materialism, the American ideal that any man can go out and make a living for himself by his own initiative and ingenuity, is a precious part of not only our American heritage, but of our continued existence as a country with a free way of life. To condemn materialism and the profit motive is striking pretty hard at America herself and the free chance her people have for making their own way in the world, "doing their own thing".

The issues at stake in the wild horse situation today look like they may go deeper than just the debate over whether or not some horses should be out there. The initial question has already been answered; the horse is now recognized as part of an important aesthetic value that is going to be preserved. There is no question about that. There are no real arguments anymore. The continued existence of the wild horse on our western ranges for posterity is assured, is an established fact.

Thus the debate, the controversy, revolves around the next question—of management and control and how many horses and burros should be out there. The ecologists, wildlife interests, environmentalists, and livestock interests recognize the need for management and control so that the horses will not ultimately destroy their range, themselves, and other values. But the extremist horse-protectors are fighting so hard for non-control (and for letting the horses outgrow their ranges and their food supply), that a person soon starts to wonder what sort of logic this is and what kind of motivation might possibly be behind it.

Another example of this kind of subtle invasion and erosion of America's resources and potentials is what has been happening to the timber industry in the last few years, and it seems to parallel the wild horse situation. In the early 1970's the U.S. Forest Service conducted a roadless area study known as Rare I. It was conducted in response to a demand by the Sierra Club and wilderness society organizations that all unroaded areas in the National Forests that were 5000 acres or larger, were, in fact, "wilderness" areas.

This was a questionable application of the Multiple Use and Sustained Yield Act and the Wilderness Act, for the impact on the National Forest System was very damaging. Litigation by the Sierra Club or its agent was started immediately after release of the Forest Service report, and vast areas of forest land were then tied up against any other use than for wilderness purposes. The timber sale program and other uses practically came to a halt.

To comply with NEPA (National Environmental Protection Act), the Forest Service began land use planning with interdisciplinary teams of researchers and reviewers on each forest. Environmental impact statements—books one to three inches thick—were published for each area, review drafts and final drafts were distributed to the public, and public meetings were held.

According to Joel Frykman, consulting forester at Ogden, Utah, "Tens of thousands of man (and woman) years were spent developing data, analyzing data, writing reports, and public participation. Most of the public input against wilderness was to no avail. They [the Sierra Club] were deaf or blind to such input. All this was done supposedly to produce a better, more equitable land management job. Little was gained except when final statements were cleared, some timber sales could be made."

Yet the vast amount of effort and expense involved in making the studies (at the taxpayer's expense) did not improve management in any way. If anything, it was a hindrance, not a help.

Frykman also has said, "President Carter has compounded the evil by appointing Dr. Rupert Cutler, an eight-year former employee of the Wilderness Society, to be assistant Secretary of Agriculture. Dr. Cutler has demanded and initiated a restudy called Rare II, of the roadless areas, claiming that the previous U.S. Forest Service Rare I interpretation of the definition of wilderness was too conservative."

In the new definition of wilderness in the new study, all kinds of permanent marks of man would be in violation of the Wilderness Act, and more than 90% of some forests would be included in roadless and wilderness type areas. The adverse effect of timber sales, mining, and people's access for any purposes, including recreation, would be devastating. It would close most of the national forest lands to the vacationer or traveler who wants to see the mountain areas from a motor vehicle (four-wheel drive vehicles, snowmobiles and trail bikes would all be prohibited). It would eventually close the mountain areas to all mining and lumbering, having a very adverse effect on our economy and raw supplies and production of lumber and paper.

There is some interesting history behind the movement. In forester Joel Frykman's words, "John Muir, when the national forests were first created under Gifford Pinchot as Chief, fought to have the newly-created forests made into national parks. Pinchot prevailed with the help of Teddy Roosevelt. However, Mr. Muir started the Sierra Club and ever since, his adherents have fought to accomplish his objective—wilderness instead of parks at present. The final objective is to include all the national forest lands into wilderness areas. Dr. Cutler's current move is a major step in this direction."

In Frykman's view, the avid preservationists don't seem to care whether excessive wilderness might contribute to the destruction of American economy. His thoughts about the forest service and timber industry are worth thinking about. The parallel that can easily be drawn here, by looking at the extremists in the wild horse movement who strongly want all other uses of our western ranges curtailed and the domestic livestock off the range, is disturbing.

The horse protection movement definitely has many sincere and dedicated people within it, who are merely misinformed. But a person wonders if some of the force behind it might be coming from people who do not have our best interests as a country at stake, people who are taking advantage of this environmental issue to suit destructive purposes. In many instances, the issue seems to be no longer over the welfare of the horses, but over power, and control of our public lands; a controversy that may well be used against us all in the end. The implications are a little frightening.

19

The Challis Trial

The Challis area, on the East Fork of the Salmon River in eastern Idaho, has been the scene of one of the dramas in the wild horse controversy, and the battle between the AHPA (and HSUS) and the BLM who wanted to gather some excess wild horses, has not yet been resolved. As of late 1978, no wild horses had yet been gathered by the BLM in the Challis district since passage of PL 92-195 in 1971.

The country around the small rural town of Challis (population 785) is a unique area in the high-desert mountains of arid eastern Idaho, where the concept of "multiple-use" for federal lands has worked fairly well for many years. The area is used for recreation, wildlife habitat, hunting and fishing, mining, live-stock grazing, watershed, lumbering, as well as having 661 wild horses (population count as of July 1978). The area is home for 600–800 mule deer, 400–500 antelope, 50 bighorn sheep (immediately adjacent to the wild horse area; their critical winter range is only half a mile from the horse area), 150 elk on critical winter range, black bear, a few cougar, coyotes, golden eagles and other raptors, small game, several kinds of grouse and other game birds. Forty ranchers have permits on the range for domestic livestock. Salmon and steelhead return up the East Fork of the Salmon River to spawn.

This area is fairly dry and the predominant vegetation is sagebrush and grass. There are valleys,

Looking at a small band of Challis wild horses through a clump of mahogany.

Looking down at farmland from one edge of the mountainous wild horse area in the Challis Planning Unit.

rolling foothills and high mountains. One reporter that came into the area said, "Considering the amount of land that could be seen with the naked eye, I realize why people would think there was plenty of land and grass to support anything that lived here. But I looked again. There was very little feed. Most of the grass was in little clumps, spaced two and three feet apart. It would take a lot of acres to support one animal. Rocky soil and sagebrush dominated the entire 15 miles I rode that day."

At present, an environmental impact statement for domestic livestock grazing programs is being completed on the Challis area, the first of 212 that the BLM must do throughout the western ranges. These statements must be done because of a suit filed against the BLM by the Natural Resources Defense Council (NRDC) and others, charging that the BLM's programmatic statement on livestock grazing (which covered the environmental impacts of livestock grazing throughout the Bureau) was not sufficient, did not comply with NEPA (National Environmental Policy Act), and should be on a more localized basis (see Chapter 18) The Challis planning Unit was chosen as the first one to be done, the EIS covering the impacts that livestock grazing has on the various other resources of the unit, including wild horses.

The wild horse area covers nearly half of the Challis Planning Unit and therefore the wild horses are a major consideration in the EIS. But, at present, the horses are having more impact on the cattle than vice versa. One of the greatest total impacts in the Challis Unit is the growing number of wild horses; the herd has grown from 150 head in 1971 to 660 in 1978—it has more than quadrupled in just seven years. The BLM had planned to round up some of the horses in the fall of 1976 (there were 490 horses at that time) and give them out for adoption. They were, that is, until the AHPA and HSUS took them to court just a week before the roundup was due to start.

The Challis herd has expanded rapidly, but it is soon doomed to winter starvation, because it has already outgrown its maximum number that the range can support. The limiting factor on this herd is not the domestic cattle that graze out there during the summer months, but the horses' winter range, which by 1977 was being used very hard at its critical period in the spring. By 1977 this range was being overgrazed, to the detriment of the future productivity of the plants. There were already too many horses, and the range could not stand any more.

As for horse and cattle competition, the Challis BLM's first wild horse specialist, James Englebright (who spent three years and well over 2000 hours of

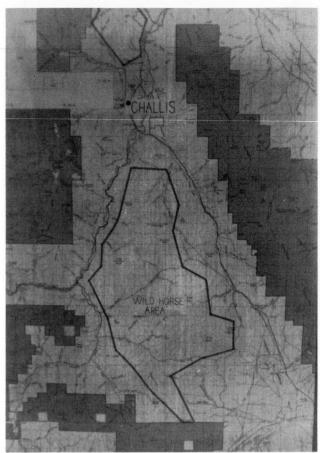

Map of the Challis Planning Unit, with the wild horse area covering roughly half of it.

field observations studying the Challis herd), has pointed out that the horses move to higher elevations in the spring and summer as the cattle move onto the range, eating the new spring grass ahead of the cows. The horses have much more impact on the cows than the cattle do on the horses. In the spring, after having wintered at lower elevations where the snow is not so deep (snow piles up 4 and 5 feet deep at higher elevations during most winters), the horses move on up as the snow melts and the new grass comes.

The lower elevation areas where the horses winter get heavy grazing pressure, for these areas are also used by wintering wildlife such as deer and antelope. These are also some of the first areas that cattle use in the spring after the horses have moved higher, and the plants simply never get a chance to recover. Loren Anderson, Challis area wildlife biologist, points out that the wild horse area is also summer range for 400-500 antelope and that the horses are competing with the antelope for food in the spring.

Areas near water are also heavily used by horses,

Wild horses on winter range near Challis.

wildlife and cattle, the horses grazing here each day on their way to water. Wet meadow areas are used heavily in early spring and fall by horses when other forage is dry. These areas are very important to other species of wildlife, and the combined use is very detrimental. These small, critical, wet meadow areas are the "lifeblood" of the cold, high desert country, and deteriorate rapidly under heavy grazing pressure. Once the plants are overgrazed and weakened, the soil mantle becomes exposed, and erosion lowers the water table, causing the meadow vegetation to die and be replaced by dry-area vegetation. Sage grouse and other small animals which depend on the succulent vegetation of these wet meadow areas cannot continue to exist.

The BLM planned a roundup, to start in August of 1976, built corrals—permanent and portable—for catching and holding the horses, and a large corral at Salmon, Idaho, for holding the horses until they could be adopted out. This roundup would have been Idaho's first since passage of the 1971 Wild Horse and Burro Act, and would reduce the herd to a number that the existing range could support. The BLM planned to round up between 130 and 260 horses. This herd had increased 28% in 1974. There were 150 horses in 1971, 214 horses in 1972, 276 in

This mare had a heavy infestation of bloodworms (Strongylus vulgaris) and was thin and weak. She did not move away when approached by photographer.

1973, 355 in 1974, 410 in 1975, 490 in 1976 and 575 in 1977. The reproduction increase rate dropped to 18% in 1975 due to a late spring and cold weather. The mares were foaling at the time, and some of the newborns died, but the increase rate climbed back up again in 1976 and 1977. Eighty-five percent of the breedable mares were producing foals.

There were more than 60 bands of horses in the

225

wild horse area, the band size ranging in number from lone animals to bands of more than 20. The average band size was six animals. Most of the horses show a fairly high incidence of strongyles (blood worms), and death loss from heavy parasite infestation was running about 2 to 5%.

The horses at Challis are largely a product of domestic stock turned out in recent years and most of the horses are fairly large because of the introduction of draft blood by early ranchers. The introduction of other types of bloodlines throughout the years by ranchers have helped thwart inbreeding. About 21% of the horses are gray and show the influence of gray Percheron stallions that were turned loose earlier. Inbreeding was not a significant problem in this herd before 1971, due to the constant introduction of new blood and the periodic roundup of young stock, but it could become a factor in the future.

The BLM's Salmon District took bids in June 1976 from contractors who were interested in doing the roundup. The District Manager stated that it was

About 21% of the Challis horses are grey, and show the influence of grey Percheron draft stallions that were turned loose on the range in earlier years.

expected "that most of the horses could be gathered into a permanent corral located within the area, but portable corrals will be installed by the Bureau in three locations to facilitate gathering in certain isolated portions of the wild horse area."

The method of capture would be limited to using saddle horses, and the successful bidder would need to furnish the manpower, saddle horses and equipment necessary for the gathering; the BLM would furnish the corrals. Transportation for the gathered horses to the central holding facility in Salmon would have to be provided by the successful bidder. The roundup was to last 90 days, beginning in late August. The contract was awarded to the low bidder, Tom Shewmaker, of Jerome, Idaho—who had gathered wild horses for the BLM for three years in Nevada.

A couple of weeks before the roundup was to start, Gail Snider, from the Bonneville Humane Society in a neighboring county, (she was also a representative of AHPA, which she did not mention), came to the BLM and asked for their wild horse management plan. A week later she and Marilyn Hall (also from the AHPA) came back and said they had been into the Challis area and had only counted 22 horses. They questioned the BLM's count of 490 horses. The BLM offered to take them on a flight to show them more horses and arranged for an airplane at BLM expense. Marilyn Hall flew with the BLM wild horse specialist and the contractor who was going to round up the horses. On the flight she repeatedly told them not to fly too close to the horses or frighten them (and she later complained in court that the pilot would not go close enough for her to take pictures). On that flight, covering roughly half of the wild horse area (and which later, in court, the two women claimed to have covered the whole wild horse area) Mr. Englebright counted 271 horses and she counted 232. The BLM personnel spent the remainder of the day showing the women the corral set-up, explaining the roundup procedure and answering their questions, some of which could only be described as harassment and animosity toward the BLM's proposed roundup.

A week later, and just a few days before the roundup was to start, the BLM learned that they were being taken to court by the AHPA and HSUS in an effort to stop the roundup. A temporary restraining order against the roundup was made by a federal Judge in Washington, D.C.

In the AHPA-HSUS complaint, it was claimed that the Wild Horse Act "elevated the status of wild horses on the public lands and has declared their preservation and protection thereon to be one of the highest beneficial uses to which the public land can be put." The proposed roundup, they declared, would be done in "90 degree heat, over mountains, steep terrain, and for distances up to four miles . . . At least one of the corrals to be used in the roundup is bordered by a barbed-wire fence, which is directly in the horses' path. The risk of injury from this fence is very high . . . Defendents have made no provisions for adequate veterinary care for injured horses. The nearest doctor of veterinary medicine will be on call in Salmon, Idaho, nearly 90 miles from the roundup site." The complaint also said that the roundup being planned to start in August was "mid-summer" rather than fall, which was to be condemned, because fall was stated to be the best time of year, according to the Challis Wild Horse Management Plan.

In the meantime, fliers were being circulated around the country by HSUS, urging people to protest the roundup by writing to the Secretary of the Interior, asking him to "stop the indescribably cruel and unnecessary roundup of 260 wild horses in Challis . . . Your letters will show that the public wants wild horses on public lands, not just cattle. Incredible as it seems, after Interior removes half of the wild horses on that range alleging that they eat too much grass, they intend to add more cattle to the 4000 already grazing. It is a windfall for cattle owners. It is inhumane to hold any roundup in the hot summer, near barbed wire fences which horses might run into as they are chased down steep inclines causing possible injury and death. No vet will be on the scene . . ."

But none of this was true. The hottest weather was past and the roundup would be conducted in the cooling days of autumn—late August through November—the best time of year for a roundup because the foals are old enough to keep up with the herd and the mares are not yet heavily pregnant. A veterinarian at Challis, about 25 miles away, would be on call at all times during the roundup. No cattle would be added to the range after removal of the horses; this range was overgrazed already and cattle were being taken off. There was no barbed-wire near the corral set-up; the corrals were well built and painstakingly thought out to be as safe as possible. The closest barbed-wire fence was half a mile downstream from the main roundup corral, on the outside of the horse capturing area and impossible for a horse to get to without first going through the corral in the canyon. The corral itself completely blocked wild horse access to this barbed-wire fence. All other wire fences on the cattle range that the horses might possibly go near were "flagged" with brightly colored material tied onto the top wire every few feet—a job that had taken the contractor

The main corral built by the BLM in the same spot used earlier by the Bradshaw family for catching wild horses. The horses would come down the canyon to the left of the photos.

and his men many long days. The horses would see the fluttering bright material and spook away instead of running into these fences. All efforts were being made to make sure that the roundup would be as humane as possible.

BLM District Manager, Harry Finlayson, said, "We have done everything we know possible as far as facilities are concerned to provide humane and safe treatment for the animals. We have avoided hazards in design and construction of the corrals and have provided canvas paneling to protect the animals from charging into the fences. We have made the corrals high enough to keep them from attempting to jump these corrals and we have built the safest chutes we know how to build. Wing fences have been set up on the ridges and the capture corral has been strengthened and camouflaged at the entrance with sagebrush."

A letter from AHPA's lawyer, Robert McCandless, to Curt Berklund, Director of BLM, opposed the roundup because the EIS had not yet been completed on the Challis Unit, and because the AHPA felt the area was not overpopulated with horses—

citing the 271 horses counted on the observation tour given Marilyn Hall by the BLM over half the wild horse area—and concluding there were thus only 271 horses in the wild horse area instead of the BLM's estimated 500. The letter went on to protest the time of year of the roundup and other conditions termed inhumane. McCandless criticized the BLM's arrangements for supervision of the roundup and for finding suitable homes for the horses. The letter ended by saying, "Ironically, it is scheduled to take place in the same area of Idaho in which 60 horses were massacred in 1973, again because of BLM's failure to obey statutory mandates. AHPA respectfully requests that this roundup be halted immediately."

In the BLM's reply to McCandless, it was pointed out that the EIS was designed for domestic livestock grazing management and not wild horse management, and that it was "neither a violation of law nor an abuse of discretion" for BLM to continue with the management of other resources such as wild horses, wildlife, minerals, recreation and timber while preparing the EIS on domestic livestock grazing.

It was also pointed out that it would be dangerous and difficult to conduct the roundup beginning in late October as AHPA recommended. Winter comes early at high elevations and bad weather would hinder the roundup. The August 10–November 7 roundup schedule would definitely be termed "fall" rather than summer, because the horses are at elevations 5400-9000 feet where fall comes much earlier than to an area such as Washington D.C. Frost in the Challis area comes in mid-August. Rain, snow and freezing temperatures can be expected any time after October 1. August and September are the "fall" months at Challis. Danger to the horses and riders because of slippery footing would increase if the roundup were not started until October.

Another requirement for a successful and humane roundup is that the dirt roads must be passable for hauling the horses out of the area, which they would not be by late October or November. The 90 degree weather spoken of by McCandless was indicative of his lack of knowledge of the area. The average monthly temperature during August recorded for the town of Challis is 65.9° F. and temperatures in the higher country where the horses are would be lower, and dropping lower as the roundup proceded into later fall.

In replying to McCandless' argument that the range was not overpopulated with horses, the BLM said that the major consideration in establishing the number of horses to retain as a viable herd is the amount of winter range in the horse area. Based on a

One of the smaller traps built by the BLM in the Challis wild horse area.

1974-75 range survey recheck of the wild horse area, it was determined that 582 horses could be supported year-around except for one factor—only about 54% of the range can be utilized by the horses during winters with heavy snowfall. Thus the area can only adequately support 314 horses (582 × 54% = 314) without deteriorating the range and losing horses. The BLM is required by law to protect both the range and the horses, and their plan was to manage the horses at a population of 150–300—to be accomplished by reducing the population to 150 about every three years and then letting it build back up. The average number of horses on that range would therefore be about 225, or 50% more than the population that existed in 1971 when PL 92-195 was passed.

In Curt Berklund's reply to McCandless he said:

Your statement that only 271 horses were observed during the flight on July 27, 1976, is correct. However, this flight, at Government expense, was certainly not an 'inventory'. An official inventory is flown in careful patterns at seasons of the year when the horses are most readily seen from the air. A complete and accurate inventory of the wild horse area of the Challis Planning Unit requires 3 to 4 hours of flying time. In an effort to be as accomodating as possible to AHPA, the Bureau offered to fly its representatives over the area. When asked if a flight over the entire wild horse area was desired, both Marilyn-Hall (who went on the flight) and Gail Snider (who did not) stated that they did not care to fly the whole area. Consequently, Marilyn Hall was given only a 1-hour "sightseeing" tour of a portion of the area. We believe that the number of horses observed during that brief flight supports our figures, if anything. Our inventory figures are carefully compiled and as accurate as inventories of this type can be. Frankly, we are surprised that AHPA would make such a serious allegation based on no more than a 1-hour sightseeing tour given by BLM to one of its representatives, especially when that representative was offered a complete 3- to 4-hour flight over the whole area and she specifically refused such a flight. Your allegation is especially surprising in view of the fact that AHPA made a similar unfounded allegation based on no more than a brief sightseeing tour approximately 1 year ago in its unsuccessful suit to stop a removal of excess horses in the Stone Cabin Valley area in Nye County, Nevada.

Berklund explained that while no overall reduction in livestock use of the area was planned, some livestock reductions would be made as a result of the grazing management plans and the EIS. "Your allegation should be put in perspective. First, domestic livestock are only allowed to graze in the wild horse area for a period of 1 to 4 months. The horses are there for the entire year. Second, domestic livestock and wildlife numbers have remained constant over the years because they are managed by grazing licenses and hunting licenses. Wild horses on the other hand, have had no management control over their numbers and have increased tremendously in the area . . ."

McCandless felt there would be inadequate supervision by the BLM during the roundup, stating that AHPA's representatives were told there would be 19 contract employees, but only one BLM employee to supervise. But according to Berklund, the AHPA representatives "were told there would be at least one Bureau supervisor at the roundup site each day. Usually there will be three to five BLM employees at the site. We do not know where you got the figure of 19 contract employees. We expect that there will be four to ten contract employees in the roundup area."

McCandless' last point was that the BLM had made no effort to find out if sufficient homes would be available for the horses and that none of the applicants had been screened for suitability. Berklund pointed out that the adoption program had had good response and that most wild horse organiza-

tions were helping the BLM in this program to provide homes for the animals. WHOA had been especially helpful, and so was Mrs. Pearl Twyne—the former president of AHPA until she resigned in 1975. Mrs. Joan Blue, current AHPA president, was briefed on the program and the procedures for screening and checking applicants, at a meeting May 14, 1976, with the BLM, but she refused their invitation to participate in the program.

In the spring of 1975, the AHPA, under its new leadership (Mrs. Blue) sent out two newsletters indicating that AHPA was against all BLM roundups of excess horses and said that, "until AHPA's legal and legislative program produces positive results" to make wild horse protection laws stronger, the AHPA "intends to take the Bureau of Land Management to court over each and every proposed roundup", with financial support from its members. It was the AHPA's intention to try to stop every proposed roundup regardless of the merits of the plan or the facts involved. The June 1976 AHPA newsletter stated:

AHPA COURT ACTION ONLY POSSIBLE WAY TO STOP MASSACRES AND ROUNDUPS PENDING CONGRESSIONAL ACTION
In recent weeks some of you may have received solicitations from AHPA asking for additional contributions in the hope we could bring one or more lawsuits to temporarily restrain or enjoin further BLM roundups this year. Some of you have responded and some of you may not have received solicitations, but we would hope that those of you who support AHPA's position to try to slow down or stop additional roundups this year would let us hear from you. Your letters of encouragement and your contributions are so greatly needed to assure that we can attempt to undertake these lawsuits.
The ultimate answer lies not in stop-gap measures such as lawsuits, but with Congress. They must be persuaded that the 1971 Wild Free Roaming Horses and Burros Act must be amended to force the BLM to protect and preserve wild horses rather than promoting their decimation and destruction by rounding them up from the public's lands. Such amendments must also include tougher penalties against both private persons and government officials who promote, allow or participate in roundups of the public's wild horses from the public's land . . . It must be an individual effort. Individual members of AHPA and other like-minded Americans must let their Representatives and Senators know that they want the 1971 Wild Horse Act amended and strengthened.
However, it is the threat to several thousand wild horses during the balance of 1976 to which AHPA and its members must address themselves. The 1971 Act will probably be upheld by the Supreme Court . . . Even so, the 1971 Act has presented enough ambiguities to other judges in our lawsuits that only by

changing it and making it explicit do we stand a chance to absolutely keep the BLM from deciding how many wild horses are enough for the public . . . [but] there is enough law . . . to at least try to persuade other federal courts to stop these roundups.

Thus, the Challis proposed roundup was chosen by the AHPA to try to stop, and to make an example of. When the restraining order was given, a stop order was issued to the contractor who was already in the area, ready with a crew of cowboys to start the roundup. A lot of interest had been expressed in the roundup, and the BLM District Manager, Harry Finlayson, went to Challis to tell the reporters, cameramen, writers, and wild horse and humane organization representatives who had gathered there that the roundup had been delayed. This is the typical course of action for AHPA, to wait until all plans are made, all people ready, and then go into action to stop the roundup, inconveniencing as many people as possible. The contractor and his men were stunned at the order to stop the roundup. "Just like that, on a one day notice?" the contractor asked. His partnership had already invested nearly $20,000 in the venture and had not yet chased a horse. The restraining order was extended to August 27.

The BLM first tried to change the place of trial, to have the court case in Idaho where the horses were, where the people involved lived, where everything relevant to the case was located. But the attorney responsible for the decision said that because two attorneys would have to be flown to Idaho at public expense, the trial would have to be in Washington D.C. (even though more than two BLM men would have to fly back there at public expense).

The court case, heard by Judge Charles Richey, and the decision that followed, was a mockery of American justice; the BLM personnel and other concerned individuals were stunned at the outcome. The only witnesses for AHPA and HSUS who had even been briefly into the wild horse area in question were Gail Snider, Marilyn Hall and F. L. Dantzler (director of field service and investigation for HSUS). Yet the judge took all of their witnesses' statements as reliable and completely disregarded the data given by the BLM men (who had worked in the area with the wild horses for several years), and affidavits from individuals like James Peek, who had been studying the wildlife in the area for several years. Most of the time during the trial was allotted to the witnesses for AHPA and HSUS; the BLM men got only a very little time at the end.

The first witness for the AHPA was Lorne Greene, of TV's "Bonanza." He stated that the horses needed to be protected, and kept dwelling on the fact that there were "4000 cattle out there" even though the BLM explained several times that the 3974 cattle were there only a short time (only 2000 are there at any given time in the summer, for some of them are on their way through BLM lands to Forest Service permits) whereas the horses are out there all year around.

Mr. Greene presented some questionable testimony and afterward the BLM men asked their lawyer why he hadn't responded to it. But the lawyer replied that it would have only hurt their case. The judge seemed so proud to have the actor, Lorne Greene, in his court room, that to have torn Mr. Greene's statements apart would have only alienated the judge.

Gail Snider tried to discredit the BLM studies in her testimony, which was mainly an emotional statement. She and Marilyn Hall tried to imply that the flight plan (from the trip over part of the wild horse area in the airplane tour) covered the entire wild horse area instead of just half of it, and tried to imply that there weren't as many horses there as the BLM claimed.

Mr. Dantzler had been in the wild horse area with Gail Snider and had looked at the BLM's corrals. He had taken photos which he used as evidence that the roundup should not proceed. Some of his photos showed some holes and depressions about 300 yards from the trap (and he tried to imply they were closer, and dangerous to the horses that would be coming into the trap) and called the whole area "densely vegetated and very rocky." He showed a photo of shale rock on the mountainside, taken at such an angle as to make it look like a cliff. This shale-rock side hill was off to the side of the trail, part of the canyon wall, and the horses would be below it, coming down the canyon past it, but he implied that the horses would be going over it, claiming that it would be another situation like the "Howe massacre" and that 50% of the horses would suffer injury or death. In actuality, the shalerock hillside would never feel a hoof—it stood beside the trail that the horses were accustomed to coming down for water, and would only serve as a "fence" to keep them coming on down the trail, around a bend and into the corral.

He also showed a photo of some bolts that he claimed were sticking out of the corral and which would injure the horses, but they were bolts up on top of a crosspiece on a high gate, higher than any horse would ever reach; he must have climbed up on the gate to take the picture. He also tried to slip a photo of some barbed-wire into his exhibit, to imply that it was part of the BLM's corral, even though it was not.

The main witness for AHPA and HSUS was Hope Ryden, a New York journalist who qualified herself as an expert on wild horses by the books she had written about them. She criticized the BLM's data, questioning the age and sex data, reproduction rate, the fact that there were some instances of mare change-over in some of the bands, and so on, even though she had never done any studies or observations herself in the Challis wild horse area. Yet her testimony convinced the judge.

Another witness for AHPA and HSUS was Dr. Porter, a race horse veterinarian from Virginia who said that the Challis roundup would be a "veterinarian's nightmare". Dr. Keiper, a wildlife biologist at Penn State University, who had done a study on feral ponies in the East, was another witness. He said he was familiar with the BLM's planning process and said that the BLM should have waited until the environmental impact statement on the area was completed before they made plans to round up any horses. But in the cross-examination it became evident that he was not familiar with range management, and he did not even know what an AUM was (Animal Unit Month, the standard grazing unit, upon which all grazing permits are based and measured; this is the basic unit in which carrying capacity of a range—the amount of feed for cows, or horses, or sheep—is determined).

The BLM had four witnesses, all BLM personnel. The chief of BLM environmental planning and coordination from Washington D.C., Robert Jones, explained their planning process and the fact that the Challis area had been through the whole proper planning procedure—he outlined in detail the planning and public hearing procedure that was taken to come up with the planned reduction in the horse herd. "With that data we felt we had a very good understanding of what the public was asking of us at that time," said Harry Finlayson, BLM District Manager (the AHPA and HSUS had said that the BLM plan for rounding up the horses was "arbitrary and capricious"). The National Mustang Association and WHOA were contacted about the roundup and had no objections to the herd reduction, but merely a few questions about the technique of the roundup.

The management framework plan for the Challis Planning Unit recommended that the horses be maintained at about the 1971 level or a little higher, because public input showed that this was the approximate number desired. This would satisfy the public's wishes about the horses, and would be compatible with the needs for soil and watershed protection, wildlife, domestic livestock, and other factors of environmental quality. The area was overstocked, and keeping the horses at 150-300 would help eliminate some of the problems. Only 6.7% of the horse area showed a stable watershed condition, 35% showed slight damage, 38%

moderate damage, and 20% critical. Since the horses use the watershed all year around, it was felt that keeping the herd at 150 or a little higher would help minimize the watershed damage.

Harry Finlayson, the Salmon District Manager in charge of the Challis area, talked about the importance of the livestock industry to the local area, the cuts in livestock numbers that the range users had already taken, and explained the dietary overlaps of horses and the other animals, wild and domestic, that use the range. He explained that the area would support very few more horses anyway, even if all the cattle were taken off, because the limiting factor on the horses was their winter range, which was already being overgrazed.

The judge brought in a special attorney to cross-examine Mr. Finlayson and asked him why the BLM hadn't considered taking the cattle off the range. Harry patiently explained that this had been one of the "alternatives" in the planning process, but that it wouldn't have solved anything in terms of the horses because the limiting factor on the horses is the winter range, not the cattle. The area might support a few more horses if all the cattle were taken off, but not very many. The question was asked why the BLM hadn't fenced off the horse's winter range from the cattle grazing area and the BLM explained that this would take 70 miles of fencing through very rough country and was not practical. The fence would also inhibit wildlife, and be a detriment to the horses themselves when they tried to move out of the winter range in the spring to summer range.

The judge kept dwelling on the "4000 cows," even though the BLM explained the situation many times. Nearly 500 horses have more impact on a range, using it year-around (especially in early spring when the plants are trying to grow, and being eaten before they get a start) than 4000 cattle in the summer, less than half of which actually use the horse area at any one time.

James Englebright, the wild horse specialist for the Salmon-Challis area, explained his studies and gave his data on age-ratios and sex ratios on the horses, reproduction rate, protein needs, dietary analysis, the fecal sample study, and other factors. He explained all of his studies and that he had spent 2½ years and over 2000 hours of actual field observations with this herd. More data had been gathered on the Challis wild horses at that time than had been gathered on any other BLM district.

Loren Anderson, wildlife biologist, showed how the horses were imposing on the critical elk winter range, had overlapping diets with deer, and how they would soon encroach on the bighorn sheep range if their numbers grew any larger. Another problem in trying to maintain the bighorn sheep

A stallion. . . .

This wild band has come down onto the Little Anderson Ranch.

. . . and his harem near Challis.

would occur if the ranchers on the East Fork were forced to sell their properties to subdividers (which would happen if the cattle were taken off the range and the ranchers were put out of business). With subdivisions and more home sites in the area and the increase in people and dogs, the mountain sheep would be lost, and the chances are high that what is left of the salmon run would also be lost. The area can be maintained more naturally and as more of a "wilderness" if the ranchers stay. If they go, their land would be "developed" and a lot more people would live in the area. "Just yanking the cows off and putting the rancher in the position of having to sell out is not the answer. From a wildlife standpoint we have to keep these people in business to keep the sheep," Anderson said.

After the presentations by the various witnesses, Judge Richey instructed the attorneys for the two sides to try to reach a compromise on the roundup. But BLM attorney John Lindskold of the U.S. Justice Department said his suggestion to cut the roundup to a maximum of 150 horses gathered was rejected by the horse protection groups, and he predicted that no compromise could be reached.

The AHPA and HSUS wanted to stop the roundup entirely.

In the summing up of the case, the attorneys for each side presented their summaries, but when it came time for the judge to give his decision, he pulled forth a paper that had already been prepared; it looked like he had made his decision earlier.

The BLM men felt they had presented a good case. It was a case that had begun over the humane issue of the roundup and the BLM had felt confident that they could win the case over this issue, because everything had been done to the best of their ability to insure humane conditions. But after the trial was over they had the feeling that it would have gone the same way—against them—whether or not they had even been in the courtroom. A court case that had started out debating the humane issue of the roundup had taken a turn, from the judge himself, to the issue of whether or not the horses should be rounded up at all—whether or not the BLM had considered all the other alternatives.

The Idaho State BLM director commented later that the judge had helped the horse protectionists develop a case, and that the cards had been stacked against the BLM. The BLM had tried to have the case heard by a judge in the West instead of in Washington, D. C. As the BLM director said, "Anything we get into the district courts in the District of Columbia we have a difficult time telling our side of the story. The environmentalists sit back and wait until a judge sympathetic to their position becomes available."

The AHPA and the HSUS had chosen to take the BLM to court over this particular roundup for two reasons. First of all, because of the unfortunate situations surrounding the "Howe roundup" and its national attention just three years before, the horse protection groups felt that if they could cast some doubts about the humane conditions of this Idaho roundup, comparing it to the "Howe massacre," they would have a lot of support from people who had been appalled by the ranchers' roundup at Howe. The only similarity between the two round-ups was that they were in the same state, but the horse protection groups felt they could capitalize on this fact and draw some other implied comparisons.

Secondly, the Challis Planning Unit was the first of 212 areas to have an environmental impact statement on livestock grazing done by the BLM, and the writing of this statement was still in progress at the time of the trial. The horse protection groups felt they could get the BLM over a barrel, because the roundup had been planned before the EIS was completed (even though the EIS was for livestock management, not wild horse management) and could also perhaps set a precedent on the wild horse situation for future areas that would have to have statements written during the next few years. Even though other BLM roundups in other areas (California, Wyoming, Nevada, and Oregon) were becoming a routine management procedure, and districts in other states were not being taken to court by protection groups, the AHPA and HSUS decided to take the BLM to court over the Challis roundup and attempt to make an example of it. The AHPA and HSUS are also good at timing their court actions in such a way as to insure that the case is tried by a judge that is sympathetic with their views.

The judge ruled that the proposed roundup violated the National Environmental Protection Act (NEPA) because the roundup would take place prior to the completion of the EIS on the proposed livestock grazing program at Challis, and violated the Wild Horse and Burro Act because it would not be conducted "under humane conditions and at the minimum feasible level." The judge claimed that the BLM had not considered the alternatives of reducing livestock numbers in favor of wild horses.

Also, he felt that the BLM had developed their roundup plan without first having reliable data on

A burro (center) runs with this harem band near Challis.

A family group.

"the size and composition of the herd"—even though the wild horse specialist had more concrete data on this particular herd than anyone else had on any other BLM district herd at that time. The judge acknowledged the fact that the BLM had made several aerial counts of the horses each year and that there were 150 horses in 1971, 214 in 1972, 276 horses in 1973, 355 horses in 1974, 407 horses in 1975, and 509 horses in 1976—an annual rate of increase of 28% in 1973, 29% in 1974. The rate dropped to 18% in 1975, but was back up above 20% in 1976.

But then the judge went on to conclude that a 25% increase was impossible and "clearly at odds with the testimony of plaintiff's expert, Ms. Ryden, whose testimony the court finds to be entirely reliable and credible, and whose testimony indicates a wide-ranging and in-depth knowledge of the subject matter of this lawsuit. On the basis of many years of studying and writing about wild horses, she testified that such a birth rate 'exceeds credibility' and would in fact be difficult to achieve in captivity. Accordingly, the Court finds that the figures computed by the defendants (BLM) must be considered meaningless data".

He said this in spite of the fact that he had already acknowledged that the Challis herd had increased 28% and 29% in 1973 and 1974.

The judge went on to say that:

"undisputed testimony of defendants' own experts indicate that there is significant dietary overlap between livestock, especially cattle, and wild horses, and the elimination of all livestock grazing on those limited parts of the Challis Unit that are considered to be critical for supplying winter range to the wild horses would enable the Challis region to sustain at least 33% more horses over the government's estimated maximum sustainable level of approximately 300 horses. In other words, the Challis Region could then support at least 400 wild horses during the critical winter months. Thus the undisputed testimony clearly indicates that the carrying capacity of the wild horses' winter range, which is undeniably the critical limiting factor upon which defendants have based their round-up plans, can be significantly increased by modifying and/or eliminating domestic livestock use of that range.

Significantly increase the carrying capacity of the horses' winter range? To 400 horses, when the horse herd had already grown to 509? And was still growing? What kind of logic is this? Fencing the winter range off from domestic cattle use (70 miles of fence to build through very rough terrain) just to make sure that the horse's winter range could carry 400 horses instead of 300, when the herd had already grown to 509 (and on up to 575 by the summer of 1977) doesn't seem to be any kind of solution at all, but rather a gross waste of time, effort and money to build the fence.

But the judge felt that the alternative of restricting livestock grazing on the winter range area by fencing them out (and how would that fence affect the wild horses when they wanted to leave their winter range in the spring and travel to higher country?) should have been considered, and that "the failure to give this alternative full and careful consideration . . . renders the proposed roundup plan arbitrary, capricious, an abuse of discretion, and otherwise not in accordance with the clear mandate of the Act (PL 92-195) to keep all management activities at the minimum feasible level."

Lorne Greene, vice chairman of the board of directors of AHPA, told the Court, "We're concerned because the wild horse is the only animal that has been selected to be rounded up." He said the horse is being "sacrificed" to save the range for cattle. He and other members of AHPA and HSUS wanted the cattle off the range, and criticized the BLM for wanting to reduce the horses without decreasing the number of cattle or deer. Livestock use of the area had already been decreased in past "cuts" in grazing permits, but the horse protection groups felt that the cattle were being "saved to benefit a small number of ranchers."

The cattle that use the Challis area for some portion of the summer months when the grass is mature, have managed on that range for many decades, producing part of the beef that feeds America. But 660 horses (1978 count), to be left to increase to even larger numbers, grazing the range all year around, eating the new green grass ahead of the cattle before it has a chance to grow, and eating browse in the winter essential to the diets of deer and elk, are making a greater impact on that range than the cattle ever did. The cattle could be taken off, but that won't be a solution. We would lose a portion of our food supply and 40 ranchers would be out of business. The horses will still continue to expand, continue to overgraze and destroy their winter range, the watershed, the native grasses, until nothing is left for even the horses to eat.

In reality, a balance of nature exists with managed use by domestic livestock and wildlife. Cow numbers and season of use are controlled. Game numbers are controlled by hunting. The horses at this point are the only animals out there not controlled, and if left to their present rate of increase they will do more damage to the land and its resources in a few short years than can be corrected in the next few decades.

Jim Bennetts, an attorney-rancher from Challis, made a statement at the April 1977 Wild Horse Forum explaining that the problem was a matter of keeping a fair balance without extinguishing any particular species or group. He also explained that the economy and tax base in the Challis area depends on the cattle. Directly or indirectly, those cattle are responsible for keeping the schools open and the roads passable.

In his statement he said, "At the present time, the wild horses are the only dwellers on the natural resource lands not being, in some manner, managed, controlled or harvested. Consequently, our herd, numbering approximately 150 head in 1971 has grown to over 500 head today (April 1977). We have a few instant experts who would like to argue with these figures, but unfortunately for them you count horses on the range, not from a lodge in Sun Valley, or the barber shop in Mackey, Idaho. The fact is, the horses are there."

He mentioned the competition with wildlife and that the range, occupied by so many horses, can't still be productive for the big game. Something will have to give, and it will be the deer, elk and bighorn doing the giving. He pointed out the studies done by James Peek in wildlife habitat and said, "I think we

A harem band pauses atop a ridge to look back at the photographer. By the summer of 1978 there were more than 660 wild horses at Challis.

should heed his warning and not sacrifice the original wild species in favor of unlimited numbers of the more recent comers to the range . . . Those of you who may think that by removing the cattle from the range the problem will miraculously be solved are misguided. In our area, the conflicts between game and horses will still be there even after the cattle are gone."

The BLM wanted to appeal the court's decision, but their superiors in the department of Interior decided not to for the time being. At this point, no one knows if or when the Challis wild horse herd can be reduced and controlled.

By the summer of 1978 there were 660 horses, and that number included 100 new foals, so the herd was still increasing at a fast rate. The winter of 1976-1977 was very mild, with very little snow (drought conditions) and as a result the horses were able to use almost all of the horse range for wintering instead of being confined to lower elevations by deep snow in the high country. The winter of 1977-78 was moderately mild. Some horses were in

poor shape by spring and a few horses died. The next winter of heavy snows will take its toll, for there are now twice as many horses as the winter range can support.

Some studies were conducted on the Challis herd, using tranquilizers, exploring the possibilities of using tranquilizers as a future means of immobilizing and capturing small groups of horses. But this action was also halted by the AHPA and HSUS. The horses continue to increase unchecked. Watching the horses destroy their range and setting themselves up for a bad winter and slow deaths by starvation is frustrating to the BLM men who are responsible for their welfare. As Harry Finlayson said, "The opponents of the Challis roundup want these animals left alone; they don't feel that starvation is inhumane, but natural attrition."

But those of us who live nearby, and the people who are responsible for the horses, don't feel that way. To us, starvation is perhaps the most cruel and inhumane fate you can inflict upon that horse herd. And so terribly unnecessary.

20

The Future

What will the future bring? That depends on how well and how quickly we can solve the problem of wild horse management on our public lands. Wild horse numbers more than tripled in the first six years after the passage of PL 92-195 to protect them. Perhaps it protected them too well from mankind, and not well enough from themselves.

According to the Wild Horse Act, allocation of forage for wild horses and burros was to be based upon the biological requirements of the animals present upon the land, and upon the nature and stability of the habitat, but there is still great controversy over how much habitat is needed for the wildlife and domestic livestock. How many domestic animals and how much wildlife should we have out there sharing the range with the horses?

Wild horse or burro numbers may be adjusted to maintain proper balance, but the law has been interpreted to mean that some horses or burros shall remain wherever they existed in 1971, regardless of the suitability of the habitat, the danger they pose to the habitat and the other animals (some of them endangered species, like desert bighorn) that depend on the habitat. Adjustments to satisfy the requirements of a horse or burro herd may mean excluding all domestic livestock in some areas, and this interpretation of the law seems impractical and

If wild horse numbers continue to increase, more and more herds will be faced with winter starvation.

nearsighted, since we are looking to the public lands to produce a good portion of our meat and wool. Also, wild horses and burros are now present on some areas where they don't have good conditions for year-long grazing. In these areas, it would seem logical, and in the interests of good range management and the horses themselves, to remove the horses entirely, but the provisions of PL 92-195 do not permit it. In addition, one wild horse on the range for 12 months can eat as much feed as 4 or 5 cows during a seasonal grazing period of 3 months.

If horse numbers continue to increase as fast as they have during the first six years of federal protection, they must either increase the size of their ranges, or die of starvation. Some ranges were already in bad shape even at the time the Wild Horse Act was passed. For instance, in an article in *Western Horseman* (June, 1973), the author told about riding through the southern Utah desert in July of 1972:

> I came upon something that will stick in my mind for a long time, something that seems likely to be seen by more people as time goes on. A yearling horse had fallen just that morning, apparently from starvation. It's head was under its body, all rolled up in a ball on the side hill. Two very thin mares were standing within ten feet of the yearling. They looked as if they, too, were waiting for death. They were big-headed, inbred horses from some wild bunch; apparently they were left to die because they couldn't keep up.

Starvation was just around the corner for several herds. The drought in late 1976-1977 brought matters to a head in more than a few areas in the West. In Oregon the lack of winter moisture forced more than 1500 wild horses in the Vale District to change their feeding habits and winter on their summer range high on the Sheepheads Mountains. Normally these horses come down out of the mountains into Alvord Basin or Barren Valley on the west side of the Owyhee River during winter— where feed is usually plentiful and potholes store water from fall rains. But in the fall of 1976 there were no rains.

In late February of 1977, Grant Baugh of the BLM said, "Usually five inches of moisture falls during the year, much of it in the winter. But the single snowstorm this year dropped less than one inch of moisture and much of that has now evaporated." The horses had no choice but to live around the waterholes in the mountains and travel long distances to find feed. In this instance they were traveling up to 15 miles each day between feed and water, cutting deep trails on their daily trips to the water holes—making trails 8 to 10 inches deep in the rocky soil. In the process of grazing summer, fall and winter in the same area, the horses had cleared the range of all edible vegetation for miles around each water source.

Burro reduction programs were proposed for the Saline Valley in California and in the Phoenix, Arizona BLM district. In April of 1977 the BLM conducted a series of five public meetings to obtain public input into a proposed emergency plan to reduce the burro numbers in the Alamo Lake region

Some of the emaciated horses gathered in Oregon during the drought of 1977.

of western Arizona, where almost all edible plants were gone. Wild Horse Annie's group, WHOA, supported these reductions. Six hundred burros were captured later that year, and all of them were adopted out by January of 1978.

In the Bakersfield District in California, plans were underway to reduce a herd of 2,500 burros down to manageable size. The National Animal Welfare League of San Francisco asked the Federal Court in Fresno to halt the burro gathering program and to require the BLM to develop a full environmental statement on burro impacts. But the court denied this request. In the hearings, the court also heard testimony from Helen Reilly, president of ISPMB. Mrs. Reilly said that ISPMB and WHOA support the BLM reduction program. She had toured the Waucoba Springs and Saline Valley areas and felt there was a vital and immediate need for burro reduction. Not only was the forage depleted, but veterinary examination of several burros showed them to be suffering from malnutrition.

Representatives from ISPMB also attended a field trip and emergency public meeting in Baker, California concerning the Lava Beds Herd Management Area. Reduction needs were critical because of lack of feed and water, but the BLM had no

Drought victims in Nevada. These wild foals died trying to get a drink of mud. Some got mired in the mudholes and could not get out. A BLM backhoe dug out the spring to provide more water for the survivors.

funds for the proposed gatherings. Mrs. Reilly contacted Washington, D.C. and pointed out the critical situation, and funds were granted for burro removal. The gathering began in mid-September, 1977. Over 200 burros were gathered by water trapping during the first 8 days of the project. The drought had caused severe water shortage and the animals were easy to trap.

In late April of 1977 one dead horse was found and six others discovered dying of thirst on the Owyhee Desert in southern Idaho where drought was severe. The six that were still alive were rescued by BLM personnel, and water was hauled out to the area for other horses. About 50 wild horses were ranging in that general area and the problem was critical. The situation had been made worse because a 150,000 acre fire in the summer of 1976 had forced the horses to move into an area where there was no natural water.

In Nevada more horses died because of the drought. The two year drought dried up many water holes, and hundreds of horses were left with nothing but mud for moisture. Many young foals died after being mired in the deep mud while trying to suck moisture from it, and some were trampled in the mud by older horses crowding in for moisture. The BLM dug out some of the springs to try to provide water for the survivors.

A May, 1977 letter from Tom Marvel, a rancher from Battle Mountain, Nevada, mentioned to me that "the number of wild horses in our area since 1971 has doubled and in some places, greater than that. This year where it is as dry as it is, much of our water is from dirt tanks on the range. We haven't had sufficient moisture and quite a lot of the horses are

dying at these waterholes for they are unable to get to live water for they are fenced off of it from management programs of the BLM [a little later that year the BLM dug a lot of these springs out for the horses]. I want to state that I am in sympathy with the BLM to some extent, because the wild horse groups have been so ignorant in their approach of understanding the management of wild horses. I will state that it is the cruelest thing, in wanting the wild horse to expand to the point of dying."

During the summer of 1977 horses were rounded up in Oregon to save them from dying of thirst and starvation. Public meetings (required by the new amendment to PL 92-195 allowing BLM use of helicopters in horse roundups) were held before starting the 1977 roundup program, and no objections were raised about the use of helicopters. The Lakeview District was the first to use the helicopter, gathering horses in July, and found it cost only $22.40 per horse to gather them, much cheaper than the previous horseback roundups. These horses were in bad shape when found, but after being captured and given water, most of them were all right within a short time. $100,000 of drought relief funds received by the BLM in Oregon in 1977 was used to reduce the numbers of wild horses in the Vale and Burns areas.

Earlier that same year Army officials were worried about 250 wild horses that looked like they might die of thirst on the Dugway Proving Grounds in Utah. By spring the drought had dried up nearly all the water holes on the Army test range, so it was planned to remove about 100 of them, after consulting with the Humane Society and the Utah State Veterinarian. A year earlier about 60 horses on the base died after natural water holes dried up and the

A survivor. BLM personnel twice pulled this two-week-old foal from the mudhole. He staggered back in after the first rescue because he was so thirsty. The BLM crew cleaned him up and bottle fed him until he was old enough to be adopted.

horses refused to drink at man-made watering troughs.

In June of 1977 part of the horse population were corralled, using helicopters to spot them and drive them toward a box canyon. Cowboys on horseback finished the roundup, herding the horses into the corral. "They were awful looking—just skin and bones. We were lucky to get them off the range when we did," said a Dugway spokesman. The horses were auctioned off as surplus Army property; they did not fall under the provisions of PL 92-195 because they spend more than half their time on the Army base.

In Nevada the lack of forage, because of drought conditions, caused some horses to eat toxic plants such as loco weed and death camas. Mike Kilpatrick, a University of Nevada range specialist, said that "in normal or good range years there is so much other growth that poisonous range plants such as loco weed and death camas are not a problem but in dry years they are." An 800 pound horse would have to eat about four pounds of camas to be poisoned, but a horse could easily eat that much in a day if there wasn't must feed and the death camas was available. With loco weed, the poison accumulates over a period of time, becoming deadly after the horse has been eating the plants for a month or so.

As summer wore on, the situation became worse and worse in drought-stricken areas of the West. In eastern Oregon horses were dying of thirst. The BLM rounded up many, and had to shoot some that were just too far gone. Dead horses were frequently seen during aerial surveys.

Then in the following winter (1977-1978), with record snowfalls on some of the western ranges, more wild horses were lost. Some were trapped by heavy snows in several areas of Montana, Nevada and California. Hay was airlifted and dropped from helicopters in an attempt to save some of the starving horses in the Pryor Mountains. There was a heavy winter loss of wild horses in Nevada. More than 270 dead horses were found in the Buffalo Hills area of the Winnemucca district, and there were winterkill losses in other districts as well.

This type of tragedy brings back unpleasant memories for some ranchers who have witnessed similar losses in other bad winters. This reminiscence by Bud Hage is worth thinking about:

It was a beautiful warm day in the early spring of 1952 . . . It was a day to make a cowman's heart glad, especially after the extra hard winter we had just come through. There had been extra heavy snow from late January through March and the seemingly unending wind had drifted the snow over fences and hay stacks. It blocked the roads, kept cattle from the feed grounds

and literally froze some stock to death. Counting the dead cows and calves had been a gruesome task and to some ranchers it had meant bankruptcy.

Today we were out looking at the condition of the range, trying to make a determination of when the grass would be able to withstand grazing. It was a welcome job after the severe ordeal of the past few months.

Enjoyable at least, until we dropped off the ridge into Beaver Creek. My saddle horse noticed it first, then Jim's horse got the scent and snorted kind of low, indicating he didn't like what was ahead.

Breaking through the willows to the far side of the creek, we came upon the grim evidence of an epic struggle for survival. Over thirty horse carcasses were lying between the willows and the base of the rimrock on the far side of the canyon. They had been trapped by the drifting snows after seeking shelter from the winter winds.

Normally these horses would have waited out the storm, then broken through the drifts to the high ridges where the wind blows the snow away and exposes grass and white sage.

This last year hadn't been normal enough. The summer had been dry with water becoming scarce in the fall. These horses had been weakened by the drought before winter set in.

The early part of winter hadn't been that unusual, but from late January on, the snows and winds came with a vengeance. In early March, high winds and drifting snow had persisted unceasingly for weeks. When it did stop, any stock that had not been on good feed when the winds began were probably dead. This bunch of wild horses had been trapped without feed.

They had eaten the willows, of course. Anything smaller than an inch in diameter and low enough to eat had been eaten down to a stub. The sagebrush, too, had been gnawed down to the ground. Then the wind, cold, and lack of feed had felled them, one by one.

Most of these carcasses had been stripped down to hide and bones. Several coyotes were lurking nearby. They were fat and their hair was shiny, showing they had wintered well.

The way the carcasses were positioned told quite a detailed story. You could see how a mare had tried to back up against the rimrock or willows to keep the coyotes from getting to her hindquarters as she fought to protect her weakened colt. The coyotes were smart enough to not really get in range of her teeth and hooves, but to continually threaten her so she would get no rest. In her already weakened condition, it didn't take long. The colt would usually go down first and the coyotes would eat him to preserve their strength while wearing the mare down. Once she collapsed, the end came quickly. Striking first at the soft underbelly and flanks, her life was quickly running out on the snow and the feast was on.

Of course, after the first few were killed, it was just a matter of finishing off the others as they dropped, in their rapidly weakening condition. When the weather cleared, the coyotes were joined by an assortment of other scavengers, buzzards, magpies and some rodents. They had cleaned up well.

This type of winter usually doesn't come very often, but when it does, the toll can be devastatingly high. Survival of the fittest, or the luckiest, had been the watchword. A combination of excessive wild horse numbers combined with summer drought and a hard winter had joined forces to establish a balance. Mother nature, contrary to popular belief, can sometimes be very cruel.

The scene recalled memories of other bad winters. During World War II, the young men from the ranches who normally spent a certain amount of time each year "mustanging" and culling the herds, were away fighting. The horse numbers built up and when the winter of '48 and '49 hit, the grizzly scene we were observing was extant on a large scale. Over 1000 horses had been found dead in the north end of Antelope Valley alone.

I could remember an old buckaroo asking me one day, "Did you ever hear a horse scream?"

"No", I replied.

He continued, "I was living in the bottom of the Owyhee River Canyon the winter of 1936. Rock cliffs rose six hundred feet on both sides of the river. The snow was deep everywhere and the wild horses had nothing to eat. After gnawing the mane and tail hair off of each other, they had attempted to reach the few blades of grass that protruded out of the broken rocks at the edge of the cliffs. Sometimes they would slip and fall. They scream just like a human while plunging to their death."

We rode on out of the canyon. There were some scattered carcasses up the creek. That scene is still vivid to me. Particularly now that it seems destined to be repeated on a massive scale. We see that deadly combination building up again, increasing horse numbers and severe drought engulfing the western range states. Today we see wild horses dying of thirst on the parched ranges.

We who have lived in the mustang country and have learned to admire and to share with the wild horses their love of independence and freedom, their need for the wide open spaces, I am fearful of what the future holds for them. It's out of the westerners' hands now. It is our hope that those who were mainly responsible for the new laws will vigorously support the "adopt a horse" program. At present it is the only viable alternative.

I, for one, would not care to see nature's grim remedy applied again.

Death by thirst, or starvation—is this the solution Americans want for the wild horse overpopulation problem? Letting the horses expand to the point of destroying their range and starving to death? Without natural predators, the herds are not going to attain a "balance" with their food supply. But a balance can be obtained by humane and flexible management procedures, rounding up excess

Death by starvation—Is this the solution Americans want for the wild horse over-population problem?

horses. Or the herds can be allowed to continue growing, overgrazing and falling victim to drought, sickness, malnutrition and starvation. This kind of death is grim, inhumane, and a slow agony for the horses. This kind of prolonged misery is much more drawn-out and cruel than any fate suffered by the horses in the 1950's that were headed for the canning plants.

Somewhere along the line we've gotten our values messed up; we may now be delivering the horse a more cruel blow than before he was "protected." The sad and frustrating thing about having these horses die slow deaths from drought and starvation is that it is so unnecessary. We can prevent these disasters. In order to truly protect the wild horse and burro, we must protect them from themselves, managing them in a manner that protects the range on which they depend for their future existence and health.

In April of 1977 a National Wild Horse Forum was held in Reno, Nevada to discuss the wild horse and burro problems. The objectives of this three-day meeting, attended by many concerned citizens, were to educate, improve communications between the various interest groups involved, and to provide a reference document and guide for future actions. Most of the groups who attended the forum agreed that there was an emergency in respect to the numbers of wild horses and burros on the range, and that immediate steps needed to be taken to correct the situation. At that time there were about 65,000 wild horses and burros in the western states, with Nevada having 35,000 head.

One of the points brought out at the forum was that the herds should remain as intended by PL 92-195, but with proper management and a more realistic harvest of excess horses. Everyone agreed that the adoption program was not working adequately as a means to get rid of the extra horses. Most agreed that shooting was much more economical, but not acceptable, and a waste of the horses. The proposal by cattle interests that the extra horses be sold, the proceeds going into range improvement funds, was received well by all groups except the HSUS and the wild horse groups. Many people felt that to be able to sell the excess horses for useful purposes would pay for the horse management program, saving the taxpayers the costly and inadequate program we now have. Helicopter use in wild horse management met with general approval except for a couple of the horse groups. Representatives from WHOA agreed that horses needed to be removed and seemed to favor some of the proposals made by the wildlife groups and livestock interests, but the AHPA and HSUS did not appear so receptive.

Roy Young, past chairman of the wild horse and burro advisory board, said that giving title to the horses would help the adoption program be more successful, for more people might take the horses. "The way it is now," he said, "there is some question as to whether a person like a cowboy could take one and use one." The horse can't be branded, so if it gets away there would be no identification that would allow the person to reclaim him. He also mentioned a wild horse allotment in Wyoming that might be a good model for future horse refuges. This allotment had no domestic livestock, and "there is a road that goes over the top of the mountain and out the other side allowing people to take their children and ride through the mountain and be able to see the wild horses. I think this is worth considering in other states. In Nevada we have an estimated 35,000 herd of horses and there is only one road (from Ely to Tonopah) where a tourist may be able to see some."

James Monroe, assistant Director for Legislation and Plans, BLM, discussed current legislation that was pending and the status of court actions concerning wild horses, and also gave a rundown on BLM management attempts, the Adopt-a-horse program, and the desperate need for a better way to control the horse population.

One of the keynote addresses given at the forum was entitled "The Role of the Wild Horse in Changing Concepts of Public Land Use in the West", by Michael J. Pontrelli, Ph.D. His address included these statements:

> The wild horse issue is probably responsible for more public awareness about public lands than any other issue, in fact, probably more than all other issues put together . . . If we take the total memberships of all of the organizations that regularly write about the protec-

tion of wild horses, assume that each membership represents a full family audience . . . we end up with a regularly informed protection oriented population of between 500,000 to 2,500,000 Americans. Also, as any of you involved in the news media know, news involving abuse to wild horses is much more likely to appear in print than questions involving abuse by wild horses . . . it's frequently true that news is printed on the basis of the greatest response expected and it is news about abuse to wild horses that brings by far the greatest response.

> If you take all the people regularly receiving information on the protection of wild horses plus all the people who respond to news about wild horse abuse (or potential abuse) and realize that this issue prompts response by letter, telegrams, etc. to their legislators, we can easily see that the West is outnumbered, if not by actual numbers then certainly by numbers of legislators directly involved.

> The following public responses are now history . . .

> The 1959 "Wild Horse Annie Law" prohibition of airborne and mechanized roundup, had "unprecedented public support". Passage in Congress was virtually without opposition.

> The 1971 "Wild Horse and Burro Law" was reportedly the heaviest mail issue of the full congressional session and passage was without opposition. Testimony shows that many of the groups now opposed to the law spoke strongly in its favor at time of passage. The week before hearings on the "Wild Horse Bill" brought 10,000 pro letters to the President's Office alone.

> The "Adopt a Horse" program of the BLM has now mailed its total 100,000 first printing and second printing is now being done.

> An extensive effort among America's school children was to name the U.S. Bicentennial Animal. It was not Ben Franklin's favorite—the wild turkey—or our magnificent bald eagle. It was overwhelmingly the wild horse. The project was dropped, I think probably because of the non-native status of the horse.

> Ok—so you know all about the popularity of wild horses. What about the public's changing concept toward the West?

> If you asked John Q. Public about public land twenty years ago, he didn't know or care about it. Public land was used and ruled by specific user groups, not because of subterfuge or illegal action but because of public ignorance and apathy. Then came the wild horse issue. Inhumane treatment of wild horses led to knowledge that these animals lived on *public land*, that vested interest user groups were dictating use on public land, that the public had the right to demand public goals on public land, and that the West would never be the same.

> Let's look at a few of the situations now before us in this wild horse issue. With each situation, I'll formulate some hypothetical statements and public responses.

> 1. *Situation*—In places there are more wild horses than can be accomodated in a thriving ecological balance.

A. Statement—These (blank blank) wild horses are eating me out of house and home, my cows are starving to death.

Or—If you have to choose between cattle, and/or deer, and horses, I'll take cattle and/or deer.

Or—I love wild horses but we have to make a choice, so the horses go.

Public response—Anger at the cattle industry; anti-hunting sentiment; recognition of some domestic livestock trespasses and overgrazing; comparison of domestic livestock and wildlife numbers versus wild horse numbers and increased controls on the livestock industry. *Increased* protection of wild horses.

B. Statement—The wild horse law was so effective in protecting our wild horses that now there may be too many. They again need our help, because too many horse eventually lead to fewer horses and fewer everything else.

Public response—Horses need management; overprotection is as bad as under-protection. Horses are part of the ecological system related to everything else.

2. *Situation*—What do we do with excess wild horses?

A. Statement—All you can see is jugheads and broomtails. A .30-30 is the solution.

Or—Mustangs make great dog food and we solve two problems.

Or—The adopt-a-horse program is a joke; it won't work.

Public response—No commercial use of horses, no private ownership; *increased* protection of wild horses.

B. Statement—We must all sit down together and discuss alternatives for excess animals.

Or—Out of 100,000 inquiries we have only 4,000 responses for Adopt-A-Horse. We have more horses than we can give away.

Public Response—Disposal of excess animals is a complex problem; many Americans know now that management is necessary and they cannot use emotion-only solutions.

3. *Situation*—Should the wild horses be a component of the range or should they only be in a few select locations?

A. Statement—Take all of them off our ranges and put those that will fit on a place where the public can see them.

Or—If we don't remove those wild horses, we are going to be out of red meat or at least we won't be able to afford it.

Public Response—The cattlemen want the range for themselves so control the livestock industry more; *increased* protection for wild horses.

B. Statement—Once we collectively decide how the western range is to be used, we must discuss the possibility of removing wild horses in all but a few special wild horse areas.

Public Response—Public learns about other range uses; public helps in the decision process.

4. *Situation*—Some people think there can never be too many horses.

A. Statement—If you let the uninformed public decide, all we will have is (blank blank) wild horses.

Public Response—Good!

B. Statement—Too many wild horses can adversely affect themselves and every other living thing.

Public Response—Knowledge that wild horses and other living things need management.

If those who are concerned about too many wild horses say their concern wrong, the wild horses win every time, unless we do have too many wild horses; then the horses and we all lose.

Milton Frei, Range Conservationist, discussed major research needs for wild horse management. He said the BLM's first priority in this area was for development of a technique to control excess wild horses at a reasonable cost and without having to physically capture them. In his view, it would entail fertility control aimed at the dominant stallions, in the form of a drug that would make them infertile while yet retaining their aggressive, dominant be-

More research needs to be done on wild horse population control. Experiments are being conducted on drugs that temporarily make a harem stallion infertile for a season.

havior (so as to keep the sub-dominant and non-harem stallions from breeding the mares). To be effective, according to Mr. Frei, the drug must be able to inhibit the production of sperm cells, not alter the stallions' aggressive behavior, and be temporary and reversible in action—affecting the stallion just for one breeding season—so that the gene pool wouldn't be irreversibly altered and the horse population can again regenerate itself when necessary. If some kind of drug could be developed that could be administered by remote injection (through use of a cap-chur gun), the stallions could be injected from helicopter or stalked from the ground. Fertility control could be a useful tool whether or not PL 92-195 is amended to allow the BLM to sell excess animals.

The BLM's second research priority involves the development of a technique for capturing and handling wild horses, a technique that could be used by individuals (such as BLM personnel) who have no real experience or expertise in capturing and handling these animals by customary physical methods. Chemical immobilization has been widely used in wildlife management for many years, but so far the drugs which can be used on wild horses have certain disadvantages, including high cost, slow knockdown time, low tolerance level by the animals (a dose that might work well on one horse might kill another, or be completely inaffective on a third), and excessive restriction on availability.

Another area of research that the BLM wants to explore is causes of natural mortality in the wild horse populations, which would help them more accurately project the rate of population increase, and would also enable them to avoid the costly removal of animals that would probably die in the near future anyway. In other words, natural mortality would harvest part of the excess horses for them.

As of 1977 the BLM was not funding any research contracts on wild horses, however. In 1974 they were able to fund two studies on wild burros, but additional funds for wild horse research were not available. Although they have requested research funds each year since 1974, the necessary funds have not been obtained, primarily because of the increased emphasis given to the range management program as the result of the NRDC lawsuit. The suit required the BLM to prepare environmental impact statements on the livestock grazing on public lands. The need for additional data for these impact statements has used all available money that might have gone into wild horse research.

William F. Hyde, a research associate for Resources for the Future, talked about resource alloca-tion and economics of wild horse management, and the problems of trying to weigh and evaluate aesthetic values as well as economic values. One of his suggestions was to create horse ranges where the wild horse would be the primary use, and where the public could view the wild horses if they wanted to. As for population control, "shooting is acceptable and there is no harm in rendering the remains. In fact rendering could be looked upon as conserving a resource as well as a means of providing additional financing for wild horse management. Of course, these thoughts . . . are my own. I have no difficulty accepting objections on ethical grounds. I do wish to point out, however, that the additional costs of other answers [expensive roundups and the adoption program, etc] imply less money is left over for other wild horse management issues, including providing for recreational viewing of the animals."

Earlier in his statement, he said, "Once we have accepted the preference of some for continued existence of wild horses then we can proceed to discuss wild horse management. And wild horses will be managed, must be managed, by humans, otherwise the horses will be managed in accordance with natural law—overpopulation and coincident destruction of the range leading to death by starvation and disease. Predators would play a role except that we have eliminated most of them. One of the co-issues in wild horse management is humane treatment. There is nothing humane about the solutions of natural law."

Bernard Shanks, a professor at the University of Nevada, made a statement about wild horses and conservation organizations. He mentioned that conservation groups (such as the Sierra Club, Wilderness Society and Audubon Society) did not actively support PL 92-195 when it was being passed in 1971. He pointed out that some of the organizations are conservative and reluctant to take an active role in public land policy issues. In recent years the wild horse focused attention on western land management, especially BLM lands, and widened the scope of some conservation groups' interests from national parks and wilderness to include the public domain lands.

The wild horse on public lands and the subject of its protection and management has much in common with other environmental issues, so why did conservationists fail to support horses? One reason is because of the horses' influence on western range conditions and soil erosion, and upon wildlife and ecological change. Many of the wildlife organizations view the horse as a threat to hunting activities because of their competition with game for habitat. A serious threat to these wildlife groups has been the arrival of animal protection groups on the western public land policy scene.

The Sierra Club has made substantial changes in its policy since the passage of PL 92-195 and the Sierra Club statement that "the wild horse is certainly not an alien". Since then, management issues of wild horses on public lands have drawn some of the conservation organizations into the wild horse controversy. Local chapters of the Sierra Club in areas with large burro populations started lengthy discussions within the Club over their burro policy and now the Club has a detailed policy statement on burro management, recognizing the need for control and even the removal of burros in some regions.

Similarly, *Audubon* magazine and the National Parks and Conservation Association printed sympathetic wild horse articles in 1969 and 1971. But by 1976 the *High Country News*, the West's best-known environmental newspaper, had an article on wild burros and the 1971 Act that showed substantial changes in conservationist attitudes toward the wild horse and burro. By 1975 the Izaak Walton League, an old and traditional conservation group, strongly supported managing and controlling these feral animals, and said their group was "deeply concerned about the actual and potential damage to wildlife and rangelands from unchecked increases in feral horse and burro populations."

Other conservation organizations support the concept of wild horses but insist on management and control to reduce the impact of wildlife. Other groups don't have a policy on wild horses and some want to avoid the issue to keep from splitting their memberships between the "purists" who don't want any horses on the public lands, and the wild horse advocates. These organizations straddle the wild horse issue and give out merely general statements about wild horse management and protection.

Chris Vosler, another speaker at the wild horse forum, and District BLM manager of the Burns, Oregon district gave a report on wild horse management and removal in the Burns district, and he emphasized that the BLM is in the horse management business, and will be for a long time to come. "This is dictated," he said, "by law, a law that I basically agree with. Of course, there are problems with the law like many others, but these problems can be worked out and hopefully this forum will be the vehicle by which some of these problems can be solved."

He said that the Burns district began horse inventory by airplane in January of 1972 and has done it yearly ever since. "Beginning in 1974," he pointed out, "we have used helicopters for our inventory work and have found the counts to be much more accurate. We count the animals during the same time period each year and calculate our increase based upon the difference between our previous year's count so that birth rate and death loss are taken care of and we don't get into the process of trying to determine how many colts were born, how many died, how many old animals died and so forth."

All horses gathered in Oregon were brought to the Burns facilities to be adopted out, and as of April 1977 over 1300 horses had been processed. Of the people who have applied to adopt horses, only one in ten actually follow through. The cost of gathering the horses has been reduced since the first roundups, but the cost of caring for the animals until their date of adoption has increased. The horses have to be vaccinated, and Coggins tested before they can be shipped out of state. The horses have to be kept in the facilities longer, generally, because the close "market" has been saturated, and the people coming to get them are coming from farther away. He closed his statement by saying "the removal and disposition of wild horses in BLM is a full time job, which requires knowledge of wild horses, of people and of vegetative resources. The hours are long, the pay isn't too bad, the dangers are great, but the job is rewarding if you are interested in the protection of wild and free-roaming horses and burros."

The Salmon River Cattlemen's Association sent a letter to the wild horse forum, explaining their own situation and expressing their views on wild horse problems. This Stockman's association is a Nevada corporation owned by 48 stockholders, who use grazing land that is a checker-board pattern of private and public land. The Utah Construction Company that sold them this grazing land had for many years run thousands of cattle and hundreds of horses, the horses being raised for use in construction work, transportation, livestock handling, and some for the U.S. Cavalry.

When the recent claiming period for free-roaming horses came about, the stockman's association was faced with a two-edged sword. A spokesman explained, "We could choose between an impractical, economically impossible method of gathering them with a trespass fee for those claimed, or relinquish ownership." In 1976 the stockholders built two large traps; labor and materials came to $11,397. Their average cost per horse gathered was approximately $248.56. "We are still concerned," he added, "with approximately 650 head remaining on the ranch. We lack the time and manpower to move them to within the trap area. Any reasoning should point to the fact this is far too many horses for the area. With our drought conditions it is becoming a disaster for the horses and our range land."

The association asked that helicopters be used for

gathering the rest of their claimed horses, and felt that the government being able to use helicopters while private ranchers could not is a double standard. They asked that helicopters be allowed, under the supervision of the BLM, to gather private horses on private allotments and deeded land.

The letter said:

Our people are minority and we are too busy making a living to compete equally with the Wild Horse Protective Association or WHOA or other groups in their lobbying techniques and publicity programs. We cannot financially compete with their propaganda campaigns through the news and TV media. We personally respect and admire Mrs. Velma Johnston and some of her associates . . . We do not deny there has been brutal handling of horses and cattle. Some of the human race hasn't progressed beyond brutal cruel treatment of their fellowman . . . The proposed rules pertaining to claimed animals is an encroachment upon our rights to manage our land and is disruptive to BLM range management plans. These rules have been forced upon us by people, who to the best of our knowlege share no financial responsibility in the actual caring for horses. We help feed the horses, water them and provide salt. The rancher is the horse's best friend. We do not subject them to the environment of a zoo. We are willing to cooperate with a reasonable amount of horses; a minimum of 40 head and a maximum of 150 head. Let them run free on our ranch. What encroachment on private land and water sources will be negligible.

The letter closed by saying:

Our 48 member group requests that the Wild Horse Adoption Plan be discontinued. It is impractical, inhumane, and economically wasteful. Since 1934 the BLM has encouraged and tried to practice good range management and through the passage of one law all this has been jeopardized. They have spent $19.00 per horse in Elko district for supervision of horses captured (claimed horses gathered by the ranchers—the ranchers paying the roundup costs). They spent $62,000.00 in Carson City Nevada for a horse adoption center. These costs with the costs of constructing traps and gathering horses add up to total financial irresponsibility. The abuse of our forage, the erosion of the soil, the waste of time, energy and fuel is inexcuseable. We feel emergency measures should be taken immediately to reduce the number of horses on our land.

Robert Wright, President of the Nevada Cattlemen's Association, made this statement at the wild horse forum:

I am a lifelong resident of Nevada and have had much association with the ranges and the wild horses that run on them.

If the wild horses were to be completely removed from the ranges I would be among the first to raise my voice in opposition to it. The wild horse is part of our American heritage and certainly needs to be preserved for future generations.

"These wild horses are fast disappearing from the American scene," states the Wild Horse Act of 1971. That statement is not valid in Nevada. The wild horse in reality is fast appearing on the scene. A systematic count by the land managing agencies in Nevada indicates a herd of some 35,000 head. The amount of forage to sustain a herd of that magnitude for one year is 360,000 AUM's or animal unit months.

There are currently recognized in Nevada 2,971,689 AUM's of public range grazing. This includes use for active, non-use, lease lands, free use, crossing and trails, exchange of use and wildlife allocations. At the present 20% rate of wild horse increase by 1987 the wild horse numbers will reach about 260,000 head and they will consume 3,120,000 AUM's of forage. This is more than the total forage now available for all uses in Nevada and will eliminate all big game wildlife and domestic livestock forage. This was not the intent nor purpose of Congress, the Wild Horse Act of 1971 nor the Federal Land Management and Policy Act of 1976.

These wild horses are far in excess of the numbers that were contemplated by the Wild Horse Act of 1971 . . . It was estimated in 1976 by the Nevada BLM that management and removal of the excess horses was going to cost the taxpayers up to the following amounts in Nevada alone:

1. Removal costs at $500 per head for 25,000 head—$12,500,000.
2. Herd management plans for the remaining 10,000 horses not removed, at $260 per head—$2,600,000.
3. Annual recurring costs for protection, surveillance, population control and management per year (10,000 head at $96.00 per head) for ten years—$960,200.

This comes to a total of $16,060,200. And if you increase the management and removal costs 20% per year from 1976 to 1987 it will cost the taxpayers of this nation $119,000,000.00 for Nevada horses alone. The cost benefit ratio cannot be justified.

A statement by John Weber, regional vice-president of the American National Cattlemen's Association included these comments:

It would be well to go back and review the enactment of the Wild Horse and Burro Act of December 15, 1971. I was told then by Congressmen that this particular legislation was the hottest thing to hit Washington in a long time. Emotions ran high as the press and television broadcast tales of large scale slaughter of wild horses on western ranges. Legislation passed under these highly emotional conditions is generally not good.

Essentially what this legislation did was to stop the gathering of wild horses and claimed horses from the public lands . . . How has the management of the wild horses fared under the Act since its enactment five years ago? I do not have the total figures of the wild horse population on all of the public lands, but I do have figures for the state of Nevada . . . During the past five years wild horses within Nevada have increased from an estimated 8,000 in 1971 to 30,000 in 1976. This is a yearly increase of 20% under the present management program of the BLM. I cannot believe how anyone can fail to see what the damage will be to our public ranges if this herd is allowed to multiply at its present rate.

Nick Theos, Chairman of the Public Land Council, had this to say:

The livestock industry didn't oppose the Wild Horse and Burro Act completely, we just wanted to see those wild horses controlled and managed like other range animals. We had a lot of faith that the wild horse advisory boards would come up with good management practices and methods of control providing the act could be changed just a bit to allow for logical methods. But it seems this has been real hard to get done because it hasn't been done yet . . . .

The Organic Act of 1976 almost had a good wild horse section to increase management. But it's such an emotional issue in Washington D.C., according to lots of congressmen, that before that land bill was passed Senator Jackson had managed to have all the good management ideas in the bill killed. What we got was just the use of helicopters in roundups. But meanwhile the courts in Washington D.C. are interpreting the Wild Horse Act and saying things like "minimum management" (which is the wording in the Wild Horse Act) means no management at all. What's the use of helicopters if the courts keep saying you can't round them up unless you can prove that you shouldn't remove all domestic livestock so there can be more horses . . . .

Very few people really have first hand knowledge about wild horses or the destruction they can have on the ranges and environment as a whole. All they can see is that news film of a few years back of that roundup when they drove them off a cliff. Sure something needed to be done about that kind of action, but like Senator Bennett Johnston of Louisiana said during the confirmation hearings for Secretary Andrus, in Louisiana they had alligators up to their you-know-whats because they were *overprotected*. He said those gators were coming up into people's backyards who lived along those rivers and bayous and eating up pet dogs, pet cats and getting way too close to small children. He said you just have to come up with some good harvest control practices if you're going to protect an animal—you can't let it get out of hand.

R. J. (Dick) Jenkins, an Oregon cattle rancher, made this statement at the wild horse forum:

We are now living during an era of great change in the United States . . . If our new President is trying to encourage an all-out effort to lower government spending and keep the truth between big government and the people, we as individuals should put out an effort on our level . . .

I have been involved in this wild horse situation all my life, and in the past few years have been one of the unfortunate operators who has been forced off his public range as well as some private property by the ever increasing numbers of wild horses. There is no way to figure exactly how many thousands of dollars I have lost in the past two years because of this situation, but under present cattle price trends as well as the impending drought, the pressure has certainly been felt. I don't mind being one of the first to be made an example of when horse herds are left uncontrolled, if something constructive comes out of it. However, up until now, I have seen quite limited progress being made towards a feasible solution.

The wild horse organizations are still blaming the ranchers for overstocking and abusing the range, and in some cases the BLM for not upholding the law in the proper order. On the other side, the ranchers are blaming the BLM for kicking them off the public lands and blaming the wild horse groups for pushing right behind.

I think that both sides of the issue have to admit that the present law and manner of upholding it are definitely not working and it looks as though it is going to get worse before it gets better. It is much easier to get a law like this in force than it is to change the weak points after it is in effect.

It all comes back to the fact that if all of the truth and facts were known before the law was sent before Congress, a lot of mistakes and hardships could have been avoided. Any time you use impressionable-age school children and misinformed adults to get a law passed, you are going to have a fallacy no one can live with. I don't mean the rancher is the only one who cannot live with the present law. We have practically reached the limit of available people to foster care for these animals, and in some cases the horses would be better off starving to death on the range than in their present foster homes . . .

It is now costing the taxpayers anywhere from $200 to $800 per head to gather and give these horses to the public to feed. Multiply that by the hundreds of horses needed to be gathered and it is reaching into the millions of dollars. We complain about our high taxes and excess government spending and turn around and support programs such as the wild horse management . . .

I have received so many letters from people who want to save the wild horses for future generations. They stated they didn't necessarily want to come and see the horses, but they just wanted to know they were there. This makes about as much sense as if the rancher were to insist that the dog catchers and dog pounds in the cities should be done away with because we like cow dogs and feel you people in the cities should be able to enjoy them also. After all, the cow dog is a western tradition, so why shouldn't the urban people be able to enjoy the dogs . . . If these people would come and see the situation first-hand they would certainly have a different outlook.

Jim Bennetts, attorney and rancher from Challis, Idaho, mentioned some of the problems associated with wild horses on his range, and the wild horse issue in general, saying "we can't afford 500 horses on a 150 head range. This kind of situation brings about the most inhumane conditions for the horses as well as on the wild life in the short term and prolonged damage to the resource in the long term. We can't afford to be so careless and thoughtless— we need management and we need control and we need it now."

He pointed out the economic factors involved.

Frankly, in my opinion, the wild horse has only an aesthetic value. Under the present situation the wild horse can not be harvested except at tremendous cost to the taxpayer and once harvested, can not be marketed in the usual sense. Other inhabitants of the range, namely cattle and the major wildlife species, show substantial economic value to the localities and the State . . . The horse, however, must make its case based upon its aesthetic value alone. I concede that it does have an aesthetic value, and therefore, a place in the scheme of things. However, it also appears to me that as we get more and more horses, the aesthetic value of each individual horse becomes less and less. For example, if the horses become so numerous that they are running around in downtown Reno, they become nuisances and in effect take on a minus value aesthetically speaking.

His final point was for more reasonable and logical methods of roundup:

Humane treatment necessarily involves control of numbers. I don't think that it follows at all, however, that the present methods of control or disposition of horses under the Adopt-a-horse program are all that humane. As a lover of horses I believe the present methods of disposition may be the most inhumane method imaginable. If those procedures can't be justified on the basis of humane treatment, they surely can't be justified on the basis of cost. Also it seems to me that by refusing to allow a more liberal use of the wild horse and by refusing to permit the animal to be processed or consumed, we are in effect denying it recognition as a valuable resource. In our state we don't even give our majestic Bighorn Ram such an untouchable status. In fact, a party who harvests a ram in Idaho and who fails to beneficially use the carcass of the animal could be held criminally accountable for malicious waste of a game animal.

I do not claim to have all the answers and some of the answers I do think I have may not be acceptable to the majority in attendance here, but I have lived a good share of my life with wild horses in my back yard. I can summarize my position in a few words. We need to be concerned with Wild and Free Roaming *Starving* Horses, as well as wild and free roaming horses. We need control of numbers and we need to reassess our methods of control from both the position of 1) humane treatment, and 2) practicality.

At a Senate hearing in May of 1977 on the wild horse issue, the suggestions ranged from slaughtering them for pet food to birth control through temporary sterilization. Some of the suggestions were for granting title to the horses to the adopters after they had had the horses one year,* horse roundups for sale to food and processing companies, calculated shooting of excess horses and burros, reintroduction of predators in areas where herds were increasing rapidly. Two bills had been introduced in Congress at that time. Charles Mathias, Senator from Maryland, had introduced a bill to include the national parks under PL 92-195, so that the horses and burros within them would be controlled either through adoption or destruction. Senator Bob Packwood of Oregon had introduced a bill to allow sale of horses for food or other commerical purposes. In eastern Oregon the horse populations as of May of 1977 were more than double proper management levels.

At a meeting held in November, 1977 on the University of Nevada Reno campus, progress was made toward forming a national group concerned with wild horses and burros. This meeting was an outgrowth of the National Wild Horse Forum held earlier that year. A steering committee was formed at the meeting, to begin forming a permanent council on wild horses and burros. Formation of the council could help fill the void created with the dissolving of the National Wild Horse and Burro Advisory Board. Various organizations and interest groups would be represented, including the livestock industry, protectionist and humane groups, state agencies, wildlife and conservation organizations, and federal agencies.

At the November meeting, three general statements were endorsed: 1. Immediate need for legislation to provide practical and humane means of disposal of wild horses and burros from deteriorating range areas where the adoption program is inadequate; 2. Under options available under present law, recommended that captured horses that cannot be disposed of through adoption within 90 days be "put down" rather than turned back on the range; 3. Recommended that any monies coming from horse disposal operations be returned to the appropriate federal agency for wild horse and range improvement.

The participants at the meeting agreed on these three statements but failed to concur in support of the Packwood Bill. Jan Bedrosia of the BLM gave a

*Several of the protectionist groups were opposed to this suggestion, feeling that people would adopt horses in large groups and then sell them after the year was up. It was pointed out that feed costs for a year would greatly exceed the price that could be gotten for the horses. Anyone attempting to keep 100 horses for a year to sell as horsemeat when the year was up, would lose several thousand dollars.

report on wild horse roundups and adoptions. As of November 1977 some 4,694 horses and 1,004 burros had been gathered. Of these, some 3,400 horses and over 1000 burros have been adopted. The remainder were mostly being held in corrals. In Nevada, 1,470 horses had been removed, with 615 still in corrals, awaiting possible adoption.

An editorial in a Nevada newspaper in 1976 said that Nevada cattlemen had understandably been at war with the federal government over the wild horse problem, but that the time had come for cattlemen and other range interests to lay aside their hostilities and join hands with the BLM to try to find a solution. Ranchers, wildlife interests and some environmentalists have argued that thousands of hungry horses increasing unchecked are overgrazing the ranges and competing with livestock and wildlife.

But public opinion remains unswayed; the wild horse protection law is here to stay. According to the editorial, the rancher, the sportsman, the conservationist should acknowledge the permanence of the law and unite together to try to make it work better. Sometimes forgotten in the bitter heat of controversy is the fact that the law itself was designed to give control of these feral populations as well as protection. It gives the BLM authority to establish optimum numbers of horses and burros, in balance with other range uses and permits the BLM to round up or destroy the surplus horses. But so far these control provisions have not worked out as well as intended. And the whole program has proved to be very expensive.

If the American people want horses on their ranges they should foot the bill. They should persuade Congress to appropriate sufficient funds for a horse control program. The horse protection law was demanded by citizens across the nation and

How will we balance the aesthetic value of the wild horse with the practical uses of our rangelands? How many horses does it take to create an aesthetic experience?

enacted by Congress, so the federal government should pay for the program. So far, the BLM has received only small appropriations for wild horse management, yet is mandated by the law to have a horse control program. Because of the size of this job and the complications and restrictions in the law, it is quite expensive, forcing the BLM to borrow from other range programs. Reforms are needed to make better control possible and workable. Stockmen, environmentalists, sportsmen, federal agents and horse lovers should all unite for this, because the need to keep horse numbers under control is an area in which they are all in complete agreement— everyone, that is, except the extremists in the horse protection movement.

In 1978 Congress worked on a range improvement bill that would also make management of wild horses easier. On June 29 the House passed the Roncalio Bill (HR 10587) and sent it to the Senate. This bill authorized $360 million over the next 20 years for range improvement. It was designed to replace the existing grazing fee formula with a seven-year trial of livestock grazing fees tied to the costs of beef production and beef prices. The sponsor of the bill, Rep. Teno Roncalio (D.-Wyoming), said the bill was "of critical importance to the western states and represents perhaps the most important legislation to the western rangelands to emerge since passage of the Taylor Grazing Act in 1934." The bill established guidelines for improvements that could be made without environmental impact statements, and stated that grazing leases would be made for a period of 10 years in most cases.

Under the sections on wild horses and burros, the bill stated that PL 92-195

continues to be successful in its goal of protecting wild free-roaming horses and burros from capture, branding, harassment, and death, and that certain amendments are necessary thereto to avoid excessive costs in the administration of the Act, and to facilitate the humane adoption or disposal of excess wild free roaming horses and burros which because they exceed the carrying capacity of the range, pose a threat to their own habitat, fish, wildlife, recreation, water and soil conservation, domestic livestock grazing, and other rangeland values.

The bill went on to state that PL 92-195 would be amended to read;

Where the Secretary of the Interior or Agriculture determines on the basis of a current inventory of lands within his jurisdiction, that an area is overpopulated with wild free-roaming horses or burros, he shall immediately cause such numbers of excess wild free-roaming horses and burros to be captured and removed for which he determines a demand exists for private adoption and maintenance by qualified individuals under humane conditions. Additional excess wild free-roaming horses and burros for which an adoption demand by qualified individuals does not exist shall be disposed of by the Secretary concerned in the most humane manner possible, so as to restore a thriving natural ecological balance on the public lands and protect the range from the deterioration associated with overpopulation.

Where excess wild free-roaming horses or burros have been transferred to a qualified individual for adoption and private maintenance, and such individual has provided humane conditions and care for such animal or animals for a period of one year, the Secretary is authorized to donate such animal or animals, to such individual at the end of the one-year period. Upon disposal, or donation as provided . . . animals shall lose their status as wild free-roaming horses and burros and shall no longer be considered as falling within the purview of this Act."

A major amendment was expected on the House floor to delete the wild horse control section and to modify the grazing fee provision. Also, the Senate Energy Committee, under Senator Henry Jackson (D.-Wash) had ignored the bill because Jackson had long been a champion of the wild horses and had been annoyed by the attempts to control them. But with the administration and environmentalists joining the livestock industry in pressing for wild horse control, Jackson could no longer ignore the impact of wild horses and burros on public lands. As the bill came up for vote in the House, expected opposition failed to materialize because the bill had widespread support. Key members of both parties, all the major livestock and farm organizations, and a number of wildlife and environmental groups publicly endorsed the bill.

But when the bill went to the Senate, there was more opposition. The Senate Energy Commission, led by Jackson, did not want to even consider the measure. At this writing (August 1978) no action had been taken on the bill in the Senate. In the House, efforts by humane groups to head off the wild horse controls were offset by statements in favor of the controls by the National Audobon Society, the Sierra Club, the National Wildlife Federation and the Wildlife Management Institute. But several facets of the bill would likely be in for lengthy debate in the Senate, and it was not known whether the bill would pass, or even be discussed. Many people feared that no range improvement or horse control bill would make it through Congress in 1978.

And, on other fronts, efforts at wild horse control were being stalemated or blocked by wild horse protection extremists.

As of this writing (August, 1978), the wild horse situation at Challis, Idaho had still not been resolved. Because of opposition by the protectionists to any kind of management, nothing had yet been done about the horse herd, which had grown to nearly 700 head. The problem was also complicated by the BLM's having to prepare a supplement to the EIS on livestock grazing, which kept ALL management of the area in a kind of limbo until the environmental statement was finished.

In September of 1977 the BLM petitioned the Federal District Court (District of Columbia) for additional time to prepare the Challis ES on the ground that there was not sufficient data available to properly analyze the environmental impacts of grazing. But on April 14, 1978, the court ruled that the BLM must complete the supplement to the Challis ES by September 30, 1978 rather than by Dec. 1, 1979, as the Bureau had requested. The supplement was needed because of a lack of data on soils and vegetative productivity in the first study. The grazing EIS issued January 10, 1977 was considered inadequate by the National Resources Defense Council. The supplement is to consider a proposed action involving allocation of forage to livestock, wild horses and wildlife.

The first public input into the updated management plan was provided by a workshop in Challis held June 6 through 9, 1978, to develop recommendations for the BLM. The committee at the workshop was composed of two representatives from the livestock industry, two from the Custer County Economic Stabilization Committee, two from the Idaho Fish and Game, and one each from the NRDC, the Idaho Environmental Council, the eastern horse protection groups and the western horse humane societies.

The committee toured the Challis area, listened to discussions by the BLM's wildlife biologists, discussed the BLM's range survey, and divided into work groups to make recommendations. The workshop closed with little or no agreement on the BLM's proposed forage allocations. The cattlemen questioned the BLM range data and criteria for determining suitability for livestock grazing and felt that cuts in cattle numbers would be a threat to family ranching operations. The Custer County Stabilization Committee felt the BLM's economic data was inadequate and asked this question: "Since the national need for food, fiber, metals, energy, preservation of local tax base and economy is becoming more apparent every day, why is the BLM so reluctant to develop, even by proven methods, all natural resources to their full potential?" The wildlife people were concerned with wild horse competition and felt that critical attention should be given to the winter ranges for elk and bighorn sheep. A man from the Soil Conservation District had this to say: "Less than 3% of the population nationwide is producing the food for 97%. Placing heavy emphasis on recreation and wild horses ahead of the harvestable food production for domestic purposes is a decision that shouldn't be made now if it is to be binding for the future."

The wild horse groups were split in their feelings. The representative from ISPMB was not against wild horse reduction but felt that additional studies would be necessary before permanent management guidelines were begun. But the eastern protection group representatives were not willing to compromise in any way. Frantz Dantzler of HSUS and Gail Snider of AHPA attended the workshop briefly and stated that the BLM's figure of 324 wild horses (the maximum that could be well supported by the horse's winter range) didn't even measure up to their minimum; they would not accept the BLM's maximum numbers as a minimum. These groups were opposed to any herd reductions.

That same year the AHPA and HSUS continued their stubborn stand against wild horse reductions in a court suit attempting to halt all roundups in Nevada. On April 5th, 1978, lawyers (McCandless and Murdaugh) for AHPA and HSUS filed a complaint against the Department of Interior and the BLM in U.S. District Court for the District of Columbia. Their complaint challenged the "mismanagement, malfeasance and cruelty" of the BLM's wild horse management program in Nevada. According to a reporter for the Las Vegas *Sun*, the suit was against the BLM and "just about everybody in the Interior Department" and charged the BLM with "about everything except Lincoln's assassination. It claims the BLM has violated the 1971 Free Roaming Horse and Burro Act, the Taylor Grazing Act, and NEPA, and contends the BLM's adoption program is leading to complete destruction of the wild herds that have roamed the Nevada desert since the Spanish Conquistadores."

The AHPA and HSUS claimed that the BLM's estimates of wild horse populations were substantially overstated. In the horse protectionists' opinions, aerial surveys are inaccurate and show an increase in population that does not exist, for in their words, the BLM had "little or no scientific data on wild horse reproduction patterns, mortality rates or behavioral patterns affecting reproduction . . . data concerning wild horse diets and feeding habits; livestock and wildlife diets and feeding habits; the extent to which livestock and wild horses overlap in terms of the plants eaten by each and the locations

that feeding takes place; the extent to which wild horse, wildlife and livestock seasonal migration affects range resources; and the extent to which livestock, wild horses and wildlife each contribute to soil compaction and sedimentation. Defendants have failed to adequately consider and analyze viable alternatives to the removal of wild horses . . . or removal of selected wild horses most likely to contribute to population increases such as dominant stallions or mares of foal bearing age. The consideration of such alternatives would disclose feasible management activities having less impact on wild horses."

The complaint also claimed that horse removal would have a significant impact on the environment and that the BLM should prepare an EIS on each grazing district before removing any horses. According to the complaint, "defendants intend to commence wild horse roundup operations in Nevada on or about June 1, 1978 . . . causing immediate and irreparable injury to plaintiff's interests, for which plaintiffs have no adequate remedy at law."

Another point of complaint was that the Palomino Valley holding facilities, where horses were held pending adoption, were operated by the BLM in a "cruel, brutal and inhumane fashion, thereby causing the horses extreme suffering, injury and death . . . As a result of this cruel and inhumane conduct, hundred of horses have died, and will die, of injury and disease . . . or will be subjected to extreme suffering. Many other horses, in good physical condition and capable of adoption, were, and will be, intentionally destroyed outright by BLM employees. The carcasses of these wild horses are, and will be, buried in a series of long trenches approximately five miles north of the Palomino Valley facility."

The AHPA and HSUS also accused the BLM of adopting out large numbers of horses to be used for "commercial exploitation", but no definition or description of this commercial exploitation was given.

The two protection groups wanted the court to declare the BLM's roundups to be in violation of NEPA and PL 91-195 and to find the BLM's "inhumane treatment" of horses at Palomino Valley and the administration of the adoption program to be in violation of PL 92-195. The protection groups wanted the court to permanently enjoin the BLM from gathering wild horses in Nevada until an EIS is prepared for each grazing district and until the holding facilities and adoption program "are operated in accordance with the law."

Mrs. Joan Blue of AHPA told reporters: "The horrible death ditches uncovered by our investigators at Palomino Valley near Reno is proof positive the BLM has decided to destroy rather than protect these symbols of our pioneer western heritage." Lorne Greene, vice-president of AHPA, said, "Anyone who sees the pictures of the death ditches dug by BLM and filled with hundreds of carcasses of wild horses will be angered at what has become our own holocaust in Nevada." The "humane" extremists ignored the hundreds of horses that had died slow miserable deaths of starvation that previous winter on over-populated ranges in Nevada and chose instead to center their outcries against the BLM's humane destruction of old, sick or injured horses from the roundups.

Conditions at Palomino Valley corrals had been bad for awhile due to wet weather and crowding (caused by delays in getting the horses adopted out; it was hard to find enough people to take the horses during the winter months). Frantz Dantzler of HSUS inspected the corrals and said he found 450 horses, some of which had been there for seven months. According to him, the corrals were full of mud and offered the horses no protection from the cold and rain. Dantzler said, "It would be very difficult to devise a worse place for wild horses. The pens had no drainage and the lower sections were flooded. The horses were overcrowded and had to eat their hay off the muddy ground."

The BLM admitted to problems but stated that some of these things had already been corrected. Some horses had died during the winter from eating dirt and sand with their hay and becoming impacted. Since then, the corrals had been cleaned and drained and feeding areas had been raised. The problem of adoption delays, however, would be helped immensely if the BLM could give title to the horses and attract more people to take them.

The BLM had planned to round up 3500 horses in Nevada during the summer of 1978, but roundup plans were suspended because of the court suit. The court did not prohibit the roundups, but the BLM's Washington office halted all but "emergency" roundups in case the judge's decision later went against them. The bureau did not want to be stuck with horses in the Palomino Valley facilities that they would be prohibited from adopting out. The BLM had been aiming for a wild horse population of about 20,000 horses in Nevada, which would mean a reduction of 15,000 (1978 population figures) but this delay would make it difficult to reach that goal because the horse numbers are continually growing.

Speaking of the halted roundups, an editorial in the Reno Evening Gazette had this to say:

Concern is mutual that the wild horse control program

should be operated properly. But at the same time, a long, unnecessary delay in the program could prove to be costly and destructive for Nevadans and other western states . . . It is now estimated that herds are increasing 20% per year . . . Wild horses are now so numerous that people are finding them in their yards and gardens. Wild horses are beautiful and a delight to behold—until they start destroying the truck garden. Then they become a nuisance. Further, steadily growing herds are chewing up and trampling Nevada rangelands into oblivion . . .

The task handed the BLM has not been a simple one or a popular one. Further, the ground rules for disposal of surplus animals are almost unworkable. Catching, holding and handling wild horses is a basically violent endeavor. When wild animals clash with civilization, accidents, injuries and deaths occur occasionally. The roundup and disposal process has been a learning situation for the BLM. No government manuals exist on the project so they have to function on common sense and the abilities of various hired experts.

Mistakes have been made and the process has suffered at times but all the staffers met at the Palomino Valley mustang holding corrals have been humane, expert and concerned individuals. They have shown a willingness to respond to suggestions and are, in fact, glad to hear from anyone who might have a "better idea" in the design of facilities and the handling of wild horses.

We suspect that the humane societies are most interested in stopping the process and blocking its resumption than they are in learning the 'environmental impact' of the operation. As the lady from Washington, D.C., who called the newspaper office, asked: What do you people out there think you are doing to OUR wild horses? Why don't you just leave them alone?

That pretty much explains the national public attitude. The public enjoys considering the fact that the wild horses are indeed public property and find great satisfaction in clamoring for their protection and preservation. On the other side of the coin, they have no awareness of, or concern for, the financial or ecological ramifications of the situation.

Possibly if Nevadans could transport a few thousand head of wild horses to Central Park or to the Mall in Washington, D.C. where they would proceed to eat up everything that grows, destroy the landscape and then stand around and starve, maybe then Nevada's fellow Americans on the East Coast could realize some of the physical realities of the situation.

The wild horse problem will not wait to be studied for the next several years. The BLM had in fact already studied and reported upon the environmental impact possibilities of action and of inaction. Further, it has acted on or responded to every responsible criticism and corrected shortcomings as they cropped up.

We would like to see the adoption program continued for what it's worth for the time being, and rules of adoption liberalized to the point of at least being

The HSUS and AHPA took the BLM to court over herd reductions, ignoring the fact that horses like these were starving to death because of overpopulation and lack of winter feed. Note the trough dug by the dying horse.

workable and effective. Also needed are some rules that permit the humane disposal of old, sick or otherwise unadoptable surplus animals. In any event, stopping the program entirely on technical grounds is not working in the right direction.

In response to this editorial, Helen Reilly, president of ISPMB, wrote a letter to the editor commending his opinions. She also said that the control and management provisions of the wild horse law have not kept pace with the need for control because of

those interests which have been fighting the Act, causing long delays in its implementation . . . What alternatives do they (AHPA and HSUS) offer? Allow the horses to starve to death. We have had a large winter loss; 292 wild horses have died as a result of starvation in the Buffalo Hills alone. What about other areas? In many areas, nearly 100% of last year's forage was consumed. This indicates that a critical situation exists in these areas, and we may expect a die-off of wild horses unless population control in initiated.

It is our position that much more can be gained for our wild horses and burros through a cooperative effort between the land management agencies and conservation organizations toward the restoration of the productivity of the public rangelands . . . It is true that sensationalism is often times the tool with which organizations increase their treasuries and their memberships and it would be sad if this were the case with the suit to stop the adoption program.

John L. Artz of the University of Nevada made this comment about the court suit: Depending on a number of factors, the next few months or longer could see the ceasing of any attempt by the BLM to remove any wild horses from Nevada ranges. As a result of the suit, the horse control program was completely halted in Nevada, and 32 horses that were remaining at the Palomino Valley corrals were released to the range.

The BLM asked for a change of venue for the trial—to have the case tried in Nevada instead of Washington, D.C. The change of venue was granted in June. Judge Aubrey Robison ruled that since the suit was directed only at BLM operations in Nevada, it should be heard there and not in Washington. This was a legal victory for the BLM because they would be more able to state their case fully and fairly.

Bill Virden, director of the San Diego County, California unit of the American Humane Association, said he believed it would be in the best interest of the horses themselves to have the case heard in Reno. "Anyplace but Washington, D.C.," he commented.

Dawn Lappin, of WHOA, agreed. "We believe that (because the case will be heard in Reno) we will be able to continue the management of the horses," she said. Many people interested in the horses and in the management of the range have felt that there has not been a fair chance of presenting a case in the earlier encounters with eastern preservationists, legislators, judges, and a biased press. In Washington, the BLM has not been able to supply many witnesses (due to budget limitations and the difficulties of sending people more than 1000 miles) and must present their case among a host of hostile witnesses before a judge that is usually ignorant of the western problems and sympathetic to the horse protectionists.

Two days of testimony for the trial was taken in late July. Witnesses for AHPA and HSUS testified the first day. The main witness was Hope Ryden, who told of her experiences on study trips to wild horse areas gathering material for her books. She testified that wild horses limit their reproduction according to the amount of feed and water available. She questioned the ranchers' and BLM complaints that horse numbers were encroaching on livestock ranges. She said deaths from old age and disease further regulate the horse herds without man having to manage them. In her opinion, wild horses seldom die from lack of food or water, and the range restores itself after they graze. But she was not sure what would happen if horses were mixed with cattle. "Alone the wild horses may cause a range to deteriorate but then their numbers will decrease and the range will recover," she said.

She disagreed with the BLM plans for future roundups to reduce the herds and said a better way to reduce them would be to water trap females only, thus reducing the male-female ration in the bands.

"They could remove a single young female, which could be adopted, and still leave the bands largely intact on their home range. Bureau plans do not include that possibility." Herd populations, in her view, should be limited by removing a single mare from a band, rather than by "atrocious" roundups.

She showed slides to support her claims that horses rounded up and taken to Palomino Valley were poorly treated. She said many ill and injured horses were trucked to nearby areas, shot and buried. "They were shot in front of other horses—an agonizing thing for the horses still to be shot," she added.

During the second day of testimony when the BLM witnesses were being questioned by the horse protectionists' attorneys, U.S. District Judge Bruce Thompson became annoyed at the attorneys' lack of knowledge of the West and questioned the witnesses himself at times. The four attorneys were from the East, and once during the questioning Thompson interrupted a plaintiff attorney and said, "You have no conception about how livestock or deer or anything else graze." He then questioned Ross Ferris, BLM wild horse specialist, himself.

Ferris told the judge that roundup plans were made according to what areas needed horse removal the most. Six different areas in Nevada were considered for roundup action after studies on the horse population, reproduction, environmental and other factors. All information was contained in environmental analysis reports. According to Ferris, the BLM must follow a multiple use concept involving the livestock, wildlife and wild horses, all which could cause problems affecting the quality of the range. "It is the bureau's contention to do roundups on the most critical areas first and if necessary take immediate action on those areas," he said.

The suit claimed that roundups were based on inaccurate, out of date and incomplete studies of the horse population and range condition. Judge Thompson asked Ferris why the BLM chose to do six different studies rather than one complete study of Nevada. Ferris replied, "No two areas are alike. The topography, water and access to each area are all different."

Bill Stewart, in charge of the Palomino Valley corrals, explained why the bad situations had occurred at the holding facilities. He admitted that the horse pens were in bad condition during the preceding winter because of an unusual amount of rain. He testified that this situation was temporary. "We cleaned the corrals as soon as we could," he said. "We knew there was a bad situation and we did everything we could to rectify it." The mud was scooped out and feeding trays were built, and raised areas were made in the pens so the horses could get to higher, drier ground. Later a better floor with good drainage was built. Shipments of horses into the pens were halted during the worst of the wet conditions.

Dr. Jack Armstrong, of the State Department of Agriculture, testified that he was in close touch with the veterinarians at Palomino Valley and saw no instances of deliberate cruelty. "I never saw intentional destruction of healthy animals there," he said. "Cruel treatment is an attempt in inflict pain, and I didn't see that." The BLM had to bury 150 horses that died, and 80 more that had to be destroyed.

The court's decision on this case came in mid-September, 1978. U.S. District Judge Bruce Thompson began his statement by reminding the plaintiffs (AHPA and HSUS) of several facts about the wild horse and burro protection Act. For instance, the Congressional Reports which led to the passage of the 1971 Act stated in part:

We believe that a comprehensive wild horse and burro management program can no longer be deferred. Consistent with sound management practice, no such program should be undertaken that does not (1) provide for the protection and preservation of healthy animals and (2) help to maintain a viable balance between the numbers of animals protected and the continued availability of suitable habitat . . . Our responsibility for management of wildlife on the public lands requires that we give consideration to the needs of all species, including some now threatened with extinction.

And he quoted from a letter of the Secretary of Interior, dated April 16, 1971, eight months prior to passage of PL 92-195:

Reliance on ranges, and particularly fenced ranges, would defeat the purpose of the legislation, i.e., the survival of wild free-roaming horses and burros, and substitute a "zoo-like" concept. The conferees are of the opinion that the confinement of these animals to such ranges, except in unusual circumstances, should be discouraged and that the animals should be considered as integral parts of the public lands, which should be administered on concepts of multiple use. The principal goal of this legislation is to provide for the protection of the animals from death and harassment at the hands of man, and not the single-use management of areas for the benefit of the wild free-roaming horses and burros. Hence, the inclusion of the phrase "in keeping with the multiple-use management concept for the public lands."

The judge's statement went on to explain that the state of Nevada, which consisted of about 110,000 square miles, was divided by the BLM into 6 grazing districts, roughly equal in size. He described these districts and the horse areas within them. The

AHPA and HSUS sought to keep the BLM from rounding up horses by contending that the roundup proposals were in violation of NEPA, in that the BLM had "unreasonably determined" that the roundups would not have significant environmental effects.

The judge pointed out that the BLM had produced an Environmental Assessment Record for each of the 6 grazing districts, and that these brought together the significant facts involved in making a decision as to whether or not numbers of wild horses should be rounded up as authorized by the Wild Horse and Burro Act. Each of the areas in question had been found by the BLM officials to be overpopulated with wild horses, and in each instance it was concluded that an EIS under NEPA need not be prepared.

AHPA and HSUS contended however, that since the grazing district is the principal BLM administrative unit, it would be appropriate "for defendants to prepare district-wide environmental impact statements concerning their wild horse roundup programs." The judge disagreed, and pointed out the immense size of the six grazing districts in relation to the relatively small area of the various wild horse areas.

In Judge Thompson's words,

the uncontradicted evidence is that the wild horse herds do not normally migrate and that they customarily range in one locality . . . The uncontradicted evidence is that no two herd areas are alike. Availability of water and forage are different. The demands of the recognized uses under the multiple use concept are different, the terrain and procedures for capturing excess wild horses are different. In sum, a study which would attempt to assess the impact of wild horse removal on a district-wide basis would be useless. The differences are evident from the Environmental Assessment Records in evidence.

Judge Thompson pointed out that a previous court case (NRDC v. the Interior Department) had established a timetable for completion of the BLM's 212 Allotment Management Plans and EIS's, ending September 1988. Assuming that an EIS is required in one or more of the Nevada areas in question, the EIS would not be due until the judgment of the District of Columbia Court says it is due, and the court did not attempt to prevent any BLM action (such as wild horse roundups) in administration of the public lands before the filing of the required EIS's.

One of the areas involved in the Nevada suit, the Stone Cabin area, had already had one case tried (when the AHPA took the BLM to court over their

roundup in 1975). In that case, it was held that a roundup of 400 horses to ease pressure on the range was not an action requiring an EIS because the roundup would not have a significant effect on the environment.

According to Judge Thompson, the BLM clearly faced an emergency in 1978, in the administration of the Wild Horse and Burro Act and in the implementation of the timetable set by the District of Columbia Court for the preparation of EIS's. In 1971 Nevada, Oregon, and Wyoming had approximately 10,000 wild horses. The object of PL 92-195 was to "insure the preservation and protection of the few remaining wild free roaming horses and burros in order to enhance and enrich the dreams and enjoyment of future generations of Americans," according to the Joint Statement of the Committee of Conference in the 92nd Congress. But wild horses in Nevada alone exceeded 35,000 by 1978, with a heavy demand on their ranges. The 1971 Act made a place for wild horses, the judge stated, but not in unlimited numbers, and not with a priority over other range uses under the multiple use concept. In the 1975 Nevada court decision concerning the Stone Cabin Valley roundup, the court inferred that the wild horse population should be maintained at about the 1971 level.

The movement to give protection and humane treatment to wild horses was led in Nevada by Wild Horse Annie. Judge Thompson pointed out that the organization she founded (WHOA) fully supported the BLM's 1978 roundup plans and procedures and found them consistent with the objectives and purpose of WHOA.

The final complaint of the plaintiffs (AHPA and HSUS) concerned the conditions at the Palomino Valley holding corrals. The judge found that evidence showed these conditions were temporary, and not deliberately established by the BLM. Plaintiffs opposed the destructions of horses that took place near Palomino Valley. Yet the wild horse law specifically states that in an overpopulated wild horse area, the Interior Secretary may order old, sick, or lame animals to be destroyed, and additional excess animals to be captured and adopted out. Healthy horses could be destroyed if that was the only practical means of disposing of them.

Because of several crucial factors, the conditions at the corrals became substandard during the fall and winter of 1977-78. There were too few corrals, and no feed racks. The corrals became overcrowded because the adopt-a-horse program was not moving the horses out as rapidly as they were coming in (not enough people wanted the horses), and the Secretary did not exercise his discretion to humanely destroy the excess animals as the only practical alternative. Unusually heavy and continuous rains made mudholes of the corrals, and some horses became sick. It is unlikely that these conditions will recur, due to additions and improvements at the corrals.

In his final decision, Judge Thompson denied the motion by AHPA and HSUS to prevent further roundups in Nevada. He also ordered that no wild horse or burro held at Palomino Valley could be destroyed, except on certificate of a veterinarian stating that the animal was injured or sick, or upon order of an authorized officer under the wild horse and burro regulations for disposing of excess animals. Destruction in all cases would be by injection of a barbiturate, rather than by shooting.

This court decision was a victory for the BLM and for the advocates of multiple use of rangelands. The BLM could resume roundup plans.

Even though nearly a year's time had been lost and the horse population had continued to grow, the BLM could go ahead with wild horse management with more confidence, now that the legal battle was behind them and the court had upheld the roundups as being in accordance with the wild horse protection law and NEPA.

But the emotional forces behind the AHPA-HSUS suit are still raging. There may be more court cases before the issue over wild horse management (or lack of it) is resolved. There are many people who cannot understand the need for wild horse management. When this management calls for reduction in horse numbers in areas of overpopulation, this bloc of people are automatically opposed to it.

The campaign to leave the horse uncontrolled is very naive and misguided. This trend in thinking has become prevalent in recent years, and some people apply this idea to wildlife as well—the idea that we must "save all wildlife". There are animal protection organizations dedicated to total preservation of wildlife and an end to all hunting. These ideas come from an urbanized society—people who are far removed from the natural world. They are well meaning people but they are ignorant of how nature works. This idea of letting these animals completely alone is probably the greatest threat to our wildlife in the last 100 years. The "Bambi complex"—wanting no wild creatures to be killed—is unrealistic because most of our wildlife today has had its environment already altered by man (reduction in predators, smaller range areas, and so on) and many species do need to be controlled.

In the words of Dr. Frank Hayes (director of the Southeastern Cooperative Wildlife Disease Project), "If you're going to compare the inhumanities of it—shooting versus nature—a deer that is literally bled to death by starvation or gradually wastes away to a rack of bones—to me that's not very humane."

The most severe example of wildlife starvation due to overpopulation occurred during the 1920's in northern Arizona (on the Grand Canyon's Kaibab Plateau) when a herd of about 3000 mule deer, totally protected by the U.S. government—even to the extent of eradication of predators—grew to more than 100,000 on a million acre sanctuary. Within 6 years the herd depleted its grazing range to the point where in most places 90% of the range was destroyed, and in the same 6 years 70,000 mule deer starved to death. The deaths from starvation continued until 1930, when there were only about 15,000 deer left. At that time annual hunting seasons were finally opened under a new agreement between the federal government and the state of Arizona. The damage from overgrazing was not just hard on the deer, but had turned the sanctuary into an eroded wasteland. The rangeland has not yet recovered.

This misguided type of thinking—that the animals should be left alone, to let nature run her course—has many advocates among wild horse enthusiasts. Many pseudo-ecologists and wild horse lovers feel that if the wild horses and burros are left alone, they will reach their natural niche in the ecosystem and become a stable component. This is an ecological theory that supposedly has application to all the living species in an ecosystem. But it must be remembered that the natural dynamics of each species are different, and each species' "niche" evolved over a long time and space, when the area or range for each species was less limited than it is today.

The horse, under totally "natural" conditions, is a plains animal, a wanderer. Under ideal conditions and with unlimited space, the horse, like the buffalo, would have plenty of room, probably not staying long enough in one place to overgraze his range. But today, with the plains settled, the horse is forced to use less natural and more limited ranges. He is bound to overgraze them unless he is controlled and managed. We cannot treat him as a native, because we have no natural native spaces for him left (the plains are farms, wheat fields, cities and highways.) It would be like asking to have the buffalo back again in a "natural existence".

Even when one considers the natural expansion of the feral horse over the southwestern plains in the late 1600's through the 1800's, we don't absolutely know that he would have reached an ecological balance on this continent without man's intervention. We'll never know, because the white man's civilization encroached upon him about the time he was expanding most rapidly. The North American plains country that the feral horse was introduced to was probably not quite the same as the land that the truly wild horse disappeared from 10,000 years ago. Were the predators and "natural" conditions of 10,000 years ago still here? The "natural" situations had probably changed in 10 thousand years. The fauna and flora of a region can change a great deal in that length of time.

When the feral horse began expanding on the western plains of the 1700's and early 1800's, there were 20 million buffalo, migrating on the plains from north to south and back. Two million horses, half of them in the Southwest, were increasing and expanding northward. Some scientists and biologists feel that the wild horse was beginning to compete with the buffalo. Another century or two of non-interference by the white man and perhaps they would have all been in trouble. We don't know. We'll never really know. We do know that there were areas on the plains that were "grazed out" by horses (see Fray Morfi's observations in Texas, 1777, Chapter 2) and this undoubtedly would have affected the buffalo. Left alone, would the horse have altered the environment enough to subsequently endanger both himself and the buffalo? How much effect would the Indian have had in this balance, as the major "predator" for both the horse and the buffalo herds? We can only guess.

But to think that we can "let the horse be" and nature will take over, is totally unrealistic today. That wouldn't work unless all of us who live in the West and Midwest took out our cities and farms and highways and disappeared. We can't. We're here. And our very existence and all of our "necessities" on this continent have limited the wild horse. So we have to use good judgment and common sense. We *can* have wild horses in some places, if we manage them for their own good and for the good of the land that supports them.

Under our present conditions, all large herbivores must be controlled, otherwise they can cause severe range damage in a short time. Even a native animal like the buffalo, who roamed freely before the coming of the white man, would be hard put to adapt to our present conditions if he were running free on our ranges; he could not live in balance with his habitat on our present ranges without some kind of management. His natural migrations would be checked by roads, cities, and farms, and he would be compelled to live the entire year in a small range area that would inevitably suffer from yearlong use. And because of lack of predators today, he would outgrow his limited range area and irreparably damage it.

Neither the horse nor the burro is native to North America, and has never had a natural niche in any known ecosystem in recent American history. The only natural controls these animals have are disease, environment, and man. The Wild Horse and Burro Act eliminated the most effective control factor, in man. Disease and environment are not acceptable nor effective natural control measures. By the time the environment is damaged enough to control the wild horse and burro population, many other things of value have been destroyed.

Thus, we must try to differentiate between fact and fiction on this wild horse situation, and provide logical and workable control measures for our wild horse and burro herds. If we don't, the Wild Horse and Burro Act will ultimately be responsible for a far-reaching catastrophe on our western ranges. The public will have to recognize that the horse and burro are large and competitive herbivores that have no effective regulatory factors in a natural biological system (in our present range set-up), except starvation.

Some BLM districts are going ahead very well with herd reduction programs, and progress is being made. But it is being done at a tremendous cost to the taxpayer, and complicated by the fact that most districts started too late—after the horses had already built up to serious proportions. And other districts, like the Salmon District that has to manage the horses at Challis, Idaho, are completely hog-tied in management attempts for an undetermined length of time. In the meantime, the over-all wild horse and burro numbers across the West continue to grow.

These increasing numbers of horses and burros are threatening the ability of the public land to produce food for our nation. Several years ago Dr. Floyd Frank, head of the Veterinary Medicine Department at University of Idaho, and chairman of the National Wild Horse Advisory Board at that time (which was discontinued in early 1977 by President Carter), expressed the view that because of the steady increase in wild horse numbers "every place that has wild horses has got a problem or will have a problem." He went on to say that "the world is on the verge of a food shortage. Every citizen has a major stake in seeing that our western range lands are stewarded in a manner which will result in minimum ecological damage and maximum utilization of forage for red meat production."

The world today has no real food reserves. Rangelands, because they furnish an annual renewable resource in the form of grass, which in turn produces red meat, may be a very valuable item in food production of the future. The idea of multiple use on our public lands began back in 1905 with

Wild horses can rapidly defoliate large areas of range forage.

James Wilson, Secretary of Agriculture, who felt that the usual production of these lands—multiple use—was for the good of all the people, under a sustained yield concept.

Over the years we have had various laws concerning sustained use for the maximum good of the nation, and Dale W. Bohmont (University of Nevada) likened these to the three blind men and the elephant. One sees the elephant from the size of his tail, another feels his side and thinks of him being like a wall, and the third feels the trunk and thinks he is like a tree. All of them are correct, but none are considering the whole. The same is true for the public lands; there has to be a lot of give and take, and a great deal of wisdom and judgment required in using these lands.

We have a great resource in these lands. Many people are beginning to feel that we can no longer look at it as though we were on this earth by ourselves; we must be aware that we are international in our responsibilities. As stewards of the land, can we actually, in good conscience, have part of our public lands not producing all that it could, or have part of our public lands supporting nothing but wild horses (or being damaged by wild horses so that future productivity is reduced), when about a third of the world is going hungry? Don't we have a responsibility to look at our range values from a larger view than our own short-term or selfish narrow interests? We want to preserve wild horses for future generations, and that is fine, but perhaps we should not let wild horses or burros dominate to such a degree that they decrease the potentials of our range for practical and necessary uses.

We are all consumers. We all need to eat. Red meat consumption is increasing around the world. We are far better fed in this country, and at a lower price, than any other nation in the world. Slightly more than 8% of our beef production and a great deal of our sheep production, comes from our federal lands, and there will be a desperate need to increase this production during the next twenty years. Right now most people aren't concerned about where the meat for the future is going to come from, but they should be. The largest percentage of our calves produced in this country come from the 17 western states, and about 58% of those come from the 11 western range states. In terms of beef and sheep production, we have a responsibility to ask ourselves whether or not we can afford to take care of certain production responsibilities, and whether or not we can really afford to neglect potentials for meat production, or let purely aesthetic uses of the range supersede them.

In a time of world food shortages, livestock use of cereal grains is considered inefficient for providing human protein, and we must make sure that the natural resource lands provide their share of forage for red meat production. We as humans cannot utilize that grass in any other way for food. And as less grain is used in finishing beef, more and more use of grass for total production of beef animals (running yearlings on the range as well as cows and calves) will be needed. These public lands are not in the best shape they could be. By curtailing overgrazing and improving range management, current estimates indicate that forage production for livestock could be increased over present levels by at least 30 percent and still maintain a balanced ecosystem on these rangelands.

It's very difficult to put a value on a beautiful view, a broad open space of natural country with no evidence of man's alterations. It's nice to have. As an affluent nation we are thinking a lot now about wilderness and pristine areas to leave for future generations and thinking less about our practical needs that can be supplied by these lands—because we now seem to have our practical needs well supplied. But for how long? The untouched expanse of land, valuable as an aesthetic resource only, is expensive. How much are we willing to pay for it in terms of production (timber, meat, wool, metals etc.) lost? Can we really afford not to utilize our natural resources in a practical way (multiple use and sustained yield, so that they will continue to produce for our practical needs indefinitely) as we continue to grow and demand more food and more raw products? Do we have a responsibility? The World Food Congress thinks we have a responsibility. They think that the affluent nations should help the underdeveloped hungry nations.

We should perhaps look at the national resources we have as opportunities to allow us to use a maximum resource for the good of the whole people. Where there are possibilities for improving red meat production, perhaps we should use them and develop them. Let's not assume that we must keep in pristine condition all of our western lands, because most of our western lands are already being "used" to some degree. The pristine people—the ecologists, environmentalists, and others that have mushroomed in the last 15 years—would like to see most of our western lands left in a "natural" untouched condition. But they still need to eat, just like the rest of us. So therefore we need to compromise. We need to keep our aesthetic values, but we need to use common sense and good judgment on how much we let these aesthetic values interfere with our practical needs.

The trend today, embodying the realization of our need to conserve and use our natural resources wisely instead of squandering them, is to produce more beef on grass alone. Cattle can utilize grass in their diets; we humans cannot. Cattle can convert grass into human-usable protein. In this time of food shortages, when part of the world is starving, the trend is to use less grain for cattle consumption (so there will be more emphasis in the future for more grass-finished beef and less grain-finished beef).

Many cattle feed-lot operators went broke in the mid-1970's because grain became too high priced to feed to cattle profitably. The future of the cattle industry lies not in more feedlots and artificial feeds for cattle, but in efficiency, better-bred beef animals that can better utilize cheap roughages, and more grass-fed beef with a shorter finishing time on expensive grains, and in some cases, no grain finishing.

As Dr. Floyd Frank has said, "The handwriting is on the wall that in the future most cereal grains will be consumed directly by humans. Grain-fed beef and lamb will be priced out of reach of the average consumer. In the future we will be consuming meat directly produced by feeding low-quality forages (grass instead of grain). Since swine and poultry cannot convert low-quality roughages to protein, the animals we will depend on for meat will be herbivorous animals, primarily cattle and sheep."

Humanity can really no longer afford the luxury of overfat, overfinished grain-fed beef. The cattle of the future must eat more grass, and our western ranges, well managed, can produce a great deal of that grass. Grass is one of our most valuable renewable resources, for properly managed (not allowing any one species to overgraze it and kill it out—whether it be cattle, sheep or horses) it will replenish itself year after year, forever.

Many BLM range managers fear that improvements in range conditions achieved during the past 40 years through careful livestock management and range revegetation will be lost in many areas if wild horse populations continue to expand without control. A lot is being heard lately about "deteriorated" range conditions and the "Nevada Report", but what usually *isn't* being heard is that the range has been *improving* steadily since 1934. The ranges have some isolated problem areas (and will have a lot more in wild horse areas, the way things are going), but are basically in the best condition they have been in during the last 50 years. Eighty percent of the range is still below its potential (it had an awfully long way to come after the overgrazing abuses by domestic livestock before the Taylor Grazing Act and by the large uncontrolled horse herds of the 1920's) but it has been steadily improving over the last 50 years. The BLM, in cooperation with range users, is continuing to try to improve it. Removal of livestock from the public lands is frequently suggested by other interest groups as a solution to undesirable range conditions, but research has shown that most ranges improve faster with regulated grazing and proper management (seed trampling at the proper time, etc.) than they do without it.

Dr. Frank has said that if PL 92-195 is modified to allow easier management of wild horses and burros, "many will say or infer it is being done in the interest of the western cattle baron. I say that it is in the interest of every citizen of this country. The rangelands are a natural resource. The Wild Horse and Burro Act in its present form is a major obstacle to proper management of that resource."

Since then, the Act has been amended to allow BLM use of helicopters in managing the horses, but it still needs to be changed to allow passage of title to people obtaining the excess horses. And the general public needs to become more aware of the importance of the other values that must coexist with wild horses and burros, and which must not be sacrificed for wild horse and burro protection.

Of all the users of the public land, the livestock

industry will feel the greatest impact from the wild horses (and wildlife ecology will feel the greatest impact from the wild burros). Adverse impact on livestock will be reflected by allotment boundary modification, forage allocations, and constraints on fencing and other range improvement projects. In rest rotation areas, the horses tend to move into the "rested" areas and eat them, negating the range management attempt to improve the range. In some situations, wild horses and burros may have to be relocated from areas where agreements cannot be negotiated with private landowners, such as in checkerboard areas where public land can't be managed independently.

According to the BLM, greater attention will be paid in the years ahead to serious range problems, by increasing supervision of the ranges and adjusting grazing privileges to bring authorized grazing use in balance with carrying capacity of the range, including a realistic apportionment of feed for use by wild life and wild horses and burros.

The federal law protecting wild horses just generally restricts logical management of them. Not only did the prohibition on use of aircraft need to be amended, but we also need loosening of restrictions and a little more flexibility on the local level. For instance, an adopted horse in Montana died and the county wouldn't allow the carcass to be put in the local dump, and PL 92-195 prohibited taking the carcass to the rendering plant. So the BLM had to pick up the carcass and take it all the way back to the Pryor Mountain Wild Horse Range and dump it out.

During the summer of 1977 at Challis, Idaho, a horse was discovered on the range with a broken leg, apparently from being kicked by another horse. But it took two weeks of unsnarling red tape before that horse could be mercifully put down. The incident was reported, then the BLM had to verify it, and it took another week to find the horse again. Then permission had to come down to the local level to destroy the horse, and by the time the poor animal was finally put out of its misery, it had endured two full weeks of suffering.

Now, the local Challis BLM official has authorization to carry a firearm and could put an animal out of its misery if the need arose again in the future, but this is a situation that could repeat itself on other districts—just one more instance of the many little problems that arise with the federal protection law. Yet any attempt to modify the law to make it more workable and flexible is viewed by many horse protectionists as a weakening of the protection, and a giving-in to local jurisdiction or western livestock interests.

But what many people still don't realize is that PL 92-195 has already proved its point; it made obvious to everyone—Western ranchers included—that the American people overwhelmingly feel that the wild horse is a valuable part of our heritage and should be preserved. The question is no longer even debatable on whether or not we should have him. Everyone in this nation will agree that he is here to stay—as a heritage animal instead of just "stray livestock" as he was classified in the past. The Wild Horse and Burro Act and all the support it had, made that clear. But the current question, is how shall we manage him? And he must be managed. There are still a lot of people in this country who apparently don't realize this, people like the members of AHPA and HSUS and other groups who have been fighting the BLM's management attempts at every turn, by fair means or foul—people who feel that PL 92-195 elevated the status of the wild horse and burro on the public lands to the highest beneficial use of the public lands. With this kind of thinking they disregard the value of the domestic livestock and the native wildlife that also must use these lands, and continue to fight for non-control on the horses—a fight that will ultimately hurt us all if it continues in the vein it has been conducted the past few years.

These horse protectionists feel that any attempts to solve some of the horse problems are just attempts to "weaken" the federal law or go back to the lax and sloppy way the horses were "managed" before it was passed. But this is not true. The people who are attempting to find a workable solution to the wild horse situation are seriously concerned people, who have the welfare of the horses in mind, as well as the welfare of our public lands and its multiplicity of values.

In a statement at the Rock Springs wild horse advisory board meeting in September 1975, AHPA representative Russ Gaspar said that the Wild Horse Act elevated the wild horses and burros to a status equivalent to the American Bald Eagle or bison—as a national symbol of our traditions and history. In his words, "To conduct wholesale roundups of wild horses from the western public lands without good reason, and to remove them forever from the range, is an act analogous to a group of citizens from the East tearing down the Lincoln Memorial. Both symbols belong to all of the citizens of the U.S. and must be preserved to be enjoyed by all."

The fallacy of this argument is that the horse roundups are conducted for good reason (even though AHPA and HSUS cannot seem to see the reasoning), and his analogy is poor because rounding up part of these horses is not destroying the symbol or the heritage value; there are still a lot of horses out there (reproducing annually), and always will be, under the protection of federal law.

He also said that "AHPA believes that the Act mandates management that interferes least with the size and location of horse herds. Rounding up wild horses and removing them permanently from federal land is rarely necessary or appropriate. Destroying them, unless for humane reasons, is never to be condoned. AHPA will continue to oppose such activities until the Wild Horse Act is amended or until a court conclusively rules that the Act is to be interpreted differently. AHPA doubts that the enormous amount of tax dollars expended to gather wild horses is well spent. If range deterioration and a lack of water are problems in wild horse management, AHPA suggests that the Board recommend a program of irrigation and range improvements rather than roundups . . . If water can be piped from the mountains to the desert floor to trap horses, it can be piped for irrigation."

These conclusions are too naive. Even if range improvements are made (and the suggestions such as irrigating the rangeland show a great lack of knowledge about western range conditions; a tiny trickle can be piped to a tank for a drinking supply, but could not possibly irrigate anything, much of these lands are semi-desert), the horses are still going to increase. Sooner or later, no matter how many range improvements are made, the horses are going to outgrow that range capacity. Sooner or later excess horses will have to be removed or destroyed. To think that the range can support ever-increasing horse herds forever is being ignorant of the basic facts of life. It would be a lot wiser to start controlling the horse herds now, instead of waiting for mother nature to show us the folly of letting them expand to the point of starving to death.

Many livestock men are deeply concerned with the turn things have taken since passage of PL 92-195. They are concerned not only for the future of livestock ranching in the West, but also for the future of the range itself. Even the ranchers involved in the Howe incident have some valid comments on the situation. In the words of Bill Robison, in 1974:

We believe that the wild horse law is written with no effective method of controlling wild horses. We believe that vast increases in horse numbers are inevitable under the present law along with the present policy of the various horse protection associations. Greater increases in numbers of horses on public lands means grazing cuts. These horse protection groups very masterfully involve the news media and use their political influence to reach their objectives regarding wild horse policy and laws.

We as ranchers realize that members of the various horse protection associations are very dedicated and sincere in their efforts to protect and preserve wild horses. We respect this dedication and we believe the wild horse does have a place as part of the American heritage, but we should be sure that horses we are working to preserve are truly wild horses and not range horses that are owned. We as stockmen don't believe any rancher is for total withdrawal of all wild horses from public lands, but we do believe that wild horse numbers must be controlled.

The government agencies that have the responsibility of managing wild horses must have a free hand to use the methods they deem necessary to do the job. We believe that livestock people along with federal and state governments and concerned citizens should work together to formulate wild horse policy which would be workable and beneficial to all rather than favor a few. The American people should be made aware of the total effects of wild horses on public lands and the total cost to them if numbers are allowed to increase beyond tolerable levels.

Dean Rhodes, at a BLM advisory board meeting in 1975, mentioned that Nevada in 1975 had 23,000 horses and 1000 burros. At a 20% increase per year (which some people feel is too low an estimate) by 1980 there would be 68,000 horses and 3000 burros (unless the BLM can start to keep pace with the increase with roundups) and these animals would need 1,700,000 AUM's of forage annually. There are currently only 1,900,000 AUM's for livestock available, and 97,000 AUM's for wildlife. By 1980, if wildlife continues to take 97,000 AUM's, livestock would have only 250,000, a reduction of 88% of the livestock use in Nevada. Rhodes asked, "Is this what the general public wants? The Nevada rancher must ask himself, is the general public sending signals back to him that they would rather see our state full of horses than eat beef at a reasonable price? If it is the signal, the traditional American way of life is in trouble. We, the livestock industry, do not believe that the people making headlines today, advocating the continued protection of the spiraling horse population explotion is the general public. There must be management of these horses."

As Dr. Frank said earlier, "We can provide for a reasonable number of horses indefinitely. However, we must be given the means for keeping wild horse numbers in line with forage. We are on the verge of repeating the serious abuses caused by domestic livestock overgrazing in the past. We must convinve the public of the seriousness of the situation at every opportunity."

We shouldn't have to eliminate all other forms of animal use of the land, just to have more wild horses. In speaking of the wild horse situation on our ranges, Len Jordan, a former U.S. Senator from Idaho, said,

Wild stallion herding his mares. We can provide for a reasonable number of these horses indefinitely—but some people are still arguing over what constitutes a "reasonable number".

"My own philosophy is that these resources should be used wisely to pass on to future generations. I would feel badly if my generation were to pass them on in a worse condition. The need for control is now obvious, for the horses compete with wildlife and livestock and are destroying the watershed."

As Dean Prosser explained in his testimony before the Subcommittee on Public Lands of the Committee on Interior and Insular Affairs, "The public lands themselves are a most important heritage of the American people and we must manage and control all animal life that uses these lands in such a manner as not to destroy the lands that belong to the American people."

Mrs. Blue of the AHPA has asked the fundamental question whether roundups of horses are necessary at all, and says "wild horses are important to Americans for much the same reason that the eagle and the bison are important. Even if an individual never sees a wild horse or a bald eagle, he feels pleasure and pride simply because he knows they exist."

Even if a person never sees a wild horse or a bald eagle . . . that's something to think about. We won't see any more bald eagles in some areas if the horses increase to the point of destroying the habitat for the rodents and small animals and birds that the eagle depends on for prey. A very broad range of conservation and wildlife groups, as well as cattlemen, are concerned about the competition of wild horses and burros and what they are doing to plant and soil reserves as well as to the food supplies and habitat of many other animals.

And if the horse is a *symbol*, the symbol of free spirit and the "historic and pioneer spirit of the west", as stated in the Wild Horse and Burro Act, what difference does it make to our aesthetic experience, really, from the point of view of the wild horse preservationist, whether there are 250 wild horses in a certain geographical area, or 600, or 1200? Two hundred and fifty healthy horses—true free spirits—or 600 thin, wretched starving horses that have ruined their range? Six hundred starving horses that are doomed to suffer and die from malnutrition. How many horses does it take to create an aesthetic experience? Perhaps by the time we have mass starvation in our wild herds, the American people will wake up and realize that this is not what they really wanted when they worked so hard for the federal protection law. But by that time it will be too late for some of the rest of our American heritage—some of the endangered wildlife, for instance, and some of the native vegetation that will have been killed completely out of some areas. Letting wild horses rape the land is no better or smarter than some of the past abuses we claim to abhor.

If we have SOME wild horses, in balance with their natural habitat and food supply, why fight for more horses at the expense of everything else out there? Instead, we should be working for a practical means to best control and manage these horses and burros for their own good, and for the health of their range and our multiple use system.

There is such a thing as stewardship of this good earth of ours, and good husbandry of our natural resources and bounty, and a certain moral obligation of mankind to take care of what has been given to him. Horse protectionists like AHPA and HSUS and a few others are fighting for just one thing—no controls on the wild horses and burros—and therefore the subsequent trampling of all the other values out there. Those of us who live here in the West and who love the range are fighting for several things— for the land itself and its natural beauty and plenty; the cattle, the sheep, the wildlife in all its varied forms, the unique vegetation, the ecology, the welfare of the wild horses and burros themselves, and perhaps, when all is said and done, the American way of life. The greed that Mrs. Blue talks about when she refers to livestockmen and sportsmen, seems to me to be a more appropriate term to fit an organization or an individual that has only one narrow, selfish objective. Multiple use of our federal lands and good husbandry of our natural resources seems to be a much wiser course.

Appendix 1

Public Law 92-195
92nd Congress, S. 1116
December 15, 1971

An Act

To require the protection, management, and control of wild free-roaming horses and burros on public lands.

Be it enacted by the Senate and House of Representatives of the United States of America in Congress assembled, That Congress finds and declares that wild free-roaming horses and burros are living symbols of the historic and pioneer spirit of the West; that they contribute to the diversity of life forms within the Nation and enrich the lives of the American people; and that these horses and burros are fast disappearing from the American scene. It is the policy of Congress that wild free-roaming horses and burros shall be protected from capture, branding, harassment, or death; and to accomplish this they are to be considered in the area where presently found, as an integral part of the natural system of the public lands.

SEC. 2. As used in this Act—

(a) "Secretary" means the Secretary of the Interior when used in connection with public lands administered by him through the Bureau of Land Management and the Secretary of Agriculture in connection with public lands administered by him through the Forest Service;

(b) "wild free-roaming horses and burros" means all unbranded and unclaimed horses and burros on public lands of the United States;

(c) "range" means the amount of land necessary to sustain an existing herd or herds of wild free-roaming horses and burros, which does not exceed their known territorial limits, and which is devoted principally but not necessarily exclusively to their welfare in keeping with the multiple-use management concept for the public lands;

(d) "herd" means one or more stallions and his mares; and

(e) "public lands" means any lands administered by the Secretary of the Interior through the Bureau of Land Management or by the Secretary of Agriculture through the Forest Service.

SEC. 3. (a) All wild free-roaming horses and burros are hereby declared to be under the jurisdiction of the Secretary for the purpose of management and protection in accordance with the provisions of this Act. The Secretary is authorized and directed to protect and manage wild free-roaming horses and burros as components of the public lands, and he may designate and maintain specific ranges on public lands as sanctuaries for their protection and preservation, where the Secretary after consultation with the wildlife agency of the State wherein any such range is proposed and with the Advisory Board established in section 7 of this Act deems such action desirable. The Secretary shall manage wild free-roaming horses and burros in a manner that is designed to achieve and maintain a thriving natural ecological balance on the public lands. He shall consider the recommendations of qualified scientists in the field of biology and ecology, some of whom shall be independent of both Federal and State agencies and may include members of the Advisory Board established in section 7 of this Act. All management activities shall be at the minimal feasible level and shall be carried out in consultation with the wildlife agency of the State wherein such lands are located in order to protect the natural ecological balance of all wildlife species which inhabit such lands, particularly endangered wildlife species. Any adjustments in forage allocations on any such lands shall take into consideration the needs of other wildlife species which inhabit such lands.

(b) Where an area is found to be overpopulated, the Secretary, after consulting with the Advisory Board, may order old, sick, or lame animals to be destroyed in the most humane manner possible, and he may cause additional excess wild free-roaming horses and burros to be captured and removed for private maintenance under humane conditions and care.

(c) The Secretary may order wild free-roaming horses or burros to be destroyed in the most humane manner possible when he deems such action to be an act of mercy or when in his judgment such action is necessary to preserve and maintain the habitat in a suitable condition for continued use. No wild free-roaming horse or burro shall be ordered to be destroyed because of overpopulation unless in the judgment of the Secretary such action is the only practical way to remove excess animals from the area.

(d) Nothing in this Act shall preclude the customary disposal of the remains of a deceased wild free-roaming horse or burro, including those in the authorized possession of private parties, but in no event shall such remains, or any part thereof, be sold for any consideration, directly or indirectly.

Sec. 4. If wild free-roaming horses or burros stray from public lands onto privately owned land, the owners of such land may inform the nearest Federal marshall or agent of the Secretary, who shall arrange to have the animals removed. In no event shall such wild free-roaming horses and burros be destroyed except by the agents of the Secretary. Nothing in this section shall be construed to prohibit a private landowner from maintaining wild free-roaming horses or burros on his private lands, or lands leased from the Government, if he does so in a manner that protects them from harassment, and if the animals were not willfully removed or enticed from the public lands. Any individuals who maintain such wild free-roaming horses or burros on their private lands or lands leased from the Government shall notify the appropriate agent of the Secretary and supply him with a reasonable approximation of the number of animals so maintained.

Sec. 5. A person claiming ownership of a horse or burro on the public lands shall be entitled to recover it only if recovery is permissible under the branding and estray laws of the State in which the animal is found.

Sec. 6. The Secretary is authorized to enter into cooperative agreements with other landowners and with the State and local governmental agencies and may issue such regulations as he deems necessary for the furtherance of the purposes of this Act.

Sec. 7. The Secretary of the Interior and the Secretary of Agriculture are authorized and directed to appoint a joint advisory borad of not more than nine members to advise them on any matter relating to wild free-roaming horses and burros and their management and protection. They shall select as advisers persons who are not employees of the Federal or State Governments and whom they deem to have special knowledge about protection of horses and burros, management of wildlife, animal husbandry, or natural resources management. Members of the board shall not receive reimbursement except for travel and other expenditures necessary in connection with their services.

Sec. 8. Any person who—

(1) willfully removes or attempts to remove a wild free-roaming horse or burro from the public lands, without authority from the Secretary, or

(2) converts a wild free-roaming horse or burro to private use, without authority from the Secretary, or

(3) maliciously causes the death or harassment of any wild free-roaming horse or burro, or

(4) processes or permits to be processed into commercial products the remains of a wild free-roaming horse or burro, or

(5) sells, directly or indirectly, a wild free-roaming horse or burro maintained on private or leased land pursuant to section 4 of this Act, or the remains thereof, or

(6) willfully violates a regulation issued pursuant to this Act, shall be subject to a fine of not more than $2,000, or imprisonment for not more than one year, or both. Any person so charged with such violation by the Secretary may be tried and sentenced by any United States commissioner or magistrate designated for that purpose by the court by which he was appointed, in the same manner and subject to the same conditions as provided for in section 3401, title 18, United States Code.

(b) Any employee designated by the Secretary of the Interior or the Secretary of Agriculture shall have power, without warrant, to arrest any person committing in the presence of such employee a violation of this Act or any regulation made pursuant thereto, and to take such person immediately for examination or trial before an officer or court of competent jurisdiction, and shall have power to execute any warrant or other process issued by an officer or court of competent jurisdiction to enforce the provisions of this Act or regulations made pursuant thereto. Any judge of a court established under the laws of the United States, or any United States magistrate may, within his respective jurisdiction, upon proper oath or affirmation showing probable cause, issue warrants in all such cases.

Sec. 9. Nothing in this Act shall be construed to authorize the Secretary to relocate wild free-roaming horses or burros to areas of the public lands where they do not presently exist.

Sec. 10. After the expiration of thirty calendar months following the date of enactment of this Act, and every twenty-four calendar months thereafter, the Secretaries of the Interior and Agriculture shall submit to Congress a joint report on the administration of this Act, including a summary of enforcement and/or other actions taken thereunder, costs, and such recommendations for legislative or other actions as he might deem appropriate.

The Secretary of the Interior and the Secretary of Agriculture shall consult with respect to the implementation and enforcement of this Act and to the maximum feasible extent coordinate the activities of their respective departments and in the implementation and enforcement of this Act. The Secretaries are authorized and directed to undertake those studies of the habits of wild free-roaming horses and burros that they may deem necessary in order to carry out the provisions of this Act.

Approved December 15, 1971.

LEGISLATIVE HISTORY:

HOUSE REPORTS: No. 92-480 accompanying H.R. 9890 (Comm. on Interior and Insular Affairs) and No. 92-681 (Comm. of Conference).

SENATE REPORT No. 92-242 (Comm. on Interior and Insular Affairs).

CONGRESSIONAL RECORD, Vol. 117 (1971):
June 29, considered and passed Senate.
Oct. 4, considered and passed House, amended, in lieu of H.R. 9890.
Dec. 2, House agreed to conference report.
Dec. 3, Senate agreed to conference report.

WEEKLY COMPILATION OF PRESIDENTIAL DOCUMENTS, Vol. 7, No. 51: Dec. 17, Presidential statement.

Appendix 2—BLM Management Regulations

Group 4700—Wild Free-Roaming Horse and Burro Management

PART 4710—WILD FREE-ROAMING HORSE AND BURRO MANAGEMENT; GENERAL

Subpart 4710—Purpose; Objective; Authority; Definitions; Policy

§ 4710.01 *Purpose*.

To implement the laws relating to wild free-roaming horses and burros on public lands.

§ 4710.0-2 *Objective*.

The objective of these regulations is to provide criteria and procedures for protecting, managing, and controlling wild free-roaming horses and burros as a recognized component of the public land environment.

§ 4710.0-3 *Authority*.

The Act of December 15, 1971 (16 U.S.C. 1331-1340), requires the protection, management, and control of wild free-roaming horses and burros on public lands.

§ 4710.0-5 *Definitions*.

(a) "Authorized Officer" means any employee of the Bureau of Land Management to whom has been delegated the authority to take actions under the regulations of this Chapter.

(b) "Wild free-roaming horses and burros" means all unbranded and unclaimed horses and burros and their progeny that have used or do use public lands as all or part of their habitat on or after December 15, 1971, including those animals given an identifying mark upon capture for live disposal by the authorized officer. Unbranded, claimed horses and burros where the claim is found to be erroneous are also considered as wild and free-roaming if they meet the criteria above. However, this definition shall not include any horse or burro introduced onto public lands on or after December 15, 1971, by accidental, negligent, or willful disregard of ownership.

(c) "Herd" means one or more stallions and their mares or jacks and their jennies.

(d) "Excess animals" means wild free-roaming horses or burros determined to be in excess of populations proper to maintain a thriving natural ecological balance and harmonious multiple-use relationship on public lands.

(e) "Problem animal" means a wild free-roaming horse or burro whose demonstrated individual habits or traits pose an undue threat to the safety or welfare of persons, wildlife, livestock, or property.

(f) "Public lands" means any lands administered by the Secretary of the Interior through the Bureau of Land Management.

(g) "Wild horse or burro range" means a specifically designated area of land necessary to sustain a herd or herds of wild free-roaming horses or burros, and which is devoted principally but not necessarily exclusively to their welfare in keeping with the multiple use management of the public lands.

(h) "Management plan" means a written program of action designed to protect, manage, and control wild free-roaming horses and burros and maintain a natural ecological balance on the public lands.

(i) "Act" means the Act of December 15, 1971 (16 U.S.C. 1331-1340).

(j) "Advisory Board" means the joint advisory board established by the Secretary of the Interior and the Secretary of Agriculture pursuant to Section 7 of the Act.

§ 4710.0-6 *Policy*.

(a) Wild free-roaming horses and burros are under the jurisdiction of the Secretary and will be managed as an integral part of the natural system of the public lands. They will be protected from unauthorized capture, branding, undue disturbance, and destruction. They and their habitat will be managed and controlled in a manner designed to achieve and maintain an ecological balance on the public lands and a population of sound, healthy individuals, all in accordance with the basic program policies for public land management set forth in subpart 1725 of this Chapter.

(b) Wild free-roaming horses and burros on the public lands will be managed by the authorized officer, with full public participation and such cooperative arrangements as he may find helpful. Management on public lands will not be assigned to any private individual or association through a grazing license, lease, or permit.

Subpart 4711—Management Coordination.

§ 4711.1 *Recommendations from the Joint National Advisory Board on Wild Free-Roaming Horses and Burros*.

Policies and guidelines relative to proposals for establishment of ranges, proposed management plans, adjustments in number, relocation and disposal of animals, and other matters relating generally to the protection, management, and control of wild free-roaming horses and burros shall be presented to the Advisory Board of recommendations.

§ 4711.2 *State Agencies*.

(a) All management activities including, but not limited to, establishment of ranges and adjustments in forage allocation shall be planned and executed in consultation with the appropriate State agency to further consider the needs of all wildlife, particularly endangered species.

(b) All actions taken in connection with private ownership claims to unbranded horses and burros shall be coordinated to the fullest extent possible with the appropriate State agency.

§ 4711.3 *Cooperative Agreements*.

The authorized officer may enter into cooperative agreements with other landowners, nonprofit organizations, and with Federal, State and local governmental agencies as he deems necessary for purposes of protecting, managing and controlling wild free-roaming horses and burros. Where the grazing patterns of the animals require utilization of lands in other ownerships or administration, the authorized officer shall seek cooperative agreements to insure continuance of such use.

Subpart 4712—Management Considerations.

§ 4712.1 *Management:General*.

§ 4712.1-1 Planning.

In planning for management, protection, and control of wild free-roaming horses and burros, including the establishment of specifically designated ranges, determination of desirable numbers and other management provisions of these regulations, the authorized officer will utilize the Bureau's multiple-use planning system with its requirements for public participation by and coordination with others.

§ 4712.1-2 *Intensity of Management*.

Wild free-roaming horse or burro herds may be managed either as one of the components of public land use or managed on a specifically designated wild horse or burro range. Management practices shall be consistent to the extent possible and practical with the maintenance of their free-roaming behavior. Management facilities should be designed and constructed to the extent possible to maintain the free-roaming behavior of the herds.

§ 4712.1-3 *Habitat Reservation and Allocation*.

The biological requirements of wild free-roaming horses and burros will be determined based upon appropriate studies or other available information. The needs for soil and watershed protection, domestic livestock, maintenance of environmental quality, wildlife and other factors will be considered along with wild free-roaming horse and burro requirements. After determining the optimum number of such horses and burros to be maintained on an area, the authorized officer shall reserve adequate forage and satisfy other biological requirements of such horses and burros and, when necessary, adjust or exclude domestic livestock use accordingly. See §§ 4115.2-1 (d) and 4121. 2-1 (a).

§ 4712.2 *Establishment of Specifically Designated Ranges or Herd Management Areas*.

§ 4712.2-1 *Designation*.

The authorized officer may designate and maintain specifically designated ranges principally for the protection and preservation of wild free-roaming horses and burros.

§ 4712.2-2 *Criteria for Designation*.

In designating specific ranges and herd management areas, the authorized officer, in addition to any other provisions of these regulations, shall:

(1) Consider only those areas utilized by wild free-roaming horses or burros on December 15, 1971.

(2) Consider those areas where self-sustaining herds can maintain themselves within their established utilization and migratory patterns.

(3) Consider those areas which are capable of being managed as a unit to ensure a sustained yield or forage without jeopardy to the resources.

(4) Develop a wild free-roaming horse or burro management plan in accordance with § 4712.2-3.

§ 4712.2-3 *Management Plan*.

The authorized officer shall, in connection with the designation of a specific range, develop a wild free-roaming horse or burro management plan designed to protect and manage wild free-roaming horses and burros on the area on a continuing basis. The authorized officer may also develop herd management plans as part of the multiple use management of areas outside of specifically designated wild horse or burro ranges. All management plans shall be developed in accordance with the Bureau's planning system and shall govern management of the area.

§ 4712.3 Removal and Relocation or Disposal of Excess Animals.

§ 4712.3-1 Method of Capture.

Under the supervision of the authorized officer animals may be captured, corraled and held under humane conditions pending disposal under the provisions of the Subpart.

§ 4712.3-2 Relocation of Animals.

(a) The authorized officer may relocate wild free-roaming horses and burros on public lands when he determines such action is necessary to: (1) relieve overgrazed areas, (2) locate animals removed from private lands in accordance with § 4712.3, (3) remove problem animals, or (4) achieve other purposes deemed to be in the interest of proper resource and herd management. Such animals relocated on public lands shall not be introduced onto areas which were not inhabited by wild free-roaming horses or burros on December 15, 1971.

(b) The authorized officer may also place animals in the custody of private persons, organizations or other governmental agencies. Custodial arrangements shall be made through a cooperative agreement which shall include provisions as necessary to maintain and protect the animals and ensure that the animals will not be used for commercial exploitation. The authorized officer may, at his discretion, mark animals placed in private custody for identification purposes.

§ 4712.3-3 Disposal.

Where the authorized officer finds it necessary, in accordance with § 4712.3-2, to remove excess animals from areas of the public lands, and he determines that the relocation of animals under § 4712.3-2 is not practical, he may destroy such animals in the most humane manner possible. No person, except the authorized officer or his authorized representative, shall destroy wild free-roaming horses and burros.

§ 4712.3-4 Acts of Mercy.

Severely injured or seriously sick animals will be destroyed in the most humane manner possible as an act of mercy.

§ 4712.3-5 Disposal of Carcasses.

Carcasses shall be disposed of in any customary manner under State sanitary statutes. In no event shall carcasses, or any part thereof, including those in the authorized possession of private parties, be sold for any consideration, directly or indirectly.

§ 4712.4 Animals on Private Lands.

§ 4712.4-1 Allowing Animals on Private Lands.

Nothing in these regulations shall preclude a private landowner from allowing wild free-roaming horses and burros to remain on his private lands so long as the animals were not willfully removed, enticed, or retained by him or his agent from the public lands.

§ 4712.4-2 Active Maintenance of Animals on Private Lands.

Any individual who actively maintains wild free-roaming horses and burros on his private lands shall notify the authorized officer and supply him with a reasonable approximation of their number and location and when required by the authorized officer a description of the animals. Thereafter, he shall furnish an annual report updating the information during the month of January. An individual will be considered to be actively maintaining wild free-roaming horses or burros if he takes measures of any kind designed to protect or enhance the welfare of the animals. No person shall maintain such animals except under cooperative agreement between the private landowner and the authorized officer setting forth the management and maintenance requirements including provisions for regulating disposal of excess animals.

§ 4712.4-3 Removal of Animals from Private Lands.

The authorized officer shall remove, as soon as he can make the necessary arrangements, wild free-roaming horses and burros from private lands at the request of the landowner where the private land is enclosed in a "legal fence." A "legal fence" for this purpose is one which complies with State standards and specifications.

Subpart 4713—Claimed and Trespass Horses and Burros

§ 4713.1 Removal of Claimed Trespass Horses and Burros

(a) All unauthorized and unbranded horses and burros on the public lands, except those introduced on or after December 15, 1971, by accident, negligence, or willful disregard of ownership, are presumed for the purpose of management to be wild free-roaming horses or burros.

(b) Any person claiming ownership of unauthorized horses or burros, either branded or unbranded, must obtain written authorization from the authorized officer to round up or remove claimed animals from public lands. Claims must be based upon acceptable proof of ownership and submitted within 90 days of the effective date of these regulations.

(c) All written authorizations to gather claimed animals shall be on a form approved by the Director. The authorized officer shall, after issuance of such public notice as he deems appropriate to notify interested parties, establish in the authorization a reasonable period of time to allow roundup of claimed animals and stipulate other conditions which he deems necessary to minimize stress on associated wild free-roaming horses and burros or protect other resources involved. Prior to removal of any gathered animals, the claimant shall substantiate proof of ownership in accordance with the criteria agreed upon between the Bureau and the appropriate State agency administering the State branding and estray laws. Such ownership shall be certified by the appropriate State official and a copy provided the authorized officer. In the absence of such agreements, ownership status will be determined by the authorized officer.

(d) Unauthorized horses or burros determined to be privately owned in accordance with the provisions of this Section will be considered to have been in trespass and may not be released until a proper trespass charge has been determined by the authorized officer in accordance with the provisions of 43 CFR.

§ 4713.2 *Removal of Other Trespass Horses and Burros.*

§ 4713.2-1 *Closures to Horse and Burro Use; Impoundment and/or Disposal of Animals.*

The authorized officer may, when conditions warrant, close any area to grazing by horses and burros and for any period of time to be specified in a notice of closure. Such closure may be made only after public notice deemed appropriate by the authorized officer. The order shall require all owners of any animals affected thereby, in accordance with provisions of the order, to remove such animals from the area under the supervision of the authorized officer. Thereafter the authorized officer shall proceed to impound, remove and dispose of any horses and burros trespassing or grazing in violation of the closing order.

§ 4713.2-2 *Notice of Public Sale.*

Following the impoundment of privately owned horses and burros, a notice of sale will be published in a local newspaper and posted at the couty courthouse and at a post office near the public land involved. The notice will describe the animals and specify the date, and place of sale. The sale date shall be at least 5 days after the publication and posting of the notice. By certified mail or by personal delivery, any known owners or agents will be notified in writing of the procedure by which the impounded animals may be redeemed prior to the sale. Proof of ownership and payments of costs will be required.

§ 4713.2-3 *Sale.*

If the horses and burros are not redeemed they may be (a) released to the State agency responsible for disposition in accordance with State law, (b) offered at public sale to the highest bidder, or (c) otherwise disposed of. Purchaser of horses and burros shall be furnished a bill of sale.

Subpart 4714—Enforcement Provisions.

§ 4714.- *Arrest.*

The Director of the Bureau of Land Managment may authorize such employees as he deems necessary to arrest without warrant, any person committing in the presence of the employee a violation of the Act or of these regulations and to take such person immediately for examination or trial before an officer or court of competent jurisdiction. Any employee so designated shall have power to execute any warrant or other process issued by a officer or court of competent jurisdiction to enforce the provisions of these regulations.

§ 4714.2 *Penalties.*

In accordance with Section 8 of the Act (16 U.S.C. 1338), any person who:

(1) willfully removes or attempts to remove a wild free-roaming horse or burro from the public lands, without authority from the authorized officer, or

(2) converts a wild free-roaming horse or burro to private use, without authority from the authorized officer, or

(3) maliciously causes the death or harassment of any wild free-roaming horse or burro, or

(4) processes or permits to be processed into commercial products the remains of a wild free-roaming horse or burro, or

(5) sells, directly or indirectly, a wild horse or burro **allowed on private or leased land pursuant to Section 4 of the Act,** or

(6) willfully violates any provisions of the regulations under Group 4700, shall be subject to a fine of not more than $2,000 or imprisonment for not more than one year, or both. Any person so charged with such violation by the authorized officer may be tried and sentenced by a United States commissioner or magistrate, designated for that purpose by the court by which he was appointed, in the same manner and subject to the same conditions as provided in Section 3401, Title 18, U.S.C.

Bibliography

I. Books

Amaral, Anthony. *Mustang; Life and Legends of Nevada's Wild Horses*. Reno: University of Nevada Press, 1977.

Denhardt, Robert M. *The Horse of the Americas*. Norman: University of Oklahoma Press, 1947.

Dobie, J. Frank. *The Mustangs*. New York: Curtis Publishing Company, 1934.

Dobie, J. Frank, M.C. Boatwright, and H.H. Ransom, ed. *Mustangs and Cow Horses*. Dallas: Southern Methodist University Press. Texas Folklore Society, 1940.

Groves, Colin P. *Horses, Asses and Zebras in the Wild*. Ralph Curtis Books, 1974.

Haines, Francis. *Horses in America*. New York: Thomas Y. Crowell Co. 1971

Henry, Marguerite. *Mustang: Wild Spirit of the West*. Skokie: Rand McNalley 1966.

Jackman, E.R., and Reub A. Long. *The Oregon Desert*. Caldwell: Idaho Caxton, 1971.

Ryden, Hope. *America's Last Wild Horses*. New York: E.P. Dutton and Co. 1970.

Ryden, Hope. *Mustangs: A Return to the Wild*. New York: Viking Press, 1972.

Ryden, Hope. *The Wild Colt*. New York: Cowards, 1972.

Stong, Phil. *Horses and Americans*. Garden City: Garden City Publishing Co. 1939.

Weiss, Ann E. *Save the Mustangs: How a Federal Law is Passed*. Julian Messner, 1974.

Wyman, Walker D. *The Wild Horse of the West*. Caldwell, Idaho Caxton, 1945.

II. Magazine articles

"Abandoned Horses on the Federal Range," *Our Public Lands*, 1958.

Amaral, Anthony. "Mustanging with Pete Barnum", *Nevada Highways and Parks*, Fall 1970.

———. "The Wild Horse—Worth Saving?" *National Parks and Conservation Magazine*, March 1971.

Barber, Ted. "Wild Horses on Welfare", *Western Horseman*, April 1974.

Bendt, R.H. "Status of Bighorn Sheep in Grand Canyon National Park and Monument", *Desert Bighorn Council Transactions*, 1957.

Blue, Joan R. "What's the True Wild Horse Picture?", *American Horseman*, October 1976.

Boone, Andrew. "The Wild Herd Passes", *Travel*, 1933.

Brandon, William. "Wild Horses of the West", *Sierra Club Bulletin*, September 1972.

Branscomb, Mary. Letter to the editor, *Chronicle of the Horse*, October 8, 1976.

Browne, Edwin H.C. "Destined for Oblivion", *American Horseman*, March 1977.

Bundy, Gus. "Rounding Up Wild Horses", *National Humane Review*, March 1953.

Burk, Adrianne. Letter to the editor, *Chronicle of the Horse*, September 10, 1976.

Cash, Peg. "Opposing Sides to the Same Story," *The Spanish Barb Quarterly*, January-June 1977.

Chambers, Gale. "Gem State Notes", *Idaho Farmer-Stockman*, July 1977.

———. "Range Users Facing Troublesome Times", *Idaho Farmer-Stockman*, November 17, 1977.

———. "Wild Horse Group Forming", *Idaho Farmer-Stockman*, December 1, 1977.

Cook, Wayne C. "Wild Horses and Burros; A New Management Problem", *Rangeman's Journal*, February 1975.

Cotterman, Dan. "Wild Horse Massacre", *Horse and Rider*, August, 1973.

———. "Wild Horse Massacre Hotline", *Horse and Rider*, October, 1973.

Dobie, J. Frank. "The Murderous Mustang of the Plains", *Saturday Evening Post*, December, 1951.

"Federal Mustang Protection Tested—Horses Brutalized in Idaho Roundup", *Mainstream* (Animal Protection Institute), 1973.

"Fight to Save Wild Horses", *Time*, July 12, 1971.

Garret, W.E. "The Grand Canyon: Are We Loving it to Death?" *National Geographic*, July, 1978.

Gibbons, Clark. "Yakima Indian Riders Round Up Wild Horses," *American Cattle Producer*, July, 1946.

Gorman, John A. and Gaydell M. Collier. "Free As . . . the Wind", *National Wildlife*, October-November 1972

Grover, Dorys Crow. "Haven for Wild Horses", *Western Horseman*, December 1964.

Haines, Francis. "How the Indian Got the Horse," *American Heritage*, February 1964.

Hall, Beverly. "The Wild Bunch", *National Wildlife*, April-May 1977.

Hansen, Richard M. and Richard E. Hubbard. "Diets of Horses, Cattle and Mule Deer in the Piceance Basin, Colorado", *Journal of Range Management*, September 1976.

Hansen, Richard M. "Foods of Free Roaming Horses in Southern New Mexico", *Journal of Range Management*, July 1976.

Hansen, Richard M. and Frank Wolsen. "Food Relationships of Wild, Free Roaming Horses to Livestock and Big Game, Red Desert, Wyoming", *Journal of Range Management*, January 1977.

Howard, Helen Addison. "Salute to the Mustang", *Horse and Horseman*, May 1977.

Idaho Cattleman, "Cattle By-Products", October 1975.

Jackson, Donald. "Mustangs", *Life*, January 1969.

James, Will. "Piñon and the Wild Ones", *Saturday Evening Post*, May 19, 1923.

Johnston, Velma B. "The Fight to Save a Memory", *Texas Law Review*, 1972.

———. "Mustang Protective Legislation", *Chronicle of the Horse*, August 7, 1970.

———. and M. J. Pontrelli. "Public Pressure and a New Dimension of Quality—Wild Horses and Burros", *Transactions of the 34th North American Wildlife and Natural Resources Conference*, March 1969.

Kania, Al. "Wild and Free Roaming", *American Horseman*, July 1974.

King, Chuck. "A Realistic Look at the Mustang-Wild Horse Situation", *Western Horseman*, May 1971.

Klataske, Ron. "Wild Horse Range", *Wyoming Wildlife*, September 1970.

"The Last Roundup?" *Newsweek*, May 13, 1968.

Libman, Joan. "A Battle in Nevada May Decide the Fate of the Wild Horse", *Wall Street Journal*, August 4, 1975.

Marshall, Larry. "Wild Horse Population Concern Mounts", *Western Livestock Journal*, September 30, 1974.

McArthur, J. Wayne. "The Wild Horse; An Asset or a Liability?" *Western Horseman*, June 1973.

McKnight, Tom. "The Wild Horse Today", *Desert*, 1959.

Moorehouse, James A. and Gene Nodine. "Wild Horse Haven," *Our Public Lands*, Fall, 1967.

Moore, Ron. "Mustangs", *Western Horseman*, May 1969.

Most, Chuck. "Wild Horses of the Pryors", *Our Public Lands*, Fall 1969.

"The Mustang Hunters", *Newsweek*, April 22, 1974.

O'Brien, Mary. "Indian Acquisition of the Horse", *Western Horseman*, October 1976.

O'Brien, Robert. "The Mustangs' Last Stand", *Reader's Digest*, December 1957.

Peterson, O. C. "Desert Horses of the 1920's", *Western Horseman*, December 1976.

Pontrelli, Michael. "Protection for Wild Mustangs," *Defenders of Wildlife News*, October-December 1969.

Reavley, William. "Wild Horse Board Suggests Sweeping Changes", *Conservation News*, November 15, 1974.

Remsberg, Charles. "One Man's Fight to Save the Mustangs", *True*, April 1967.

Rhodes, Richard. "How the West Was Lost", *Esquire*, May 1972.

Riley, J. "The Mustangers", *Los Angeles Times*, July 27, 1969.

Robertson, Anna. "Can 50,000 Wild Horses Be Wrong?" *Horse and Rider*, March 1976.

Ryden, Hope. "On the Track of the West's Wild Horses", *National Geographic*, January 1971.

———. "Goodby to the Wild Horse?" *Reader's Digest*, May 1971.

Santee, Ross. "The Last Run", *Arizona Highways*, November 1958.

Scher, Zeke. "Reprieve for the Mustangs", *Empire (Denver Post)* October 12, 1969.

Schwartz, Barney. "A Kingdom for Wild Horses", *Nature Magazine*, 1949.

Scott, Jim. "Attack on Freedom", *Horse and Rider*, September 1975.

Simmons, Diane C. "What is Humane?"

———. "Born Wild", *American Horseman*, October 1977.

Spencer, Dick. "Plight of the Mustang", *Sports Afield*, December 1959.

Sumner, L. "Effects of Wild Burros on Bighorn in Death Valley National Monument", *Desert Bighorn Council Transactions* 1959.

Thomas, Heather. "A Cattle Rancher Views the Wild Horses", *American Horseman*, March, 1977.

———. "Adopting a Wild Horse", *Horse Illustrated*, February, 1978.

———. "Plight of the Mustangs", *Horse and Rider Yearbook*, 1976.

———. "Survival of the Wild Horse Part II", *Horse Illustrated*, Volume 4, 1977.

———. "The Bowman Ranch", *Western Livestock Reporter Annual*, 1974.

———. "The Wild Horse Problem", *American Horseman*, June 1976.

Trueblood, Ted. "Disaster on the Western Range", *Field and Stream*, January 1975.

Vasiloff, Mary Jean. "My Views on Adopting a Wild Horse", *Chronicle of the Horse*, November 5, 1976.

Walters, Beverly. "Wild Horse Annie Fights to Save the Mustangs", *Desert*, June 1959.

Weaver, Richard A. "Effects of Burros on Desert Water Supplies", *Desert Bighorn Council Transactions*, 1959.

Welles, R. E. "The Feral Burro in Death Valley," *Desert Bighorn Council Transactions*, 1961.

———. "Status of the Bighorn Sheep in Death Valley", *Desert Bighorn Council Transactions*, 1957.

Weiskopf, Herman. "Wild West Showdown", *Sports Illustrated*, May 5, 1975.

"Wild Horse Annie", *Time*, July 27, 1959.

"Wild Horse Rights; Return of the Mustangs?" *Colorado Business*, November 15, 1973.

"Wild Horses . . . Or Are They?" *Western Livestock Journal*, November 1974.

Wilson, George C. "Slaughter of Wild Horses", *Defenders of Wildlife News*, April 1974.

Wood, Nancy. "The Wild Horse—Heritage or Pest?" *Audubon*, Nov. 1969.

Worcester, D. E. "Spanish Horses Among the Plains Tribes", *Pacific Historical Review*, 1945.

———. "The Spread of Spanish Horses in the Southwest", *New Mexico Historical Review*, 1944.

Wright, George M. "Big Game of Our National Parks", *Scientific Monthly*, 1935.

III. Newspaper articles

Battle Mountain Bugle, July 5, 1978, "Humane Society Accuses BLM of Wild Horse Abuse."

Chicago Tribune, June 9, 1974, "The Roundup That Became A Slaughter".

Conservation Report No. 2, January 30, 1976, "Hearings Held on Amendments to Wild Horse Act".

High Country News, November 8, 1974, "Nevada Report May Change the West; BLM Exposes Own Grazing Abuses", by Bruce Hamilton.

High Country News, January 30, 1976, "Donkey Dilemma Damages Public Land; America's Sacred Cow?" by Miriam A. Romero.

Idaho Free Press, July 11, 1974, "Woman Opposes Wild Horse Policy".

Idaho Free Press, March 1976, "BLM Responds to Complaints; Mustangs to Head for New Home".

Idahonian, December 4, 1974, "Judge Dismisses Suit in Bloody Roundup".

Idaho State Journal, March 3, 1973, "Humane Society Offers Files to U.S. Attorney".

———, March 5, 1973, "Officials Inspect Roundup Scene".

———, March 6, 1973, "Horse Roundup Investigation Underway".

———, March 7, 1973, "BLM Director Reports Horses Found Alive".

———, March 8, 1973, "Horse Herd Found Awaiting Slaughter".

———, March 15, 1973, "Reward Offered in Horse Deaths".

Idaho Statesman, May 23, 1971, "Emotions Over Saving of Mustangs Ride High as Passage of Bill Nears."

———, October 6, 1971, "Congress Passes Bill to Protect Wild Horses".

———, November 18, 1971, "Wild Horses Rescued from Montana Winter; Herds Thinned by Roundup, Not Bullets".

———, December 21, 1972, "Wild Horse, Burro Act Assessed."

———, January 13, 1973, "Wild Horse Board Ends First Meeting on Herd Protection".

———, March 2, 1973, "Society Probes Aerial Roundup of Horse Herds."

———, March 4, 1973, "Idaho Horse Roundup Called Massacre."

———, March 4, 1973, "Roaming Wild Burros Pose Desert Dilemma."

———, March 5, 1973, "BLM Reports Urging Ranchers to Round Up Lost River Horses".

———, March 7, 1973, "Lost River Horse Roundup Could Spur State Charges".

———, March 8, 1973, "30 Horses Involved in Roundup Located in Nebraska."

———, March 9, 1973, "Lemhi Horses Said Starving".

———, March 14, 1973, "BLM Board told Horse Round-up Got Public Eye after Initial Miss."

———, June 6, 1973, "BLM Supervises Jarbridge Roundup".

———, June 7, 1973, "Charges Studied for Roundup of Wild Horses".

———, July 28, 1973, "Sierra Club Assails BLM Wild Horse Study for Generality".

———, August 13, 1973, "Winter Hunger Perils 17,000 Mustangs in Western States".

———, August 16, 1973, "BLM Orders To Show Range Horse Ownership".

———, September 14, 1973, "Four Meetings to Air Wild Horse Rules".

———, September 29, 1973, "Wild Horses Fill Montana Ranges; Law Limits Methods to Thin Herds".

———, September 27, 1973, "Owyhee Ranchers Briefed on Wild Horse Regulations".

———, October 14, 1973, "19 Mustangs Returned to Idaho".

———, October 25, 1973, "BLM Prepares Return of Wild Horses to Idaho".

———, October 26, 1973, "Move Rejected for Horse Case".

———, November 7, 1973, "Rescued Herd of Wild Horses to Return Home".

———, November 10, 1973, "Horses Leave by Truck for Idaho".

———, November 12, 1973, "Howe Mustangs May Face Last Roundup".

———, November 14, 1973, "Rancher Files Claim for 14 'Wild' Horses".

———, November 16, 1973, "Finale Greets Horses".

———, November 19, 1973, "New Mexicans Plan to Claim Mustangs".

———, December 5, 1973, "Ranchers Give Their Side of 'Wild' Horse Roundup to Congressional Aides".

———, January 1, 1974, "Judge Demands Reports of Wild Horse Roundup".

———, January 21, 1974, "BLM to Clear Open Range for Mustangs".

———, March 6, 1974, "Growing Mustang Tally Alarms West's Stockmen".

———, March 27, 1974, "BLM Accused of Bungling Mustang Laws".

———, March 28, 1974, "Idaho Mustang Roundup 'Appalls' U.S. Horse Panel".

———, April 25, 1974, "BLM Counts 600 Wild Horses".

———, June 19, 1974, "Lawyer Told to Hasten in Horse Roundup Lawsuit".

———, June 20, 1974, "Horses Outgrow Limits of Range".

———, June 26, 1974, "Hearing to Settle Fate of Horses Caught at Howe".

———, June 28, 1974, "Witnesses on Private Ownership Dominate Mustang Hearing".

———, July 7, 1974, "Wild Horses in Oregon Thinned to Save Range".

———, August 20, 1974, "Decision on Howe Horses May Aid in Settling Fate on Wild Status".

———, September 4, 1974, "Status as Private Property Conferred on Howe Horses".

———, September 22, 1974, "Wild Colt Becomes Present for Ill Boy".

———, October 11, 1974, "Last Steens Mountain Mustangs Rounded up for Custodial Care".

———, October 20, 1974, "Wild Horses' Ability to Survive Poses Problems in Owyhee Breaks".

———, October 31, 1974, "Roundups to Drive Mustangs Home".

———, November 9, 1974, "Dismissal of Howe Suit Asked".

———, November 10, 1974, "Wild Horses Termed Threat to U.S. Food".

———, November 26, 1974, "Horse Trespassing Problem Bedevils BLM—For Awhile".

———, December 4, 1974, "Mustang Suit Denied".

———, December 5, 1974, "Losers in Howe Horse Roundup Suit Ponder Future Action".

———, December 6, 1974, "Howe Rancher Promises Public Horse Auction".

———, December 7, 1974, "Horse Protectors Begin Appeal".

———, December 25, 1974, "Trespassing Horses Returned to Owners".

———, January 5, 1975, "Old West Methods Slow Roundups of Wild Horses".

———, February 4, 1975, "Wild Horse Laws Require Changing, BLM Chief Says".

———, March 5, 1975, "Mustang 'Slaughter' Predicted".

———, March 6, 1975, "Wild Horse Decision Leaves Equines, Officials, in Confusion".

———, March 20, 1975, "BLM Claims Slaying of Mustangs Continue".

———, March 23, 1975, "BLM Still Watches Wild Horses Despite Confusion".

———, April 3, 1975, "Slaughter Feared After Horse Ruling".

———, April 15, 1975, "Mail Asks Governor Rampton to Protect Wild Horses".

———, April 21, 1975, "Wild Horses Frustrate BLM Crews".

———, May 29, 1975, "BLM Gets Low Bid on Capturing Horses".

———, June 4, 1975, "Packwood Seeks to Allow Copters

to Chase Horses".

———, July 29, 1975, "Nevada Confiscates BLM Mustang Herd".

———, August 1, 1975, "BLM May Resume Roundup of Horses".

———, August 5, 1975, "Nevada Asks BLM to Waive Fees on Trespassing Horses".

———, August 6, 1975, "BLM to Release Horses in Nevada".

———, August 7, 1975, "75 Wild Horses Freed in Nevada".

———, August 13, 1975, "Cowboys Begin Oregon Roundup of Wild Horses".

———, September 4, 1975, "Mustang Roundup to Resume".

———, September 17, 1975, "BLM Crew Charged with Cruelty in Roundup of Nevada Mustangs".

———, October 2, 1975, "Derogatory Pictures of Roundup Attacked as Deliberately Staged".

———, October 7, 1975, "Court to Review Wild Horse Act".

———, October 11, 1975, "Roundup of Wild Horses Planned in Vale District".

———, October 12, 1975, "Wild Mare, Yearling, Called 'Too Cagey', Outlast Utah Roundup".

———, October 18, 1975, "Vale Roundup Nets 15 Horses on Second Day".

———, October 19, 1975, "Minor Space Age Conveniences Aid Oregon Wild Horse Roundup".

———, November 19, 1975, "New Homes Run Low for Captured Horses".

———, December 14, 1975, "Wild Horse, Burro Numbers Cause Concern Over Range Use".

———, December 16, 1975, "Increase in Wild Horses Worries Advisory Head".

———, August 15, 1976, "Mustangers Ride Out Roundup Wait".

———, September 1, 1976, "Wild Horse Roundup Decision Expected Today".

———, September 17, 1976, "BLM Drops Plan to Destroy Horses".

———, January 6, 1977, "Three Humane Groups Oppose Burro Kill".

———, February 3, 1977, "U.S. Gets Last Say on Grazing Horses".

———, March 1, 1977, "Drought Forces Horses to Roam Summer Range".

———, March 16, 1977, "Helicopter Roundups Lauded".

———, April 27, 1977, "BLM Water Haul Spares Wild Horses From Death".

———, May 7, 1977, "Drought Help for Cattlemen Called Paltry, Late in Oregon".

———, May 20, 1977, "11 Unbranded Howe Horses Set

for Adoption; '73 Horse Roundup Dispute Resolved".

———, May 24, 1977, "Wild Equine Populations Debated".

———, May 26, 1977, "Helicopter Roundups Ok'd".

———, June 8, 1977, "Starving Mustangs Corralled".

———, July 1, 1977, "Park Marksmen Kill More Burros".

———, July 6, 1977, "Roundups Set To Save Horses from Drought".

———, July 16, 1977, "Meeting Accepts BLM Roundup Plan".

———, July 28, 1977, "Drought Kills Oregon Mustangs".

———, November 23, 1976, "BLM Rounds up 139 Horses".

———, October 3, 1977, "They Shoot Horses".

———, September 11, 1977, "Wild Horse Roundup".

———, September 13, 1977, "BLM Rounds up 144 Wild Horses".

———, September 28, 1977, "BLM Finds New Homes for Wild Horses".

———, September 29, 1977, "U.S. Agency May Shoot Wild Horses".

———, November 15, 1977, "BLM to Ship Last of 1397 Wild Horses".

———, January 7, 1978, "Adopted Wild Horses Return to BLM Care".

———, March 13, 1978, "Custer County Seeks Solution to Wild Horses".

Illustrated London News, 1949, "Horse Roundup by Aircraft".

Las Vegas *Sun*, July 25, 1978, "Horse Case Starts".

Las Vegas *Sun*, July 27, 1978, "Court to Hear Plight of Wild Horses".

Lewiston Morning Tribune, March 16, 1973, "Idaho Roundup; Criminal Prosecution Seen in Deaths of Wild Horses".

Lincoln County *Record*, August 24, 1972, "The Vanity of Protecting Wild Horses".

The Lovell Chronicle, March 29, 1973, "Idaho Horse Cruelty Uncovered; Annie Asks Changes in Legislation".

Nevada State Journal, April 6, 1973, "Suit Filed in Deaths of Horses".

Nevada State Journal, July 1, 1977, Editorial.

Nevada State Journal, June 29, 1978, "Break Seen in Mustang Stalemate".

Nevada State Journal, July 25, 1978, "Dispute over Wild Horses Headed for Federal Court".

Nevada State Journal, July 28, 1978, "Naturalist Testifies at Wild Horse Roundup Trial".

Nevada State Journal, July 29, 1978, "Horse Trial Judge Questions Witnesses".

Nevada State Journal, July 31, 1978, "Official Defends BLM Horse Roundup Policy".

Nevada Rancher, August 1978, "Wild Horse Trial".

Mason Valley News (Yerington, Nevada), July 2, 1976, "Public Lands States Future Endangered".

Nevada State Journal, July 8, 1976, "Wild Horse Annie Sets the Record Straight".

New York Times, November 19, 1973, "New Mexico Defies Law on Wild Horses".

New York Times, February 24, 1974, "Jackson Demands Probe on Operation of Wild Horse Act".

Oakland Tribune, May 21, 1977, "Death Stalks Nevada's Wild Horses".

The Post Register, October 16, 1974, "Howe Horses Remaining Under BLM Supervision".

Record Herald (Salmon, Idaho), May 20, 1976, "Wanted: Foster Homes for Wild Horses".

Recorder Herald, 1976, "Wild Horses Create Impact on Challis Unit Range".

Recorder Herald, June 1976, "Physical Makeup Detailed of Challis Planning Unit".

Recorder Herald, June 22, 1976, "Wild Horses Impact BLM Planning Unit".

Recorder Herald, June, 1976, "BLM Plans Roundup".

Recorder Herald, August, 1976, "BLM Faces Suit Over Horses".

Recorder Herald, August 12, 1976, "Court Action Delays Wild Horse Roundup".

Recorder Herald, August 26, 1976, "Official Finds Facilities For Wild Horses Adequate".

Recorder Herald, March 3, 1977, "Interior Proposes Rules for Use of Helicopters in Wild Horse Roundups".

Recorder Herald, March 3, 1977, "Wild Horse Explosion Threatens Several Big Game Species".

Recorder Herald, June 30, 1977, "Wild Horse Annie Dies".

Recorder Herald, August 11, 1977, "Consulting Forester Cites Threat to Forest Use".

Recorder Herald, June 8, 1978, "Beef Council Aide Discusses Industry".

Recorder Herald, March 13, 1978, "Custer County Seeks Solution to Wild Horses".

Recorder Herald, June 8, 1978, "BLM Launches Major Effort to Complete Challis Statement".

Recorder Herald, May 25, 1978, "BLM Challis Unit Impact Statement Due September 30".

Recorder Herald, August 17, 1978, "Fish and Game Survey Antelope Ranges".

Reno, Nevada, September 21, 1974, "Refuge for Wild Horses Urged by National Board".

Reno Evening Gazette, July 8, 1976 "Those Wild Horses". Editorial.

Reno Evening Gazette, July 9, 1976 "A United Front". Editorial.

Reno Evening Gazette, August 16, 1976, "Not the Enemy". Editorial.

Reno Evening Gazette, May 9, 1978, "Law Suit Halts Horse Roundup".

Reno Evening Gazette, May 10, 1978, Editorial: "Wild Horse Crisis Grows".

Reno Evening Reveille, May 12, 1978, Letters: "Wild Horse Protections", by Helen A. Reilly.

Reno Evening Gazette, May 12, 1978, "Removal of Horses May be Halted".

Sunday London Times, January 20, 1974, "The Last Sad Roundup".

Times (Ely, Nevada), June 28, 1976, "Horse Protection Causes Problems".

Times-News (Twin Falls, Idaho), March 6, 1973, "Lemhi Ranchers 'Fast One' Scored".

The Valley Times (Las Vegas), July 28, 1976, "Angling With Glassburn; Wild Horses Blitz Herds".

Washington Post, January 17, 1974, "Their Fate May Depend On Courtroom".

Washington Post, April 30, 1974, "Wild Horse Protectors Win Their First Round".

Washington Post, May 12, 1974, "The Bloody Roundup—Wild Horse Slaughter Detailed".

Washington Post, May 26, 1974, "Wild Horses—A Bill Trampled".

Western Livestock Reporter, November 14, 1974, "Wild Horses and Special Problems go Hand in Hand".

Western Livestock Reporter, July 6, 1978 "Range Bill Passes House".

The Wyoming Eagle, September 16, 1969 "Wild Horse Refuge".

IV. Organizations' Newsletters and Brochures

Wild Horse Organized Assistance (WHOA)
Information letter, December 15, 1971.
Newsletter, December 1972.
———, March 1973.
———, June 1973.
———, January 1974.
———, January 1975.
———, June 1975.
News Bulletin, October 1975.
Newsletter, June 1977.
Letter to George L. Turcott, Associate BLM Director.

International Society for the Protection of Mustangs and Burros (ISPMB)
Newsletter, December 1972.
———, and special bulletin March 1975.
———, August 18, 1975.
———, January 12, 1977.
———, October 1977.
———, February 1978.
———, May 1978.
———, July 1978.

National Mustang Association
Newsletter, "The Mustang", February-March 1977

American Horse Protection Association (AHPA)

undated brochures
newsletter, Spring 1975
———, February-March, 1975.
———, June 1976.
Booklet, "Introducing the American Mustang; The Horse That Made America", American Mustang Association, Inc.
"Inspection Procedure", American Mustang Association.
Booklet: "Spanish Barb Breeders Association," *The Spanish Barb Quarterly*, January-June, 1977.
Booklet: "The Spanish Barb".
Brochure: "Wild Horse Research Farm".
Booklet: "The Good Things We Get From Cattle Besides Beef", Idaho Beef Council.

V. Government Publications

Annotated Bibliography and Technical Note on Wild Horses and Burros, USDA, USDI, 1977.
Bakersfield District Saline Valley Burro Plan, BLM
BLM News Sheet, March 28, 1975.
BLM News Beat (California State Office), April 1977.
BLM News Release (Idaho State Office), March 6, 1973.
BLM (Salmon District) notes on Challis Workshop, June 6-9, 1978
Brewer, Clyde E. *Susanville District Wild Horse and Burros Management Plan*, June 1976.
Cleary, Rex. Billings District, "A Myth About Wild Horses," Feb. 8, 1973.
Comacho, Steve, and John Kingston. "Early Livestock Grazing in the Home Camp/Tuledad Units", Susanville District, January 1977.
Englebright, James. *Challis Wild Horse Management Plan* 1976.
Fact Sheet: "Roundup of Horses From Public Lands Near Howe, Idaho," BLM, March 19, 1976.
Fact Sheet: "Wild Horses", USDI-BLM (1969?).
Fort Churchill-Clan Alpine Land Use Guides, BLM, Carson City, Nevada.
"Four Years of Wild Horse Law Reviewed", BLM news release, Dec. 15, 1975.
Hall, Ron. *Wild Horse–Biology and Alternatives for Management; Pryor Mountain Wild Horse Range* (Wildlife Biologist, Billings Dist.)
Hearing Before the Committee on Interior and Insular Affairs; United States Senate, Ninety-Third Congress, Second Session, On the Administration of PL 92-195—The Wild Free-Roaming Horse and Burros Protection Act of 1971, June 26, 1974.
Information Sheet: Pryor Mountain Horse Area, USDI, BLM, 1968.
Letter to Robert McCandless from George Turcott, Associate BLM Director.
Inyo National Forest News: "Inyo National Forest Announces Completion of Wild Horse Management Plan".

"Little Bookliff Wild Horse Area" (mimeo sheet).
Mitchell, Michael C. *Wild Horse and Burro Proposed Management Plan*, Battle Mountain District, BLM, March 1975.
"Murderers Creek Wild Horse Herd Control Action Plan", BLM-FS
"Murderers Creek Wild Horse Roundup", by Al Myer, District Ranger, Bear Valley Ranger District, Malheur National Forest.
Pine-Nut-Markleeville Land Use Guides, Carson City BLM District.
Public Land News, June 29, 1978 and July 13, 1978
Pyramid-Long Valley Land Use Guides, Carson City BLM District
"Rock Springs Horse Removal Plan", Rock Springs, Wyoming, BLM.
Stateline Land Use Guide, Las Vegas BLM District.
USDA-USFS *Environmental Statement for the Secretary of Agriculture's Proposed Regulations for the Protection, Management and Control of Wild Free-Roaming Horses and Burros.*
USDA, *Livestock and Meat Statistics*, Supplement for 1976.
USDA, Office of the General Counsel, Memo to John R. McGuire, Chief of Forest Service, Subject: Wild Free-Roaming Horses and Burros.
USDA, "Requirements for Hauling Wild Horses", Bear Valley Ranger District, Malheur National Forest.
USDA, Forest Service, "You Asked About Acquiring A Wild Horse", Bear Valley Ranger District, Malheur National Forest.
USDA-USDI, *A Report to Congress by the Secretary of the Interior And the Secretary of Agriculture on Administration of the Wild Free-Roaming Horse and Burro Act*, June, 1974.
USDA-USDI *Second Report to Congres; Administration of the Wild Free-Roaming Horse and Burro Act*, 1976.
USDI, BLM, *Final Environmental Statement, Proposed Wild Free-Roaming Horse and Burro Management Regulations.*
USDI, *In Touch With People; U.S. Department of the Interior Conservation Yearbook Series No. 9*, 1973.
USDI, Memorandum to District BLM Manager from Wild Horse Specialist, Susanville, California, District, June 28, 1976. Subject: "Recommendations on Environmental Statement regarding the District wild horse and burro EAR".
USDI-BLM, *Proceedings; National Advisory Board*, September 8-10, Elko, Nev.
Statements:
Jack Hull, Nevada Cattleman's Association
George W. Abbot, Attorney
Curt Berklund, BLM Director
Dale W. Bohmont, University of Nevada
Lloyd Sorenson, Stockman
Von Sorenson, Rancher
John Weber, Public Lands Council

Kay Wilkes, Chief, Division of Range, BLM

USDI-BLM, *Public Land Statistics*, 1976

USDI, *Status Report; Wild Horses and Burros, Susanville District BLM Virgin Valley Land Use Guide*, Las Vegas District, BLM.

Welles, R.E. and F.B. Welles, "The Bighorn of Death Valley", U.S. Fauna Series No. 6, USDI, National Park Service, 1961.

VI. National Advisory Board for Wild, Free-Roaming Horses and Burros, Proceedings

Proceedings: First Meeting, January 12-13, 1973 Salt Lake City, Utah.
2nd Meeting, March 21-22, 1973, Denver, Colorado.
3rd Meeting, July 16-17, 1973, Billings, Montana.
4th Meeting, November 6-8, 1973 Lake Havasu City, Arizona.
5th Meeting, March 26-27, 1974, Washington, D.C.
6th Meeting, September 18-20, 1974 Reno, Nevada.
7th Meeting, September 4-5, 1975, Rock Springs, Wyoming.
8th Meeting, December 5-6, 1975, NWC, China Lake, California.
9th Meeting, June 3-4, 1976, John Day, Oregon.

Statements of Individuals or group representatives at national wild horse and burro advisory board meetings:

Ayers, Kathy. "Wild Horses of the White Mountains".

Barling, Tilly, Natural Resource Specialist, China Lake Naval Weapons Center, "Burros on and adjacent to the China Lake Naval Weapons Center".

Bibles, Dean, District BLM Manager, Susanville, California, "Wild Horses".

Box, Dr. Thadis, "Ecological Impact of Wild Horses".

Clark, Dean, Oregon Department of Agriculture.

Dantzler, F.L. Humane Society of the United States.

DeDecker, Mary.

DeForge, Jim, Desert Bighorn Council.

Fletcher, Dr. Milford, "Burros in Bandelier National Monument".

Gaspar, Russ, American Horse Protection Association.

Hampton, Kenneth R. National Wildlife Federation.

Johnston, Velma B. Wild Horse Organized Assistance.

Jones, Fred L. Chief, Division of Lands and Water Conservation Fund, Bureau of Outdoor Recreation, USDI, "Competition".

Kania, Al, Feral Organized Assistance League.

Lowe, Jesse R. Wyoming State Report.

Lutz, Dr. Loren, "Burros and Burrocrats".

Mouras, Belton, Animal Protection Institute.

Nevada Woolgrowers Association.

Navel Weapons Center Natural Resources Advisory Council, Department of the Navy, NWC.

Ohmart, Dr. Robert, Arizona State University, "The Ecological Impact of Wild Burros on the Public Lands".

Pontrelli, Michael.

Powell, Walter B. Chairman, Land Use Committee, California Wildlife Federation.

Radtkey, Bill, Wildlife Biologist, BLM, California State Office, "Burros on Public Lands".

Rice, Carl M. Range Management specialist, California State BLM, Sacramento, "Animal Diseases".

Rhodes, Dean, Public Lands Council.

Romero, Miriam, statement regarding implementation of PL 92-195.

Russo, John P. Chief, Game Management, Arizona Game and Fish Department, "Burro Food, Habits and Competition".

Sanchez, Pete, Resource Management Specialist at Death Valley National Monument, "Burros and Wildlife in Death Valley".

Seater, Steve, Fund for Animals.

Sierra Club.

Smith, Pat, American Horse Protection Association.

Springer, Robert L. Bureau of Land Management.

Swarthout, Donald M. "The Other Side of the Burro".

Thompson, James B. National Park Service, "Burros in Death Valley National Monument".

Turcott, George, Associate BLM Director.

Weaver, Richard A. Associate Wildlife Manager and Biologist, California Fish and Game, "Census and Management of Burros".

Woody, Pat, rancher's wife, Howe, Idaho.

Wright, William, rancher, Deeth, Nevada.

VII. Master of Science Theses

Blakeslee, Jodean Kay. 1974 *Mother-Young Relationships and Related Behavior Among Free-Ranging Appaloosa Horses.* M.S. Thesis, Idaho State University.

Feist, James Dean. 1971. *Behavior of Feral Horses in the Pryor Mountain Wild Horse Range.* M.S. Thesis, University of Michigan.

McMichael, T.J. 1964 *Studies of the Relationship Between Desert Bighorn and Feral Burro in the Black Mountains of Northwestern Arizona.* M.S. Thesis, University of Arizona, Tucson.

Pellegrini, Steven W. 1971 *Home Range, Territoriality and Movement Patterns of Wild Horses in the Wassuk Range of Western Nevada.* M.S. Thesis, University of Nevada, Reno.

Rey, Mark Edward. 1975 *A Critique of the BLM Management Program for Wild Horses and Burros in the*

Western United States. M.S. Thesis, University of Michigan.

VIII. Personal Interviews, telephone interviews, and conversations

Bailey, Jim. Retired horseman and mustanger, Salmon, Idaho.

Bedrosia, Jan. BLM, Reno, Nevada.

Beers, Gail. Participant in Adopt-A-Horse program. Reno, Nevada.

Bowman, Chester. Rancher, Salmon, Idaho.

Bradshaw, Ken. Rancher, Challis, Idaho.

Englebright, Jim. Wild Horse specialist, BLM, Salmon, Idaho.

Finlayson, Harry. BLM District Manager, Salmon, Idaho.

Fischer, Frances, Participant in Adopt-A-Horse program. Carson City, Nevada.

Gaston, Sandy. Participant in Adopt-A-Horse program. Reno, Nevada.

Gidlund, Carl. Chief, Public Affairs, BLM, Reno, Nevada.

Gossey, Don, and Ray Gossey, Ranchers, Challis, Idaho.

Gregory, Sally. Assistant Manager, Challis-Mackay Area, BLM, Salmon, Ida.

Larkin, Robert. Wild Horse Specialist, BLM, Salmon, Idaho.

Pyron, Charlene. Participant in Adopt-A-Horse program, Atlanta, Georgia.

Smith, Don. Challis-Mackay Area Manager, BLM, Salmon, Idaho.

Thomas, Charles, Rancher, Salmon, Idaho.

IX. Correspondence

Applegate, L. Paul, BLM District Manager, Carson City, Nevada, January 11, 1977.

Babbit, Jim, Spanish Mustang Registry, Inc. May 3, 1977.

Boyles, John S. BLM District Manager, Las Vegas, Nevada, January 13, 1977, April 28, 1977.

Buck, John A. Acting District Manager, BLM, Grand Junction, Colorado, February 13, 1977.

Cleary, C. Rex. BLM District Manager, Susanville, California, January 21, 1977, June 7, 1977.

Conard, Chester E. BLM District Manager, Winnemucca, Nevada, January 27, 1977, August 19, 1977.

Cropper, George, Acting District Manager, BLM, Ely, Nevada, February 9, 1977.

Fischer, Frances, Carson City, Nevada, November 7, 1977.

Frank, Dr. Floyd, Head of Veterinary Medicine, University of Idaho, Moscow, Idaho, May 25, 1977.

Frei, Milton, Range Conservationist, BLM, Denver Service Center, January 19, 1977, May 11, 1977.

Freitag, Peg, Spanish Barb Breeders Association, June 12, 1977, Sept. 6, 1977.

Fuener, Donald C. Information Specialist, USDA, Agricultural Marketing Service, Midwest Regional Information Office, June 14, 1977.

Gidlund, Carl A. Chief, Public Affairs, BLM Nevada State Office, January 11, 1977, May 12, 1977.

Johnston, Velma B. WHOA, June 6, 1972, November 29, 1976.

Lappin, Dawn, WHOA, August 3, 1977.

Lawhorn, Leo W. Wild Horse Specialist, BLM, Meeder, Colorado, May 17, 1977.

Marvel, Tom, Nevada rancher, Battle Mountain, Nevada, May 22, 1977.

Matthews, William L. BLM, Idaho State Director, Boise, Idaho January 11, 1977, April 21, 1977.

Moore, A.E. BLM District Manager, Elko, Nevada, January 7, 1977, March 31, 1978.

Morck, Neil F. BLM District Manager, Rock Springs, Wyoming, January 11, 1977, April 28, 1977, May 10, 1977.

Nevada Cattlemen's Association, Elko, Nevada, April 22, 1977.

Pickering, Ruth S. Secretary, National Mustang Association, Newcastle, Utah, Aug. 29, 1977.

Phillips, Willard P. Drewsey Area Manager, BLM, Burns, Oregon January 11, 1977.

Weaver, Richard A. Associate Wildlife Manager-Biologist, California Dept. of Fish and Game, November 16, 1977.

X. Miscellaneous

Brief of Amicus Curiae, State of Idaho, in the Supreme Court of the United States, October Term, 1974, No. 74-1488.

Brief of New Mexico, in the Supreme Court of the United States, October Term, 1974, No. 74-1488.

Complaint for Declaratory Judgment and Injunctive Relief; United States District Court for the District of Columbia, American Horse Protection Association, Inc. and The Humane Society of the United States, Plaintiffs, versus Thomas Kleppe, Secretary of the U.S. Department of Interior, *et al.* August 4, 1976.

Complaint; United States District Court for the District of Columbia, American Horse Protection Association, Inc. and The Humane Society of the United States, Plaintiffs, versus Cecil Andrus, *et al.* Civil Action File no. 78-0606. April 5, 1978.

Affidavit of James M. Peek, Moscow, Idaho, in AHPA v. Thomas Kleppe.

Syllabus, Supreme Court of the United States; Kleppe, Secretary of the Interior, versus New Mexico, *et al.* Argued March 23, 1976. Decided June 17, 1976.

Testimony of Dean T. Prosser, Jr., Chief Brand Inspector, Wyoming Stock Growers Association, before the Subcommittee on Public Lands, of the Committee on Interior and Insular Affairs, of the U.S. House of Representatives, Billings, Montana, August 12, 1975.

United States District Court for the District of Columbia, Findings of Fact and Conclusions of Law, American Horse Portection Association, Inc. *et al*, Plaintiffs, versus Thomas Kleppe, *et al*, Defendants, September 9, 1976.

"Feral Burro and Wildlife", by Richard Weaver, Associate Wildlife Manager-Biologist, California Department of Fish and Game (presented at the Vertebrate Pest Conference, Anaheim, California, March 5-7, 1974).

Senate bill S.2475, 95th Congress, 2nd Session.

XL. Wild Horse Forum (April 5-7, 1977)

Bennetts, Jim. Challis, Idaho rancher and attorney.

Cleary, Rex. BLM, Susanville, California.

Dantzler, F. L. "Statement of HSUS concerning Wild Horses, their Management, Current Problems and Statement of Policy".

Fisher, Charles. Range Conservationist. "Horses on Indian Reservations".

Frei, Milton N. Range Conservationist, Division of Standards and Technology, BLM, Denver, Colorado. "Wild Horse Research Needs".

Green, Nancy F. and Howard D. Green, Humboldt State University, Arcata, California, "The Wild Horse Population of Stone Cabin Valley, Nevada".

Hyde, William F. Research Associate, Resources for the Future, Washington, D.C. "The Wild Horse and Allocations of Public Resources".

Jenkens, R.J. (Dick). Cattleman.

Pontrelli, Michael J. "The Role of the Wild Horse in Changing Concepts of Public Land Use in the West".

Reynolds, Douglas A. Extension Horse Specialist, University of Nevada, Reno. "Hoofbeats and Heartbeats".

Shanks, Bernard. Associate Professor, University of Nevada, Reno, "Wild Horses and Conservation Organizations".

Shewmaker, Lloyd E. Salmon River Cattleman's Association, Inc.

Snider, Gail Krandall. Statement of AHPA.

Teyens, Roger Van. Field Consultant of American Humane Association.

Theos, Nick. Chairman of Public Lands Council.

Vosler, Christian, BLM District Manager, Burns, Oregon. "Removal and Disposition Program of Wild Horses in the Burns District".

Weber, John. Regional Vice President of American National Cattleman's Association.

Wright, Robert. President, Nevada Cattleman's Association.

Young, Roy, Nevada rancher and former Wild Horse Advisory Board Chairman.

Index

279

helicopter roundups, 164–65, 167; assertion of federal power over free-roaming animals, 169, 173; attempts to amend, 142, 149, 157, 247–49; burro management under, in California, 181, 188; Congressional reports leading up to, 253; constitutionally challenged, 155, 168–75; rule unconstitutional, 169–70; constitutionality upheld, 175; costs of wild horse management under, in Nevada, 245; definition and characteristics of, 102–4, 138; environmental impact statements on, 105–110; expansion of wild horses after protection, 108, 151–52, 166; influence in Howe roundup, 117; immediate problems, 103–4; increased adverse impact on range management, 259–61; lack of funding, 104, 139, 243, 248; legislation leading up to, 98–101; management attempts of BLM, 151–67; management regulations, 105–6, 138–39; need for amending, 150–51, 241–42, 246–48, 251–52; research, 139; restrictions on management, 150–51, 210, 258–59, 236; Sierra Club recommendation it apply only to horses, 188; violations and investigations, 140

Wild Horse Forum, 201, 213, 234, 240–47: claiming problems, 244–45; conservation groups and wild horses, 243–44; economic factors in population control, 243, 247; emotion versus facts in the wild horse controversy, 241–42; horse management at Burns, Oregon, 244; needs for research, 242–43; review of PL 92-195, 245–47; wild horse increases in Nevada, and costs of management, 245; wild horse ranges, 243

Wildlife versus wild horses, 96, 108, 110, 142, 144, 163, 190–95, 261: at Challis, Idaho, 224, 231, 234–35; wildlife and burro competition, 178, 183–89

Wildlife Management Institute, 172

Williams, Lynn, 100

Williamson, Bob (Forest Service, Range Management), 169

Wilson, James (Secretary of Agriculture), 257

Winnemucca District (BLM), 159–60: starvation of wild horses in, 239

Winter range, 42, 86, 199: at Challis, Idaho, 224, 228

Wood, Verne, 63

Woodard, Larry (Associate State BLM Director, Idaho), 130

Woodie, Pat (rancher's wife), 122, 204

World War I, 39

World War II, 43, 62, 64, 240

Wright, James (Texas Congressman), 69

Wright, Robert (Nevada Cattleman's Association), 245

Wright, Roy (rancher, conservationist), 61

Wright, William (mustanger), 112

Wyman, Walker D. (*Wild Horse of the West*), 43

Wyoming: gathering claimed horses, 133–34, 162; horse roundups, 40, 42; wild horses and mustanging, 50–51; wild horse problems, 163

Yearsley, Bill (Idaho rancher), 117–19, 120

Young, Roy (advisory board), 241

Zebra, 93